Encyclopedia of Modern Ethnic Conflicts

Edited by Joseph R. Rudolph, Jr.

Greenwood Press
Westport, Connecticut · London

Library of Congress Cataloging-in-Publication Data

Encyclopedia of modern ethnic conflicts / edited by Joseph R. Rudolph, Jr.
     p.   cm.
   Includes bibliographical references and index.
   ISBN 0–313–31381–4 (alk. paper)
     1. Ethnic relations—Political aspects—Encyclopedias. 2. Cultural conflict—Encyclopedias.
   3. World politics—1995–2005—Encyclopedias. I. Rudolph, Joseph R. (Joseph Russell),
   1942–
   GN496.E56   2003
   305.8′003—dc21   2002070025

British Library Cataloguing in Publication Data is available.

Library of Congress Catalog Card Number: 2002070025
ISBN: 0–313–31381–4

First published in 2003

Greenwood Press, 88 Post Road West, Westport, CT 06881
An imprint of Greenwood Publishing Group, Inc.
www.greenwood.com

Printed in the United States of America

The paper used in this book complies with the
Permanent Paper Standard issued by the National
Information Standards Organization (Z39.48-1984).

10   9   8   7   6   5   4   3   2   1

To those members of the American melting pot who have blessed my life: my Irish-English-American mother, my German-American father, my Italian-American daughter, Alexandra, and my German-Polish-Lithuanian-American wife, Sabrina.

CONTENTS

ACKNOWLEDGMENTS

For a work of this nature, acknowledgments must necessarily be brief or comprehensive beyond almost any allotted manuscript length. Hence, I will err on the brief side, beginning with grateful thanks to my family, colleagues at Towson University, and editors at Greenwood Press for their equal doses of encouragement and patience along the way. Second, my obvious thanks to all who contributed to this volume whose well-written essays made the editing work so easy. Within this category, special thanks go to Stuart Kaufman for his suggestions and assistance in the final structuring of this volume. Last, my deep gratitude to the wider academic community without whose assistance in selecting the case studies and finding the contributors to write them this book would still occupy only a tiny space on my computer's hard drive.

MOROCCO
TUNISIA
ALGERIA
LIBYA
EGYPT
Western
Sahara
MAURITANIA
MALI
NIGER
CHAD
THE SUDAN
ERITREA
SENEGAL
GAMBIA
BURKINA
FASO
GUINEA
BISSAU
GUINEA
BENIN
NIGERIA
ETHIOPIA
SIERRA
LEONE
IVORY
COAST
GHANA
TOGO
CENTRAL AFRICAN
REPUBLIC
SOMALIA
LIBERIA
CAMEROON
EQUATORIAL
GUINEA
GABON
CONGO
CONGO
DEMOCRATIC
REPUBLIC
UGANDA
KENYA
INDIAN
OCEAN
TANGANYIKA
ATLANTIC
OCEAN
ANGOLA
ZAMBIA
MALAWI
MOZAMBIQUE
ZIMBABWE
MADAGASCAR
NAMIBIA
BOTSWANA
N
SOUTH
AFRICA

Case Studies in Africa

1 Ethnic Conflict in Multinational West Africa

2 Hutu–Tutsi Conflict and Genocide in Central Africa

3 Ethnic Conflict in the Sudan

4 Ethnic Conflict and the 20th Century's Last Colonial War

0   1000 km
0   1000 miles

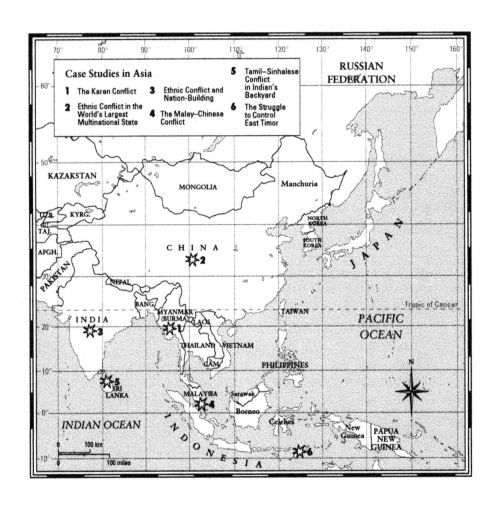

Case Studies in
The Americas

1 Canada: The Nationalist
Movement in Québec

2 Mexico: The Zapatista
Rebellion in Chiapas

3 The Struggle for Survival
and Equality of the
First Americans

4 Racial Violence, 1900–1919

5 Race and the Civil Rights
Struggle in Post-World
War II America

6 The U.S.–Puerto Rico
Relationship

7 Bolivia: Ethnicized
Peasant Conflict

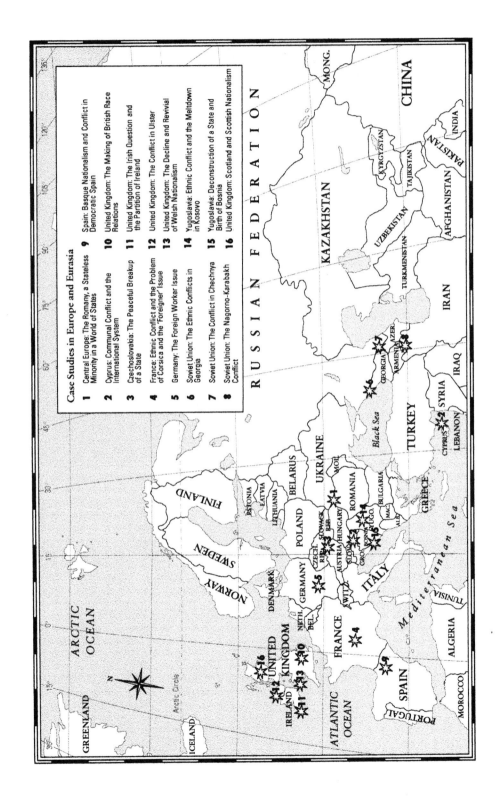

Case Studies in Europe and Eurasia

1. Central Europe: The Romany, a Stateless Minority in a World of States
2. Cyprus: Communal Conflict and the International System
3. Czechoslovakia: The Peaceful Breakup of a State
4. France: Ethnic Conflict and the Problem of Corsica and the 'Foreigner' Issue
5. Germany: The Foreign Worker Issue
6. Soviet Union: The Ethnic Conflicts in Georgia
7. Soviet Union: The Conflict in Chechnya
8. Soviet Union: The Nagorno-Karabakh Conflict
9. Spain: Basque Nationalism and Conflict in Democratic Spain
10. United Kingdom: The Making of British Race Relations
11. United Kingdom: The Irish Question and the Partition of Ireland
12. United Kingdom: The Conflict in Ulster
13. United Kingdom: The Decline and Revival of Welsh Nationalism
14. Yugoslavia: Ethnic Conflict and the Meltdown in Kosovo
15. Yugoslavia: Deconstruction of a State and Birth of Bosnia
16. United Kingdom: Scotland and Scottish Nationalism

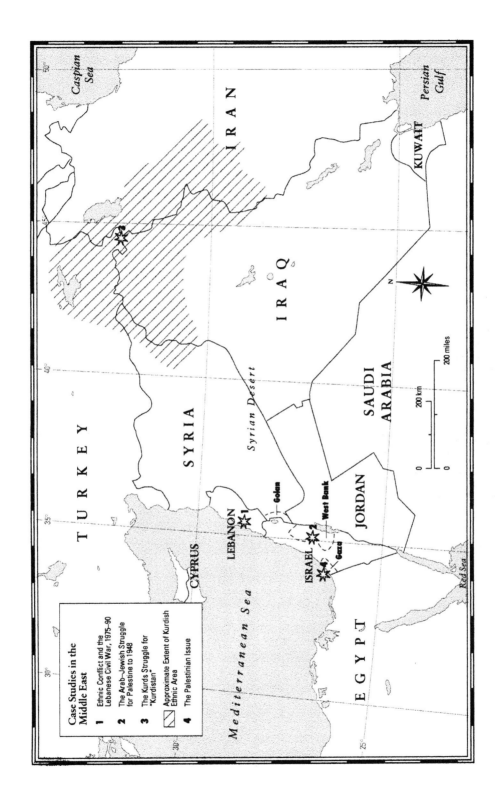

Case Studies in the Middle East

1   Ethnic Conflict and the
    Lebanese Civil War, 1975–90
2   The Arab–Jewish Struggle
    for Palestine to 1948
3   The Kurds Struggle for
    "Kurdistan"
    Approximate Extent of Kurdish
    Ethnic Area
4   The Palestinian Issue

INTRODUCTION

The literature on ethnicity is both voluminous and multidisciplinary, with particularly significant contributions drawn from history, sociology, and political science. Even the portion of it that focuses on the meaning of ethnicity is vast and continues to grow. There is, nonetheless, a consensus concerning both the general nature of an ethnic group and the ongoing political importance of ethnicity.

ETHNICITY, NATIONALISM, AND POLITICS

Defined broadly—as opposed to narrowly in terms of biological similarities—an ethnic group consists of a people "who identify themselves or are identified by others in cultural terms, such as language, religion, tribe, nationality, and possibly race."[1] As such, ethnicity has long been a basis of political as well as social association. Moreover, defying the prognostications of the Marxists who a century ago were predicting that social class would replace such primordial bases of political association as ethnicity and language, ethnic identity continues to be very much a part of politics in the modern world. Indeed, as the twentieth century drew to a close, ethnicity had not only proven to be an extraordinarily resilient factor but remained one of the most virulent political forces in the world. In domestic and international politics, in developed and developing countries, in democracies and autocracies, peacefully and violently, ethnopolitical actors and issues often commanded center stage, sometimes destroying states and societies.

Even where ethnicity functions in the context of a multiethnic society with an overarching sense of national identity, as in the United States, self-conscious ethnic identity can exert a powerful impact upon a political process, as is indicated by the chapters in this volume that treat African Americans' struggle for civil rights. In the twentieth century, however, the most significant manifestations of ethnicity occurred where it became the building block of nations either seeking self-determination or attempting to preserve their ethnic purity.

Using Rupert Emerson's still eminently serviceable definition of a nation as "the largest community which, when the chips are down, effectively commands men's loyalty, overriding the claims both of the lesser communities within it and those which cut across it or potentially enfold it within a still greater society,"[2] the link between an ethnic group and a nation becomes obvious. People usually develop this paramount level of identification only with those with whom they already have much in common. In turn, once aware of their distinctiveness, a nation is apt to develop a desire for political self-determination (nationalism, or—more precisely—what Walker Connor labels "ethnonationalism"[3]). It is in this form that ethnicity made its greatest mark in the latter half of the twentieth century, frequently prompting groups with a territorial base to press demands—both peacefully and otherwise—for autonomy or even independence against the leaders of the broader political systems housing their communities.

The chapters that follow, within the space restrictions allotted them,[4] catalog a significant number of conflicts involving both territorialized and geographically intermingled ethnic groups.

THE CASE STUDIES

Given the pervasiveness of the ethnic factor and the extensive number of instances in which ethnicity had a pivotal impact on political developments during the twentieth century, this volume makes no pretense of being comprehensive in cataloging all of the ethnic conflicts of the past hundred years. Nor do the chapter pretend to be comprehensive analyses of their individual case studies. Rather, as Thomas Spira observed in his *Nationalism and Ethnicity Terminologies: an Encyclopedic Dictionary and Research Guide,* "Encyclopedias and dictionaries are designed as consultation guides, and not as primary or secondary research sources."[5] Thus, this book is envisional in a starting point. Each case study includes a preliminary bibliography for follow-up research, as well as a list of the related case studies to be found in this volume.

At the same time, the selection of case studies was not a haphazard process. Organized alphabetically on the basis of the country or geographical area in which they unfolded during the twentieth century, each study follows a common organizational format focusing on (1) the history and issues involved in each case, (2) the efforts pursued to manage the conflict, and (3) the significance of the conflict in terms of its impact on politics in the area in question or the illumination it sheds on the general nature of twentieth-century ethnic conflict and the strategies—including violent repression—employed to control it.

Similarly, several explicit criteria were used in selecting the entries. First and foremost, each study represents an important example of twentieth-century ethnic conflict measured in terms of its longevity, level of violence, and/or impact on the political process housing it. To these criteria others were added. A conscious effort, for example, was made to include studies illustrative of the variety *and* the geographical scope of twentieth-century ethnic conflicts, although some areas do receive far greater attention than others.[6] This tilt reflects the fact that certain types of ethnic conflict are far more salient in some regions of the world than in others, as well as the editor's desire to include examples of both the different faces which the same type of ethnic conflict can adopt across time and space and the different forms in which ethnic conflict can occur in the same political system.

The studies are also chronologically skewed in the sense that a significant majority of them are drawn from the second half of the twentieth century, when two broad but separate developments produced a sharp increase in ethnic conflict in large portions of the globe: (1) the steady increase in the number of self-governing, multinational states in the world and the growing political assertiveness of their minority communities and (2) the equally steady increase in the forces of globalization and accompanying mass migrations of peoples to ethnically different, economically more advanced countries. Ethnic conflict as we experience it today is, consequently, predominantly a creature of the second half of the last century, albeit one owing a significant debt to Woodrow Wilson's World War I popularization of the twin ideals of national self-determination and the protection of minority rights.[7]

The Multiplication of Multinational States

The single most important factor accounting for the mushrooming of multinational states and ethnonational politics during the latter half of the twentieth century resulted from the state-making legacy of colonialism. When the twentieth century dawned, 84 percent of the earth's surface was under the control of Europeans.[8] Part of that surface was Europe itself. An even greater landmass was composed of non-European areas which had been settled by Europeans and had already achieved self-government, for example, the United States and Canada in North America and New Zealand and Australia in the Southern Hemisphere. The greatest amount of this territory at the turn of the twentieth century, however, housed the non-self-governing parts of the empires of European states. In most instances, the boundaries of these possessions were constructed with little or no attention to the ethnic makeup of the included populations. Occasionally, individual ethnic communities were split apart and consigned to two or more separate colonies. More frequently, the result was to encapsulate in the same colonial possession numerous ethnonational groups with different languages, religions, precolonial histories and ways of life, and to widen the differences separating these peoples via the uneven impact upon them of such forces associated with European colonialism as Christianization, Westernization, and urbanization.

When these predominantly Third World areas began to achieve their independence in large numbers after World War II (approximately 30 new states emerged in Africa alone in 1960), they overwhelmingly did so within those boundaries drawn by their European rulers during the colonial era. As a consequence, the vast majority of the independent states which emerged in postwar Africa and Asia tended to be multinational—often extensively so. Moreover, once independence was achieved—the indigenous independence struggles are excluded from this volume on the grounds that they were primarily anti-imperialist struggles, not ethnic conflicts per se between the ruled and their European rulers—the minority ethnic groups in these newly self-governing countries began to assert their right to national self-determination against the other ethnic fellows now governing their respective countries. The demand of India's Tamil-speaking minority for their own state, raised only a few years after India achieved independence in 1947, soon proved to be a harbinger of things to come throughout emergent multinational states (see, for example, the chapters on India, Nigeria, Burma, and Indonesia). It also initiated a series of challenges to India's internal stability which have bedeviled India's government in New Delhi ever since and have on occasion cost India's prime ministers their lives.

Meanwhile, at approximately the same time that the decolonization process began to unfold in earnest in the Southern Hemisphere, a significant resurgence of ethnopolitical identity and activity began to emerge in the multinational states of the developed world. This phenomenon resulted largely from the simultaneous convergence of several propitious factors during the 1945–1970 period, especially (1) the diminishing status of the national capitals in Europe following their liquidation of empire, (2) the desire of the governed throughout the developed world for less remote, less bureaucratic government, which was reinforced by the ethnic factor in the ethnoterritorially distinct regions of such states as Britain (Scotland, Wales) and France (Alsace, Brittany, Corsica), (3) the feelings of minority regions that they were being economically neglected or exploited by the majority groups controlling them (Basque Spain, Quebec in Canada), and often (4) the surfacing of visible threats to the survival of minority cultures in postwar Europe (the declining numbers speaking Welsh in Wales, for example). In coping with these developments, political leaders in numerous states were forced to reconsider and, sometimes, drastically revise their constitutions. The case studies of federalization in post–Franco Spain, Canada's constitutional debates and referendums on the status of Quebec, and the creation of assemblies in Wales and Scotland in Britain and Corsica in France examine this development, but by no means exhaustively.

Finally, and again increasing the *number* of multinational states, ethnopolitics in the developed world received a significant, end-of-the-century boost from the collapse of communism and the subsequent resurfacing inside the former Soviet Union and Central Europe of ethnic hostilities which had long been kept more or less under control. The violent breakup of Yugoslavia, chronicled here in separate entries on the birth of Bosnia and the struggle for self-government in Kosovo, provided the most dramatic example of this resultant ethnic conflict. Other examples abound, some of which—like the intensification of the Armenian-Azerbaijan conflict over an Armenian enclave in Azerbaijan, the more peaceful breakup of Czechoslovakia, and the upsurge in political violence against the Romany in most of post-Communist Central Europe—are included in this work.

The Age of Globalization and Mass Migration

Incidents of ethnopolitical conflict also multiplied during the twentieth century as a result of the steady increase in global interdependence. Revolutionary developments in the fields of transportation and communication, the relative global peace following World War II, and the eras of economic expansion in the developed world which date from the postwar period combined during the second half of the twentieth century to produce a new diversity in numerous states. This was particularly true of the relatively ethnically homogeneous states of the developed Western world, into which large numbers of immigrants and foreign workers moved from culturally remote areas in search of jobs. Reinforcing this development was the large influx of refugees and asylum seekers entering the stable Western democracies during the 1990s from politically dangerous areas, including countries embroiled in interethnic civil wars as a result of the collapse of the Soviet Union and Yugoslavia. In virtually all instances, this growing ethnic diversity in Northern Hemisphere states begat political conflict between the host populations and the incoming peoples. As early as 1971, West Germany closed its borders to additional "guest workers"; however, the presence of non-Germans within Germany's workforce and borders remains a major issue in the reunified Germany of today. In a similar manner, the movement of foreign workers from the former French empire in North Africa to jobs in France and the flood of immigrants from the "coloured commonwealth" who settled in Britain during the 1950s and 1960s has made a heavy imprint on the politics as well as the populations of these states.

ETHNIC CONFLICT AND THE HUMAN CONDITION

It was precisely this steady growth in the incidence and significance of ethnic conflict throughout the twentieth century that made the compiling of this volume so difficult. Conflicts not primarily rooted in ethnic or national differences had to be excluded, including some well-known recent conflicts—like those in Afghanistan and Somalia—which have ethnic dimensions but are not fundamentally ethnic conflicts.[9] Likewise, many legitimate candidates for inclusion had to be omitted either because of space restrictions or idiosyncratic elements too numerous and diverse to list. Thus, the limited success of Welsh nationalists in squeezing an assembly out of London is included, but not the story of Belgium's almost complete metamorphosis from being Western Europe's most centralized unitary state in 1970 to its least centralized state by century's end. Likewise, Biafra's unsuccessful bid for independence is discussed as a part of Nigeria's postindependence struggle with the incompatible ethnopolitical demands emanating from its principal tribal groups, but not the successful effort of Bangladesh (previously East Pakistan) to win independence from (West) Pakistan.[10] To those who would have included these and other important instances of twentieth-century ethnic conflict, the editor tenders his understanding and regrets. We can hope, perhaps not very realistically, that subsequent, similar compendiums will have fewer choices to make. Certainly few voices are predicting the imminent demise of ethnic conflict in the face of global interdependency, the war against terrorism, or any of the other forces so seemingly strong in the early years of this new century.

Americans are frequently, and not necessarily incorrectly, faulted for having too little sense of history—for being too prone to forget the lessons which even recent history has to offer. Other cultures seem to have a deeper historical memory, and it can be an important building block in generating patriotism and forging a political community. The statue erected in Budapest in honor of the courageous Hungarian prime minister who led his country's 1956 effort to break away from Soviet control and who was killed by the Soviets after they brutally crushed that rebellion, for example, symbolizes the new, post-Communist Hungary of today. It has been adorned with flowers by ordinary Hungarians since its erection.

Dwelling too deeply on the past, however, can also be a problem, especially in multiethnic polities. There are times when discussions can still be heard in

RADOVIC, KOSOVO. Memorial to Albanian Kosovars who died in Kosovo's struggle for autonomy. Like others throughout the province, it is daily adorned with fresh flowers. Photo courtesy of the author.

the Catholic pubs of Northern Ireland of the 1690 Battle of the Boyne like it was last week's hurling match, not the more than 300-year-old battle in which Ireland definitively fell under the rule of Protestant Britain. And sometimes history can cut both ways, building identity and hostilities at the same time, as in the Balkans, where the twentieth century opened and closed with bloody wars resulting from Serb dreams of a greater Serbia. Monuments to freshly fallen heroes can be found throughout the region today—in Tuzla and other parts of Bosnia, in Rahovec and elsewhere in Kosovo, and in numerous sites in Croatia. Recently erected in these would-be twenty-first-century, multinational democracies (which still contain Serb minorities) to honor those Bosnian Muslim, Albanian, and Croatian citizens who died at Serbian hands in their efforts to win their provinces' freedom from Belgrade's control, they too are daily adorned with fresh flowers.

NOTES

1. Thomas Spira, *Nationalism and Ethnicity Terminologies: An Encyclopedic Dictionary and Research Guide,* vol. I (Gulf Breeze, Fla. Academic International Press, 1999), 207, with specific reference to Rodolfo Stavenhagen's definition in *Conflicts, Development and Human Rights* (Tokyo: United Nations University, 1990).
2. Rupert Emerson, *From Empire to Nation: The Rise to Self-Assertion of Asian and African Peoples* (Cambridge, Mass: Harvard University Press, 1960), 95–96.
3. See especially Walker Connor's landmark essay "The Politics of Ethnonationalism," *Journal of International Affairs* 22, no. 1 (1973): 1–21.
4. All but three entries were limited to between 3,500 and 4,000 words. The only exceptions were James S. Wunsch's chapter on Nigeria, which is essentially a double study of Nigeria before and after that country's civil war; James A. Reilly's chapter on the highly complex and lengthy period leading to the partition of Palestine and birth of Israel; and Martin Smith's account of the many threads of ethnic conflict in Burma.
5. Spira, *Nationalism and Ethnicity Terminologies,* ix.
6. The case studies cover instances of ethnic conflict on all continents except Australia, where a considerable degree of anti-Asian immigration politics—similar to the anti-foreigner sentiment in France chronicled in this volume—could be found at century's end.
7. At President Woodrow Wilson's insistence, clauses were explicitly inserted in the postwar accords to protect the religious and ethnic minorities in those states destined to be carved out of the defunct Ottoman and Austrian-Hungarian empires in Central Europe. The League of Nations was charged with guaranteeing the majorities' compliance with these provisions.
8. Daniel R. Headrick, *The Tools of Empire: Technology and European Imperialism in the Nineteenth Century* (New York: Oxford University Press, 1981), 3.
9. Although there has been limited political unrest among ethnic minorities located along Somalia's borders, Somalia has been principally troubled by clan and intraclan conflict within its Hamitic community, which comprises 85 percent of its population.

   A much better case can be made for including Afghanistan, which houses four major ethnic groups including the Pashtuns, who accounted for approximately half of the country's people prior to the population dislocations that began with the Soviet invasion of Afghanistan in December 1979. On the other hand, the bloody conflicts that dominated Afghanistan's politics during the last quarter of the twentieth century centered not on ethnicity but on the persistent feuds of regional warlords within its dominant ethnic group, the ideological and international conflict resulting from the Soviet Union's 1979–1989 effort to maintain a pro-Soviet government in Kapul, and the bloody, quasi-religious warfare that involved the fundamentalist Taliban's acquisition of power in the 1990s and ouster from power in 2001.

   Statistics are drawn from the *National Intelligence Survey: Basic Intelligence Factbook* (Washington, D.C.: Central Intelligence Agency, 1971), page 1 for Afghanistan, page 305 for Somalia. For a general discussion of the nature of politics in Somalia, see Jeffrey Clark,

"Debacle in Somalia: Failure of the Collective Response," in Lori Fisler Damrosch, ed., *Enforcing Restraint: Collective Inervention in Internal Conflicts* (New York: Council on Foreign Relations Press, 1993), 205–240. Afghanistan's short, turbulent history is summarized in Cathal J. Noland, *The Longman Guide to World Affairs* (White Plains, N.Y.: Longman Publishers, 1995), 3–4.

10. For a short but excellent discussion of tribal identity as one of the major categories of ethnicity, see Cynthia Enloe, *Ethnic Conflict and Political Development* (Boston: Little Brown, 1973).

Bolivia

Ethnicized Peasant Conflict

David W. Dent

We are governed by the Whites [descendants of Spanish conquistadores] who have stolen our power and land.

Felipe Quispe, Aymara peasant leader, October 2000[1]

TIMELINE

1200 Rise of Aymara kingdoms in Andes Altiplano regions.

1519–1540 Main period of Spanish conquest of pre-Columbian civilizations, including the Incas, Aztecs, and Mayas in the Americas.

1780–1782 Indigenous rebellions break out in Bolivian highlands, led by Tupac Amaru and Tupac Katari. Rebellion ends when Tupac Katari is executed by colonial rulers for challenging Spanish authority.

1825 Bolivian independence; country is named after the liberator, Simón Bolívar.

1874 Law of Expropriation dramatically alters the prevailing pattern of landownership from communal to individual private property; peasant organization and resistance leads to repeal of the law in 1902.

1880 Bolivia is defeated in War of Pacific and loses territory and its outlet to the sea.

1882–1930 Land seizures lead to the creation of neofeudal estates (haciendas), eliminating lands controlled by indigenous communities and making Indians dependent on white European bosses and a few mestizos.

1894 Rubber boom adds to the devastation of Indian villages.

1902 Tin replaces silver as Bolivia's major export.

1932–1935 Bolivia is defeated in Chaco War, resulting in more loss of national territory.

1942 National Revolutionary Movement (Movimiento Nacionalista Revolucionario, MNR) is founded as a vehicle for instituting major reforms.

1945 First National Congress of Peasants is held in La Paz.

1952 Bolivian revolution begins, led by Víctor Paz Estenssoro and Hernán Siles Suazo of the MNR and backed by armed mine workers and ethnicized peasants. Revolution nationalizes tin mines, initiates massive land-reform program, and legislates universal suffrage and labor rights.

1953 Agrarian reform legislation divides land into thousands of parcels, leading to the disintegration of many indigenous communities.

1964–1970 Period of populist military governments.

1966–1967 Che Guevara tries to instigate a Cuban-style revolution among the Bolivian peasantry, but he is captured and executed in 1967.

1973 Katarista movement protests ethnic and class exploitation with a formal manifesto; movement links the contemporary quest for Indian rights with the earlier struggles of Tupac Katari.

1979 Katarista movement organizes massive roadblocks to protest government's neglect of indigenous communities and repression of Indian demands.

1982 Semblance of democracy is restored after almost twenty years of conservative military rule.

1990 March for Land and Dignity, involving 800 indigenous peasants in a 330-mile walk from Trinidad to La Paz, protests government's inaction in preventing the exploitation of the Amazon Basin's resources.

1992 Indigenous communities adopt the slogan 500 Years of Resistance to protest the 500th anniversary of Christopher Columbus's arrival in the Americas. Indian communities are given additional encouragement when an Indian human rights activist, Rigoberto Menchú, is awarded the Nobel Peace Prize.

1993 United Nation Year of Indigenous Peoples: working group includes protocol for a universal declaration of indigenous rights and protection of minorities. Vice President Víctor Hugo Cárdenas becomes first indigenous person to assume executive powers, while Bolivia's elected president was outside of the country on an official visit, in the Americas since nineteenth-century presidency of Benito Juarez in Mexico.

1995 United Nation Decade of Indigenous Peoples (1995–2004) begins.

2000 Ethnic conflict increases with government-supported globalization, coca eradication, and economic liberalization programs considered harmful by workers, environmentalists, ethnicized peasants, neighborhood organizations, and others to their economic well-being.

2001 Ethnic protests continue, despite government efforts to buy time by agreeing to many of demonstrators' demands. With inexpensive mobile telephones, protest organization and coordination become easier and more effective.

Bolivia, a multiethnic society, evolved from a clash of indigenous cultures in the Andes of South America and Spanish explorers in search of mineral wealth in the sixteenth century. From the beginning, the Iberian conquest (1519–1540) and expansion brought excessive levels of cruelty, deprivation, and death to the native populations, aided by smallpox and the exploitation of the original inhabitants. The majority of the indigenous population in Bolivia today are Quechua-speaking (30 percent) and Aymara-speaking (25 percent) Indians who live in the highlands of South America's poorest country. The rest of Bolivia's population is made up of citizens of European descent (15 percent) or mixed European and Indian ancestry (30 percent). With a total population of approximately 8 million in 2000, Bolivia is sharply divided between its Indian and non-Indian populations, which is the source of most of the country's struggle over Indian rights, class and political power, and overall economic well-being.

Bolivian society is divided into three major classes, depending on ancestral composition and level of assimilation. At the top of the power structure are the small minority of whites of European ancestry who are commonly referred to as *gente decente* or *refinado,* which means decent or refined people. Citizens who are of mixed blood (European and Indian), or who have adapted to the norms and culture of the dominant elites, are considered *cholos,* neither Indian nor *gente decente*. Those at the bottom of the social pyramid are members of the indigenous population, mostly Indians or campesinos (or both) who are unassimilated, poor, and discriminated against by the rest of society. The *gente decente* live in urban areas such as La Paz or Cochabamba, while *cholos* and *indios* live in mostly rural, agricultural areas or in very poor urban enclaves.

Bolivia is the most Indian of the countries in Latin America that experienced over 300 years of Spanish colonialism. For the past 500 years, ethnic conflict in Bolivia has been rooted in the differences—language, culture, tradition, and economic and political power—between Indian and non-Indian segments of the population. Until the twentieth century, the white upper class of Spanish-speaking, Western-oriented elites were successful in containing Indian uprisings that demanded land, autonomy, bilingual education, and many political rights, including the right to vote. Since the 1940s, Indian communities have been transformed into organized political actors capable of making demands—primarily through antigovernment protests—on elected governments that have often neglected the indigenous population. With effective leadership, new political parties, ethnic organization, and improved resistance strategies, Bolivia's ethnic majority has been able to force the government to recognize the legitimacy of its demands for basic rights and communal autonomy by utilizing relatively low levels of violence.

HISTORICAL BACKGROUND

Since the arrival of the Spanish conquistadores, indigenous communities in Bolivia have endured with astonishing reserve a multitude of intrusions and indignities. However, the restraint exhibited by tribal or indigenous communities over the centuries has often been interrupted by cycles of rebellion and state repression, compounded by violent confrontations between Indian organizations and the state. The exploitation of Indian communities led to indigenous rebellions in the highlands, including the 1780–1782 revolt led by Tupac Amaru and Tupac Katari. Before he was killed by the Spaniards in 1782, Tupac Katari offered this prophetic statement to his executioners: "I will return and I will be millions." As Indian communities faced repeated discrimination by the state, they gradually realized the potent symbolism of Tupac Katari's struggle and martyrdom to challenge the authority of the state.

From independence from Spain in 1825 to the middle of the twentieth century, Bolivia lost a considerable amount of its national territory in wars with its neighbors (including its outlet to the sea) and settled landownership battles through the creation of neofeudal estates that reduced the communal ownership of land by Indian communities. The internationalization of the Bolivian economy—particularly the rubber boom in the 1890s and the emergence of tin as a major export at the turn of the twentieth century—contributed further to the concentration of power in the hands of a white minority and a few mestizos who continued to resist the demands for reform by mine workers and Indian peasants.

Indigenous communities formed rural unions in the 1940s to settle the question of growing inequality in land ownership. By 1950 Bolivia's large landowners controlled over 92 percent of all land, and Indians were forced to work on the land they considered theirs under traditional communal laws of ownership. The Bolivian revolution of 1952—one of the defining events in modern Bolivian history—decreed a major land redistribution, universal suffrage that gave Indians the right to vote for the first time, and the nationalization of the mining industry. Under the leadership of Víctor Paz Estenssoro, a moderate leftist who decades later turned into a conservative during the economic and political turmoil of the 1980s, Bolivia responded positively to Indian demands for the first time during the 1950s.

The 1952 Bolivian revolution addressed some of the concerns of indigenous groups—particularly the land ownership issue, citizenry, and the right to vote—but the goal of the National Revolutionary Movement (MNR) was to *assimilate* Indians by eliminating their cultural autonomy and distinct living patterns. Furthermore, Indians continued to face discrimination and were denied many political rights enjoyed by non-Indians. During the 1960s, indigenous communities began to organize to resist efforts by the state to assimilate them into Bolivian society. The indigenous movement identified with Tupac Katari, a former Aymara leader who led the 1780–1782 anticolonial uprising; mobilized around the banner of the traditional multicolored scarf (*wiphala*); and placed a considerable emphasis on traditional dress, medicine, oral history, bilingualism, and historical monuments and ceremonies to symbolize the national unity of Bolivia's diverse ethnic movements.

The recognition of Tupac Katari's early resistance to state authority led to the creation of the Unitary Union Confederation of Bolivian Workers and Peasants (CSUTCB) in 1979 and other local and regional organizations to represent highland indigenous demands. The most successful of these was the Movimiento Indio Tupac Katari (MITKA), an Indian political party formed in 1978. Although it captured 2 percent of the vote in the 1979 congressional election in La Paz, it soon split into MITKA-1 and MITKA, which undermined its electoral strength. After MITKA was organized, the Tupac Katari Revolutionary Movement (MRTK) was formed as a political party to represent indigenous

and rural peasants. Waves of protests against government policies—privatization of water utilities, a proposal to construct three military bases, and a United States–backed plan to eradicate coca crops—have paralyzed much of the country recently because roadblocks have been set up to cut off supplies to the nation's capital. The conflict over the production and consumption of coca is an important part of the ethnic conflict in Bolivia since coca, unlike its potent derivative cocaine, has been consumed by indigenous communities in the Andes for over 2,000 years to alleviate hunger, fatigue, and altitude sickness.

In response, the national government has countered with states of siege, using combined army and police forces to neutralize the effects of the Indian protests. During several protests in 2000, twenty people were shot to death and more than 150 were injured in confrontations between civilians and military forces. During the last decade of the twentieth century, Indian communities have grown increasingly defiant of state authority as indigenous territorial and human rights have been violated. While interethnic conflict in Bolivia has led to greater recognition and protection through constitutional and legal reforms, Indian communities continue to suffer the most from poverty, government neglect, and human rights abuses. Bolivians elected Víctor Hugo Cárdenas, an Aymara Indian, as vice president in 1993, and new laws recognizing the political rights and land needs of Indians followed. However, this political change had little effect on the everyday political and social reality of the indigenous people. Since the United States–backed war on drugs was instituted in the 1980s, coca producers have had to put up with escalating human rights abuses and waves of unrealized promises of development schemes and improved living conditions.

THE CONFLICT

At the heart of the interethnic conflict in Bolivia is the right to retain lands Indian communities have controlled for generations and the right to control that land communally. As Donna Lee Van Cott argues in a recent study, "It [land] provides the basis for the re-creation of the indigenous community as a social organization—the medium through which native peoples pass their culture and their identity to their descendants."[2] The dramatic increase in Indian political mobilization—and interethnic conflict—over the past twenty years is associated with the following factors: (1) government efforts to eliminate legal protections of communal lands and other ethnic rights; (2) the demise of military dictatorships and increasing democratization; (3) foreign debt, globalization, and a new model of economic development based on structural adjustment, privatization, and free-market principles; (4) the war on drugs, particularly the United States–backed coca eradication program and a proposed construction of three United States–financed military bases in the Chapare area; (5) territorial intrusions by international actors such as loggers, ranchers, missionaries, multinational corporations, and the military; and (6) the international recognition of indigenous peoples by the United Nations and other organizations. While the degree of internationalization of Bolivia's indigenous communities is moderate, and levels of ethnic violence are low, the underlying cause of much of the protest is that Indian villages remain deeply impoverished and poorly educated, despite almost twenty years of democratic government and more than 15 years of World Bank and International Monetary Fund–backed structural reforms. The efforts made by indigenous communities to build a stronger sense of identity based on a shared past, govern-

ment neglect and abuse, and the threats posed by hostile outsiders are at the root of much of the new social protest and the increase in the government's use of repressive force.

Neoliberal economic policies—implemented by elected governments starved for resources and encouraged by international lending agencies—have threatened the existence of Indian communities by privatizing water rights, removing protections from communal lands, and threatening campesino agricultural interests. Indigenous leaders throughout Latin America have met to consider the implications of the North American Free Trade Agreement (NAFTA) and pending free-trade agreements on Indian communities. Representatives of the Zapatista movement in southern Mexico have traveled to Bolivia to meet with Indian leaders to coordinate strategies for improving the condition of indigenous communities. Of particular concern is access to land and natural resources, unbalanced economic development, and efforts to weaken the identity of indigenous peoples through a multitude of assimilation strategies. When Aymara leader Felipe Quispe states that Indians have lost power and land to upper-class whites who govern with little accountability, he is speaking for the poorest and most defenseless members of Bolivian society.

Bolivia's new wave of protest is linked to the determination of the U.S. and the Bolivian governments to eradicate what was once the largest coca-growing area in the world and one of the few sources of income for ethnicized peasants. Coca growers (*cocaleros*) are angry at the Bolivian government's willingness to go along with U.S. efforts forcibly to reduce coca production to only that needed for domestic consumption by 2002 and the militarization of the drug war as part of U.S. antinarcotics strategy in the Andean region. As a result of Bolivia's drug-eradication strategy, some peasant coca growers have left the Chapare region or have stopped growing coca bushes to cultivate less profitable, legal crops. Until recently, close to 500,000 indigenous farmers were involved in growing coca leaf, a legal plant used for medicinal or traditional purposes, and were represented by a well-organized and militant trade union, the National Association of Coca Producers (ANAPCOCA).

Under pressure from the U.S. government, President Hugo Bánzer made the elimination of drugs by 2002 a national policy, making Bolivia the first country in the recent drug wars to eliminate itself effectively as a producer. Between 1997 and 2001, the total acreage devoted to coca growing in the Chapare was reduced from 78,000 acres to about 4,000. As the size of the coca fields has shrunk drastically, the resistance of a hard core of an estimated 2,000 ethnicized peasant families has organized in opposition to the eradication effort. In October 2000, a three-week-long road blockade by coca growers did serious damage to U.S.–Bolivian efforts to encourage alternative agricultural develop-

ment projects. Leaders of the coca growers threatened armed conflict if they were restricted from growing at least small amounts of legal coca. With the growing militancy of ethnic peasants, the government is worried about the effects of peasant and labor unrest on economic and political stability. However, despite the costs of the radical eradication efforts in Bolivia, the supply of cocaine in local markets has changed little, as traffickers have transferred the growing and production of coca/cocaine to Colombia and Peru over the past five years. Despite the growing protests over drug policy, the Bolivian government is planning to move its eradication efforts to the Yungas, an area where the government will face an even bigger challenge since the ethnicized peasants are more firmly attached to their crops because of the medicinal and ceremonial functions they have served for centuries. Moreover, the Yungas region is served by a single-lane mountain road, which will make it considerably easier to engineer roadblocks to prevent government forces from entering the region.

VILLA TUNARI, BOLIVIA. Bolivian police officers threaten the leader of coca growers, Evo Morales, during an altercation on September 21, 2000. Growers were blocking a highway to reverse the government's anti-drug policies to eradicate all coca plantations in the Chapare region, forcing farmers to abandon their traditional crop. AFP/CORBIS/Conzalo Espinoza.

MANAGEMENT OF THE CONFLICT

The recent clashes between dissatisfied highland Indians and the state have produced relatively low levels of violence, despite protest marches, the forceful eradication of coca plants, and the heavy use of military and police to quash Indian demands. These low levels of violence—in deaths and property destruction—reflect both the methods of protest made by the indigenous peasants and the government's fear of acting too forcefully and provoking more violence, hence the government's tendency to pursue both accommodative gestures and repression in responding to native demands. Recent government efforts to respond to Indian demands through tax cuts and increased spending on roads have not brought much relief to impoverished rural communities; other accommodative agreements designed to revise the land reform laws and reduce the cost of water rights to the poor will take time to implement fully. Similarly, the government's continuation of coca-eradication efforts has alienated thousands of coca-growing peasants who have watched one of their major sources of income evaporate and are using road blockades and protests to make their demands, the same strategy employed by Tupac Katari over 200 years ago. Nevertheless, Indian protests are becoming more violent largely because of an increase in the state's use of repressive force to stop such antigovernment activities.

President Hugo Bánzer's (1997–2002) ability to exercise legitimate authority has been undermined by his inability to respond effectively to protests made by ethnicized peasants who have repeatedly paralyzed much of the country in the process. With Indian peasants demanding changes in a land law, the elimination of a proposed law that would privatize water utilities, and opposition to the construction of three military bases tied to the eradication of coca crops, 2000 was a particularly bad year for the president, a former military dictator turned "democrat" during his second term in office. In April 2000, the president decreed a state of siege that resulted in the deaths of five Indian protesters. In September of the same year, Felipe Quispe, head of the CSUTCB, instructed his followers to "lay siege" to La Paz in the "same way that Tupac Katari and his Aymara followers did during colonial times. Although President Bánzer called out troops to line the highways leading to the capital, La Paz, Quispe's Indian peasant followers succeeded in isolating the city and cutting off food supplies from neighboring regions. Between September and November 2000, more than twenty

people were killed and more than 100 were injured in clashes between coca-leaf producers, schoolteachers, students, and government forces made up of the army and police. The government's repeated use of the constitutional state of siege has had little effect on reducing ethnic violence.

SIGNIFICANCE

The conflict between ethnicized peasants and the Bolivian government, which for decades centered on land ownership and rights, has been compounded by the forces of modernization and globalization. The coca economy and United States' efforts to stop the supply of illicit drugs through coca eradication, local crop substitution, and various kinds of rural development efforts have all intensified ethnic politics in Bolivia. As Indians have been affected by declining prices for tin and coca-eradication efforts, they have organized ethnic-based organizations and marches to protest government initiatives. However, by declaring states of siege, arresting union leaders, and using the military to block marches by disgruntled Indians, government responses have contributed to the mobilization of Indian communities and the prolongation of the ethnic conflict. Although levels of indigenous violence remained low until the 1970s, Bolivia's indigenous communities have relied on nonviolent protest rather than armed insurrection. In any case, recent conflicts involving ethnicized peasants and an embattled state suggest that neoliberal economic reforms and forced eradication of the traditional coca leaf are likely to heighten the frustration among indigenous communities and continue the mobilized resistance to globalization and structural adjustment programs. Some observers predict that civil strife may become worse unless the United States and repressive Bolivian governments put an end to crop-eradication programs and face the more serious issues of poverty and the political marginalization of Bolivia's large indigenous communities.

See also Indonesia: The Struggle to Control East Timor; and Mexico: The Zapatista Rebellion in Chiapas.

NOTES

1. "Bolivia: Inca Nation," *The Economist* (October 28, 2000): 36.
2. Donna Lee Van Cott, *The Friendly Liquidation of the Past: The Politics of Diversity in Latin America* (Pittsburgh, Pa.: University of Pittsburgh Press, 2000), 2.

SUGGESTED READINGS

Albó, Xavier. "Ethnic Violence: The Case of Bolivia." In *The Culture of Violence,* edited by K. Rupesinghe and M. Rubio C. New York: United Nations University Press, 1994.
———. "From MNRistas to Kataristas to Katari." In *Resistance, Rebellion, and Consciousness in the Andean Peasant World: 18th to 20th Centuries,* edited by Steven J. Stein. Madison: University of Wisconsin Press, 1987.

Brysk, Alison. *From Tribal Village to Global Village: Indian Rights and International Relations in Latin America.* Stanford, Calif.: Stanford University Press, 2000.
Farthing, Linda, and Ben Kohl. "Bolivia's New Wave of Protest." *NACLA Report on the Americas* 34, no. 5 (March/April 2001).
Gamarra, Eduardo A. "The United States and Bolivia: Fighting the Drug War." In *The United States and Latin America: The New Agenda,* edited by Victor Bulmer-Thomas and James Dunkerley. London: Institute of Latin American Studies, 1999.
Gill, Leslie. *Teetering on the Rim: Global Restructuring, Daily Life, and the Armed Retreat of the Bolivian State.* New York: Columbia University Press, 2000.
Klein, Herbert S. *Bolivia: The Evolution of a Multi-Ethnic Society,* 2d ed. New York: Oxford University Press, 1992.
Strobele-Gregor, J. "From Indio to Mestizo to Indio: New Indianist Movements in Bolivia." *Latin American Perspectives* 21, no. 2 (Spring 1994): 106–23.
Van Cott, Donna Lee. *The Friendly Liquidation of the Past: The Politics of Diversity in Latin America.* Pittsburgh, Pa.: University of Pittsburgh Press, 2000.

Burma

The Karen Conflict

Martin Smith

TIMELINE

800 + Karen-speaking peoples begin migrating into lower and southeast Burma.

1752 A series of wars start during Alaunghpaya's rule that extend Burma's borders to its present shape under the Konbaung dynasty.

1824–1826 The British annex Arakan and Tenasserim in the first Anglo-Burmese war.

1830 The Karen language is put into writing by Christian missionaries.

1852–1853 Karen guides support British forces in the second Anglo-Burmese war.

1875 The independence of western Karenni is recognized by the British and the Burman king, Mindon.

1881 The Karen National Association is formed to promote Karen progress.

1885–1886 Burma is incorporated into the British India Empire following the third Anglo-Burmese war.

1928 Dr. San C. Po makes the first proposal for a Karen state; however, the Karen-inhabited areas are divided into several territories within British Burma.

1930–1932 The Saya San rebellion highlights the growing resistance movement among the Burman majority.

1937 Burma is separated from British India.

1941–1945 Communal violence breaks out between Burmans and Karens during the Japanese occupation of Burma in World War II.

1947 The Karen National Union (KNU) is formed but boycotts elections to the Constituent Assembly. Political situation further deteriorates after Burma's nationalist hero Aung San is assassinated by a rival.

1948 Burma gains independence from Great Britain, but the insurrection of the Communist Party of Burma (CPB) breaks out. Fighting also begins in the Karenni state.

1949 The KNU takes up arms, along with its Karenni and Pao cousins. The Antigovernment conflict spreads to other ethnic groups.

1953 The Pro-Communist Karen National United Party (KNUP) is formed; it later splits from the KNU.

1958–1960 General Ne Win takes control of the country under a "military caretaker" administration. Army officers hold unsuccessful peace talks with the KNU before Ne Win gives power to Prime Minister U Nu.

1959–1961 New ethnic insurgencies erupt in Shan and Kachin states.

1962 General Ne Win seizes power in a military coup and imposes his Burmese Way to Socialism.

1963–1964 Karen leader Saw Hunter Tha Hmwe agrees to a cease-fire with the government in a nationwide peace parley, but most other KNU and KNUP forces reject the deal. Insurgencies escalate elsewhere in the country.

1967–1975 The KNU is reorganized in the Thai borderlands and briefly allies with U Nu. The KNUP is destroyed in the Delta and Pegu Yoma regions by Burmese army operations.

1976 The KNU becomes a founding member of the ethnic minority National Democratic Front (NDF), which seeks a federal union of Burma.

1988 Ne Win resigns and the government collapses during prodemocracy protests. In September the Burmese armed forces reassume control through the State Law and Order Restoration Council (SLORC). The KNU supports a new generation of opposition fronts, with Burman and urban activists who had fled into its territory.

1989 The CPB collapses due to ethnic mutinies. The ruling military council introduces a new cease-fire policy toward ethnic minority forces.

1990 Aung San Suu Kyi's National League for Democracy (NLD) wins Burma's first general election in three decades. The SLORC arrests NLD supporters after the party tries to call a parliament.

1991 Pao and other NDF members begin to negotiate cease-fires with the SLORC.

1993 The SLORC initiates a national convention to draw up a new constitution.

1994 Newly formed Democratic Karen Buddhist Army secedes from the KNU. Ethnic Karenni and Kayan factions make truces with the SLORC.

1995–1996 KNU holds its first peace talks with the Burmese army since 1963–1964. The negotiations fail.

1997 The KNU loses most of its remaining base areas in government offensives. The number of Karen refugees in Thailand surpasses 100,000. The SLORC is superseded by the State Peace and Development Council (SPDC).

2000–2001 Under international pressure, the SPDC begins talks with Aung San Suu Kyi. The United Nation supports the concept of a tripartite dialogue. The KNU and other ethnic organizations agree with this aim.

The Karen peoples of Burma (Myanmar[1]) are not only the largest minority population in mainland Southeast Asia who have failed to gain political recognition in an independent nation-state, but they have also been at the center of one of the longest-running armed conflicts in the world.[2] From the outbreak of fighting during 1948–1949, a variety of Karen groups have waged armed struggle against successive governments in Rangoon for greater autonomy and ethnic rights.

In general, these conflicts are reflective of the greater problems in the country at large. Burma is one of the most ethnically diverse and strife-torn countries in Asia. With the Karen insurgency continuing into the twenty-first century, history shows that settlement of the Karen question remains one of the most critical challenges facing Burma's peoples. The legacy of the Karen conflict has long underpinned ethnic discontent in general within the country.

HISTORICAL BACKGROUND

Along with the Shans (Tai), the Karens constitute the largest ethnic minority group among the 52 million inhabitants of Burma, but many aspects of Karen history and culture remain clouded in controversy. This lack of interethnic understanding has often fueled the conflict. Even Karen population statistics are disputed; rebel leaders' estimates are over 7 million Karens in modern-day Burma, but government figures are less than half that number.[3]

Part of these differences can be attributed to the broad spread and diversity of the Karen peoples. There are also increasing numbers of Buddhist Karens who speak only Burmese, the predominant language of the country.[4] But perhaps the major reason for such disagreements is that, until the British annexation of Burma in the nineteenth century, the Karens were largely a hill or forest-dwelling people without a written literature; they enjoyed only oral traditions. As a result, the Karens appear as an ethnic group very much on the fringes of recorded history.

In fact, the ancestors of the Karens were probably among the first inhabitants of Burma in the early centuries C.E. To reach upper Burma, Karen legend tells of a journey from across the "River of Shifting Sands," believed by some observers to be the Gobi Desert in Mongolia. The Karen language, however, offers few clues as to ethnic origins: unlike other languages in Burma, it has been classified in a Karenic, Sino-Tibetan, or Sino-Karen, a category of its own.[5]

Only after the ninth century C.E. does the historical record begin to clear. Modern theory suggests that, with the arrival of Burman migrants from the north, the Karens resumed their long journey southward. This sense of the Karens as a nomadic and often persecuted people, without a recognized home, may well date back to these times. The poor (and crafty) orphan, along with tales of wanderings and lost riches, remain distinctive features of Karen mythology.[6]

Under such pressures, the Karens descended into lower Burma over the following centuries into lands then inhabited by the Mons and now disappeared Pyu. On their travels, they are presumed to have followed the valleys of three main rivers: the Chindwin-Irrawaddy, Sittang, and Salween. These different routes probably ac-

count for the disparate spread of Karen-speaking peoples in modern Burma. Around 20 subgroups have been identified. Of these, the largest are the majority Sgaw and Pwo in the Irrawaddy Delta, Pegu Yoma hills, and Thai borderlands; the Pao (Taungthu) and "long-necked" Kayan (Padaung) in southwest Shan state; and the Kayah, who are the most numerous of the Karenni (Red Karen) subgroups in the eastern state of that name.[7]

In precolonial times, the Karens do not appear to have built up political structures beyond the village or local levels, in contrast with their Burman, Mon, Rakhine, and Shan neighbors who established Buddhist city kingdoms in the valleys and plains. A degree of cultural interchange did take place; for example, the Karenni chieftains assimilated the *sawbwa* (princely ruler) system of their Shan neighbors. Most Pao communities—and many Pwo—began to practice Buddhism. However early Western travelers in Burma in the eighteenth century wrote of the Karens as a reclusive people, living in small villages, who appeared determined to retain their own customs and traditions.[8]

Karen history was about to change drastically. Beginning in 1740, the Karens found themselves in the middle of a series of devastating wars that wracked the country for decades. Karen villages were plundered, and the inhabitants were conscripted as porters. Meanwhile, the great Burman king Alaunghpaya and his successors overran Arakan and the Mon kingdom of Pegu, vied with neighboring Siam (modern Thailand) and China, and extended the authority of the Konbaung dynasty to borders approximating the shape of modern Burma. Shortly afterward, the British seized Arakan and Tenasserim in the first Anglo-Burmese war of 1824–1826. The growth of a Karen national consciousness—as well as modern political problems—can probably be traced to these days.

Until the present, this juxtaposition of the eighteenth-century wars and the British annexation that followed have led to some very different perceptions of Burma's history. In particular, Karen villagers, many of whom regarded the British as "liberators" from Burman domination, served as guides for the colonial forces in the war of 1824–1826 and the second annexation campaign of 1852–1853. Subsequently, Karen levies helped subdue Burman resistance in the final war of 1885–1886, as well as the Saya San rebellion in 1930–1932, leaving a legacy of Burman resentment against Karen collaboration with "imperialist designs."[9]

These divisive perceptions were further compounded when the colonial government, in a policy of divide and rule, preferred Karens, along with minority Kachins and Chins, to ethnic Burmans for recruitment into the British Burmese army. It was also believed that the British encouraged Christianity among the Karens to "separate them culturally" from their Burman neighbors.[10] Like the Burmans, most Karens are, in fact, Buddhists.[11] But certainly, inspired by Christian Karens, the advocacy of Karen nationalism and identity grew rapidly under British rule.

Education, especially, proved a major stimulus, and many villagers moved closer to the towns. In 1830 an American missionary, Dr. Wade, transcribed the Karen language to writing, and in 1841 the first Karen-language newspaper appeared. In 1881 the Karen National Association (KNA), the forerunner of the modern-day Karen National Union (KNU), was formed to promote the advancement of all Karens, regardless of religion or location. Subsequently, in 1928, the Karen leader, Dr. San C. Po, first called for the creation of a Karen state or homeland. The model he envisaged was similar to Wales in Great Britain.[12]

Whether the Karens were truly privileged under British rule is debatable. Far from being governed as a nationality group, Karen-inhabited areas were divided among five political districts under a complicated two-tier system of administration, separated between Ministerial Burma, which was dominated by the Burman majority, and the ethnic minority Frontier Areas Administration.[13] Ultimately, such divisions did much to undermine the unity of the Karen cause. Indeed there is evidence that, during the anti-British agitations of the 1930s, Karen-Burman relations were improving among a younger generation who, recognizing the need for interethnic harmony, was ready to work together for the future progress of Burma. The belated separation of Burma from British India in 1937 further highlighted this need.

Such cooperation, however, rapidly disappeared during World War II. While the Burman nationalists of the Burma Independence Army (BIA), headed by Aung San, initially fought on the side of Imperial Japan, the Karens stayed mostly loyal to the British. As a result, there were serious outbreaks of communal violence in which Karen communities came off very much the worse. Disturbing atrocities included the killing of over 1,800 Karens in Myaungmya district and the execution of Karen hostages in the eastern hills.[14] In 1945, as the British reinvaded Burma from the north, Aung San and the Burma National Army (the former BIA) turned against the Japanese, but it was Karen and Karenni units, who believed that they had been promised independence by the British, that inflicted the heaviest casualties on the retreating Japanese army.

Such antipathies were never resolved in the hurried British departure from Burma in 1948. There were now diehards on all sides who were ready to take up arms in support of their goals. At the war's end, nationalist demands for an independent Karen state, federated to Burma and including Karenni blood brothers, were proclaimed in a series of public meetings. But although communicated to the British, they were never fully discussed with Aung San and their Burman counterparts. A dangerous sense of rift was developing.

In February 1947, the Karen National Union (KNU) was formed, but it did not take formal part in the historic Panglong Conference, where the Shan, Kachin, and Chin minorities agreed to join the forthcoming Union of Burma. Instead, the KNU began boycott tactics, refusing to stand in elections to the Constituent Assembly that drew up Burma's new constitution. As late as October 1947, the cabinet of the Anti-Fascist People's Freedom League (AFPFL) coalition, which had won the 1947 election, was still prepared to offer a large nationality state to Karen parties that incorporated most Karen-inhabited areas in the eastern hills, including the Karenni and Kayan.[15] For the Delta Karens, a Karen Affairs Council was suggested.

Such proposals, however, were rejected by the KNU which not only wanted a seaport but claimed much of the Irrawaddy Delta as well. This latter issue alienated many British sympathizers as being too large a demand. Moreover, in another unexpected strategy, the KNU supported their Karenni and Pao cousins, putting forward their own cases for political autonomy separately. Such pluralism was partly out of respect for the right of ethnic self-determination, but also because lawyers in the KNU leadership believed that such broad representation would numerically and politically strengthen the Karen cause. In particular, Karen and Karenni leaders were very aware that the Karenni states had never been fully incorporated into British Burma.[16] Whatever the reasons, the result of such stratagems and thinking is that no pan-Karen movement has ever transpired.[17]

In any event, the Karen question was completely overshadowed by other emergencies that year. In July 1947, Aung San

was assassinated, along with most of his cabinet, by the gang of a political rival. He is still widely regarded as the one political leader who could have united Burma's different nationalities after the distrust and devastation of the war.

Subsequently, a hasty attempt was made to resolve the Karen question through a variety of constitutional arrangements. The Pao and Kayan were to remain in Shan state under the traditional Shan *sawbwas*, while the Karenni states, like the Shan, were to be constituted as one with the right of secession after a 10-year trial period. However, for the majority of Karens, the exact demarcation and rights of a Karen state—known by nationalists as Kawthoolei—were left to be decided until after Burma's independence. Significantly, unlike the Shan and Karenni states, it would not have the right of secession.

As a gesture of goodwill, a Karen, Smith Dun, was appointed Burmese army chief and another Karen, Shi Sho, the head of the air force. Cabinet posts were also offered to Karens. However, as the hour of the British departure drew near, few observers believed that such ad hoc arrangements would address Karen aspirations.

The Karen question, indeed, was just one of a number of political time bombs that were now ticking ominously.

THE CONFLICT

Burma's independence was born out of conflict. Certainly, political violence in the country has never been simply an interethnic affair. Within three months of the British exodus, the Communist Party of Burma (CPB) began its long insurrection against the central government and was quickly joined by mutinies from the fledgling Burmese army. Then, in August 1948, fighting broke out in the Karenni state after the nationalist leader, U Bee Tu Re, was murdered by union military police. Finally, the breakdown into chaos became complete in January 1949 when, to a backdrop of communal violence, Saw Ba U Gyi and the KNU leaders made the decision to take up arms. This opened the ethnic flood-gates, and, in the following decade, armed opposition quickly spread to other nation-ality groups, including the Mon, Rakhine, Chin, and, eventually, Shan and Kachin.

The AFPFL government, led by prime minister U Nu, barely survived. Supported by the defection of Karen units from the Burmese army, the KNU seized vast areas of the country, including Mandalay, Toun-goo, and Twante. However, after a 112-day siege at Insein on the doorstep of Ran-goon, the KNU was gradually pushed back. With the fall of Papun in 1955, the KNU lost the last major town it controlled.

Despite these setbacks, throughout the parliamentary era of the 1950s, KNU forces controlled much of lower and south-east Burma, with 15,000 well-equipped troops organized into two divisions: the Delta and Eastern. Party officials moved freely across the Irrawaddy Delta from the Arakan Yoma to the Thai borderlands. The KNU also worked closely with Pao and Karenni allies, and, during this period, the four nationality-political groupings by which Karen identity is largely represented today evolved: the mainstream Karen (Kayin) and the smaller Pao, Karenni, and Kayan movements. However political and ethnic relations remained close and, in the 1950s, both the present-day Pao National Organization (PNO) and the Karenni Na-tional Progressive Party (KNPP) were es-tablished with KNU support.[18]

Local armed Mon groups were also important allies, and, in the early 1950s, KNU, Mon, and Karenni forces briefly al-lied with remnant Kuomintang (KMT) units, which had invaded parts of Shan state after the Communist victory in China. It was, however, the KNU's increas-ingly close contacts with the CPB in the Irrawaddy Delta region that fueled the most controversy. In 1953 the borrowing

of Mao Zedong's "people's warfare" tac-tics from the CPB inspired the formation of the pro-Marxist Karen National United Party (KNUP), which eventually took con-trol of the KNU's Delta division. This shift to the political left caused a growing split with the more conservative leaders of the KNU in the eastern hills, especially after the KNUP (and KNPP) allied with the CPB in a Communist-inspired National Democratic United Front in 1959.[19]

These divisions came to a head in 1963–1964, shortly after General Ne Win had seized control of the country, when the KNU's most prominent leader, Saw Hunter Tha Hmwe, made a unilateral peace agree-ment with the military government and came in with several hundred troops from the eastern hills. The majority of KNU/ KNUP forces quickly rejected Ne Win's idiosyncratic Burmese Way to Socialism, but the nationalist movement never truly recovered from the damaging schisms of these years. More than a decade of armed struggle was beginning to take its political toll.

In a further split in 1967, several KNUP leaders, headed by Mahn Ba Zan, quit the KNUP organization in the Delta and rejoined the eastern KNU where lead-ership had been taken over by Bo Mya, a formidable hill Karen commander. In 1970 this reunited KNU leadership briefly allied in the National United Liberation Front (1970–1974) with deposed Prime Minister U Nu who, in a dramatic change in politi-cal alignments, also took up arms against Ne Win in the Karen-Mon borderlands.[20]

Such changes, however, left KNUP forces dangerously isolated in their Delta and Pegu Yoma strongholds, and, by 1975, they had been destroyed by the govern-ment's constant counterinsurgency opera-tions. Under Ne Win's Burma Socialist Program Party (BSPP), there was a defi-nite harshening in military tactics. Par-ticularly notorious was the Four Cuts campaign, first introduced in 1966, under which large areas were declared virtual free-fire zones in an attempt to flush out guerrillas from the civilian population. In subsequent decades, the Four Cuts was successively introduced in other war zones of the country.

Despite the demise of Karen forces in the Delta, the BSPP era (1962–1988), somewhat paradoxically, marked the high point in KNU fortunes in the east. Invigorated by control of the burgeoning black-market trade with Thailand, the KNU increased again in strength to around 10,000 men under arms. Bo Mya replaced Mahn Ba Zan in 1976 as KNU president, and, rejecting alliances with U Nu, the CPB, and other Burman-led parties, KNU leaders instead sought to improve collaboration with other ethnic minority forces.

For two decades, the KNU's headquarters at Mannerplaw on the Thai border was the political hub of ethnic insurgency in Burma. The main political vehicle was the nine-party National Democratic Front (NDF) established in 1976, which sought the creation of a new federal union of Burma. It was a symbolic moment. For the first time since independence, united goals had been agreed on by all the main ethnic opposition groups in the country.[21] In the following years, the Burmese army did launch attacks against KNU strongholds along the Thai border, but these were largely repulsed. Rather, confronted by countrywide insurgencies, it was Ne Win's Burmese Way to Socialism that was on the point of economic and political collapse.

It was against this backdrop, in July 1988, that General Ne Win resigned as BSPP chairman. In response, millions of protestors took to the streets across the country to call for democracy. In September of that year, Ne Win loyalists suppressed demonstrations and reassumed control through a military State Law and Order Restoration Council (SLORC), which was superseded in 1997 by the State Peace and Development Council (SPDC).

KNU fortunes initially appeared enhanced during the SLORC-SPDC era when thousands of students and democracy activists fled into KNU-controlled territories in the aftermath of the 1988 clampdown. A new generation of opposition fronts was established at Mannerplaw, heralded by the 23-party Democratic Alliance of Burma (DAB) in November 1988. Two years later, the KNU's linkup with urban-based groups appeared even more potent after a dozen Members of Parliament from Aung San Suu Kyi's National League for Democracy (NLD), which had won the 1990 general election, also fled into KNU territory, where they formed the exile National Coalition Government Union of Burma (NCGUB). The zenith of this unexpected realignment occurred in 1992 when Bo Mya was named joint head of a new National Council Union of Burma (NCUB), which linked all such antigovernment groups in the borderland world, including the NDF, DAB, and NCGUB.[22]

In the mid-1990s, however, the KNU's revival went into a sudden decline. Younger activists believed that the KNU's aging leadership, many of whom were veterans from the days of the British, found it difficult to cope with the fast-changing world of the post–Cold War era. Significantly, the KNU's longtime rival, the CPB, also collapsed during this unpredictable time. Long tolerated as a "buffer" force by Thai officials along their western border, the KNU's position was very vulnerable to change as the SLORC-SPDC tentatively opened the door to the outside world.

Three factors now intensified the pressures on the KNU. First, after 1988, the KNU found itself increasingly marginalized as official Thailand-Burma relations began to improve; logging deals and gas pipelines through Karen territory to Thailand were only the most obvious examples of the new political order. Eventually, in 1997, Burma joined Thailand in the Association of South East Asian Nations, leaving the KNU and other insurgent groups very isolated as "illegal" or "terrorist" groups in the region's governmental vocabulary.

Second, in another unexpected development, during the 1990s a growing number of the KNU's ethnic minority allies, including its Pao, Kayan, and Karenni cousins,[23] began to turn their backs on the DAB and other antigovernment fronts and, instead, negotiated cease-fires with the SLORC-SPDC. The impact on the military balance in the field was dramatic, and, as a result, the Burmese army was able to concentrate ever greater firepower against the remaining, non-cease-fire groups, especially the KNU. This was reflected in the growing numbers of Karen refugees from rural areas fleeing into Thailand.

Without doubt, however, the third and greatest setback to the KNU was a serious internal split in its central strongholds during 1994 which saw the breakaway of a 1,000-strong Democratic Karen Buddhist Army (DKBA) which accused KNU leaders, most of whom are Christians, of human rights abuses against local Buddhists in the Paan area. In the ensuing fighting, Mannerplaw quickly fell to the Burmese army, which supported the DKBA mutineers.

Such disunity within its ranks was a devastating blow to KNU morale. Factionalism has always been a serious problem in Burmese politics,[24] but, after the KNUP split in the early 1960s, the KNU had largely been able to avoid any further divisions.

During 1995 and 1996, KNU leaders entered into peace talks with the SLORC-SPDC to try to relieve some of these pressures. Their failure, however, was followed by more frontline mutinies, and, within just four years, the KNU had lost almost all its permanent base areas. Perhaps no incident was more poignant than the formation of the short-lived Karen God's Army, led by twin boys, that briefly staged

guerrilla attacks and gained international media attention after local KNU forces in its Fourth Brigade had collapsed in the southernmost Tenasserim division.[25]

Still under great pressure, at the end of the 1990s, KNU loyalists on the Thai border tried to regroup and reverted to a guerrilla-based strategy. During early 2001, attacks on various transport and military targets by KNU units were still being reported in remote districts of southeast Burma. But it was clear that, five decades after its inception, the KNU was struggling for its survival.

The organization, however, had not been defeated, and the Karen question remained to be settled. Indeed, the victory of the NLD in the 1990 election and the SLORC-SPDC's cease-fires with other ethnic minority forces merely served to focus international attention on the need for political reform and peace in the country. Acknowledging these realities, younger KNU leaders conceded that armed struggle alone was never going to provide the answers. Their urgent need to find a new political platform was reflected in the year 2000 by the replacement of Bo Mya (who remained military commander) with Padoh Ba Thin, a civilian, as KNU president.

There was also another imperative. Years of warfare had inflicted an alarming social cost. Indeed, with over 100,000 Karen refugees in Thailand and even larger numbers internally displaced inside Burma, many Karen leaders feared for the very future of their people. As the emergency escalated in the late 1990s, conflict resolution became an increasingly voiced concern. The humanitarian crisis in many communities was now desperate.

MANAGEMENT OF THE CONFLICT

Since independence in 1948, insurgency and military politics have been virtual ways of life in Burma. As a result, the

Karen conflict—including its conduct and the failure to find peace—needs to be seen as part of the broader political and ethnic problems within the country. Every part of Burma has been affected by armed conflict at some stage. Indeed, even at the beginning of the twenty-first century, the KNU and over 20 ethnic groups remained under arms, while an estimated 40 percent of the national budget was being spent on the Burmese armed forces by a military hierarchy that had been in power since 1962.

Tragically, the accumulative results of such a long-standing deadlock are the disturbing humanitarian and economic consequences that have long underpinned the country's malaise. Loss of life, refugees, internal displacement, forced labor and other human rights abuses, illicit narcotics, and HIV/AIDS—the list is long. As a result, by the 1990s, concern over Burma's many grave problems was moving to the center of the international stage.[26]

What, however, is perhaps most remarkable in the Karen case is how little effort has been made to end the conflict by peaceful means. In the first fifty years of fighting, only four real attempts at dialogue were made: in 1949, 1960, 1963–1964, and 1995–1996. Instead, chastened by these failures, the KNU and its allies concentrated through the intervening years on maintaining extensive liberated zones, with separate governments, armies, education, and health systems of their own. The symbolism of such self-government has been crucial. Through such tactics, the KNU and other parties not only functioned as opposition parties to governments in Rangoon, but also kept alive, in both concept and form, very different visions of political rights and ethnic identity.

For the Karens and other minorities, this has been especially important in priority areas like language rights, where minority languages are the first subject taught in ethnic opposition schools but never used beyond fourth grade (if at all) in those run by the government. In government schools, the Burmese language is usually exclusive.

Over the years, such competing systems, combined with the perennial lack of dialogue, witnessed a growing polarization among the different sides, which, on the rare occasions of talks, made discussing even common issues extremely difficult. In consequence, by the beginning of the twenty-first century, the political vocabulary and room for maneuver in Burma had become very restricted. A state of siege mentality was deeply ingrained on all sides.

In political terms, the evolution of the Karen conflict can be divided into three governmental periods: the parliamentary (1948–1962), the BSPP (1962–1988), and the SLORC-SPDC (post-1988). During the parliamentary era, the conflict was very much over the demarcation of Karen territories and political rights. In recent years, veteran KNU leaders have admitted that some of their early land claims during 1945–1949, including the right of secession, were always intended as bargaining chips; much of the Karen population, they recognize, is too intermingled with the Burmans, Mons, and other ethnic groups to make a complete breakaway of the Karen population a serious proposition. In clarification, what they say they originally wanted at independence in 1948 was the recognition of a nationality state substantial enough to reflect and safeguard the political and cultural identity of all Karens, wherever they live in Burma.

The precipitate outbreak of fighting, however, prevented any further discussion of such issues. Antipathies swiftly deepened, and Karen leaders contend that a number of measures undertaken by the AFPFL government illustrate that Burman-led parties were never sincere in dealing with Karen aspirations, even during the democratic era of the 1950s. First, it took until 1952 for a Karen state to be demarcated, which then was much smaller than Karen demands. With a capital at the then village of Paan, it did not include even one quarter of the Karens in Burma. Nationality progress, KNU supporters argue, will always be limited if Karen political identity is restricted to this backwater.

A second grievance concerned the Karenni state, which, in something of an anomaly, had been granted the right of secession in the 1947 constitution.[27] The territory was renamed Kayah state by the AFPFL government in 1951 in an apparent bid to remove a name that has historical connotations of independence and also to separate the Karennis from other Karens in Burma.[28] In 1959 the Karenni *sawbwas*, along with their Shan neighbors, renounced their traditional rights during Ne Win's interim military caretaker administration, and pressures immediately began to abolish the right of secession altogether. Four decades later, the issue is still a contentious one, and the Karenni National Progressive Party and other nationalist forces remain under arms seeking the restoration of the Karenni name and identity. The KNU continues to support this position.

Perhaps the greatest resentment in the 1950s, however, was over the use of force to suppress Karen opposition and demands. Atrocities were doubtless committed on all sides, but after the talks between Saw Ba U Gyi and U Nu, mediated by Anglican Bishop West, failed at Insein in 1949, it was over a decade before the KNU sat down with government officials again—and then only briefly during Ne Win's military caretaker administration.[29] In the meantime, countless lives had been lost, and grave harm had been done to intercommunal relations.

In many respects, the situation worsened during the second governmental period: the BSPP era of General Ne Win. On an analytical level, the complexities of Burmese politics appeared simplified. After the breakdown of a nationwide peace parley during 1963–1964,[30] the conflicts in Burma largely developed into a three-cornered struggle between the Ne Win government, the China-backed CPB, and the KNU and other armed ethnic groups which, in 1976, allied in the National Democratic Front.

Under the BSPP's 1974 constitution, the political map of Burma was redrawn into seven divisions in which the Burman majority predominated and seven states representing the largest minorities: the Karen, Kayah (Karenni), Shan, Kachin, Mon, Rakhine, and Chin. It was always clear, however, that the one-party dogma of the BSPP was never likely to satisfy ethnic minority demands. Indeed, as the schools, media, and large sectors of the economy became nationalized, Ne Win's Burmese Way to Socialism became synonymous to many ethnic minorities with "Burmanization." In short, the BSPP government was even less popular than the AFPFL, and this was reflected in the escalation of ethnic insurgencies throughout the Ne Win era.

Isolated from the outside world for 26 years, Burma under Ne Win entered something of a time warp that ended only with economic collapse and the prodemocracy upheavals of 1988. Three events now followed in quick succession that dramatically rearranged the political landscape: the 1988 collapse of the BSPP; ethnic mutinies in 1989, which saw the breakup of the CPB's 15,000-strong People's Army (and final ending of China's support); and the NLD's victory, along with 19 ethnic minority parties, in the 1990 election. The hermetic era of Ne Win's Burmese Way to Socialism was apparently at an end.

Once the dust had settled, the political confrontation in Burma had emerged as a new three-cornered struggle among the new military government of the SLORC-SPDC, the NLD, and the various ethnic minority parties. Recognizing these configurations, tripartite dialogue became a key objective of the first initiatives at national reconciliation in Burma undertaken by the United Nations. In the early 2000s, these initiatives were still continuing through a UN special representative, Mr. Razmali Ismail of Malaysia.

On paper, all sides, including the SLORC-SPDC, agreed that they were committed to a new era of multiparty democracy and free-market reform. Not for the first time, however, the course of Burmese politics defied many predictions.

On the national stage, the military government insisted that the 1990 election, Burma's first in three decades, was only to prepare the way for a national convention to draw up a new constitution, the country's third since independence. This body belatedly got under way in 1993. Although greater ethnic rights were promised (including a Pao and other new self-administered areas), the model it supported was the military-dominated democracy of Indonesia in the President Suharto era. Burma's turbulent history, military leaders argued, justified the right of the Burmese armed forces to be guaranteed the leading role in national political life.

In contrast, the NLD and other elected parties have always insisted that the 1990 election was for a new parliament and government, and periodic attempts to assemble these bodies were repeatedly suppressed by the SLORC-SPDC. Throughout the 1990s, hundreds of democracy supporters, including Aung San Suu Kyi and many NLD Members of Parliament-elect, were detained or imprisoned on various security and treason charges.[31] Under such pressures, it was difficult for the NLD to clarify specific goals. Although the party promised greater attention to ethnic minority concerns, its main aims were the achievement of office and a reversal to the democratic ideals of the 1947 constitution, which was federal in principle, if not in name.

For armed opposition groups, the situation was equally difficult. Few Karens attempted to revive aboveground politics in the 1990 election and, like other minorities, most voted for the NLD.[32] In general, such voting echoed the position of the KNU which had welcomed the revival of the democracy movement in 1988 and became the main host for the students and prodemocracy exiles who took sanctuary in Burma's borderlands after the SLORC crackdown.

This strategy of democratic solidarity, however, was to cost the KNU dearly. After 1988 the KNU came under some of the most sustained offensives from the Burmese army since the Delta counterinsurgency campaigns in the 1960s. Compounding its difficulties, the KNU was caught off guard in 1989 when the military government unveiled its new cease-fire policy following the CPB's collapse. Instigated by the SLORC-SPDC's first secretary, Lieutenant General Khin Nyunt, the peace terms offered were very much on a military basis. Politics were not discussed, but it was agreed that ethnic cease-fire groups would be allowed to engage in politics and business, as well as keep their arms and territories, until a new constitution could be introduced.

Long isolated in the forests, many war-weary parties were quick to agree to such an offer of peace. The first to agree to terms were four breakaway forces from the CPB; by the mid-1990s, cease-fires had spread to another dozen of the most important insurgent groups in the country, including the Pao National Organization, the Kayan New Land Party, and some of the KNU's closest allies from the NDF. The Karenni National Progressive Party, long a staunch KNU friend, also concluded a cease-fire in 1995, though this quickly broke down.

Inevitably, such dramatic changes in strategies and alignment attracted much criticism and controversy—as well as many accusations of opportunism. In particular, there was concern over money laundering and increased illicit narcotics production in areas controlled by the Wa and cease-fire groups along the Chinese border. Leaders of the cease-fire groups, such as the veteran Pao leader Aung Kham Hti, a former Buddhist monk, were adamant that they wanted to find a new way to enter the process of transition and dialogue after so many years of inconclusive warfare.[33]

KNU leaders shared many of the same aspirations, but a serious difference of opinions now emerged with many of its former allies over the question of peace talks. By the mid-1990s, it was clear to even the most diehard Karen nationalists that peace talks with the military government were inevitable sooner or later. Under pressure from the Thai authorities and shattered by the DKBA mutinies, Bo Mya and the KNU leaders knew that they were increasingly isolated. Although refugees were well cared for by international aid agencies in cross-border camps in Thailand, the DAB and NCUB alliances had brought scant relief for Karen communities in the front line of the conflict. Indeed, in fifty years of warfare, no foreign government had ever come to the KNU's aid.

It was in this environment that the peace talks between the KNU and SLORC-SPDC finally began. These were brokered by a go-between team of Karen elders, including veteran Karen state leader Saw Alfonzo. In total, seven meetings were held with Burmese army officials during 1995–1996. However, unlike the talks with other armed opposition groups, these broke down after the KNU refused to accept two basic conditions: that the KNU enter the legal fold and that it lay down its arms after Burma's new constitution was introduced. After five decades of conflict, KNU veterans analyzed such terms as tantamount to surrender—virtually the same conditions that the KNU had

rejected at the Insein talks in 1949. In particular, KNU leaders were insistent that something in the form of a political agreement was needed on the table—not only as a guarantee of reform but also to justify the sacrifices of the many who had died. Anything less, they argued, would be a betrayal.[34]

Thus a different strategy in conflict resolution emerged among the various opposition groups in Burma. In essence, this could be categorized as a difference between a politics-first demand, which was advocated by the KNU and the NLD, and the peace-through-development policy of mutual trust building that had been reached in the negotiations between the military government and the ethnic cease-fire groups. By the turn of the century, this had resulted in some very different images of contemporary Burma, with the continuing fighting and loss of life in the Karen, Karenni, Shan, and several other borderlands contrasting with the first peace programs in former war zones in decades, especially in the northeast of the country.[35]

Perhaps the clearest reflection of these different outlooks was the 1997 Mae Hta Raw Tha declaration (from the village of that name) in which the KNU called, after its peace talks broke down, for support for the NLD, strengthening united fronts, and the overthrow of the military government.[36] In response, the SLORC-SPDC demanded that this statement, which was cosigned by a number of smaller ethnic parties in the borderlands, be withdrawn before any future talks could take place.

Nothing, however, has been set in stone, and, as the SLORC-SPDC government entered its second decade, the international and domestic pressures for reform remained intense. In particular, great hopes were raised in 2001 when, as a result of continuing UN efforts at mediation, the SPDC and Aung San Suu Kyi began to engage in unpublicized talks. This immediately cast the spotlight on the KNU and other ethnic groups. Whether as legal parties, in cease-fires, or still engaged in fighting, all sides recognized that the ethnic minority question was an equally important part of the country's tripartite debate.

With the KNU marginalized and the nationalist movement badly fragmented, this tripartite equation posed serious problems for Karen leaders. The KNU had come to its weakest point in 50 years, and many long-standing ethnic allies, including the Pao and Kayan, were in cease-fires with the government. Nevertheless the new century began with the same responsibilities and challenges facing all the political protagonists in Burma as they had at independence in 1948. Whatever the difficulties, a just and equitable solution was still needed for the Karens if the country was ever truly to progress. Indeed, the Karen dilemma was only a reflection of the ethnic challenges in the country at large.

Blame, however, could not be put all on one side after five decades of conflict. In private, encouraged by the 1990 election result, many Karens argued that the KNU had to show that it, too, was part of the solutions—not the problems. A generational change was under way in Burma, and, after so many years of suffering, the need had long been urgent to resolve what the KNU called the father-to-son war.

The challenge now was to achieve real dialogue, and this time—whatever the format—the dialogue would have to be inclusive if Burma was not to be condemned to another fifty years of conflict. The lessons from history give very stark warnings of the price of failure.

SIGNIFICANCE

Although little reported in the outside world, there are many aspects to the Karen conflict in Burma that make resolution essential. First, as one of the longest-running armed struggles in the world, the human and social costs that have built up over the past five decades are extremely disturbing. At the beginning of the twenty-first century, the more than 100,000 Karen and Karenni refugees in camps in Thailand are only the most visible evidence of the long years of suffering within the country. Many communities and families have been torn apart, and there has been a heavy loss of life on all sides of the conflict.

Second, as an ethnic minority people who have often been described under international definitions by such terms as "indigenous" or "tribal," the Karens have made perhaps the most persistent effort of any such group in east or south Asia to achieve the identity of a state which acknowledges their rights as a nationality. As with many other "non-state" minorities, this lack of ethnic recognition is a major handicap. Not only governments but intergovernmental bodies, including the United Nations, continue to have problems addressing the aspirations of such marginalized peoples as the Kurds, Hmongs, and Nagas. As the KNU once declared, "The Karens are much more than a national minority. We are a nation."[37]

This central position of the nationality question is emphasized by a third key feature of the Karen conflict: its pivotal role in postcolonial Burmese politics. Far from being a short-lived or peripheral rebellion, the Karen struggle has been a long ideological journey that has encompassed three different eras of government over six decades. During this time, Karen parties have embraced both pro-Communist and anti-Communist philosophies, fought both against and alongside Burman majority parties, and constantly tried to forge unity with other ethnic groups in the country. Modern Burma is indeed one of the most complex and ethnically troubled lands in Asia, and the long struggle of the Karens needs to be seen against this hazardous backdrop.

Related to this, a fourth feature of the Karen conflict is the perennial extent to

BURMA. Karen National Union (KNU) leaders in 2001, including KNU chief of staff, Tamla Baw (second from left) and, next to him, the KNU's veteran leader, Bo Mya. Photo courtesy of the author.

which armed struggle has been sustained. Outside aid has been minimal, but for over fifty years various armed nationalist movements of the Karens, with considerable sacrifice and ingenuity, have been able to support standing armies and control large rural territories.

Among the peoples of Burma, the realities of rebellion are no cause for celebration. After so many years of conflict, no side has truly won. Rather, a culture of the economics and politics of survival has come to dominate in the country, and this, in turn, has long hindered the search for solutions. Whether in government or opposition, Burma at the beginning of the twenty-first century is one of the most militarized countries in the world, and the ethnic insurgencies must be seen as an integral part of the country's problems. Demilitarization, resettlement, reconcilia-

tion, and development are all long-term tasks for the future.

Finally, perhaps the most remarkable feature of the Karen conflict is how few talks of any substance have taken place between the different protagonists since the outbreak of conflict in 1948–1949. The reasons for these failures must be assessed and resolved. From land and language rights to health and education, many vital issues underpin the long-standing conflict. The problems and aspirations of the Karens are not different, in essence, from those of any other nationality group in Burma, but they are unlikely to be addressed until there is dialogue and peace.

The cycle of conflict has long since needed to be broken. At independence in 1948, ethnic Karens were among the country's leaders, but today few Karens (or any other minority) are in any leading position on the national stage. As the failure of KNU-SLORC talks in 1995–1996 once again warned, the long-standing task remains to move from talking about peace to achieving reform.

See also India: Ethnic Conflict and Nation-building in a Multiethnic State; Malaysia: The Malay-Chinese Conflict; and Sri Lanka: Tamil-Sinhalese Conflict in India's Backyard.

NOTES

1. The changing of Burma's official name to Myanmar by the State Law and Order Restoration Council government in 1989 remains a matter of controversy. While recognized by the United Nations, it is rejected by many prodemocracy and ethnic opposition groups.

2. It can be argued that the ethnopolitical identity of the other large minority group in Burma, the Shan (Tai), is reflected in the existence of Thailand.

3. Many of the ethnic and political issues in this chapter are discussed more fully by the author in Martin Smith, *Burma: Insurgency and the Politics of Ethnicity*, 2d ed. (London: Zed Books, 1999). For a discussion of populations, see pp. 29–31.

4. "Burmese" generally refers to language and citizenship, while "Burman" refers to the majority ethnic group who constitute about two-thirds of the country's population: someone can be an ethnic Karen, Mon, or Burman but a Burmese citizen.

5. Most of the more then 100 languages and dialects in Burma, including those of the Kachin and Chin subgroups, are classified in the Tibeto-Burmese linguistic group. The other large language families in Burma are Mon-Khmer and Tai (Shan).

6. The story of the lost "Golden Book" of all knowledge is especially popular in recent history. This book was reputedly stolen by the younger "white brother" of the Karens. The arrival of the Western missionaries with the Bible was therefore interpreted by some observers as the returning of this book.

7. The 1931 census, which was the last attempt at a detailed breakdown, estimated the Sgaw and Pwo at just over 35 percent each in a Karen population of 1,367,673, the Pao at 16.5 percent, the Kayah at 2.3 percent, and the Kayan at 1.4 percent. The subgroups, however, do not live in distinct blocks. There is, for example, a large Pao community in Thaton district, quite removed from the main areas of Pao habitation in Shan state.

8. See Father Sangermano, *A Description of the Burmese Empire* (Rome, 1833; reprint, Rangoon: Government Press, 1885), 42–44.

9. Such criticisms were often expressed in the twentieth century. See Government of the Union of Burma, *KNDO Insurrection* (Rangoon: Government Printing and Stationery, 1949), 35; and *The Guardian* (Rangoon), September 19, 1987, in which the insurgent Karen National Union was accused by the state-run media of "craving for colonial servitude, yearning for their distant relative over and above their own mother."

10. U Ba Swe, prime minister of Burma (1956–1957), as quoted in F. R. Von Der Mehden, *Religion and Nationalism in Southeast Asia: Burma, Indonesia, the Philippines* (Madison: University of Wisconsin Press, 1963), 191.

11. There are no accurate figures on modern-day religions among the Karens. In the 1960s, the Burma Baptist Convention estimated Christians as around one-sixth of the Karen population, but Christian numbers are probably still growing. In contrast, traditional spirit-worship has rapidly declined during the last 100 years. An unusual phenomenon in rural areas is the millenial sect, which combines aspects of Buddhism and Christianity. See Smith, *Burma: Insurgency*, 454–56 and note 25.

12. Dr. San Crombie Po, *Burma and the Karens* (London: Eliott Stock, 1928), 79–83.

13. Ministerial Burma, Parts I and II of the "Scheduled" Frontier Areas, the Karenni states, and southwestern Shan states. In Ministerial Burma, where a limited form of democratic home rule was introduced in the 1920s, 12 communal seats were allotted to the Karens. The other four areas, in contrast, remained under the British governor, but local chiefs and rulers were allowed to retain their traditional positions.

14. For a wartime description of Karen areas, see Ian Morrison, *Grandfather Longlegs: The Life and Gallant Death of Maj. H. P. Seagrim* (London: Faber and Faber, 1947). For this and following events in the 1941–1948 era, see also Smith, *Burma: Insurgency*, 60–87.

15. Smith, *Burma: Insurgency*, 86. The Kayan territory was the Shan substate of Mongpai (Mobye), which is largely inhabited by Kayans (Padaungs).

16. The basis for this was an 1875 treaty between the British and Burman king Mindon under

which the independence of the western Karenni region was mutually recognized.

17. Most Karen-related groups, including the Pao and Karenni, are still aware of their common "Karen" heritage. There has been much interaction between the different parties. In 1950, for example, the presidency of the KNU was offered to Pao leader "Thaton" Hla Pe. Nevertheless, over the decades, different Karen, Pao, Karenni, and Kayan identities have become increasingly fixed in contemporary political terms. This chapter therefore largely concentrates on modern "Karen" and KNU histories.

18. Smith, *Burma: Insurgency,* 172–73. In 2001 one organizer sent up by the KNU, Tha Kalei, a Sgaw Karen, still headed a later PNO faction, the Shan State Nationalities Liberation Organization, while a Pwo Karen, Aung Than Lay, remained a senior leader of the KNPP.

19. The National Democratic United Front (1959–1975) initially consisted of the CPB, KNUP, KNPP, Chin National Vanguard Party, and New Mon State Party.

20. The National United Liberation Front members were the KNU, New Mon State Party, Chin Democracy Party, and U Nu's short-lived Parliamentary Democracy Party.

21. The founding groups of the NDF were KNU, KNPP, PNO, Kayan New Land Party, Arakan Liberation Party, Kachin Independence Organization, Lahu National United Party, Palaung State Liberation Party, and Shan State Progress Party. Subsequently, some parties left and others joined. In 2001, although much reduced in effectiveness, the NDF still existed in name.

22. The other NCUB leaders were Aung San Suu Kyi's cousin, Dr. Sein Win MP-elect (NCGUB), Brang Seng (Kachin Independence Organization), and Nai Shwe Kyin (New Mon State Party).

23. The PNO, an NDF member, was the first to make a cease-fire in 1991. In 1994 three forces, which had previously been allied with the CPB, also entered into cease-fires: the Kayan New Land Party, established in 1964; the Karenni State Nationalities Liberation Front, which was a 1978 breakaway group from the KNPP; and the (Pao majority) Shan State Nationalities Liberation Organisation, which was a longtime rival to the PNO. For the histories of these groups, see Smith, *Burma: Insurgency,* 336–39, 344–47, 353–54. Though numbers fluctuated over the years, each group usually maintained several hundred troops under arms.

24. See e.g., Ibid.

25. See Terry McCarthy, "Leading God's Army,"

Time (Magazine), February 7, 2000. See also note 11. Since the 1960s, KNU forces were organized in seven main "brigade" areas in the Karen state and Tenasserim division. By the end of the 1990s, each was considerably under strength, usually consisting of between 100 and 200 armed regulars in each.

26. For international human rights concerns, see, for example, *Situation of Human Rights in Myanmar: Report of Special Rapporteur, Mr Rajsoomer Lallah* (Geneva: UN Mission on Human Rights, January 15, 1998); for humanitarian dimensions, see, for exmaple, Martin Smith, *Fatal Silence? Freedom of Expression and the Right to Health in Burma* (London: Article 19, 1996).

27. See note 16.

28. The Kayah are, in fact, only the largest of the dozen Karen-related groups in the state, including Kayan, Kayow, and Paku. In political terms, most inhabitants have preferred the collective name of Karenni for their territory and identity.

29. The KNU team was led by Kaw Htoo, Skaw Ler Taw, and Kyin Pe. On the government side were Brigadiers Aung Gyi and Aung Shwe, both of whom joined the NLD in 1988 (Aung Gyi later resigned). Smith, *Burma: Insurgency,* 186.

30. Ibid., 206–13.

31. See, for example, Amnesty International, *Myanmar: Prisoners of Political Repression* (London: International, 2001).

32. Newly formed ethnic Pao, Kayan, and Kayah (Karenni) parties did stand in the election and won several seats.

33. Interview with author, February 18, 1998.

34. This analysis is based on a series of interviews made over the years with different KNU leaders, including Bo Mya and Padoh Ba Thin.

35. For a discussion, see, for example, Martin Smith, "Ethnic Conflict and the Challenge of Civil Society in Burma," in *Strengthening Civil Society in Burma: Possibilities and Dilemmas for International NGOs,* ed. Barma Center Netherlands (Chieng Mai: Silkworm Books, 1999), 15–53.

36. Smith, *Burma: Insurgency,* 449.

37. The Government of Kawthoolei, *The Karens and Their Struggle for Independence* (Mergui-Iavoy, Burma: KNU Publishing, 1984), 2–3.

SUGGESTED READINGS

Amnesty International. *Myanmar: The Kayin (Karen) State: Militarization and Human Rights.* London: Amnesty International, 1999.

Falla, Jonathon. *True Love and Bartholomew: Rebels on the Burmese Border*. Cambridge: England: Cambridge University Press, 1991.

Keyes, Charles, ed. *Ethnic Adaptation and Identity: The Karen on the Thai Frontier with Burma*. Philadelphia: Institute for the Study of Human Issues, 1979.

Lehman, Frederick. "Burma: Kayah Society as a Function of the Shan-Burman-Karen Context." In *Contemporary Change in Traditional Societies*, edited by J. Steward. Urbana: University of Illinois, 1967, 1–104.

Morrison, Ian. *Grandfather Longlegs: The Life and Gallant Death of Maj. H. P. Seagrim*. London: Faber and Faber, 1947.

San Crombie Po, Dr. *Burma and the Karens*. London: Elliot Stock, 1928.

Silverstein, Josef. *Burmese Politics: The Dilemma of National Unity*. New Brunswick, N.J.: Rutgers University Press, 1980.

Smith, Martin. *Burma: Insurgency and the Politics of Ethnicity,* 2d ed. (London: Zed Books, 1999).

———. *Ethnic Groups in Burma: Democracy, Development and Human Rights*. London: Anti-Slavery International, 1994.

Stern, Theodore. "*Ariya* and the Golden Book: A Millenarian Buddhist Sect Among the Karen." *Journal of Asian Studies* 27, no. 2 (1968): 297–327.

Canada

The Nationalist Movement in Quebec

Saul Newman

TIMELINE

1534 Jacques Cartier explores the Saint Lawrence River and claims the region for France.

1608 Samuel de Champlain establishes a trading post in the area that later becomes known as Quebec City.

1670 England grants a charter to the Hudson's Bay Company that increases English settlement and later results in economic and military conflict with New France.

1759 British troops defeat New France at the Plains of Abraham in Quebec City, finally wresting control of Canada from France.

1774 The Quebec Act preserves French civil codes, the system of landholding, and the freedom of the Catholic Church.

1837 The *Patriotes* of Louis-Joseph Papineau lead a rebellion for more political power for French Canadians, but they are defeated.

1841 Act of Union combines Ontario and Quebec into one province, based on the recommendations of Governor-General Lord Durham that internal self-government be coupled with efforts to Anglicize Quebec.

1867 The British North America Act creates the confederation of Canada.

1885 Louis Riel is hung after his second rebellion on behalf of Francophones of indigenous and European ancestry.

1917 Conscription for World War I is bitterly opposed by French Canadians.

1936 Maurice Duplessis, the leader of the Union Nationale, is elected premier of Quebec.

1944 World War II ushers in a second conscription crisis.

1960 Jean Lesage of the Liberal Party is elected premier of Quebec; the Quiet Revolution begins.

1968 René Lévesque, a former television reporter and Lesage cabinet member, forms the Parti Québécois (PQ), which is committed to sovereignty for Quebec.

1970 The Front de Libération du Québec (FLQ) kidnaps and kills Quebec's minister of labor. Canada responds with the War Measures Act, which temporarily suspends some civil liberties in Quebec.

1976 The PQ wins the Quebec provincial elections and Lévesque becomes premier.

1977 The National Assembly passes Bill 101, designed to make French the language of business and social mobility in Quebec.

1980 Quebec holds its first referendum on giving the PQ government the authority to negotiate sovereignty-association with Canada. It is defeated when nearly two-thirds of Quebec's voters vote against it.

1981 The PQ is reelected to a second term.

1982 Prime Minister Pierre Trudeau negotiates the repatriation of the Canadian constitution without the support of Quebec's government.

1985 Lévesque retires and the PQ is defeated by the Parti Liberal du Québec (PLQ).

1987 The Meech Lake Accord is negotiated. Among other things, the accord recognizes Quebec as a "distinct society."

1990 Unable to receive ratification from all provinces, the Meech Lake Accord is defeated; in response, support for sovereignty among *Québécois* soars.

1992 A second attempt to negotiate a new constitutional agreement, the Charlottetown Accord, is brought before Canadians in a national referendum and is convincingly rejected.

1994 The PQ is returned to power with Jacques Parizeau, a committed sovereigntist, as the new premier.

1995 A second provincial referendum committing Quebec's government to negotiate Quebec's separation from Canada loses by a vote of 50.6 percent to 49.4 percent.

1996 Lucien Bouchard becomes PQ leader and premier.

1998 The PQ is reelected.

2001 Bouchard resigns and is replaced as PQ leader and Quebec Premier by Bernard Landry.

Although the origins of the conflict between French speakers, or Francophones, and English speakers, or Anglophones, in Canada date back to the seventeenth century, the patterns of this political conflict are constantly evolving. The area of North America that became known as Canada was first explored and settled by the French. With greater imperial might Great Britain defeated New France and took control of Canada. As British subjects, French

Canadians were treated reasonably well by colonial standards, but because they were a numerical minority with little economic leverage, they retained little political power of their own. When, in 1837, the Francophones rebelled, the British responded by encouraging both Canadian self-government and the dissolution of Francophone culture and identity in Anglophone Canada in order to alleviate "two nations warring in the bosom of a single state."[1]

In 1867 Canada received from the British Parliament the power to govern itself in a confederation of provinces. For several generations French-Canadian nationalism was embodied in the ideology of *la survivance*. This entailed a glorification of rural French-Canadian agrarian life, the conservative social dominance of a Catholic Church, and an attempt to maintain a social and economic isolationism from all things Anglophone, urban, and industrial. With the economic modernization of Quebec after World War II, the ideology of *la survivance* became unsustainable. Instead, during the Quiet Revolution of the early 1960s, when Quebec experienced a burst of social and cultural turbulence and political and institutional change, the French Canadians began to expand their political power by modernizing the provincial government of the only province in which they were a majority: Quebec. This became known as *rattrapage*, or catching up.

Mobilized by both the successes and failures of the Quiet Revolution, some *Québécois* demanded that they truly become *maîtres chez nous*, masters in our own house, through Quebec's independence. Although nationalism was channeled through the Parti Québécois (PQ) resulting in growing political, economic, and cultural power for the Québécois, the PQ has not yet succeeded in achieving its raison d'être, Quebec's independence. This growing power has weakened the nationalist argument that Quebec needs to be independent, while strengthening the belief that Quebec is strong enough to succeed as an independent state. The nationalist struggle continues not through the isolationist ideology of *la survivance,* nor the intense effort of *rattrapage,* but in the confidence that Quebec has the capacity to be a thriving, independent state.

HISTORICAL BACKGROUND

The origins of the present conflict in Quebec are rooted in the mercantilism, imperialism, and power politics of a bygone era. In 1534 Jacques Cartier was the first documented European to explore the region now known as Quebec for France. Although conditions were extremely harsh in New France, other explorers and settlers followed. In 1608 Samuel de Champlain established a trading post in what today is the capital of Quebec, Quebec City. The early French settlers made a living in fur trading. French Jesuit missionaries who arrived in New France established the Church institutions that would later structure Quebec's social life. In 1670 England granted a charter to Hudson's Bay Company that increased English settlement in New France. As Great Britain and France struggled for supremacy in Europe and throughout their empires, European conflicts spilled over into lands far from the European continent. In 1759 British troops fought and defeated the French settlers in New France at the Plains of Abraham in Quebec City. This battle, which finally wrested control of Canada from France, became etched in the collective memory of the defeated French Canadians.

Britain's colonial governance of French Canada was a mixture of tolerance, indifference, and imperialism. The Quebec Act of 1774 preserved French civil legal codes, the French-Canadian system of landholding, and the freedom of the Catholic Church. The Constitutional Act of 1791 divided Upper Canada (Ontario)

from Lower Canada (Quebec) and granted both elected assemblies. This show of tolerance was, in fact, a veneer for translating the Anglophone numerical majority and control over coercive force into English Canada's economic and political dominance over French Canada. After the *Patriotes* of Louis-Joseph Papineau were defeated in their rebellion for more political power for French Canadians in 1837, Lord Durham was appointed by the British government to investigate the causes of the rebellion and recommend long-term solutions to the problems of governance in Canada.

Durham recommended that internal self-government be coupled with efforts to Anglicize Quebec so as to remove the source of the conflict: French-Canadian identity and culture. The Act of Union of 1841 was designed to implement this policy by combining Ontario and Quebec into one unit so as to swamp the Francophones with a huge Anglophone majority. This continued until 1867 when the British Parliament passed the British North America Act giving the confederation of Canada effective self-governance if not de jure independence. Canada was divided into provinces, each with substantial powers within the confederation. French Canadians were scattered minorities in several provinces and a small but significant minority throughout Canada. Only in Quebec did they constitute a majority.

Although French Canadians occasionally rebelled against the dominance of English Canada, they by and large developed a cogent, if potentially self-destructive, mechanism for coping with their minority status. In the 1880s Louis Riel led two small rebellions, and French Canadians in Quebec resisted conscription in both world wars; however, these acts of resistance were the exception rather than the rule from the time of the British North America Act until the Quiet Revolution, which began in 1960. During this 93-year period, a

French-Canadian survival strategy evolved known appropriately as *la survivance*. *La survivance* rested on the almost mythological belief that the survival of French Canada depended on the preservation of its rural Catholic identity as a devout agrarian society made up of small family farms. This identity was perpetuated from the depression onward by the Catholic Church and the Quebec government of Maurice Duplessis. Duplessis believed that the preservation of faith, language, and race required minimal government intervention in social and economic affairs. The provincial government supported the social dominance of the Church. The Church operated the educational system and the limited social welfare system. The government of Quebec sold, at a discount, provincial mining permits and minerals to Anglophone companies to keep Francophones out of industry. It broke the backs of union members, both figuratively and literally, to keep Francophones from being exposed to progressive ideologies.

Duplessis considered himself a French-Canadian nationalist. This nationalism, however, did not involve support for an independent Quebec. Instead,

> he believed in the obligation to respect the terms of Confederation whereby the two founding nations should coexist peacefully and ensure the political stability of the country. This view rested in turn on the historical assumption that each partner had been given a vocation conforming to its aptitudes and interests. The English-speaking community occupied the domain of industry and finance and was said to be moved mainly by economic considerations. The French, on the other hand, would willingly remain a rural society steeped in religion and cultural pursuits.[2]

Before an independence movement could develop in Quebec, the *Québécois,*

the French Canadians of Quebec, had to throw off the political and ideological chains of Maurice Duplessis.

THE CONFLICT

The modern independence movement in Quebec grew out of the collapse of *la survivance* and the successes and failures of the Quiet Revolution of the early 1960s. *La survivance* collapsed because it no longer had any basis in reality. In 1941, 41 percent of Francophone *Québécois* lived on farms; in 1961, only 13 percent of Francophone *Québécois* lived on farms.[3] This and other social changes made this ideology appear increasingly anachronistic. Quebec was becoming urbanized and industrialized. Political elites began to realize that the Church could not provide adequate social welfare and educational programs for Quebeckers. Moreover, despite constituting 80 percent of the population of Quebec, Francophones were the poor neighbors of Quebec's Anglophones. In 1961 the per capita income of *Québécois* was \$3,185.[4] Non-Francophones earned \$4,605. These realities led to the defeat of Duplessis's Union Nationale and the victory of Jean Lesage and the Liberals who were committed to undertaking a Quiet Revolution in Quebec politics.

The Quiet Revolution transformed the provincial government into *the* progressive force in Quebec. The role of the Parti Liberal du Québec, or PLQ, government was to make the *Québécois* "masters in our own house." The government was committed to rationalizing and expanding its educational and social welfare responsibilities. It was also committed to developing Quebec's economy while opening up new occupational opportunities to the *Québécois.* For some nationalists, however, the Quiet Revolution did not go far enough. Only independence would eliminate the cultural division of labor, protect the French-Canadian language and identity, and give the *Québécois* the tools to manage their own destiny in their own house. This new *Québécois,* or Quebec-centered, nationalism, as opposed to the old survivalist French-Canadian nationalism, manifested itself through many different organizations in the late 1960s. Animated by a speech given by French President Charles de Gaulle in 1967, blessing "a free Quebec" with long life, political parties organized along with the Front de Libération du Québec (FLQ), modeled on Third World and black liberation movements. When, in 1970, the FLQ kidnapped and murdered the Quebec minister of labor, Pierre Laporte, provoking the Canadian government to institute the War Measures Act, curtail civil liberties, and bring armed troops to the streets of Quebec, support for violent nationalism quickly dissipated. Instead, nationalist activism was channeled through the newly created Parti Québécois (PQ). The story of Quebec nationalism since 1970 has been woven into the evolution of the PQ.

MANAGEMENT OF THE CONFLICT

The PQ, which quickly became the focus for the nationalist movement, was founded in 1968 by René Lévesque, a former television reporter and Lesage cabinet member. In its first few years, the PQ was a combative home for many different strands of the nationalist movement. As the PQ grew electorally in the early 1970s, Lévesque was able to direct and control the party together with his clique of technocratic advisors. Realizing that a majority of Quebeckers did not support outright separation from Canada, Lévesque coaxed the PQ into adopting an *etapiste,* or stepwise, approach toward sovereignty-association. The PQ promised that if elected it would not unilaterally declare independence but would provide good government in the hope of building support for sovereignty-association, independence with an economic union with Canada. If elected it promised it would first hold a referendum before proceeding with moves toward sovereignty-association. While the PQ remained an independence party, Lévesque sought to convince those skeptical about independence that a vote for the PQ would not set in motion the inevitable separation from Canada.

Etapisme worked. On November 15, 1976, the PQ, a party committed to the dissolution of Canada, was elected to govern Quebec. Lévesque became premier of Quebec and set out to introduce good government through moderate social reforms. The most important legislation of the PQ's first term was Bill 101. This legislation required that French be used for all communications involving provincial or local governments. The law also limited English-language instruction to schoolchildren whose parents or older siblings were educated in English in Quebec. External business advertising and shop floor communications had to be in French. Over the years this law has succeeded in making French, rather than English, the language of social and economic mobility in Quebec. But Lévesque's biggest challenge lay ahead.

On May 20, 1980, the government of Quebec held a referendum on the complicated question of whether the people of Quebec gave the provincial government a "mandate to negotiate" sovereignty-association with Canada. Despite the "softness" of the question, it was not a vote for immediate independence; the "no" side turned the vote into a stark choice between Quebec or Canada. In a memorable series of speeches, Canada's prime minister, Pierre Elliot Trudeau, a Quebecker with a Francophone father and Anglophone mother, argued that Canada would not negotiate with a Quebec that voted "yes" but would offer the province a new version of federalism if it voted "no." The "yes" side tried to reassure the *Québécois* that Quebec had as much right and ability to be a thriving independent state as other northern, resource-rich countries with small populations, such as Denmark, Norway, and Finland. The "no" side won convincingly with over 59 percent of the vote.

The defeat of the referendum deeply affected the PQ and Quebec. To win the 1981 provincial elections, the PQ had to commit itself to not holding another referendum in its second term. Even though the PQ was reelected, it was severely weakened. Trudeau saw in this an opportunity to fulfill a life's dream: the repatriation of the Canadian constitution from Great Britain and de jure independence for Canada. He hoped that now he could enshrine in the new constitution a strong Canadian federalism that would bind all the provinces, including Quebec, to an invigorated Canada. The negotiation for repatriation took place among Trudeau and the provincial premiers. Although initially Lévesque led a coalition of provincial premiers in demanding greater provincial powers in the new constitution, Trudeau was able artfully to break apart this coalition and convince the other premiers to sign on to a new constitution without the support of Quebec. Canada had a new constitution, and the British House of Commons rescinded their legal authority over Canada, but Quebec, feeling that certain provisions undermined its provincial authority, was not a signatory. Lévesque returned to Quebec dejected and embittered by what became known among Quebec nationalists as the "Night of the Long Knives." In 1985 Lévesque retired from politics and was replaced by a new leadership, which, despite further watering down the PQ's commitment to sovereignty, was defeated in the provincial elections.

In 1987 a new progressive conservative prime minister who was also a Quebecker, Brian Mulroney, decided to reinvigorate negotiations to bring Quebec into the Canadian constitution. Mulroney and the provincial premiers, including Quebec's Liberal premier, Robert Bourassa, negotiated the Meech Lake Accord, which, among other things, recognized Quebec as a "distinct society" within Canada. Although this was designed to ameliorate the concerns of Quebec nationalists by giving Quebec a unique status in Canada, the agreement was not ratified by the provinces of Newfoundland and Manitoba, which intensified the anger in Quebec and resulted in polls showing, for the first time, majority support for Quebec sovereignty.

Desperate to save Canada from collapse, Mulroney and the premiers met again in 1990 and negotiated the Charlottetown Accord, a second attempt at creating a constitution acceptable to Quebec. This time the agreement was submitted to a national referendum. The population of each province would have to vote in favor of the accord for it to be approved. Six provinces, including Quebec, voted against it.

The defeat of the Meech Lake and Charlottetown Accords transformed the nationalist movement in Quebec. The events of the early 1980s had made it a shadow of its former self, afraid to campaign for independence. Canada's "rejection" of Quebec in the late 1980s and early 1990s reinvigorated the movement. Leadership of the PQ passed to Jacques Parizeau, a former minister in Lévesque's governments and an outspoken *indépendantiste*. Moreover, a *Québécois* minister in Mulroney's cabinet, Lucien Bouchard, resigned from the federal Progressive Conservative Party to form and lead the Bloc Québécois (BQ), a party committed to Quebec's sovereignty that competed in federal elections. In a dramatic set of elections, the federal Liberals led by Jean Chrétien, a federalist *Québécois* and a former minister and close advisor to Trudeau, were elected to govern Canada in 1993. The BQ and Bouchard became the official opposition, and in 1994 the PQ and Parizeau were elected to govern Quebec. From the nationalist perspective, with Parizeau, committed to independence, in power in Quebec City, and Chrétien, the betrayer of Quebec, in power in Ottawa, the time was ripe for the PQ to hold another referendum on independence.

The referendum campaign of 1995 was a tense affair. This time the referendum was worded so as to give the provincial government the authority to negotiate sovereignty and a possible economic association with Canada as well as the authority to move toward a unilateral declaration of independence should those talks fail. Unable to inspire new support for independence, Parizeau relinquished the central campaign role to the more charismatic Bouchard. Since the 1970s the provincial government had extensively expanded its powers and had improved the relative conditions of the *Québécois* so the PQ found it difficult to campaign on the socioeconomic need for independence. Instead Bouchard focused on the political offences of Canada against Quebec through the 1980s and 1990s while arguing that Quebec had the capacity to be independent rather than the economic *need* to be independent. In an election night cliffhanger, with well over 90 percent of eligible voters going to the polls, and a majority of Francophones voting "yes," the

referendum was defeated 50.6 percent to 49.4 percent. In what some saw as a bitter speech on the night of the defeat, Parizeau blamed the results on "money and the ethnic vote." This allowed the opponents of sovereignty to paint the PQ and Parizeau as less the party of all Quebec than the party of Francophones. Parizeau resigned as PQ leader and was replaced by Bouchard.

Since 1998, when Bouchard and the PQ were reelected, both supporters and opponents of sovereignty have been jockeying for position. With support for sovereignty well below a majority in Quebec, Bouchard has committed to holding the next referendum when his side has "winning conditions." Federalists have now become resigned to the potential of a "neverendum referendum," continuous referenda until a majority votes for independence. Faced with this prospect, the federal government has tried to define under what conditions it would recognize the results in favor of sovereignty and would negotiate the dissolution of Canada. In response, Bouchard has tried to mobilize opposition within Quebec to this supposed infringement of Quebec's right to determine its own future in the hopes this might forge his "winning conditions." As of yet, this has not happened.

SIGNIFICANCE

For all its contentiousness, the struggle between Quebec and Canada has been a remarkably peaceful affair. In Northern Ireland, Catholics and Protestants, divided by religion alone, have fought a protracted low-intensity civil war. In Quebec the protagonists have been divided by religion and language. Although one might expect these more intense and potentially less reconcilable differences would serve as the fodder an of even more violent conflict, since 1970 the battle has been fought en-

QUEBEC, CANADA. Bilingual stop sign in French and English in Quebec. Corbis © 2002.

tirely with ballots rather than bullets. Why did this conflict result in bitter social divisions between the two populations, the creation of two solitudes, a cultural division of labor that guaranteed Anglophone dominance, national political domination by Anglophones, and a superiority complex that manifested itself in attempts at assimilation but did not take the form of repressive legislation, usurpation of property, or the denial of religious and political rights that could serve as the basis of sectarian political domination? There are two reasons why repressive political sectarianism did not develop in Canada. Anglophone Canada required the support of Francophone Canada in its struggle against the expansionist United States and its culture.[5] More important, the lack of a feudal past and the existence of an expanding frontier undermined the need for a repressive political structure. In Ireland, a primarily agricultural settlement, land was at a premium on a small island. In contrast, Canada was an agricultural and mercantile economy where a native population had been subdued and a huge landmass was available for exploitation by merchants and free farmers. Neither ethnic group needed to institutionalize repression in order to maintain their economic livelihood.

This tolerance, however, has had a paradoxical impact on nationalism in Quebec. Neither elite bargaining among Canada's prime ministers and the provincial premiers nor the votes of the citizens of Quebec have resolved the dispute over the political identities of Canada and Quebec. As the pot continues to simmer, however, the success of nationalist governments in expanding provincial powers has made an independent state more viable but in some ways less necessary. As one trenchant Canadian scholar and government official has incisively observed, the better conditions are for the *Québécois* the more they think they can be independent but the less they

feel they need it, but the worse things are the more they want to be independent and the less they think they can be independent.[6] In order to resolve this paradox, the PQ has evolved from a social democratic party to a more liberal free-market party that sees its independent economic future tied to its participation in the global international trading order defined by treaties such as the North American Free Trade Agreement (NAFTA). The PQ has argued this will allow Quebec to be a viable independent state regardless of its political relationship with Canada. This, of course, may be the ultimate irony. However stifling Quebec may feel the fairly benign stewardship of Anglophone Canada to have been, its influence would pale by comparison to the cultural and economic force the United States would likely exert on a small, independent, French-speaking enclave in North America.

See also Czechoslovakia: The Peaceful Breakup of a State; France: Ethnic Conflict and the Problem of Corsica; Spain: Basque Nationalism and Conflict in Democratic Spain; and United Kingdom: The Irish Question and the Partition of Ireland.

NOTES

1. Gerald M. Craig, ed., *Lord Durham's Report* (Toronto: McClelland and Stewart, 1963), 22–23.
2. Dominique Clift, *Quebec Nationalism in Crisis* (Kingston: McGill-Queen's University Press, 1982), 13.
3. Kenneth McRoberts and Dale Posgate, *Quebec: Social Change and Political Crisis*, 3d ed. (Toronto: McClelland and Stewart, 1988), 38–40.
4. In Canadian dollars. *Comité de documentation du Parti Québécois, La souveraineté et l'economie (Mars 1970)*, 22–23.
5. Katherine O'Sullivan, *First World Nationalisms: Class and Ethnic Politics in Northern Ireland and Quebec* (Chicago: University of Chicago Press, 1986), 58.
6. Stephane Dion, "Why Is Secession Difficult in Well-Established Democracies? Lessons from Quebec," *British Journal of Political Science* 26, no. 1 (April 1996): 269–83.

SUGGESTED READINGS

Cook, Ramsey. *Canada, Quebec and the Uses of Nationalism,* 2d ed. Toronto: McClelland and Stewart, 1995.

Dion, Stephane. "Why Is Secession Difficult in Well-Established Democracies? Lessons from Quebec." *British Journal of Political Science* 26, no. 1 (April 1996): 269–83.

Howe, Paul. "Rationality and Sovereignty Support in Quebec." *Canadian Journal of Political Science* 31, no. 1 (March 1998): 31–59.

Keating, Michael. "Stateless Nation-Building: Quebec, Catalonia and Scotland in the Changing State System." *Nations and Nationalism* 3, no. 4. (October 1997): 689–717.

Lévesque, René. *Memoirs.* Toronto: McClelland and Stewart, 1986.

McRoberts, Kenneth, and Dale Posgate. *Quebec: Social Change and Political Crisis,* 3d ed. Toronto: McClelland and Stewart, 1988.

McRoberts, Kenneth. *Misconceiving Canada: The Struggle for National Unity.* Toronto: Oxford University Press, 1997.

Meadwell, Hudson. "The Politics of Nationalism in Quebec." *World Politics* 45, no. 1 (January 1993): 203–41.

Pinard, Maurice. "The Dramatic Reemergence of the Quebec Independence Movement." *Journal of International Affairs* 45, no. 2 (Winter 1992): 471–97.

Pinard, Maurice, Robert Bernier, and Vincent Lemieux. *Un combat inachevé.* Sainte-Foy: Presses de l Université du Québec, 1997.

Young, Robert A. *The Struggle for Quebec: From Referendum to Referendum?* Montreal: McGill-Queen's University Press, 1999.

Central Europe

The Romany, a Stateless Minority in a World of States

Joseph R. Rudolph, Jr.

TIMELINE

c. 1300 Arrival of Roma in Europe.

14th c. Recorded arrival of Roma in Serbia, Croatia, Bulgaria, Greece, Romania, and Hungary.

1407 Romany first recorded in modern-day Germany.

1416 Romany expelled from Meissen region of Germany.

1418–1427 Romany recorded in modern France, Belgium, Holland, Italy, and Slovakia.

1449 Romany driven from Frankfurt, Germany.

1471 Anti-Gypsy laws are passed in Lucerne, Switzerland; 17,000 Romany are deported to Moldavia as slave labor.

1482–1492 First anti-Gypsy laws are enacted in Brandenburg (1482) and Spain (1492).

1493 Romany are expelled from Milan, Italy.

1504 Louis XII prohibits Roma from living in France.

1512 Romany are recorded in Sweden; Catalonia expels Roma.

1526 First anti-Gypsy laws are passed in Holland and Portugal.

1532 England introduces its first laws expelling Gypsies.

1540 Gypsies are allowed to live under own laws in Scotland.

1541 First anti-Gypsy laws are passed in Scotland; Romany, blamed for a rash of fires, are attacked in Prague, Czechoslovakia.

1549 First anti-Gypsy law is passed in Bohemia (Czech lands).

1568 The pope expels Romany from the domain of the Catholic Church.

1589 Denmark condemns to death any Romany not leaving country.

1619 Spain bans all *Gitanos,* as well as Gypsy dress, names, and languages under penalty of death.

1637 First anti-Gypsy laws are passed in Sweden; expulsion is ordered under penalty of death.

1650s Last known execution in England for being a Gypsy.

1666 Louis XIV, the Sun King, orders severe punishment for any "Bohemian" found in France.

1685 Portugal bans Romany language and deports Romany to Brazil.

1710 Prague orders hanging without trial of adult Romany men; women and boys are to be mutilated.

1721 Austro-Hungarian Empire orders extermination of Romany throughout its domain.

1733 Russia forbids Romany from settling as serfs on land.

1759 Romany banned from Saint Petersburg, Russia.

1761 Maria Theresa, empress of Hungary, makes first European attempt to settle and assimilate the Roma.

1773 Maria Theresa orders taking of Romany children over five years of age from parents for assignment to foster homes.

1776 Prince of Moldavia prohibits marriages to Romany.

1782 200 Romany charged with cannibalism in Hungary.

1800s Gypsy hunts become popular sport in Germany.

1803 Napoléon Bonaparte prohibits Romany from residing in France.

1830 Nordhausen, Germany, removes Romany children from families for rearing by non-Roma families.

1842 Moldavian Church liberates its Romany slaves.

1856 Abolition of Romany slavery (the *Slobuzenia*) in Europe.

1880s Argentina bars Romany from entering country.

1885 Romany excluded from entry into the United States.

1886 Otto von Bismarck encourages German states to deport non-German-born Romany.

1908 England requires public education of Gypsy children.

1914 Sweden prohibits further Romany immigration.

1919 Weimar Republic gives Romany full citizenship rights.

1921 Czechoslovakia recognizes Romany as separate "nationality"; legislation later repealed.

1924 Romany tried for cannibalism in Slovakia.

1926 Bavaria mandates registration of all Romany.

1927 Czechoslovakia prohibits Romany nomadism and permits taking Gypsy children from parents for foster care.

1928 Bavaria places Romany under permanent surveillance.

1931 Moscow Gypsy Theater opens (it still exists).

1933 In July, Adolf Hitler orders sterilization of Gypsies; citizenship of Gypsies and Eastern Jews revoked. In September, Law Against Habitual Criminals orders arrest of Romany.

1934 Sweden passes sterilization law to keep Swedish pure.

1934–1937 German Romany sent to processing camps; sterilization orders are gradually replaced by extermination orders.

1938 June 12–18: Roundup of Romany in Germany and Austria.

1941 Concentration camps opened in Poland, Croatia, Ukraine, and Serbia.

1944 On August 2, 4,000 Romany are gassed and cremated at Auschwitz in a single action.

1945 World War II ends.

1946–1990 Central European Communist regimes target Romany for assimilation.

1953 Roma are readmitted to Denmark.

1969 Segregated schools are established for Romany in Bulgaria.

1971 First World Romany Congress is held; delegates from 14 countries adopt the Romany flag and anthem.

1972 International Romany Union (IRU) affiliates with the Council of Europe; Czechoslovakia initiates sterilization program for Romany and bans Romany associations.

1975 Belgium permits Belgian-born Romany to naturalize.

1976 Indira Gandhi supports Romany demand to be recognized as a national minority of Indian origin.

1979 IRU given consultative status by UNESCO.

1981 Yugoslavia grants Romany national status on equal footing with other minorities.

1986 IRU becomes member of UN Children's Fund (UNICEF).

1990 IRU participates in European Conference on Security and Cooperation.

1991 Macedonia gives Romany equal rights.

1993 Macedonia introduces use of Romany languages in schools; Austria recognizes Roma as an ethnic group.

1994 England abolishes caravan (trailer) sites; 3,000 Roma are left without legal homes; numerous anti-Gypsy acts occur in the Czech Republic and Slovakia despite Romany's improved legal status.

1995 Union of Romany Political Parties is formed in Slovakia.

1996 European Roma Rights Center is established in Budapest; 5,000 Roma are evicted from their quarters in Istanbul, Turkey.

1997 Romany refugees from Slovakia arrive in England seeking asylum and meet with negative reaction.

1998 New Jersey rescinds the last anti-Roma law in the United States.

2001 Czech Roma establish patrols of Roma areas to protect themselves from attacks by Czechs.

2002 Dorking, England, district council distributes leaflets advertising forthcoming performance of Budapest's 100 Gypsies Ensemble as "the only time you want to see 100 Gypsies on your doorstep."

Discrimination against immigrants and other outsiders is neither uncommon nor new. The unfriendly, sometimes violent environment faced by North Africans, Turks, and immigrants from the "coloured commonwealth" in, respectively, contemporary France, Germany, and Britain echoes the hostility immigrants from Asia and Mexico faced in the United States at the turn of the twentieth century.[1]

In the short term, immigrant and other foreign groups have often found assistance in protecting their rights and lives in an unlikely quarter: their country of origin. Thus, one of the United States' oldest civil rights organizations, the Anti-Defamation League, owes its origin at least in part to the urging of the government of Italy, which was deeply concerned about the wave of lynchings aimed at Catholic Italian immigrants in the heavily Protestant South of post–Civil War America. Likewise, concern with the physical safety of Algerians working in post–World War II France prompted the government of Algeria in the early 1970s to halt the flow of Algerian workers into France. More recently, Budapest's concern over Slovakia's treatment of its large Hungarian minority prompted the Hungarian government to hold up Slovakia's application for membership in the Council of Europe during the middle 1990s until Slovakia's government agreed to respect the rights of those of Hungarian descent living in the Slovak Republic.

In the longer term, most immigrants, refugees, and other foreign groups historically have found relief from local persecution by assimilating, as much as possible, into the culture of their host country. Hence, most groups migrating from continental Europe to the United States before World War I embraced not just the language of the English who colonized the original thirteen colonies but their attire, style of living, and political creed. The integrative efforts of Russian immigrants in France after the 1917 fall of the czar offers a similar example of survival through assimilation.

What happens if the migrating group refuses to settle permanently, to divest itself of its distinct culture, or to assimilate even after centuries? What if it lacks an outside protector to champion its cause? An unpleasant answer to these questions can be found in the Romany's six-hundred-year history of enslavement, persecution, banishment, and even genocide in the Western world.

HISTORICAL BACKGROUND

The Romany people have been known by many names in the countries to and through which they have traveled, including the generic term Gypsy and such more specific references as *Gitanos, Sinti, Romanichal,* and "Egyptians." For a long time, there were nearly as many explanations of their origin as there were names attached to them. Relatively recent linguistic analyses, however, have produced a general consensus that the Roma, whose Indo-Aryan language is very close to the Sanskrit-based languages spoken in the Punjab and Gujarat areas of India, probably originated in ths northwestern area of the Indian subcontinent.

Beginning in the eleventh century, it appears, the spread of Islam into that region caused numerous local tribes to move north and westward ahead of the invading Muslim conquerors. Among those fleeing were various Romany groups, who by the early 1300s had reached the southeastern edge of Europe. A hundred years later, they had spread into Southern and Central Europe, and by 1427 their presence had been recorded in modern-day Serbia, Greece, Hungary, Germany, Slovakia, Italy, France, Belgium, and Holland. Shortly thereafter emerged the pattern of Romani arrival/local rejection, which has been their history ever since.

During the following centuries, the Roma have been most grievously treated in Germany—where Gypsy hunts were organized during the nineteenth century and the Romany Holocaust was carried out during Adolf Hitler's era—and most consistently discriminated against in the Czech and Slovak regions of Central Europe, which still constituted the epicenter of anti-Romany activity at the end of the twentieth century. At some time or another, the Roma have been enslaved, expelled, murdered, or otherwise discriminated against by virtually every state in Europe, including Switzerland, which in 1471 deported 17,000 Roma as slave labor to Moldavia; England, which passed its first expulsion laws in 1532; Scotland, which permitted Gypsies to reside under own their own law in Scotland in 1540 and then passed its first anti-Gypsy law the following year; the Vatican, which in 1568 ordered their expulsion from the entire domain of the Roman Catholic Church; Denmark, which in 1589 prescribed the death penalty for any Roma not leaving the country; Prague, which in 1710 ordered the hanging without trial of any adult Gypsy male found in its domain; and the Austro-Hungarian Empire, which in 1721 ordered the extermination of Roma throughout its realm. Nor did their lot improve greatly in the nineteenth and early twentieth centuries. As early as the 1830s Germany was removing children from their Romany families to be reared in non-Romany homes, and although Romany slavery was abolished in Europe in 1856 as late as 1924 Roma were being tried for cannibalism in Slovakia. In between, many states simply closed their borders to them, including Argentina (1880s), the United States (1885), and Sweden (1914).

Then came the rise of fascism and notions of racial purity in Europe. In Germany, the Roma were first required to register and later placed under constant surveillance (Bavaria, 1926–1928), then subjected to forced sterilization (all of Germany in 1933, but also in Sweden in 1934 in order to keep the Swedish race pure), then dispatched to work camps for processing (in Germany, 1934–1937), and finally targeted for extermination (in Germany, 1938; German-occupied Poland, Croatia, the Ukraine, and Serbia in 1941). The data are unreliable, but certainly by the time Germany was defeated and the Roma Holocaust ended in 1945, between 50,000 and 500,000 Roma had died,[2] and their Central European area of concentration was about to fall under the rule of Communist regimes controlled by the Soviet Union.

The Romany under Communist Rule

The descent of the Iron Curtain, which separated Communist Central Europe from Western Europe for two generations (ca. 1950–1990), had a profound if uneven impact on the lot of Central Europe's large (at least 6 million) Roma population.[3] In the economic sphere, communism guaranteed employment to all people and thereby opened some seams in the "invisible" curtain that had often made it difficult to impossible for Romani to obtain employment in the national job markets of Czechoslovakia, Hungary, Poland, and elsewhere in Central Europe. On the other hand, these Communist regimes also proscribed many of the market economy and shady but formerly legal occupations from which the Roma traditionally derived income, including fortune-telling, horse-trading, and merchandising used clothes.

The policies with the most significant impact on the Romani were those that affected their pattern of living, not their way of making a living. The closure of borders, including those between the Communist states themselves, halted the traditional, nomadic lifestyle of various Roma tribes and resulted in the buildup of a large, more or less permanent Gypsy population in the states of Central Europe. Meanwhile, inside their individual borders, the Communist regimes attempted to settle, educate, and otherwise assimilate the Roma into their societies. Of course, the Romani had historically been targeted for assimilation by numerous European governments, most notably by Empress Maria Theresa in the 1760s; however, never before had these efforts been pursued with the routes of escape so solidly sealed.

The policies, frequently harsh in nature and heavy handed in their execution, were usually enforced by locals who had no love for the Roma element. Thus, compulsory education was usually meted out in segregated schools, frequently with the Roma children consigned to remedial classes because of lack of fluency in the national languages. Romany associations were often banned, and Romany women were disproportionally targeted for sterilization, not by being forced into the programs but by being offered more incentives than were extended to nationals.

Less draconian were the housing and economic programs designed to integrate the Roma into society and the economy by placing them in normal occupations. Czechoslovakia's second policy of resettlement and integration, launched in 1958, provides a fairly typical example of the efforts made to mesh Roma integration policies with general policy needs. The nomadic lifestyle of the Roma was outlawed, and large numbers of Roma were relocated from the rural regions of Slovakia, which they favored, to the industrialized region of the Czech lands to help revive that area's economy by filling, with low-cost Roma labor, the jobs vacated by the Germans who had long lived in the area but who were summarily expelled after World War II. One spinoff of this policy was a significant growth in the number of (largely self-segregated) Roma enclaves in Central European cities and towns. Another was the significant degree to which the Communist effort to integrate socially (schools) and economically (jobs) the Roma into the host population repeatedly raised tensions between the Roma and the local populations. Invariably the locals felt that the Roma were getting preferential treatment in their governments' housing and employment policies.

With the fall of communism, the limited protection that the Romany had enjoyed vanished, and the resentment against them boiled into the open throughout much of Central Europe, whose citizens continued to view the Romany with a mixture of open hostility and lingering prejudices.[4]

THE CONFLICT

At its core, the conflict is uncomplicated but virtually irreconcilable. The Roma want to be allowed to live their lifestyle and stay or travel without restriction; the host population, more often than not, wants them to leave. Failing that, the host populations generally want to regulate their existence (sometimes in order to harass them into departing) and, more rarely, to integrate them into their populations in order to control them. At the root of these opposing positions lie two equally simple points of view. The Roma want to preserve their ancient way of life, and they have historical reasons not to trust their hosts; the indigenous populations have deep-seated prejudices against the Roma and—when pushed into a corner to defend these prejudices—can cite recent, objective data to support their point of view.

Even without these prejudices bedeviling them, it would be difficult for the Romany to achieve their basic objective—the status of a legally protected ethnic minority in the countries where they live—or their more pedestrian goals, such as access to better housing and employment and the right to home school their children. Few in number, disenfranchised as noncitizens in many states, and fragmented among dozens of different tribes, even on a level playing field the Roma would have difficulty amassing the political clout necessary to be politically effective. Their nomadic lifestyle and other manifestations of otherness daily feed the biased prisms through which they are viewed, and make it difficult for them to alter the hostility with which they are so frequently greeted. Their unwillingness to assimilate and their disproportionate contribution to crime in the areas they frequent exacerbate the situation.

The crime issue is a particularly sensitive one, dovetailing as it does with the issue of the high unemployment rate among the Roma in post–Communist Europe. The staggeringly high unemployment rate of from 60 to 70 percent throughout the region, according to the Roma, is the result of discrimination. In contrast, local populations argue that these rates merely reflect the disinterest of the Roma in legitimate employment. To support this view they note that, although only 10 percent of Hungary's population, the Roma accounted for over half of all the crime in that country during the last decade. Similar figures exist for other Central European states; however, sociologists are more inclined to explain the disproportionately high level of (generally nonviolent) crime committed by Roma in terms of their low level of education, high unemployment, and poor living conditions than to the innate dishonesty that Central Europeans ascribe to the Roma.

MANAGEMENT OF
THE CONFLICT

Efforts to manage the conflict between the Romany on the one hand and the peoples and governments of the states in which they live on the other were proceeding during the twentieth century's final days in two quite different directions involving three sets of actors.

First, there are the policies of the governments in those states housing significant numbers of Romany. Their approach has very often been in the traditional mode of managing the "Roma problem" by controlling or expelling their Roma people. To be sure, there are no current policies even remotely akin to the excessive devices historically aimed at Europe's Roma population. On the other hand, because the Roma Holocaust never received the same publicity as Hitler's final solution to Germany's "Jewish problem," it has been easier for

European democracies to discriminate against their Roma peoples in ways which would be politically unthinkable if aimed at members of the Jewish community. Thus, even the carefully watched democratizing states in post-Communist Europe have enacted policies openly prejudicial to Romany interests. In 1994, for example, Britain summarily abolished its Caravan Sites Act, leaving nearly 5,000 mostly Roma families homeless. Moreover, by the mid-1990s, Britain, Belgium, and other Western states were reexamining their asylum policies to the disadvantage of the Roma on the grounds that the recent movement of large numbers of Roma into their states reflected more the Romany desire to obtain the generous welfare benefits available to them while their asylum applications were being processed than flight from actual persecution in post-Communist Central Europe.

Second, the 1990s witnessed numerous self-help efforts made by the Roma to increase their political clout both in the states of their residence and at the European level. Typical of their action at the state level were their efforts to group fragmented Romany organizations under a single umbrella organization in each Central European country—for example, the 1995 formation of the Union of Romany Political Parties in Slovakia. At the same time, the Roma were equally active at the international level seeking to publicize their cause and enlist international support for their objectives. The International Romany Union (IRU), for example, the most influential of Europe's Romany organizations, essentially achieved consultation status in the European Conference on Security and Cooperation in 1990 and in 1996 participated in the birth of its own watch-dog and publicity arm, the Budapest-based European Roma Rights Center.

Finally, in a different domain, discrimination against the Romany has been has been mitigated by (1) the gradual emergence of an internationally recognized, albeit implicit taboo against such action, (2) precedents granting the Romany equality in areas that once discriminated against them, and (3) the monitoring and lobbying efforts of a growing number of international agencies concerned with the behavior of European governments toward their Roma minorities. Beginning in 1976, for example, the prime minister of India, Indira Gandhi, pledged her country's support for the Roma demand that the Romany be officially recognized in their countries of residence as a national minority of Indian origin. Fifteen years later, one of the first acts of Yugoslavia's breakaway Republic of Macedonia was to give its Roma rights equal to those of its Macedonian and Albanian citizens. Elsewhere, in 1998, New Jersey became the last state in the United States to purge its statutes of anti-Gypsy laws, and even in Hungary, the late 1990s found the Ministry of Education contemplating the withdrawal of textbooks containing racist descriptions of Hungary's Roma peoples.[5]

This incremental effort toward getting the Roma accepted as a recognized ethnic minority throughout the developed democratic and democratizing world has received significant boosts from several international organizations. The United Nations Committee on the Elimination of Racial Discrimination, for example, in 2000 issued a stinging indictment of the continuing persecution of and "reprisal attacks on" Roma in Kosovo and other conflict-torn areas of Central and Eastern Europe. Meanwhile, in Central Europe, the Organization for Security and Cooperation in Europe (OSCE), which has overseen many elections in post–Communist Europe (including Bosnia, Kosovo, and Bulgaria), has made serious efforts to register and turn out the vote of the Romany electorate. The most persistent efforts, however, have probably been those of the Council of Europe, which maintains active

MONTENEGRO. A much needed food shipment arrives at a Kosovo Romany refugee camp outside Podgorica, Montenegro, November 2001. Photo courtesy of the author.

programs in three areas of top priority to Europe's Roma: protecting minorities, combating racial intolerance, and fighting against policies of social exclusion in Europe.

Still, old outlooks and behavioral patterns persist throughout Europe. Policies of intolerance toward the Roma are still easy to find, especially in Southern Europe and post–Communist Central Europe. Thus, in Istanbul, 5,000 Roma were evicted from their quarters the same year that the European Roma Human Rights Center was established in Budapest. Similarly, in Serbia, the Roma displaced by 1998–1999 conflict in Kosovo remain without welcome or even clear legal status. In Slovakia, in September 2000, an upsurge in attacks on the Roma drove several Romany to seek asylum at the U.S. embassy in Bratislava.

SIGNIFICANCE

Case studies sometimes reveal the worst in human nature and experience. The implements of conflict—knives, clubs, pointed blades, and projectile instruments—are universally among the anthropological artifacts of humanity. In a like manner ethnicity has proven to be equally durable as a basis for association and discrimination over time and space. Furthermore, very often—as the history of the Roma attests—minorities receive their worst treatment at the hands of those who have themselves been the object of discriminatory rule. Abuse continued to be the lot of the Roma throughout the twentieth century, although in a far gentler form as the twenty-first century dawned. And nowhere were the Roma more ill-treated than in Slovakia, whose majority had hardly achieved self-rule after generations of oppression by the Hungarians before World War I and seventy-five years of standing in the shadow of the more numerous Czechs in Czechoslovakia before taking prejudicial action against Slovakia's Hungarian and Roma minorities.

The better news is that both the human condition and our concepts of acceptable levels of civility do evolve. Many countries as well as numerous American states now view capital punishment as a cruel and unusual act. The treatment of Native Americans has become a source of shame in American history. Numerous countries during the 1990s apologized to and compensated ethnic communities previously abused by them. The gains achieved by the Roma in the waning years of the twentieth century may fit into this pattern. If so, the twenty-first century may witness substantial progress on the part of the Roma in achieving official recognition and equality in Europe. For all their internal fragmentation, they are, after all, the only truly transnational ethnic group in a uniting Europe committed to becoming a democratic Europe without borders.

See also France: The "Foreigner" Issue; Germany: The Foreign Worker Issue; United Kingdom: The Making of British Race Relations; and United States: The Struggle for Survival and Equality of the First Americans

NOTES

1. The "Yellow Peril" campaign conducted against Japanese immigrants in the United States, for example, began in 1899—only one year after the United States Supreme Court found it necessary to affirm the citizenship of U.S.-born Chinese.

2. Roma estimates of the number of Romany Holocaust victims run as high as 1.5 million.
3. The number of Roma in Central Europe can only be estimated. Central European states have historically undercounted their Roma population, especially during the Communist era when efforts were being made to assimilate the officially "small" Romani element. Conversely, Roma spokesmen have tended to exaggerate their numbers. The best estimates currently are that there are from 12 to 15 million Roma worldwide, and that nearly half live in Central Europe, with the largest concentrations in Romania (2–3 million in a country of 20 million when communism fell), and prepartition Czechoslovakia, pre–civil war Yugoslavia, Hungary, and Bulgaria (600,000–800,000 each).
4. Many of the names by which the Roma have become known in Europe, especially *Tshingani* and *Cziganye,* are derived from the Byzantine word *atsinganoi,* which means "untouchable" in the sense of being beyond the influence of those around them. Tracy Brand, "Eastern Europe's Gypsy Minority" (master's thesis, Johns Hopkins University (1996), 18.
5. One book, for example, claimed that many Gypsies "were unable to and did not even want to adapt to a civilized European way of life" and that "the life of Romany is marked by crime." Cited in *Budapest Sun,* September 6, 2000, p. 3.

SUGGESTED READINGS

Crowe, David M. *A History of the Gypsies of Eastern Europe and Russia.* New York: St. Martin's Griffin, 1996.

Fings, Karola. *The Gypsies During the Second World War.* Hatfield, United Kingdom: Gypsie Research Centre, University of Hertfordshire Press, 1997.

Puxon, Grattan. *Roma, Europe's Gypsies.* London: Minority Rights Group, 1987.

Ringold, Dena. *Roma and the Transition in Central and Eastern Europe: Trends and Challenges.* Washington, D.C.: World Bank, 2000.

Tong, Diane, ed. *Gypsies: An Interdisciplinary Reader.* New York: Garland, 1998.

China

Ethnic Conflict in the World's Largest Multinational State

Katherine Palmer Kaup

TIMELINE

211 B.C. China is unified for the first time in history.

1279–1368 The (Mongol) Yuan Dynasty rules.

1368–1644 The (Han) Ming Dynasty rules.

1644–1911 The (Manchu) Qing Dynasty rules.

1884 Xinjiang is incorporated as a Chinese province.

1904 The Anglo-Tibetan Treaty grants British trade concessions in Tibet.

1911 The dynastic order ends.

1912 The Dalai Lama declares Tibetan independence.

1914 Tibet, Great Britain, and China attend the Simla Convention.

1910–1949 The Republican Era, Nationalist (KMT) rule.

1933 The East Turkestan Republic is established.

1935 The fourteenth Dalai Lama is born.

1944–1949 The second Eastern Turkestan Republic is established.

1947 The Inner Mongolia Autonomous Region is established.

1949 Mao Zedong proclaims the establishment of the People's Republic of China.

1950 The Communist Party's People's Liberation Army declares the "liberation of Tibet."

1951 Tibetan delegation signs the 17-Point Agreement.

1956 Popular uprising occurs in Tibet.

1959 Major rebellion against Chinese occurs in Tibet. The Dalai Lama flees Tibet for India with more than 50,000 followers.

1966–1976 The Cultural Revolution: China's "Ten Lost Years."

1976 Mao Zedong dies.

1978 Deng Xiaoping becomes China's paramount leader.

1979 Deng Xiaoping launches new economic and political reforms.

1981 The Communist Party announces new development program in Inner Mongolia.

1987 The Dalai Lama internationalizes the campaign to free Tibet.

1988 The Dalai Lama revokes call for independence with the Strasbourg Proposal.

1989 Riots erupt in Tibet: martial law is declared.

1990 The Baren uprising results in martial law.

1991 The Union of Soviet Socialist Republics (Soviet Union) is dissolved.

1997 The Yining uprising occurs; several arrests follow.

1999 China, Russia, Kazakhstan, Tajikistan, and Kyrgyzstan sign agreement to fight Islamic insurgency.

2000–2001 China wins 2008 Summer Olympics bid.

Scholars often refer to China as an "ethnic mosaic," and the preamble of the People's Republic of China's constitution declares the country a "multinational unitary state." The Chinese Communist Party officially recognizes 56 different nationalities, although the state's efforts to classify and label the hundreds of smaller ethnic groups into neat categories belies the extremely complex ethnic makeup of China's population. The minorities are diverse, speaking nearly one hundred separate languages that belong to at least five independent language families. Different minority groups adhere to all of the world's major religions; some practice religions unique to their own ethnic group.

The majority population, the Han, account for nearly 92 percent of the country's total population. Securing amiable relations among China's numerous ethnic groups has played a far more important role to successful state rule than the minorities' mere numbers would suggest. Minority communities are spread across roughly 65 percent of China's total landmass, 20 percent of the nation's arable land, 90 percent of the grasslands plains, and 40 percent of the national forests. Over 90 percent of China's international borders fall within minority territory, and these borders arbitrarily divide more than 30 Chinese nationalities from their counterparts in adjacent states. While some of the minority groups have historically cooperated with the Han and have adopted many of their customs, others have long traditions of open conflict and warfare with the Han majority. The history of ethnic conflict since the fall of the dynastic order in 1911 has primarily been between the Han and the Tibetans, Uygurs, and Mongols.

HISTORICAL BACKGROUND

The Ethnic Context Prior to Communist Rule

Prior to the twentieth century, no Chinese government had successfully integrated the hundreds of ethnic groups living within its imperial administrative domain. The history of pre-twentieth-century China is riddled with bloody conflicts between various minority groups and the majority Han population; the best-known and largest resulted in the rule of the Mongols over the entire country from 1279 to 1367 and of the Manchus from 1644 to 1911. To prevent open conflict between the imperial authorities and the various ethnic groups, the Chinese leadership allowed minorities to govern themselves in exchange for nominal tutelage to the emperor.

The Republican government that came to power in 1911 abolished the office of the emperor after more than 2,000 years. The new Nationalist, or KMT, government recognized only five nationalities (Han, Manchu, Mongol, Tibetan, and Turkic Muslim) and generally practiced a policy of forced assimilation. In fact, KMT leader Sun Yat-sen once proclaimed, "We must facilitate the *dying out* of all names of individual peoples inhabiting China, i.e., Manchus, Tibetans, etc. . . . we must satisfy the demands of all races and unite them in a single cultural and political whole."[1]

The Ethnic Context under CCP Rule

The Chinese Communist Party (CCP) radically restructured relations between the minorities and the ruling party. Bent on fully integrating the diverse groups into a unified state for the first time, the CCP ironically implemented a policy of regional autonomy for the minorities and promised to protect their unique cultures, languages, religions, and right to self-rule. The CCP's Regional Autonomy Policy grants the minorities a number of special economic, political, and social privileges. Economically, the minorities receive greater control over local budgets than Han areas, preferential tax terms, scholarships and loans restricted from the Han, and extra investment funds for capital development. Politically, the CCP grants the minorities proportional representation on legislative bodies, limits the lead state political post in minority areas to a member of the titular group, and allows minority areas to adjust central directives to "suit local minority traditions." Socially, the CCP's accommodative policies officially encourage the minorities to develop their own languages and promote their own cultural and religious practices.

The CCP's minority policy was formulated in keeping with the Marxist contention that nationality is a reflection of class relations and will die out as communism takes root. The CCP believed that its policy would both satisfy the nationalities' demands for unique recognition, and ultimately make these pressures obsolete. Unfortunately, in Tibet, the northwestern region of Xinjiang, and Inner Mongolia, CCP policy not only failed to obviate demands for independence from the local nationalities, but also led to increased tensions between the Han and their ethnic charges. Many among these ethnic groups are demanding outright independence; nearly all are demanding at least increased government economic assistance and greater autonomy.[2] Despite official pledges to reduce economic inequality, economic reforms since 1979 have significantly exacerbated the economic disparity between the minorities and the Han, radicalizing ethnic demands on the state. The difference between Han and non-Han areas' agricultural and industrial per capita production more than tripled in the first decade of the reforms alone.[3] Although the nationalities constitute only 8 percent of China's total population, over half of the counties below the abject poverty line are minority areas.

THE CONFLICT

The "Liberation" of Tibet

On October 7, 1950, almost a year to the day after seizing control of China, the Chinese Communist Party's People's Liberation Army (PLA) began its assault on Tibet. The PLA declared that it was liberating the Tibetan people from the "feudal oppression" raging throughout Tibet and assured the Tibetan people that only through joining the Communist movement could their rights and culture truly be protected. The Tibetans, for their part, claimed that the Chinese forces were invading the independent nation of Tibet and appealed to the United Nations for assistance.

The legal status of Tibet on the eve of the Communist takeover is contentiously debated and rarely presented objectively by either side. Whether or not Tibet was an independent state at the time of the PLA penetration, however, largely determines whether the Chinese Communist Party has the right to govern Tibet. The CCP itself condemns the use of force in acquiring territory and bases its claim to rule on the pre-1950 status of Tibet as a province of China, not on its military acquisition of Tibet in 1950. International jurists, scholars, and politicians all can present compelling arguments both to support and refute Tibet's legal claims to independent statehood. What is not debated, even among Chinese officials, is that often extreme counter-insurgency measures have been taken against the Tibetans, including— according to groups such as Amnesty International—"cruel and degrading treatment of children" and the torture of both adults and children to extract confessions.[4]

The Chinese government claims that Tibet was formally incorporated into the Chinese state during the Yuan Dynasty (1279–1367). The Yuan Dynasty was established by Mongol ruler Kublai Khan, who asserted his control over the majority Han population and the smaller nationalities within the territory now known as China and stretched his Mongol Empire as far west as the gates of Vienna. The Chinese government argues that the Mongol incorporation of Tibet into Chinese territory was formalized through inter alia the Yuan demarcation of Tibetan administrative boundaries, the appointment of local officials, the collection of taxes, and the imperial preceptor system in which a Tibetan religious leader served as a direct spiritual advisor to the Mongol supreme leader. Chinese control continued, according to the official Chinese stance, throughout the Ming Dynasty (1368–1644) and strengthened significantly under the Qing Dynasty (1644–1911), another non-Han dynasty controlled by the Manchus. China contends that the British government forced the Chinese into an unequal treaty in 1904 that relinquished Chinese "rightful control" over Tibet. When the Tibetan spiritual and secular leader, the Dalai Lama, declared Tibet independent in 1912, he violated international law, according to the Chinese. Tibet's declaration of independence cannot, therefore, be used to justify contemporary Tibetan claims to independence.

The Tibetan government in exile, however, claims that Tibet has been an independent nation for over 2,000 years, although it experienced brief periods of foreign influence in the thirteenth and eighteenth centuries when the Mongol Empire and the Manchu Qing Dynasty forced its will on Tibet. According to many Tibetans, the Mongol Empire was a world empire, and whatever ties Tibet had with the Mongol leadership ended with the fall of the empire and the reestablishment of the Han leadership under the Ming Dynasty. Practically no relationship was maintained with the Ming Dynasty, and the Qing dynasty was again a non-Chinese empire and ties with it cannot be used to justify the current Han Chinese government's claims to rule. Furthermore, the Tibetans argue, virtually throughout Tibet maintained all of the qualifications for statehood required by international law, including a stable population, territory, independent government, and the ability to engage in diplomatic relations with international players. Treaties concluded between an independent Tibet and Great Britain in 1904 and at the Simla Convention in 1914, as well as treaties reached between Tibet and the neighboring countries of Nepal and Bhutan, all show evidence of Tibet's independent status and ability to engage in diplomatic relations without the involvement of the Chinese.

Nearly all of the Tibetan population adheres to a unique form of Buddhism, which blends the monastic discipline of early Theravada Buddhism with some shamanistic features of the indigenous Tibetan religion known as Bon. The Dalai Lama is the spiritual head of the Tibetan community and the secular leader of the Tibetan government in exile. Although the CCP formally acknowledges the Tibetans' right to practice their religion, the party's official orthodoxy still follows the Marxist view that religion is a false ideology, an "opiate of the masses." The appeal and power of the Dalai Lama fundamentally

TIBET. Young Tibetan Buddhist monks. Corbis © 2002.

contrasts with the party's self-depiction as the sole representative of the masses. The CCP also demands that all citizens within the People's Republic of China accept the sole authority of the Chinese Communist Party and unitary rule of the multinational state. Managing some type of reconciliation between these two radically opposed worldviews, then, has been anything but smooth.

The Xinjiang Uygur Autonomous Region

China's northwest province of Xinjiang is home to more than 8 million Turkic-Muslims, many of whom have been struggling for independence from the linguistically, ethnically, and culturally distinct Han for decades. Like the Tibetans, the Uygurs, and several of the other Turkic nationalities in Xinjiang, are deeply committed to their religion. Maintaining control over this region has been much more important to the CCP than in Tibet because Xinjiang is China's largest province, contains a wealth of natural resources (including oil and coal reserves estimated at more than three times that in the entire United States), and borders several Islamic states dominated by ethnic groups also found in Xinjiang.

Although the region has been of crucial importance to the Chinese for centuries as a crossing point for caravans shipping goods between China and the Middle East, Xinjiang was not formally incorporated into China as a province until 1884. The local population frequently asserted its independence from the Chinese over the next several decades, establishing an independent East Turkestan Republic in 1933, which lasted only briefly, and again in 1944. The second republic was dismantled in 1949 when the PLA took control of Xinjiang. In September 1955 the area was renamed the Xinjiang Uygur Autonomous Region. Hundreds of thousands of Han Chinese migrated to the region with the CCP-created Xinjiang Production and Construction Corps, and by 1997 Han Chinese made up 38 percent of Xinjiang's population compared to the 6 percent they constituted in 1950. As in Tibet, the region's religion was attacked violently during the chaotic Cultural Revolution from 1966 to 1976. Muslim clerics were forced to raise pigs and often were paraded through the streets with pig heads strapped around their necks.

Although tensions eased for a while during the 1980s after the loosening of controls by the new Chinese leader, Deng Xiaoping, the breakup of the Soviet Union in 1991 gave Uygur nationalists cause to hope that China might similarly collapse along ethnic lines. Turkic separatists also hoped for support from the new Central Asian states, many of which bore the names of the nationalities living within Xinjiang, including Uzbekistan, Turkmenistan, Kyrgyzstan, and Kazakhstan. Incidents of violent demonstrations in Xinjiang and outside of it by separatists increased exponentially in the 1990s, causing the governor of Xinjiang to estimate them in the thousands. In 1997 a major anti-Han riot erupted in Yining, Xinjiang, leaving nine dead and more than 200 wounded. The Han crackdown following the Yining uprising was swift and forceful: Amnesty International reported that 210 Uygur were sentenced to death between January 1997 and April 1999.[5]

The Inner Mongolia Autonomous Region

Relations between the Han Chinese and the non-Han nomads to the north have historically been strained. Repelling northern invasion inspired the first emperor of China to begin construction of the Great Wall over 2,000 years ago. The Mongol Empire reached its height in the thirteenth century, and China fell under the control of the Mongol Yuan Dynasty from 1279 to 1367. Periodic fighting erupted between the Mongols and the Han-ruled Ming Dynasty (1368–1643), though the Manchu-dominated Qing Dynasty (1644–1911) was able to control the Mongol territories loosely.

Mongol separatists assert that ties with China were severed with the fall of the Manchu dynasty in 1911. The northern regions of Mongolia declared their independence in 1921, and the Mongolian People's Republic was established with the support of the Soviet Union in 1924. Southern Mongolia, now called Inner Mongolia, fell under the control of the Chinese. The KMT leadership sought to divide the area and restricted autonomous power. The Chinese Communist Party exploited the Mongol resentment of KMT policy, promising the Mongols true autonomy and establishing the Inner Mongolia Autonomous Region in 1947.

Inner Mongolia enjoyed relative autonomy and a high level of state development assistance until the Cultural Revolution (1966 to 1976). Mongol customs were then attacked, and the autonomous privileges were rescinded during the Ten Lost Years. Subsequently, Deng Xiaoping offered to compensate some of the Mongol families who had been wrongly attacked during the Cultural Revolution; however, when the CCP announced a new development program for the region in 1981, including the transport of a large contingent of trained Han developers, Mongol students took to the streets in protest. The CCP reacted quickly, and several accused separatists were arrested. Another large-scale independence movement erupted in 1990, again resulting in several arrests and reportedly 200 deaths.

MANAGEMENT OF THE CONFLICT

Managing the Tibetan Conflict

When the PLA began invading Tibet, it claimed to be overthrowing centuries of feudalist oppression of the Tibetan masses. The Chinese forces easily vanquished the ill-equipped Tibetan army and, in May 1951, forced a Tibetan delegation in Beijing to sign the 17-Point Agreement for the Peaceful Liberation of Tibet. The 17-point agreement recognized Chinese sovereignty over Tibet while purportedly giving the Dalai Lama's government the right to administer Tibet. It promised religious freedom throughout the territory. As reports of Chinese discriminatory policies toward Tibetans and the suppression of the Tibetan religion began circulating throughout Tibet in the years following the 17-point agreement, however, Tibetans took up arms against the Chinese in a major uprising in 1956 and in another larger-scale revolt in 1959. The Dalai Lama fled Tibet for neighboring India in 1959 with an entourage of more than 50,000. During the Cultural Revolution, the Chinese tightened their control throughout Tibet and waged a mass campaign to root out Tibetan religion and culture.

Tensions between the Tibetans and Han eased somewhat after Deng Xiaoping took control of China in 1978. Deng allowed a Tibetan delegation from outside of China to tour the Autonomous Region in 1979 and, to the chagrin of the CCP, Tibetans flocked by the tens of thousands to greet the delegates and express concern for the Dalai Lama. Although officially refusing to negotiate, the Chinese government and the Dalai Lama met secretly twice in the early 1980s, once in 1982 and again in 1984. The Tibetan government in exile demanded not only the right for true political autonomy within Tibet, but for the creation of Greater Tibet, including large portions of Sichuan, Qinghai, and Yunnan provinces.

In 1987 the Dalai Lama decided to internationalize the campaign to free Tibet and began meeting with top officials and policy makers throughout the world. At a meeting before the European Parliament in Strasbourg in 1988, he abandoned his demands for full independence and agreed to allow CCP control over Tibet's external affairs in exchange for allowing true autonomy within Tibet, including the right to have a Tibetan-led constitutional democracy with open, competitive elections. As more foreign governments seemed interested in the Tibetan cause and with the move toward negotiations between the Dalai Lama and the Chinese, many Tibetans within Tibet felt inspired to demonstrate their desire for greater control from the Han Chinese. Several riots erupted in Lhasa and, after the fourth major incident, Beijing declared martial law in April 1989.

As the twenty-first century dawned, the Dalai Lama continued to assert that Tibetans would be willing to accept Chinese sovereignty were Tibetans given true autonomy, including the right to hold competitive elections and establish the rule of law. This demand, however, is not tenable to the Chinese regime, which contends that the CCP must be the guiding party throughout the country and that all regional governments must rule in accordance with Beijing's unitary state policies. Analysts disagree on which side time favors. Beijing may be biding its time until the popular 67-year-old fourteenth Dalai Lama passes away. As Beijing seeks to enter the global community, however, it may be faced with increasing pressure to ease its grip on Tibet.

The Xinjiang Uygur and the Inner Mongolia Autonomous Regions

Neither Xinjiang nor Inner Mongolia has received the type of international exposure or support received by the Tibetan independence movement. Uygur hopes for assistance from the newly independent Central Asian countries seemed dashed when China, Russia, Kazakhstan, Tajikistan, and Kyrgyzstan signed an agreement in August 1999 to fight Islamic insurgency. The Chinese Communist Party is banking on the fact that economic development will increase the commitment of the national minorities to the People's Republic of China and their inclusion therein. Massive amounts of investment capital have been shipped into the areas, though Uygur and Mongol advocates claim that nearly all of the investment favors either the Chinese state or the Han immigrants to the area. The Xinjiang Production and Construction Corps, which has an annual revenue of U.S. $2.05 billion, runs nearly all aspects of the region's industrial and commercial development, yet over 97 percent of the Corps' 2.4 million employees are Han Chinese. Unemployment rates among the minority nationalities are radically higher than those of the Han.[6]

During the last two or three years of the twentieth century, the Chinese press began attacking "separatists and splittists" with new vigor and frequency. Current policy is to integrate the regions with the rest of the country economically, praise China's cultural diversity, and to repress any calls for independence with whatever means necessary. For their part, the Uygur and Mongol separatist groups are seeking to increase both Chinese popular domestic and international awareness of the ethnic demands and to "struggle to expose China's criminal communist-colonial policy."[7]

SIGNIFICANCE

Finding an acceptable solution to the Tibetan, Uygur, and Mongol challenges is one of the more vexing problems facing the Chinese regime today. Although these territories cover vast areas and are home to rich natural resources, their significance is heightened as the Chinese Communist Party seeks to maintain its legitimacy as the sole representative of the broad Chinese masses. China must also prove that it can provide true autonomy to its contingent parts if it hopes ever to lure Taiwan into reuniting with the motherland. It may prove more difficult to integrate these areas fully over the next decade, as the central Beijing government is likely to funnel vast resources into Beijing and coastal-city development in preparation for the 2008 Olympics, leaving the more remote western regions relatively disadvantaged.

See also Burma: The Karen Conflict; India: Ethnic Conflict and Nation-building in a Multiethnic State; and Western Sahara: Ethnic Conflict and the Twentieth Century's Last Colonial War.

NOTES

1. Sun Yat-sen, *Memoirs of a Chinese Revolutionary* (Taipei: China Cultural Service, 1953), 180.
2. Katherine P. Kaup, *Creating the Zhuang: Ethnic Politics in China* (Boulder, Colo.: Lynne Rienner Publishers, 2000), chaps 1 and 7.
3. Ibid., 10.
4. "China Accused of Horrors in Tibet," Associated Press dispatch filed on an Amnesty Interna-

tional report released on May 30, 1995, available online at http://www. christusrex. org/www1/sdc/ tibet/html.
5. Amnesty International also reported 190 executions of Uygurs (alternate spelling, Uyghurs) in the territory during the same period. Other monitoring organizations have released comparable figures. See "Chinese Government Executed at least 114 Uyghurs, Sentenced to Death Another 3 in Two Years," at http://www. uyghuramerican. org/HumanRights/executions. html.
6. Naer Hasan, "China's Forgotten Dissenters," *Harvard International Review* 22, no. 3 (Fall 2000): 38–41, 39.
7. G. Tsengelt, "The Nationality Question: Inner Mongolia and the Ethnic Opposition," Radical Party Web site, http://www. radicalparty. org/ humanrights/mon_doc2. htm#4.

SUGGESTED READINGS

Benson, Linda. *The Ili Rebellion: The Moslem Challenge to Chinese Authority in Xinjiang*. London: M. E. Sharpe, 1990.

Gladney, Dru. *Ethnic Identity in China: The Making of a Muslim Minority Nationality*. Fort Worth, Tex.: Harcourt Brace College Publishers, 1998.

Goldstein, Melvyn C. *The Snow Lion and the Dragon: China, Tibet, and the Dalai Lama*. Berkeley: University of California Press, 1999.

Grunfeld, A. Tom. *The Making of Modern Tibet*. New York: M. E. Sharpe, 1996.

Harrell, Stevan, ed. *Cultural Encounters on China's Ethnic Frontiers*. Seattle: University of Washington Press, 1995.

Kaup, Katherine P. *Creating the Zhuang: Ethnic Politics in China*. Boulder, Colo.: Lynne Rienner Publishers, 2000.

Ma Yin. *China's Minority Nationalities*. Beijing: Foreign Languages Press, 1994.

Mackerras, Colin. *China's Minorities: Integration and Modernization in the Twentieth Century*. Hong Kong: Oxford University Press, 1994.

Safran, William. *Nationalism and Ethnoregional Identities in China*. London: Frank Cass, 1998.

Sneath, David. *Changing Inner Mongolia: Pastoral Mongolian Society and the Chinese State*. Oxford, England: Oxford University Press, 2000.

Cyprus

Communal Conflict and the International System

Joseph R. Rudolph, Jr.

TIMELINE

1600 B.C. Beginning of 600 years of Greek influence in Cyprus.

700 B.C. Island becomes part of Mediterranean struggle for power; at various times during next 650 years falls under Assyrian, Egyptian, and Persian control.

58 B.C. Cyprus becomes part of the Roman Empire and later the East Roman (Byzantine) Empire.

1489 Venetian Empire establishes outpost in Cyprus.

1571 Beginning of Ottoman (Turkish) influence.

1875–1878 Cyprus essentially passes to Britain under terms of Cyprus Convention in return for Britain's promise to aid Turkey should czarist Russia attack the Ottoman Empire.

1914 Britain formally annexes Cyprus.

1925 Cyprus becomes a British crown colony.

1960 In August, Cyprus achieves independence; Turkey and Greece agree not to interfere in affairs of the new state.

1963 On November 30, President Makarios proposes a constitutional change that would have effectively barred Turkish

Cypriots from political power. In December, intercommunal conflict prompts Britain to intervene to restore order and preempt intervention by Turkey or Greece.

1964 In March, UN Security Council creates UN peacekeeping force in Cyprus to replace British forces and help local officials maintain order. Uneasy peace resumes.

1967 Colonels' dictatorial rule begins in Greece.

1974 Talks between Greek and Turkish Cypriots on establishing a unitary Cyprus with strong local government proceeding well at midyear. In July, colonels propose *enosis,* the annexation of Cyprus by Greece, as an answer to the ethnic conflict in Cyprus. On July 15, Makarios government in Cyprus is overthrown by pro-*enosis* regime in coup led by Cyprus National Guard, under control of officers from mainland Greece. Turkey invades island to protect Turkish Cypriots. Colonels' regime falls in Greece.

1974–1975 Turkey's invasion triggers massive, often forced migration of Greek Cypriots to the island's south, Turk Cypriots to the island's north; de facto partition of Cyprus.

1975 On June 8, Turkish Cypriots vote to form a separate federal state in north as step toward creating a biregional Federal Republic of Cyprus. Remaining Greek Cypriots are expelled from the north.

1983 On November 15, Turkish Cypriot region tries to secede, declaring itself the Turkish Republic of Northern Cyprus (TRNC).

1988 First significant discussions are held between leaders of two communities in Cyprus on the topic of resolving communal conflict.

1989 A limited pullback of TRNC, Turkish, and Republic of Cyprus forces is achieved.

1990 In March, talks collapse as a result of Turkish demand for amended constitution recognizing minority's "right to self-determination."

1990s Applications of Cyprus and Turkey for EU membership necessitate the settlement of ethnic conflict on Cyprus and offer encouragement it will be resolved.

2000 Turkish Cypriot leader says TRNC will not continue negotiations with Greek Cypriots or outside mediators until its independence is recognized.

2001 In December, under European Union pressure to resolve their conflict or see Cyprus passed over when the EU next expands, the leaders of Turkish and Greek communities agree to begin a new round of efforts to resolve the conflict.

Cyprus, the third largest island in the Mediterranean Sea, lies approximately 250 miles east of the Greek Archipelago and 50 miles south of Turkey. Its geographical location explains much of its history and the composition of its people. Likewise, much of its history since receiving independence in 1960 has revolved around the fact that the country of origin of the 18 percent Turkish Cypriot minority on this island of slightly over 700,000 people is both much nearer and much more militarily powerful than the country of origin of its 80 percent Greek Cypriot majority.[1]

HISTORICAL BACKGROUND

The Greek Cypriots can trace their roots back in time to more than 3,500 years ago, when Greek civilization and culture began to exert nine centuries of influence on the island. Thereafter, the island fell under the control of a series of foreign conquerors and cultures, over time becoming a part of the Assyrian, Egyptian, Persian, and Roman empires. Its majority, however, retained their Greek identity. Indeed, it was not until Cyprus fell under Turkey's control and became a part of the Ottoman Empire (1571–1878) that a significantly large foreign community began to emerge on the island. Even then, however, the Greek religious and social foundations of the island largely survived under the administrative (*millet*) system applied by the Ottomans, which allowed non-Muslim peoples to be governed by their own religious institutions. As a result, the rule of Cyprus by the Turkish outsiders had the practical result of increasing the solidarity of its Greek community and the political as well as religious position of the Greek Orthodox Church in Cyprus. At the same time, the island also acquired its minority presence, the Turkish Cypriots.

Although Britain did not formally annex Cyprus until World War I (1914), the island essentially passed from the Ottomans into British hands in the late 1870s in return for the British promise to aid Turkey in the event of an attack by czarist Russia. Neither then, nor in 1925 when Cyprus became a crown colony, were the political preferences of its majority or minority formally consulted. Likewise, little attention was given to the interests of Greece or Turkey at the time. In fact, as a loser in World War I, Turkey had been forced to renounce all claims to Cyprus under terms of the Treaty of Lausanne in 1923.

Greek-Turkish ethnic unrest on the island, which predated British colonialism, intensified during the period of Britain's rule over Cyprus. The Ottoman Empire left its mark on intercommunal relations in Cyprus, and under British rule economic disparities were added to the reinforcing religious, ethnic, and linguistic separating dividing the Greek and Turkish Cypriots. Although the island remained largely agricultural and—by European standards at the time—poor, by the 1950s Greek Cypriots in general were visibly better off economically than the Turkish minority.

In August 1960, Cyprus received independence as a bicommunal state, under a constitution that guaranteed the rights of the Greek and Turkish Cypriots. As British rule wound down, Greece lobbied for *enosis* (incorporating Cyprus into Greece's political system) as a solution to post-empire Britain's problem of what to do with Cyprus. The proposal, however, was strenuously opposed by the Turkish minority, and the final settlement was a broad, international one involving Britain, Greece, and Turkey as guarantors of Cyprus's independence.

An uneasy three years followed Britain's withdrawal. As a result, the residential pattern of geographically intermingled communities that existed when Cyprus became independent altered as an increasing number of ethnic enclaves began to develop throughout island. In November 1963 President (Archbishop) Makarios proposed rewriting the constitution in order to curtail the political rights and influence of the Turkish Cypriots. Within a month, intercommunal violence had increased to the point where the British found it necessary to intervene to restore order. The following March, at the request of all parties (including Greece and Turkey), the United Nations Peacekeeping Forces in Cyprus (UNFICYP) was established to replace the British forces with a multinational peacekeeping unit in which Britain remained as a contributing member.

UNFICYP's presence enabled the Makarios government manage ethnic tensions in Cyprus for nearly a decade. In the early 1970s, Makarios even seemed to have moved Cyprus's two national communities toward a more tranquil state of cohabitation on the island. If so, the fruits of his work disappeared in summer of 1974, when the military rulers controlling Greece publicly endorsed *enosis* as solution to Cyprus's continuing ethnic tension and instigated the attempted overthrow of the Makarios government by like-minded Greek Cypriots spearheaded by a Cyprus National Guard under the control of officers from mainland Greece. Amidst the resultant turmoil, including the false rumor of Makarios's death, the Turkish Cypriots looked to Turkey for aid. Turkey responded by landing troops in Northern Cyprus. By the time their subsequent battle with the Greek Cypriot National Guard had ended, the northern 37 percent of the island was under Turkish control.

THE CONFLICT

Turkey's intervention—or invasion, in the eyes of the Greek Cypriots—radically redefined the political environment of politics on the island. By mid-1975, the northern area had acquired de facto autonomy, its inhabitants had voted (on June 8) to form a separate federal state in northern Cyprus as a step toward creating a future biregional Federal Republic of Cyprus, and both the north and south of Cyprus were well on their way to becoming ethnically homogeneous. In the north, 200,000 Greek Cypriots were forced to move to the south by Turkish troops and Turkish Cypriots, and 40,000 Turkish Cypriots in the south found it prudent, under the circumstances, to migrate northward.[2] The resultant homogenization of

Cyprus's previously intermingled communities and elevation of tensions between the island's Greek majority and Turkish minority also redefined UNFICYP's mission. Instead of providing daily street mediation between the intermixing national groups, UNFICYP's mission was now focused on policing a buffer zone between the Greek and Turkish Cypriots. Known as the Green Line, this 110-mile-long border continues to exist, from 4 to 12 miles wide at most points but only a few blocks wide or less in Nicosia.

Above all, since the events of 1974, the issues surrounding ethnic conflict on Cyprus have expanded steadily—from the original, Turkish minority's desire for empowerment to the continuing presence of Turkish troops in Cyprus, the fate of the 1,619 Greeks missing since Turkey's intervention, to territorial autonomy for the north [which on November 15, 1983, tried to secede as the independent Turkish Republic of Northern Cyprus (TRNC) but gained diplomatic recognition only from Turkey], and the resettlement of the Greek Cypriots driven from their homes in 1974–1975. Additionally, there have been the international dimensions of the conflict: primarily avoiding a confrontation between two key members of the North Atlantic Treaty Organization (NATO), Greece and Turkey, and determining when and under what circumstances United Nations peacekeeping forces can withdraw from the island without the conflict reigniting.

MANAGEMENT OF
THE CONFLICT

There is little evidence in the island's twentieth-century history that the leaders of either its Greek or Turkish communities, before or after independence, devoted much energy to preventing the linguistic, ethnic, religious, and other differences separating their peoples from disrupting politics in Cyprus. Rather, the evidence indicates that prior to the system's breakdown in 1974, these differences were consistently exploited by communal partisans to politicize Cyprus's ethnocultural distinctions in order to shape Cyprus politics in their respective favor. Since 1974 these lines of cleavage have further hardened, dooming the dozens of diplomatic initiatives launched by outside negotiators during the last quarter of the twentieth century in an effort to get Cyprus's two communities to accept a unified federal Cyprus Republic.

For all but four years of its history as an independent state, the management of ethnic conflict in Cyprus has thus been in the hands of the international peacekeeping forces that patrolled its streets from 1963 to 1974 and have policed the cease-fire line separating Greek and Turkish Cypriots since 1974. On the whole, these forces have been remarkably successful in maintaining intercommunal peace, despite the strong emotions on both sides of the cease-fire line, the complicating presence of troops and settlers from Turkey in the north, and a Greek Cypriot National Guard largely commanded by officers from Greece in the south.

On the other hand, despite the territorialized nature of the Greek and Turkish communities, the United Nations has had little success in capitalizing on its peacekeeping accomplishments to broker a political settlement between the two nations of Cyprus. Ostensibly, the principal obstacle to conflict resolution remains the presence of Turkey military forces in the north. The government of Cyprus—which effectively rules only the southern 63 percent of the island—has steadfastly refused to relinquish its claim to the island as a whole and has refused to negotiate a federalist compromise with the TRNC until Turkey's forces withdraw. More basically, little headway has been possible because the leaders of the TRNC are essentially content with the existing situation. To be sure, they would like to be recognized as an independent state by the world community and to receive the greater outside investment which such recognition might bring; however, from the territorial perspective, they are satisfied. They have no desire to expand the TRNC's borders, and they remain secure in those borders because—as long as Turkey's army is deployed in the north—the greater military force is on their side.[3]

As the twentieth century ended, however, one light could be dimly seen at the end of the long tunnel of protracted ethnic conflict in Cyprus, radiating from yet another international actor affected by and seeking to influence Greek-Turkish conflict in Cyprus. During the 1990s, the European Union (EU) held numerous discussions on the subject of its future enlargement. The fall of communism in the Soviet Union and Central Europe enabled Western countries such as Austria and Sweden, who had hitherto found it desirable on security grounds to remain outside of Western political and military organizations, to join an integrating Europe. It also produced a long list of newly democratizing countries in Central Europe petitioning for EU membership, making it possible for the leaders of the European Union to envision it truly becoming European in scope rather than a predominantly Western European union. Within this framework, Cyprus was repeatedly placed on the EU's list of potential future members; however, only as a single state. Whether the lure of EU membership will provide the needed extra inducement to get Turkey (which actively sought admission to the EU throughout the 1990s) and the Greek and Turkish Cypriot leaders to settle their conflict remains to be seen.

SIGNIFICANCE

Because so much of Cyprus's history has revolved around the presence of peacekeeping forces on the island, perhaps the greatest significance of the Cyprus case is the light it sheds on the utility of peacekeeping as a means of conflict management and resolution. UNFICYP is the oldest of all the UN peacekeeping operations; yet, when the twentieth century ended, the jury was still debating the value of its thirty-six-year presence in Cyprus.

There is little disagreement that UNFICYP has been a great success as a tool of preventive diplomacy; that is, a means of preventing Greek-Turkish conflict in Cyprus from erupting again or spreading into a regional war between Greece and Turkey. Its presence from 1964 to 1974 clearly contributed to the control of numerous communal conflicts that might otherwise have escalated into violent intercommunal strife "in such a mixed, distrustful, and trigger happy state as Cyprus."[4] Subsequently, it has maintained the truce achieved in 1974, and it has done so with relatively few personnel compared to the tens of thousands of peacekeeping forces deployed in Sri Lanka during the 1980s and in Bosnia and Kosovo during the 1990s.[5]

There is less consensus concerning UNFICYP's value to conflict resolution in Cyprus. Many political observers of events in Cyprus continue to believe that the diplomatic stalemate in Cyprus persists pre-

TURKISH REPUBLIC OF NORTHERN CYPRUS. Government headquarters. Photo courtesy of the Turkish Republic of Northern Cyprus Washington, D.C., Bureau.

cisely because of UNFICYP's stabilizing presence there, which "has also made it less necessary, unfortunately, to find a lasting solution."[6]

There are other factors, however, that have made it difficult for the governments in Cyprus and the outside mediators to resolve the ethnic conflict on the island. Thus, Cyprus's experience also underscores the degree to which the presence of outside states sharing the ethnic identity of one or more of the rival communities in a multinational political system can complicate the process of conflict management. Where a country's ethnic minority is also the ethnic majority in the broader region—the Turkish Cypriots, for example, or the Celtic Catholics who are the minority in Northern Ireland but majority in Ireland as a whole, and the Tamil minority in Sri Lanka who live just a short distance away from the tens of millions of Tamils in southern India—the already complex nature of any ethnic conflict typically increases. So, too, does the difficulty of peacefully resolving it. And when the outsiders meddle in that country's ethnopolitical affairs the likelihood of peaceful conflict resolution becomes even more remote.

Finally, the Cyprus case indicates the extent to which conflict resolution can be persistently blocked by the refugee issue. As in such other centers of national conflict as Bosnia and Kosovo, the problem of resettling those driven from their homes during military action has made it difficult for Greek and Turkish Cypriot leaders to move toward a comprehensive settlement of the political issues dividing them.

See also Sri Lanka: Tamil-Sinhalese Conflict in India's Backyard; United Kingdom: The Conflict in Ulster; Yugoslavia: The Deconstruction of a State and Birth of Bosnia; and Yugoslavia: Ethnic Conflict and the Meltdown in Kosovo.

NOTES

1. The percentages are approximate. What is definite is the fact that ethnicity, language, and religion reinforce one another in separating the island's two communities. The majority—78 percent of the population in 1974—are Greek ethnically and linguistically, and Greek Orthodox in religion; the minority is Turkish in language and ethnicity, Muslim in faith.
2. It is estimated that by the 1990s fewer than 100 Turkish Cypriots remained in the south, and only about 600 Greek Cypriots lived in the north.
3. The military force on the TRNC side of the border is conservatively estimated at 22,000 men, 17,000 of which are from Turkey. The Republic of Cyprus National Guard on other side is estimated at, again conservatively, 11,000.
4. Alan James, "The UN Force in Cypress," *International Affairs* 65, no. 3 (Summer 1989): 481–500.
5. When initially deployed, the UNFICYP was 6,300 strong. It had shrunk to 2,300 by the time of Turkey's 1974 invasion, when it was rebuilt to approximately 4,000. During the 1990s, it kept the peace with only about 2,000 men in uniform.
6. Matthew Nimetz, "The Cyprus Problem Revisited," *Mediterranean Quarterly* 2, no. 1 (Winter 1991): 61.

SUGGESTED READINGS

Bahcheli, Tozun. "Searching for a Cyprus Settlement: Considering Options for Creating a Federation, Confederation, or Two Independent States." *Publius* 30, no. 1–2 (Winter/Spring 2000): 203–16.

Borowiec, Andrew. *Cyprus, a Troubled Island*. New York: Praeger, 2000.

James, Alan. "The UN Force in Cyprus." *International Affairs* 65, no. 3 (Summer 1989): 481–500.

Joseph, Joseph S. *Cyprus: Ethnic Conflict and International Politics*. New York: St. Martin's Press, 1997.

Salem, Norma, ed. *Cyprus: A Regional Conflict and Its Resolution*. New York: St. Martin's Press, 1992.

Stefanidis, Joannis D. *Isle of Discord: Nationalism, Imperialism, and the Making of the Cyprus Problem*. New York: New York University Press, 1999.

Theophanous, Andreas. "Prospects for Solving the Cyprus Problem and the Role of the European Union." *Publius* 30, no. 1–2 (Winter/Spring 2000): 217–41.

Czechoslovakia

The Peaceful Breakup of a State

Joseph R. Rudolph, Jr.

TIMELINE

1000 Slovakia becomes a part of the Hungarian state.

1467 The university in Bratislava (Academia Istropolitana) is founded.

1530 The Turkish invasion occur.

1780 Beginning of Slovak national revival.

1792 Hungarianization process begins.

1843 Legalization of the Slovak literary language.

1918 Czechoslovakia is established following World War I as the First Czechoslovak Republic.

1938 Munich Accords sanction loss of Czechoslovakia's Sudeten region to Germany; Vienna Award gives Slovakia to Hungary.

1939 Germany establishes the Czech lands as a German protectorate and makes Slovakia a separate state (the Slovak Republic, 1939–1945) under German sponsorship.

1944 Slovak national uprising against German rule occurs.

1945 World War II ends; Czechoslovakia is reunited; the second Czechoslovak Republic (1945–1948) begins.

1948 Communists seize power in February and establish a Communist regime in Czechoslovakia.

1968 Prague Spring of reform is ended by a summer invasion by the Soviet Union. In the aftermath, Czechoslovakia is restructured from a unitary to a federal state (1969).

1989 The Velvet Revolution in November ends Communist rule.

1992 Nationalists emerge as the dominant parties in Slovakia's summer state elections; fall negotiations between the federal government in Prague and government in Slovakia fail to find a formula for keeping the country together.

1993 On January 1, Czechoslovakia is dissolved into two sovereign states: the Czech Republic and the Slovak Republic.

1997 The Czech Republic is invited to join NATO and is placed on the fast track for membership in the European Union; the Slovak Republic is not due to allegations that the Meciar government in Bratislava is abusing fundamental democratic rights, especially with respect to Slovakia's Hungarian minority.

1998 The Meciar government fails to win reelection; a new coalition government is formed and includes the leaders of three parties representing the Hungarians in Slovakia.

Czechoslovakia had a short history of self-rule following its creation in the aftermath of World War I. Launched as one of the century's great experiments in state building, Czechoslovakia was meant to unite two linguistically similar but culturally distinct, Slavic-speaking communities in Central Europe: the more numerous Czechs living west of the Moravia River and their "Little Brothers," the Slovaks, to the east. Scarcely was the state in place, however, before tensions developed between the two, and the Slovaks began to lobby for a state of their own, where they would be free to teach their own cultural heritage, control their own political institutions, and pursue their own future. Scarcely had the debate over Slovak self-determination begun before the Great Depression and the prelude to World War II deprived Czechoslovakia's leaders of the opportunity to address the separatist issue directly or, alternately, to build durable political institutions and a durable political community out of the two Slavic peoples composing the state. Then came the twin traumas of German occupation during the war and post–World War II Soviet control. Consequently, it was not until the Velvet Revolution, a peaceful overthrow of the Communist regime in Czechoslovakia in 1989, that the Czechs and Slovaks had the opportunity to decide themselves what they wanted do with their union. Within three years, they decided to end it.

HISTORICAL BACKGROUND

When Czechoslovakia split apart on January 1, 1993, the leaders of the newly created Czech Republic and Slovak Republic alike heralded the breakup as a "Velvet Divorce"—an amiable decision by all parties to go their separate ways. The self-congratulatory announcement was a considerable overstatement.

The Origins of Czechoslovakia

The story of the demise of Czechoslovakia begins with a brief exploration of its origins seventy-five years earlier. The marriage contract that led to the creation of Czechoslovakia in 1918 owed its existence to several factors. First was the general ambiance created by U.S. President Woodrow Wilson's wartime rhetoric of making the world safe for democracy and promise to erect a postwar order based on the principle of national self-determination. To be sure, his idea of national self-determination was never intended to be evenly implemented. It was never meant to apply, for example, to the Irish seeking independence from our wartime ally Great Britain. Likewise, it received very short treatment when the leaders of the wartime victors (Britain, France, and the United States) gathered at Versailles Palace outside Paris in 1918–1919 to determine the fate of the Arabs previously governed by the Ottoman Empire centered in Turkey. By the time the conferences concluded, most of these peoples found their land carved up to enlarge the French and British empires in the Middle East. The principle was, however, meant to be applied to the Central European possessions of the vast Austrian-Hungarian Empire, which also ended the war on the losing side, and that knowledge led to the outside lobbying for the creation of Czechoslovakia. Even before the war ended, Slavic immigrants in the United States and political exiles from the region living in America and France were petitioning the governments in Washington and Paris to join together into one sovereign Slavic state the Slovaks and Czechs who, for centuries, had been, respectively, under the rule of the Austria-Hungarian Empire's twin capitals, Budapest and Vienna.

The proposal made more sense from the Czech perspective than from the Slovak. The nineteenth century had seen a flowering of nationalist movements among the various Slavic peoples under the heavy-handed rule of Hungary or the less oppressive but still very real control of the Austrians. Both the Czechs and Slovaks had participated in this nationalist revivalism, but in significantly different ways. Czech nationalists stressed the commonality of the Czech and Slovak peoples to the point where Czech propagandists wrote frequently but with little historical evidence of a common history and ancestry linking the Czechs and Slovaks;[1] Slovak nationalism stressed the long and unique history of the Slovak people, their rural traditions, and their distinctive folk culture. Czech nationalists stressed the historical accomplishments of the Czechs even when under the control of their German and later Austrian conquerors—the achievements of Czech kings, the success of their merchants, the grandeur of Prague, still one of the most beautiful European cities. A corollary to this strand of nineteenth-century Czech nationalism was the argument that the Czechs had an obligation, through merger, to aid their unfortunate Slovak kin, whose culture was being attacked by their Hungarian masters. Slovak nationalism focused on the injustices done to the Slovak peoples by their oppressors, and on the sacrifices and efforts of Slovaks to do right; for example, Janocik, a Robin Hood–like folk hero who stole from Slovakia's rich, foreign tyrants and gave the gold to poor Slovaks before he was betrayed by a comrade and hung. Above all, Slovak nationalism stressed self-help, not dependency on others.

Given the different outlooks and motivations of Slovak and Czech nationalists, the founding of Czechoslovakia can be largely described as an Old World marriage of convenience. Instead of lust and passion, each of the contracting parties brought to the marriage an important dowry defined in terms of ethnic group mathematics. For the Slovaks in the eastern portion of the projected state, Czecho-slovakia was a means of escaping from the influence of Budapest by joining with a larger ethnic group with whom they already shared a language and common history. The merger allowed them to return to their Slavic heritage after centuries of repression and forced Hungarianization. Conversely, even if offered national self-determination for themselves at Versailles, Slovak leaders saw little chance of a small Slovak state containing a large Hungarian minority located on the northern border of Hungary being able to establish, quickly and securely, its own identity.

For the Czechs, the mathematics of the pairing were even more important. The Czech lands of Bohemia and Moravia, adjacent to or near Germany, had a minority problem of their own; they contained very large number of Germans (33 percent of the population of Bohemia and 20.9 percent of the population of Moravia in 1921). A merger with the economically backward Slovaks, whose chief appeal to many Czech leaders was that they were not German, would decidedly tilt the numbers inside a Czechoslovak state in the Slavic direction, with the Slovaks providing a significant counterweight to the German presence in the Czech lands of Bohemia and Moravia.

Czech-Slovak Conflict, the Formative Years

Scarcely was the union born before tensions sharpened between the Czech and Slovak communities inside the new state. Economics as well as numbers consigned the Slovaks to a minority status in Czechoslovakia. Not only were they outnumbered two to one by the Czechs, but the economy of Slovakia was poor and still rooted in agriculture, which accounted for nearly three jobs in four (72.3 percent) in the Slovak lands in 1910. By contrast, the Czech lands enjoyed significant social and economic prosperity under Austrian rule and possessed a diverse, modern economy by the time of World War I, with more of their workforce in industry than in agriculture by 1910. Most important, the Czech lands already possessed a large number of professionals and public sector workers on the eve of World War I (12.3 percent of the 1910 Czech workforce) and were thus much better prepared to take the helm of the new state than Slovakia, which had been under the direct and intrusive rule of Budapest and where less than one Slovak worker in fifty (1.9 percent) was employed either in the public sector or a professional field.[2]

A minority status of this ilk would have been difficult for any ethnic group to have accepted, but it was particularly grating to the Slovaks. Years of humiliation and subjection to Hungarianization had left them with a deep sense of inferiority and defensiveness. Consequently, when Czechoslovakia's (basically Czech) leaders in Prague first rejected regional autonomy for Slovakia in organizing the state and then launched a Czech culture–based educational program to close the social and economic gaps between the Czech lands and Slovakia, large numbers of Slovaks mobilized around nationalist banners and began to press for the independent Slovakia of which they dreamed, but which they did not pursue, in 1918.

By the mid-1930s Czech-Slovak relations had deteriorated to the point where estranged Slovak nationalists were openly negotiating with Germany, offering to support Adolf Hitler in his confrontation with Prague over its treatment of the Germans living in Bohemia in return for his promise to create an independent Slovak Republic should Germany invade Czechoslovakia. Their ill-considered venture haunted Czech-Slovak relations for years. Hitler did invade Czechoslovakia in 1939, effectively ending the First Republic of Czechoslovakia. The invasion also led to the creation of the First Slovak Republic, but it quickly proved bogus: a Third Reich

creation whose existence depended entirely on German military support. In 1944 the Slovaks launched a failed uprising against Slovakia's German occupiers. After World War II, the Soviet Union's Red Army occupied and converted Czechoslovakia into a Soviet satellite state. These developments did not end Czech efforts to punish Slovakia for the wartime collaboration of some of its leaders with Germany. Assertions of Slovak national identity were severely punished by the Communists in Prague as an assertion of "bourgeois nationalism." Slovak political parties were either banned or enfolded into the Czech-dominated Communist Party of Czechoslovakia, and the First Slovak Republic disappeared in the Communist state created in Czechoslovakia under Moscow's supervision.

In the long term, however, communism in Czechoslovakia advanced the cause of Slovak nationalism in important ways. The Marxist answer to the socioeconomic gap separating the Slovaks and Czechs was not education but economics: the industrialization of Slovakia. The program had only limited success—the Czech head start in industrialization, more educated and sophisticated population, and forward location on the edge of Western Europe gave the Czechs a competitive advantage over Slovakia that could not be overcome by the relatively meager resources invested in modernizing Slovakia's economy. Nevertheless, by the time of the Velvet Revolution, Slovakia had at last developed the type of mixed (agricultural-industrial-service) economy necessary for survival in the modern world, and Slovak nationalists could realistically talk of an economically viable, independent Slovakia, complete with a modern, urbanized capital city in Bratislava.

Meanwhile, in 1968, Czech intellectuals and politicians instituted a minirevolution called the "Prague Spring" in an effort to establish a more democratic po-

BRATISLAVA, SLOVAK REPUBLIC. Hero's Square, erected during communist rule to honor the heroes of the 1944 Slovak uprising, was subsequently the scene of the principal Slovak protests against Soviet and Czech domination. Photo courtesy of the author.

litical process. Moscow summarily ended the reform movement by invading Czechoslovakia in the summer of 1968 and arresting the architects of the Prague Spring. Moscow's ability to continue to control the country with minimum costs forced it to engineer some reforms of its own in Czechoslovakia. A centerpiece of these reforms involved courting the Slovaks by restructuring the country along federalist lines, creating a Slovak regional government in Bratislava, and regularly appointing Slovaks to important ministerial positions in the federal government in Prague. The strategy appears to have worked. In return for their economic and political gains, the Slovaks supported their Communist rulers to a far greater extent than the Czechs did. Prague Spring had been a Czech movement, with scant echoes in

Slovakia. Similarly, the Charter 77 movement, which was launched in 1977 when a petition drawn up by dissidents to protest the government's continued suppression of intellectual discourse, obtained more than a thousand signatures in the Czech lands but attracted only one Slovak signature. Even the Velvet Revolution of 1989 was largely a Czech phenomenon, both in organization and execution. As communism began to crumble elsewhere in Central Europe, beginning with the dramatic collapse of the regime in East Germany in October 1989 and the fall of the Communist government in Bulgaria in early November, hundreds of thousands filled the streets of Prague on November 24, 1989, to protest communism's continued rule of Czechoslovakia, but only a few thousand gathered in Bratislava to call for the end of communism. When the Velvet Revolution succeeded and the Communist Party began a two-month-long process of turning over the control of the Czechoslovakian government to the coalition of opposition forces known as the Civic Forum, the scene of the action was Prague. Except for Miroslav Kusy, who became President Vaclav Havel's agent in Bratislava following the transfer of power and who had been the one Slovak to sign the Charter 77 petition, Slovaks again found themselves largely the observers of political events, not participants in shaping their own destiny.

THE CONFLICT

The fall of Communist rule in the Soviet Union—which began in the mid-1980s when Soviet leader Mikhail Gorbachev began to liberalize the Soviet Union's economic system and tolerate the discussion of political reform, and which effectively concluded with the failure of the August 1991 attempt by Communist hard-liners to overthrow Gorbachev—opened the door in Czechoslovakia to a quickly developing debate over the future of that country. Fueled by old grievances on both sides, the debate essentially had only one dimension: whether Slovakia should remain a federally autonomous region in a Czech-Slovak Federal Republic (CSFR) or should secede and form a separate, independent country. The decisive showdown between the federalists and nationalists came in the June 1992 national and regional elections, in which a nationalist coalition, headed by the former Communist/born-again-nationalist Vladimir Meciar, gained control of Slovakia's regional assembly. Claiming that the election provided him with a mandate to pursue the Slovaks' long-standing dream of national self-determination, Meciar immediately began negotiations with the prime minister of Czechoslovakia, Vaclav Klaus, over the future of Slovakia.

MANAGEMENT OF THE CONFLICT

Scholars are still debating whether Meciar was single-minded in his desire for Slovak independence or, as seems more likely, was only using the threat of secession to induce Prague into widening Slovakia's federal autonomy and pumping more investment capital into Slovakia. If Meciar saw the separation talks as a bargaining ploy, he grievously overplayed his hand. It takes two sides willing to compromise for reconciliation to occur in such dramatic moments, and at least three factors worked against the Czechs making any major concessions during these negotiations. At the top of this list was the fact that the Slovak economy still lagged well behind that of the Czech lands. In the minds of the Czech leadership in Prague, an independent Czech Republic would be poised for early admission into the European Union whereas continuing the union with Slovakia would delay admission and force Prague to spend considerable resources on economically developing eastern Slovakia. In short, the union with lovakia had become, at best, an economic inconvenience.

Second, the Czechs saw no compelling political reasons for retaining their association with the Slovaks. The German minority that had existed in the Czech lands when Czechoslovakia was created and that made union with the Slovaks attractive at that time had been unceremoniously booted out of the country after World War II. A Slovak counterweight was no longer needed. Nor were there any partisan political reasons for clinging to Slovakia. Following the Velvet Revolution, the Czechs developed a party system similar to that of most democratic states in the West; that is, a class-based system in which the parties primarily disagree about the acceptable limits of government intervention in the economy and society. By contrast, after 1992, Slovakia's party system was dominated by nationalist and federalist organizations less concerned with economic policy than redefining Slovakia's political relationship with Prague. The parties in power in Prague no longer had regional wings in Slovakia to protect.

Finally, there was a personal element at work in the Klaus-Meciar talks that made the Czechs less than enthusiastic about compromising with Slovakia's leaders. The government in Prague was widely staffed by the Czechs who had formed the backbone of the resistance to Communist rule from the days of the Prague Spring to the Velvet Revolution. For them, many of those years had been spent in jail or on state work farms. Slovakia's rulers were, overwhelmingly, former Communists who had once been a part of the establishment that had jailed them.

Fortunately, it also takes two irresolute sides for a civil war to occur: one side willing to fight to leave and another willing to fight to preserve the union. The Czechs were no more interested in fighting to keep Slovakia in the union than they were interested in bribing Slovakia into staying. Hence, the negotiations concluded by setting an early date for the dissolution of the Czech-Slovak Federal Republic: January 1, 1993, less than seven months after the summer elections brought the Slovak nationalists to power and less than three months after the conclusion of the Klaus-Meciar talks.

SIGNIFICANCE

On the one hand, the relative calm and peacefulness with which the elected leaders of the Czech and Slovak communities agreed to divide their state seems to testify to the ability of reason to overcome the emotionalism of national identity. Certainly the decision to split Czechoslovakia into two states stands in stark contrast to the violent end of the former Yugoslavia.

Equally assuredly, the voluntary decision by all parties to split an existing state into two independent countries was unique in the annals of ethnopolitics.

On the other hand, the details surrounding the breakup of Czechoslovakia do not support the conclusion that even under highly propitious circumstances nationalism can be easily separated from its emotional content and function in a world of tranquil, cost-benefit analysis. Viewed objectively, there was no significant reason for the Slovaks and Czechs to divorce, much less engage in such postdivorce shows of sovereignty as forcing their citizens to choose a single citizenship. The predominantly industrial economy of the Czech lands and the still largely agricultural economy of Slovakia complement each other; their respective citizens speak a shared language with approximately the same degree of deviation you find between American and British English. They have been intermarrying and living on opposite sides of the new frontier for centuries. The explanation for the breakup lies primarily in Meciar's self-serving exploitation of the nationalist issue to retain power in post-Communist Slovakia. To do so, he launched a movement for an independent Slovakia that gained such momentum that he could not halt it or withdraw his separatist demands when the Czechs refused to offer Slovakia incentives to remain. Thus, even though at the time of the Meciar-Klaus talks, a majority in both the Czech and Slovak communities seemed opposed to dissolution, it was by then too late to stop the flow of events. To return to the Velvet Divorce metaphor, without consulting the children (via formal opinion polls or a referendum), the Czech and Slovak leaders split the marital property and went their separate ways, perhaps to cohabit again in the future as members of an expanded European Union.

In the meantime, both sides have learned since the division of Czechoslovakia that in politics as in private lives, truly velvet divorces are very rare. Recriminations rebounded throughout Meciar's years as Slovakia's prime minister (1993–1998), and at the turn of the millennium neither the Czech nor the Slovak economy was as strong as it had been at the time of the Velvet Revolution. The Czechs did gain the prize of a fast-track entry into NATO and of becoming one of the states on the first short list of post-Communist countries eligible for membership in the European Union. Membership in NATO, however, soon led them into an unwanted war in Kosovo, and the new millennium found them still waiting for an offer to join the EU.

For their part, the Slovaks gained their own state, complete with its own passports, currency, border patrol posts, and a territorialized (Hungarian) ethnic minority demanding its autonomy.

See also Middle East: The Arab-Jewish Struggle for Palestine to 1948; United Kingdom: The Conflict in Ulster; and Yugoslavia: The Deconstruction of a State and Birth of Bosnia.

NOTES

1. See David Shot, "The Use and Abuse of the Language Argument in Mid-Nineteenth-Century 'Czechoslovakism': An Appraisal of a Propaganda Milestone," in *The Literature of Nationalism: Essays on East European Identity*, edited by Robert B. Pynsent (New York: St. Martin's Press, 1996), 40–65, esp. 52–55.
2. For a more extensive discussion of the demographic and economic conditions in the Czech and Slovak lands at the time of the creation of Czechoslovakia, see Carol Skalnik Leff, *National Conflict in Czechoslovakia: The Making and Remaking of a State, 1918–1987* (Princeton, N.J.: Princeton University Press, 1988), 13–21.

SUGGESTED READINGS

Dedek, Oldrich, et al. *The Breakup of Czechoslovakia: An In-depth Economic Analysis.* Aldershot, England: Avebury, 1996.

Fitzmaurice, John. *Politics and Government in the Visegrad Countries: Poland, Hungary, the Czech Republic, and Slovakia.* New York: St. Martin's Press, 1998.

Golan, Galia. *Reform Rule I Czechoslovakia: The Dubcek Era, 1968–1969.* Cambridge, England: Cambridge University Press, 1973.

Goldman, Minton F. *Slovakia Since Independence: A Struggle for Democracy.* Westport, Conn.: Praeger, 1999.

Kirschbaum, Stanislav J. "Czechoslovakia: The Creation, Federalization and Dissolution of a Nation State," in *The Territorial Management of Ethnic Conflict,* edited by John Coakley, 69–95. London: Frank Cass, 1993.

———. *A History of Slovakia: The Struggle for Survival.* New York: St. Martin's Griffin, 1995.

Kirschbaum, Stanislav J., ed. *Slovak Politics.* Cleveland, Ohio: Slovak Institute, 1983.

Leff, Carol Skalnik. *National Conflict in Czechoslovakia: The Making and Remaking of a State, 1918–1987.* Princeton, N.J.: Princeton University Press, 1988.

Musil, Jiri, ed. *The End of Czechoslovakia.* New York: Central European University Press, 1995.

Olivova, Vera, and George Theiner, trans. *The Doomed Democracy: Czechoslovakia in a Disrupted Europe, 1914–1938.* Montreal: McGill-Queen's University Press, 1972.

Preece, Jennifer Jackson. *National Minorities and the European Nation-States System.* Oxford, England: Clarendon Press, 1998.

Pynsent, Robert B., ed. *The Literature of Nationalism: Essays on East European Identity.* New York: St. Martin's Press, 1996.

Steiner, Eugen. *The Slovak Dilemma.* Cambridge; England: Cambridge University Press, 1973.

Szayna, Thomas S. "Ultra-Nationalism in Central Europe." *Orbis* 37, no. 4 (Fall 1993): 527–52.

France

Ethnic Conflict and the Problem of Corsica

Sue Ellen Charlton

TIMELINE

1209 Albigensian crusade begins; leads to transfer of territory in the south of France from the counts of Toulouse to the French monarchy.

1481 Provence is bequeathed to the king of France.

1532 Brittany is acquired by France through royal marriage.

1635 The Academie française is established.

1648 Alsace is attached to France by the Treaty of Westphalia.

1729 Corsican rebellion against Genoa begins.

1752 Corsica wins nominal independence from Genoa.

1755 Pasquale Paoli becomes chief of the Corsican nation.

1768 Corsica is ceded to France.

1789 The French Revolution begins.

1794 Two years of quasi-independence for Corsica begins.

1860 Savoy becomes part of France.

1871 Alsace is given to Germany as a result of the Franco-Prussian War.

1918 Alsace is returned to French sovereignty after World War II.

1962 Algeria gains independence from France; many French Algerians immigrate to Corsica.

1965 The Front regionaliste corse (FRC) is established.

1967 The Action regionaliste corse (ARC) is established; evolved into the *Action pour la renaissance de la Corse* in the early 1970s.

1976 Corsican National Liberation Front established.

1982 A special statute for Corsica is adopted, creating the Corsican Assembly.

1993 Additional powers are decentralized to Corsica.

2000 The third step in the devolution of power to Corsica is made by the French government.

Most people consider France one of the oldest, most unified, most stable of Europe's nation-states. In many ways it is, although this image must be qualified by the reality of a number of regional conflicts that are grounded in ethnic—and particularly language—differences. In the second half of the twentieth century, dozens of regional movements and political parties, most very small, demanded that the central government in Paris recognize their claims to regional distinctiveness. Some lobbied for greater decentralization of government activities and support for the teaching of regional languages in the public schools. Others went farther and demanded autonomy or even independence.

The most important of these autonomy-seeking movements were located in Brittany in western France, the Pyrenees region in the extreme southwest on the Spanish border, Occitania in the south, and on the island of Corsica. Occasionally members of some of these movements resorted to violence to call attention to their grievances, but most often they used elections and other legal processes to pursue their goals. By the beginning of the twenty-first century, Corsica was the only region still employing sporadic violence to draw attention to ethnic demands. In order to deal with the instability in Corsica, the French central government followed precedents set elsewhere in Western Europe and negotiated an agreement to decentralize powers to a Corsican assembly. Whether this agreement would resolve the conflict was unknown. Also unanswered was the question of whether the Corsican arrangement would encourage a renaissance of ethnic demands and claims for special treatment in other regions of France.

HISTORICAL BACKGROUND

The origins of ethnic conflict in France, as elsewhere in Europe, lie in the construction of the modern territorial nation-state, a process that by definition meant the elimination of smaller feudal states and local loyalties, as well as the breakup of large empires. The boundaries of France were not always what they are today. Although by the time of the French

Revolution of 1789, French kings claimed a lineage dating back a thousand years, most of the land under the control of the reigning Bourbon monarchy was incorporated into the expanding French kingdom only during the previous three centuries.

Building the French State and Nation

Modern ethnonationalists argue that the French nation-state was constructed by the forcible incorporation of independent political entities and diverse local cultures into the expanding realm of centralizing Paris-based monarchies before 1789, and by the bureaucrats and politicians of the French republics after 1789. This expansion of control from Paris was composed of two overlapping processes that occurred over a long period. The first process was the construction of a modern state with clearly defined territorial boundaries and centralized political, military, and economic institutions. The second process was the elimination of the regional loyalties, customs, and languages that persisted even after political sovereignty was transferred to the kings of France. This process was one of nation-building or, as Eugen Weber called it in his rich historical study of France, a process of turning *Peasants into Frenchmen* (1976).

The construction of the modern French state required the physical incorporation of diverse regions into the control of the central monarchy. The expansion of French borders from the Paris region to the configuration we know today began in the early thirteenth century and continued into the twentieth century with war, dynastic marriages, and diplomacy all playing a role. State-building politics mixed with religion and later with "great-power" diplomacy on a broad European scale. For example, much of contemporary southwestern France, the modern regions of Midi-Pyrénées and Languedoc-Roussillon, the area that ethnonationalists call Occitania, was under the authority of the counts of Toulouse by the thirteenth century. The destruction of the region's autonomy was a result of the Albigensian crusade in southern France. The crusade targeted a dissident Christian sect branded as heretical by the Catholic Church and a regional count who was accused of being sympathatic toward this heresy. The viciousness of the crusade, which began in 1209, followed by the incorporation of the possessions of the counts of Toulouse into the realm of the French crown has led some modern ethnic nationalists to interpret the events of the thirteenth century as a political conspiracy designed to destroy a rich culture.

Through the course of state building, most of southern France to the east of Languedoc, in the region now known as Provence, officially became part of France in the fifteenth century; the west and far southwest were incorporated piecemeal by the monarchs from the fifteenth to the seventeenth centuries; and Brittany became part of France in 1532 through royal marriage. Alsace, on the border with Germany in the east, was officially attached to France in 1648 by the Treaty of Westphalia, but was turned over to Germany as a result of the Franco-Prussian War in 1871. After Germany's defeat in World War I in 1918, Alsace returned to French sovereignty until it was annexed by Germany at the beginning of World War II, only to be ceded again to France after the war. Corsica, as explained below, did not become part of France until the eighteenth century, and its annexation was a result of great-power politics, not religion or dynastic marriages. Finally, Savoy, in the far southeast, was added to France in the mid-nineteenth century.

After formal annexation, the agencies of the king and state undertook to integrate the peripheral territories through a variety of policies. These policies included the elimination of regional armies, the estab-lishment of state-controlled manufacturing enterprises (such as salt), a centralized taxation system, the abolition of local tolls, the creation of a common system of weights and measures, and, in the nineteenth century, centralized systems of law, railroads, and education. From as early as the seventeenth century, a policy of subordinating the cultures of the newly incorporated territories complemented the institutions of economic and political control. This policy was exemplified by the Académie française, which was founded in 1635 to publish a standardized dictionary of French and which still exists today as an official monitor of the French language. Other national and regional academies for the arts and sciences were subsequently established in the seventeenth and eighteenth centuries. The primary objective of these academies was to foster the linguistic and cultural unification of France in the wake of territorial expansion. Although the academies did not eliminate regional languages, they did contribute to the erosion of regional identity by co-opting educated local elites and undermining the acceptability of local cultures and languages.

Corsica

Corsica was one of the last regions whose sovereignty was officially transferred to the French state. This fact, along with the island's relative geographical isolation and the circumstances under which France took control, helps account for the persistence of a strong Corsican identity and demands for political autonomy.

After the fall of the Roman Empire in the fifth century, Corsica was subjected to successive invasions by various peoples and armies competing for power after Rome's fall. Then the island became a pawn in the competition for power between the Italian city-states. Finally, control fell to the city-state of Genoa, which nominally ruled Corsica for most of the period from the late thirteenth century to the middle of the eighteenth century. During this time, raids against the island, combined with the notoriously corrupt Genoese rule, prompted several rebellions by Corsicans. In 1729 Corsicans launched a war of independence that eventually resulted in nominal independence from 1752 to 1768. In 1755 Pasquale (Pascal) Paoli was chosen general in chief of the Corsican nation, a position which earned him a place in history as Corsica's first acknowledged nationalist. Ironically, Napoléon Bonaparte, one of France's most famous leaders, was born in Corsica during this period, in 1769, the year after Corsica was formally ceded to France.

Meanwhile, France, an expanding military power in the eighteenth century, was embroiled in strategic competition with England. This was the era of great-power politics and dynastic wars in Europe, and France sought to expand its influence throughout the Mediterranean region. It proposed to Paoli a protectorate over Corsica, a proposal that was rejected. In response, France simply bought the island from Genoa in 1768 and, in 1769, sent its troops to Corsica to make a point about the authority of the new owners. Corsica was now officially part of France. Except for a brief period from 1794 to 1796 when, during the tumult that followed the French Revolution of 1789, Paoli again led a Corsican state (under British protection), and again during World War II, when the island was occupied by Italian and German troops, Corsica has belonged to France.

The Rise of Ethnic Consciousness

The rise of ethnic consciousness in the twentieth century is rooted in the economic, social, and political changes of nineteenth-century France. Industrialization reduced the economic isolation of outlying regions, while also sharpening regional differences as some areas remained largely rural and agricultural and others

became major centers of manufacturing. Textile production, for example, was concentrated in the north, while Brittany in the west and much of southern France remained underdeveloped. Regions which had been peripheral in a political and cultural sense now became peripheral in the economic sense. In the twentieth century, the relative poverty of the outlying regions would merge with issues centered in the survival of regional language and culture to stimulate movements drawing on ethnic distinctiveness, especially language, as well as economic grievances. Corsica is a good example of this fusion.

During the mid-1970s, when Corsican autonomy movements peaked, the French government estimated that 173,000 of the 240,000 people (72 percent) on the island still spoke Corsican, a language more closely related to Italian than French. Lying in the Mediterranean sea 100 miles south of France, Corsica is actually closer to Italy, which lies 50 miles to its east. The island's physical and linguistic detachment from metropolitan France was underscored throughout most of the twentieth century by the persistence on the island of a unique social structure and distinctive culture. Corsican society historically has been organized around extended-family clans, marked by strongly differentiated gender roles, codes of honor and the vendetta, and occultism.

Ethnic distinctiveness, as well as a long history of outside control and the cultivated historical memory of a brief period of independence in the eighteenth century, are central to the ideology of Corsican autonomy movements. Economic grievances and the structure of political power on the island have fueled these movements. The French government undertook no significant economic development policies in Corsica until the 1950s, and when it did promote development, its policies benefited newcomers more than the local population. Thus, investments designed to support agriculture primarily helped the French who left Algeria in the 1960s in the wake of Algeria's successful war of independence against France. Many of these French Algerians migrated to Corsica, where their expanding economic and social presence contributed to Corsican resentment of outsiders.

Corsican economic grievances were not imaginary. The island's population was smaller in the early 1970s than at the end of the nineteenth century. The island's depopulation was typical of many rural, poor French administrative areas (departments) from which people migrated to richer areas to find work. Although the central government in Paris has pursued concentrated strategies of economic development for Corsica since the 1960s, and despite substantial aid from the European Union, the island remains among the least developed regions of France and—more generally—Europe.

The earliest Corsican nationalist movements followed a pattern found elsewhere among French ethnic groups by focusing on literary and language questions. Explicit political organization dates from the post–World War I period, when the Autonomous Corsican Party (Partitu Corsu Autonomista) was founded. The most important growth period for the Corsican movement was in the 1960s, when several nationalist political organizations were established. The most influential of these were the socialist Corsican Regionalist Front (Front régionaliste corse), established in 1965, and an autonomist organization which became the Action pour la renaissance de la Corse (ARC) or Action for Corsican Renaissance. All of these organizations became more radical after 1968, a year of great social, economic, and political turbulence for France in general, and the number of violent incidents provoked by autonomist and separatist Corsican groups escalated from the late 1960s to the mid-1970s. By 1976 there were four

legal and at least two illegal autonomist Corsican organizations. The most important of the clandestine movements, both in terms of size and longevity, was the Corsican National Liberation Front (FLNC), which was established in 1976.

THE CONFLICT

By the end of the twentieth century, Corsica's autonomist groups and their demands had evolved considerably. Some groups disappeared or merged; some moved into mainstream politics; a few still operated clandestinely. A variety of goals have fueled these groups, and the groups themselves have been fragmented, thereby making it difficult to identify one or two central issues that could be addressed in the political process.[1]

At the core of the island's autonomy demands is the identity stemming from the Corsican language, or Corsu, which developed from the colloquial Latin spoken during the Roman Empire. Over the centuries, the language became infused with Italian dialects from Pisa and Genoa. Although today French is more widely spoken on the island than Corsu, the language has become the most prominent and acceptable marker of cultural identity. Corsu has been an optional language in the schools, but most nationalist groups have wanted its study to be mandatory—a demand that runs up against the central government's long tradition of insisting on French as the only legitimate national language.

In addition to language, ethnic identity is characterized by the cultural traits noted above, such as the wide acceptance of and reliance on clan lineages, political clientelism, and patronage in social and political matters. Most observers link clans, in turn, to codes of honor, blood feuds, and the vendatta, which have long been part of the island's social fabric. The resulting tradition of violence has led outsiders, including politicians based on the mainland, to claim that the ethnic conflict on Corsica has had more to do with vendettas and banditry than goals of political autonomy or a language renaissance.

During the 1960s and 1970s, a coherent nationalist doctrine came to characterize the ideology of the various branches of the nationalist movement, however much they disagreed on political strategies. Under this doctrine, the history of the island was formulated in terms of colonial exploitation: Corsica was exploited first by Genoa, then by the French state, with the result that a Corsican identity was repressed, and the island was subjected to perpetual underdevelopment.

By the 1980s, the language of "Corsican specificity," which maintained the necessity of defending Corsican culture and identity, had become central to the political discourse of a broad range of political leaders and groups. Not all agreed, however, on the implications of this specificity in terms of the political strategies needed to deal with the institutions of the French state.

MANAGEMENT OF THE CONFLICT

The policy of the central government has focused on decentralizing political authority to the island in the expectation that decentralization, combined with economic development, will undercut the residual politically motivated violence that still occasionally plagues the island. Put differently, the formula is decentralization plus economic growth yields diminished violence. The questions that remain, of course, are how much decentralization and what kind of economic growth.

The central government has pursued the strategy of political decentralization in three major steps. In 1982 a newly elected Socialist government sought to decentral-

ize government authority throughout France by a series of institutional reforms. One of the first reforms targeted Corsica, where a directly elected Corsican Assembly was established. The assembly was given wide powers in executive decision making for the island in the areas of education, economic development, agriculture, transportation, and housing policy. In recognition of the importance of historical memory to Corsican sensibilities, a new university named for Pasquale Paoli was established, and the building used by Paoli's government in the 1760s became the home of the new Center for Corsican Studies.

In 1993 the central government undertook a second institutional reform package for Corsica by expanding the authority of the Corsican regional government and establishing an executive directly elected by regional councilors. At the same time, both the French government and the European Union invested heavily in the island's economic development. Although key indicators, such as per capita gross national product and unemployment figures, showed Corsica still lagging behind most French regions by the close of the twentieth century, commitments made in 1999 in both Paris and Brussels, headquarters of the European Union, promised gradually to close the gap. The progress made on the economic front, combined with the promises of more development assistance to come, suggested that the sources of the still ongoing conflicts over Corsica owed more to politics than economics.[2]

It was in this context that the third major initiative of decentralization was undertaken in 2000. The French government, led by Socialist premier Lionel Jospin, negotiated a further devolution of legislative power to Corsica. The accord also provided for the obligatory instruction of the Corsican language in the public schools and reaffirmed a variety of fiscal and economic measures designed to strengthen the Corsican economy. Although the terms of the accord were ratified overwhelmingly by a formal vote in the Corsican Assembly, the extremist wing of the nationalist movement was not unanimous in its approval of the reforms. The majority supported the peace process and, while raising questions about the implications of the government initiatives, were prepared to wait for the unfolding of the proposed changes before passing final judgment. A notable exception were several small political factions, two of which appeared in 1999 and claimed responsibility for terrorist attacks that included assassinations and the bombings of public buildings at the end of the decade.

SIGNIFICANCE

Even as the process of devolving power to Corsica was well under way, sporadic political violence—most of it targeting symbols of the French state—continued. Typically, a small splinter group of a nationalist movement would bomb a building, concentrating its attack on property damage. In 1998 the new prefect for Corsica, Claude Erignac, was assassinated; and two years later, two moderate Corsica nationalists were shot. The more recent violence, which occurred after the government's decentralization agreement of 2000, suggests that a further complication in the Corsican situation is the division between moderates and extremists in the nationalist movement over the strategy of accommodation with the central government. These kinds of divisions could make future negotiations more difficult, as they have in Northern Ireland.

Another factor complicating the future is the structure of political authority on the island. Traditionally in Corsica, local "notables" built their political influence by using personal connections to gain access to government resources such as education and employment opportunities and local infrastructure improvement projects. These resources became increasingly important as the central government poured more money into Corsica's economic development. By the 1990s, for example, one-fourth of all employment was in public sector jobs. This economic expansion provided ongoing opportunities for political elites with traditional bases of power; these same elites resisted any institutional changes that would have expanded access for new groups—those formerly excluded from political power. Unlike most mainland regions, including those that experienced nationalist movements in the 1960s and 1970s, official politics and government patronage in Corsica have been dominated by the conservative parties with a vested interest in maintaining the status quo—and their monopoly of government resources.[3] Leftist parties that might open up the political process to new groups, including nationalists, have generally been excluded from mainline politics. Consequently, the central government's strategy of decentralization largely failed to co-opt the nationalist groups. Whether the reforms of 2000 would conform to this pattern or set a new course for inclusion of formerly excluded groups was the key question at the turn of the century.

See also Canada: The Nationalist Movement in Quebec; Czechoslovakia: The Peaceful Breakup of a State; Spain: Basque Nationalism and Conflict in Democratic Spain; and United Kingdom: The Irish Question and the Partition of Ireland.

NOTES

1. Vanina, *La Renvendication institutionnelle en Corse: Collectivité territoriale et movement nationaliste* (La Bussière, France: Acratie, 1995) explores this diversity by examining seven different groupings found in the Corsican movement.
2. *Le Monde,* July 29, 2000, 7.

3. Jean-Louis Briquet, "Le problème corse," *Regards sur l'actualité* 240 (April 1998): 25–37.

SUGGESTED READINGS

Braudel, Fernand. *The Identity of France,* Vol. I; *History and Environment*. Trans. Sian Reynolds. New York: Harper & Row, 1988.

Carrington, Dorothy. *Corsica: Portrait of a Granite Island*. New York: John Day, 1974.

———. *The Dream Hunters of Corsica*. London: Weidenfield and Nicolson, 1995.

Northcutt, Wayne. *The Regions of France: A Reference Guide to History and Culture*. Westport, Conn.: Greenwood Press, 1996.

Weber, Eugen Joseph. *Peasants into Frenchmen: The Modernization of Rural France, 1870–1914*. Stanford, Calif.: Stanford University Press, 1976.

France

The "Foreigner" Issue

Joseph R. Rudolph, Jr.

1989 A national furor occurs when three North African students in Paris refuse to remove traditional head coverings worn by Muslim women. Government responds by announcing strict border controls and control of immigrants already in country.

1990 Constitutional Counsel refuses to rule that all forms of discrimination are unconstitutional. In Lyon, immigrants riot in a model redevelopment area, attacking police and looting shops.

1993 New anti-immigration law is enacted to reduce the numbers of illegal immigrants.

1995 Jacques Chirac, a Gaullist and mayor of Paris, is elected president on a platform that stresses a new toughness toward illegal immigrants in France.

1996 One week after the UN Human Rights Commission denounces a "wave of xenophobia and racism" in France, France adopts new laws regulating immigration and asylum entry into France, illegal immigrants inside France, and access of legal immigrants to French health care, education, and other services.

1997 In March, new restrictions on foreigners in France are passed; in April, the Constitutional Counsel sets aside the section of the act withdrawing the residence rights of longtime residents on the grounds of being a danger to the public order. In December, Socialists now controlling the French Assembly grant automatic citizenship to children born in France of foreign parents when they reach the age of 18.

1998 FN wins 15 percent of the vote in regional elections, forcing center-right parties to form alliances with the FN as the "party of governance" in three regions.

Conflict between indigenous peoples or older immigrant communities and more recent immigrants is not new in the world of ethnic politics. Similarly, racial prejudice has long exerted an important influence on public policy toward aliens. Historically, however, race has been an infrequent element in conflicts between diverse ethnic communities *inside* a country, primarily because racial considerations normally lead to the creation of legal barriers against immigrants coming from culturally "unacceptable" parts of the world. Thus, although much of the nineteenth-century history of America's largest cities can be written in terms of the often acrimonious battles for jobs and influence between the early and later arriving immigrant groups from Europe, conflict between European and Asian communities was minimized by immigration laws that severely restricted the ability of Chinese, Japanese, and other Asians to enter the United States.

The "foreigner" issue has unfolded differently in contemporary Western Europe. As a result of the post–World War II efforts of national leaders there to recruit workers from Southern and Central Europe, Asia and Africa, a high level of conflict has recently emerged between the indigenous populations on the one hand and, on the other, refugees, foreign workers, and immigrants from ethnically and often racially different backgrounds who are already present in large numbers within these countries. The political debate revolving around these groups has consequently become a significant and volatile element in politics throughout Western Europe, and nowhere has this debate been sharper or more influential on national politics than in France.

HISTORICAL BACKGROUND

Despite the fact that France has traditionally projected to the world an image of "one people, one language, one country," its population has historically exhibited considerable ethnic and cultural diversity. Modern France is the product of the centralizing policies of French kings who for centuries prior to the French Revolution of 1789 used both dynastic intermarriage and military conquest to establish Paris's control over regions that neither spoke French nor thought of themselves as French. By the time of the French Revolution, the populace of France spoke more than thirty different dialects and languages, and this situation lingered well into the nineteenth century. As late as 1870, despite a national school system created in 1794 to teach all children the French language, millions still conversed in Breton, Alsacian, Catalan, Flemish, or Basque, and one child in four could still not write in French. It was not until the twentieth century that the language and culture of Paris finally displaced the regional tongues in daily use, and even today French leaders must occasionally address the demands of regionalized minorities desiring greater cultural and political autonomy inside France.

The migration of people from neighboring states also contributed historically to France's cultural and ethnic diversity. During the twentieth century this traditional flow was augmented by the arrival of refugees from ever more remote areas in Europe. For the most part, however, these groups were absorbed with little political fallout. They were overwhelmingly European, frequently shared the Catholic faith of the French, arrived in relatively small numbers, and normally settled in Paris, where tens of thousands could be absorbed without altering the city's French nature. Most important, they were willing to assimilate to the French way of life.

The Emergence of the Foreigner Issue

In contrast to these earlier immigrants, the million who legally entered France between 1946 and 1974 were overwhelmingly non-European in origin, dispersed widely throughout the country, and—except for the Vietnamese whose numbers became significant after the French withdrew from Indochina in 1954—have been slow or unwilling to assimilate. Also unlike their predecessors, their presence has become a major issue in French politics.

The development of this "foreigner" problem can be substantially explained in terms of four factors, starting with the sheer size of the non-European element in contemporary French society. France had a desperate need for labor in 1945. Not only had the country's economy been disrupted by the war and many of its factories destroyed during the war, but even before the war France's chronic shortage of manpower had precluded the country from fully participating in the Industrial Revolution. The numbers are striking. In 1870 France, with 38 million people, was the largest country in Europe except for Russia, with its vast Eurasian plain. Seventy years later, despite the arrival of substantial numbers of immigrants from elsewhere in Europe, its population was only 40 million. In the intervening period, during which its economy only grew 70 percent (versus Britain's 350 percent and Germany's 500 percent), a series of small colonial conflicts and two great wars with Germany (the Franco-Prussian War of 1870–1871 and World War I, 1914–1918) had cost France awesome numbers of its young men and created a climate of insecurity that discouraged others from having large families. World War II again cost France large numbers of its young men. Consequently, one of the first acts of the postwar Fourth French Republic (1946–1958) was to create a department to recruit foreign labor from France's overseas empire in Indochina, North Africa, and West Africa. The principal hunting grounds were its possessions in nearby North Africa.

By 1995 France's foreign nationals from Algeria, Tunisia, and Morocco alone accounted for 1.5 million of the 58,027,308 people officially estimated to be living legally in France, and almost without exception they arrived as practicing Moslems. Overall, the Muslim, North African contingent constitutes approximately 3 percent of the population and almost half (45.8 percent) of the country's legal, alien population, and "legal" is the operative term with respect to these statistics.[1] In 1974 the French government began to limit the number of foreign workers permitted to enter France and began to restrict other forms of immigration. The principal effect of these measures was to turn the trickle of illegal immigrants previously entering the country into a torrent. False papers have rarely been necessary, given the relative ease with which even small craft can cross the Mediterranean Sea at night and the length of France's southern coastline. The French government officially estimates that there are 3.5 million illegal residents in France. Most commentators place that number closer to 5 million, 70 percent of whom come from North Africa.[2] Most alarming to those French concerned with preserving the French way of life is the fact that, when the list of legal and illegal foreigners is adjusted to include the children and grandchildren of the foreign-born (most of whom are French citizens by birth), the number of foreigners in the country jumps to nearly 25 percent of the population. Furthermore, their share of the population is likely to continue to increase even if France can successfully seal its borders. By the mid-1990s, France's foreign residents were responsible for 12.7 percent of all births even though they accounted for only 6.3 percent of the population.[3]

The growing size of the North African population created the visible mass necessary to awaken the French to the cultural distance separating them from the tens of thousands of Moslems arriving annually from France's former empire in North Africa. The reluctance of these immigrants to close that gap by adhering to the assimilationist path taken by prior immigrants made their presence an issue. In Paris and those areas of Mediterranean France into which they settled in large numbers, North Africans refused to renounce their overseas citizenships, erected their own markets and mosques, and continued to wear their traditional apparel. Resistance to their presence became increasingly visible in the French political process and on the street. In 1972 Jean-Marie Le Pen founded an anti-immigrant party, the Front National (FN), to give a political voice to the growing anti-immigrant sentiment in France. By 1973 physical attacks on foreign workers had become sufficiently common to prompt Algeria to halt the flow of its citizens into the French workforce.

The economic conditions of the late 1970s and the 1980s significantly intensified this emerging conflict between France's foreign residents and their French hosts. Like virtually all other European countries and Japan, France had rebuilt its economy after World War II on Middle Eastern oil—a near-at-hand energy source more efficient, more useful (in transportation, home heating, and industry), and less expensive than the coal which met France's energy needs prior to the war. During approximately the period from 1945 to 1960, the United States became a net oil importer despite remaining one of the world's leading producers of oil. For the first time in history, civilizations (in this case, Western civilization) became dependent on an essential, and not readily replaceable, energy source they did not control. Until the late 1960s the event went largely unnoticed because oil was plentiful and cheap in what was for much of the time a buyer's market; however, twice during the 1970s that dependency on imported energy came back to haunt them.

By the time the October 1973 (Yom Kippur) war broke out between Israel and its neighboring Arab states, a prolonged period of economic growth in Europe, Japan, and the United States had turned the international petroleum trade into a seller's market. When the Organization of Arab Petroleum Exporting Countries (OAPEC), which forms the inner core of the Organization of Petroleum Exporting Countries (OPEC) cartel, responded to that war by threatening to withhold oil from any country supporting Israel, panic swept the market. As NATO allies competed against one another to purchase available petroleum, the price of OPEC oil increased fourfold in less than a week, from under $3 per 42-gallon barrel of oil to nearly $12 per barrel. The process repeated itself in 1979 when the fall of the shah of Iran in January and the start of a war between Iran and Iraq in September produced a temporary shortage of oil on the market, this time more than doubling the price of OPEC oil to $36 per barrel in eight months. In both instances the result was the same. The rising cost of oil produced enormous inflationary pressures to which governments responded by raising interest rates even at the cost of increasing unemployment.

The energy crises of 1973 and 1979 ushered in a decade of global "stagflation" that was particularly hard on France. As the French unemployment rate soared from 1.8 percent in 1973 to 9 percent by 1982 and 12.2 percent by 1993, and as the numbers of unemployed doubled to over 3 million between 1973 and 1993,[4] economic issues reinforced the displeasure which the French already felt toward their foreign guests and those citizens born in France of North African parents. The foreign workers quickly became the target of French animosity even though there was scant evidence to support the argument that these workers were stealing jobs from the French. The foreign workers essentially performed those menial, unpleasant, and unsafe jobs that the French would not take at the prevailing market wages, and they continue to do so. Nevertheless, in the post–oil crisis world the argument had a

powerful appeal, especially to the nearly one in three workers entering the job market after 1973 who were not able to find employment.

Weaving these elements into a politically explosive package was the anti-immigrant Front National party. It had enjoyed very little electoral success during its first decade of existence, but France's growing unemployment rate gave it a new issue during the 1980s, and the FN took advantage of it. Blaming French economic woes on the country's large foreign population, the party began regularly to garner between 10 and 15 percent of the vote, a significant amount in a country whose voters were already divided among four nationally organized parties. In turn, the FN's growing voter base and electoral success, which continued long after the energy crises subsided and culminated in 1998 when the FN became a part of the governing coalition in three of France's regional government, has kept the foreigner issue in the forefront of the French political process and has pushed the leaders of France's principal parties into adopting much of the FN's rhetoric and several of its proposals for dealing with the foreigner problem.

THE CONFLICT

The principal characteristic of the debate concerning France's immigrant communities has been its one-sided nature. Although the immigrants have no shortage of grievances—they often live in substandard housing, for example, and unless naturalized they cannot apply for a lengthy list of jobs—political discussion has focused on these communities as the only problem requiring remedial action. The main complaints are the size of the foreign population and the unwillingness of these residents to adopt the French way of life. Critics claim that foreign workers are responsible for the high level of unemployment plaguing French workers. The issues of social nonconformity have ranged from the refusal of North African girls to follow the dress codes in the public schools, to the immigrant groups' occasionally violent protests of their living conditions and their refusal to give up their native nationalities and naturalize. Assimilation has long been the cornerstone of French immigration policy and, for that matter, social policy in France. It was not until after the presidency of Charles de Gaulle, the founder and first president (1958–1969) of the Fifth French Republic, that the government for the first time officially acknowledged that it contained any "minorities," despite the continued presence in France of linguistic minorities in such regions as Alsace, Brittany, and Corsica. Hence, the Deixonne Law, which in 1951 authorized the limited teaching of regional tongues in French public schools, explicitly excluded Alsacien, the German dialect spoken daily by the citizens in Alsace, and Corse, the Italian-based language of Corsica, as "corrupt" languages not entitled to the benefits of the law. It is therefore not surprising that any example of the unwillingness of the current immigrant communities to embrace assimilation is broadly perceived by both the French government and the French citizens socialized in the assimilationist tradition as evidence that the foreigners do not belong in France.

Meanwhile, from the perspective of France's Muslim communities, the ethnocultural collision between their lifestyle and that of their hosts is definitely two-sided. In addition to their specific grievances over such issues as housing and access to jobs, practicing Moslems tend to view Western civilization in general and the French lifestyle in particular as offensive and debased. Its crass consumerism affords them job opportunities they would not have in their homelands, but at the cost of raising their families in a society where alcohol is a part of meals and where women appear in public barely dressed. To

them, the dwelling enclaves in which they live and the markets and mosques they erect are not so much efforts to resist assimilation as oases in which they can continue to adhere to a faith that is an all-embracing guide to life.

MANAGEMENT OF THE CONFLICT

Given the nature of the foreigner debate, public policy has been far less concerned with addressing immigrant grievances than assuring the French public that the government shares their concerns. Within this framework, public policy has altered with the growing importance of the foreigner issue and the issues of the moment. During the period from 1945 to 1968, when the foreign workers began to arrive, the immigrants received little policy attention. Nothing was done to prepare the French populace for the arrival of large numbers of culturally different peoples or to help the immigrants settle in France. The fact that most of the arrivals entered as foreign workers on temporary visas rather than as immigrants destined for future citizenship seemed to make such policies unnecessary. It was not until the number of foreign workers had grown large enough to become an issue that the government began to reassess the situation. Then, at approximately the time of the FN's founding, visa requirements were tightened to the point where the loss of a job would result in the immediate withdrawal of a foreign worker's visa.

When the foreigner issue intensified after the 1973 oil crisis, government action became more aggressive. In 1974 a temporary stoppage order was imposed on all immigration originating outside of the European Community (now the European Union). The temporary ban soon became permanent. Three years later, broad categories of foreign workers were offered a free ticket home and a bonus of 10,000 francs (approximately $2,000 at the time) to leave the country. Although very few (only 5 percent of the unemployed foreign workers) took advantage of the offer, the proposal aligned public policy with public opinion and probably contributed to the FN's initial difficulty in finding electoral support. Thereafter, except for a brief period during the 1980s—when the Socialist Party controlled both the presidency and the legislature, committed itself to an image of a multicultural France not shared by the French masses, liberalized naturalization requirements, and attempted to equalize the wages and other benefits of foreign and indigenous workers—the politics of restrictionism have dominated public policy toward the foreign communities.

This pattern is particularly evident when the immigrant communities call attention to themselves; for example, in the aftermath of the immigrant riots in Lyon in 1990 and during the furor caused the previous year when three North African girls attending public school in Paris refused to remove the scarfs traditionally worn by Moslem women in order to conform to the official French dress codes. Even without such provocation, however, except for the 1997 law granting automatic citizenship at 18 to children born in France

of foreign parents, the broad course of public policy since 1990 has been decidedly biased against foreigners seeking to enter France or living in France. The Constitutional Council has refused to rule that all forms of discrimination against immigrants are unconstitutional. Border checks and other efforts to limit illegal immigration have been expanded, most notably in the 1993 Pasqual laws. Illegal immigrants have been increasingly deported with little opportunity to appeal the action despite a 1997 ruling of the Constitutional Counsel that longtime residents may not be deported solely on the vague grounds of constituting a danger to the public order. Most far reaching, in 1996—one year after Jacques Chirac was elected to the presidency on a platform that stressed a new toughness toward illegal immigrants and one week after the United Nations Human Rights Commission decried the "wave of xenophobia and racism" in France—laws were enacted to deny asylum to anyone without identity papers, to require the fingerprinting of all visa applicants from "high immigration risk countries," to impose harsh fines on those employing workers without valid work permits, and to limit the rights of even legal resident aliens to health care, education, and other social services.[5] In each instance, the policy goal has not so much been to manage the conflict between the French and the foreign communities as to (1) stem the FN's further electoral growth, (2) placate the antiforeigner opinions held to some degree by the vast majority of France's citizens, and (3) keep the traditional parties in office.

SIGNIFICANCE

The ethnic conflict involving France's North African communities, although not particularly violent or long in duration, is illustrative of the debate concerning foreign workers, refugees, asylum seekers, and/or immigrants in such other Western

FRANCE. Front National founder and party leader Jean-Marie Le Pen inaugurates his 2002 campaign for the French presidency. Photo courtesy of Front National Web site, www.frontnational.com.

European countries as Austria, Belgium, Germany, and Sweden. In each instance, the foreigner issue has unfolded in much the same pattern as in France, and in several countries it has propelled antiforeigner parties like the FN into parliamentary seats. Furthermore, the issue has enormous potential to disrupt and redefine French politics in the foreseeable future. Indicators of this development can already be found, for example, in the FN's growing electoral support in those portions of southern France with high concentrations of North Africans and in the resultant weakening of the major parties' hold over the regional governments in these areas. It is worth remembering in this context that the French word for foreigner, *l'étranger,* literally means one who is strange or different. As long as the North African contingent continues to reject cultural assimilation, it is unlikely that the conflict between the native French and the North Africans will abate. On the contrary, as the number of North Africans increases, the conflict is apt to grow, even if an increasing number of these foreigners are, in fact, French citizens by birth or naturalization.

See also Germany: The Foreign Worker Issue; and United Kingdom: The Making of British Race Relations.

NOTES

1. Http//www.France.diplomatic.fr/France/geo/popu.gb.html, July 1, 1997.
2. Milton J. Esman, *Ethnic Politics* (Ithaca, N.Y.: Cornell University Press, 1997), 199.
3. Http//www.France.diplomatic.fr/France/geo/popu.gb.html, July 1, 1997.
4. For a comparative discussion of the economic impact of the energy crises on France, see Jean Saint-Geours, "The Social Contract Under Stress in Western Europe," in Daniel Yergin and Martin Hillenbrand, eds., *Global Insecurity: A Strategy for Energy and Economic Renewal* (New York: Penguin Books, 1983): 230–64. Unemployment figures for the 1973–1982 period are taken from Saint-Geours, 256. The 1993 data can be found at http://www.nato.int/ccms/general/countrydb/france.htm.
5. Julie Read, "Rift over French Immigration Laws," *The European,* April 18–24, 1996.

SUGGESTED READINGS

Fysh, Peter, and Jim Wolfreys. "Le Pen, the National Front, and the Extreme Right in France." *Parliamentary Affairs* 45, no. 3 (July 1992): 309–25.

Heisler, Martin O., and Barbara Schmitter Heisler, eds. *From Foreign Workers to Settlers? Transnational Migration and the Emergence of the New Minorities.* Beverly Hills, Calif.: Sage Publications. *The Annals of the American Academy of Political and Social Sciences,* v. 485, 1986).

Horowitz, Donald L., and Gerrard Noiriel, eds. *Immigrants in Two Democracies: French and American Experience.* New York: New York University Press, 1992.

Messina, Anthony M., ed. *Ethnic and Racial Minorities in Advanced Industrial Democracies.* New York: Greenwood Press, 1992.

Ogden, Philip. "Immigration to France Since 1945: Myth and Reality." *Ethnic and Racial Studies* 14, no. 3 (July 1991): 294–17.

Tiersky, Ronald. *France in the New Europe.* Belmont, Calif.: Wadsworth, 1994.

Vaughan, Michalina. "The Extreme Right in France: 'Lepenisme,' or the Politics of Fear." In *The Far Right in Western and Eastern Europe,* edited by Luciano Cheles, Ronnie Ferguson, and Michalina Vaughan. New York: Longman, 1995.

Viorst, Milton. "The Muslims of France." *Foreign Affairs* 75, no. 5 (September/October 1996): 78–96.

Weiner, Myron. *The Global Immigration Crisis: Challenge to States and to Human Rights.* New York: HarperCollins, 1995.

Wolfreys, Jim. "The Programme of the French Front National." *Parliamentary Affairs* 46, no. 3 (July 1993): 415–29.

Germany

The Foreign Worker Issue

John S. Bendix

TIMELINE

1848 First attempt is made at German unification.

1871 German unification is accomplished.

1913 German Citizenship Law is adopted.

1945 Allied occupation occurs; zonal division soon leads to creation of West and East Germany.

1953 Federal Expellee Law is enacted.

1955 West Germany regains sovereignty; recruitment of Italian foreign workers begins.

1961 Berlin Wall is built; a worker recruitment agreement is concluded with Turkey.

1973 "Oil Shock"; official recruitment ends.

1989 German reunification occurs.

1999–2002 No subsequent, equally significant developments shaping Germany's policies. Lesser events include a constitutional amendment in 1993 and new set of laws in 2002, tightening the requirements for asylum, and half-hearted efforts in 1999 and 2001 to offer German citizenship to foreigners born in Germany.

In the United States, the term "ethnic" calls attention to a history of immigration to the country by people who differed substantially from one another by national origin, religious faith, or cultural practices, as well as to the segregation and persecution of those who came to the United States involuntarily as slaves or who were Native Americans. "Ethnicity" implies differentiation and raises the question whether those who claim to belong to an ethnic group should have particular group rights. Even so, there is an overarching faith that being an American is a greater and more inclusive identity, and that the unity of the American nation is created out of its diversity.

In Germany, ethnic has referred instead to the majority culture and to a largely nineteenth-century idea of the unity and community of the German people (or *Volk*). Minority groups of both non-German and German background exist, but American-style assertions of minority group interests or "identity politics" have been barely evident. Conflicts instead have circled around economics and cultural difference, and they are often framed as a debate between those on the political right arguing that long-term residents from non-German national, religious, or cultural backgrounds need to integrate into and adapt to German culture, and those on the political left arguing that there is de facto diversity and de facto immigration, and that non-Germans have brought many benefits to Germany. The ethnic view has been top down, emphasizing what the government or the Germans think minorities need to do to accommodate Germany, not the other way around.

HISTORICAL BACKGROUND

The emphasis on a specifically German identity was a response to the need to find cultural unity among the 39 kingdoms, duchies, principalities, and free cities that were politically unified as the German Confederation in 1815, but it was also a reaction to the new idea of a "nation," which emerged from the French Revolution. Protestant, militaristic, imperial Prussia in the north and west was by far the largest and most powerful of the sovereign, autonomous territories in this confederation, but it had a strong rival in the Catholic kingdom of Bavaria in the south. Each member of the confederation had its own currency, weights and measures, and passport controls, so the natives of one territory were treated as foreigners when they traveled to a neighboring territory. The first steps toward German unity were the creation of a customs union to level barriers and establish free trade; however, a first attempt to create a common political system failed in 1848. Only in 1871 would the German Empire be called into life under the leadership of Prussian Emperor William I and Chancellor Otto von Bismarck.

If most of the nineteenth century was consumed with the effort to create a cohesive German political state, the effort to define what was German about the Germans was even more protracted. As early as the 1660s, the German language was exalted as natural and organic, as well as ancient, pure, and incomparable. That leg-

acy fed into the Romantic notions of Johann Gottfried Herder in the 1770s of a poetic "soul of the folk" that he linked to an organic idea of the nation and the use of language. By 1810 Friedrich Ludwig Jahn was writing about the *Volk* as the "organic body of common life," and equating folk traditions (*Volkstum*) with Germanness. He used a kind of mystifying language that spoke of the "inner consolidation of folk traditions" and the idea of a German collective spirit (*Geist*) that would give life to what was still a very fragmented collection of German-speaking people. Over the next decades, as part of the process of nation building, scholars like the Brothers Grimm engaged in intensive examinations of the origins of the language, as well as of popular myths, beliefs, and folk tales, and in the process helped create a sense of a unique people with a common culture, character, history, and future. One still hears echoes of Romantic mystification in claims that terms like *Heimat* or *Gemeinschaft* cannot be translated or understood by non-Germans.

Herder wrote that "nature obliges us to learn only our native tongue," and the consequence of scholarly efforts like that of the Grimms was to standardize German and make that standard the only language of school instruction.[1] While this certainly made communication easier across the politically fragmented territories, it also devalued dialects and discouraged the use of any language but German. Herder also wrote that people held nothing dearer than the language of their fathers, and to deprive them of it was to deprive a people "of its only immortal possession."[2] Yet such deprivation seems to have been practiced on the Slavic peoples who lived in Prussia, which in its eastern and largely rural territory stretched all the way across northern Poland into Lithuania. With the rise of industrial employment in the late nineteenth century, rural Poles with Prussian citizenship migrated to work in the coal mines of the Ruhr river basin far to the west to escape the drudgery of agricultural work on the estates of the large eastern landowners.

Prussia actively sought to Germanize these ethnic Polish Prussians, even though they resisted, while simultaneously strengthening its eastern borders to keep Russians out. This dual approach laid the groundwork for a policy pursued ever since to favor "natives" (*Inländer*) over "foreigners" (*Ausländer,* literally, those outside the territory). It also set the stage for the 1913 Reich German Citizenship Law, large parts of which are still in effect today, which establishes descent by blood (*jus sanguinis*) as the basis for citizenship. Merely living in Germany (*jus soli*) has been far less important for citizenship than the efforts foreigners make to assimilate and become culturally, politically, socially, and linguistically German.

Because homogeneity and the sharing of a common cultural heritage were the key elements of German ethnicity, the minority group of German Jews (many of whom were middle class, urban, and highly assimilated into German culture, economics, and social life) were bewildered by their rapid segregation after the Nazis came to power in 1933. Jews as well as other groups unpalatable to Nazi ideology were pushed out of many professions, deprived of their possessions and businesses, subjected to punitive taxes, and by Nazi law (rescinded in 1945) declared to not be part of the German *Volk.* Thousands of the persecuted had fled the country by 1939, but nearly all of the German Jews who could not leave were murdered or died as a result of disease or deprivation in various labor, concentration, and killing camps throughout the Third Reich over the next six years.

The horrors of the war, coupled with military defeat, occupation, and the creation of new political institutions after 1945 in both West and East Germany deeply affected the German sense of identity to the point where there was a nearly allergic reaction in law, politics, and society to anything that even faintly smelled of nationalism. Pride in West Germany was taken in technological achievements, in the robust economy, and the sound Deutschmark currency, or in Johann Sebastian Bach and Martin Luther. Until the mid-1980s, even flag-waving and national anthem-singing smacked of fanaticism and the ruin brought about by Adolf Hitler.

During World War II, hundreds of thousands of people lost their citizenship, were driven from, fled from, or evacuated from their homes. About 7 million foreigners, including Jews and prisoners of war, were employed in the Third Reich by 1944, many—though not all—unwillingly. In 1945, between 5 and 7 million "displaced persons" were in Allied-occupied Germany, living in a territory where half the buildings were damaged or destroyed.[3] By 1955 many displaced persons had been repatriated, replaced in West Germany by those fleeing East Germany and by those of German background who found themselves less than welcome in Communist East Europe. By 1961 as many as 13 million displaced persons, refugees, and expellees may have been added to the West German population.[4] Because many of these were of the "right" (that is, German) ethnicity, their integration was aided by public laws and private efforts, although that, in turn, created some resentment among resident Germans who felt passed over despite their own needs.

West Germany, newly sovereign in 1955, began to move into a phase of rapid economic growth, and with it came labor shortages (migration from the east had come to a halt in 1961 with the building of the Berlin Wall). To meet the need, the government in 1955 negotiated a contract with Italy to bring agricultural workers temporarily to West Germany; however, the needs of industry for longer-term laborers soon led to recruitment agreements with Greece and Spain (both in 1960), Turkey (1961), Portugal (1964), and Yugoslavia (1968). Limited arrangements were also made to bring in Tunisians and Moroccans (1965, 1966), as well as Japanese, Korean, and Chilean coal miners (1962–1965). Labor demand was so strong that at least one-third of the foreign workers arriving in Germany were circumventing official recruitment entirely and simply arriving with a visa and looking for work. By 1973 nearly 12 percent (or 2.5 million workers) of the German workforce was foreign.[5]

Though the German government assumed foreign workers would return home at the end of their labor contracts, and some indeed did, many remained even after official recruitment halted in 1973. Because the German constitution accords special protection to families, settled foreign workers were able to have their families join them in Germany if they met certain criteria. However, as this minority grew while the economy stagnated, some politicians in the mid-1980s suggested appropriate financial incentives might persuade long-term resident foreign families to return to their home countries permanently. Most foreign families were not tempted, and political opposition was sufficiently intense that this idea was soon dropped. At the same time, the inclusion of Greece, Spain, and Portugal into the European Union (EU) by 1986 meant labor migration barriers for some previously recruited Europeans were vanishing. When additional measures to "make an ever closer European Union" passed in 1992, Germans had to start thinking of, if not treating, fellow-EU citizens more like *Inländer;* Turks and Yugoslavs (and a growing number of political asylum seekers from the Middle East and Asia) remained *Ausländer.* The alienness of the *Ausländer* was reinforced by German reunification in 1989, when West Germans suddenly discovered there were thousands of resident foreign workers from such socialist countries as Vietnam, Mozambique, or Cuba living in East Germany.

THE CONFLICT

One major arena of conflict has been economic: when economic times are good or there are special labor needs, foreigners are recruited to come and work, but when economic times are bad, they are accused of taking jobs away and are encouraged to leave the country. Readily forgotten is that many foreigners began in the 1960s by working in menial service or repetitive industrial jobs to *replace* German natives who were only too happy to move up to better positions. With time, entire low-wage employment categories—for example, trash collection or assembly-line work—became associated with low-status foreigners, so it is very odd in economic downturns for Germans then to claim foreigners are *displacing* them, since even if these foreigners left, many Germans would not want the foreign worker jobs again that they had long ago abandoned. Competition for jobs since 1992 has increasingly been between EU workers, all of whom have priority over non-EU workers (including Turks), and not between Germans and foreigners. To complicate matters further, at least in the industrial workplace—and perhaps because the main focus there is on tasks to be completed rather than on cultural differences between workers—workers from various ethnicities (including Germans) have managed to get along with one another. Competition *for* the job does not preclude cooperation when *on* the job.

The cultural conflicts have been the most visible. Some are minor, as when Italian workers in the early 1960s complained that their German employers always served potatoes and not pasta—an amusing complaint today, now that Italian cuisine is ubiquitous in German cities. Other conflicts have been more serious, with mutually held stereotypes having behavioral and workplace consequences. A 1961 German list of pointers for dealing with Italian, Spanish, and Greek foreign workers stated that "some Southerners do not yet have a proper sense of cleanliness and order," and "communication difficulties tempt foreign workers from the South into telling white lies . . . (and) as a result one can not always or immediately believe what they say." On the other side of the coin, there are those like the Italian worker who in 1960 said, "For the Germans, I'm a tool, like a spade or a hoe. I'm supposed to work and keep my trap shut."[6]

The most enduring cultural conflict has been between the Germans and the Turkish Muslims. Germans have found some Turkish religious practices, such as those followed during Ramadan, hard to accept or understand. In addition, some cultural practices with respect to women—such as the wearing of head scarves and prohibiting daughters from school activities out of fear for their modesty—are widely judged as incompatible with German gender norms. The fact that many labor migrants came from rural Anatolia in the 1960s supported the stereotype that Turks in Germany were uneducated (if not uncivilized) peasants. The irony in the (sometimes violent) reactions even to how Turks appear in public is that Germany until recently was quite rural, German peasant women wore head scarves, and German patriarchs ruled the home. But if Turks unconsciously remind Germans of a part of their past they would like to leave behind, Muslim Turks may be equally reluctant to accommodate German mores, since for some Turks accommodation is the first step toward Christianization and the abandoning of their faith.

It has not helped that German attitudes toward foreign workers in the 1970s and 1980s were whipped up by fears of *Über-* *fremdung* (literally, "overforeignization") and political talk about how West Germany had reached its limits in its ability to take in foreigners. Those limits seem pretty low, given that foreigners remained a steady 7 to 8 percent of the population from 1973 to 1989 (and since reunification, from 9 to 10 percent). Fears are worsened by the fact that disproportionate numbers of both foreigners and press reporters are concentrated in large cities. Thus, even though only 7 million of Germany's 82 million residents are foreigners (2 million of them Turks), 29 percent of Frankfurt's population was foreign by 1995.[7] A Frankfurt reporter looking for a story on foreigners forgets that the city has triple the national average.

Open expression of *Ausländerfeindlichkeit* (hostility toward foreigners) is all too frequent, and to the bullies willing to use violence against Turks, Vietnamese, or black Africans, these foreigners are defined as competitors taking away German jobs, sapping German society and threatening the integrity and order of German culture. These are old nationalistic canards, though evidently newly discovered in the eastern German states since 1989— ironically, the regions where the fewest foreigners are to be found, though also some of the economically most depressed areas in reunified Germany. Against these culturally based, emotional claims from the violent political right, many Germans point to the economic benefits foreign workers have brought, and some argue that Germany has been socially and culturally enriched by their presence.

MANAGEMENT OF THE CONFLICT

The management of the conflict for many years has been characterized by deep denial. Politicians have argued at least since the mid-1960s that Germany is not a country of immigration, which aside from being historically inaccurate willfully ignores the fact that in 1995 one-sixth of the 7 million foreign nationals in Germany were born in Germany, and that more than half of all resident foreigners had lived in Germany for more than 10 years by that time.[8] The standard term used, *Ausländerpolitik* (policy toward foreigners), linguistically upholds the century-old distinction between native and foreigner and ignores immigration. Other forms of denial exist, including Chancellor Helmut Kohl's refusal in 1992 to go to Mölln (the site of a horrific murder of long-resident Turks), and the thinking that by banning a few, small, extreme right-wing political parties one can somehow address the problems of xenophobia.

Another form of management is more invidious. To both public and private agencies, it sounds good to try to "integrate" foreigners by providing special German-language classes or encouraging them to form associations like sports clubs (but not political associations). The ultimate point is to have foreigners adapt to the German way of life. Conflicts are thereby "managed" by teaching non-natives to behave more like natives—another form of Germanizing—rather than having Germans adapt to the customs and habits of the foreigners living among them, or at least for both natives and foreigners to develop new, joint forms of social behavior. Even though some academics have tried to promote it, the idea of dual citizenship or a U.S.–style ethnic hyphenation (e.g., a Turkish-German or a German-Serb) has received very little support, although some legal changes to improve access to citizenship for the children of foreign workers were enacted on the eve of the twenty-first century.

SIGNIFICANCE

Social science and historical studies suggest that the perception of cultural similarity has a large effect on the German acceptance of foreigners: the more similar a group seems to the German by language, religion, race, customs, and history, the more accepted it is. Physical proximity can also play a role: cosmopolitan city dwellers find ways to cope with their foreign neighbors; it is the suburban or rural residents with little contact who are the ones who most fear and dislike foreigners. Feared and disliked groups, unfortunately, are also ready objects for projection, and those labeled different have in many cultures become scapegoats whenever personal or political matters take a turn for the worse.

The importance of not leaving current cultural and economic conflicts unresolved is evident for both demographic and nationalistic reasons. Given the low birthrate among Germans and the demographic projections of current population growth among non-Germans, even conservative estimates foresee a doubling in the proportion of foreign nationals by 2030.[9] If the concentration of foreigners in larger cities persists, then some urban areas may soon have nearly half their population as disenfranchised, second-class residents. The potential for social and political conflict with a population that large who continue to be held at arm's length from German decision making and public positions looms large.

Yet, at the same time, Germany is running headlong into the arms of Europe, coordinating its economics to the point of giving up the Deutschmark currency, a core symbol of postwar identity, in favor of the abstraction of the Euro. Political and social coordination with other EU nations has been slower, but the direction seems inexorable: it will mean less of Germany and more of Europe. One unnoted area is legal coordination: EU law already supercedes national law, a situation that could well have an impact on minority group rights within EU countries. In response to these impending changes, some Germans cling to an older sense of Germanness and fight a kind of rearguard action to hold on to an older, imagined identity. Perhaps, like those who have left their home countries and chosen to move to Germany themselves, Germans should find this movement toward Europe less a threat than an opportunity.

See also France: The "Foreigner" Issue; and United Kingdom: The Making of British Race Relations.

NOTES

1. Johann Gottfried Herder, *Sämmtliche Werke,* ed. Bernard Suphan et al. (33 volumes, Berlin: Weichmann, 1877–1913) vol. 17: 58, cited in Hans Kohn, *The Idea of Nationalism* (New York: Collier Books, 1967): 432.
2. Herder, loc. cit., vol. 1: 21, cited in Kohn, 423–33.
3. Frank Grube and Gerhard Richter, *Die Gründerjahre der Bundesrepublik—Deutschland zwischen 1945 und 1955* (Hamburg: Hoffman and Campe, 1981): SR-27.
4. Robert Mueller, *West Germany Under Construction* (Ann Arbor: University of Michigan Press, 1997), 54.
5. More precisely, 11.9 percent or 2,595,000 workers were foreign, according to the "Anwerbung und Vermittlung Ausländischer Arbeitnehmer—Erfahrungsbericht 1973" (pp. 70–1), an annual survey report on foreign worker recruitment and employment that was published by the *Bundesanstalt für Arbeit* [the German Federal Employment Administration] in Nürnberg from 1961 to 1973. Hartmut Esser, "Gastarbeiter" gives a slightly different figure (11.6 percent of the employed population was foreign in 1973) in Wolfgang Benz, hg., *Die Geschichte der Bundesrepublik Deutschland: Wirtschaft (Vol. 2)* (Frankfurt: Fischer Verlag, 1989), pp. 332–33.
6. This is the title quote in Gerhard Mauz, "Ich bin fur die Deutschen wie Gerat, wie Spaten, hacke," *Die Welt,* August 22, 1960: 1.
7. The best recent source in English is Klaus Bade and Myron Weiner, *Migration Past, Migration Future: Germany and the United States (Vol. 1)* (Oxford: Berghahn Books, 1997). Figure 3.4, Foreigners and Foreign Labor in Germany 1960–1994, p. 80, provides population numbers and trends; Table 3.5, German Cities with the Highest Share of Foreign Population, p. 97, provides breakdowns for the major cities, giving the Frankfurt percentage in 1993 as 27.9 percent. These figures are from official publications from the Federal Statistics Office (Statistisches Bundesamt) and from the Federal Employment Administration (Bundesanstalt für Arbeit). As of 1999, at http://www.bafl.de/bafl/template/migration/content_migration_auslaenderanteil_bundeslaender.htm (citing official statistics), Frankfurt had 30.1 percent foreigners.

   According to "Ausländer im Bundesgebiet seit 1960," Table 1 of "Facts and Figures on the Situation of Foreigners in the Federal Republic of Germany" available at http://www.bundesauslaenderbeauftragte.de/daten/index.stm, there were just under 7.3 million foreigners in Germany in 2000, or 8.9 percent of the population; 1,998,534 of these were Turks. The "Bundesausländerbeauftragte" is the Federal Commissioner for Foreigners.
8. According to the latest statistics (available 2000), this figure is even higher: 22.1 percent (or 1,613,778) of the 7,296,817 foreigners (e.g., more than one-fifth) of the foreigner population was born in Germany. The source is "Die ausländische Bevölkerung in der Bundesrepublik Deutschland am 31. Dezember 2000 nach Altersgruppen und in Deutschland Geborene," Table 4 of "Facts and Figures on the Situation of Foreigners in the Federal Republic of Germany" available at http://www.bundesauslaenderbeauftragte.de/daten/index.stm
9. Extracted from a lengthy discussion of demographic and migration trends of both Germans and foreigners in Germany, in Rainer Münz and Ralf Ulrich, "Migration und zukünftige Bevölkerungsentwicklung in Deutschland," in Klaus Bade and Rainer Münz, eds. *Migrationsreport 2000: Fakten—Analysen—Perspektiven* (Frankfurt: Campus Verlag, 2000): 23–58.

SUGGESTED READINGS

Bade, Klaus, and Myron Weiner, eds. *Migration Past, Migration Future: Germany and the United States.* Providence, R.I.: Berghahn, 1997.

Barbieri, William. *Ethics of Citizenship.* Durham, N.C.: Duke University Press, 1998.

Bendix, John. *Importing Foreign Workers: A Comparison of German and American Policy.* New York: Peter Lang, 1990.

Brubaker, Rogers. *Citizenship and Nationhood in France and Germany.* Cambridge, Mass.: Harvard University Press, 1992.

Cordell, Karl, ed. *Ethnicity and Democratization in the New Europe.* London: Routledge, 1999.

Fetzer, Joel. *Public Attitudes Toward Immigration in the United States, France, and Germany.*

Cambridge, England: Cambridge University Press, 2000.

Finzsch, Norbert, and Dietmar Schirmer, eds. *Identity and Intolerance: Nationalism, Racism, and Xenophobia in Germany and the United States.* Cambridge, England: Cambridge University Press, 1998.

Homze, Edward. *Foreign Labor in Nazi Germany.* Princeton, N.J.: Princeton University Press, 1967.

Kohn, Hans. *The Idea of Nationalism.* New York: Collier, 1967.

Moeller, Robert. *West Germany Under Construction: Politics, Society, and Culture in the Adenauer Era.* Ann Arbor; Mich.: University of Michigan Press, 1997.

Panayi, Panikos. *Ethnic Minorities in Nineteenth and Twentieth Century Germany: Jews, Gypsies, Poles, Turks and Others.* London: Longman, 2000.

India

Ethnic Conflict and Nation-building in a Multiethnic State

Maya Chadda

TIMELINE

1947 Partition of India into India and Pakistan occurs.

1956 Indian Federation is reorganized essentially on a linguistic state basis.

1963 Nagaland is created.

1972 Breakup of Assam occurs.

1973 Anandpur Sahib Resolution is passed by Akali Dal in Punjab.

1980 The Congress Party under Indira Gandhi returns to power at the center.

1984 Followers of Jarnail Singh Bhindranwale confront the Indian army in the Sikh Golden Temple; Indira Gandhi is assassinated.

1985 Rajiv Gandhi and the Congress Party win a landslide victory; Rajiv Gandhi signs an agreement involving Punjab with Akali Dal leader Harchandsingh Longowale.

1989 Insurgency breaks out in Kashmir.

1992 In elections held in Punjab, the Akali Dal wins a majority.

2000 In August, three additional states are carved out of the Punjab state in an effort to manage ethnic conflict in northern India.

2002 In the spring, Pakistan's alleged support of insurgents in Kashmir brings India and Pakistan to brink of war.

The press and media reporting on India is usually dominated by stories of religious and ethnic violence. Ever since India gained its independence in 1947, scholars of India have regularly predicted India's demise. In popular perceptions, India's unity is forever in question. Fortunately, these forebodings have failed to materialize, but their origin is not difficult to understand. How can a country of subcontinent proportions, comprising 325 distinctive languages, several separate religions, endemic poverty, and a century and a half of colonial subjugation, become a coherent nation-state? It is not surprising that many regard ethnic conflict as a threat to India's modern and democratic political system. Yet, as one looks back from the beginning of the new millennium, India has been remarkably successful in welding together a coherent political community out of a welter of unintegrated and often mutually antagonistic regions and provinces. This is not to deny the destructive impact of ethnic violence in India—which has marked much of its recent history—but to suggest that ethnic conflicts and their accommodations need to be viewed within a single perspective that accounts for both India's success and failures. India's experience suggests an answer to the critical question of our times: how to accommodate multiethnic communities within a single territorial nation while retaining a broadly democratic framework?

HISTORICAL BACKGROUND

India's ethnic map has been shaped by many factors. The rise and fall of empires, the Mughal and then the British, led to the crystallization of ethnic consciousness in several regions of the Indian subcontinent. Before the British arrived on the scene, India was ruled by several large and small kingdoms, each multiethnic and multireligious but with one or two linguistic groups that had gained dominance because of royal patronage and size. The British had absorbed these kingdoms into their empire by 1857 but largely stayed away from the way in which local communities defined themselves. British policies nevertheless had a profound impact on the self-definition of ethnic communities. The introduction of census and recruitment in the colonial army along ethnic and religious lines reinforced ethnic identities. For instance, the British believed that certain ethnic groups made better soldiers than others. The Punjabi-speaking Sikhs and the Marathas who spoke Marathi were considered martial races. In contrast, the Bengali-speaking people of Bengal, perceived to be soft and artistic, were viewed as good civil servants but poor soldiers. Hence, the British created the Sikh regiment exclusively for the Sikhs and recruited other communities into the army along ethnic, caste, and religious lines. As demand for self-rule grew among Indian nationalists, the British created special electorates for the "minority" communities—the Muslims and Sikhs—in India. These policies gradually become a part of the ethnic history and the British perceptions, a part of the ethnic folklore. Both carried beyond the British rule into the political life of independent India.

The rise of India's nationalist movement and the way in which it came to be organized was the second factor to shape ethnic identity. The rise of nationalism in the nineteenth century had initiated a search for indigenous histories and cultural pride in which "they" the British were separated from "we" the Indians, but the "we" consisted of many ethnic communities with distinctive histories and languages. These were fully formed by the time the idea of separate electorates got its first push in the 1930s. The gradual welding of pan-Indian nationalism was then mediated through ethnic identities which had firm roots in particular regions of India. In its mass mobilization phase (the 1940s), the Indian national movement gathered support by appealing to ethnic pride. By the time India became independent, it was a land of politicized ethnic and religious identities that had lent support to win independence and were ready to bargain with the new pan-Indian nation-state. Since 1947 the management of these identities has become the principal preoccupation of every central government in India.

THE CONFLICT

Not all ethnic groups demanded equal status or a separate state. Why did some seek integration while others demanded separation? First, particular ethnolinguistic communities are concentrated in and constitute a numerical majority in particular regions. For instance, the Gujarati-speaking people dominate the western regions of historical Gujarat, and the Tamil-speaking people dominate the southeastern region of Tamilnadu. There is a correlation, though not a perfect fit, between the ethnic "homeland" and the ethnic identity. Possessing many of the features of a nation, these ethnic communities have sought cultural and political autonomy. This has often been the cause of tension between the government in New Delhi and the ethnic community. Other ethnolinguistic groups have also constituted a significant presence in the same province. Conflict can develop if one group believes it is being discriminated against while its rival is favored with power, office, and status.

Second, ethnic groups can be divided into core and periphery groups in India. The former are a part of the Indian heartland; the latter reside on the state's outer boundaries and frequently share kinship and identity with fellow ethnic groups across borders. The Indian Kashmiris and the Kashmiris across the border in Pakistan, the Tamils in India and in Sri Lanka,

the Bengalis in West Bengal and in what is now Bangladesh, and the Nagas on both sides of the India-Myanmar border are only a few examples of these overlapping, cross-border ethnic identities. Such ethnic group overlaps have been used by one or more countries in the region to intervene in the domestic politics of a neighboring state. Pakistan uses the Kashmiris to wage clandestine warfare against India; India has used its Bengali and Tamil ethnic nationalities to mount interventions against Pakistan and Sri Lanka. The distinction between the core and the periphery may blur where demands for autonomy give way to demands for separation, which can happen if frustrated ethnic groups seek out and receive arms and safe havens across the border.

Third, as most popular movements are prone to do, ethnic conflicts have a rhythm; they rise and fall. Ethnic communities are known to move from auton-

NEW DELHI, INDIA. New Delhi, India's modern capital and, with a population of nearly 10 million people, the third-largest city in India. Photo courtesy of Vijayendra Kumar.

omy to separatist militancy and then back to autonomy. The separatist movement in Punjab followed this rhythm between 1970s and 1990s.

Fourth, electoral expansion and economic growth have contributed to and shaped ethnic tensions. Growth has produced a sense of relative deprivation among rival ethnic groups. For instance, the separatist movement in Punjab was nurtured by the perception that the central government had neglected Punjab in its allocation of industrial investments. Modernity and growth are the goals of both the pan-Indian and ethnic leaders in India. Ethnicity is not a primordial construct driven by the impulse to return to some form of nativity. Political activism of one ethnic community can often spark parallel activism in a proximate ethnic group. For instance, the Bodos, who constitute a relatively small ethnic group (about 5 million) within the Assam province, demanded protection from the central government when a movement calling for "Assam to the Assamese" reached a violent stage.

Finally, but most important, party competition and rivalry for office and position have heightened ethnic tensions. Ethnic leaders belonging to national as well as provincial parties have fomented ethnic sentiments to win elections. Clearly no single cause explains the reasons for the ethnic conflicts that have marked India's federal evolution since 1947.

MANAGEMENT OF THE CONFLICT

To achieve and preserve unity within this environment, governments in New Delhi have sought to centralize power. Anxious to retain cultural and political autonomy, ethnic identity has been mobilized to resist the center. The past 55 years of independent India can be divided into three broad phases: from 1950 to 1980, a period marked largely by accommodation,

although after the middle of 1970s the spirit of compromise faded; from 1980 to 1990, a period in which violent ethnic conflict resurrected the fears of disintegration; and from 1990 to the present, a period in which the balance has been restored in favor of accommodation.

The first order of required business for independent India was to weld its disparate regions and many layers of rule and jurisdictions into a single, coherent political system. That task was accomplished by merging the approximately 500 princely states and regions directly under British rule into the Indian state. The unification of the new nation-state was not an easy task given that the princely states possessed nominal sovereignty and had been given a choice between India, Pakistan, and independence by the departing British authorities. The Hindu-Muslim riots of 1946–1947, the communal carnage that accompanied the division of British India, and the outbreak of war over Kashmir immediately following the division all made Indian leaders fearful that a heterogenous India might not hold together. By the same token, India was too large and too diverse to fit into a unitary design. The Indian leaders thus created a constitution that sought to balance the need for unification against those of autonomy. India was to be a secular federal democracy with a strong central government that possessed vast powers over its federal units, especially in the event of a local or national emergency. The constitution, however, did not define the criterion by which India's federal units were to be created. Originally, the Indian federation was to be structured primarily on the basis of administrative efficiency.

The initial reaction to the administrative division between the center and the federal units occurred in Andhra in 1953. Setting the pattern for future demands, it took the form of a demand for a linguistically defined Andhra province. Other large and numerically dominant ethnolinguistic groups lacking states of their own soon followed Andhra's lead. By 1954 ethnic agitation had spread far and wide. The central government of Prime Minister Jawaharlal Nehru was, nevertheless, reluctant to divide India on the basis of language or religion. The trauma of the 1947 partition had clearly left a mark. Nehru sought to calm ethnic tempers by appointing the State Reorganization Commission to look into the problem and make recommendations. In 1956, after much foot dragging, the Nehru government implemented the commission's recommendations and reorganized the Indian federation along ethnolinguistic lines.[1] However, as already noted, there was no perfect fit to be found in India between ethnicity and territory. The region of Punjab and Bombay could not be divided neatly along ethnolinguistic lines because the province of Bombay comprised Marathi- and Gujarati-speaking communities, both with legitimate claims to the most important commercial city in India, Bombay. Similarly, the province of Punjab, included Sikhs and Hindus who both spoke Punjabi but worshiped at separate temples. Nor could any reasonable linguistic criterion be applied to the country's northeast.

The Conflict in the Punjab

In the Punjab, communal religious rivalries were exploited by both the Hindu and Sikh leaders. The Sikh leader, Master Tara Singh, argued that religion made the Sikhs a distinctive people who could be safe only in an autonomous Punjab. The Nehru government refused to recognize religion as the basis for division. That, in his view, undermined the secular foundations of independent India. In the reorganized Punjab, which had been made larger by adding adjacent regions to it, the Sikhs had become a minority and could not win enough seats to form the provincial government there. The Indian National Congress Party, nonetheless, remained popular

with the Sikhs. Meanwhile, when it failed to garner support for the religious argument, the Akali Dal Party, which represented a segment of the Sikhs, shifted to language as the basis for demanding a provincial state of Punjab. In 1965 it was partially rewarded for this tactic when Indira Gandhi, India's third prime minster, created three new states out of the former Punjab: Haryana, a Hindu majority state; Punjab, a Sikh majority state; and Himachal Pradesh.

Although the Sikhs became a majority in the newly restructured Punjab state, the Hindus remained a significant minority. That might not have been a problem had the Akali Dal fulfilled its dream of winning assembly elections and forming a provincial level government. Throughout the decades of 1960s and 1970s, however, the Congress Party continued to dominate Punjab in elections. The Akali Dal repeatedly appealed to the religious sentiments of the Sikhs but, until the 1980s, a large number among them remained impervious to such appeals. The Punjabi Hindus generally supported the right-wing political party, the Jan Sangh. In the 1960s and early part of the 1970s, the Congress had managed to hold the balance between the Hindus and Sikhs by forging an alliance across religious, class, and ethnic lines. By the end of 1970s, though, the political economy of Punjab had changed, with profound implications for politics in that state.[2] A whole new class of peasant proprietors had emerged in the previous decade to take control of the Akali Dal. This was the product of the agricultural development commonly known as the Green Revolution. Economic expansion in rural Punjab intensified class disparities and eventually destroyed the cross-communal alliance created by the Congress Party in Punjab.

To shore up its slipping majority, the Congress Party also appealed to Sikh religious sentiments. Efforts were also made to divide the Akali Dal through outright bribery and co-optation (that is, the offer of public office). The tensions between the Congress and the Akali Dal mounted to dangerous levels throughout the early 1970s. Each party kept edging to the extreme in its efforts to outdo the other. The Akalis led demonstrations and strikes, passed the famous Anandpur Sahib Resolution of 1973, which demanded that the Punjab state be given jurisdiction over all subjects except foreign policy, defense, and currency.

Tensions between the center and the state parties were momentarily defused in 1977, when the Congress Party lost the general elections; however, the Congress Party and Indira Gandhi returned to power in 1980. The forces that had paralyzed Punjab previously—party competition, religious extremism, tensions over power sharing—once again picked up steam and plunged the province into confrontation with the center. This time the struggle revolved around Jarnail Singh Bhindranwale, an obscure Sikh preacher pushed to the center stage by the Congress leaders in order to split the Akali Dal and weaken its hold on Punjab. Bhindranwale's religious rhetoric not only split the Akali Dal but also gained him enough of a following to swing free of his erstwhile Congress supporters and demand the creation of "Khalistan"—a separate Sikh state free of Hindu dominance.

Bhindranwale soon fomented an insurgency, which led to the assassination of several Indian officials and political leaders. A series of tragic events then ensued: an army assault on the Sikh Golden Temple in June 1984, the holiest of all Sikh shrines; the death of Bhindranwale; and the assassination of Prime Minister Indira Gandhi in November 1984 by her Sikh bodyguard. Riding on the wave of sympathy for his assassinated mother, Rajiv Gandhi and the Congress Party won the 1985 elections with a landslide, and Rajiv

Gandhi's first step as prime minister was to sign an agreement with the moderate Akali Dal leader Harchandsingh Longowale to bring peace to Punjab. Two months after the agreement, however, Longowale was assassinated, and the strategy fell apart. It was not until after thousands of deaths, popular fatigue with the militancy of the conflict, and the physical elimination of many militant leaders that elections could again be held (in 1992). In fact, the militancy might not have ended had there not been two dramatic shifts in Indian politics in general: the steady erosion of the Congress Party and the rise of coalition governments reflecting the growing weight of ethnic and regional political parties in the 1990s.

Conflict in the Northeast and Kashmir

The conflicts in the northeast and Kashmir can be traced to many of the same factors influencing the conflict in the Punjab—arbitrary centralization of power, the center's denial of political autonomy, and the rise of nativist, ethnic, and religious tensions in the region. All were a result of modernization, uneven economic growth, and party competition. In the 1980s, however, a new element was added to the list: intervention by neighboring states in India's domestic ethnic conflicts. The link between terrorism in Punjab and Pakistan did not have an impact until 1987. The Naga and Mizo tribal communities in the northeast had, on the other hand, forged a connection with Burma and China in the 1960s. The Kashmir insurgents began to receive systematic support in the mid-1980s. Each of these developments had a different impact on the course of ethnic conflict.

The Northeast

The northeast was poorly integrated into the British Raj and then independent India. Linked to India by a slim corridor, it is populated by many hill tribes who have a language and culture distinct from those residing in the plains of Assam. The Nagas were the first to demand separation from Assam, and India created Nagaland in 1963. Once the Nagas got a state, others with claims to an equally distinctive identity could not be denied a state within the Indian federation. Between 1972 and 1987, the original province of Assam was divided into seven separate federal province-states. This division brought temporary respite, but the northeast remained subject to separatist violence fueled by economic and political frustrations.[3] More than most, the northeast defies a rational division on ethnic or religious lines. There are culturally distinctive communities surrounded by other equally distinctive communities whose lives have been closely intertwined. Thus ethnic awakening created a cascading effect. The example of Bodos in Assam has already been mentioned. The Indian government has tried to manage the cascading effect by creating autonomous district councils for territorially compact tribal communities. However, these councils have worked less than perfectly.

Jammu and Kashmir

Ethnic insurgency erupted somewhat suddenly in the state of Jammu and Kashmir in 1989 although the demand for independence had been voiced on many occasions in Kashmir. The kingdom of Kashmir was divided in 1947 into Pakistan-held and India-held parts as a result of the first India-Pakistan war. Pakistan has continued to claim the entire kingdom of Kashmir on the argument that, prior to the partition of the Indian subcontinent into India and Pakistan in 1947, Kashmir was a Muslim majority state and that India coerced its maharajah into ceding the kingdom in India's favor. India has argued that the maharajah of Kashmir voluntarily ceded Kashmir to India and that Pakistani presence in Kashmir is therefore

a violation of Indian territory. These opposite arguments have led to three wars and frequent confrontations, not to mention armed subversion and clashes along the disputed sectors of Indo-Pakistan borders.[4]

During the last decade of the twentieth century, the Kashmir dispute came to combine most of the elements, domestic and international, that can make a localized ethnic struggle into a wider regional conflict. The collapse of Afghanistan and the rise of the Taliban in the 1990s has made Kashmir, Pakistan, and Afghanistan a single battlefield where regional actors have engaged in fierce warfare. While Pakistan's interference has aggravated the Kashmir conflict, the causes of Kashmir's alienation lie in the erosion of its autonomy. In a series of actions, the governments in New Delhi took away the autonomy granted to Kashmir in 1953 by a special amendment to the Indian constitution known as article 370.

Overall, the Kashmir conflict has claimed more than 60,000 lives over the past decade. A negotiated solution seems unlikely, at least in the near future, because moderate Kashmiri nationalists have lost control of the state to the Islamic insurgents located in Pakistan. India cannot reenact its Punjab strategy—use of coercion followed by elections—to recapture Kashmir. Rivalry among the separatists makes negotiated agreement almost impossible. In stark contrast to Kashmir, ethnic conflict has diminished elsewhere in India. This is mainly because of full participation of ethnically based parties in forming governments at the center. While ethnic conflicts have paralyzed specific parts of India from time to time, the rest has coalesced into a single state with a common political system. Punjab, the northeast, and Kashmir, it is important to note, do not account for all of the ethnic conflict in India. Other regions—Tamilnadu and lately parts of Uttar Pradesh,

Madhya Pradesh, and Bihar—have struggled for autonomy, sometimes violently and sometimes in a more peaceful manner lending itself to accommodation. In this vein, the latter three states were carved up in August 2000 to create three new states in northern India in an effort to continue control ethnic conflict by redrawing India's federal system.

SIGNIFICANCE

The success and failures of ethnic struggles in India and the central government's efforts to manage them suggest that ethnic conflicts in general are episodic. They rise and fall and are amenable to creative power-sharing arrangements. India's experience with ethnopolitics also suggests that ethnic identity is not a static, unchangeable primordial construct; rather, it is formed and reinforced by modern nationalism and the policies of the state. Nor are identities forged by any one factor. Finally, India's history of coping with ethnic demands indicates that ethnic identities can be vehicles by which peoples can be mobilized, democracy can be expanded, and distinctive regions and people can be federally integrated into larger territorial entities—whether a subcontinental nation-state such as India or the European Union—provided power-sharing arrangements evolve out of negotiations between truly representative agencies at the various levels of government.

See also Burma: The Karen Conflict; Malaysia: The Malay-Chinese Conflict; and Sri Lanka: Tamil-Sinhalese Conflict in India's Backyard.

NOTES

1. *Report of the Reorganization Commission* (New Delhi: Government of India, 1955), 46.
2. Maya Chadda, *Ethnicity, Security, and Separatism in India* (New York: Columbia University Press, 1997), 58.
3. See Sanjib Baruah, "Immigration, Ethnic Conflict and Political Turmoil—Assam 1979–1985," *Asian Survey* 26 (November 1986): 1184–1206.
4. For an overview of rival arguments, see Raju G. C. Thomas, ed., *Perspectives on Kashmir: The Roots of Conflict* (Boulder, Colo., Westview Press, 1992).

SUGGESTED READINGS

Babulal, Fadia. *State Politics in India,* 2 vols. New Delhi: Radiant, 1984.

Baruah, Sanjib. *India Against Itself, Assam and the Politics of Nationality*. Philadelphia: University of Pennsylvania Press, 1999.

Chadda, Maya. *Building Democracy in South Asia, India, Pakistan, Nepal*. (Boulder, Colo.: Lynne Rienner Publishers, 2000.

———. *Ethnicity, Security, and Separatism in India*. New York: Columbia University Press, 1997.

Jha, Prem Shankar. *Kashmir 1947, Rival Versions of History*. New Delhi: Oxford University Press, 1996.

Thomas, Raju G. C. *Democracy, Security and Development in India*. New York: St. Martins Press, 1996.

Indonesia

The Struggle to Control East Timor

Stephen Zunes

TIMELINE

1974 In April, the Portugese Carnation Revolution overthrows that country's dictatorship. The new government begins to reduce its far-flung colonies, including East Timor, which had been controlled by Portugal for 400 years.

1975 In September, Indonesia provokes a civil war between rival East Timorese factions. On December 6, U.S. President Gerald Ford and Secretary of State Henry Kissinger meet Indonesian dictator Suharto and give an apparent green light for an Indonesian invasion of East Timor. On December 7, Indonesia launches an all-out invasion of East Timor, killing thousands in the first weeks.

1977 Carter administration authorizes military sales to Indonesia, including counterinsurgency aircraft; widespread massacres and forced starvation of East Timor's civilian population follow.

1991 On November 12, Santa Cruz massacre occurs in Dili, where Indonesian troops kill more than 270 unarmed civilians with U.S.–supplied weapons. Western journalists with cameras escape country and give eyewitness testimony.

1996 On October 11, the Nobel Peace Prize is awarded to Bishop Carlos Filipe Xi-

menes Belo and de facto foreign minister in exile Jose Ramos Horta.

1998 In May, President Suharto resigns in face of mass demonstrations held by prodemocracy students and others in Jakarta.

1999 In January, President Habibie offers East Timorese a vote on independence. In April, Falintil, the armed East Timorese guerrilla resistance, announces a ceasefire despite mounting attacks by Indonesian-backed anti-independence militia. On May 5, Portugal and Indonesia sign an agreement in New York that sends United Nations personnel into East Timor to prepare for an August plebiscite. Indonesia is granted responsibility for security arrangements on the ground. On August 30, in plebiscite with a 98.5 percent turnout, 78 percent of East Timorese vote for independence. In September, Indonesian troops and allied militia rampage against the civilian population, destroying buildings, displacing thousands, and killing an estimated 1,500 civilians. On September 14, United States suspends all military ties with Indonesia and threatens to block multilateral aid; Indonesia immediately halts assaults and allows Australian-led UN forces to enter. In October, all Indonesian forces and allied militia withdraw.

The invasion by Indonesia of the tiny island nation of East Timor in 1975 and the subsequent occupation constituted one of the most serious breaches of international law and human rights of the second half of the twentieth century. The 24-year rule over East Timor was quietly supported by major world powers desiring close relations with Indonesia, itself a vast, ethnically diverse country of over 200 million people. Efforts to assimilate the East Timorese, a Roman Catholic Melanesian people, by the largely Muslim Malay Indonesian government and military were unsuccessful, despite a combination of propaganda, repression, and incentives, coupled with the colonization of the territory by Indonesian civilians. For years, the Indonesian conquest was depicted as a triumph of realpolitik: brute force rather than morality or rule of law was the most decisive element in international relations and ethnic and political divisions could be suppressed by conventional power calculations. However, a serious economic downturn, the end of the 34-year dictatorship of President Suharto, and the international mobilization of human rights groups and other nongovernmental organizations (NGOs) forced the Indonesians to permit a free vote on the territory's future in 1999. When the overwhelming percentage of the population opted for independence, the Indonesians formally gave up control of the island, although the Indonesian military and allied East Timorese militias massacred thousands and destroyed much of the country's infrastructure in the process of their withdrawal.

HISTORICAL BACKGROUND

The island of Timor, along with other parts of the East Indies, was the subject of the competing colonial interests of the Netherlands and Portugal as far back as the sixteenth century. By the mid-nineteenth century, Timor had been formally partitioned, with the Dutch controlling most of the western half of the island and the Portuguese controlling the eastern half, along with an enclave on the northwest coast, totaling approximately 13,000 square miles. The divisions coincidentally approximated the precolonial division of the island between two confederations of kingdoms.[1] Despite the ensuing nearly 400 years of formal colonialism, Timor's kingdoms preserved a high level of autonomy much of the time, maintaining their historic trade links with other islands of the archipelago. These kingdoms, which consisted of loosely knit localized territorial groups with a hierarchy of clans, were ruled by chiefs who received tribute and arranged marital alliances with neighboring clans.[2] Though Portuguese rule included many of the standard abuses by European imperial powers, there was also a degree of benign neglect. Although Portuguese became the common language among educated East Timorese and increasing numbers of the indigenous population converted to Catholicism, the colonial imprint was weaker than in many colonized parts of the world.

The East Timorese are primarily of Melanesian stock—although Malays and, more recently, Chinese, Arabs, Africans, and Portuguese have added to the racial mix—with a population approximating 600,000 at the time of the Portuguese withdrawal in 1975. There were virtually no cultural, ethnic, or religious linkages with the Javanese, who dominate Indonesian politics and society and who control the country's government and armed forces. Java is not the largest island in size, but it constitutes more than half of Indonesia's population; it is the location of Jakarta, the country's capital and largest city; and it is the center of commercial and cultural life.

Precolonial ties between Timor and Java were limited to some trade. Even during the height of Javanese power between the tenth and fifteenth centuries, there was no political or even significant cultural influence. While unity of the entire Dutch East Indies under Jakarta's rule has been a demand of virtually every Indonesian nationalist, and President Sukarno for a time articulated Indonesian claims for such adjacent British possessions as Malaysia, Singapore, and Brunei during the 1950s and early 1960s, the small Portuguese colony was never much of an issue. When East Timor first became an item in international forums on decolonization in the early 1960s, the Indonesians explicitly discounted any territorial claims over the Portuguese colony, though there were some contradictory statements that did indicate interest among some sectors of the Indonesian leadership.[3] Even during the struggle with the Dutch over Irian Jaya in the early 1960s, the question of East Timor was never raised.

By the late 1960s and early 1970s, however, following Sukarno's ouster, the army's intelligence agency, BAKIN (Badan Koordinasi Intel), began covert support for a prointegrationist group in East Timor. The official line at that time was still that of noninterference in the country's affairs. There appears to have been internal disagreements within the Indonesian government regarding their position; BAKIN led the lobbying for annexation. BAKIN's role proved to be a decisive one. Its officers and their network of allies formed the backbone of Suharto's New Order regime and were thus able to influence government policy.[4]

In April 1974, Portugal's nonviolent Carnation Revolution overthrew that country's fascist dictatorship. The new government began to ease out of its far-flung colonies, including East Timor, which had been under Portuguese control for 400 years. As political parties sprang up inside East Timor, the Indonesian military launched an intelligence operation that backed the tiny pro-Indonesian party Apodeti and encouraged divisions between the two major proindependence parties, resulting in a brief civil war in the summer of 1975. The Indonesian army also engaged in a series of cross-border attacks.

President Suharto, the Indonesian dictator, was reluctant to push the matter too fast, despite being encouraged by his general, Benny Murdani, to launch a full-scale invasion of East Timor. An August 20, 1975, Central Intelligence Agency (CIA) cable noted that "a major consideration on [Suharto's] part is that an invasion of Timor, if it comes, must be justified as an act of defense of Indonesian security. He is acutely aware that conditions of United States military assistance to Indonesia specifically limit the use of this equipment to defensive purposes."[5]

In December 1975, President Gerald Ford and Secretary of State Henry Kissinger visited Jakarta. In meeting with President Suharto, Ford—who later referred to East Timor as a "lower-echelon priority" in United States–Indonesia relations—conceded that "the Indonesians were anxious for greater military help and assistance"[6] and gave them what a CIA official stationed in Jakarta at the time called "the green light" for a full-scale invasion.[7] The invasion of East Timor was launched just sixteen hours after Ford and Kissinger left Indonesia, on December 7.

Kissinger publicly stated that the United States "understands Indonesia's position on East Timor"; namely, that it not be allowed its right of self-determination under international law. Behind closed doors, his recommendation was to suspend arms sales "for a few weeks and then open it up again." To justify continued military backing for Jakarta, he asked his staff, "Can't we construe a communist government in the middle of Asia as self-defense?" Kissinger also instructed U.S. Ambassador David Newsom to avoid discussion of East Timor and limit embassy reporting, thus allowing "events to take their course."[8]

While the United Nations Security Council voted unanimously for Indonesia to halt its invasion and withdraw to within its internationally recognized borders, the United States blocked the UN from imposing economic sanctions or any other means of enforcing its mandate. The U.S. ambassador to the United Nations, at that time Daniel Patrick Moynihan, later bragged how, under State Department instructions, he had made the United Nations totally ineffectual in bringing a halt to the invasion. As he wrote in his memoirs,

The United States wished things to turn out as they did, and I worked to bring this about. The Department of State desired that the United Nations prove utterly ineffective in whatever measures it undertook. This task was given me, and I carried it forward with no inconsiderable success.[9]

From the beginning of the 1975 invasion, the scale of killing carried out by the invading Indonesian military was staggering. Hundreds were lined up on a dock in the East Timorese capital of Dili and shot into the sea, even ethnic Chinese merchants and others who initially welcomed the takeover. In the first few months of the occupation, the Indonesian military slaughtered more than 60,000 East Timorese. The Indonesian military faced unexpectedly tenacious resistance from the East Timorese, however, and hundreds of thousands of people managed to survive in the mountains. President Jimmy Carter, during his first year in office in 1977, authorized $112 million worth of military sales to Indonesia, up from just $13 million the year before. These sales included deliveries of counterinsurgency OV-10 Bronco aircraft, which allowed a dramatic expansion of the air war—with devastating consequences.[10] By the decade's end, as many as 200,000 East Timorese—more than one-third of the island nation's preinvasion population—were dead as a result of aerial bombing, massacres, forced starvation, and preventable diseases, especially in the detention camps where tens of thousands were eventually herded.[11]

THE CONFLICT

In many respects, the occupation was more of a political, nationalist struggle than a purely ethnic one. Ethnically, the East Timorese were very similar to the people of the western half of the island, who were largely assimilated into Indonesia. While the East Timorese were overwhelmingly Catholic, as compared with largely Muslim Indonesia, the sizable Christian minority in Indonesia largely supported the takeover of East Timor as much as the Muslim majority.

Yet there was clearly an ethnic component that helped the Indonesians justify their occupation and helped fuel the widespread opposition. The East Timorese were regarded by the Indonesians as a backward Melanesian race whom they had liberated from the Portuguese. The 24-year Indonesian occupation was defended in terms of improvements in infrastructure—such as roads and bridges—which the Indonesians had brought, along with education and housing, after centuries of Portuguese colonial neglect. Propaganda from the Indonesian government justified the occupation as a kind of *mission civilisatrice*. In many respects, such improvements were made largely better to impose Indonesian rule and to win the support of the population. Winning hearts and minds was largely unsuccessful, however, so Indonesia managed the conflict largely through political repression, in the knowledge that the international community would not want to risk losing close relations with this large, strategically located, resource-rich nation.

MANAGEMENT OF
THE CONFLICT

The Indonesians tried to control the East Timorese population by indoctrinating them in the official ideology of the Suharto dictatorship and by stressing the unity of the archipelago under Javanese rule. For the first thirteen years of the occupation, there was virtually no contact with the outside world; foreigners were largely forbidden to visit the territory. Promising East Timorese students were educated at Indonesian universities in the hopes that they would identify themselves as Indonesians rather than East Timorese. Bahasa Indonesian was taught in the schools. Meanwhile, the Indonesians brought thousands of colonists into the country to encourage integration still further. Any public expression of nationalism or of ethnic identity distinct from Indonesia was ruthlessly suppressed. A small class of collaborators came into being, some of whom evolved into militias that collaborated closely with the Indonesian armed forces.

Despite being granted scholarships to Indonesian universities and offered other incentives to secure their loyalty, few East Timorese gave up on the nationalist cause, and many became involved in underground proindependence organizations within Indonesia proper. By the early 1990s, there had been a rather dramatic growth in awareness of the East Timor situation among prodemocracy activists in Indonesia, though the concern was often focused upon improving the human rights conditions, not on recognizing the right of the East Timorese to self-determination. The most significant opposition movements criticized the repressive, overcentralized governance of East Timor by the Suharto regime, but still favored the country's integration into Indonesia and the suppression of any distinct ethnic or na-

tional identity. The democratic movement in Indonesia included many strong nationalists. Nationalism, in the Indonesian context, included uniting all the islands, which, for most, included East Timor. Covert intervention by the United States in the late 1950s against the nationalist Sukarno government focused upon encouraging secessionist movements in Aceh in northwestern Sumatra and some outer islands in the east.[12] Centralized rule from Java and bitter opposition to independence or even to a more federalistic system thus became ingrained across the ideological spectrum in the Indonesian national consciousness. Expression of a distinct ethnic identity was seen as an act of national disloyalty. In the 1950s and early 1960s, the charismatic Sukarno used anti-imperialist rhetoric as a substitute for coherent economic or political planning; internal opposition was defined as a threat by external neocolonial interests.[13] Later, the fact that the colonial power of the disputed territory was a fascist European state helped give the appearance of a moral imperative for Indonesia to "liberate" the country from colonial rule. Indeed, any effort at expressing a distinct ethnic or national identity was depicted as an outside imperialist plot.

Indonesia's military regime appears to have been motivated by the desire to consolidate the fragile national unity of the country through an example of strength and firmness against East Timorese efforts at independence.[14] There was an enormous fear that allowing East Timor to be an independent state run by the East Timorese would create a precedent that would lead to breakaway movements elsewhere in the archipelago. Legally, there was a significant difference in that the other regions and ethnic minorities restive for greater autonomy or independence were all part of the Dutch East Indies, and were recognized as part of Indonesia at independence, whereas East Timor was invaded and placed under foreign military occupation in violation of international law and two UN Security Council resolutions. Yet there was no guarantee that every Indonesian would appreciate that distinction. Therefore, while in many respects the Indonesian–East Timorese conflict was not primarily an ethnic conflict, because its fate was linked to the fear of a breakup of the country on ethnic or regional lines, it took on an ethnic significance.

SIGNIFICANCE

The conflict over East Timor was significant on several levels. First of all, in terms of loss of life, Indonesia's occupation was one of the most costly in recent decades. Indeed, in terms of the percentage of the population killed, it was the deadliest conflict since World War II, surpassing even the carnage of the Khmer Rouge rule in Cambodia in the late 1970s.

Another significant factor is how much of the international community ignored the gross violations of international law and human rights. Indeed, such major outside powers as the United States, Great Britain, and Australia openly backed Indonesia's occupation and supplied much of

VIQUEQUE, EAST TIMOR. Falantil (Armed Forces for the Liberation of East Timor) soldiers drill in Waimori guerilla camp, August 1999. Photo by Damen Whiteside, © Reuters NewMedia Inc./CORBIS.

the weaponry for the occupation forces. Most of Indonesian's Asian neighbors and most of the Muslim world also backed the suppression of East Timoreses independence. For many years, students of international relations saw the conflict as the classic triumph of realpolitik over international legal norms and principles. Yet the mobilization of NGOs—particularly in the United States, Great Britain, Australia, and Canada—created a situation where it became difficult for these important allied governments to provide Indonesia with its accustomed military aid, financial loans, and other support. This forced the Indonesian government to realize that good relations with the international community—particularly important after the collapse of its stock market and currency in 1997—were far more important than holding onto this small territory. Indeed, in 2000, they decided to cut their losses, albeit with a series of massacres and destruction of property during the final weeks of occupation. Therefore, perhaps the greatest significance of the case of East Timor is that it is a demonstration of the way in which NGOs from throughout the international community can successfully mobilize to support an oppressed minority or captive nation despite the narrowly defined strategic and economic interests of world powers.

See also Burma: The Karen Conflict; Malaysia: The Malay-Chinese Conflict; Sri Lanka: Tamil-Sinhalese Conflict in India's Backyard; and Yugoslavia: The Deconstruction of a State and Birth of Bosnia.

NOTES

1. Antonio Barbedo de Magalhaes, *East Timor: Land of Hope* (Oporto, Portugal: University of Oporto, 1990), 17.
2. John G. Taylor, *Indonesia's Forgotten War: The Hidden History of East Timor* (London: Zed Books, 1991), 2.

3. Ibid., 20–21.

4. Ibid., 23, 25, 30.

5. Cited by Allan Nairn in foreword to Constancio Pinto and Matthew Jardine, *East Timor's Unfinished Struggle: Inside the Timorese Resistance* (Boston: South End Press, 1997), xii.

6. Ibid., xiii.

7. Cited in an interview by John Pilger from Philip Liechty in documentary *Death of a Nation: The Timor Conspiracy,* directed by David Munro, Great Britain, 1994. 76 min.

8. Cited in Walter Isaacson, *Kissinger: A Biography* (New York: Simon and Schuster, 1992), 680.

9. Daniel Patrick Moynihan, *A Dangerous Place* (Boston: Little, Brown, 1980), 247.

10. Matthew Jardine, *East Timor: Genocide in Paradise,* 2d ed. (Monrue, Maine: Odonian Press, 1999), 42.

11. Asia Watch, "Human Rights in Indonesia and East Timor," *Human Rights Watch* (New York: Human Rights Watch, 1989), 253.

12. See Audrey Kahin and George Kahin, *Subversion as Foreign Policy: The Secret Eisenhower and Dulles Debacle in Indonesia* (New York: W. W. Norton, 1995).

13. Taylor, *Indonesia's Forgotten War,* 20.

14. Barbedo, *East Timor,* 23.

SUGGESTED READINGS

Budiardjo, Carmel, and Lem Soei Liong. *The War Against East Timor*. London: Zed Books, 1984.

Cotton, James. "The Emergence of an Independent East Timor: National and Regional Challenges." *Contemporary Southeast Asia* 22, no. 1 (April 2000), 1–22.

Jardine, Matthew. *East Timor: Genocide in Paradise*. Tucson, Ariz.: Odonian Press, 1995.

Kohen, Arnold S. *From the Place of the Dead: The Epic Struggle of Bishop Belo of East Timor*. New York: St. Martin's Press, 1999.

Pinto, Constancio, and Matthew Jardine. *East Timor's Unfinished Struggle: Inside the Timorese Resistance*. Boston: South End Press, 1997.

Schulze, Kirsten. "The East Timorese Referendum Crisis and Its Impact on Indonesian Politics." *Studies in Conflict and Terrorism* 24, no. 1 (January–February 2001), 77–82.

Taylor, John G. *Indonesia's Forgotten War: The Hidden History of East Timor*. London: Zed Books, 1991.

Zunes, Stephen. "Indigestible Lands? Comparing the Fates of the Western Sahara and East Timor." In *Rightsizing the State: The Politics of Moving Borders,* edited by Brendan O' Leary and Ian Lustick. Oxford, England: Oxford University Press, 2001.

Lebanon

Ethnic Conflict and the Lebanese Civil War, 1975–1990

Marie-Joelle Zahar

TIMELINE

1943 Lebanon achieves independence and the National Pact is formulated.

1958 The first postindependence civil war occurs.

1967 Palestinians establish guerrilla bases in Lebanon.

1969 The Cairo Agreement on Palestinian activities in Lebanon is established.

1975 Civil war begins.

1976 Syrian troops enter Lebanon.

1977 The Arab Deterrent Force is sent to Lebanon.

1978 Clashes occur between Syrian troops and Christian militias. Israel launches Operation Litani. United Nations Security Council Resolution 425 creates the UN Interim Force in Lebanon (UNIFIL).

1982 Israel launches Operation Peace for Galilee. Bashir Jumayyil is elected president of the Lebanese Republic.

1983 The May 17 Agreement is reached. The Battle of the Mountain between Christian and Muslim combatants occurs. National reconciliation talks are held in Geneva.

1984 Clashes occur between the Lebanese Army and the Shia and Druze militias. A follow-up meeting of the Geneva conference is held in Lausanne, Switzerland. The Battle of Iqlim al-Kharrub and Eastern Sidon occurs between Amal and Lebanese Forces fighters.

1985 Syria sponsors the Tripartite Agreement.

1986 The Tripartite Agreement fails.

1988 Lebanon fails to hold presidential elections; a military government of transition is set.

1989 Army Commander Michel 'Awn launches a war of liberation against the Syrian troops. Representatives of the Arab League mediate a cease-fire. Lebanese parliamentarians meet in Ta'if are produce the Ta'if Accord. General 'Awn rejects the Ta'if Accord.

1990 'Awn is ousted from power, and Ta'if implementation begins.

The Lebanese civil war (1975–1990) is one of the most complex internal conflicts of the twentieth century.[1] At least three ethnoreligious groups fought for political supremacy, committing ethnic cleansing in the course of the conflict. Domestic political issues became entangled with larger regional issues, notably strategic relations between Syria and Israel. Between 1975 and 1989, repeated attempts at international mediation failed. Yet, in September 1989, members of the Lebanese parliament gathered in Ta'if, Saudi Arabia, and reached a negotiated settlement that endures.

Only 15 percent of civil wars end in negotiated settlements. Ethnoreligious conflicts are said to be the least likely candidates, even when not converted into "international civil wars" by the presence of outside powers. During the civil war, Lebanon was a collapsed state "where the structure, authority (legitimate power), law, and political order have fallen apart."[2] When collapse accompanies civil conflict, conflict resolution becomes arduous. Yet, the Ta'if Accord ended a 15-year-long ethnoreligious war in a collapsed state. In other words, Lebanon's civil war is unusual.

HISTORICAL BACKGROUND

Following the Allied victory in World War I, France was offered a mandate over present-day Syria and Lebanon. In 1920 the French high commissioner, General Gouraud, proclaimed the creation of Grand Liban (Greater Lebanon). The new state included the prewar autonomous province of Mount Lebanon as well as the towns and surrounding districts of Beirut, Tripoli, Sur (Tyre), and Saida (Sidon); the wheat-producing regions of Baalbek and the Biqa'; and the districts of Rashayya and Hasbayya. The Maronites, the main Christian community in Mount Lebanon, deemed this geographic expansion necessary for the new state's viability.

Greater Lebanon gained in economic viability but lost in social homogeneity. Profound demographic changes accompanied the expansion. Maronites were a clear majority in Mount Lebanon, but not in the new state. The Druze lost their position as the dominant Muslim sect to the Sunnis, who emerged as the main challengers to Maronite numerical and political preponderance. Nor did the various communities equally desire a separate Lebanese state. For Maronites and Catholics, this was a dream come true. They had always asserted Mount Lebanon's cultural and historical uniqueness and had attempted to dissociate it from the Arab world. Sunnis, influenced by Arab nationalist ideas, were "unwilling to accept the change from being part of the political community of the Ottoman Empire to being only one community among others."[3] Druze and Shia Muslims preferred union with Syria but were partially attracted to a separate Lebanon because of their status as minority sects in the Sunni Arab world.

The Institutionalization of Confessional Politics

The loss of social homogeneity propelled the various communities into direct competition over government posts and services. This state of affairs was exacerbated in 1926 when the French promulgated a new constitution. According to Article 95, "By temporary right and with a view to justice and harmony, the communities shall be equitably represented in public employment and in the formation of the ministry, without prejudice, however, to the welfare of the State." Thus, confessional politics were enshrined in state institutions.

Upon gaining independence in 1943, the Maronites sought to gain control of the machinery of government to serve their (mainly) commercial interests. Sunnis, on the other hand, sought independence from the French mandate. The first postindependence president and prime minister, Bishara al-Khuri (a Maronite) and Ryad al-Sulh (a Sunni), reconciled these divergent interests in the National Pact (*Al-mithaq al-watani*). This informal gentlemen's agreement supplemented the formal constitution. Under the terms of the pact, Maronites renounced French tutelage in return for key political, security, and military positions while Sunnis renounced joining Syria and consented to Lebanon's independence, provided the Lebanese state considered itself part of the Arab world. Institutionally, the National Pact reaffirmed two principles: segmental proportionality, or the representation of the religious communities in the political system on the basis of demographic weight; and segmental autonomy, or the recognition of the religious communities' right to conduct their internal affairs—notably in the realms of personal status and education—without state interference.

The National Pact solidified religious identities, but it gave the advantage to Christian Lebanese. Indeed, a 1932 census used to allocate posts in the new state's institutions returned a proportion of six Christians for every five Muslims in Lebanon. Christians were also granted the presidency of the republic, the high command of the army, and top administrative positions. Nonetheless, the system was designed to encourage intercommunal cooperation. Seats in the parliament were distributed on the basis of religious affiliation, but the electoral law divided the country into religiously mixed geographical districts where candidates needed to appeal to voters outside their own sect to be elected. This electoral device fulfilled its purpose, but not for long.

Postindependence Challenges to Lebanon's Stability

The volatile regional environment played an important role in destabilizing the Lebanese consociational formula. The Arab-Israeli conflict produced, among others, two phenomena of consequence for the stability of the Lebanese political system: the rise of Arab nationalism and the emergence of Palestinian guerrillas.

Whenever they felt threatened, each of the communities sought to promote its vision of Lebanon by relying on outside support. The resulting linkage between domestic politics and regional conflicts became a hallmark of Lebanese politics.

Prior to 1975, two crises illustrated this entanglement. In the mid-1950s, Egyptian President Gamal Abdel-Nasser issued calls for Arab unity that spurred the creation of revolutionary movements and threatened conservative regimes across the Arab world. Concerned about the fate of its conservative allies in the region, the United States established the U.S.–led Baghdad Pact, which Lebanon's president Camille Chamoun decided to join. This decision was strongly opposed by the Lebanese National Movement (LNM), an umbrella organization of opposition parties, which identified with the Egyptian president's discourse. This disagreement sparked a crisis over the extensive prerogatives granted to Lebanon's Maronite president by the constitution. The opposition demanded political reforms to prevent the Maronite vision of Lebanon from dominating. A mini-civil war, the country's first postindependence violent breakdown, ensued in 1958, and the United States dispatched U.S. Marines to back Chamoun. Ultimately the crisis was resolved on the basis of a return to the status quo.

In 1967, after Israel's defeat of the Arab armies, Palestinians began conducting guerrilla warfare, and they started operating from Lebanon. The Christian leadership considered the guerrillas a threat to Lebanon's stability. The LNM parties wanted Lebanon to embrace the Palestinian cause. Once again, differences on regional issues sparked an internal crisis in 1969 when the Lebanese army confronted the guerrillas. The move was applauded by Christians and condemned by the LNM. Egypt mediated a settlement, the Cairo Agreement, which gave the guerrillas a wide margin in which to maneuver.[4]

These two pre–civil war crises and the state's attempt to resolve them through conciliation led Christian leaders to infer that the state was weak and the army unable to defend the country. Consequently, they formed and trained paramilitaries to defend the status quo and preserve the Maronite-dominated power-sharing formula. The Lebanese Phalanges (Al-Kata'ib al-Lubnaniyya), the largest Maronite political party and an outspoken proponent of the Christian vision of Lebanon, took the lead.[5] Other groups armed themselves in response. By the mid-1970s almost every party in Lebanon had its own militia. The stage was set for the eruption of the civil war.

THE CONFLICT

On April 13, 1975, as they rode a bus through a Christian neighborhood, 26 Palestinians were gunned down in retaliation for an attempt made earlier that day on the life of the Kata'ib leader, Pierre Jumayyil. This event ignited the civil war. Grand conspiracy theory explanations of Lebanon's breakdown abound. Many analysts contend that the conflict was a "war for others" fought on Lebanese soil. But, in spite of the catalyst provided by foreign intervention, internal factors are to blame for the breakdown of the political system.

The two warring factions are often labeled Christian and Muslim; however, at the outset of the conflict, this was only partially correct. It is more accurate to describe them as pro– and anti–status quo with the main areas of disagreement revolving around Lebanon's foreign policy and demands for the renegotiation of the Lebanese power-sharing formula. Those in favor of the status quo came to be known as the Lebanese Front.[6] The anti–status quo forces revolved around the LNM and some Palestinian guerrillas. The commonly held notion that this was a religious conflict masked the fact that religious divisions roughly overlapped with power and wealth differentials. The more powerful traditional elites (mostly Maronites) fought to maintain their privileges; the more socioeconomically disadvantaged groups (mostly Shia) fought for power and access to state resources.

As the conflict continued, however, it acquired an increasingly ethnic coloration. Warring factions gradually represented religious communities rather than political persuasions. The Lebanese Front forces (LF), led by Pierre Jumayyil's son, Bashir, emerged as the most powerful Christian militia. Whereas the LNM was an umbrella organization of various (though mostly Muslim) political forces with shared goals, its successors stood for specific communities. The Amal Movement was the first Shia political party in Lebanon. The Progressive Socialist Party (PSP), a largely Druze party, was created by LNM leader Kamal Junblatt. By 1983 these three groups were the most influential actors in the conflict.

Although carried out on a smaller scale than in the former Yugoslavia, ethnic cleansing was practiced in Lebanon, providing another indication that the war had taken on an ethnic dimension. The most sadly famous instances remain the massacres of Palestinians by Maronite Lebanese Force militiamen in the refugee camps of Sabra and Shatila shortly after the 1982 Israeli invasion of Lebanon. During the 1983 Battle of the Mountain, the Druze PSP militia ethnically cleansed the Shuf of Christian presence. In 1985 the battles of Iqlim al-Kharrub and Eastern Sidon between the LF and the Amal Movement resulted in the displacement of the majority of the area's Christian population. By the mid-1980s, sectarian-based acts of violence against civilians had driven the Christians to seek refuge among coreligionists dividing the country into largely religiously homogenous enclaves.

The battles of the first two years (1975–1976) roughly determined the military map. The Lebanese Forces controlled East Beirut, the northern Metn and Kisrwan mountain ranges, and the coastal strip extending from Beirut north to Jubayl. The PSP's fiefdom extended from the southern Metn to the Shuf with a substantial presence in West Beirut. The Amal Movement was in control of southern Lebanon, the Biqa' valley and parts of West Beirut (later disputed between Amal and its Shia rival, Hizballah). After the Israeli invasion in 1982, the various forces reached a military equilibrium. A number of major confrontations did occur afterward, notably the 1983 Battle of the Mountain, the 1984 *intifada* (upheaval) in West Beirut when Amal and PSP militiamen fought the Lebanese army to protest the policies of President Amin Jumayyil, and the 1985 battle of the Iqlim and Eastern Sidon. These battles did not drastically modify the military map, nor did they seriously tip the balance of power. Their net effect was to homogenize local zones of control by ridding them of pockets of "enemy" presence. They were instrumental in the establishment of compact territorial enclaves in which the militias asserted their control. As of the early 1980s, the Lebanese Forces, Amal, and the PSP effectively governed their respective zones of control.

In the summer of 1988 this stalemate was rocked by a political crisis when the warring factions failed to agree on a compromise candidate to the presidency of the republic. Until that time, Lebanon's executive had continued to function although it did not possess effective control on the ground. The ensuing deadlock created a constitutional crisis, and outgoing President Amin Jumayyil appointed a military government of transition under the leadership of Army Commander General Michel 'Awn. The Muslim leaders objected; 'Awn was a Maronite, and customary practice reserved the premiership for the Sunnis. Instead, they extended recog-

nition to Jumayyil's last prime minister, Salim al-Huss. The situation was unprecedented: the presidency was vacant, there were two parallel governments, and the army split along confessional lines with troops loyal to 'Awn and others closing ranks with Huss. In January 1989, the Arab League launched an unsuccessful attempt to mediate between the parties. Against this backdrop, 'Awn started a war of liberation from Syrian occupation. The military escalation drew international attention. In May 1989, a Tripartite Committee of the Arab League launched a second mediation effort.[7] The seven-point truce plan stipulated that a cease-fire would come into effect on August 29, followed by a meeting of the Lebanese parliamentarians in Ta'if.

MANAGEMENT OF
THE CONFLICT

Lebanon's civil war elicited numerous mediation and peacekeeping efforts. In October 1976, the Riyadh conference sought to find a solution to the Lebanese civil war. In January 1977, an Arab Deterrent Force of 30,000 men was positioned in Lebanon. The Arab League and several Arab countries, notably Saudi Arabia, Morocco, and Algeria, later attempted to mediate among the various factions. The Ta'if Accord Agreement is the result of such good offices. Western countries also intervened to end the war. In 1983 they sent a multinational force to help the state reestablish its authority.[8] However, no country played as influential and sustained a role as Syria. Syria's behavior during the Lebanese civil war seems inconsistent. Initially Damascus supported the LNM and Palestinian fighters; a year later, Syria backed the Maronite conservative forces. This shifting pattern of alliances is understandable only when evaluated against the background of Syria's larger concerns. An unstable Lebanon could harbor political movements hostile to the Asad regime; it could also become a security liability in the conflict with Israel. Syria's military and political intervention in the Lebanese civil war attempted to address these two concerns.

Military Intervention

Beginning in January 1976, Syria mediated cease-fires in the civil war. In late 1975 and 1976, as the conflict took a confessional coloring, Syria played the role of balancer. In 1976 President Suleyman Franjiyya and the Lebanese Front requested the deployment of Syrian forces to prevent an all-out victory of the LNM and its allies. In May 1976, the first Syrian forces of interposition entered Lebanon. Their presence was further legitimized a few months later when the Riyadh conference established the (mainly Syrian-manned) Arab Deterrent Force. Syria's willingness to intervene militarily in support of the Christian forces (and against its own allies) spoke to Damascus's concerns over the partition or disintegration of Lebanon. Syrian authorities worried that partition would result in the establishment of a mini–Christian state allied with Israel. The prospect of Lebanon's disintegration also posed grave threats to Syria's security since Lebanon is a buffer between Syria's long and most vulnerable western border and Israel.

The Camp David peace treaty between Egypt and Israel changed Syrian calculations in Lebanon. In 1977 Syria initiated a rapprochement with the Palestine Liberation Organization (PLO) to reunite the Arab front. This rapprochement starkly contrasted with mounting strains in Syrian-Maronite relations. The leading Maronite faction, represented by Bashir Jumayyil, wanted nothing short of political predominance. Otherwise it advocated the creation of a Christian mini-state. The Syrian government, on the other hand, sought to bring the Lebanese Front and the LNM

together in a pro-Syrian Lebanese government.

In March 1978, Israeli troops launched Operation Litani, an invasion of South Lebanon, in retaliation for a guerrilla attack on a bus near Tel Aviv. United Nations Security Council Resolution 425 called on Israel to withdraw, and United Nations Interim Forces in Lebanon (UNIFIL) were sent to replace the Israelis as they pulled back. However, Israel retained a ten-kilometer "security belt" entrusted to a Lebanese client, the (mainly Christian) South Lebanon Army. This military incursion was accompanied by the creation of a formal alliance between the Israelis and the Lebanese Front. While the Maronite-Israeli alliance was being consolidated, Maronite-Syrian fighting erupted between February and October 1978.

The potential establishment in Lebanon of a regime friendly to Israel had long been of concern to Syria. When Israel invaded Lebanon in 1982, the Israelis secured the election of their Maronite ally, Bashir Jumayyil, to the presidency of the republic.[9] Jumayyil's election was highly criticized by Damascus. When Jumayyil was assassinated two weeks before assuming his office, his brother, Amin, was elected to the presidency. Under U.S. auspices, Amin Jumayyil negotiated the May 17 Agreement with Israel. Among other things, the agreement called for the withdrawal of Israeli and Syrian troops from the country. Damascus expressed its rejection of these terms by applying military pressure on the Christian enclave. Syria's allies in the Lebanese parliament blocked the treaty's ratification, and the resumption of national reconciliation talks in Switzerland was conditioned upon the treaty's abrogation.

The Syrian military presence in Lebanon remained a bone of contention in Christian political circles. It was at the heart of the War of Liberation launched in 1989 by the head of the interim military cabinet, General 'Awn, and emerged as a central issue at the negotiating table in Ta'if.

Political Intervention

Syria's role in the elaboration of several conflict-resolution blueprints reflects the general Syrian policy in Lebanon. Syria sought peace agreements that would maintain the regional strategic balance. The Syrian regime did not want the partition of Lebanon, but it was weary of Lebanese leaders who did not ascribe to Syrian strategic concerns. Damascus thus sought to promote a modification of the Lebanese power-sharing formula with an eye on giving pro-Syrian communities more power in decision making.

The first Syrian mediation attempt, the 1976 Constitutional Document, conceded some of the internal reforms sought by the LNM but did not alter the confessional character of the top decision-making elites. In counterpart for Maronite acceptance of the document, Syria offered guarantees that the PLO would respect the terms of the 1969 Cairo Agreement. In 1980 the Fourteen Points for Reconciliation called for the reestablishment of Lebanese sovereignty, an equilibrated system of power sharing, close cooperation with Syria, and support for the Palestinian cause. In late 1983–early 1984, the national reconciliation talks in Geneva and Lausanne produced a cabinet of national unity that confirmed Lebanon's full affiliation to the Arab world, projected the redistribution of parliamentary seats on a 50:50 basis, and planned the deconfessionalization of most of the Lebanese civil service.

In all three instances, Christian political forces ultimately rejected the Syrian mediation efforts arguing that Syria's intervention in Lebanese domestic affairs revealed an intent to alter the nature of Lebanon.

The Tripartite Accord, signed in Damascus on December 28, 1985, was the principal Syrian mediation effort. The agreement thrust Lebanon at the heart of Syria's policy of strategic parity with Israel. To prevent Lebanon from serving as a gateway between Israel and Syria, Syria would station troops at strategic positions in Lebanese territory. The agreement also curtailed the powers of the president and transferred executive power to the cabinet. Although the leader of the LF at that time, Ilyas Hubeiqa, was one of its signatories, the agreement failed to secure support in Christian ranks. Maronites especially perceived the settlement as bringing Lebanon under Syrian tutelage. Two weeks after the agreement was signed, Hubeiqa was overthrown by an upheaval within the ranks of the Lebanese Forces.

SIGNIFICANCE

Against all odds, Lebanon's civil war ended in a negotiated settlement. The Ta'if Accord has endured for a decade albeit with ups and downs. General 'Awn attempted to spoil the agreement, but in October 1990 Syrian troops assisted the state in ending the general's rebellion. The agreement recalibrated power sharing among the various communities, and it clarified the nature of Syrian-Lebanese relations. Ta'if sought to succeed where the National Pact failed: find an acceptable compromise among all the Lebanese factions and limit foreign intervention in Lebanese domestic political affairs. This second objective has largely failed because Lebanese domestic politics remain hostage to the Syrian-Israeli conflict. However, the resort to domestic violence has increasingly become an unlikely option. Furthermore, if we note the relative success of Lebanon's post–conflict reconstruction where many similar experiments are still faltering, it speaks to the significance of this case study for all students of ethnic conflict.

BEIRUT, LEBANON, 1996. Bombed-out buildings continue to straddle the Green Line. Photo courtesy of Deborah J. Gerner.

See also Middle East: The Arab-Jewish Struggle for Palestine to 1948; and Middle East: The Palestinian Issue.

NOTES

1. By my count, there were seven major and six minor internal factions. The conflict also involved at least five Palestinian guerrilla factions. Two regional actors, Syria and Israel, were militarily embroiled in the war. Lebanon received peace-keeping assistance from the UN Intervention Force in Lebanon (UNIFIL), the Arab Deterrent Force, and the Multi-National Force (MNF), each of which involved militaries from at least three different countries. Finally, external mediators in Lebanon included, among others, France, the Vatican, the United States, the Arab League, Saudi Arabia, and Syria.

2. I. William Zartman, "Introduction: Posing the Problem of State Collapse," in *Collapsed States: The Disintegration and Restoration of Legitimate Authority*, ed. I. William Zartman, (Boulder, Colo.: Lynne Rienner, 1995), 1.

3. Albert Hourani, "Lebanon: The Development of a Political Society," in *Toward a Viable Lebanon* (London: Croom Helm; Washington, D.C.: Center for Contemporary Arab Studies, Georgetown University, 1988), Halim Barakat, ed. 25.

4. The PLO had to coordinate activities with the Lebanese army. Some territorial restrictions were placed on the guerrillas. In exchange, the Lebanese government recognized the legitimacy of a Palestinian armed presence in Lebanon and the PLO's right to establish autonomous institutions in the camps.

5. Founded in 1936 by Pierre Jumayyil, al-Kata'ib fought for Lebanon's independence before becoming a constitutional party in 1952.

6. The Lebanese Front included political forces associated with Maronite traditional political families, the Jumayyils (the Kata'ib party), the Chamouns (the National Liberal Party), and the Franjiyyas (the Marada), in addition to the militias of Maronite religious orders.

7. The Tripartite Committee included the kings of Morocco and Saudi Arabia and the president of Algeria.

8. The multinational force was composed of U.S. Marines, French paratroopers, and Italian soldiers. It withdrew from Lebanon after simultaneous attacks on the American and French barracks claimed a high casualty toll.

9. Operation Peace for Galilee followed a PLO self-imposed six-month moratorium on guerrilla attacks into Israel.

SUGGESTED READINGS

Collings, Deirdre, ed. *Peace for Lebanon? From War to Reconstruction.* Boulder, Colo.: Lynne Rienner, 1994.

Hourani, Albert. "Visions of Lebanon" in *Toward a Viable Lebanon,* edited by Halim Barakat. London: Croom Helm; Washington, D.C.: Center for Contemporary Arab Studies, Georgetown University, 1988.

Picard, Elizabeth, and Franklin Philip, trans. *Lebanon, a Shattered Country: Myths and Realities of the Wars in Lebanon.* New York: Holmes and Meier, 1996.

Salem, Paul, ed. *Conflict Resolution in the Arab World: Selected Essays.* Beirut: American University of Beirut, 1997.

Salibi, Kamal. *Crossroads to Civil War: Lebanon 1958–1976.* Delmar, N.Y.: Caravan Books, 1976.

Schiff, Ze'ev, and Ehud Ya'ari. *Israel's Lebanon War.* Edited and translated by Ina Friedman. New York: Simon and Schuster, 1984.

Shehadi, Nadim, and Dana Haffar Mills, eds. *Lebanon: A History of Conflict and Consensus.* London: Centre for Lebanese Studies, I. B. Tauris, 1988.

Sirriyeh, Hussein. *Lebanon: Dimensions of Conflict.* Adelphi Papers no. 243. London: International Institute of Strategic Studies, 1989.

Malaysia

The Malay-Chinese Conflict

Amy L. Freedman

TIMELINE

1400 Chinese traders begin arriving on the Malay Peninsula.

1860 Significant numbers of Chinese begin to migrate to the (now) British colonies on the Malay Peninsula. Migration ends in approximately 1930.

1911 The Qing Dynasty in China is overthrown.

1919 May 4th Movement occurs in China: intellectual protest movement against corruption and foreign influence.

1942–1945 Japanese occupy British Malaya.

1942–1948 Insurgency is waged by the Malayan Communist Party.

1945–1946 Military rule is established by the British.

1948 Emergency rule is declared by the British to eliminate Communist insurgents.

1957 The Independence Constitution is drafted for the Federation of Malaya.

1963 The Federation of Malaysia is created with the merger of the Federation of Malaya states Singapore, Sarawak, and North Borneo (Sabah).

1965 Singapore is separated from the Federation of Malaysia.

1969 Riots on May 13 against ethnic Chinese lead to two years of emergency rule in Malaysia.

1971 New Economic Policy is adopted.

1987 In October, demonstrations are held and the Internal Security Act is passed to contain the opposition forces challenging government.

1998 An economic crisis in Southeast Asia, in general, produces demonstrations against the regime in Malaysia; Malaysian Chinese seem to avoid protests.

1999 General elections are held, and the leading coalition retains power with support from the ethnic Chinese.

2001 In June, the Malaysian Chinese Association president is criticized for the party's purchase of the two largest Chinese language newspapers, and Chinese disappointment with the party intensifies.

Post-September 11, the Malaysian government cracks down on Al Qaeda–linked Islamic groups. The move increases Chinese support for the ruling Malay party and is supported by moderate Malays.

2002 On June 25, Prime Minister Mahatir Mohamad announces that he will retire in October 2003 and be replaced by his deputy prime minister, Abdullah Ahmad Badawi.

Malaysia is a multiethnic society sandwiched between Buddhist Thailand, which is mostly peaceful, and Muslim-dominated Indonesia, which was plagued with serious ethnic and religious violence as the twentieth century ended (1996–2000). Malaysia's population is roughly 60 percent ethnic Malay, 29 percent Chinese, and 11 percent Indian. With a few exceptions, Malaysia has been known more for its ethnic accommodation and harmony than for ethnic conflict. Such a reputation, however, makes light of the significant conflict that has occurred, and it minimizes the very real tension that still exists between the dominant Malays, on the one hand, and the Chinese and Indian populations in Malaysia, on the other—especially between the federation's Malay and Chinese inhabitants.

Overall, Malaysian politics remains highly ethnicized. Political parties represent the three largest ethnic groups and are supposed to channel ethnic interests to prevent violence. Few issues are not, in some manner, linked to ethnic relations. What is most compelling about ethnic relations in Malaysia is that, from the 1950s through the 1970s, ethnic conflict was violent; however, since the 1970s, this violence has virtually disappeared. In general, this lack of overt conflict has come at the expense of equality and a public discourse about political rights and Malaysian identity.

HISTORICAL BACKGROUND

Ethnic relations in the Malay Peninsula can be basically viewed as falling into four distinct periods: (1) the period during British colonialism, (2) the era covering the post–World War II transition from colonial rule to independence, (3) the turbulent early years of independent Malaya/ Malaysia's existence (1957–1969), and the period stretching from 1969 until the present. Throughout, the Chinese in Malaysia have been a dynamic economic force and, because they make up close to 30 percent of the current population, they have long been perceived as a political threat by the indigenous Malays.

The Malay Peninsula has always been ethnically mixed, with indigenous and Malay inhabitants. This pluralism increased when the Chinese began coming to western Malaysia (around 1400), especially in the mid-nineteenth century when Chinese settlement in the peninsula became significant. Most immigrants came from Guangdong and Fujian and spoke one of five major Chinese dialects: Hokkien, Hakka, Cantonese, Teochiu, or Hainanese. Like elsewhere in the Chinese diaspora, Chinese in Malaysia were socially and politically organized into myriad common-origin associations, for example, the Guangdong Association, the Fujian Association, and so on. The British colonial administration relied on the Kapitan Cina (Chinese secret society heads with financial power and ties to local Malay chiefs) to administer revenue farms, develop tin mining and plantation economies, and keep the peace in Chinese communities.[1] During colonial rule, conflict between Malay and Chinese inhabitants was kept to a minimum. Ethnic groups were segmented by employment, place of residence, and place of education. Colonial authorities kept in place the Malay sultanates, and they relied on Malay elites to staff the civil service. Chinese were utilized as economic middleman.

The Chinese under British Rule

As the British gained administrative control over Malaya, the Chinese lost some of their ability to govern themselves. Under British rule, Chinese participation in the colonial regime was highly limited. Fear of Chinese political agitation increased after the fall of the Qing Dynasty in China in 1911. Since 1911 Chinese involvement in Malaysian politics has been linked to fears of Chinese Nationalist or Communist Party influence. Moreover, under colonialism, Chinese immigrants were allowed to organize and run their own schools, and the curriculum offered tended to reflect a growing sense of Chinese nationalism. Emphasis was placed on creating military spirit, and drilling, uniforms, and patriotic songs were incorporated into the school day. Shortly after the May 4th Movement of 1919 in China (a protest movement led by intellectuals against the corruption of the new republican regime), Sun Yat-sen's three principles (nationalism, democracy, and livelihood) became mandatory political components of the already militarized curriculum. This alarmed both Malay elites and the British. Chinese schools and communal organizations would later serve as targets of ethnic conflict.

The Transition to Independence

While Malaysia was under Japanese occupation during World War II, the (overwhelmingly Chinese) Communists in Malaya succeeded in organizing the only viable underground resistance. In doing so, they gathered widespread cooperation and support from the Chinese (and from some Malays), and they tried to position themselves to assume political power following the war. Indeed, after the Japanese surrender in 1945 the Malayan Communist Party (MCP) operated as a parallel government to the British Military Administration, which returned after the war ended. As the British solidified their rule, however, they took steps to reduce the MCP's power. By 1948 police raids and arrests had destroyed the labor movement, and the party was being shut out of newly formed advisory councils. The MCP opted for armed insurrection, and the colonial government initiated a drive to eliminate the Communist insurgents. During this period, known as *the emergency,* the Chinese were suspected of participating in the Communist campaigns, and those suppor-

tive of the movement were targeted for education campaigns, detentions, and massive relocation efforts.

The late 1940s and 1950s were a turbulent time for ethnic relations in Malaysia. Ethnic Malays were determined to win independence from the British, and they wanted to ensure that the new nation would be Malay in character. They feared the Chinese for two, somewhat contradictory, reasons. First, the Chinese Communist Party was well organized and well funded, and the British were reluctant to leave the peninsula if it looked as though the MCP was too powerful. Second, the Chinese were a significant source of capital. If Malaysia were to be independent, Chinese business interests would have to be incorporated in the new government. If not, there was a fear of capital flight that the soon-to-be-independent nation could ill afford. The Malayan Chinese Association (MCA), known as the *Malaysian* Chinese Association after 1963 (when the addition of Singapore, Sarawak, and North Borneo transformed the Federation of Malaya into the Federation of Malaysia), was formed at this time as a conservative, business-oriented organization that would work with the British and Malay elites to redirect Chinese support away from the Communists. It was in the economic and political interest of this class to work against fellow Chinese Communists. The negotiations among interethnic actors in working toward independence would create a pattern for elite cooperation that would last until 1969.

The Early Years of Independence, 1957–1989

The concern over non-Malay privilege and ambition (in the form of Chinese economic dominance) led to the institutionalization of Malay special rights in the Independence Constitution of 1957. These rights evolved as part of complex negotiations for multiethnic rule in postcolonial

Malaysia that left the Chinese community dismayed at how Malays were favored by legitimizing the primacy of the Malay identity within the constitution. At the same time, the Chinese were willing to compromise on this in exchange for concessions on citizenship eligibility and moderate protection of the Chinese vernacular education.[2]

There had previously been a brief window of time during decolonization in 1946–1947 when it seemed that the Chinese might be accorded equal political and economic rights. However, intense opposition from the newly formed United Malays National Organization (UMNO) prevented it. The British then proposed a federal system that guaranteed Malay sovereignty and contained strict citizenship requirements for non-Malays. The UMNO clearly favored this arrangement, and decolonization moved forward.

Thus, although the Independence Constitution was drawn up by Malay and non-Malay members of a multiethnic coalition (called the Alliance Party), the final document clearly favored ethnic Malays. The constitution defines a Malay as a Muslim, a Malay speaker, and a follower of Malay custom. Non-Malay culture is not defined. The Chinese in Malaysia were (and still are) Buddhist, Confucian, or Christian. Because few practice Islam, Chinese can never be "Malay" according to the constitution, and in part for this reason the constitution has been subsequently pointed to as a justification for pro-Malay policies. In return for allowing the Malays to retain their political preeminence, it was agreed that the economic position of the Chinese would be undisturbed and that Chinese and Indians would be permitted to maintain their cultures and traditions.

For the first ten years of independence, the ruling Alliance coalition was able to maintain about 60 percent of the votes and keep control both of parliament and the state governments, although Malay-

Chinese tensions in the early 1960s led to the expulsion from the Federation of Malaysia of the overwhelmingly Chinese city-state of Singapore in 1965. In 1969, however, the system broke down. A riot erupted on May 13, after general elections in which the Alliance won only 48 percent of the votes, down 10 percent from 1964. Victory parades were held after the election, which were perceived as abusive to Malay sensibilities. Rioting ensued in which thousands (mostly Chinese) were killed, and property was burned and looted. After 1969 a consensus evolved that the disturbance was caused by an economic imbalance between the wealthier Chinese and the less-well-off native Malays.[3] A countrywide state of emergency was proclaimed, and parliamentary rule was suspended for nearly two years (1969–1971).

The Recent Era, 1969–2000

The race riots marked the rise of Malay leadership dedicated to the translation of Malay constitutional privileges into actual policies. This opened the door to a massive shift in economic and social policies to boost the position of Malays within their own country. The New Economic Policy (NEP) was created. Adopted in 1971 as the first act of business of the newly reconstituted parliament, the NEP's aim was to redistribute wealth from the Chinese to the Malays and other indigenous races. A secondary goal was to eliminate the link between race and economic function. In other words, it aimed at bringing the *bumiputras* (sons of the soil, or ethnic Malays) into sectors of the economy previously dominated by Chinese. It gave preference to Malays in job allocation, scholarships abroad, and university seats, and it required that Malays be given larger ownership stakes in Malaysian companies. In order for this legislation to go forward, however, there needed to be an agreement between Malays and Chinese on the necessity of addressing ethnic income disparity. There was, however, little discussion at the time of the distribution of power within the institutions of power and how the NEP would concern various groups in society. Given the nature and results of the bargaining which took place at independence and the fact that the constitution accords Malays political primacy, many Malays feel that they should control the political process. Any political opposition by ethnic Chinese was—and largely remains—viewed as a threat to Malay political dominance.

THE CONFLICT

From 1957 to 1969, there was a tacit understanding among elites of all ethnic groups that the Chinese would be left alone to prosper economically while the Malays would control the political institutions even though the Chinese slightly outnumbered the Malays in the Federation of Malaysia during the brief period when Singapore was a part of it. Over time the violence and relocation efforts against Chinese suspected of affiliation with the Malaysian Communist Party died down. A fragile stability was created but was shattered later by the riots of 1969. While there has not been a second period of violent conflict since 1969, ethnic tension lies just below the surface of ethnic tranquility. The NEP was designed to address economic inequalities through affirmative action for ethnic Malays. This severely disadvantaged Chinese and Indians, particularly in university admissions, government jobs, and corporate ownership. Small political issues have occasionally brought Malaysia to the brink of renewed conflict. For example, in October 1987, a series of demonstrations were held following the government's appointment of more than 100 Chinese teachers to high administrative positions within Chinese primary schools. Although Chinese, these teachers did not possess Mandarin Chinese qualifications.

To the Chinese community, this seemed like yet another move to undermine the Chinese schools. The Democratic Action Party (DAP), a Chinese opposition party, quickly mobilized support for a protest. Fearing that the DAP would garner greater leverage from the event, the MCA (which is part of the ruling coalition) also participated in the protest meeting held in Kuala Lumpur on October 11, 1987. At that meeting, and despite the fact that the government had already decided to reassign the teachers, the leaders agreed to call for a boycott of schools if the appointments were not withdrawn by October 14. The boycott went ahead on October 15.

The Malay response to the DAP/MCA cooperation was dramatic. The youth wing of the UMNO held a huge rally denouncing the MCA and Chinese in general. People in the capital feared a repeat of May 13, 1969. Thus, when several leaders in the UMNO advocated further mass demonstrations, Prime Minister Mahathir Mohamad put an end to the plans and called for the detainment of activists under the Internal Security Act. Both Chinese and Malay leaders were arrested. While many were released quickly, opposition leaders were given much longer sentences.

This incident illustrates two important points. Feeling pressure from internal and external challenges, both the MCA and the UMNO were inclined to racialize the issue to mobilize support. Second, although the government may have justly feared renewed communal conflict, they used the crisis to achieve partisan goals. By arresting DAP leaders, the government not only removed the most strenuous backers of Chinese interests, but also put an end to criticism from the opposition on other issues. Repression of dissent as a mode of conflict management has continued to this day.

Meanwhile, from 1987 until 1998, Malaysia's economy boomed. While there was resentment among many Chinese

PENANG, MALAYSIA. Outside a Chinese Temple in Penang, in 1996. Photo courtesy of the author.

about their quasi second-class status and about the fact that the NEP favored Malays in education, employment, and government service, with a rising economy disgruntlement was successfully managed. In 1998 Malaysia, like the rest of Southeast Asia, suffered a serious economic crisis. For a short time in the summer and fall of 1998 it looked as though the economic turmoil would result in a political backlash against the Mahathir regime. Protestors took to the streets complaining about the political ousting of Deputy Prime Minister Anwar Ibrahim on trumped-up charges of corruption and sodomy. Many wondered if there would also be violence against ethnic Chinese, as was occurring at the time in Indonesia. The demonstrations were not ethnically motivated, however, and there was no racial violence. Malaysian Chinese, for the most part, refrained from participating in the demonstrations against the regime. In fact, in the general elections

held in the fall of 1999, the Chinese were some of the strongest supporters of the ruling coalition.

MANAGEMENT OF THE CONFLICT

Malaysia's political system is responsible both for managing ethnic conflict and for perpetuating ethnic inequalities. How can one best characterize the Malaysian political system? Is it democratic or authoritarian? It contains clear elements of both. There are regularly scheduled, free, and fair elections, and opposition parties contest a large number of seats. However, the major media outlets, particularly the Malay and English newspapers, are owned in part by the major political parties. There is also some amount of regulation and suppression of nongovernmental activity, and critics and opposition groups endure close scrutiny by the government.

In addition to such repressive elements in the operation of Malaysian democracy, the organs of the state are stacked in favor of the Malays. The political party system is structured to reflect ethnic divisions. Chinese and Indians have representation through communal parties in the ruling coalition: the Malaysian Chinese Association and the Malaysian Indian Congress. These parties are supposed to represent the interests of each ethnic group. From 1957 until the mid-1960s, people perceived that these parties did indeed represent the needs of their constituents. After the passage of the NEP in 1971, however, many Chinese and Indians felt that these parties came to represent only the interests of those in power, not necessarily the desires of the communities as a whole.

Malaysia's electoral system has also limited the power of Chinese and Indian interests. Since 1957 national elections have been held every five years[4] for the lower house of parliament, the Dewan Rakyat, and for state assemblies. In each election the ruling coalition, the National Front (Barisan Nasional, or BN), has won at least a two-thirds majority, and the conventional wisdom is that if the elections were not so one sided, they would not be held. By winning two-thirds of the seats in the legislature, the BN is able to change the constitution at will.

The Malaysian parliamentary system is also highly gerrymandered. Electoral constituencies both enhance the representation of (rural) Malay voters and give overwhelming leverage to the plurality in each district. Malays constitute a majority in 70 percent of the parliamentary constituencies (versus their 60 percent share in the population as a whole). This severely disadvantages non-Malay voters and minimizes their electoral representation while promoting the political fortunes of the BN coalition. This is perhaps the greatest institutional constraint to Chinese political power.

Between 1969 until 1999, the facade of influence being shared across all three major ethnic groups faded. With the creation of a newly rich, middle and upper class of Malays, and through the continued gerrymandering of electoral districts, there was less of an electoral incentive for the UMNO to cater to Chinese constituents either for funding or for electoral support. Ironically, this situation may have changed with the general election of 1999. In the face of a newly politicized (Malay) electorate, the ruling coalition turned to Chinese citizens for support. By many accounts, the Chinese voted in larger numbers for the ruling parties than they had since the mid-1960s. There are two reasons for this support. First, the major beneficiary of Malay anger against the regime was the Islamic Party of Malaysia (*Partai Se Islam di Malaysia,* or PAS), a Muslim opposition party. Since few Malaysian Chinese are Muslim, many felt that the ruling coalition was preferable to Islamic rule. Second, in light of the riots and violence targeted against the ethnic Chinese in Indonesia, many Malaysian Chinese felt that stability and the continued leadership of Mahathir was better than the risk of the chaos that could result from toppling the regime.

SIGNIFICANCE

Ethnic conflict in Malaysia has occurred when cooperation between elites has broken down. Prior to 1969, the Chinese community was mobilized to participate in the political process by the MCA. The MCA represented Chinese business interests, and its leaders were able to work with Malay and Indian elites because they shared the common goals of achieving independence from the British and combating communism. Although Malay interests were privileged, the interests of other groups were addressed in significant and tangible ways. This accommodation deteriorated after the riots of 1969. Heightened ethnic demands and interethnic tensions after 1969 made the bargaining process more costly. The rise of stronger opposition parties and the less homogenous nature of the second generation of leaders within the ruling coalition made it more difficult to secure the support of constituents and less possible to reach accommodation through elite negotiation. In many ways, the fallout from the riots of 1969 included both a weakening of Chinese political power, and an increase in the power of the government over all potential opposition. While it seems that the Chinese community in Malaysia has been willing to trade equality of opportunity and political power for protection of their economic rights and stability, there is a growing sense that this trade-off may not last. As democracy continues to spread both globally and within Southeast Asia, there is a sense that Malaysia's political system will not be able to avoid reforming its nondemocratic elements. While Malaysia's political system has successfully managed ethnic conflict by giving incentives to ethnic leaders to cooperate, a more democratic system could empower new groups within the ethnic communities. This could result in a multiethnic power-sharing arrangement, or it could result in more blatant Malay dominance. This could once again create an atmosphere of ethnic polarization and conflict from which no one would benefit.

See also India: Ethnic Conflict and Nation-building in a Multiethnic State.

NOTES

1. Secret societies were not actually secret until they were banned in 1890. For more information on the secret societies in Malay, and for a longer discussion on the Kapitan Cina system, see Lynn Pan, ed., *The Encyclopedia of the Chinese Over-* *seas* (Cambridge, Mass.: Harvard University Press, 1999), 173.

2. The Malaysian Indian Congress represents Indians in Malaysia. Indians have lagged behind both Malay and Chinese in economic and political standing.

3. In 1970 the average per capita household income for Chinese was M$1,032 as compared with M$492 for a Malay household.

4. In 1969 riots erupted following preliminary election results, and voting was suspended before the election was completed. The results were eventually allowed to be tabulated, and the period of emergency rule did not upset the regular pattern of elections.

SUGGESTED READINGS

Brown, David. *The State and Ethnic Politics in Southeast Asia*. New York: Routledge Press, 1994.

Crouch, Harold A. *Government and Society in Malaysia*. Ithaca, N.Y.: Cornell University Press, 1996.

Freedman, Amy L. *Political Participation and Ethnic Minorities: Chinese Overseas in Malaysia, Indonesia, the United States*. New York: Routledge Press, 2000.

Jalali, Rita, and Seymour Martin Lipset. "Racial and Ethnic Conflicts: A Global Perspective." *Political Science Quarterly* 107, no. 4 (1992/1993), 585–606.

Jayasankaran, S. "Malaysia: Surprise Attack." *Far Eastern Economic Review* (November 18, 1999), 16–18.

Kahn, Joel, and Francis Lo Kok Wah. *Fragmented Vision: Culture and Politics in Contemporary Malaysia*. Honolulu: University of Hawaii Press, 1992.

Lee, Raymond, ed. *Ethnicity and Ethnic Relations in Malaysia*. Normal, Ill.: Center on Southeast Asian Studies, Monograph Series on Southeast Asia, Northern Illinois University, Occasional Paper no. 12, 1986.

Means, Gordon P. *Malaysian Politics: The Second Generation*. Singapore: Oxford University Press, 1991.

Munro-Kua, Anne. *Authoritarian Populism in Malaysia*. New York: St. Martins' Press, 1996.

Pan, Lynn. ed. *The Encyclopedia of the Chinese Overseas*. Cambridge, Mass.: Harvard University Press, 1999.

Skeldon, Rondald. "The Last Half Century of Chinese Overseas (1945–1994): Comparative Perspectives." *International Migration Review* 29, no. 2 (1996), 576–79.

Mexico

The Zapatista Rebellion in Chiapas

Richard Stahler-Sholk

TIMELINE

1542 Dominican friar Bartolomé de Las Casas is named Bishop of Chiapas after his *Very Brief Account of the Destruction of the Indies* persuades the Spanish crown to enact new laws ending the enslavement of Indians.

1712 Tzeltal revolt in Cancuc in the highlands is suppressed by troops arriving from Guatemala.

1821 Independence is gained from Spain; Guatemala and elites request annexation by Mexico.

1869 Caste war rebellion ends in a massacre of Tzotzil Indians in highlands of Chiapas.

1910–1920 Mexican Revolution; rights of communal landholding (*ejidos*) are guaranteed to peasant and indigenous communities under Article 27 of the 1917 constitution.

1934–1940 President Lázaro Cárdenas undertakes land redistributions, some of which finally reach Chiapas; National Indigenous Institute (INI) is founded to promote assimilationist policies.

1974 Indigenous Congress in San Cristóbal de Las Casas becomes a catalyst for grassroots organizing by Maoists and Liberation Theology catechists influenced by Bishop Samuel Ruiz.

1983 A tiny band of guerrilla organizers arrives in Lacandón Forest of Chiapas and founds forerunner of Zapatista Army of National Liberation (EZLN).

1991 Article 27 of the constitution is reformed, allowing *ejido* lands to be put on market.

1992 In March and April, Ch'ol organization Xi = Nich ("Ant people") marches from Palenque to Mexico City to protest repression. On October 12, National Emiliano Zapata Independent Peasant Alliance (ANCIEZ) leads protest march in San Cristóbal de Las Casas.

1994 Zapatista rebellion occurs on January 1 when North American Free Trade Agreement (NAFTA) goes into effect; the army counterattack leaves 150 dead by January 12 cease-fire. In August, Zapatistas convene National Democratic Convention (CND) in Lacandón Forest, which is attended by thousands.

1995 In February, a government military offensive, which breaks the cease-fire, fails to capture EZLN leadership.

1996 In February government and EZLN sign the San Andrés Accords on indigenous rights and culture.

In July, Zapatistas host international forum against neoliberalism.

1997 On December, 22, 46 Tzotzil Indians are massacred by paramilitaries in the highlands village of Acteal.

2000 On July 2, the Partido Revolucionario Institutional (PRI) party loses presidency after 71 years to Partido Acción Nacional (PAN) candidate Vicente Fox.

2001 In February and March, Zapatista leaders caravan from Chiapas to Mexico City, where they hold a mass rally and address Congress, calling for indigenous rights legislation.

In July, a revised indigenous rights law is ratified by a majority of state legislatures but denounced as a sham by the Zapatistas and by national and international human rights groups and subject to a constitutional challenge.

2002 Local violence continues in Chiapas, and international human rights organizations criticize Mexico's record. The administration of President Vincente Fox promises the "Puebla-Panama Plan" of multibillion dollar investment to attract foreign investments in export assemby industries in southern Mexico.

The 1994 Zapatista rebellion in the southernmost Mexican state of Chiapas was locally rooted in indigenous Mayan communities, but it was timed for the day when the North American Free Trade Agreement (NAFTA) took effect, and it soon became a symbol of creative resistance to neoliberal globalization. The Zapatista Army of National Liberation (EZLN), an unorthodox rebel group, refused vanguard status and set aside the armed struggle for state power in favor of building a nonviolent social movement, using more guerrilla theater than guerrilla warfare. Pipe-puffing Subcommander Marcos, the Zapatista spokesperson and icon, was not indigenous to the region, but the heart of the rebellion was the resistance of indigenous communities in the eastern Lacandón Forest, northern zone, and central highlands of Chiapas. They did not seek secession, but rather autonomy, appealing to universal principles of indigenous and human rights and democracy.

The rebel cry of "*¡Ya basta!*" (Enough is enough!) resonated strongly with indigenous and other marginalized peoples in Chiapas and the rest of "deep Mexico,"[1] buffeted by a changing political economy since the 1970s oil boom and 1980s debt crisis. Opening to the world market provoked social upheaval, which could no longer be contained by the dominant-party authoritarian rule of the Institutional Revolutionary Party (PRI). Marcos's ironic style prompted some to label this the world's "first postmodern rebellion." Yet the rebellion focused on concrete social and political realities related to land, markets, and state policies, and it departed from the historical reference point of peasant leader Emiliano Zapata and the Mexican Revolution.

HISTORICAL BACKGROUND

The Colonial Era and Beyond

Chiapas is "Mexico's Mississippi,"[2] a backwater since the colonial period when it languished at the northern fringe of Spanish administration based in Guatemala. Oppressive labor requirements were imposed on the indigenous populations in the Spanish-colonized Americas, prompting sixteenth-century Dominican friar Bartolomé de Las Casas to persuade the crown to end the *encomienda* system of royal "trusts" or grants of Indian labor to Spanish settlers. De Las Casas was appointed protector of the Indians and was sent in the 1540s as Bishop of Chiapas, where he battled local clerics, *encomenderos,* and Guatemalan authorities until his death in 1566.

The colonial era saw continued conflict as the local Ladino (non-Indian) oligarchy, headquartered in the provincial capital of Ciudad Real de Los Altos (later renamed San Cristóbal), sought to control Indian labor and, eventually, to institutionalize labor migration. Amid clashes between Ladino factions and periodic agricultural crises, Indian uprisings such as the 1712 Tzeltal revolt in Cancuc were crushed. Disease, forced labor, and cultural and religious imposition decimated the indigenous populations. After independence was gained from Spain in 1821, the local oligarchy chose annexation by the more powerful Mexico rather than Guatemala. The Indians suffered in the battles between Conservative and Liberal elites. When the Liberals gained the upper hand in Mexico, following the defeat of Emperor Maximilian, Tzotzil communities resisted a Liberal government's head tax in the 1860s and sought greater independence in the highlands, which led to a massacre of Tzotzil peoples that Ladinos insisted was a "caste war."[3]

Liberal reforms in the 1800s brought encroachment by Ladino landowners into previously communal indigenous areas of the central valley and highlands. Modernization also saw the transfer of the state capital in 1858 from San Cristóbal, bastion of the Conservative oligarchy, westward to Tuxtla Gutiérrez. The expansion of commercial agriculture was accelerated by foreign investment, including German immigrants from Guatemala planting coffee in the southern Soconusco region. Debt peonage, vagrancy laws, and other forms of disguised servitude recruited Indians displaced from the highlands for labor in the central valley and southern Pacific coastal plantations.

Revolution, Indians, and National Identity

The Mexican Revolution of 1910 brought about a realignment of the political elites in Chiapas, but a fundamental transformation of social relations did not immediately reach the indigenous peasants. The 1917 constitution did not specifically recognize indigenous rights; however, it did incorporate peasant leader Emiliano Zapata's *Plan de Ayala* in the form of Article 27, which established peasant rights to *ejidos,* or community-managed landholdings. For indigenous communities in Chiapas, the revolution really came during the 1934–1940 presidency of Lázaro Cárdenas. Agrarian reform significantly expanded the *ejido* sector, with credit and management structures increasingly tying the communities to a corporatist state controlled by the PRI. The *ejidatarios* remained desperately poor, in contrast to commercial agriculture in the central valley and the Soconusco.

A National Indigenous Institute (INI) began to promote *indigenismo,* the postrevolution official ideology that Indians were not inferior but rather made a positive contribution to the national "cosmic race," celebrated in a book of that title written by education minister José Vasconcelos and in the heroic depictions of dark-skinned Mexicans in the murals of Diego Rivera, David Siqueiros, and José Clemente Orozco. In the highlands of Chiapas, Indian agencies and agrarian committees superimposed a national PRI-controlled clientelism on the indigenous communities' cargo system of religious and political hierarchy controlled by local caciques (bosses). The resulting system of political control made the small, poor state of Chiapas a bedrock of electoral support for the 71-year reign of the PRI.

Political Economy of the Late Twentieth Century

Changing market conditions produced an economic expansion in Chiapas from 1950 to 1980, dominated by wealthy cattle ranchers and timber companies. As unresolved agrarian reform claims rose, a growing flow of indigenous landless peasants and former plantation workers began to migrate eastward to the agricultural frontier of the Lacandón Forest. These migrants included Tzotzil, Tzeltal and Ch'ol Indians from the central, eastern, and northern highlands, and some Tojolabal moving eastward into the southern Lacandón. They streamed into the canyons of the Lacandón, quadrupling that region's population between 1950 and 1980. Economic opportunities offered by the expansion of commercial agriculture, the escape valve of migration to the Lacandón agricultural frontier, and the oil boom of the 1970s all proved to be limited, and land conflicts had escalated by the 1980s. Repression escalated under state governors Absalón Castellanos (1982–1988), a former general, and Patrocinio González (1988–1994), who favored wealthy Ladino landowners and ranchers and their private guntoting *guardias blancas* (white guards).

Several new organizing initiatives arose among the primarily indigenous poor peasants of Chiapas in the 1970s and 1980s. The *Plan de Ayala* National Coordinating Committee (CNPA), formed in 1979; the Emiliano Zapata Peasant Organization (OCEZ), established in 1982, and the National Union of Regional Autonomous Peasant Organizations (UNORCA), founded in 1985, all promoted agrarian reform independently of the PRI-controlled National Peasant Confederation (CNC). The national Independent Confederation of Agricultural Workers and Peasants (CIOAC), linked to the Mexican Communist Party, began operating in Chiapas in 1976. Another form of organizing had its origins in unions of *ejidos* (UE) created to incorporate peasants into government rural development projects in the late 1970s. These were later linked to form a Union of Unions (UU) and Rural Collective Interest Associations (ARIC), which broke free of PRI control to press for broader autonomy in production, credit,

and marketing decisions. Participants in these initiatives were radicalized through alternating government attempts made at co-optation and repression.

Various ideological influences shaped the mobilization of poor indigenous communities in the central highlands, north, and eastern Lacandón regions of Chiapas. Samuel Ruiz, a Roman Catholic bishop since 1960 of the diocese of San Cristóbal covering the northeastern half of the state, became inspired by the Liberation Theology movement in the Latin American Catholic Church. The movement called for a "preferential option for the poor." The diocese, which trained indigenous catechists and community organizers, found fertile terrain among the uprooted and transplanted colonists in the canyons of the Lacandón. Protestant missionaries also organized in these new communities, but their converts were often expelled from highlands communities by traditional Catholic caciques, who resented such escape routes from their ironclad religious-civil hierarchies. Joining the mix were a handful of Maoists, many of whom were survivors of the repressed 1968 student movement, who began arriving in Chiapas in the mid-1970s. Some were from a group called Popular Politics (PP), which had been active in several northern Mexican cities. They joined a broader effort called Proletarian Line (LP), which made organizing inroads in the late 1970s in the northern highlands and Lacandón.

A key catalyst for indigenous and peasant organizing in Chiapas was the 1974 Indigenous Congress held in San Cristóbal de Las Casas. The congress was initially called by the state governor to mark the five-hundredth anniversary of the birth of Bartolomé de Las Casas, but owing to the state's limited organizational presence in indigenous areas, preparation was turned over to Bishop Samuel Ruiz. The congress brought together representatives of hundreds of Tzotzil, Tzeltal,

Ch'ol, and Tojolabal communities, whose demands resisted co-optation by the PRI. It also sharpened consciousness of overlapping ethnic and class issues and laid the groundwork for overcoming mutual suspicions between Maoist organizers and religious catechists. The congress also reinforced a growing sense of cross-ethnic indigenous identity among the pioneers in the new communities on the agricultural frontier.

Around 1983 members of a tiny clandestine movement called the Forces of National Liberation (FLN), including one who later became known as the rebel spokesperson Marcos, began working in the Lacandón. They recruited first among the UU, and in 1991 they organized the National Emiliano Zapata Independent Peasant Alliance (ANCIEZ). They also clandestinely trained armed units for community self-defense against the forces of the ranchers and the repressive state government, at a time when many communities were becoming radicalized in the struggle for survival. Neoliberal reform in the late 1980s and early 1990s had led to the dissolution of the state coffee marketing board and the collapse of coffee prices, the withdrawal of price supports for corn and bean producers, credit cutbacks, and the prospect of a flood of cheap U.S. agribusiness imports further devastating local markets when NAFTA took effect in 1994.

In 1991–1992 President Carlos Salinas introduced reforms to Article 27 of the constitution in preparation for NAFTA, ending land redistribution and allowing private sale of *ejido* land. This assault on one of the pillars of the Mexican Revolution, akin to revoking the Bill of Rights in the U.S. Constitution, sent shock waves throughout the peasantry. ANCIEZ spearheaded the opposition in the state that had the largest share of unresolved agrarian reform land claims. In mid-1992 the indige-nous communities met to discuss armed struggle, and they decided, as a trial run, to have ANCIEZ lead a peaceful indigenous march into San Cristóbal on October 12 in defiance of the Columbus Day quincentenary, shocking the Ladino oligarchy. In early 1993, a Clandestine Revolutionary Indigenous Committee-General Command (CCRI-CG) was formed, with Marcos as military secretary of what was by then called the Zapatista Army of National Liberation (EZLN), and the decision was made to organize an armed rebellion. With preparations for war under way, in May 1993, a Mexican army patrol discovered an EZLN camp and a battle ensued, which the government covered up to avoid jeopardizing passage of NAFTA in the U.S. Congress.

On the eve of the rebellion, Chiapas produced half of Mexico's hydroelectric power and a significant amount of oil and gas, but most of its indigenous regions lacked electricity. Over half the state's population suffered from malnutrition, and illiteracy was three times the national average. Along with the southern Pacific states of Guerrero and Oaxaca, the population of Chiapas ranks among the poorest in Mexico, with among the highest concentrations of indigenous peoples who have endured centuries of racism. The Zapatistas, who affirmed the historically felt rights of indigenous people and Mexican peasants, organized across ethnic groups and religions and asserted women's rights. Their rebellion also tapped into historical struggles against an authoritarian party-state that was increasingly seen as having betrayed the revolutionary promise of free elections, worker and social rights, agrarian reform, and national control of resources. More broadly, the Zapatista movement was embraced by many who felt excluded by the neoliberal model of opening to the powerful forces of the global market.

THE CONFLICT

The Zapatistas chose January 1, 1994—the date NAFTA went into effect—to emerge from the jungle in an armed takeover of San Cristóbal, Ocosingo, and five other municipal seats in southeastern Chiapas. Their First Declaration of the Lacandón Jungle asserted that the dispossessed had suffered injustice and betrayal at the hands of the political elite, cited the Mexican constitution and the people's inalienable right to alter or modify their form of government, and demanded "work, land, housing, food, health care, education, independence, freedom, democracy, justice, and peace." The Mexican military responded with ground forces and aerial strafing, driving the insurgents back into the jungle and leaving some 150 dead before a cease-fire was declared on January 12. Intermittent negotiations ensued over the next seven years, along with a steadily increasing military presence in Chiapas and the proliferation of paramilitaries in a counterinsurgency campaign that killed a few hundred (mainly indigenous Zapatista sympathizers) each year.

MANAGEMENT OF THE CONFLICT

The Zapatista rebellion caught the PRI party, which had ruled Mexico since the 1920s, at a time of deep internal division. The PRI was still recovering from its electoral nadir of 1988, when center-left opposition candidate Cuahtémoc Cárdenas of the Party of the Democratic Revolution (PRD) had possibly won the presidency, and the PRI resorted to massive fraud to claim victory. The PRI was divided between the "technocrats," who promoted neoliberal reforms, and the "dinosaurs," who controlled the old patronage machinery. President Carlos Salinas (1988–1994), who had engineered the NAFTA signing and aspired to head the World Trade Organization when his term ended, hoped to bring a quick end to the uprising. He sent Manuel Camacho Solís, a party reformer with his own presidential ambitions, to negotiate with the Zapatistas. Meanwhile, PRI presidential candidate Luis Donaldo Colosio was assassinated in March 1994, and the compromise successor candidate was a colorless technocrat, Ernesto Zedillo. The Zapatistas submitted Camacho's tepid proposal for study commissions and more government programs to a vote in their support communities, where it was roundly rejected.

The EZLN then organized a National Democratic Convention (CND) in August 1994 in the Lacandón, where thousands of dissident organizations from all over Mexico assembled to consider democratic alternatives. They built bleachers in a jungle clearing and called the place Aguascalientes, after the site of the constitutional convention in the Mexican Revolution. When the army later dismantled the locale, the EZLN built five more and called them all Aguascalientes, turning them into cultural and multiservice centers of resistance for surrounding communities of Zapatista supporters.

In October 1994, Bishop Ruiz formed the National Mediation Commission (CONAI) to try to jump-start negotiations. Tensions mounted in December as the army began closing a circle around the region of presumed Zapatista strongholds, and the EZLN peacefully occupied 38 municipalities to demonstrate their support outside the area of encirclement. The Mexican peso collapsed, and investor pressure mounted for a quick solution. In February 1995, the government launched a major military offensive in violation of its own cease-fire, failing to capture the EZLN leadership but accelerating the flow of internally displaced people fleeing the army. In March 1995, the Mexican Congress formed a Commission of Concord and

SELVA LACANDONA, CHIAPAS MEXICO. Trotzil women meeting on the fifth anniversary of the Zapatista rebellion, January 1, 1999. Photo courtesy of the author.

Pacification (COCOPA), and protracted negotiations finally produced an Accord on Indigenous Rights and Culture, signed in February 1996 in the highlands town of San Andrés Larráinzar. However, continued attempts by the executive branch unilaterally to modify the content of the San Andrés Accords, with COCOPA proposing compromise language to salvage them, finally led to a breakdown in peace talks in August 1996 with no actual legislation to implement the accords.

The conflict continued to reverberate, both locally and beyond. The Zapatistas advanced their autonomy project in supportive communities, rejected government projects in favor of self-help, and invited international solidarity and human rights observers. The government sent in between 40,000 and 70,000 troops, up to one-third of the federal army, into a poor state with only 3 percent of the country's population, while channeling aid to PRI supporters and promoting paramilitaries in a classic low-intensity warfare strategy. Growing numbers of Mexican soldiers received counterinsurgency training at the U.S. Army School of the Americas. Many communities were divided among Zapatista supporters, PRI loyalists, and groups that supported Zapatista aims but renounced violence. By the end of the 1990s, there were some 14 paramilitary groups operating, one of which conducted a particularly gruesome massacre of unarmed Tzotzil villagers in the highlands community of Acteal in December 1997.

After the initial uprising, the Zapatistas focused on mobilizing national and international civil society support. In July 1996, they hosted an international forum for humanity and against neoliberalism, followed by a September 1997 journey of

1,111 unarmed Zapatistas to Mexico City to found a civic Zapatista Front for National Liberation (FZLN). In March 1999, 5,000 Zapatistas dispersed throughout Mexico to organize a national consultation, or informal referendum on the San Andrés Accords; 3 million Mexicans participated. In July 2000 the political panorama shifted when Vicente Fox, a conservative populist businessman from the National Action Party (PAN), won the presidential election, the first PRI defeat since the party's founding 71 years before. Fox's campaign promises stressed clean government and an end to the Chiapas conflict "in 15 minutes," though he promoted the same neoliberal policies that were anathema to the Zapatistas. In February and March 2001, the Zapatista leadership traveled in a three-week caravan from Chiapas to Mexico City, addressing rallies of supporters along the way. The caravan culminated in an enormous gathering in the capital's *zócalo* (main plaza) and an historic address given by rebel Commander Esther to Congress, calling for indigenous rights legislation. The government response was equivocal, but observers compared the political impact to the celebrated March on Washington during the U.S. civil rights movement.

SIGNIFICANCE

The Zapatista rebellion awakened the indigenous rights movement not only in Chiapas, but throughout Mexico, with a National Indigenous Congress (CNI) endorsing the principles in the San Andrés Accords and insisting, "Never again a Mexico without us." By stressing grassroots democracy in their community-based autonomy movement, and by rejecting vanguardism in favor of an open invitation for civil society participation, the rebels played a significant role in the possible democratization of Mexico.

The Zapatista movement reflects a wider Latin American indigenous revival, partly in reaction to the neoliberal model which reduces rights to a series of individual contracts in the marketplace. The Zapatistas also creatively used the Internet and other networks of globalization, positioning themselves within a transnational social movement.

See also Bolivia: Ethnicized Peasant Conflict; and Indonesia: The Struggle to Control East Timor.

NOTES

1. This phrase, referring to the submerged identity of the country's indigenous poor, originates from the classic work by Mexican anthropologist Guillermo Bonfil Batalla, *México Profundo: Reclaiming a Civilization* (Austin: University of Texas Press, 1996).
2. John Womack, Jr., *Rebellion in Chiapas: An Historical Reader* (New York: New Press, 1999), 4.
3. Jan Rus, "Whose Caste War? Indians, Ladinos, and the Chiapas 'Caste War' of 1869," in *Spaniards and Indians in Southeastern Mesoamerica: Essays on the History of Ethnic Relations*, ed. Murdo J. MacLeod and Robert Wasserstrom (Lincoln: University of Nebraska Press, 1983), 144–56.

SUGGESTED READINGS

Bardacke, Frank, et al., eds. *Shadows of Tender Fury: The Letters and Communiqués of Subcomandante Marcos and the Zapatista Army of National Liberation.* New York: Monthly Review Press, 1995.

Benjamin, Thomas. *A Rich Land, a Poor People: Politics and Society in Modern Chiapas,* 2d ed. Albuquerque: University of New Mexico Press, 1996.

Collier, George, with Elizabeth Lowery Quaratiello. *Basta! Land and the Zapatista Rebellion in Chiapas,* 2d ed. Oakland, Calif: Institute for Food and Development Policy, 1999.

Harvey, Neil. *The Chiapas Rebellion: The Struggle for Land and Democracy.* Durham, N.C.: Duke University Press, 1998.

———. *Rebellion in Chiapas: Rural Reforms, Campesino Radicalism, and the Limits of Sal-*

inismo, 2d ed. San Diego: U.C.–San Diego Center for U.S.–Mexico Studies, 1994.

LaBotz, Dan. *Democracy in Mexico: Peasant Rebellion and Political Reform.* Boston: South End Press, 1995.

Nash, June, C. *Mayan Visions; The Quest for Autonomy in an Age of Globallzation.* New York: Routledge, 2001.

Ponce de León, Juana, ed. *Our Word Is Our Weapon: Selected Writings, Subcomandante Marcos.* New York: Seven Stories Press, 2001.

Ross, John. *Rebellion from the Roots: Indian Uprising in Chiapas.* Monroe, Maine: Common Courage Press, 1995.

———. *The War Against Oblivion: The Zapatista Chronicles.* Monroe, Maine: Common Courage Press, 2000.

Rus, Jan. "The 'Comunidad Revolucionaria Institucional': The Subversion of Native Government in Highland Chiapas, 1936–1968." In *Everyday Forms of State Formation: Revolution and the Negotiation of Rule in Modern Mexico,* edited by Gilbert M. Joseph and Daniel Nugent, 265–300. Durham, N.C.: Duke University Press, 1994.

Rus, Jan, Aída Hernández Castillo, and Shannan L. Mattiace, eds. "The Indigenous People of Chiapas and the State in the Time of Zapatismo: Remaking Culture, Renegotiating Power." Special issue of *Latin American Perspectives* 28, no. 2 (March 2001): 3–170. [Expanded edition forthcoming, *Land, Liberty and Autonomy: Zapatismo and the Indigenous Peoples of Chiapas* (Lanham, Md.: Rowman and Littlefield, 2002)]

Stahler-Sholk, Richard. "Massacre in Chiapas." *Latin American Perspectives* 25, no. 4 (July 1998): 63–75.

Weinberg, Bill. *Homage to Chiapas: The New Indigenous Struggles in Mexico.* New York: Verso, 2000.

Womack, Jr., John. *Rebellion in Chiapas: An Historical Reader.* New York: New Press, 1999.

Middle East

The Arab-Jewish Struggle for Palestine to 1948

James A. Reilly

TIMELINE

142 B.C. Palestine's last independent Jewish kingdom is established.

63 B.C. Rome conquers Palestine; end of Jewish independence.

70 C.E. Romans destroy the Jewish temple in Jerusalem.

312 C.E. Palestine is under Christian (Roman and Byzantine) rule.

638 Muslim Arabs conquer Palestine.

691 Arab rulers build Dome of the Rock in Jerusalem.

1099–1291 Crusader principalities are established in and around Palestine.

1517 The Ottoman Turks seize Palestine from Mamluk sultans of Egypt.

1881 The first Zionist society is founded in Russia.

1888 Ottomans give Jerusalem special administrative status.

1897 The World Zionist Organization is formed.

1908–1914 Arab press articulates sentiments of Arab nationalism and Palestinian patriotism.

1914–1918 World War I is fought.

1916 Britain and France agree to partition Ottoman lands.

1917 Balfour Declaration commits Britain to supporting "a national home for the Jewish people" in Palestine.

1920 British civil administration is established in Palestine; Arab-Jewish violence flares.

1921 British appoint al-Hajj Amin al-Husayni as mufti of Jerusalem.

1929 Major intercommunal violence is sparked by tensions surrounding the Western (Wailing) Wall.

1930 Official British commission recommends a pro-Arab policy tilt; British government declines to accept the recommendations.

1933 Adolf Hitler and the Nazi Party come to power in Germany.

1935 Sheikh 'Izz al-Din al-Qassam dies in a gunbattle with British police. David Ben-Gurion assumes leadership of the Jewish self-governing body.

1936 An Arab general strike and subsequent armed revolt are undertaken to oppose British rule and Jewish nationalism.

1937 The official British commission recommends the partition of Palestine into a

Jewish state and an Arab region. The Arab revolt intensifies. British arrest Arab leadership, and al-Hajj Amin al-Husayni flees into exile.

1939 The Arab revolt is suppressed; British declare intention to give Palestine independence as a unitary, Arab-majority state within ten years.

1939–1945 World War II is fought.

1941–1945 Nazi Germany's genocide policy kills approximately 6 million European Jews.

1946 Irgun militia (Jewish) destroys a wing of the King David Hotel in Jerusalem.

1947 The United Nations General Assembly votes to partition Palestine.

1948 In April, intercommunal warfare intensifies, triggering massive Palestinian Arab flight. In May, British evacuate Palestine, and Jewish leadership declares State of Israel.

The conflict between Arabs and Jews for political sovereignty in Palestine illustrates a number of themes in recent world history. An old, multinational empire was broken up and replaced by a state system whose source of legitimacy was deemed to be the principle of national self-determination. In the scramble to establish political rights and to foster modern national consciousness in a newly demarcated territory, rival political movements asserted their connection to ancient peoples, histories, and myths. European and Western imperial states sought to manipulate and guide local politics, provoking an anticolonial national movement. The two world wars marked decisive turning points in the development of this conflict, which took on an international (not merely local or regional) dimension from its early days. All of this was played out against an evocative backdrop: Palestine, Jerusalem, and the Holy Land. Other colonial and postcolonial wars and conflicts in South Asia and parts of Africa might have been fiercer

and bloodier, but none attracted the attention and mobilized the sentiments of the people around the world like the Arab-Jewish conflict over Palestine.

HISTORICAL BACKGROUND

The country of Palestine (the Land of Israel in Jewish tradition) loomed large in the religious and historical imaginations of Jews, Christians, and Muslims. It was the locale of most of the stories in Jewish and Christian scripture. Islam subsumed these earlier monotheistic traditions into its own narrative. The sacred histories of all three faiths reserved a special place for Jerusalem. Ancient Jewish kingdoms rose and fell in Palestine, but Jewish political sovereignty came to an end at the time of the Roman Empire. Rome's successor, the Eastern Roman (Byzantine) Empire, emphasized Palestine's place in Christianity through the identification of holy sites associated with the career of Jesus of Nazareth. Muslim Arabs swept the Byzantines from the country in 638 C.E. In the centuries that followed, Palestine became a predominantly Muslim, Arabic-speaking country. The Islamization of Palestine accelerated in the wake of the medieval crusades, a doomed effort by Western Europeans to create Christian colonies along the shore of the Eastern Mediterranean (eleventh to thirteenth centuries). Throughout these episodes, significant communities of Jews and Christians continued to live in Palestine. The last premodern sovereign in Palestine was the Ottoman Empire, a nonnational Islamic sultanate based in Istanbul (old Constantinople). The Ottomans established their 400-year reign in Palestine in 1517.

Under Ottoman rule the peoples of Palestine were governed by officials appointed from Istanbul, as well as by their local sheikhs, chieftains, and strongmen who served as intermediaries between the

JERUSALEM. Dome of the Rock, established by the area's Arab rulers in 691. Photo courtesy of Deborah J. Gerner.

Ottomans and the local population. The internal affairs of Palestine's Jews and Christians were left mostly in the hands of their respective religious officials. The majority Muslim population were served by their own religious hierarchy. Ottoman rule in Palestine was not seriously challenged until the nineteenth century. From the 1850s onward, the expanding power of the European states and the growth of national movements hostile to nonnational monarchies like that of the Ottomans combined to undermine the foundations of the political status quo in Palestine.

THE CONFLICT

The emergence of what came to be known as the Jewish Question in nineteenth-century Europe provided the first articulation of territorial-national goals in Palestine. Prior to the Enlightenment and the French Revolution (eighteenth century), European Jews occupied a defined, subordinate, and sometimes barely tolerated place in societies that defined themselves as "Christian." However, the intellectual movement of the Enlightenment, the political triumph of the French Revolution (1789), and the spread of liberal values in general caused a fundamental rethinking about the place of Jews in European society. According to Enlightenment thinkers and liberal revolutionaries, all men are created equal, and (adult male) members of national communities should be able to participate in government and society on an equitable basis. Therefore, while Christianity remained the majority religion in Europe, more and more European states were hesitant to define rights and responsibilities in their societies along religious lines. Instead, loyalty to and affiliation with the state and the nation became a citizen's or a subject's basis of participation in public life.

This change of paradigm presented European Jews with both a challenge and an opportunity. Their old, well-defined cultural, communal, and social roles now appeared anachronistic to many Jews. For the first time, they were being invited to participate in predominantly Gentile societies on an equal basis. But to take up this invitation, they would have to subordinate their Jewish identity and culture to their civic identity and culture as Englishmen, Frenchmen, Germans, and so on. If Jews were no longer a subordinate and well-defined religious and communal group, then what were they?

Some European Jews sought to assimilate into Gentile society, to become wholly French, English, or German by formally abandoning Judaism. Others entirely rejected the blandishments of assimilation and modernity and clung ever more tightly to their older religious and communal traditions. The majority of European Jews searched for a middle ground that would allow them to express both their older Jewish and their modern national identities. One consequence was a Hebrew literary revival in the nineteenth century among intellectuals, and these writers subtly redefined Jews as a "people" with their own national history, linked to but distinct from the concept of a "religious community" defined mainly by its adherence to communal rules and structures.

Liberal governments and movements promised Jews equality in a secular community; however, these promises often proved hollow. As European societies were rapidly transformed by political and economic revolutions in the nineteenth century, older forms of social consciousness based on religion became less prominent. New forms of consciousness based on nationality, race, and ethnicity came to the fore. If "the nation" was now seen as the

basis of human history, were Jews part of "the nation" or not? If they were not, what were they? Right-wing and populist movements in France, Germany, and Austria-Hungary began propounding a new ideology, anti-Semitism, which asserted that Jews were not and could not be full members of the national community. Anti-Semitic demagogues laid the disruptions of capitalism and of industrial society at the feet of the Jews. Anti-Semitism found a receptive audience among people who faced difficulty or hardship as a consequence of the dramatic social and cultural changes of the period. Even in liberal France, anti-Semitism proved a powerful force. Its spread disillusioned many Jews who had hoped that they could share in society on a basis of equality.

In the Eastern European lands of tsarist Russia, the situation was even worse. In a bid to strengthen itself in the era of nationalism, the Russian monarchy after 1881 allied itself with Slavic nationalists who defined the large Jewish community within Russia's frontiers as foreign and alien. The Russian regime supported or tolerated violent attacks (pogroms) against Jewish communities. Moreover, Jews in the Russian Empire faced a range of legal handicaps limiting where they could live and restricting their access to modern state institutions, including universities. (It was under these circumstances that the mass Russian Jewish emigration to the United States began.) Jews radicalized by tsarist repression joined revolutionary societies. Some of these espoused socialism or communism; others advocated Jewish nationalism.

Thus anti-Semitism in both Eastern and Western Europe encouraged the formation of Jewish nationalist (Zionist) societies, whose members linked the Hebrew cultural revival to the articulation of a modern Jewish *national* claim to Palestine, at the time still under Ottoman rule. From 1882 onward there was a small but steady inflow of immigration into Palestine of secular European Jews, who moved there in order to establish a modern national (as opposed to traditional religious) Jewish presence. In 1897 the World Zionist Organization (WZO) was created as a coordinating body for grassroots Jewish nationalist organizations. The WZO set itself the task of establishing a Jewish national homeland—a state—in Palestine with great power (European) support.

A significant point for understanding the future of the Arab-Jewish conflict is that these aspirations for a Jewish homeland or a Jewish state in Palestine emanated from Europe. They were a response to the problems and challenges facing Jews in France, Germany, and Russia. Middle Eastern Jews, in contrast, were still largely enfolded within their traditional communities and structures. They lived under the tolerant but inegalitarian Ottoman government. Ottoman Jews had communal rights and privileges, but they were not and could not be equal citizens of the officially Muslim Ottoman state. The modern secular ideology of Jewish nationalism scarcely touched the indigenous Jews of the Ottoman Empire and the Middle East prior to 1914.

The bulk of the population of Ottoman Palestine were Arabic-speaking Muslims and Christians. Similar to other people coming to terms with the demands of the modern state, the Arabs of Palestine were forced to redefine and to reconsider their political identities and status in the nineteenth century. The Ottoman Empire itself was facing crisis after crisis in its rich Balkan provinces, where national movements among its Christian subjects (Greeks, Serbs, Bulgarians) combined with European support for secessionist or nationalist movements to challenge the security and the identity of the empire. Like its contemporary counterparts in Austria-Hungary, Russia, and Japan, the Ottoman monarchy in the second half of the nineteenth cen-

tury tried to strengthen its bases of support and legitimacy by forging new ties to its subject population. Because the empire remained multiethnic, the Ottoman monarchy's modern basis of legitimacy could not be defined in ethnic national terms. However, with the loss of its Christian Balkan provinces, the Ottoman population was increasingly Muslim. Therefore, in the second half of the nineteenth century, the Ottoman sultanate emphasized its Islamic identity, and a type of "national" identity based on religion was promoted by the Ottoman state in Palestine and elsewhere in its domains.

The introduction of print technology and the spread of modern education in the Ottoman lands led to literary revivals and movements among the subject populations. An Arabic literary revival is noticeable from the mid-nineteenth century onward. Arabic-speaking intellectuals placed new emphasis on the Arabic language and on the identity of themselves as "Arabs," that is, users of the majority language of the Fertile Crescent. These Arab thinkers included both Muslims and Christians. Muslims emphasized the Arabs' contribution to Islam and the importance of the Arabic language in Islamic law and scripture. Christians interpreted classical Islam as the shared heritage of Arabs no matter what their religion, and they sought to define a new sense of community based on shared language and culture. Different Arabic-speaking regions began to be identified as homelands in the modern sense. By the eve of World War I in 1914, the older Muslim and Christian Arab understandings of the Holy Land and Palestine had acquired political connotations.

By this time, Arabs were aware of European Jewish national claims on the country, and sentiments of Palestinian patriotism were expressed in the Arabic press and among Arab deputies in the Ottoman parliament. Arab politicians and community leaders feared that the Ottoman state was not equal to the challenge of defending their community and their homeland from the Zionist movement. Since Jewish nationalism aimed to settle Jews in Palestine and to create a Jewish government there, Arabs interpreted Zionism as another face of European colonialism. Arabs' apprehensions of European conquest were further fueled by French, British, and Italian expansion into various regions of the Arab and Muslim worlds.

Jewish nationalism prescribed Jewish sovereignty and a Jewish state as a remedy to the problem of anti-Semitism, especially as it affected the Jews of Europe. Palestinian Arab nationalism sought to defend the national community and homeland against European colonization and conquest. These fundamental ideological attitudes were in place prior to World War I. Throughout the rest of the twentieth century, they remained basic ingredients in the respective worldviews of Jewish and Palestinian Arab nationalists.

MANAGEMENT OF
THE CONFLICT

The Zionist movement made little headway with the European great powers prior to World War I. European governments received Zionist emissaries with greater or lesser degrees of sympathy, but prior to the outbreak of the war, no great power believed its interests would be served by advocating a Jewish state in this Ottoman province. The beleaguered Ottoman government itself was strongly opposed to any movement that threatened to weaken further its own hold on the Holy Land. The outbreak of a general war in 1914 changed the political situation dramatically. Hoping to regain lands it had lost earlier to Britain and Russia, the Ottoman government allied itself with Germany and Austria-Hungary in World War I. The Allied powers of Britain, France, and Russia consequently projected the

breakup of the Ottoman Empire in the event of an Allied victory. To this end, Britain, France, and Russia each put forward claims to Palestine. When Russia was on the verge of being knocked out of the war (November 1917), Britain sought to trump France by issuing the Balfour Declaration, proclaiming Britain's support for a "Jewish national home" in Palestine. The Balfour Declaration, the British government hoped, would lend weight to its efforts to establish Britain as the sole great power in Palestine once the war was over. Britain was particularly concerned with Palestine owing to its proximity to Britain's strategic lifeline, the Suez Canal.

The Paris Peace Conference
and the British Mandate

At the Paris Peace Conference held after the war (1919–1920), Britain and France agreed to divide the former Ottoman lands in the Fertile Crescent. Britain obtained Palestine in return for agreeing to allow France a free hand in Syria. These newly demarcated and defined countries were called "mandates" of Britain and France. According to the theory of the mandate system, Britain and France were to govern those territories on behalf of the newly established League of Nations (1919). The mandatory powers were to prepare their mandated territories for self-government. When Britain obtained the mandate for Palestine, the language of the Balfour Declaration was incorporated into the documents that legalized Britain's rule. Therefore, at the end of World War I, the question of Palestine had acquired an international dimension, and Jewish national rights in Palestine were recognized in international law.

Palestinian Arab opinion was outraged by the creation of the mandate, particularly by the provisions for the construction of a Jewish national home in Palestine. Palestinian Arabs argued that they were a majority in Palestine (90 percent of the population in 1920), and that Britain did not have the right to promote a Jewish national home and Jewish self-government in the country. Right or wrong, the Arabs were unable to force Britain and the League of Nations to alter the terms of the Palestine mandate in their favor. The first serious incidents of intercommunal Jewish-Arab violence occurred in 1920–1921 as the personnel and institutions of the British mandate were being put into place.

During the early years of the mandate in the 1920s, British officials were confident that they could manage and contain Arab-Jewish rivalry. Even after Britain's attempts to establish an Arab-Jewish government under British supervision failed, the British believed that they would be able to find the right formula to allow the development of a Jewish national home (rather than a state), while reassuring the Arabs that their rights and position in the country would not be threatened. Political tranquillity in Palestine in the mid-1920s lulled the British government into thinking that this divide-and-rule policy—or balance-and-contain policy—could work. However, Arab-Jewish violence flared up anew in a dispute over the status of the Western (or Wailing) Wall, which became a symbolic flashpoint for the larger political conflict.

The Western Wall is the last remnant of the ancient Jewish temple, and in Ottoman times pious Jews had prayed there at the sufferance of the Muslim religious authorities. The major Muslim monuments of Jerusalem were built on the platform above the Western Wall, near the spot where the Jewish temple had once stood. This platform is usually referred to as the Temple Mount in English, or *al-Haram al-Sharif* (the Noble Sanctuary) in Arabic. Islam's first major monument, the Dome of the Rock, was built there in 691 C.E. The Dome of the Rock encloses Mount Moriah, identified in both the Jewish and Muslim traditions as the spot where Abraham

prepared to sacrifice his son. In addition, Muslims associate the site with a passage in the Koran that recounts a mystical heavenly journey undertaken by the Prophet Muhammad. The Western Wall itself was part of a Muslim religious endowment.

The status of the Western Wall was deeply emotive. Jewish leaders argued that, because the Jewish people were building their national home in Palestine by right, it was inappropriate that they should require anyone's permission to pray there. Jews challenged the religious status quo by trying to introduce unilaterally, in the teeth of Muslim opposition, symbolic changes to the prayer space in front of the Western Wall. Muslims regarded these measures as an attack on their religious and political prerogatives, not only as it related to the Western Wall but as it pertained to Palestine as a whole. The Western Wall became a flashpoint of communal demonstrations. In August 1929, this tension exploded into violence. In the wake of this outburst, Britain dispatched a committee of inquiry to ascertain what had gone wrong and to make policy recommendations for the Palestine mandate.

The violence at the Western Wall demonstrated several points that were to become ever more visible in the remaining years of the mandate. First, symbols of religious communal identity became nationalized. The Zionist movement was predominantly secular, and in fact it represented a rejection of Jewish religious traditionalism. Yet the Western Wall was important to the Zionist movement as a national symbol, as a symbol of the Jewish people's history and of their aspirations for political sovereignty in the Land of Israel. For Arabs (Muslims and Christians alike), the Western Wall (which they called *al-Buraq*) represented the Arab and Islamic identity of Jerusalem and of Palestine. From this point on the leading Muslim religious official in Palestine, the mufti of Jerusalem, al-Hajj Amin al-Husayni

(d. 1974), became the leading Palestinian political figure as he attempted to mobilize Muslim and Christian Arabs, plus other Muslims throughout the world, around the symbol of *al-Haram al-Sharif*. Second, the Arab-Jewish conflict had irretrievably taken on an intercommunal character. The bloodshed of 1929 was not the first time that Jews and Arabs had randomly attacked one another, but the ferocity of the violence and the fact that non-Zionist Jews bore the brunt of Arab attacks indicated that the political boundaries were clearly drawn between Jews and Arabs. This gulf would widen in the ensuing decades, spurred on by a British colonial policy that encouraged the separate political, economic, and cultural development of Jews and Arabs in Palestine.

The British commission of inquiry concluded that Arab fears of Zionism were justified. The British commissioners reported that Jewish immigration, land purchase and acquisition, and the construction of separate Jewish political structures had led to legitimate fears among Arabs that they faced dispossession and marginalization. The British commission recommended that Britain sharply restrict Jewish immigration and land purchases in the future. Conservative, pro-British Arab leaders, who had been hoping for a change in British policy, were delighted with this recommendation. The Zionist leadership, on the other hand, felt that Britain was about to betray them, in violation of the Balfour Declaration and of Britain's commitments under international law through the mandate system. Jewish activists in Britain mobilized a public campaign to prevent the British government from reneging on its commitment to the Jewish national home. In 1931 the British prime minister announced that the pro-Arab recommendations of the official commission would not be implemented. Now it was the turn of the Arabs to feel betrayed.

Both Arabs and Jews had increasing reason to be skeptical of Britain as the decade of the 1930s dawned. Pro-British figures among the Arab leadership were discredited among their own population. Likewise, pro-British figures within the Zionist movement lost influence. A new, activist Jewish leadership emerged that was based in Palestine itself, symbolized by David Ben-Gurion (d. 1973), a leader in the Zionist Labor movement. On the Arab side, the mufti of Jerusalem, al-Hajj Amin al-Husayni, found it increasingly difficult to walk the political tightrope between the British authorities (who had appointed him to his post) and an increasingly radicalized Arab public opinion.

Tensions in Palestine during the 1930s were aggravated by two developments whose origins lay outside of the country: the rise of Nazism in Germany and the Great Depression which was engulfing the world economy. The Nazi party's takeover of Germany in 1933 produced a rapid worsening of the situation of German Jews. Pathologically anti-Semitic, the Nazi regime introduced a series of discriminatory laws aimed at humiliating German Jews and pushing them into emigration. (The formulation of the Nazi's genocidal Final Solution to the Jewish Question would not occur until later, in 1941.) Indeed, the Zionist movement and the German government agreed to allow selected German Jews to immigrate to Palestine and take their liquid assets with them. As a consequence of these pressures, the Jewish population of Palestine doubled in three short years (1933–1936). The bulk of the new arrivals were middle-class Central Europeans, and their arrival significantly boosted the demographic and economic presence of the Jewish community in Palestine.

Meanwhile, the predominantly rural Arab society was in crisis as world agricultural prices fell. Cash-strapped Arab landowners (who often were political leaders or were linked to Arab political leaders) sold off bits and pieces of their landed estates to Jewish institutions. Increasing numbers of Arab villagers became landless and unable to make a living in the countryside, either because of Jewish land purchases or because of bankruptcy and land loss brought about by their debts to Arab landowners. This was a combustible social and political mixture, and both communities (Jewish and Arab) began to arm in preparation for a showdown. The Jewish authorities had organized a clandestine militia, the Haganah, in 1920. Though technically illegal, it was tolerated by the British authorities. The polycentric Arab militias and armed groups reflected the regionally fragmented politics of the Arab population.

Grassroots radicalization in this period was represented by the Muslim sheikh and religious leader 'Izz al-Din al-Qassam (d. 1935). After leading a struggle against French colonial rule in his home country, Syria, al-Qassam had arrived in Palestine where he worked for Muslim religious institutions in the northern port of Haifa. As registrar of marriages in the Islamic court, al-Qassam had the opportunity to travel the countryside in Haifa's hinterland. What set al-Qassam apart from other urban Arab leaders was his genuine interest in and work with the poor and the displaced of Arab society. Al-Qassam developed a following among those who had been the most direct victims of the crisis in the Palestinian countryside. He preached a heady mixture of nationalism, religious revivalism, and dignity through work and sober morals. Unlike the traditional landowning Arab leadership, al-Qassam argued that the British mandate itself, not just the Jewish national home, was the fundamental problem facing Arab society. He encouraged militant, armed action, and in 1935 he was killed in a confrontation with British police.

Al-Qassam's death galvanized Arab opinion and led to increasing popular movements against both the British government and the Jewish community. In an attempt to keep control of the situation, the established Arab leadership (including al-Hajj Amin) called for a general strike in 1936 to compel a change of British policy.

The First Partition Plan and the Arab Revolt

In response, the British sent yet another commission to Palestine. This time (1937) they recommended the partition of Palestine into a small Jewish state and a larger Arab entity which would be linked to neighboring, British-ruled Transjordan. The Jewish leadership interpreted this recommendation as an important political victory. Although the projected Jewish state would be quite small, it nevertheless represented the first time that an official British body had publicly endorsed the concept of a Jewish state in Palestine, rather than the more nebulous concept of a national home. Arab reaction to the partition recommendation was hostile. Most Arabs opposed partition in principle. They argued that they were a majority in the country (still more than two-thirds of the population at this time), and that Britain had no right to slice off a part of the country for the benefit of foreign colonists (i.e., the Jews). Even the minority of Arab leaders who might have accepted partition in some form could not accept the specific recommendations of the 1937 commission. Although the projected Jewish state would have been small, it would have included the predominantly Arab region of the Western Galilee. The British commission had recommended that the Arab population of the Western Galilee be removed in order to facilitate the creation of the Jewish state. This was the first time that the removal of part of the Arab population was officially debated, and this element made it impossible for any Arabs of consequence to accept the plan.

An armed Arab uprising against the British and the Jews broke out anew with great ferocity. At the revolt's peak, Arab guerrillas controlled most of the countryside and dominated the Arab towns. Britain was compelled to bring additional troops from Europe, as well as enlist Jewish auxiliaries from the Haganah, to suppress the Arab revolt. Despite its early successes, the revolt suffered from internal divisions and weaknesses, symptomatic of an Arab society in crisis. The rank and file of the rebels were usually villagers and peasants, and they had scores to settle with Arab landowners whom they regarded as the coauthors of their misfortunes. Peasant guerrilla bands used their power to impose exactions on urban or well-to-do people in Arab communities. By the end of the revolt (1939), some Arab landowners had armed counterrevolutionary militias who cooperated with Britain in the restoration of government authority. The upshot was a defeated, divided, and disarmed Arab population. Elements of the Jewish Haganah, meanwhile, had gained some useful training and military experience through their cooperation with the British.

The immediate aftermath of the Arab revolt appeared to mark a major setback for Zionist hopes of establishing a Jewish state. Arab opinion throughout the Middle East was increasingly mobilized by the question of Palestine, and Britain feared for the security of its imperial position in areas of vital strategic importance, such as Egypt (the Suez Canal) and Iraq (air bases and oil fields). The British government retreated from its own recommendation to partition Palestine and invited representatives of the Jewish and Arab communities to London in the summer of 1939 to find a solution to the Palestine impasse. When common ground between Jews and Arabs was forthcoming, Britain announced yet another unilateral change of policy: Palestine, London announced, would be granted its independence within ten years. In the meantime, Jewish immigration and land purchase would be restricted to en-

sure that this independent Palestine would retain an Arab majority. Britain hoped that its announcement would reduce anti-British Arab nationalist agitation in the Middle East on the eve of an expected new war with Germany. David Ben-Gurion and the Zionists were stung by this latest British reversal and betrayal, but they had no choice except to support Britain in its forthcoming war with Nazi Germany. The political question of the future of Palestine would be put off until World War II was over.

Mandate's End

Just as World War I had put the question of Palestine on the international agenda, World War II paved the way for the creation of a Jewish state. Britain, the ruling power in Palestine, emerged from World War II victorious but weakened. The postwar international system was dominated by two powers with little stake in the preservation of the older European empires: the United States and the Soviet Union. The genocide of some 6 million European Jews in Nazi-controlled Europe during the war had given a new urgency to Zionist efforts to establish a Jewish state in Palestine. The United States supported the immediate entry of 100,000 displaced European Jews into the country, oblivious to British worries about the political impact that this influx would have on British-Arab relations. Zionist parties, meanwhile, identified Britain as the principal obstacle to the creation of a Jewish state and launched a political and guerrilla campaign against British rule—marked most spectacularly by the bombing of the British headquarters at the King David Hotel in Jerusalem in 1946. The Soviet Union supported the campaign for a Jewish state, seeing this as a way to reduce British influence in the Middle East.

Palestinian Arabs, meanwhile, were weakened, divided, and effectively leaderless. Al-Hajj Amin had fled Palestine into exile in 1937 following the Arabs' rejection of Britain's partition plan and the outbreak of the Arab insurrection. He resided in various places in the Middle East before turning up in Berlin in 1941 where he lent propaganda support to the German war effort. After the war, he moved to Cairo from where he attempted to influence Palestinian politics.

The United Nations and the Birth of Israel

The British despaired of ever resolving the impossible Palestine situation, and they turned the matter over to the new United Nations. Britain hoped in this way to confront the United States with its responsibilities, rather than be subject to unceasing U.S. criticism of British policies in Palestine. American political leaders, including President Harry S. Truman, were sensitive to the Jewish vote in key states. These electoral considerations, combined with their sympathy for the Jewish national cause provoked by the Nazi genocide, caused the American leadership to pressure Britain regarding Palestine in favor of Jewish aspirations.

The UN General Assembly, dominated by the victorious superpowers, voted to partition Palestine in November 1947 into two states: one Jewish and one Arab. Under this plan, a majority of the surface area of the country would be incorporated into a Jewish state, and the holy cities of Jerusalem and Bethlehem would be placed under international administration. Jewish nationalists welcomed the UN partition resolution because international endorsement of Jewish sovereignty in their national homeland marked a major political and diplomatic triumph. Arabs rejected the resolution, fearful of the consequences for the large Arab minority that would remain in the Jewish state and resenting the handover of the majority of their country to a foreign, Jewish minority. Britain announced that it would not try to implement the partition resolution, and prepared to withdraw unilaterally from Palestine by May 1948. Arabs and Jews would be left to fight it out to determine the country's future.

The first shots in the civil war between the Jews and Arabs of Palestine erupted within days of the November 1947 partition resolution. By January 1948, a renewed pattern of intercommunal violence was firmly established, with both Jewish and Arab paramilitary groups attacking population centers and workplaces identified with the other community. In the clashes of the first three months of 1948, the Palestinian Arabs, assisted by militiamen from neighboring Arab countries, had the upper hand. The Arabs attempted, with some success, to isolate distant Jewish communities and settlements from the main bloc of Jewish population in the coastal plain between Tel Aviv and Haifa. The Arabs were most successful in cutting off the mountain road that linked Jewish neighborhoods in Jerusalem to the coast.

As they continued their withdrawal from different regions of Palestine, British garrison commanders handed over control to whichever local community or militia was locally the strongest. With their experience of self-government under the mandate, Jewish authorities in Jewish towns and cities were able to step into Britain's shoes with a minimum of disruption. But no centralized Arab authority existed, so power in Arab areas devolved to diffuse local committees or militia groups. The spreading violence and insecurity of the months between November 1947 and March 1948 caused many of the better-off Arab families to leave Palestine for safety elsewhere. This outflow of people, who might otherwise have formed a kernel or nucleus of communal leadership, further hindered efforts to construct a coherent Palestinian Arab administration in areas from which Britain withdrew.

In April 1948 a new and decisive phase of the Jewish-Arab civil war opened.

With the British mandate in its final weeks and with British forces reduced to a token number, the Jewish leadership opted to launch a war of movement in order to capture and secure territory needed for the creation and consolidation of a Jewish state. Breaking the Arab siege of Jerusalem was a top priority. In this context, the Haganah undertook an operation known as Plan D, which called for clearing out Arab military and population centers that stood astride or threatened Jewish routes of communication. As Jewish forces seized Arab villagers, the Palestinian inhabitants fled or were driven out. Panic set in among the Arab population as news spread of a massacre committed by Jewish militias in the Arab village of Deir Yasin west of Jerusalem. Accounts of Deir Yasin, spread both by Arabs (as an atrocity report) and Jews (as a psychological warfare tactic), triggered a panicky Arab exodus from areas of the country where Jewish forces were advancing. The flood of Arab refugees alarmed Palestine's Arab neighbors and strained their resources. In keeping with the spirit of intercommunal warfare, Arab militias retaliated for Deir Yasin by attacking a medical convoy in Jerusalem a few days later that killed a number of Jewish medical workers. Jewish depopulation of Arab villages had its counterpart in the Arab seizure of Gush Etzion and the execution of its surviving Jewish defenders in May 1948.

The British mandate ended, and the State of Israel was proclaimed on May 15, 1948. By that time Palestine was already engulfed in war (a civil or intercommunal war between the country's Jews and Arabs). With the proclamation of the Jewish state, the conflict took on an interstate dimension as neighboring Arab countries prepared to send their armies into Palestine, ostensibly to rescue their defeated Palestinian brethren but, equally important, to pursue their own particular goals as well.

SIGNIFICANCE

The Jewish-Arab conflict in Palestine up to 1948 illustrates a number of themes common to the history of the developing world in the last century. A modern ethnic and national conflict arose between two peoples with long histories. Jews and Palestinian Arabs began to define themselves in national terms as they struggled for control of a new state. The modern boundaries of Palestine were drawn by the imperial powers of Great Britain and France in the service of imperial interests. The previously imprecise understanding of Palestine/the Land of Israel thereby acquired a concrete, geopolitical meaning. The struggle between Jews and Arabs focused on the illegitimacy of each other's claims, and both parties appealed to history and to religion to create a sense of historical continuity between the national present and the historical or mythical past. The Jewish nationalists, mainly Europeans, adopted colonial techniques in order to carve out a place for themselves in a predominantly Arab country. Palestinian Arabs responded as many native populations did in similar circumstances. At times of crisis and armed conflict, Arab militants made little effort to distinguish between "good" colonists and "bad," between combatant Jews and noncombatant Jews. For their part, confronting what they perceived as a wall of native hostility, Jewish nationalists defined Arabs as an alien, hostile population whose expulsion and exile from contested lands was justified in the name of self-defense. The entire conflict unfolded in an international context that was molded by World War I and II, and events of these wars had a direct impact on the conflict's course and development. The Arab-Jewish struggle in Palestine was not, and is not, a slice of exotica disconnected from the mainstream of world history. Instead it is very much both a product and an emblem of the bloody twentieth century.

See also Lebanon: Ethnic Conflict and the Lebanese Civil War, 1975–1990; and Middle East: The Palestinian Issue.

SUGGESTED READINGS

Beit-Hallahmi, Benjamin. *Original Sins: Reflections on the History of Zionism and Israel.* London: Pluto Press, 1992.

Kurzman, Dan. *Ben-Gurion: Prophet of Fire.* New York: Simon and Schuster, 1983.

Mattar, Philip. *The Mufti of Jerusalem: Al-Hajj Amin al-Husayni and the Palestinian National Movement.* New York: Columbia University Press, 1988.

Morris, Benny. *Righteous Victims: A History of the Zionist-Arab Conflict 1881–1999.* New York: Knopf, 1999.

Smith, Charles D. *Palestine and the Arab-Israeli Conflict.* New York: St. Martin's Press, 1996.

Tessler, Mark A. *A History of the Israeli-Palestinian Conflict.* Bloomington: Indiana University Press, 1994.

Middle East

The Kurds Struggle for "Kurdistan"

Michael M. Gunter

TIMELINE

401 B.C. Kardouchoi harass retreating Greeks as recorded by Xenophon in *Anabasis*.

A.D. 600s Kurds are Islamicized in mid-century.

1137–1193 Era of Saladin, the most famous Kurd.

1847 Bedr Khan Beg, ruler of last semi-independent Kurdish emirate, surrenders to Ottomans.

1880 Sheikh Obeidullah conducts an unsuccessful revolt.

1891 Ottoman Sultan Abdulhamid II creates *Hamidiye* Kurdish cavalry.

1914–1918 Kurds support Ottomans in World War I.

1918 U.S. President Woodrow Wilson proposes the Fourteen Points.

1919 British create Iraq; Sheikh Mahmud begins decade of unsuccessful revolts in Iraq.

1919–1922 Kurds support Turkish War of Independence.

1920 Stillborn Treaty of Sèvres provides for possible Kurdish independence.

1923 Definitive Treaty of Lausanne fails to mention Kurds.

1925 Turks crush Sheikh Said's rebellion. "Mountain Turks" (Kurds) are repressed.

1926 Iranian Kurdish leader Ismail Agha Simko is assassinated.

1930 Turks crush Kurdish rebellion in Ararat area.

1931 Mulla Mustafa Barzani (1903–1979) begins to emerge in Iraq as the preeminent Kurdish leader of the twentieth century.

1936–1938 Turks crush Kurdish rebellion in Dersim (Tunceli).

1946 Kurdistan Democratic Party (KDP) (Iraq) is formed on August 16.

1946–1947 Mahabad Republic of Kurdistan is organized in Iran.

1947 Qazi Muhammad is hanged by Iranians on March 31.

1970 March Manifesto in Iraq theoretically promises Kurdish autonomy.

1975 Mulla Mustafa Barzani is defeated. His son, Massoud Barzani, eventually emerges as his successor. On June 1, Jalal Talabani (1933–) creates (Iraqi) Patriotic Union of Kurdistan (PUK).

1978 On November 27, Abdullah (Apo) Ocalan creates Kurdistan Workers Party (PKK) in Turkey.

1982 Current Turkish constitution contains several provisions repressing Kurds.

1984 In August, a PKK insurgency in Turkey begins.

1987–1988 Saddam Hussein conducts genocidal *Anfal* campaigns against Iraqi Kurds.

1989 Iranian Kurdish leader Abdul Rahman Ghassemlou is assassinated.

1991 Gulf War is fought. Iraqi Kurdish uprising occurs, and mass refugee flight takes place. United States creates safe haven and no-fly zone resulting in a de facto Kurdish state in northern Iraq. UN Security Council Resolution 688 condemns Iraqi repression of Kurds. An antiterrorism law (Turkey) makes the peaceful advocacy of Kurdish rights a crime.

1994 Peoples Democracy Party (HADEP) is created as the legal Kurdish party in Turkey.

1994–1998 KDP-PUK civil war is conducted in Iraqi Kurdistan.

1995 In PKK attacks the KDP in northern Iraq.

1998 In October, Syria expels Ocalan.

1999 In February, the Turks capture Ocalan; and, in June, Ocalan is sentenced to death. In December, the European Union accepts Turkey as a candidate member. Ocalan's death sentence put on hold.

2000 Reform-minded Ahmet Necdet Sezar is elected president in Turkey.

Although they form a large majority within the mountainous Middle East where Turkey, Iran, Iraq, and Syria meet, the Kurds have been gerrymandered into being mere minorities within the existing states they inhabit. They constitute the largest nation or ethnic group in the world without its own independent state. The desire of many Kurds for statehood, or at least cultural autonomy within the states they now inhabit, has led to an almost continuous series of Kurdish revolts since the creation of the modern Middle East fol-

lowing World War I. This situation is the basis of the Kurdish problem or question.

The Kurds are a largely Sunni Muslim, Indo-European-speaking people. Thus, they are quite distinct ethnically from the Turks and Arabs, but they are related to the Iranians with whom they share the *Newroz* (new year) holiday at the beginning of spring. No reliable estimates of the Kurdish population exist because most Kurds tend to exaggerate their numbers, while the states in which they live undercount them for political reasons. In addition, a significant number of Kurds have been partially or fully assimilated into the larger Arab, Turkish, or Iranian populations surrounding them. Furthermore, debate continues concerning whether such groups as the Lurs, Bakhtiyaris, and others are Kurds or not. Thus, there is not even complete agreement on who is a Kurd.

Nevertheless, a reasonable estimate is that there may be as many as 12 to 15 million Kurds in Turkey (18 to 21 percent of the population), 6 million in Iran (11 percent), 3.5 to 4 million in Iraq (20 to 23 percent), and 800,000 in Syria (7 percent). At least 100,000 Kurds also live in parts of the former Soviet Union, and recently a Kurdish diaspora of more than 1 million has risen in Western Europe. More than half of this diaspora is concentrated in Germany. Some 20,000 Kurds live in the United States.[1]

In the Middle East, Kurdistan (Land of the Kurds) is blessed with water and oil, but the Kurds themselves are divided geographically, politically, linguistically, tribally, and ideologically. Although a Kurdish adage warns that the Kurds have no friends but the mountains, these very mountains and valleys divide them as much as they ethnically stamp them. The Kurdish problem or question is vast, extremely complicated, and can quickly become very emotional. What follows, therefore, is only a brief introduction.

HISTORICAL BACKGROUND

The origin of the Kurds is uncertain, although some scholars believe them to be the descendants of various Indo-European tribes that settled in the area perhaps 4,000 years ago. The Kurds themselves claim to be the descendants of the Medes, who helped overthrow the Assyrian Empire in 612 B.C., and they recite interesting myths about their origins involving King Solomon, jinni, and other magical agents. Many believe that the Kardouchoi, mentioned in the *Anabasis* by Xenophon as having given his 10,000 such a mauling that they retreated from Persia in 401 B.C., were the ancestors of the Kurds.

In the seventh century A.D., the conquering Arabs applied the name "Kurds" to the mountainous people they Islamicized in the region, and history also records that the famous Saladin (Salah ad-Din, 1137–1193), who fought so chivalrously and successfully against the Christian Crusaders and Richard the Lionhearted, was a Kurd.

Whatever their exact origin, it is clear that racially the Kurds today constitute a mixture of various groupings, the result of earlier invasions and migrations. The Kurdish language too (which is related to Iranian) has two main variants: Kurmanji (or Bahdinani), spoken mainly in the northwest of Kurdistan (Turkey and the Bahdinan or Barzani area of northwest Iraqi Kurdistan); and Sorani, spoken mainly in the southeast of Kurdistan. In addition, Dimili (Zaza) is also spoken in parts of Turkish Kurdistan, while Gurani is spoken in sections of Iraqi and Iranian Kurdistan. Finally, there are numerous subdialects of each one of these four main dialects. These Kurdish language variants are only partially mutually understandable, a situation that adds to the many divisions in Kurdish society.

Tribalism too has prevented Kurdish unity. Indeed, it is probably true that the tribe has received more loyalty than any sense of Kurdish nationalism. In all of the Kurdish revolts of the twentieth century, for example, significant numbers of Kurds have supported the government because of their tribal antipathies for those rebelling. In Iraq these pro-government Kurds have been derisively referred to as *josh* (little donkeys), while in recent years the Turkish government created a pro-government militia of Kurds called village guards. Similarly, the *aghas* (feudal landlords or tribal chieftains) and sheikhs (religious leaders) continue to command allegiances inconsistent with the full development of a modern sense of nationalism.

Early in the sixteenth century, most of the Kurds loosely fell under Ottoman Turkish rule, while the remainder were placed under the Persians. Bedr Khan Beg, the ruler of the last semi-independent Kurdish emirate of Botan, surrendered to the Ottomans in 1847. Some scholars argue that Sheikh Obeidullah's unsuccessful revolt in 1880 represented the first indication of modern Kurdish nationalism; others consider it to be little more than a tribal-religious disturbance.

Turkey

In 1891 Ottoman sultan Abdulhamid II created the *Hamidiye,* a modern pro-government Kurdish cavalry that proved to be an important stage in the emergence of modern Kurdish nationalism. Nevertheless, the Kurds supported the Ottomans in World War I and Mustafa Kemal (Ataturk) during the Turkish War of Independence following that conflict.

During World War I, one of U.S. President Woodrow Wilson's Fourteen Points (number 12) declared that the non-Turkish minorities of the Ottoman Empire should be granted the right of "autonomous development." The stillborn Treaty of Sèvres, signed in August 1920, provided for "local autonomy for the predominantly Kurdish areas" (Article 62), and in Article

64 even looked forward to the possibility that "the Kurdish peoples" might be granted "independence from Turkey." Turkey's quick revival under Ataturk—ironically enough with considerable Kurdish help as the Turks played well on the theme of Islamic unity—altered the entire situation. The subsequent and definitive Treaty of Lausanne in July 1923 recognized the modern Republic of Turkey without any special provisions for the Turkish Kurds.

Ataturk's creation of a secular and purely Turkish state led to the first of three great Kurdish revolts: the rising in 1925 of Sheikh Said, the hereditary chief of the powerful Naqshbandi dervish Islamic sect. Sheikh Said's rebellion was both nationalistic and religious in as much as it favored the reinstatement of the caliphate. After some initial successes, Sheikh Said's forces were crushed, and he was hanged. In 1930 Khoyboun (Independence), a transnational Kurdish party, which had been founded a year earlier in Lebanon, launched a major uprising under General Ihsan Nuri Pasha in the Ararat area. This uprising was completely crushed, this time with Iranian cooperation. Finally, the Dersim (now called Tunceli) rebellion, led by Sheikh Sayyid Rida from 1936 to the end of 1938, also ended in a total Kurdish defeat.

Although many Kurdish tribes either supported the Turkish government or were at least neutral in these rebellions, the Turkish authorities decided to eliminate anything that might suggest a separate Kurdish nation. A broad battery of social and constitutional devices was employed to achieve this goal. In some cases, what can only be termed pseudo-theoretical justifications were offered to defend what was being done. Thus, the so-called sun theory taught that all languages derived from one original primeval Turkic language in central Asia. Isolated in the mountain fastnesses of eastern Anatolia, the Kurds had simply forgotten their mother tongue. The

much-abused and criticized appellation "mountain Turks," when referring to the Turkish Kurds, served as a code term for these actions. Everything that recalled a separate Kurdish identity was to be abolished: language, clothing, names, and so on.

Continuing this trend, the current (1982) Turkish constitution contains a number of specific provisions that seek to limit even speaking or writing in Kurdish. Its preamble, for example, declares, "The determination that no protection shall be afforded to thoughts or opinions contrary to Turkish national interests, the principle of the existence of Turkey as an indivisible entity." Two articles ban the spoken and written usage of the Kurdish language without specifically naming it.

Although restrictions on the usage of the Kurdish language were eased following the Gulf War in 1991, Article 8 of a new antiterrorism law, which became enforced in April 1991, made it possible to consider academics, intellectuals, or journalists who were speaking up peacefully for Kurdish rights to be engaging in a terrorist act. Similarly, under Article 312 of the Turkish Penal Code, mere verbal or written support of Kurdish rights could lead one to be charged with "provoking hatred or animosity between groups of different race, religion, region, or social class." Yasar Kemal, one of Turkey's most famous novelists and an ethnic Kurd, was indicted in 1995 for violating these provisions of what some have termed a "thought crime."

Iraq

The Kurds in Iraq have been in an almost constant state of revolt ever since Britain artificially created Iraq—according to the Sykes-Picot Agreement of World War I—out of the former Ottoman *vilayets* (provinces) of Mosul, Baghdad, and Basra. There are three major reasons for this rebellious situation.

First, the Kurds in Iraq long constituted a greater proportion of the population than they did in any other state they inhabited. Accordingly, despite their smaller absolute numbers, they represented a larger critical mass in Iraq than elsewhere, a situation that enabled them to play a more important role there than in Turkey or Iran. Second, as an artificial, new state, Iraq had less legitimacy as a political entity than Turkey and Iran, two states that had existed in one form or another for many centuries despite their large Kurdish minorities. Thus, discontent and rebellion came easier for the Iraqi Kurds. Third, Iraq was further divided by a Sunni-Shiite Muslim division not present in Turkey or Iran. This predicament called into question Iraq's future.

For its part, the Iraqi government has always feared the possibility of Kurdish separatism. Kurdish secession would not only deplete the Iraqi population, it would set a precedent that the Shiites, some 55 percent of the population, might follow and threaten the very future of the Iraqi state. In addition, since approximately two-thirds of oil production and reserves, as well as much of the fertile land, are located in the Kurdish area, the government is concerned that Kurdish secession would strike at the economic heart of the state. Thus were sown the seeds of a seemingly irreconcilable struggle between Iraq and its Kurdish minority.

To further their goals, the British, who held Iraq as a mandate from the League of Nations, invited a local Kurdish leader, Sheikh Mahmud Barzinji of Sulaymaniya, to act as their governor in the Kurdish *vilayet* of Mosul. Despite his inability to overcome the division among the Kurds, Sheikh Mahmud almost immediately proclaimed himself "king of Kurdistan," revolted against British rule, and began to conduct secret dealings with the Turks. In a precursor to subsequent defeats at the hands of the Iraqi government in Baghdad,

the British Royal Air Force successfully bombed the sheikh's forces, putting down several of his uprisings during the 1920s.

Although the Treaty of Sèvres (1920) held out the possibility of Kurdish independence, as mentioned above, the definitive Treaty of Lausanne (1923) made no mention of the Kurds. What is more, the British already had decided to attach the largely Kurdish *vilayet* of Mosul to Iraq because of its vast oil resources. The British felt that this was the only way Iraq could be made viable.

With the final defeat of Sheikh Mahmud in 1931, Mulla Mustafa Barzani (1903–1979) began to emerge as the leader almost synonymous with the Kurdish movement in Iraq. Although the Barzanis's power was originally founded on their religious authority as Naqshbandi sheikhs, they also became noted for their fighting abilities, and they still wear a distinctive turban with red stripes. For more than a half a century, Barzani fought the Iraqi government in one way or another. Despite his inherent conservatism and tribal mentality, he was the guiding spirit of the Kurdistan Democratic Party (KDP) founded on August 16, 1946. He spent a decade of exile in the Soviet Union (1947–1958) and, at the height of his power in the early 1970s, he negotiated the March Manifesto of 1970, which theoretically provided for Kurdish autonomy under his rule. Intra-Kurdish infighting against such other leaders as Ibrahim Ahmad (1914–2000) and his son-in-law, Jalal Talabani (1933–   ), and continuing government opposition, however, finally helped lead to Barzani's ultimate defeat in 1975. Barzani's defeat also occurred because the United States and Iran withdrew their support in return for Iraqi concessions, an action U.S. President Richard Nixon's national security advisor, and later secretary of state, Henry Kissinger cynically explained as necessary covert action not to be confused with missionary work.

Following Barzani's collapse in March 1975, his son, Massoud Barzani, eventually emerged as the new leader of the KDP, while Talabani established his Patriotic Union of Kurdistan (PUK) on June 1, 1975. Divided by philosophy, geography, dialect, and ambition, Barzani's KDP and Talabani's PUK have alternated between cooperation and bloody conflict ever since. They also have suffered greviously from such horrific repression as Saddam Hussein's genocidal *Anfal* campaigns of 1987–1988, launched against Iraq's Kurds to punish them for supporting Iran during the 1979–1989 Iran-Iraqi War.

After the Gulf War and the failure of the ensuing Kurdish uprising in March 1991, the mass flight of Kurdish refugees to the mountains forced the United States to reluctantly create a safe haven and no-fly zone in which a de facto Kurdish state began to develop. In addition, the unprecedented UN Security Council Resolution 688 of April 5, 1991, condemned "the repression of the Iraqi civilian population . . . in Kurdish populated areas" and demanded "that Iraq . . . immediately end this repression." As symbolic as it may have been, never before had the Kurds received such official international mention and protection.

Despite the de facto Kurdish state that emerged in northern Iraq following Saddam Hussein's defeat in the Gulf War, the KDP and PUK actually fought a civil war against each other from 1994 to 1998, for which the United States finally brokered an unsteady cease-fire by bringing Barzani and Talabani together in Washington, D.C., in September 1998. As a result of this internal Kurdish fighting, there are now two separate rump governments in Iraqi Kurdistan: the KDP's government in Irbil and the PUK's in Sulaymaniya. Inevitably the resulting instability and power vacuum have drawn in neighboring Turkey and Iran, among others such as the United States, Syria, and, of course, Iraq, since for reasons of state none of the powers wants to see a Kurdish state established in northern Iraq.

Iran

Although twice as many Kurds live in Iran as do in Iraq, the Kurdish national movement in Iran has enjoyed much less success due in part to the relatively greater long-term strength of the Iranian government. This, however, did not prevent Ismail Agha Simko from leading major Kurdish revolts in the 1920s that ended only when the Iranian government treacherously assassinated him under false pretenses of negotiation in 1926. This Iranian technique of solving its Kurdish problem was used again in August 1989 when Iranian agents assassinated the leader of the Kurdistan Democratic Party of Iran (KDPI), Abdul Rahman Ghassemlou, in Vienna while supposedly negotiating with him. Three years later, Iranian agents assassinated Ghassemlou's successor, Sadegh Sharafkandi, while he was dining at a restaurant in Berlin. Earlier, the KDPI's revolt against the Ayatollah Khomeini's new government had been completely smashed by the superior Iranian forces by 1981.

Despite these failures, the Iranian Kurds are famous among their Kurdish brethren for having established the only Kurdish state in the twentieth century; the short-lived Mahabad Republic of Kurdistan (1946–1947). When this rump Kurdish state was destroyed, however, its president, Qazi Muhammad, was summarily hanged on March 31, 1947, a blow from which the Iranian Kurds still have not completely recovered.

THE CONFLICT

During the 1980s in Turkey and—as described above—the 1990s in Iraq, the Kurdish conflict reached its greatest heights to date. In Turkey, an increasingly significant portion of the country's population of ethnic Kurds has actively demanded cultural, linguistic, and political rights as Kurds. The government has ruthlessly suppressed these demands for fear they would lead to the breakup of the state itself. This official refusal to brook any moderate Kurdish opposition helped encourage extremism and the creation of the Partiya Karkaren Kurdistan (PKK), or Kurdistan Workers Party, headed by Abdullah (Apo) Ocalan on November 27, 1978. In August 1984, the PKK officially launched an insurgency that, by the beginning of 2000, had resulted in more than 36,500 deaths, as many as 3,000 villages partially or completely destroyed, and some 3,000,000 people internally displaced.

For a short period in the early 1990s, Ocalan actually seemed close to achieving a certain degree of military success. In the end, however, he overextended himself, while the Turkish military spared no excesses in containing him. Slowly but steadily, the Turks marginalized the PKK's military threat. Ocalan's ill-advised decision in August 1995 also to attack Barzani's KDP in northern Iraq because of its support for Turkey further sapped his strength. The final blow came when Turkey threatened to go to war against Syria in October 1998 unless Damascus expelled Ocalan from his long-time sanctuary in that country.

Ocalan fled to Italy, where U.S. pressure on behalf of its NATO ally Turkey led Italy and others to reject Ocalan as a terrorist undeserving of political asylum. For years the United States had given Turkey intelligence training and weapons to battle against what it saw as the "bad" Kurds of Turkey, while ironically supporting the "good" Kurds of Iraq against Saddam Hussein. Ocalan was finally captured in Kenya, flown back to Turkey for a sensational trial, and sentenced to death for treason.

MANAGEMENT OF THE CONFLICT

Instead of making a hard-line appeal for a renewed struggle during his trial, Ocalan issued a remarkable statement that called for the implementation of true democracy to solve the Kurdish problem within the existing borders of a unitary Turkey. He also ordered his guerrillas to evacuate Turkey to demonstrate his sincerity. Thus, far from ending Turkey's Kurdish problem, Ocalan's capture began a process of moving away from the policy of relying almost entirely on military suppression of Kurdish nationalism toward a conflict-management policy involving at least implicit bargaining between the state and many of its citizens of Kurdish ethnic heritage, as represented by the PKK and the Peoples Democracy Party (HADEP). The HADEP, founded in 1994 as a legal Kurdish party, had elected numerous mayors in the Kurdish areas during the local elections held shortly after Ocalan's capture.

At the same time, Harold Hongju Koh, the U.S. assistant secretary of state for democracy, human rights, and labor, visited Turkey and met with a wide variety of people. Although he recognized Turkey's right to defend itself against the PKK, he also argued that one could oppose terrorism and still support human rights. He further maintained that, far from hurting Turkey's territorial integrity, now that the PKK's military threat had been defeated, an inclusive policy that acknowledged human rights would strengthen the Turkish state by giving its Kurdish ethnic community a genuine stake in their country's future.

At this point, Turkish candidacy for membership in the European Union (EU) entered the picture when, in December, 1999, the EU finally accepted Turkey as a candidate member. If implemented, EU membership would fulfill Ataturk's ultimate hope for a strong, united, and dem-

SYRIA. Female PKK guerillas at a locale near Damascus in March 1998. Photo courtesy of the author.

ocratic Turkey joined to the West. Until Turkey successfully implements the Copenhagen Criteria of minority rights for its Kurdish ethnic population and suspends Ocalan's death sentence to conform with EU standards, which ban capital punishment, Turkey's long-treasured candidacy would be only a pipe dream. Although the election of Ahmet Necdet Sezar, a reform-minded judge, as Turkey's new president in May 2000 demonstrated a willingness to seek new, bolder approaches, there are unfortunately still powerful forces in Turkey that do not seek further democratization nor even an end to what for them continues to be a profitable war.

Despite the seemingly ceaseless conflicts of the past century, most Kurds in Turkey would probably still be satisfied with meaningful cultural rights and real democracy. In Iran and Syria, the lesser-developed Kurdish movements would also be more than pleased with such a result. In Iraq, on the other hand—owing to the in-

credible incompetence of Saddam Hussein in calling forth the Gulf War of 1991 upon himself and thus the resulting institution of a de facto Kurdish state in northern Iraq—the Iraqi Kurds will probably be satisfied with nothing less than a federal solution in any post–Saddam Hussein Iraq.

SIGNIFICANCE

The approximately 25 million Kurds constitute the largest nation in the world without its own independent state. In recent years, the Kurdish issue has become increasingly important in Middle Eastern and even international politics for the reasons touched upon above. Should the Arab-Israeli dispute ever be resolved, the Kurdish issue will bid to replace it as the leading factor of instability in the geo-strategically important Middle East. Furthermore, since the Kurds sit on a great deal of the Middle East's oil and possibly even more important water resources, the

Kurdish issue will become even more important in the twenty-first century.

See also Central Europe: The Romany, a Stateless Minority in a World of States; Middle East: The Arab-Jewish Struggle for Palestine to 1948; and Middle East: The Palestinian Issue.

NOTE

1. Because Kurdish leaders exaggerate their numbers and the governments of the states housing them normally undercount them to downplay their importance, their numbers must necessarily be estimated. The figures offered here are estimates based on the author's field work. See Michael Gunter, *The Kurds and the Future of Turkey* (New York: St. Martin's Press, 1997) and Michael Gunter, *The Kurdish Predicament in Iraq: A Political Analysis* (New York: St. Martin's Press, 1999).

SUGGESTED READINGS

Barkey, Henri J., and Graham E. Fuller. *Turkey's Kurdish Question*. New York: Rowman and Littlefield, 1998.

Bruinessen, Martin van. *Agha, Shaikh and State: On the Social and Political Organization of Kurdistan*. London: Zed Books, 1992.

Chaliand, Gerard, ed. *A People Without a Country: The Kurds and Kurdistan*. New York: Olive Branch Press, 1993.

Ghareeb, Edmund. *The Kurdish Question in Iraq*. Syracuse, N.Y.: Syracuse University Press, 1981.

Gunter, Michael. *The Kurdish Predicament in Iraq: A Political Analysis*. New York: St. Martin's Press, 1999.

———. *The Kurds and the Future of Turkey*. New York: St. Martin's Press, 1997.

Izady, Mehrdad. *The Kurds: A Concise Handbook*. Washington, D.C.: Crane Russak, 1992.

Kirisci, Kemal, and Gareth M. Winrow. *The Kurdish Question and Turkey: An Example of a Transstate Conflict*. London: Frank Cass, 1997.

Kreyenbroek, Philip G., and Stefan Sperl, eds. *The Kurds: A Contemporary Overview*. London: Routledge, 1992.

McDowall, David. *A Modern History of the Kurds*. London: I. B. Tauris, 1996.

Meho, Lokman I., comp. *The Kurds and Kurdistan: A Selective and Annotated Bibliography*. Westport, Conn.: Greenwood Press, 1997.

Meiselas, Susan. *Kurdistan: In the Shadow of History*. New York: Random House, 1997.

Olson, Robert. *The Emergence of Kurdish Nationalism and the Sheikh Said Rebellion, 1880–1925*. Austin: University of Texas Press, 1989.

Randal, Jonathan C. *After Such Knowledge What Forgiveness? My Encounters with Kurdistan*. New York: Farrar, Straus and Giroux, 1997.

Washington Kurdish Institute (USA). http://www.kurd.org/kurd.

Middle East

The Palestinian Issue

Deborah J. Gerner

TIMELINE

1880s The Arab independence movement begins.

1881 Russian pogroms against Jews are initiated (1881–1903); the first wave of Russian Jewish immigration to Palestine occurs.

1914–1918 World War I is fought. Britain makes conflicting commitments regarding Palestine.

1936–1939 Arab revolt against British rule takes place.

1947 United Nations General Assembly enacts Resolution 181 on the partition of Palestine.

1948–1949 First Arab-Israeli War occurs; Israel declares independence; Palestinian *nakba* (catastrophe) results.

1964 The Palestine Liberation Organization (PLO) is established.

1967 During the Six-Day War, Israel occupies the Sinai, Gaza Strip, Golan Heights, and West Bank. UN Security Council Resolution 242 is passed.

1973 October War occurs. UN Security Council passes Resolution 338.

1978 Camp David Accords are signed by Israel, Egypt, and the United States.

1982 Israelis invade Lebanon; massacre occurs at Palestinian refugee camps near Beirut.

1987 The Palestinian *intifada* begins.

1988 Yasir Arafat condemns terrorism and recognizes the State of Israel. The United States opens direct discussions with the PLO.

1991 United States leads war against Iraq's invasion of Kuwait; Arab-Israeli peace conference is held in Madrid, Spain.

1993 Declaration of Principles on interim Palestinian self-government arrangements is proposed.

1994 Cairo Agreement is signed; Arafat establishes his headquarters in Gaza.

1995 Oslo II Accords passed; Israeli Prime Minister Yitzhak Rabin is assassinated.

1996 Palestinian elections are held.

1998 Wye River Memorandum is issued.

2000 Camp David II summit and negotiations end in failure; a new Palestinian uprising begins.

2001 Taba negotiations fail; "Mitchell Report" is issued.

2002 New *intifada* begins, and amid mounting violence on both sides, including wave after wave of suicide bombings by Palestinians, the Israel military occupies much of the Palestinian West Bank and threatens to exile Arafat.

The Palestinian issue remains one of the most significant and difficult dilemmas facing the international community. The ongoing conflict between Israelis and Palestinians—a struggle over land and political control—is the result of a search for national identity and self-determination by two ethnonationalist groups in the context of nineteenth-century European imperialism, twentieth-century decolonization, and evolving international understandings of statehood and nationalism. Israeli-Palestinian hostility has directly or indirectly spawned half a dozen regional wars in the past five decades, threatened Western access to critical petroleum resources, provided a justification for increased militarization throughout the region, and led to civilian deaths as a result of terrorism by both state and nonstate actors. The United States, the Soviet Union/Russia, the European states (particularly Great Britain), and the Arab countries have all attempted to manipulate or control the Israeli-Palestinian conflict in order to enhance their own perceived national interests. The United Nations has also been involved. It has passed numerous resolutions and has sent peacekeeping forces to patrol the Egyptian, Syrian, and Lebanese borders with Israel, but it has been kept out of an active mediation role. Overall, the policies of actors external to the conflict have frequently exacerbated rather than reduced tensions between the principal participants.

HISTORICAL BACKGROUND

At the start of the twentieth century, the Ottoman Empire ruled much of the Arab world, including Palestine, the area now referred to as Israel, the West Bank of the Jordan River, and the Gaza Strip. With the Allied victory in World War I, Pales-

tine came under the control of the British, who made contradictory promises to French, Arab, and European Zionist leaders about how—and by whom—the area was to be governed. In a series of letters exchanged in 1915 and 1916, Sharif Hussein, head of the Hashemite family and governor of Mecca, and Sir Henry McMahon, the British high commissioner of Egypt, discussed the terms under which the Arabs would assist the British war effort by revolting against their Ottoman rulers. Britain promised that, in exchange for this support, the Arabs would receive independence after the war ended. At the same time, European Zionists (Jewish nationalists) felt that the 1917 Balfour Declaration, which called for a "Jewish national home in Palestine," provided international sanction for Jewish political aspirations to be fulfilled in the same small territory. In addition, Britain had signed a secret agreement with France specifying how these two countries would divide control over the Arab parts of the Ottoman Empire once the latter had been defeated.

Not surprisingly, these irreconcilable commitments led to tensions within Palestine between the Jewish and Palestinian communities. In 1922 about 88 percent of the population of Palestine was Arab (Muslim, Christian, or Druze). The Jewish community included a small group of long-time residents (living mostly in Hebron, Safad, Tiberias, and Jerusalem), older immigrants who had fled persecution in Russia in the late 1800s, and more recent immigrants (particularly Zionists from Central Europe). The number of recent immigrants increased dramatically in size following Adolf Hitler's rise to power in Germany, leading Palestinians to fear that a Jewish homeland would indeed be created—at Palestinian expense. Between 1936 and 1939, Palestinians engaged in a massive revolt against British rule. Initially the rebellion was nonviolent; however, after a British commission recommended splitting Palestine, the revolt flared again in a much more violent form. The commission's proposal was widely rejected and was not implemented. Instead, Britain issued a new, equally problematic, policy that limited Jewish immigration and land purchases.

In the aftermath of World War II and the near destruction of European Jewry, on November 29, 1947, the United Nations General Assembly voted in favor of Resolution 181, which called for the creation of two states—one Jewish, one Arab— within a partitioned Palestine as soon as the British mandate ended in May 1948. The plan gave the proposed Jewish state 56 percent of the territory, including most of the fertile coastal area, although at this point the Jewish community owned only 6 to 8 percent of the total land and made up about a third of the population. Jerusalem and Bethlehem were designated as international zones. Fighting between Palestinian and Jewish inhabitants began almost immediately after the United Nations announced its vote. Although small in number, the Zionist military forces were well-trained, well-armed, and well-organized; the Palestinians were not. By the time Britain withdrew and Israel declared independence, Zionist troops had conquered most of the areas allocated to Israel as well as some additional lands intended for the Palestinians. The surrounding Arab countries, which had territorial aspirations of their own and no interest in allowing a Palestinian state to come into existence, intervened militarily and took over those parts of Palestine not occupied by Israel. When armistice agreements were finally signed in 1949, Israel held 77 percent of Palestine, Egypt controlled the Gaza Strip, and Jordan claimed sovereignty over East Jerusalem and the hilly West Bank. The name "Palestine" was wiped off the political map of the world.

Only about 150,000 Palestinians remained in what became Israel. A second, much larger, group of Palestinians—over 700,000 people by most accounts—who had fled the fighting found themselves refugees at the end of the war. Forbidden to return to their homes in Israel, many remained in refugee camps in the West Bank, the Gaza Strip, and nearby Arab countries; others traveled to the Gulf, Europe, or the United States in search of work. Finally, a significant number of Palestinians who were living in the West Bank and Gaza Strip before the war remained there and came under Jordanian or Egyptian rule.

The Palestinian *nakba* (catastrophe), with its massive dislocation, dispossession, and economic deprivation, stunned Palestinians and created an immediate and profound crisis for the Palestinian nation. Until the mid-1960s, most Palestinians within Israel were ruled under strict military regulations, many first imposed during the years of British rule. They had to obtain permission to travel in or out of their immediate area, faced restrictions on their economic activities, and were subject to arrest or even expulsion for political reasons. Egypt and Jordan pressured Palestinians in the West Bank and the Gaza Strip not to challenge the status quo or engage in acts of resistance against Israel. Demoralized and without effective political or military direction (since Britain had expelled most Palestinian leaders in the late 1930s as part of the suppression of the Arab revolt), the Palestinian community entered into a period of political quietude that lasted well into the 1960s.

Less than 20 years after *al nakba*, during the June 1967 Six-Day War, Israel conquered the rest of the former mandate of Palestine as well the Egyptian Sinai (since returned to Egypt) and the Syrian Golan Heights. In the aftermath, Palestinians faced further dislocation and economic hardship as well as renewed shock and disappointment in the failures of the Arab military forces. Whereas the Palestinians had been completely disheartened by the events of 1948 and to a large extent withdrew from political activities, this time their response was one of active resistance, born out of the conviction that none of the Arab states could be relied upon to help. In Gaza, women and men engaged in an insurrection that began in 1968 and lasted for three years. In the West Bank, charitable organizations provided an organizational structure through which Palestinians could undertake resistance activities. Outside the borders of mandatory Palestine, nationalist guerrilla groups took over the Palestine Liberation Organization (PLO), which was established by the Arab states in 1964, and in 1969 elected Yasir Arafat chairman.

The mid-1970s, after the October War of 1973, was a period of increased international awareness of and support for the Palestinian national movement and for the PLO specifically. In October 1974, at the Arab League conference held in Rabat, Morocco, the Arab states acknowledged the PLO as the "sole legitimate representative of the Palestinian people." The next month, PLO leader Yasir Arafat was invited to address the members of the United Nations; after his speech, the United Nations granted the PLO observer status within the organization. Despite these political victories, the Palestinians still lacked the ability to determine their own destiny rather than serving as pawns in the political games of the superpowers and the Arab countries. This was made brutally clear when Egypt and Israel signed the Camp David Accords in 1978 and followed this with a peace treaty the next year, despite the failure of the accords to resolve any aspect of the Israeli-Palestinian conflict. The message was reinforced when Israel invaded Lebanon in 1982 to eliminate the PLO's political and military infrastructure in that country (where the PLO had relocated after being expelled from Jordan in 1970).

The outbreak in December 1987 of the Palestinian *intifada* (uprising) marked the beginning of a community-wide mobilization against the lengthy Israeli occupation. Strikes, demonstrations, tax resistance, boycotts of Israeli products, and other acts of civil disobedience were coordinated through locally based popular committees. Palestinian resistance activities also included stone throwing and the creation of barricades to hinder the movement of Israeli forces. Massive Israeli arrests of Palestinians (over 100,000 by the end of 1993), the "administration detention" of more than 18,000 suspected activists for periods of six months to several years, deportations, curfews and closures, and the sealing or destruction of hundreds of homes affected virtually the entire population. In addition, more than 300 Pa-

HEBRON, WEST BANK. Memorial to intifada martyrs. "Those who were killed by the sake of Allah are not dead but are alive with Allah." Photo courtesy of the author.

lestinians and 11 Israelis were killed in the first year of the *intifada;* by the end of the *intifada,* Palestinian deaths numbered over 1,000.[1]

On July 31, 1988, Jordan renounced its claim to the West Bank, creating new political opportunities for the Palestinians, and in November 1988 the Palestine National Council met and declared the independence of the State of Palestine. The following month, Arafat, in addressing the United Nations General Assembly, committed the PLO to "a comprehensive settlement among the parties concerned in the Arab-Israeli conflict, including the state of Palestine and Israel and other neighbors within the framework of . . . Resolutions 242 and 338."[2] Arafat's explicit and very public declaration was an irrevocable act that changed forever the framework of the conflict and set the stage for the U.S.–sponsored Madrid Conference, the Oslo Agreement, and subsequent Israeli-Palestinian negotiations aimed at resolving the conflict.

THE CONFLICT

The core issues dividing the Israeli and Palestinian ethnonational communities have remained relatively constant over the years. They include the following:

- Borders: specific, fixed, agreed-upon boundaries for Israel and for the Arab states in the region, including whatever form of Palestinian state or political entity is created
- Status of Jerusalem
- Settlers and settlements: the political, civil, and national status of approximately 400,000 Jewish Israelis currently living on occupied land within the West Bank (including East Jerusalem) and the Gaza Strip
- Refugees and the right of return: the political, civil, and national status of Palestinians currently living outside the borders of the historic Palestine

- Compensation for Palestinians and Israelis who were forced to leave their homes and property as a direct result of the Israeli-Palestinian conflict
- Natural resources: the allocation of resources such as water among the region's peoples
- Assurance of mutual security for all states and all peoples in the region
- Political, civil, and national status of Palestinians currently living within Israel
- Economic viability of all the states in the region
- Role of the international community in supervising a negotiated settlement.

Each of these points reflects a significant and controversial aspect of Israeli-Palestinian relations that must be addressed before their conflict can be fully resolved.

MANAGEMENT OF THE CONFLICT

Throughout the twentieth century, various efforts were made to arbitrate the dispute between Palestinians and Israelis. The United Nations was heavily involved in the years following its vote to partition Palestine. It created the United Nations Relief and Works Agency to take responsibility for Palestinian refugees, sent mediators to the region throughout the 1940s, 1950s, and 1960s, and passed dozens of General Assembly and Security Council resolutions calling for cease-fires, condemning aggressive actions by each of the parties, and suggesting approaches for conflict resolution.

In recent decades, the United States has attempted to take a leading role in managing the conflict and has worked to exclude the United Nations from participation. The close relationship between Israel and the United States has hampered the ability of the United States to serve as a neutral mediator, however. Furthermore, for 13 years, the United States refused to acknowledge or deal officially with the PLO because of a promise the United States made to Israel in 1975:

> The United States will continue to adhere to its present policy with respect to the Palestine Liberation Organization [PLO], whereby it will not recognize or negotiate with the Palestine Liberation Organization so long as the Palestine Liberation Organization does not recognize Israel's right to exist and does not accept Security Council Resolutions 242 and 338.[3]

The two UN Security Council resolutions referred to—242 and 338—marked the end of the June 1967 and October 1973 Arab-Israeli wars, respectively. Palestinians maintained these resolutions were an inadequate basis for negotiation because, among other issues, they did not address Palestinian demands for self-determination, referring instead only to a "settlement of the refugee problem." Later, in 1984, Congress wrote the 1975 pledge into law and added that the PLO had to renounce the use of terrorism before there would be any formal diplomatic discussions between the two parties. In the absence of relations with the PLO, the United States was forced to rely on other Arab states to represent Palestinian interests, a task these countries did poorly and without enthusiasm. After Arafat's conciliatory statements in December 1988, the United States opened direct contacts with the PLO.

The inability of the United States and the international community to resolve the Palestinian situation became a problem for the United States when Iraq overran Kuwait in August 1990. There were urgent calls for Iraq to withdraw, and the United States immediately began to put together a coalition to reverse the invasion. Palestinians were livid, asking why the Iraqi occupation was instantly condemned while Israel's occupation of Palestinian lands was ignored and, in the case of the United States, implicitly supported through U.S.

economic and military assistance to Israel. In order to build a broad coalition against Iraq—one that included a number of Arab states—the United States committed itself to addressing the Israeli-Palestinian conflict once the war ended. Throughout the spring and summer of 1991, the United States undertook a series of meetings with Arab and Israeli leaders that culminated in a regional peace conference, cosponsored by the United States and the former Soviet Union, in Madrid, Spain.

Over the next two years, the Madrid negotiations, now moved to Washington, D.C., dragged on with a series of bilateral and multilateral meetings that accomplished little. A U.S. commitment to Israel guaranteed that the United Nations would have no role in the process. Unexpectedly, at the end of August 1993, the Israeli government and the PLO announced they had been meeting secretly in Norway and had reached an interim agreement for Palestinian self-government. The Declaration of Principles (DoP), signed in September, outlined a process for transforming the nature of the Israeli occupation but left numerous issues unresolved, including the status of Jerusalem, the right of return for Palestinian refugees, the disposition of Israeli settlements, security arrangements, and final borders between Israel and a Palestinian state.

Under the DoP, Israel was to relinquish day-to-day civil authority over parts of the Gaza Strip and West Bank to a newly created Palestinian National Authority headed by Arafat, who returned to Gaza in 1994. Ultimate power, however, remained with Israel, which exercised its control by sealing off the Palestinian-governed areas from the rest of the Occupied Territories and from Israel for extended periods of time, an action that devastated a Palestinian economy already weakened by years of occupation. In addition, Israel continued to confiscate land and to build settlements and roads that served to separate Palestinian cities, towns, and villages from each other, exacerbating the fragmentation of the West Bank and Gaza.

Subsequent agreements in 1994 (Cairo Agreement), 1995 (Oslo II), 1998 (Wye River I), and 1999 (Wye River II) failed to address the fundamental weaknesses of the DoP. The 314 pages of the Oslo II agreement, for instance, extended Palestinian civilian jurisdiction over major population areas, specified the form that Palestinian elections for a legislative council and president would take, and set May 4, 1996, as the deadline to begin final status negotiations that would deal with outstanding issues. It did not, however, indicate the consequences of a failure to meet the May deadline. Nor did Oslo II contain provisions to halt the creation of new "facts on the ground" that would influence the final form of any eventual agreement. The Wye I agreement, which took nineteen months to achieve in part due to the assassination of Israeli Prime Minister Yitzhak Rabin by a Jewish Israeli, simply rearticulated how Israel and the Palestinians were to carry out what they had already agreed to in Oslo II and were supposed to have finished more than a year earlier: interim steps toward a final status agreement. Wye River II set a new target date of September 10, 2000, for a permanent peace agreement.

With Palestinian-Israeli negotiations stalled and the final status talks not yet begun, U.S. President Bill Clinton called a summit at Camp David in July 2000. After two weeks of tense discussion, the conference ended without a deal, and by late September—following a provocative visit by Israeli Likud Party leader Ariel Sharon to the Noble Sanctuary/Temple Mount site— a second Palestinian *intifada* had begun. The massive and widespread violence rapidly dwarfed what had been seen during the first uprising. The Israel Defense Force killed alleged Palestinian militants, regularly shelled Palestinian police stations and

other government buildings, and bulldozed Palestinian houses and crops, creating barren swaths of land. Israel also tightened its control around the Palestinian population enclaves and sent tanks and troops into areas that previously had been turned over to Palestinian control. Palestinian suicide bombings inside Israel and attacks on Israeli settlements reflected the increased level of violence. The U.S. "Mitchell Report"—released on April 30, 2001—called for a halt to the violence, a complete end to Israeli settlement expansion, and a return to what it called the "normal" conditions that existed before September 27, 2000. It had no impact. By late September 2001, more than 600 Palestinians and 170 Israelis had been killed. Few outside the region noticed the first anniversary of the uprising, however. Two weeks earlier, on September 11, 2001, nineteen men hijacked four commercial planes leaving New York City and Boston and crashed them into the World Trade Center, the Pentagon Building in Washington, D.C., and a field in Pennsylvania, killing about 3,000 people from dozens of countries. As the United States and its allies prepared for a war on terrorism, management of the Israeli-Palestinian conflict no longer seems to be a priority, even as the ground situation in the middle east steadily deteriorated to the point where it became necessary in the spring of 2002 to dispatch Secretary of State Colin Powell to a region shattered by almost daily Palestinian bombings and Israeli military reprisals, in a forlorn effort to paste together a new peace.

SIGNIFICANCE

Strife between Israeli Jews and Palestinian Muslims, Christians, and Druze has now lasted more than a century. It is an archetypal example of a protracted, ethnonational conflict. None of the problems created by Britain's irreconcilable World

War I promises, the partition of Palestine in 1948, and Israel's conquest of the West Bank and Gaza Strip in 1967 are close to resolution. Despite its military superiority and support from the world's most powerful country, Israel has failed to crush Palestinian nationalism. Nor have the Palestinians succeeded in advancing their cause significantly, despite political support from other states in the region and the vast majority of United Nations member countries. There is a stalemate: neither can defeat the other, yet the terms under which each is willing to end their conflict are unacceptable to the other side.

The importance of this area—the Holy Land—to Judaism, Christianity, and Islam guarantees that, until the conflict is resolved, it will continue to occupy a position of importance internationally far beyond what would be expected given the small territory, resources, and population involved. Furthermore, the failure of the United States to resolve this ongoing dispute challenges its stature and credibility as a world leader. While international law could provide guidance regarding the shape a permanent resolution might take, it is frequently ignored—a situation unlikely to change as long as the United States maintains its dominant position in negotiations. The conflict over Palestine is a dangerous situation that shows little evidence of being resolved in the near future.

See also Lebanon: Ethnic Conflict and the Lebanese Civil War, 1975–1990; and Middle East: The Arab-Jewish Struggle for Palestine to 1948.

NOTES

1. The data on Palestinian human rights violations come from the Palestine Human Rights Information Center (Chicago and Jerusalem).
2. "Yasser Arafat, Speech at UN General Assembly, Geneva, General Assembly 13 December 1988," *Le Monde diplomatique,* online at http://Monde Diplo.com/focus/mideast/arafat88.en.
3. U.S. Congress, House Subcommittee on Europe

and the Middle East, *The Search for Peace in the Middle East: Documents and Statements, 1967–1979.* Prepared by the Foreign Affairs and National Defense Division, Congressional Research Service, Library of Congress (Washington, D.C.: U.S. Government Printing Office, 1979), 15.

SUGGESTED READINGS

Abu-Lughod, Ibrahim, ed. *The Transformation of Palestine.* Evanston, Ill.: Northwestern University Press, 1971; reprint, 1987.

Beinin, Joel, and Lisa Hajjar. *Palestine, Israel and the Arab-Israeli Conflict: A Primer.* Washington, D.C.: Middle East Research and Information Project, 2001. http://www.merip.org/palestine-israel_primer.

Farsoun, Samih K., with Christina E. Zacharia. *Palestine and the Palestinians.* Boulder, Colo.: Westview Press, 1997.

Gerner, Deborah J. *One Land, Two Peoples: The Conflict over Palestine.* Boulder, Colo.: Westview Press, 1994.

Hass, Amira. *Drinking the Sea at Gaza: Days and Nights in a Land Under Siege.* Translated by Elana Wesley and Maxine Kaufman-Lacusta. New York: Metropolitan Books, 1999.

Khalidi, Rashid. *Palestinian Identity: The Construction of Modern National Consciousness.* New York: Columbia University Press, 1997.

Kimmerling, Baruch, and Joel S. Migdal. *Palestinians: The Making of a People.* Cambridge, Mass.: Harvard University Press, 1994.

Mattar, Philip, ed. *Encyclopedia of the Palestinians.* New York: Facts on File, 2000.

Quandt, William B. *Peace Process: American Diplomacy and the Arab-Israeli Conflict Since 1967.* Los Angeles: University of California Press, 1993.

Robinson, Glenn E. *Building a Palestinian State: The Incomplete Revolution.* Bloomington: Indiana University Press, 1997.

Rouhana, Nadim N. *Palestinian Citizens in an Ethnic Jewish State.* New Haven, Conn.: Yale University Press, 1997.

Said, Edward. *The Question of Palestine.* New York: Vintage, 1980.

Sayigh, Yezid. *Armed Struggle and the Search for State: The Palestinian National Movement, 1949–1993.* Oxford, England: Clarendon Press, 1997.

Sharoni, Simona, and Mohammed Abu-Nimer. "The Israeli-Palestinian Conflict: Analysis and Prospects for Resolution." In *Understanding the Contemporary Middle East,* edited by Deborah J. Gerner. Boulder, Colo.: Lynne Rienner, 2000.

Nigeria

Ethnic Conflict in Multinational West Africa

James S. Wunsch

TIMELINE

1804 Usman dan Fodio begins Fulani jihad in northern parts of modern Nigeria.

1807 Fodio completes conquest of major northern Hausa states.

1900 Northern Nigeria becomes a British protectorate.

1906 Lagos and Niger Coast colonies are amalgamated by Britain to form the colony of South Nigeria.

1914 Northern and Southern Nigeria are amalgamated under a single governor, Lord Lugard.

1951 Initial postwar constitution is established with a weak regional system.

1954 Second postwar constitution, the Richard's Constitution, is established with three strong regions under a federal government.

1956–1957 Elections, which take place in the three regions, are won, respectively, by the three regional parties, each with a core tribal base. Regional internal self-government begins under these parties, and all major parties participate in the transitional central government.

1959 Federal elections establish the (northern) Northern Peoples Congress (NPC) as the strongest party, which joins with the (east's) National Congress of Nigerian Citizens (NCNC) to form a coalition government, with Sir Abubakar Tafawa Balewa as prime minister.

1960 Nigeria attains independence.

1962 Chief Obafemi Awolowo, leader of the (western region's dominant) Action Group (AG) party and of the opposition in the federal parliament, is convicted of "treasonable felony" and sentenced to ten years in prison. His rival, Chief Akintola, takes control of the AG.

1963 The midwest region is created by carving out the eastern portion of the western region. It comes under NCNC control.

1964 A disputed census gives the northern region an absolute majority of the population of Nigeria. A general strike in the south is one of the results. Federal elections give the NPC an absolute majority in the federal parliament. It forms a coalition with the AG, now led by Chief Akintola.

1965 October regional elections in the western region, contested between Akintola and Awolowo's followers, are marred by violence and fraud. Most observers agree Awowolo would have won a fair election, but Akintola officially wins. Violent protests and insurrections occur.

1966 *January 14–15:* A group of junior officers, largely Igbo, launch a coup against the federal, western, and northern regional governments. Casualities include many senior, non-Igbo leaders. An Igbo, General Aguiyi-Ironsi, takes control.

May 24: General Aguiyi-Ironsi, in Decree no. 34, abolishes the federal system and establishes a strong unitary government.

May 27–30: Riots in the north kill numerous Igbo civilians.

July 28–29: Northern soldiers mutiny and kill Ironsi and another 200 Igbo officers and soldiers.

August 1: Lt. Col. Yakuba Gowon, a middle-belter and a Christian, having asserted control over the mutinous troops, is recognized by fellow officers as head of state. He reaffirms federalism and paradons and releases Chief Awolowo from prison.

September 1: Decree no. 34 is formally repealed.

September 29: Wholesale slaughter of Igbo civilians begins in north. Authorities fail to stop it, and 30,000 are killed; thousands flee to the eastern region.

October–May 1967: Various negotiations are pursued to revise the Nigerian constitution to make it acceptable to all four regions. They are not successful.

1967 *May 27:* Gowon announces a division of Nigeria into 12 states with a strong federal center, the opposite of the regional confederation demanded by the east.

May 30: The east secedes as Biafra.

July: Federal troops cross into Biafra; war ensues.

1970 In January, Biafra surrenders to the federal government.

1975 In July, General Gowon is removed by a military coup led by General Murtala Muhammad.

1979 Nigeria's second republic begins under the recently elected Shehu Shagari, a Hausa-Fulani.

1983 President Shagari wins reelection in an election tainted by accusations of fraud

and corruption. On December 31, Shagari is removed in a coup led by General Muhammadu Buhari.

1984 In April, significant religious rioting occurs in two states.

1985 In April, General Buhari is removed in a coup led by General Ibrahim Babangida. In December, Babangida presents the Structural Adjustment Program (SAP). Implementation begins the following June.

1987 In March, Muslim-Christian rioting occurs in Kafanchan.

1989 In April, the constitution for the third republic is presented by the Constitutional Assembly.

1990 In April, an attempted coup, led by middle-belt minority officers, is aimed explicitly at ending northern (i.e., Hausa-Fulani/Muslim/emirate) domination. The coup is put down, and 69 plotters are eventually executed.

1991 In April, hundreds are killed and hundreds are arrested in religious rioting in Bauchi State.

1993 *June 12:* Elections are held for the presidency of Nigeria's third republic. Mashood Abiola, a Yourba Muslim from the west, appears to win the election (58.5 percent to 41.5 percent). Abiola wins 19 of 30 states.

June 15: Babangida suspends counting of returns when extent of Abiola's victory becomes apparent.

June 23: Election is nullified by Babangida.

July 5–7: Large-scale strikes and civil disorder occur in the southwest in reaction to election nullification.

August 26: Pressure from such persons as the sultan of Sokoto and retired generals lead to Babangida's resignation and the appointment of Chief Ernest Shonekan to head an interim government.

November 15: General Sani Abacha, a Northern Muslim/Kanuri seizes power and declares himself head of state.

1994 In May, Abiola returns to Nigeria, declares himself president, and is arrested and imprisoned by Abacha.

1995 Ken Saro-Wiwa and eight other Ogoni activists are hanged after convicted in a court of questionable neutrality and legitimacy.

1998 In June, Abacha dies suddenly. General Abdulsalami Abubakar assumes power and declares there will be a swift return to civilian rule.

1999 In February, retired General Olusegun Obasanjo, a Christian/Yourba from the south, who was sentenced to death under Abacha, is elected president of Nigeria's third republic with a majority of more than 60 percent.

2000 Several northern states formally adopt the Sharia as their legal code.

Understanding ethnic conflict in Nigeria requires attention to multiple and changing factors. These include events from precolonial history, diverse aspects of British colonial policy, and the way in which Nigeria's people were affected by and adapted to them, and the political structure with which Nigeria began independence. They also include the military's repeated proclivity to intervene and stay in high political office, repeated attempts to design new political frameworks, key choices made regarding economic development policy, and the impact of Nigeria's oil wealth. Together these create a context in which the central state's massive control over wealth has intensified a variety of ethnic, religious, and regional identities in the competition for that wealth. This competition has never been simply along a single dimension, nor has it been among entirely cohesive groups, nor has it lacked important economic class–related issues. For all these reasons, conflict in Nigeria since independence, while always sharp and frequently intense, has never simply conformed to ethnic or tribal groups. Indeed, most observers agree that of the fissures in Nigeria (regional, religious, and group size), only one of them is truly "ethnic" in the usual sense of the word, and it has been dynamic over time.

HISTORICAL BACKGROUND

History sets the stage for ethnic, regional, and religious coalitions and competition in contemporary Nigeria: via precolonial relations among Nigeria's peoples, and via the policies of the British. Regarding the first, the epochal historical event for precolonial Nigeria was the Fulani jihad (holy war) and the conquests of Usman dan Fodio early in the nineteenth century. Sweeping across northwestern Nigeria, this intensely reformist Islamic movement established the Fulani-Hausa city-state (emirate) system, which created an aristocratic political class and political structures that adapted and maintained political and economic power throughout the colonial period, and well into the independence era in the north. Some analysts maintain that its power is unchecked to this day. The Fulani jihad also established a purist form of Islam in the northwest, which divides it culturally from the less intensely Islamic northeast of Kanem-Bornu, and has historically led to fears among Christians (in the middle-belt and southern areas) of Islamic religious chauvinism and dominance. Finally, the Fulani jihad led the Yoruba, whose northernmost area of Ilorin was conquered and came under emirate control; the middle-belters; and the Kanuri of the northeast to be wary to this day of renewed northern political imperialism.

The British Legacy

History also affects the contemporary Nigerian conflict through the policies of the British colonial government. In a variety of ways, the British intensified the north-south divide which became, perhaps, the most persistent, most stubborn political demarcation in modern Nigeria; at the same time, it encouraged ethnic identities and coalitions to form out of the inchoate peoples who lived throughout the regions. Key British decisions included amalgamating Northern and Southern Nigeria in 1914, while continuing to administer them separately. The first decision helped ensure Nigeria would reach independence as a single state. The second helped ensure that north and south would have vast differences from one another, ones which would lead to political competition, then to ethnic conflict, and then to the regional balancing and competition involved in all governments, military and civilian, since independence.

Specifically, separate administrations led to different institutions and policies for the two portions of Nigeria. The south was more exposed to education from the missionaries, to cash cropping, commerce, and trade, and to the beginning of investment, and that exposure continued at an increasing pace. The north was governed by a theocratic and feudal aristocracy, which was continued via indirect rule, and it remained insulated from Western education by the British decision to keep Christian missionaries out of the emirates and other Islamic areas. At independence the educational and economic gaps between north and south were enormous. This motivated the northerners to seek to capture and hold firmly to control of the Nigerian state to avoid dominance by the southerners, and to use state power to close that gap. It led southerners to resent what they saw as a monopoly political power and economic exploitation by the north.

At the same time that British policy was intensifying, the economic and social differences between north and south, the colonial government's efforts to organize various areas into administrative units, and the missionaries' efforts to codify languages for religious and educational purposes began to narrow the differences among culturally related peoples living in various areas. Similarly, establishing structures of indirect rule tended to group peoples who hitherto had regarded one another as rivals into single administrative

entities. Also, as some peoples gained educational advantages and migrated into other less modern areas to work in the colonial bureaucracy or the petite bourgeoisie, the formation of group identities among the less educated peoples was accelerated. Igbo identity grew largely in reaction to non-Igbo, and it was also stimulated by the media-based and organizational efforts of Nnamdi Azikiwe in the 1930s. Many explain the rapid rise of a Yoruba identity in the post–World War II era by the impact upon them of educated and economically active Igbo migrants. The Igbos seem to have had a similar impact on the Hausa-Fulani in the 1950s and 1960s. A Hausa identity was hardly contemplated until the Hausa-Fulani felt it necessary to organize in the 1950s to deal with the threat independence posed because of the potential for political dominance by southerners. The southerners, in turn, existed then, and now, as a coherent identity only in the minds of northerners. It was only in the context of these and other events that peoples and communities within these three groups, which had regarded one another as competitors, rivals, and even, at times, enemies, began to see themselves as peoples who shared something.

The constitutional legacy of the British also powerfully affected regional and ethnic identities. In the late 1940s, the British created the three-territory scheme with which Nigeria was to begin its political independence. The northern region remained intact, but the southern region was divided into two parts: the eastern and western regions. This decision stimulated several dynamic processes which echo in Nigeria to this day. First, it further coalesced the three largest protoethnic groups—the Igbo, Yoruba, and Hausa—since the elites among them believed that each elite group had the potential to capture and benefit from control of one of the regions and sought to capitalize on ethnicity to build a winning coalition to do just that. Second, it unleashed a pattern of majority-minority ethnic domination in which each of the big three, or majority groups, clearly dominated the many smaller minority groups in their areas. Third, it stimulated intense competition among the three groups, and the political parties organized by their leaders, for control over the Nigerian federal government, once independence arrived in 1960.[1] Even then, those identities and the coalitions among them were tenuous because intense competition for resources within the ethnic groups continued right along with their cooperation to pursue political and economic goods at the national level.[2]

THE CONFLICT

Ethnic relations in Nigeria cannot be understood outside of the pursuit of economic advantage by regional elites and, given the economic power of the state, outside of the pursuit of political access and control. The latter factor means the political structure, which has varied much in the four decades of independence, always affects the nature and course of ethnic conflicts. In spite of media stereotypes, these relations have been far more instrumental and flexible in their reaction to events, structures, and conditions than they have been primordial and rigid. Indeed, even today, one really ought not to speak of ethnic "groups" per se in Nigeria; one will better understand it and its history if one thinks of them as ethnic "coalitions."

The First Republic and the Biafran War

The three-region/three-party/three-ethnic-group dynamic of the first republic, for example, catalyzed the intense ethnic consciousness and conflict in Nigeria that led eventually to civil war. This grew from the historical factors discussed above and the ways in which they affected the competi-

tion for political power during Nigeria's first six years. Together these created a climate in the first republic in which political defeat was seen as a threat to the vital interests of each region's political elite, whose access to wealth came entirely through political power.[3] The excessive, at times violent, political conflict among these groups—and between them and the minority groups in their regions—ultimately led to a growing unity within the various ethnic coalitions, to an intense north-south rivalry over control of the center and fear for the security of each region, to the secession of the eastern region, or Biafra, to a civil war drawn along clear ethnic lines, and to a process of majority-minority ethnic competition which continues to this day. The details of the events that occurred during this era go beyond the limits of this chapter. The key facts, dynamics, and events, however, are as follows.

In spite of the historical gap and uneasiness between the northwest and the northeast, and between the north and the south, a coalition government was established in 1960 which united virtually all of the north under the Northern Peoples Congress (NPC) and the east under the National Congress of Nigerian Citizens (NCNC). The west, under the Action Group (AG), took the role of opposition. Each region was governed by a party that drew the bulk of its support and its leadership from the largest group in the region: in the north by a Hausa-Kanuri alliance, in the east by the Igbo, and in the west by the Yoruba. Because of the substantial resources controlled by the regional governments, the privileges these gave to the elites controlling each region, as well as the opportunities these resources gave for patron-clientage, control of one's regional government was considered critical to survival as a ruling party and as members of the political elite. Being out of the federal coalition was unfortunate; losing control of the regional government would be a disaster. For that reason, each party's leadership sought to maintain uncontested control over its own region. Non-primary groups (non-Hausa, non-Yoruba, non-Igbo) or minorities, however, were regarded by each party's leadership in other regions as the entry point by which it could win seats in those regions; conversely, they regarded the minority groups in their own regions as "Trojan horses" through which other parties could challenge them. This raised the political stakes regarding control over one's own region, and during this time there were probably poorer relations between dominant regional groups and regional minorities than there were among the three major groups.[4]

The strongest advocate of this Trojan horse strategy, Chief Obafemi Awolowo of the western region, was jailed and convicted of "treason" in 1962, in what most Yoruba and AG leaders considered a political response to this strategy, and a move to weaken the AG's challenge elsewhere in Nigeria. His rival, Chief Akintola, continued as premier of the west, and he took over leadership of the AG. During the same period, a disputed census was announced which would have maintained the north's population edge over the rest of the country, and a portion of the western region was separated from it, further weakening the Yoruba and creating a new midwest region that was controlled by the Igbo NCNC party. In this climate, the federal election of 1964 was marred by substantial irregularities, including violence, designed to weaken challenges to the dominant parties in each region.

In the federal election of 1964, the northern party, or NPC, allied with the "rump" AG of the western region under Chief Akintola, won control of the federal parliament. This left the NCNC (controlling the eastern and midwest regions) in opposition. They were joined in an alliance by Awolowo's followers, now out of

power in the west. Awolowo and his followers were eyeing a return to power in the west in the regional elections of October 1965, and they hoped for his release from jail if they won that election. However, Chief Akintola defeated them through what has generally been accepted as blatant rigging of the election, and an insurrection broke out throughout much of the western region. As a result of Akintola's tainted victory, the trumped-up treason convictions, a disputed census, a general strike in 1964 over wage issues, increasing election irregularities and violence, and the federal government's desultory response to insurrection in the west over the election, the legitimacy of the Nigerian state was rapidly eroding.

On January 15, 1966, a group of largely Igbo officers executed several non-Igbo leaders of the first republic (including Prime Minister Akubakar Tafawa Balewa), most of the senior officers from the north, Chief Akintola, and the sardauna (Sultan) of Sokoto, who was the political and religious leader of the Hausa. Twenty-seven of the thirty-two leaders of the coup were Igbo. It is important to note, however, that up to this point even the intense conflict over control of federal and regional governments was largely among political elites and largely concerned regional interests, not the general population. To be sure, the leaders of each party were of the region's largest ethnic group. But so were many of those who had become allied to parties from other regions that challenged the region's dominant party. Even the coup, many still argue, was far more a modernist and nationalist coup than an ethnic coup, in spite of the Igbo "flavor" of its leaders. It was in the ethnic *appearance* of the coup, and the move to a unitary form of government that followed soon after it made by General Aguiyi-Ironsi (also an Igbo), that threatened northerners with southern domination. General Aguiyi-Ironsi announced his Decree no. 34 on

May 24, 1966, which abolished the federal system and with it the autonomy the major tribe had over their own affairs at the state (regional) level. Five days later, riots, directed at Igbos, broke out in the north, and many were killed. These events led to the July 29, 1966, military mutiny and countercoup by northern troops, whose actions spoke both of vengeance and a desire to strike at the specter of the southern domination.

In that coup, some 200 Igbo officers and rank-and-file soldiers were clearly sought out by coup leaders and swiftly executed. A few weeks later, on September 29, during a violent pogrom in the north, some 30,000 Igbos were slaughtered, and many others were driven from their homes and fled to the east. Elite conflict thus became a widespread, violent, and grassroots conflict. Negotiations among military governors of the four regions held to design a mutually acceptable constitutional framework continued throughout 1966 and well into 1967, but they were all unsuccessful. The east seceded as Biafra in May 1967. A few days later, the head of state, Colonel Yakuba Gowon, announced a 12-state, strong federal system for Nigeria. This was the exact opposite of the loose confederation demanded by Igbo leaders, and the Nigerian civil war ensued.

LAGOS, NIGERIA, January 13, 1970. Jubilant Nigerians parade through the streets following the announcement of the cease-fire ending the nation's 31-month civil war. © Bettmann/CORBIS.

After harsh combat and an estimated 600,000 deaths, Biafra was defeated. The rapid reintegration and reconciliation of the Igbos that followed suggests this was more a political than an ethnic war. No punitive measures were pursued against the Igbos or their leaders. Even though the Igbo people stood alone at the end, the issue was whether they could secede, and once the issue was settled, most Nigerians seemed able to put the war behind them and move on. Still, many Igbos to this day feel like second-class citizens in Nigeria.

MANAGEMENT OF THE CONFLICT

Nigeria's primary overt ethnic problem in the postwar era has been the status of the smaller ethnic groups in the new multistate system. Since none of the big three groups could expect to dominate the federal government as long as electoral and constitutional governance was followed, none seriously feared domination by either of the others, though coalitions could still rule. This notched down the intense conflict of 1960, at least until the northerners began dominating the federal government during the military governments of the mid-1980s onward. Also, the larger ethnic minorities, such as the Tiv, Kanuri, Ijaw, Bini, Efik, Nupe, and others, were granted control of their own states, which satisfied them. Groups too small to win their own state, and even some larger groups who were divided among several states, were unhappy with their status. Religious conflict developed during this period, and regional fears and conflict continued, though their public manifestations were frequently hidden by the repressive nature of military rule. Often, there appeared to be implicit ethnic issues in these conflicts: feelings by Igbo and Yoruba that their fair political share was still being blocked by northerners, whether they be Hausa or other groups. Similarly, northerners have seemed intent on keeping southerners out of power.

As Nigeria grew in 1967 to 12 states, and then progressively to 36 in 1995, the clamor for even more states never ceased. As other federal systems have discovered, such as Yugoslavia and India, as each demand is answered with a new state, a new group feels itself to be a conspicuous and deprived minority. Soon it clamors for own state. Nigeria has not been able to solve this; particular frustration has been expressed by the Ogoni and others in the oil-producing areas; the many non-Hausa, non-Islamic smaller groups in Kaduna and Kano states; minority groups in the middle belt, such as the Idoma; and others. One author estimates that there are demands on the table for 40 additional states to help address these problems in such states as Benue, Delta, Akwa-Ibom, Kaduna, Kogi, Niger, Plateau, Rivers, and Taraba.[5] Interestingly enough, in some cases, such as the call by the Idoma for their own state, minorities *within* an ethnic group or coalition have complained of marginalization. Thus calls for even more states are likely to continue.

The desire for statehood grows from the political power it grants to the new majority group it creates, and the economic and professional opportunities for the group's elites in staffing and operating it. Intensifying this is the "federal character" principle. First asserted in the 1975 constitution, this requires that public offices, public investments, appointments to the civil service, scholarships to university, and just about any other goods controlled by the federal government, be distributed in a way that all states receive a fair share: one that thereby maintains Nigeria's federal character.

Of course, this makes a powerful incentive to demand one's own state. Had the federal character been defined in ethnic rather than state grounds, there probably would have been much less pressure.[6] As it was, however, the majority-minority dynamic within states, the political and eco-nomic advantages of statehood, and the fact that minority groups were not sharing in these federal resources developed this issue into a widespread sense of grievance.[7]

The importance of minority exclusion from the federal character principle was accentuated by Nigeria's vast oil wealth and the fact that federal and state governments controlled it. One can hardly read or hear a Nigerian political debate without seeing or hearing reference to the claim for shares of the "federal cake." As oil money flooded Nigeria, the roles of agriculture, industry, and commerce in generating wealth were eclipsed by the vastly more lucrative and essentially passive occupation of capturing a share of the oil windfall. The states as a result, became far less self-sufficient in revenues. Since the federal government controlled the oil-money flow, access to the federal government was critical. The formula used to allocate oil money was literally the formula to win shares of the Nigerian jackpot. How the factors of "derivation" (where the revenues were generated), population, area, equality, poverty, and so on were used, was seen as a game in which the rules were constantly changing to strengthen some to the disadvantage of others. Who had influence in government was critical, and thus the more politically powerful became better off in what was, in reality, a zero-sum game usually lost by the less powerful. Minorities, of course, had no power. Economic conflict became political conflict and, given the political weakness of small ethnic groups, it became ethnic conflict as well, which sometimes turned violent.

Intensifying this situation was the nationalist economic strategy Nigeria chose in the 1970s. It required foreign firms to sell substantial shares in their enterprises to Nigerians at well below market value rather than choosing an entreprenual strategy such as encouraging development of new enterprises that would generate new jobs and economic growth. This policy re-inforced the importance of controlling the state or, more specifically, of having access to those who distributed these lucrative opportunities. Had Nigeria pursued eco-nomic policies which dispersed opportu-nity and influence more broadly across so-ciety and concentrated less of them in the hands of those who controlled the state, the differences between those groups with political power and those groups without would have been less stark and perhaps less consequential. In the adverse eco-nomic climate of the post–Structural Ad-justment Policy (SAP) of the mid-1980s, in the midst of the vast looting of the state by the military governments of Ibrahim Babangida and Sani Abacha, and with other sectors of the economy neglected and worn down during the oil boom, the competition for an ever-shrinking federal cake was intense. Groups, including smaller ethnic groups, which did poorly in this felt seriously aggrieved, and ethnicity became one of the more potent strategies to mobilize the populace and compete for whatever was left at the federal table.[8]

Ethnic conflict has not been the only grounds of conflict in the era. There were certainly class-related aspects of economic and political deprivation during this time. The rural and urban poor, wage earners, agriculturists, and increasingly the salaried middle classes all saw their economic for-tunes plummet in the 1980s and 1990s. However, their misfortunes did not lead to organized political resistance, although the widespread protest in the southwest and among the Yoruba when the 1993 election of Mashood Abiola (a Yoruba from the southwest) was nullified by a military government led by a northerner, probably reflects a merger of widespread class grievances and ethnic and regional resent-ment. Given the obstacles to widespread class organization, such as distance, ethnic divisions, state boundaries, and the federal government's ability to suppress or co-opt

as needed, the failure of class organization is probably not surprising.

Instead, what has grown more intense in the past two decades has been religious conflict. This was not a major source of conflict during the first republic. For ex-ample, the entirely Islamic- and Hausa-led NPC was in alliance with the Christian and Igbo NCNC; the AG—mixed Islamic and Christian—and the middle-belt peoples—mixed Christian and traditional religion—were in opposition. Similarly, it was largely the Christian officers who led the army in the war against the Christian Biafra. However, in the last 20 years, rhetoric has been harsh along Christian-Islamic lines, and political battles have been intense over such issues as the role of *Sharia* (Islamic) law, and violence claming several thousand lives broke out repeatedly in the north. Southerners, frus-trated by the continued grip of northern Muslims on the position of head of state, have blamed this on a conspiracy of the "Kaduna Mafia." The Christian Associa-tion of Nigeria (CAN), an umbrella group of most of the Christian denominations, was founded and has flourished in this cli-mate, and it has regularly exchanged harsh rhetoric with Islamic leaders. More re-cently, the spread of northern states adopt-ing the *Sharia* since 2000 has led to much tension, which exploded in riots between Hausa and Yoruba in Kaduna in February and May 2000, and which claimed an es-timated 2,000 lives. Lurking behind this religious conflict is the continued fear, by both north and south, of domination by the other region.[9]

Much of the conflict in Nigeria, while it may be presented in religious or ethnic terms, is really at heart over economic re-sources or political power. In many cases, such as the violence in the central part of the southwest among the Ife and Modak-eke communities (both of them Yoruba), this takes the form of which group is the indigenous and which is the settlers, and whether one group owes another rent for use of land, which should hold the seat of a local government authority, and so on. In other cases, such as the pitched warfare between the Tiv and the Jukun in Taraba state, it is whether one group's monarch rules the others. Finally, in many cases, such as in Kafanchan in Kaduna state, it is over the autonomy of non-Hausa groups versus claims of political control by the various Hausa emirates. These and other conflicts, while rarely reaching the international media, have cost thousands of lives, have occurred often since precolonial times, and will probably continue. These issues are exacerbated by current economic stagnation and joblessness, which leads many to seek scapegoats and maintains large numbers of jobless and angry youths available for violence. Ethnic, regional, and religious differences are handy identities for mobilizing people. These may be the media of conflict, but it is control over land, trade, and political power which is generally its fuel.

Overall, most observers agree that military rule, far from managing conflict, has seriously exacerbated ethnic and other conflict in Nigeria. While the military was able, in 1966, summarily to end the regional standoff that civilian politicians had shown no interest or stomach in facing, the military's defects far outweigh that one accomplishment. The defects include its tendency to act arbitrarily and without broad investigation or consultation in establishing new states and local government authorities; its suppression of the deliberative, negotiation, and conflict-resolution bodies and processes typical of democracies (political parties, legislatures, independent judicial bodies); and its repeated flouting of the rule of law and the general insecurity this engendered. It destroyed Nigeria's federal system, as it centralized ever-more power into military command–type governance, which, among other things, reaffirmed in Nigerians the fear of dominance by a single region, religion, or ethnic group.[10] Finally, the military deliberately neglected and eventually enfeebled bodies established to protect minority rights, such as the Human Rights Commission, the Federal Character Commission, and the Public Complaints Commission. The military also badly mishandled or deliberately chose to inflame religious and regional antagonisms, through such loaded religious actions such as instituting a national *Sharia* court, instituting the *Sharia* code in some northern states, and joining the Organization of Islamic Conference in January 1986.[11]

During this time, ethnic and ethnically related conflict burst forth in several instances of mass violence: the Ogoni protests throughout the 1990s; the Maitatsine riots of the early 1980s; the Kafanchan, Zaria, and Bauchi riots of 1987; and the April 22, 1990, coup led by middle-belt minorities that "expelled" from Nigeria the states of Bauchi, Sokoto, Kano, Katsina, and Borno (the supposed bastions of northern domination). The fact that the leadership of the post-Gowon military governments has virtually always been heavily dominated by northerners and Muslims makes southerners and non-Muslims suspicious of it. Its dominant reaction to this and other public discontent has been intimidation and suppression, which reinforced suspicion into a deep distrust. The revisions it made in the allocation formula for oil money consistently favored the north, another grounds for the resentment and distrust of the south and the intensification of regional and religious suspicions and hostilities. During the 1980s and 1990s, numerous civil society organizations, such as the Association of Minority Oil Producing States, the Southern Minorities Forum, and Ethnic Minority Rights Organization of Nigeria, developed. These were largely expressions of minority groups' belief that the Nigerian government, particularly the military, was unresponsive to them. Unfortunately, the response of the military government was to ban these and other similar organizations in December 4, 1992, as threats to "the peace, order and good governance of the federation."[12] These events culminated in the execution in 1995 of the Ogoni leader, Ken Saro-Wiwa and eight other Ogoni activists. These harsh and rigid responses did nothing to respond to the disadvantages, fears, and at times genuine suffering of many groups.

The scale of corruption under the last two decades of military rule exacerbated the conflict in Nigeria. As the economy sank deeper under military mismanagement and its monumental theft, the scramble for economic survival grew more intense, just as the capacity of the state to regulate and moderate that conflict eroded. Lack of resources, the flight overseas of competent civil servants, and the blight of corruption all degraded the state and its legitimacy toward the end of the regime. It seemed that the military would do anything, including consciously stimulating regional and religious conflict, to stay in power.

The election of 1993 was a decisive rejection of continued military rule. In a broadly based victory over the candidate of the north and the military, Mashood Abiola, an Islamic Yoruba from the southwest, drew significant support from *all* regions of Nigeria. Before General Babangida suspended and then rejected the electoral count, it appeared Abiola had won by a margin of 58.5 to 41.5 percent. The return of democracy and constitutional government was delayed another six years, but soon after Babangida's successor, General Abacha, died, the military bowed to its deep unpopularity and returned power to an elected civilian government led by a southern Yoruba, a Christian, Olusegun Obasanjo.[13]

Obasanjo's government is supported by southerners, middle-belters, some nor-

theasterners, and the international community. Nonetheless, Hausa-Fulani northerners have continued to push the *Sharia* issue. This suggests Obasanjo has no easy solution to religiously based conflict. It also suggests that the northern elite, out of power now for the first time in many years, is willing to inflame regional/religious sentiments to destabilize his administration. Similarly, there has as yet been no resolution of lingering minority group issues, particularly in the oil-producing regions, nor has the Nigerian state withdrawn from its central role in the economy. Thus, it is not clear what to expect next regarding ethnic and other conflict. Nonetheless, removing the military has substantially eased the general climate of fear, intimidation, and gross corruption that hindered all progress on these issues prior to 1999.

In summary, most participants in ethnic conflict in the post-Biafra era are groups that are minorities in the new states. While dividing Nigeria into 36 states freed many larger minority groups (Tiv, Kanuri, Ijaw) from majority group domination by the Igbo, Yoruba, or Hausa-Fulani, it left a multitude of smaller groups in these new states and groups divided across several states. The political restructuring did reduce the tug-of-war among the three largest groups, and the federal character required by the constitution of 1979 assured that offices and opportunities would be divided among the states to ensure Nigerian federal character would be maintained. But these were monopolized by the various states' dominant ethnic groups, leaving the smaller ones without their share of the federal cake. Military mishandling, corruption, and perhaps divide-and-rule strategies intensified these conflicts and led to an increase in regional and religious problems.

The "theft" of the presidency from Abiola seriously inflamed regional sentiment among the Yoruba. This event, along with a widespread sense among the Yorubas of the southwest that they had been deprived of leadership opportunities in the federal government and squeezed economically by the increasing control by the center, led to the rise of the Oduduwa Peoples Congress (OPC). This is a broadly supported movement among the Yoruba, both Christian and Muslim, to weaken the federal system, or to move to a confederation. There are similar, though weaker, organizations among the Igbo.

There is an interesting parallel in the religious/regional conflict of the 1980s, 1990s, and 2000s with the political/regional conflict of the 1960s. In the 1960s, the Hausa-Fulani elite won control of Nigeria through control of the northern region, then a single political unit. After the multiple-state reforms, an evolving northern elite had to find a new way to unite a large enough group around it to control Nigeria. The most direct route was to inflame fears among northerners of religious and economic domination of the south and to stimulate southerners to act in ways that intensified those fears, such as the actions and words of the CAN. The fact that Abacha, a non-Hausa Kanuri, followed the same strategy only suggests a different faction of the political/economic elite of the north was trying to control the Nigerian body politic, but via the same methods. Finally, the use of the *Sharia* issue in the Obasanjo era may be an attempt to follow this same path. As in the first republic, regional political elites appear to be using communalism of one sort or another to try to unite the public behind them against a supposed outside threat, so they can take and hold power.

SIGNIFICANCE

The Nigerian experience suggests several important lessons for students of ethnicity and ethnic conflict. In general, it shows how often ethnic consciousness and conflict are stimulated by political and economic structures. These have worked to divide some groups from others (north and south); enhance the awareness of ethnicity, the rewards for ethnic organization, and the incentive to suppress other ethnic groups (the three-region system of the first republic); increase the advantages of majority and other larger ethnic groups (the federal character principle, the growth of states, the economic nationalist policy, manipulating the revenue-sharing formulas); channel the impact of the political economy (the federally controlled tide of oil money); and influence the impact of extraconstitutional and nondemocratic governance (repression; institutional erosion caused by, lack of accountability of, and propensity to manipulate or deal poorly with religious divisions of military rule). As individuals sought to pursue their interests in the context of these structures and conditions, groups increasingly thought of themselves as having cultural and linguistic ties (as "ethnic") and considered these ties relevant to the pursuit of other goods they sought. While these identities and perceptions have generally been able to coexist peacefully with one another, at times they have led to perceptions of zero-sum relations among the groups where some were consistent losers in the contest. Occasionally they led to severe conflict, which at times burst into physical violence.

The lessons of Nigeria are several. First, conflict was never inevitable in Nigeria. Primordial hatreds are rare, and even spates of severe violence, as in the 1960s, have passed when the structures and policies that caused them were changed. Second, and less encouraging, the factors that caused conflicts are several, are intertwined with the interests of those who are living in the situation, probably transcend the authority or power of any identifiable actors to change, and are tied into such eternal human problems as greed, scarcity, and ambition. These may have been hindering the civilian government of Obasanjo as it tried at century's end to manage and make progress on these and other problems. Third, political elites in Nigeria have often pursued their personal interests in power and wealth through the medium of ethnic, regional, and religious suspicion and conflict. They have rarely been responsible in this to the larger issue of the Nigerian peoples' well-being. Fourth, and finally, the interactions among structure, policy, institutions, and autonomous actors that create ethnic conflict are too complex reliably to predict, and therefore to avoid. This leaves us with an all-too-familiar dilemma: while any single ethnic conflict is not inevitable, there is enough confusion, error, and selfishness in human existence that some conflict probably is inevitable.

See also Burma: The Karen Conflict; India: Ethnic Conflict and Nation-building in a Multiethnic State; Rwanda: Hutu-Tutsi Conflict and Genocide in Central Africa; and Sri Lanka: Tamil-Sinhalese Conflict in India's Backyard.

NOTES

1. Walter Schwarz, *Nigeria* (New York: Praeger, 1968).
2. Audrey C. Smock, *Ibo Politics: The Role of Ethnic Unions in Eastern Nigeria* (Cambridge, Mass.: Harvard University Press, 1971); Howard Wolpe, *Urban Politics in Nigeria: A Study of Port Harcourt* (Los Angeles: University of California Press, 1974).
3. P. C. Lloyd, "The Ethnic Background to the Nigerian Crisis," in *Nigerian Politics and Military Rule: The Prelude to Civil War,* ed. K. Panter-Brick (London: Athlone Press, 1970).
4. Kenneth Post and Michael Vickers, *Structure and Conflict in Nigeria, 1960–1966* (London: Heinemann, 1977).
5. Rotimi Suberu, "Federalism, Ethnicity, and Regionalism in Nigeria," in *Dilemmas of Democracy in Nigeria*, Paul Beckett and Crawford Young, ed. (Rochester, N.Y.: University of Rochester Press, 1997).
6. See *Nigeria—Report of the Commissions Appointed to Enquire into the Fears of the Minorities and the Means of Allaying Them* (London: Her Majesty's Stationery Office, cmnd. 505, 1958).
7. Eghosa Osaghae, "Managing Multiple Minority Problems in a Divided Society: The Nigerian Experience," *Journal of Modern African Studies* 36, no. 1 (1998): 1–24.
8. Ibid.
9. Toyin Falola, "Christian Radicalism and Nigerian Politics," in *Dilemmas of Democracy in Nigeria,* ed. Paul Beckett and Crawford Young (Rochester, N.Y.: Rochester University Press, 1997). Also, Sabo Bako, "Muslims, State and the Struggle for Democratic Transitions in Nigeria: From Cooperation to Conflict," in Beckett and Young, *Dilemmas of Democracy.*
10. Richard Joseph, "Democratization Under Military Rule and Repression in Nigeria," in Beckett and Young, *Dilemmas of Democracy.*
11. Osaghae, "Managing Multiple Minority Problems."
12. Ibid.
13. John Paden, "Nigerian Unity and the Tension of Democracy: Geo-cultural Zones and North-South Legacies," in Beckett and Young, *Dilemmas of Democracy.*

SUGGESTED READINGS

Beckett, Paul, and Crawford Young, eds. *Dilemmas of Democracy in Nigeria.* Rochester, N.Y.: Rochester University Press, 1997.

Diamond, Larry, Anthony Kirk-Greene, and Oyeleye Oyediran, eds. *Transition Without End: Nigerian Politics and Civil Society Under Babangida.* Boulder, Colo.: Lynne Rienner, 1997.

Dudley, B. J. *An Introduction to Nigerian Government and Politics.* London: 1992.

Ekwe-Ekwe, Herbert. *Issues in Nigerian Politics Since the Fall of the Second Republic.* Lewiston, N.Y.: Edwin Meller Press, 1991.

Joseph, Richard. *Democracy and Prebendal Politics in Nigeria: The Rise and Fall of the Second Republic.* Cambridge; England: Cambridge University Press, 1987.

Kasfelt, Wiels. *Religion and Politics in Nigeria.* London: British Academic Press, 1994.

Laitin, David. "The Sharia Debate and the Origins of Nigeria's Second Republic." *Journal of Modern African Studies* 20, no. 3 (1982): 411–30.

Maier, Karl. *This House Has Fallen: Midnight in Nigeria.* New York: Public Affairs, 2000.

Osaghae, Eghosa E. "Managing Multiple Minority Problems in a Divided Society: The Nigerian

Experience," *Journal of Modern African Studies* 36, no. 1 (1998): 1–24.

———. "The Ogoni Uprising: Oil Politics, Minority Nationalism and the Future of the Nigerian State." *African Affairs* 93, no. 376 (1995): 325–44.

———. *Structural Adjustment and Ethnicity in Nigeria*. Uppsala, Sweden: Scandinavian Institute of African Studies, Research Report no. 98, 1995.

Panter-Brick, S. K., ed. *Nigerian Politics and Military Rule: Prelude to the Civil War*. London: Athlone Press, 1970.

Rothchild, Donald S. *Managing Ethnic Conflict in Africa: Pressures and Incentives for Cooperation*. Washington, D.C.: Brookings, 1997.

Rwanda

Hutu-Tutsi Conflict and Genocide in Central Africa

Stephen D. Wrage

TIMELINE

ca. 1500 Bantu and Nilotic peoples migrate into Rwanda and displace the aboriginal pygmy Twa.

1894 The first Caucasian enters the kingdom of Rwanda.

1919 Rwanda passes from German colonial rule to Belgian.

1926 Belgian colonial rulers issue identity cards that label all Rwandans as Hutu (85 percent), Tutsi (14 percent), or Twa (1 percent).

1959 A Tutsi king dies, and thousands of Tutsi are killed by Hutus.

1962 Belgian colonial rulers depart from Rwanda. More killing of Tutsi follows independence, and many flee to neighboring countries.

1963–1967 Tutsis suffer from unusually heavy violence.

1973 Hutu military chief Juvenal Habyarimana seizes power in the wake of violence against Tutsis. Under his new government, exclusion laws ban Tutsis from such institutions as universities, deprive them of political rights, and limit their representation in government jobs to 9 percent.

1989 The first of several years of drought occurs. Agricultural production drops. At the same time, coffee and tea prices decline, suppressing Rwanda's foreign earnings.

1989 The Habyarimana government comes under pressure from the United States and other aid-granting governments to democratize. (About 60 percent of the Rwandan budget comes from foreign aid.)

1990 The Tutsi Rwandan Patriotic Front (RPF) invades Rwanda from Uganda. French troops assist the Habyarimana regime in driving the RPF back across the border. Many Tutsi are killed in reprisal for the invasion.

1993 *February:* an RPF offensive is stopped near Kigali by a combined force of Rwandan government troops and French troops. The RPF continues to hold significant territory.

August 4: Habyarimana's government and the RPF achieve a peace agreement in Arusha, Tanzania.

October 3: 18 American Army Rangers are killed in an ambush in Mogadishu, Somalia.

October: United Nations Security Council approves the UN Assistance Mission to Rwanda (UNAMIR). Between October 1993 and March 1994, UNAMIR forces are built up to about 2,500 troops from Tunisia, Belgium, Bangladesh, and Ghana. The USS *Harlan County* is turned away from the docks of Port au Prince, Haiti.

1994 On April 6, President Juvenal Habyarimana is killed when his plane is destroyed by a missile. The same day, genocidal slaughter begins in Rwanda and continues for 100 days. Rwandan Prime Minister Agathe Uwilingiyimana is tortured and murdered along with ten Belgian soldiers sent to protect her.

April 7: The UN begins a six-week debate on how to respond to the slaughter in Rwanda. The use of the word "genocide" is avoided because the UN would be required to intervene in a genocide.

April 16: UN Security Council reduces UNAMIR forces by roughly 90 percent to approximately 250.

May 17: UN Security Council decides to enlarge and strengthen UNAMIR to 5,500 men. Decisions on financing and operational issues are delayed until late July.

May 25: UN Human Rights Commission meets in Geneva and passes a resolution that implies that the slaughter is a "genocide."

July 6: Kigali is taken by the RPA.

July 18: A cease-fire is announced, and a new government, headed by Pasteur Bizimungu, as president, and Faustin Twagiramungu, as prime minister, both Hutu, is established. The real power, however, rests with the Tutsi commander of the RPF, General Paul Kagame, who holds the posts of vice president and minister of defense.

Post 1994 In November, the UN Security Council establishes the International Criminal Tribunal for Rwanda (ICTR).

1998 On September 4, the ICTR hands down first rulings, marking the first time that an international court has applied the Genocide Convention of 1948. The Rwandan prime minister at the time of the massacre was found guilty of genocide and sentenced to life in prison.

In the hundred days following April 6, 1994, the people of Rwanda engaged in an orgy of slaughter that left 800,000 people dead.[1] The Hutu majority set out to exterminate the Tutsi minority, and, at the same time, killed many Hutu moderates. The Hutus carried out this project with stunning ruthlessness and unprecedented speed. They made little effort to conceal their actions, yet they were able to proceed almost entirely without interference from the United Nations, from the other countries of Africa, or from the rest of the world.

HISTORICAL BACKGROUND

Few countries are less strategically significant than Rwanda. No precious or strategic minerals have been discovered there, no oil lies beneath it, and it is not located on any "arc of crisis" or near any choke point for navigation. It is a small, mountainous state in south central Africa, no larger than Maryland, bordered by Uganda, Tanzania, Burundi, and the Congo. It has no access to the sea, and the nearest port is more than 600 miles away. Coffee and tea are the source of two-thirds of its foreign currency, but most of its citizens live largely outside the money economy, by practicing subsistence agriculture or herding or by trading by barter, earning the equivalent of about $290 per year.

The population of Rwanda is divided into three groups: the Hutu, the Tutsi, and the Twa, whose proportions in 1985 were roughly 88 percent, 11 percent, and 1 percent, respectively.[2] The Twa, a pygmy people who dwelt in caves in the mountains of Rwanda from time immemorial, were conquered and displaced by Hutu or Tutsi invaders in the fifteenth or sixteenth century. It is not clear whether the Tutsi or the Hutu arrived first (or even whether they constitute two distinct ethnic groups), but each group claims to have arrived before the other and labels the other as late-coming invaders.

Some ethnographers assert that the Hutu are a Bantu people who came from the south and west and that the Tutsi are a Nilotic people who came from the north and east. Other ethnographers and linguists maintain that there is no demonstrable difference between Tutsis and Hutus in appearance or language or genetic background and assert that the divide between the two groups is based on imaginary distinctions.[3]

There may be no genetic distinction between the Hutu and Tutsi, but there is an economic divide. The Hutu traditionally have been tillers of the earth; the Tutsi, herdsmen. Over time the Tutsi came to be the wealthier, dominant class, even though the Hutu were eight times as numerous. The colonial rulers of Rwanda treated the Tutsi as a superior caste of aristocrats and the Hutu as their vassals.

Rwanda was subjected to colonization later than most of Africa, reflecting the fact that it had been a coherent, powerful kingdom. British explorer Sir Henry Morton Stanley attempted to visit Rwanda but was repulsed by warriors. The first Caucasian to enter the kingdom was Count Von Gotzen of Germany who did not arrive until 1894, 36 years after British explorer John Hanning Speke had first reached Lake Victoria. Rwanda was first a German colony, then a Belgian one, passing from one power to the other in the game of colonial checkers that followed the German defeat in World War I.

The Belgian colonial authorities[4] also strongly favored the Tutsi, who they perceived to be taller, finer-featured, natural aristocrats, and they abetted and encouraged the Tutsis' often harsh treatment of the supposedly shorter, darker Hutu as serfs. In 1929 the Belgians helped deepen and perpetuate the divide between Hutus and Tutsis by establishing an identity card system that labeled every citizen of Rwanda a Hutu, a Tutsi, or a Twa. As the Belgians began to pare down their pres-

ence in Rwanda preparatory to their total withdrawal in 1962, Hutu extremists unleashed violent attacks on the Tutsis, killing several thousand.

Such attacks continued sporadically under the long dictatorship of Hutu General Juvenal Habyarimana, who seized power in a bloody coup in 1973 and ruled until the day the genocide began in 1994. The Habyarimana regime overtly favored the Hutu majority, and by 1990 more than a million Tutsi had left the country, about half of them fleeing to armed camps across the border to the north in Uganda. Although conditions for Tutsi were always oppressive and intermittently lethal under Habyarimana's 21-year rule, Rwanda prospered to a considerable degree. In the 1970s and 1980s, its record of economic growth was far more favorable than that of other former French and Belgian colonies in Africa.

THE CONFLICT

By the late 1980s, Habyarimana's hold on power was slipping. The years 1989, 1991, and 1993 were all years of grave drought. Starting in 1990, the Rwandan Patriotic Front (or RPF, as the Tutsi rebels based in Uganda called themselves) launched numerous attacks across the border. Habyarimana's domination of the political scene waned as political parties proliferated. Most of these parties were affiliated with the cause of Hutu Power.

Hutu Power proponents backed a series of Tutsi exclusion laws limiting Tutsis' rights to own property, banning marriage to non-Tutsis, and denying the right to travel or to join most organizations or to form political parties. Hutu Power newspapers and radio programs warned that the Tutsi insurgents would overrun Rwanda and enslave and murder all Hutus, and they preached the need to organize for self-defense.

The most notable of these radio preachers was Hassan Ngeze, "a former bus-fare collector who had established himself as an entrepreneur, selling newspapers and drinks outside a gas station."[5] He popularized the term *inyenzi* (which means "cockroaches") to refer to Tutsi and warned everyone to be ready to defend themselves against *inyenzi* and their "accomplices," meaning moderate Hutus. In December 1990, Ngeze issued the "Ten Hutu Commandments," the last of which was "Hutus must stop having mercy on the Tutsis."[6]

The Hutu Power parties sponsored youth militias, many of them based on soccer clubs. The largest of these militias was called *Interahamwe,* meaning "those who attack together":

> The *interahamwe,* and the various copycat groups that were eventually subsumed into it, promoted genocide as a carnival romp. Hutu Power youth leaders, jetting around on motorbikes and sporting pop hairstyles, dark glasses, and flamboyantly colored pajama suits and robes, preached ethnic solidarity and civil defense to increasingly packed rallies, where alcohol usually flowed freely, giant banners splashed with hagiographic portraits of Habyarimana flapped in the breeze, and paramilitary drills were conducted like the latest hot dance moves. The president and his wife often turned out to be cheered at these spectacles, while in private the members of the *interahamwe* were organized into small neighborhood bands, drew up lists of Tutsis, and went on retreats to practice burning houses, tossing grenades, and hacking dummies up with machetes.[7]

When the RPF scored successes in the north, Habyarimana chose a path of negotiation. On August 4, 1993, he signed a peace agreement with the insurgents in the Tanzanian town of Arusha. Under the Arusha Accords, Tutsi refugees would come home, the RPF would be included in a new transition government, elections would be held, and a United Nations peacekeeping force would be sent to observe the process.

The prospect of sharing power divided the old Habyarimana oligarchy and cost the dictator many long-term supporters. At the same time, the promise of moderation outraged the Hutu Power extremists. An end to RPF attacks in the north threatened to rob them of their militias' rationale for preparing violence against the Tutsis. Just across the southern border in Burundi, however, events occurred that strengthened the Hutu Power cause. In August 1993, an election had ended thirty years of Tutsi rule and installed the country's first democratically chosen president, a Hutu. In November of that year, however, four Tutsi army officers assassinated him. In the violence that followed, over 50,000 persons, most of them Hutus, were killed.

In keeping with the Arusha Accords, the UN Security Council approved the United Nations Assistance Mission to Rwanda (UNAMIR) and, in October 1993, sent a multinational force of 2,500 troops to Kigali. Within days of the UN deployment, Hutu Power propagandist Hassan Ngeze was warning in his broadcasts that UNAMIR was nothing but a device "to help the RPF take power by force. . . . If the RPF has decided to kill us, then let's kill each other. Let whatever is smoldering erupt. . . . At such a time, a lot of blood will be spilled."[8] On January 11, 1994, Ngeze's newspaper declared UNAMIR ought to "consider its danger."[9]

On April 6, 1994, President Habyarimana was returning by plane from a follow-on meeting with RPF representatives in Arusha. As the plane approached Kigali, it was destroyed by a surface-to-air missile fired from near the airport. All aboard were killed. Hutu Power radio announced that RPF forces had infiltrated the country and were responsible for the attack and that it was time to strike back in self-defense. There is little doubt today that Hutu Power forces actually destroyed the plane.[10]

The killing began in Kigali and was carried out by squads working from lists.

They visited the home and work addresses of prominent Tutsis and moderate Hutus and took them to warehouses and army bases where they were executed. There was little rape or looting at the start, and the victims were primarily adult males.

In two or three days, after the Tutsi political, intellectual, and social elites had been nearly eliminated and the moderate Hutu leadership had been killed, the Hutu extremists shifted their tactics to terrorizing large numbers of people in the cities, driving them into the countryside, straining them through roadblocks on the way, and selecting those whose names appeared on lists for execution. At this point, the Hutu militias and Rwandan military began exterminating entire families and seizing their property.[11]

In the countryside, the murders typically were committed in schoolyards and churchyards. Government radio announced that churches would be sanctuaries to encourage potential victims to concentrate themselves there. The churches were then surrounded by militias who often set up barbed wire and watch fires. Tutsis who defended themselves with sticks and rocks sometimes were able to make standoffs last for days or weeks, even after water and food supplies were cut off. Finally experienced killers armed with rifles and grenades would be sent to the town to organize the slaughter. These *interahamwe* professionals often found willing executioners among the locals, but they also took care to compel as many people as possible to "do their duty" with a machete.

Because committing murder with a machete is exhausting, the militias were organized to work in shifts. At the day's end, the Achilles tendons of unprocessed victims were sometimes cut before the murderers retired to rest, to feast on the victims' cattle, and to drink. Victims sometimes begged to be allowed to pay to die from a bullet and so to avoid a death by being hacked with a hoe or a machete.

NAYARBUYE, RWANDA. Scene at the site of a 1994 massacre of hundreds of Tutsis by Hutu militia at a countryside village church in the southeast corner of Rwanda. © David Turnley/CORBIS.

The following description of the process of slaughter comes from the London *Economist*:

Using the organizational skills of the local civil service and the muscle of the army, it was easy for the Hutu militiamen to herd 5,000 members of the minority Tutsi tribe, and some Hutu members of opposition parties, into the church of St. Vincent—and then to kill them all. . . . Militiamen controlled by the ruling party had been asking every local council to organize 'local security meetings' since December. These were widely taken as means of identifying Tutsis for murder later on. 'The Tutsis did not go, and those Hutu who refused would find themselves on a death list,' says a UN consultant until recently based in Kigali.

. . . With the help of the army, the victims were then crowded into St. Vincent, a few yards away. Then the militiamen were let loose. They tossed grenades in through the windows, sprayed machine gun bullets from next to the altar, and finally went in—with their wives and children—to finish the slaughter with machetes. The local council's earth-moving equipment was used to bury the bodies of the maybe 5,000 victims in a neat mass grave.[12]

The genocide continued with astonishing speed. Although the killing was "low tech," usually performed with a machete or a hoe, and although it was carried out in large part by amateurs (often the neighbors and workmates of the victims), "the dead of Rwanda accumulated at nearly three times the rate of Jewish dead during the Holocaust."[13]

MANAGEMENT OF THE CONFLICT

The remnants of the Habyarimana regime collaborated openly with the Hutu extremists.[14] They supported the genocidal militias with weapons and uniformed troops and argued abroad that the events were an internal matter protected by sovereignty from intervention. They had little difficulty getting the rest of the world to look the other way.

The United States was loathe to intervene. A few months earlier, in October 1993, 18 U.S. Army Rangers had been killed in Somalia as part of a peacekeeping mission that had gone terribly wrong. In the very months that the situation in Rwanda was unfolding, a campaign to oust a dictatorship in Haiti was coming to a climax and would result, in September 1994, in an invasion of Haiti using 20,000 troops. The Clinton administration was determined not to be drawn into a third such intervention and so responded to news of the slaughter with implausible evasions and long delays.

As Rwandans were murdered at the rate of 1,000 per day, U.S. policy makers refused to use the obvious term "genocide." Instead, they spoke of "acts of ethnic violence" and maintained that the United States had no obligation to act even though it is a signatory to the United Nations Convention Against Genocide.

The United Nations was no more effective than the United States; in fact, the United States worked there to forestall any response beyond debate and expressions of concern. On April 6, 1994, the day the violence began, Hutu militia killed ten Belgian soldiers attached to UNAMIR who had been sent to guard the office of the prime minister. The Belgians immediately withdrew their forces, depriving the UN force of its best-trained, best-equipped unit, and began to lobby other UN members to terminate UNAMIR entirely.

For six weeks, from April 7, 1994, through May 17, the UN Security Council debated its response to Rwanda. Its only decisive act came on April 16, ten days after Habyarimana's assassination, when the Security Council voted to cut the size of the forces committed to UNAMIR by almost 90 percent, leaving about 250 troops in Rwanda, a force too small even to monitor the slaughter. During this period, corpses were accumulating at about 8,000 per day.

Finally, on May 17, the UN Security Council declared an intention to increase the UNAMIR forces to about 5,000, but decisions regarding the size, source, and logistical support of the various national contingents were delayed until late July. On May 25, 1994, Secretary General Boutros-Ghali told a news conference in New York, "It is a failure not only of the United Nations. . . . It is a failure of the international community. It is a genocide. More than 200,000 people have been killed and we are still discussing what to do."[15]

The Tutsi Rwandan Patriotic Front brought the genocide to an end. By early July, the RPF had pushed to the outskirts of Kigali. On July 6, the city fell, and on July 18, the Tutsi forces imposed a cease-fire and set up a puppet government headed by two Hutu figures.

Three years later, on March 25, 1998, President Clinton stopped at the airport in Kigali to apologize for American indifference at the time of the genocide.

> During the ninety days that began on April 6, 1994, Rwanda experienced the most intensive slaughter in this blood-filled century. It is important that the world know that these killings were not spontaneous or accidental . . . they were most certainly not the result of ancient tribal struggles. . . . These events grew from a policy aimed at the systematic destruction of a people.[16]

SIGNIFICANCE

The record of the hundred days of slaughter in Rwanda raises at least three points important to students of ethnic conflict in the twentieth century. First, mass murder occurred in Rwanda at a rate unprecedented in history. With between 800,000 and 1 million dead in 100 days, an average of 8,000 to 10,000 persons died every day. This rate of killing exceeded past epochal acts in the obliteration of humanity, including the Crusaders' sack of Jerusalem, Tamerlane's destruction of Delhi, and the incineration of Dresden, Hiroshima, and Nagasaki.[17] In those cases the death toll may have been very great for several days, but the profligate destruction of human life was not sustained for as long as it was in Rwanda.

Second, there is excellent reason to doubt that any biologically verifiable ethnic distinction actually existed between the murderers and their victims. Though almost every Rwandan citizen carried an identity card labeling him or her a Hutu or a Tutsi, ethnographers can make only a weak case for distinguishing the two groups as they do not differ significantly in appearance, language, traditions, or in other ways. The murderers and their victims appear to have been ethnically identical, and the massive crime of hundreds of thousands of murders seems to have been carried out on the basis of an imaginary distinction.

Finally, the mass murder required and was the result of years of propaganda. Over the course of a decade, the minds of both the killers and their victims had been prepared through the teachings of the Hutu Power movement. During the 100 days, the Hutu Power leaders directed the slaughter like a horrific movie with a cast of millions. In short, the genocide in Rwanda did not just happen, nor was it an inexplicable episode of mass frenzy. Rather, it was the product of a program that was successfully implemented in Rwanda and might be initiated elsewhere.

See also Nigeria: Ethnic Conflict in Multinational West Africa; and Yugoslavia: The Deconstruction of a State and Birth of Bosnia.

NOTES

1. Estimates of the number of violent deaths range from 800,000 to over 1,000,000. When the number of fatalities caused by disease and hardship in refugee camps is added, the estimated totals nearly double.
2. Richard F. Nyropp, *Rwanda: A Country Study* (Washington, D.C.: United States Government Printing Office, 1985), 3.
3. Philip Gourevitch, author of the best book-length account of the genocide in Rwanda, is skeptical of any ethnic distinction:

    With time, Hutus and Tutsis spoke the same language, followed the same religion, intermarried, and lived intermingled, without territorial distinctions, on the same hills, sharing the same social and political culture in small chiefdoms. The chiefs were called Mwamis, and some of them were Hutus, some Tutsis; Hutus and Tutsis fought together in the Mwamis' armies; through marriage and clientage, Hutus could become hereditary Tutsis, and Tutsis could become hereditary Hutus. Because of all this mixing, ethnographers have come to agree that Hutus and Tutsis cannot properly be called distinct ethnic groups.

    We Wish to Inform You That Tomorrow We Will Be Killed with Our Families: Stories from

Rwanda (New York: Farrar Straus and Giroux, 1998), 47–48.

4. On the dismal Belgian record of rule, see Adam Hochschild, *King Leopold's Ghost: A Story of Greed, Terror, and Heroism in Colonial Africa* (New York: Houghton Mifflin, 1998).

5. Gourevitch, *We Wish to Inform You,* 85.

6. See Gary Rosen, "Can We Prevent Genocide?" *Commentary* February 1999, 52.

7. See Gourevitch, *We Wish to Inform You,* 93. Between 1990 and 1994, the Habyarimana government imported massive shipments of machetes from China and rifles and grenades from France and distributed them to these militias.

8. See Gourevitch, *We Wish to Inform You,* 100.

9. Ibid., 103.

10. For a discussion of the identity of the assassins, see Gerard Prunier, *The Rwanda Crisis: History of a Genocide* (New York: Columbia University Press, 1995), 213–29, 223. Prunier identifies Hutu extremists as the likeliest culprits and observes, "The plane was shot down at around 8:30 PM, and by 9:15 there were already *Interahamwe* roadblocks everywhere in town and houses were being searched."

11. As early as the first week, rape was deployed as a weapon to humiliate Tutsi women and destroy Tutsi families. Twa men were employed as rapists since there was an additional stigma attached to rape by a man of the pygmy race. See Gourevitch, *We Wish to Inform You,* 8.

12. *The Economist* (London), "Rwanda: The Art of Death," May 28, 1994: 35.

13. See Gourevitch, *We Wish to Inform You,* 3. Prunier, *The Rwanda Crisis*, 261: "The daily killing rate was at least five times that of the Nazi death camps."

14. Government ministers did nothing to prevent the slaughter. Dr. Rwamakuba, a medical doctor, and secretary for primary and secondary education, shouted during a recent interview: "We have tried to protect the minority [Tutsis] for 15 years. But they don't want protection, they want war." Meanwhile two miles away helpless Tutsis were being murdered. *The Economist,* "Rwanda: The Art of Death," May 28, 1994. 35.

15. Boutros-Ghali Angrily Condemns All Sides for Not Saving Rwanda," *New York Times,* May 26, 1994, late edition: A1.

16. "Clinton's Painful Words of Sorrow and Chagrin," *New York Times,* March 26, 1998, late edition: A12.

17. The Nazis' efforts at mass murder have led many writers to conclude that genocide was a peculiarly twentieth-century crime requiring the use of modern technology. Events in Rwanda demonstrate that this is not the case.

SUGGESTED READINGS

Feil, Scott R. *Preventing Genocide: How the Early Use of Force Might Have Succeeded in Rwanda.* New York: Carnegie Commission on Preventing Deadly Conflict, 1998.

Gourevitch, Philip. *We Wish to Inform You That Tomorrow We Will Be Killed with Our Families: Stories from Rwanda.* New York: Farrar Straus and Giroux, 1998.

Hochschild, Adam. *King Leopold's Ghost: A Story of Greed, Terror, and Heroism in Colonial Africa.* New York: Houghton Mifflin, 1998.

Klinghoffer, Arthur J. *The International Dimension of Genocide in Rwanda.* New York : New York University Press, 1998.

Kuperman, Alan J. "Rwanda in Retrospect." *Foreign Affairs* 79, no. 1 (January/February 2000): 94–118.

Prunier, Gerard. *The Rwanda Crisis: A History of Genocide.* New York: Columbia University Press, 1995.

Rosen, Gary. "Can We Prevent Genocide?" *Commentary* (February 1999): 51–56.

Speke, John Hanning. *Journal of the Discovery of the Source of the Nile.* New York: Harper, 1864.

United Nations. *The United Nations and Rwanda, 1993–1996.* New York: Department of Public Information of the United Nations, 1996.

Soviet Union

The Conflict in Chechnya

Robert Bruce Ware

TIMELINE

1831 Russia encounters fierce resistance from Islamic warriors in the northeast Caucasus.

1835 Immam Shamil leads resistance.

1859 Shamil surrenders.

1922 Chechen Autonomous Republic established.

1934 Checheno-Ingush Republic established.

1944 Chechens and other Caucasian nationalities deported to Central Asia.

1957 Chechens allowed to return to Chechnya.

1990 Chechen National Congress held in Grozny.

1991 Djohar Dudayev elected president of Chechnya.

1992 Declaration of independent Chechen Republic; Chechnya does not sign Russian Federation treaty; Chechnya and Ingushetia separated; federal troops withdrawn from Chechnya.

1993 Dudayev disbands Chechen Parliament and decrees presidential rule.

1994 Civil war in Chechnya; Ruslan Labazanov and Beslan Gantimirov attack Grozny; Russia invades.

1995 Federal troops take Grozny; Basayev attacks Budenovsk; Basayev announces cesium-137 located in a Moscow park.

1996 Salman Raduyev attacks Kizlyar, Dagestan; Russian troops attack Raduyev's fighters and their hostages in Pervomayskoye; Dudayev killed; Chechen fighters capture Grozny and other cities; Khasavyurt Accord signed; ICRC workers killed.

1997 Aslan Maskhadov elected president of Chechnya.

1998 Kidnapping and other criminal activities increase; British telecom workers beheaded.

1999 Basayev and Khattab invade Dagestan; Vladimir Putin becomes Russian prime minister; hundreds die in four Russian apartment block explosions; Russian troops invade Chechnya and attack Grozny.

2000 Tailban recognizes Chechen sovereignty and declares that Afghan fighters are in Chechnya; Chechen fighters abandon Grozny; Basayev undergoes amputation; Putin elected Russian president; Akhmed Kadyrov appointed by Moscow to head Chechnya administration.

2001 Arbi Bareyev killed; Eduard Shevardnadze states that Chechen militants are in Georgia's Pankisi Gorge; American presidential spokesperson says Al Qaeda terrorist organization is active in Chechnya.

2002 United States troops train Georgian forces to combat Al Qaeda in Pankisi Gorge.

The militarized, nationalist conflict in Chechnya is the latest installment of more than two hundred years of intermittent hostilities in Russia's Caucasus region between the Russians and the Chechens, who differ from one another in terms of language, ethnicity, and religion. Many of those hostilities have been distinguished by their extreme brutality, and the present conflict is no exception. Yet the current conflict derives special significance from the role it has played in the geopolitical realignments that have occurred since 1990. The site of the largest conflict in Europe since World War II, Chechnya has also been the scene of the worst violence to occur in the former Soviet territories. It has divided Russian public opinion and depleted Russia's resources at a crucial point in its history. It has tarnished Russia's rehabilitation, interfered with its efforts to join the West, and isolated it at times from much of the international community. It has led to social, economic, and moral devastation in Chechnya, and it has been a source of protracted suffering throughout the Caucasus region. It has outraged Muslims around the world, attracted radical Islamist support, and peripherally engaged the American campaign against terrorism. It is a conflict that often has seemed to defy resolution and that may culminate in the exhaustion of all sides.

HISTORICAL BACKGROUND

Beginning in 1831, Russia's southward expansion encountered fierce resistance from Muslim warriors in Chechnya and the neighboring region of Dagestan. A charismatic Dagestani leader, Immam Shamil, drove the resistance from 1835 until his surrender in 1859.

In 1922 the Chechens were granted an autonomous territory within the Soviet state, but in 1934 it was combined with that of the Ingush people to the west. Following charges of collaboration with German troops, the Chechens—along with the Ingush and other Caucasian nationalities—were deported en masse to Central Asia on February 23, 1944. Their return to the Chechen homeland occurred surreptitiously throughout the 1950s and openly after their official rehabilitation in 1957.

In 1990, Communist authorities permitted the convocation of a Chechen National Congress, largely as a release for social tensions that were accumulating during the period of Soviet reform. The Congress was attended by Djohar Dudayev, a Chechen who was then stationed in Estonia as a general in the Soviet military and who gained attention at the Congress when he made a fiery nationalistic speech.

On October 27, 1991, the Checheno-Ingushetian presidential election was marred by irregularities, but Dudayev took the presidential oath on November 9. Despite a referendum supporting participation in the Russian Federation, the Chechen Republic adopted a constitution declaring itself an independent secular state on March 12, 1992, and it did not join other republics in signing the Russian treaty of federation. The Chechen and Ingush Republics were formally separated on June 4, 1992, and four days later the last Russian Federation troops were withdrawn from Chechnya.

Dudayev's radical nationalism increasingly led to conflicts with moderates in his government. After a vote of nonconfidence, Dudayev dissolved the Chechen parliament and declared presidential rule. On April 18, 1993, the remnants of the Chechen parliament began impeachment proceedings, and the Chechen constitutional court ruled Dudayev's action unconstitutional. The ensuing struggle pitted Dudayev's supporters against a series of opposition figures, including Ruslan Labazanov and Beslan Gantimirov. Growing chaos led to violence in Chechnya and criminal raids into surrounding Russian territories. Chechnya sank into civil war in the autumn of 1994, and a Russian team began planning a two-week invasion for December.

THE CONFLICT

Russian troops crossed into Chechnya on December 10, 1994, and, on New Year's eve, began a difficult two-month assault on the capital of Grozny. Dudayev's forces withdrew from Grozny in March to wage a guerrilla war in the rugged Caucasus Mountains of southern Chechnya. Throughout March and April, the Russian army took the major towns to the south and west of Grozny. After April 19, 1995, when Russian troops captured Bamut, the last rebel stronghold in the Chechen lowlands, Russian Prime Minister Victor Chernomyrdin declared that Moscow was ready to talk to Chechen field commanders without preconditions and announced a general amnesty for all Chechen fighters who had not been involved in serious crimes. Moscow declared a unilateral cease-fire to commence on May 1, but on April 29, Dudayev rejected the cease-fire, and Moscow withdrew its offer after Dudayev's forces shot down a Russian Su-25 aircraft. Russian forces launched a major offensive on May 24, seeking to engage Chechen resistance in the mountains. Between June 4 and 13, federal forces captured the towns of Vedeno, Shatoi, and Nozhay-Yurt, Dudayev's last highland strongholds.

At the same time, Chechen field commander Shamil Basayev infiltrated the neighboring Russian province of Stavropol with a band of 150 men. More than 200 kilometers north of Chechnya, Basayev attacked the town of Budenovsk on June 14, causing numerous fatalities and eventually taking hundreds of Russian civilians hostage in a maternity hospital. Basayev demanded an end to military operations in Chechnya and called for immediate talks with the Russian prime minister. Chernomyrdin assumed control of negotiations and reached an agreement with Basayev on June 19. Many hostages were released directly, but others were forced to flee with Basayev on a dramatic bus ride to the mountains of Chechnya, where Basayev was hailed as a hero and the remaining hostages were freed the next day.

On the same day that Basayev released his hostages, negotiators in Grozny agreed on a three-day cease-fire, and arrived subsequently at a military agreement. Dudayev's forces would be disarmed in three stages, and the Chechen side promised to turn over Basayev. Moscow agreed to grant a general amnesty to all who surrendered their weapons and to withdraw all Russian troops except for an Interior Ministry brigade. The next day Dudayev condemned the peace talks and claimed that representatives had no authority to speak for the Chechen side. Despite Dudayev's protests, the agreement was signed on June 30 and approved by the Chechen Defense Committee on August 1, 1995. The next day, Chernomyrdin announced that the Chechen war had ended.

Several groups of Chechen fighters surrendered their weapons on the 16th and 17th of August, but on the 19th a group of hard-liners attacked a Russian Interior Ministry building in the Chechen town of Argun. Fighting raged for three days before the building was recaptured. Accusations were traded, and Dudayev's forces boycotted a conference designed to get the peace agreement back on track. On October 13, Russian President Yeltsin reiterated his commitment to a peaceful settlement; however, during the next two weeks fighting resumed and quickly escalated. On November 23, a container of radioactive cesium-137 was unearthed in a Moscow park after Basayev announced its location in a television interview. He claimed to have another four containers.

On January 9, 1996, Chechen gunmen, led by Salman Raduyev, attacked a small air base near the Dagestani city of Kislyar and forced nearly 3,000 civilian hostages into a hospital. After tense negotiations with Dagestani officials, Raduyev departed for Chechnya with about 160 hostages. When federal troops attacked their convoy just short of the Chechen border, Raduyev's men, along with their hostages, sought refuge in the Dagestani village of Pervomayskoye. Federal troops began a three-day bombardment of the village on January 15, killing 153 of the raiders and more than 50 of their hostages. Raduyev escaped to Chechnya.

On the April 16, 1996, 73 federal troops were killed in ambush near the mountain town of Shatoi. The attack was significant because it was led by a Saudi-Jordanian commander known as Emir al Khattab, who had come to Chechnya with a contingent of foreign fighters. Five days later, President Dudayev was killed in a directed federal airstrike targeted to the frequency of his cellular phone. He was succeeded by Vice President Zelimkhan Yandarbiyev.

Dissension over the conflict increased throughout 1995, and by February 1996, political leaders across Russia were calling for an end to the war. Yeltsin and Yandarbiyev met in Moscow on May 27 and agreed to conclude hostilities as of June 1. On June 10, federal and Dudayevist negotiators signed an agreement on the withdrawal of Russian forces by the end of August. Yeltsin announced the beginning of the troop withdrawal on the 25th of June.

On August 6, 1996, Chechen fighters led by Ruslan Gelayev attacked Grozny. Simultaneously, other contingents attacked the cities of Gudermes and Argun. Once in Grozny, the rebels were able to pin down approximately 12,000 Russian troops scattered in pockets throughout the city. Six days later the rebels controlled Grozny and Argun, and a federal battalion was ambushed near Vedeno. The breathtaking success of the August offensive, and the slaughter of Russia's unprepared and ill-equipped conscripts, persuaded many in Russia that the war was futile.

General Alexander Lebed was appointed Yeltsin's special envoy to Chechnya, and he began to meet with rebel leaders on August 11. On August 31, 1996, a comprehensive agreement for ending the war was signed by Lebed and Aslan Maskhadov, the Chechen chief commander. Known as the "Khasavyurt Accord," for the Dagestani city in which it was signed, it left the political status of Chechnya to be determined over the next five years. On January 5, 1997, Moscow stated that all its troops were out of Chechnya.

Violence nevertheless continued among Chechen factions as Chechen society rapidly descended into chaos and criminality. On December 17, 1996, six foreign medical personnel working for the International Committee of the Red Cross (ICRC) were killed in a hospital in the Chechen town of Nove Atagi. The ICRC announced that it was suspending operations in Chechnya, and other international relief organizations pulled out of the area. Murders increased, and kidnapping spiraled into an organized criminal industry that targeted foreigners and preyed increasingly upon locals throughout the region. The hostage industry stifled what little opportunity there may have been for foreign investment in Chechnya's devastated economy. Transit fees from a pipeline carrying Caspian oil to the Black Sea port of Novorossisk were lost when relentless thefts from the line led to Russia's construction of an alternate route.

During the same period, from late 1996 to early 1997, the region saw an increase in violent incidents involving militant Islamists, who were described by their local opponents as "*Wahhabis*." The name suggests a connection to the fundamentalist Islam associated with the Persian Gulf. *Wahhabism* initially appeared in Dagestan in the early 1990s and later spread to Chechnya. Its growth in the region may be attributed to Caucasian Muslims making pilgrimages to Saudi Arabia or studying abroad in Islamic universities, to funding from Persian Gulf organizations, to foreign Islamist fighters who came to the region during and after the first Chechen war, to local political alienation, and to a lack of economic opportunities.

Against this background, presidential and parliamentary elections were held in Chechnya on January 27, 1997. Maskhadov received 59 percent of the vote to beat a field of candidates that included Basayev and Yandarbiyev. His inauguration on February 12 was widely hailed as a victory for moderation. Kremlin leaders were confident that they could work with him.

Maskhadov joined with traditional Islamic leaders, such as Akhmed Kadyrov, to stem the spread of *Wahhabism*. He attempted to resist the hostage industry and to break up organized crime. Some members of his administration, however, were involved in criminal activities, and those who genuinely worked against crime encountered stiff, sometimes fatal, resistance. Despite Maskhadov's efforts, *Wahhabism* and criminal activities proliferated, feeding together on conditions of social disintegration and economic collapse. In early 1998, several foreign aid workers were kidnapped, as was Valentin Vlasov, Yeltsin's envoy to Chechnya. In December, the heads of four foreign telecom workers were found beside a road.

From the end of 1997 onward, Maskhadov encountered radical opposition within Chechnya. He disbanded his government on January 1, 1998, and again on October 1, 1998, appointing supporters who included several members of his own clan. Increasingly, Maskhadov found himself in tense opposition with numerous warlords, such as Basayev and Raduyev, many of whom were making radically nationalist and Islamist appeals for authority.

On August 17, 1997, representatives from several Caucasian republics gathered in Grozny to attend the founding congress of the Caucasus Confederation. Under the leadership of Yandarbiyev and other Chechens, the Confederation aimed to unite all political forces of the Caucasus in a struggle of liberation against "Russian colonialism" and to create a confederation of independent Caucasian states. In April 1998, Basayev was elected president of a "Congress of Chechen and Dagestani Peoples." At a meeting of the Congress in April 1999, Basayev affirmed his interest in the unification of Chechnya and Dagestan and described his organization of an Islamic "Peacekeeping Brigade," trained at bases established with foreign funding and located near Chechnya's border with Dagestan.

Beginning in 1996, that border had become the scene of numerous raids from Chechnya, often involving skirmishes with Dagestanis and ending with the capture of hostages who were held in Chechnya for ransom. On December 22, 1997, Chechen

WASHINGTON, D.C. Chechen President Aslan Maskhadov during his visit to Washington. Photo courtesy of Albert Digaev/Chechen Republic Online. www.amina.com.

raiders joined with *Wahhabis* from the Dagestani village of Karamakhi (where Khattab had married a Dagestani woman) to attack a Russian tank garrison near the Dagestani city of Buinaksk.

The next important escalation in the conflict occurred on August 2, 1999, when Basayev and Khattab led more than a thousand militants, including many Dagestani *Wahhabis,* into Dagestan. The militants occupied numerous villages, especially in the Botlikh and Tsumadinsky regions of Dagestan. Dagestani citizen militias quickly organized to resist the invaders, receiving federal artillery and air support as early as August 7. On August 10, the "Islamic Shura of Dagestan" in Grozny declared the establishment of an independent Islamic state in Dagestan, but Maskhadov denied that his government was connected to the fighting. By August 22 the insurgents were in retreat and Moscow was declaring success. On August 25, the Russian federation attacked targets in Chechnya, including the bases from which the insurgents had originated.

Thereafter attention turned to the *Wahhabi* enclave that had developed around the central Dagestani village of Karamakhi. When Dagestani police proved ineffective in addressing the problem, Russian artillery attacked. Then, on September 4, an apartment building in nearby Buinaksk was destroyed in an explosion that killed more than 60 people. The next day insurgents led by Basayev and Khattab crossed the border into Dagestan's Novolaksky region. They appeared to be driving toward the city of Khasavyurt, but their line of attack led to speculation that they might have been interested in pushing beyond the city toward the Caspian Sea. There was also speculation that they aimed to relieve Karamakhi. By September 12, however, Basayev and Khattab had been pushed back out of Dagestan, and four days later Karamakhi was subdued. Altogether, 32,000 Dagestani refugees found themselves without assistance from any international relief organization.

Meanwhile in Moscow, on September 9, a nine-story apartment building was leveled by an explosion that killed 94 people. Four days later, 118 died in another Moscow blast. Just three days after that, 17 people died when a bomb exploded in a truck parked near an apartment building in Volgodonsk. Russia's recently appointed prime minister, Vladimir Putin, declared that the bombings revealed a "Chechen connection." Maskhadov denied it, and doubts about the accuracy of the charge were aired after September 22, when another suspected bomb turned out to be part of a "training exercise" for federal security services. The next day Russian aircraft bombed the Grozny airport.

On October 1, Russian troops entered Chechnya and rolled quickly across its northern plains. Five days later Putin announced that the northern third of the republic was under federal control. Federal troops crossed the Terek River on October 21, the same day that many people were killed by an explosion in a Grozny market that was blamed on a Russian missile. Thousands of Chechen refugees fled to squalid camps in Ingushetia and to the Pankisi Gorge in northern Georgia. Yet Dagestan, which had taken in 130,000 Chechen refugees during the first war, now not only refused to accept any refugees but began expelling Chechens who resided there illegally.

By November 12, local residents helped federal forces to control Gudermes, Chechnya's second largest city. That month an Abu Dabhi newspaper quoted Chechya's supreme Islamic leader, Akhmed Kadyrov, as refusing to proclaim *jihad* against Russia on Maskhadov's orders because he considered it counter to the interests of the Chechen people. Kadyrov condemned the "alien" religious creed of Khattab and Basayev.

By December 6 Russian troops had

surrounded Grozny and were dropping leaflets there urging civilians to depart by way of "safe corridors" before December 11. On December 14, following a devastating bombardment of the city, federal forces entered Grozny and began weeks of fierce urban warfare. By January 20, 2000, federal forces were pressing toward the center of the city from several directions and Chechen fighters were conceding heavy losses. During the siege of Grozny, the Taliban government of Afghanistan formally recognized the Chechen Republic—Ichkeria—and announced that a group of Taliban was fighting in Chechnya.

Aslambek Ismailov, who commanded the Grozny defense, was killed when Chechen fighters retreated from Grozny on February 1, 2000. Many rebels were killed or wounded as they retreated across a minefield under a federal artillery barrage. Basayev's lower leg was amputated as a consequence of a wound he suffered in the minefield.

On February 6, Putin declared Grozny under the control of federal forces, but the city was utterly devastated. Human rights organizations accused Russian troops of abuses including summary executions and torture.

On June 12, Putin appointed Kadyrov to head an interim administration in Chechnya. Kadyrov declared that his first priority was to stop the fighting, and he offered to talk to anyone except "those who made slave trading and hostage-taking their business."

On January 26, 2001, Maskhadov declared that he was ready for "unconditional" peace talks with Moscow, yet he was unable to control militants such as Shamil Basayev, Arbi Barayev, Ruslan Gelayev, and Khattab. Amid numerous reports that Russian troops were regularly abusing noncombatants, a mass grave was discovered near the federal military base at Khankala, outside Grozny. The grave contained several dozen bodies, including those of women and children.

That June the notorious warlord and kidnapper, Arbi Barayev, was killed by Russian troops, and Georgian President Eduard Shevardnadze conceded that Chechen militants were among 7,000 Chechen refugees in the Pankisi Gorge. On September 26, 2001, President Bush's press secretary stated, "there are terrorists' organizations in Chechnya that have ties to Osama bin Laden." The follow-up action came in February 2002, when Washington officials announced that dozens of fighters from the Al Qaeda terrorist organization were among Chechen refugees in the Pankisi Gorge, and that American forces would deploy in Georgia on a mission to train Georgian troops to establish order in the region.

MANAGEMENT OF THE CONFLICT

As of early 2002, it was difficult to identify a realistic strategy for the management of the conflict in Chechnya. Calls for a political solution to the conflict faced several difficulties. First, there is the legacy of the recent past to be overcome. A political settlement was attempted in Khasavyurt in 1996 with catastrophic results. Second, since the early 1990s, Chechen society has been fragmented to the point that there has been no one capable of guaranteeing any settlement with Russia that might be achieved. Third, an international peacekeeping force in Chechnya seems unlikely to be effective and likely to suffer from the hostage industry. Similarly, proposals to establish a *cordon sanitaire* around Chechnya appeared unrealistic because of the ruggedness of the highland terrain and the regional propensity for bribing border guards.

The conflict in Chechnya reached this impasse due to its tragic mismanagement at nearly every turn, by nearly all concerned. Dudayev's radical nationalism wrecked repeated opportunities for compromise and reconciliation. Basayev's 1995 raid on Budenovsk rallied his comrades and confounded his enemies, but 1,500 hostages in a maternity hospital proved difficult for Russians to forget. Raduyev's meaningless imitation of Basayev's raid undermined Dagestani sympathy for Chechnya, and Basayev's subsequent invasions of Dagestan in 1999 were deeply contrary to Chechen interests. The foreign fighters who joined Chechnya's radicals, and the foreign organizations who funded them, compromised the goals of Chechen separatism with those of radical Islam and compounded the suffering of the people they claimed to assist. Yet Russian military and political leaders also undermined their own objectives in Chechnya by regular atrocities that turned Chechen civilians against federal forces and turned Western leaders against Moscow.

SIGNIFICANCE

The conflict in Chechnya has, so far, primarily produced lessons of a negative nature. Western efforts to influence Moscow's policies were often undercut by their own one-sided focus on Russian abuses. For example, human rights organizations were important in exposing Russian atrocities in Chechnya, but they failed to attend to abuses on the other side, including the hostage industry, and thereby relinquished the moral authority requisite for leveraging Moscow's tactics.

Players of every stripe plied their interests without genuine understanding or regard for the people of the region, while some established personal stakes in the perpetuation of the conflict. Russian troops, for example, colluded with Chechen criminals in the sale of pilfered petroleum products. All sides in the conflict undercut their own objectives, and the people of Chechnya were victimized by the illusions of all concerned, not least of which were their own.

See also Soviet Union: The Ethnic Conflicts in Georgia; Soviet Union: The Nagorno-Karabakh Conflict; and Spain: Basque Nationalism and Conflict in Democratic Spain.

SUGGESTED READINGS

Dunlop, John. *Russia Confronts Chechnya*. Cambridge: Cambridge University Press, 1998.

Gall, Carlotta, and Tom de Waal. *Chechnya*. New York: New York University Press, 1998.

Lieven, Anatol. *Chechnya: Tombstone of Russian Power*. New Haven: Yale University Press, 1998.

Nivat, Anne. *Chienne de Guerre: A Woman Reporter Behind the Lines of the War in Chechnya*. Susan Darnton, translator. New York: Public Affairs, 2001.

Politkovskaya, Anna. *A Dirty War: A Russian Reporter in Chechnya*. John Crowfoot, translator. London: Harvill Press, 2001.

Ware, Robert Bruce, and Enver Kisriev. "Political Stability in Dagestan: Ethnic Parity and Religious Polarization." *Problems of Post Communism* 47, no. 2 (March/April 2000).

Soviet Union

The Ethnic Conflicts in Georgia

Stuart J. Kaufman

TIMELINE

ca. A.D. 780 Abkhazia achieves independence from Byzantium.

1008 Georgia is unified under Abkhazian ruler Bagrat III.

1089 Reign of David the Builder (1089–1125) begins.

1184 Reign of Queen Tamar (1184–1212) begins.

17th century Abkhazia achieves independence from fragmented Georgia; main Ossetian migration to Georgia takes place.

1801–1810 Russia annexes Georgian principalities and Abkhazia.

1866–1877 Abkhazian uprisings against Russia occur after abolition of local autonomy provokes mass expulsion of Abkhazians by Russia (*mohajirstvo*).

1918 Georgia receives independence during Russian civil war; fights rebellions in Abkhazia and South Ossetia.

1921 Georgia is annexed by Soviet Russia; Abkhazia is set up as a separate Soviet republic.

1931 Abkhazia is subordinated to Georgia as an autonomous republic.

1978 Nationalist rallies take place in Georgia and Abkhazia.

1986–1988 Georgian nationalist and Abkhazian movements reemerge.

1989 April 9 massacre occurs in Tbilisi. First ethnic violence takes place in Abkhazia and South Ossetia.

1990 Georgian elections bring nationalist leader Zviad Gamsakhurdia to power. South Ossetia declares independence from Georgia; Georgia dissolves South Ossetian autonomy.

1991 War in South Ossetia begins; new autonomous government is established in Abkhazia. Soviet Union collapses. An effort is made to create a Commonwealth of Independent States (CIS) out of the former component pieces.

1992 Gamsakhurdia is ousted, sparking an intra-Georgian civil war. Eduard Shevardnadze returns to power in Georgia and ends fighting in South Ossetia. Georgia invades Abkhazia.

1993 Abkhazia war ends with Abkhazian military victory. Most Georgians flee Abkhazia. United Nations observer mission UNOMIG is inaugurated.

1994 A Russian-dominated CIS peacekeeping force is introduced.

1998 Remaining Georgians in Abkhazia flee after renewed fighting occurs in May.

The Republic of Georgia, formerly the Georgian Soviet Socialist Republic (SSR), was one of the Soviet Union's fifteen constituent parts, located between Russia and Turkey in the South Caucasus region. As was often done in the Soviet system, Moscow created three autonomous regions for minority groups within the ethnically diverse Georgian SSR: the Abkhazian Autonomous Soviet Socialist Republic (ASSR), the Ajarian ASSR, and the South Ossetian Autonomous Region. As Georgian nationalist sentiment began to revive in the late Gorbachev period, all three minority regions began calling for increased autonomy of their own. Whereas the Georgians increasingly demanded independence, the Ossetians and Abkhazians wanted to stay with Russia: the Ossetians because they had ethnic kin in Russia and the Abkhazians because they feared Georgian assimilationist pressure. Ajaria, led by strongman Aslan Abashidze, kept its demands more moderate, slipping out of the grasp of the Georgian government in Tbilisi while avoiding violence.

Abkhazia, South Ossetia, and the rest of Georgia were not so fortunate. Indeed, within a year of independence, the luckless people of Georgia faced more separate (if interconnected) civil wars than any other former Soviet republic. South Ossetia was the first to see violence, when Georgian militias began mobilizing against the increasingly assertive Ossetian separatist movement in 1989–1990. Next, a civil war engulfed the ethnic Georgian heartland, as Georgia's temperamental warlords united against the increasingly unstable and despotic rule of Georgia's first elected president, Zviad Gamsakhurdia, sparking continuing violence between the "Zviadists" and their adversaries. In the context of a campaign against the Zviadists, the new Georgian authorities, under the still-shaky leadership of former Soviet Foreign Minister Eduard Shevardnadze, invaded Abkhazia, sparking the bloodiest, most disastrous of Georgia's civil wars. While Shevardnadze managed to reestablish a fragile peace and stability in Georgia in the mid- and late-1990s, the century ended with all three former autonomous regions outside the effective control of the Georgian government.

HISTORICAL BACKGROUND

The Georgians, among the original inhabitants of the South Caucasus region, trace their history back to the ancient civilization of Colchis, the source of the Golden Fleece of Greek myth. The Georgian nation includes speakers of several related but distinct languages in the Caucasian language family. The most important of these are Kartuli, or Georgian proper, the basis of the Georgian literary language; and Mingrelian, the spoken language of the inhabitants of the western Georgian region of Mingrelia. Most Georgians are traditionally Orthodox Christian in religion, but Ajaria is distinguished by its concentration of Georgian-speaking Sunni Muslims.

The Abkhazians, speakers of a Caucasian language related distantly, if at all, to Georgian, are also autochthonous inhabitants of their land, which lies in the northwestern corner of Georgia. Compared to these groups, the Ossetians are the relative newcomers, descendants of Iranian speakers who first entered what is now Georgia in the thirteenth century.

The historical relationship among these groups is hotly contested. The Georgians insist that Abkhazia and South Ossetia are traditionally and inseparably Georgian lands—indeed, they reject the very name South Ossetia, calling it instead Inner Kartli. The Ossetians insist on the validity of their eponymous region. And the Abkhazians argue that Abkhazia was traditionally a separate unit from Georgia, only occasionally united in a single state.

The truth, though murky, seems to be somewhere in between. Ancient and medieval western Georgian kingdoms, variously named Colchis, Lazica, and Egrisi, sometimes included Abkhazia and sometimes excluded it, but they were almost always separate from eastern Georgian kingdoms before the eleventh century. The first durably united Georgian kingdom came about when a prince of Abkhazia in the early eleventh century fell heir first to the other lands of western Georgia, then to the eastern Georgian kingdom of Kartli. What followed was a two-century golden age of Georgian unity punctuated by the reign of Georgia's most celebrated rulers, David the Builder (1089–1125) and Queen Tamar (1184–1212): both members of the originally Abkhazian royal house. Independent Georgia was then shattered by the Mongol invasion, and eventually it broke down into an eastern Georgian kingdom led by Kartli, and a series of quabbling principalities in western Georgia, one of which was Abkhazia. Western Georgia, including Abkhazia, soon came under Ottoman suzerainty, while eastern Georgia fell into the Iranian sphere. Both halves then fell to Russia in the early nineteenth century. The Georgians accepted Russian rule, but the Abkhazians repeatedly rebelled, prompting the Russian authorities to expel most of them in a series of great migrations the Abkhazians remember as the *mohajirstvo,* a tragedy with near-genocidal effects for their people.

The period of the Russian civil war (1918–1921) gave Georgia's ethnic conflicts their modern form. Georgia emerged as an independent state in 1918 and swiftly took control of both Abkhazia and South Ossetia. However, some in both regions resisted, aided by the Russian Bolsheviks. The Georgian government brutally suppressed these risings, prompting hostile memories that would last for decades. In March 1921, Soviet Russia invaded and took control of Georgia, briefly making Abkhazia a separate Soviet republic before subordinating it to Georgia in 1931. In the decades that followed, the Soviet government under Joseph Stalin and his henchman Lavrenty Beria—both ethnic Georgians—promoted policies that forced Georgia's minorities to learn Georgian and encouraged the migration of ethnic Georgians into sparsely populated Abkhazia.

After the deaths of Stalin and Beria in 1953, Abkhazians launched a series of protests against these Georgianization policies, finally winning a package of economic and cultural concessions after a round of enormous mass rallies conducted in 1978. Still, by 1989, Abkhazians constituted only 17.8 percent of the population of Abkhazia—hardly 2 percent of Georgia's population—so they continued to see themselves as being on the brink of extinction. While the South Ossetians were less inclined to mobilize as an ethnic group, they were also badly neglected in Georgia's economic development and social welfare budgets.

THE CONFLICT

In the late 1980s, Soviet leader Mikhail Gorbachev's reforms made it possible for the peoples of Georgia to begin expressing their political demands. Fiery Georgian nationalist dissidents, such as Zviad Gamsakhurdia, roused their audiences with emotional rhetoric claiming that Soviet repression and the demographic growth of Georgia's Muslim minorities threatened the very existence of the Georgian nation. By early 1989, Abkhazian and South Ossetian nationalist activists were increasingly concerned about this Georgian nationalist mood; the Abkhazians responded in a mass rally some 30,000 strong in March 1989 demanding independence from Georgia (though still within the Soviet Union). Georgians, considering this demand a threat to dismember their republic, responded with massive nationalist demonstrations that soon turned to demanding Georgian independence from the Soviet Union. With the demonstrations growing daily, the Communist government responded by forcibly suppressing a demonstration in Ibilisi on the night of April 9. Nineteen demonstrators were killed, sixteen of them women. The effect was to destroy the credibility of Georgia's Communist government, weakening its ability to rule.

Soon after these events occurred, ethnic Georgians living in Abkhazia began demanding separate institutions for themselves in all walks of life, undermining the Abkhazian cultural institutions created after the 1978 protests. The Abkhaz resisted, sparking a series of violent confrontations in July 1989 after Georgian and Abkhaz crowds clashed over a Georgian effort to divide Abkhaz State University. Two weeks of intermittent violence left at least 15 dead and 500 wounded.

This violence impelled both sides, and the Ossetians as well, to further nationalist mobilization. In August, the Georgian parliament passed a restrictive language law, prompting defiance from the South Ossetian parliament, which in turn prompted violent clashes between Georgians and Ossetians. Meanwhile, the Georgian nationalist movement had forced the holding of free elections in October 1990, which were won handily by nationalist leader Gamsakhurdia's Round Table/Free Georgia bloc. The extreme nationalist rhetoric of Gamsakhurdia and his even more extremist opponents further raised Ossetians' alarm, prompting South Ossetia to call for separation from Georgia. Georgian militants, loosely organized in a cluster of militia groups, responded by clamping a blockade around the South Ossetian capital of Tskhinvali in February 1991. Soviet authorities reacted at first by aiding the South Ossetians as a source of pressure on Gamsakhurdia's independence-minded government, but a few months later, Soviet Interior Ministry troops imposed a brief calm on the region. The status of those troops was, however, immediately put into sharp question when, in April 1991, the new Georgian parliament unanimously passed a declaration of independence from the Soviet Union.

Meanwhile, Gamsakhurdia's increasingly erratic behavior began to alienate large segments of the Georgian elite. When his attempts to establish dictatorial control over the Georgian government and media were criticized, he became increasingly paranoid, accusing virtually all critics of being traitors presumptively in the employ of the Soviet government. The crisis came in August, when first his premier, Tengiz Sigua, then the commander of his military force, National Guard commander Tengiz Kitovani, swung over to the opposition, with Kitovani taking most of his troops with him. Fighting over the course of the winter destroyed the center of Tbilisi and resulted in the deaths of more than 200 people before Gamaskhurdia was finally allowed to flee in January. Sigua, Kitovani, and warlord Jaba Ioseliani now formed a ruling council, and in March 1992 they invited former Soviet Foreign Minister Eduard Shevardnadze, Georgia's elder statesman, to join them to lend respectability to their regime. By May, Shevardnadze had negotiated a cease-fire with the Ossetians, though at the cost of conceding their de facto independence from Georgia.

Gamsakhurdia's mystical charismatic appeal, however, combined with Georgia's fractured regionalism to spark a civil war. Since Gamsakhurdia's family came from Mingrelia, his Zviadist movement found a base of support in that region, launching a persistent rebellion. Worse, when Kitovani and Ioseliani were sent to suppress the rebellion, the widespread looting committed by their ill-disciplined troops further alienated the Mingrelians from the Tbilisi authorities. Also, the large population of Mingrelians in Abkhazia gave the Zviadists a significant base in the eastern part of that region, a fact that would later spark the outbreak of the Georgian-Abkhazian war.

The stage for the conflict had been set earlier. In response to the discriminatory language law passed by the Georgian parliament in August 1990, the Abkhazian parliament—or, rather, its non-Georgian members—had voted to declare Abkhazian "sovereignty," as many other autonomous republics in Russia were doing. There followed a "war of laws" as Georgian authorities tried repeatedly to establish their authority over Abkhazia, while the Abkhazians moved increasingly toward complete separation from Georgia. The election of Gamaskhurdia in October, followed by the December elevation of Abkhazian firebrand Vladislav Ardzinba to leadership in Abkhazia, boded ill for compromise, as did the increasingly violent rhetoric on both sides. However, in the summer of 1991, Gamsakhurdia and Ardzinba agreed on a new governing scheme for Abkhazia, weighted to give disproportionate representation to ethnic Abkhaz. Fall elections confirmed Ardzinba and his nationalist followers in power in Abkhazia.

The new Abkhazian government immediately faced three crises: the breakup of the Soviet Union, the ouster of Gamsakhurdia and resulting intra-Georgian war on Abkhazia's border, and the obstinate opposition of Abkhazia's ethnic Georgians to the new political system. With Abkhazia's Georgians refusing to cooperate with his government at all, Ardzinba chose to ignore the Georgians' theoretical veto right and move increasingly toward full independence from Georgia. Meanwhile, in February 1992, Georgia returned to its 1921 constitution, which had no provision for Abkhazian autonomy. Abkhazia responded in July by returning to its 1925 constitution, according to which Abkhazia

was virtually independent of Georgia. Abkhazian offers to form a loose confederation were ignored.

Instead, Georgian warlords Kitovani and Ioseliani invaded Abkhazia in August 1992 under the pretense of searching for some Georgian officials kidnapped by Zviadists. Bypassing the alleged location of the hostage takers, however, Kitovani immediately marched on the Abkhazian capital of Sukhumi, while other Georgian troops made an amphibious landing near Gagra at Abkhazia's northwestern end, near the border with Russia. The Georgians quickly occupied the capital and five out of six of Abkhazia's districts, indulging as they had in Mingrelia in an orgy of looting, arson (aimed especially at Abkhazian cultural artifacts), rape, and murder. They also began clashing with the Russian troops who had been sent to evacuate Russian vacationers from Abkhazian resorts, causing casualties among Russian civilians.

After the initial Georgian advances, the conflict became deadlocked while the Abkhazians built up their strength with assistance from their ethnic kin in the North Caucasus, especially the well-armed, warlike Chechens, as well as Russian Cossack volunteers and the Abkhazian exile community (descendants of the *mohajirstvo* victims) in Turkey. Russian military and intelligence services also helped, in part to pressure Georgia into abandoning its anti-Russian foreign policy. With this help, the Abkhazians ended a brief September cease-fire with an early October counteroffensive that recaptured Gagra and the rest of northwestern Abkhazia. A December 1992 incident, in which Georgian forces shot down a Russian helicopter evacuating Russian refugees, further spurred the Russians into helping the Abkhaz. Russian warships began shelling Georgian targets, and Russian planes bombarded Georgian positions.

With the balance shifting, the Georgians agreed in July 1993 to another cease-fire, and in accordance with its terms they pulled back their heavy weapons from the front near Sukhumi. Two months later, the Abkhazians launched another counteroffensive, sweeping the Georgian forces out of Abkhazia and expelling most Georgians from the region, generating some 200,000 refugees amidst appalling atrocities. Resurgent Zviadist forces then disarmed the fleeing Georgian troops. Shevardnadze now submitted to Russia, joining the Russian-led Commonwealth of Independent States (CIS) and accepting the stationing of Russian troops in Georgia. In exchange, Russia provided logistical support enabling Georgian forces to defeat the Zviadists in the fall of 1993. A December 1993 Georgian-Abkhazian cease-fire agreement stopped most fighting in Abkhazia. Georgian partisans reopened the fighting in the late 1990s, however, prompting a May 1998 Abkhazian counteroffensive that expelled the remaining Georgians from Abkhazia's easternmost Gali district.

MANAGEMENT OF THE CONFLICT

The management of Georgia's conflicts by the Soviet authorities before the Soviet collapse included a number of notable successes, but also enormous failures. One success was Moscow's dispatch of Interior Ministry troops to Abkhazia in July 1989, which not only ended the rioting in the region, but also set the stage for three years of ethnic peace, if not calm. The refusal to grant Abkhazia's demands for separation from Georgia was necessary, and indeed it was part of the success: there were more Georgians than Abkhazians in Abkhazia, so any revision of Abkhazia's status clearly had to involve Georgian acquiescence and continued links to Georgia. Similarly, after flirting with support for the South Ossetians, the forceful Soviet government intervention in South

Ossetia in the spring of 1991 temporarily ended the violence in that region as well.

Moscow's biggest failure in conflict management was in its response to the nonviolent protests of the Georgians. Feeling besieged by the nationalist protesters demanding Georgian independence, Georgia's Communist leadership panicked, requesting the deployment of troops to suppress the demonstrators. The result was the April 9, 1989, crackdown in Tbilisi that discredited the government that had ordered it, while also demonstrating that the Communist authorities lacked the determination to maintain the repression. At that point, the victory of proindependence Georgian politicians became virtually inevitable.

Once the Soviet Union collapsed, Moscow turned from peacemaker to troublemaker. It was Russian help that enabled the South Ossetians to withstand Georgian pressure, and to force a cease-fire that maintained South Ossetia's de facto independence from Tbilisi's authority—though Moscow did kindly broker that cease-fire, which the Organization for Security and Cooperation in Europe (OSCE) helped to maintain. In Abkhazia, Russian actions were more ambiguous, but again it was increasing support from Russia that made possible the Abkhazians' military victory. However, the final Abkhazian offensive came when Moscow was preoccupied with a violent confrontation between President Boris Yeltsin and Russia's opposition-dominated parliament, so that offensive may not have been entirely Moscow's idea. On the other hand, the suspicious success and quick collapse of resurgent Zviadist forces in Mingrelia in the summer and fall of 1993 strongly hint at Russian involvement.

With the war effectively over, Russia turned its efforts to securing its influence on the peace. After Shevardnadze's submission to Russian influence, including the reintroduction of Russian military

ABKHAZIA, GEORGIA, 2002. Bombed apartment building in the heart of the city. Photo courtesy of Brad Camp and Dustin Bickle.

bases, Russian aid allowed Georgia quickly to suppress the Zviadists again. Without entirely ending its support for the Abkhazians, Russia clamped an economic blockade on Abkhazia. In May 1994, the Russians further secured the introduction of a Russian-dominated peacekeeping force in the region, under the auspices of the CIS but with the approval of the United Nations.

The UN's own diplomatic interventions were mostly ineffective. The UN secretary general appointed in May 1993 a special envoy for Georgia who brokered the July 1993 cease-fire, but it was the terms of that cease-fire that eventually facilitated the victory of the September Abkhazian offensive. The introduction of a small UN Observer Mission in Georgia (UNOMIG) to observe the cease-fire could do nothing to prevent its collapse, as the Abkhazians were determined to fight. The UN did, however, sponsor the negotiations leading to the December 1, 1993, Georgian-

Abkhazian cease-fire agreement and the May 1994 Separation of Forces agreement, which provided for the CIS peacekeepers and the reintroduction of UNOMIG. Those peacekeepers and observers helped keep the peace in the following years, though UN diplomacy achieved only minimal progress during the remainder of the decade.

SIGNIFICANCE

The troubles in Georgia affected mainly the peoples of Georgia. South Ossetia turned into an impoverished, informal appendage to Russia, while Abkhazia, blockaded from both sides, was reduced to a destitute, unrecognized microstate entirely dependent on smuggling for the survival of its diminishing population. While Georgia had achieved some political stability and some tenuous economic growth by the late 1980s, the blockade of Abkhazia closed its only direct rail link with

Russia, and Ajarian separatism deprived it of most customs revenue from its trade with Turkey. Georgia's ability to serve as a transit corridor for Caspian oil and gas resources en route to Turkey provided a glimmer of economic hope at century's end, but the unresolved separatist troubles, combined with government corruption and instability, severely handicap its future promise.

The only neighboring country seriously affected by Georgia's troubles was, ironically, Russia. By arming and training Chechen fighters in Abkhazia, Russia sowed the seeds of its own problems when those same Chechens led the resistance to Russia in Russia's Chechnya wars of the 1990s. Moreover, Russia could never rid itself of the suspicion that Georgia was helping the Chechens, embittering Russian-Georgian relations throughout the decade.

See also Soviet Union: The Nagorno-Karabakh Conflict; and Spain: Basque Nationalism and Conflict in Democratic Spain.

SUGGESTED READINGS

Chervonnaya, Svetlana. *Conflict in the Caucasus.* Translated by Ariane Chanturia. Glastonbury, England: Gothic Image Publications, 1994.

Goldenberg, Suzanne. *Pride of Small Nations: The Caucasus and Post-Soviet Disorder.* London: Zed Books, 1994.

Hewitt, George, ed. *The Abkhazians: A Handbook.* New York: St. Martin's Press, 1998.

Hunter, Shireen T. *The Transcausasus in Transition: Nation Building and Conflict.* Washington, D.C.: Center for Strategic and International Studies, 1994.

Jones, Stephen F. "Georgia: A Failed Democratic Transition." In *Nations and Politics in the Soviet Successor States,* edited by Ian Bremmer and Ray Taras. New York: Cambridge University Press, 1993.

Kaufman, Stuart J. *Modern Hatreds: The Symbolic Politics of Ethnic War.* Ithaca, N.Y.: Cornell University Press, 2001.

Lang, David Marshall. *A Modern History of Georgia.* New York: Grove Press, 1962.

Nasmyth, Peter. *Georgia: A Rebel in the Caucasus.* London: Cassell, 1992.

Ozhiganov, Edward. "The Republic of Georgia: Conflict in Abkhazia and South Ossetia." In *Managing Conflict in the Former Soviet Union: Russian and American Perspectives,* edited by Alexei Arbatov et al. Cambridge, Mass.: MIT Press, 1997.

Slider, Darrell. "Crisis and Response in Soviet Nationality Policy: The Case of Abkhazia." *Central Asian Survey* 4, no. 4 (1985): 51–68.

Suny, Ronald Grigor. *The Making of the Georgian Nation.* Bloomington: Indiana University Press, 1988.

Wright, John F., Suzanne Goldenberg, and Richard Schofield, eds. *Transcaucasian Boundaries.* New York: St. Martin's Press, 1996.

Soviet Union

The Nagorno-Karabakh Conflict

Stuart J. Kaufman

TIMELINE

95–55 B.C. Reign of King Tigran I, the greatest Armenian king.

A.D. 100s Caucasian Albanian kingdom emerges on the territory of modern Azerbaijan.

301–314 Armenia becomes the first country to adopt Christianity as national religion.

ca. 700 Arab invasion extinguishes Armenian autonomy and introduces Islam to the region.

1000s Seljuk Turks subjugate Armenia and begin a large-scale Turkic settlement of Azerbaijan.

1300s Five Armenian principalities in Karabakh achieve autonomy under the Persians and maintain it through the 1700s.

1813–1828 Russia annexes Azerbaijan and Armenia in Treaties of Gulistan and Turkmenchai.

1894–1896 Armenian uprising against Ottomans leads to large-scale massacres of Armenians.

1905–1906 Armeno-Tatar war, a guerrilla conflict between Armenians and Azerbaijanis, takes place.

1915 Ottoman government–organized genocide of Armenians commences.

1918–1920 Independent Armenia and Azerbaijan fight war over Karabakh and other regions.

1920–1921 Soviet Russia annexes Armenia and Azerbaijan and awards Karabakh to Azerbaijan.

1923 Nagorno-Karabakh Autonomous Oblast established within Soviet Azerbaijan.

1986 Beginning of glasnost prompts calls in Nagorno-Karabakh for transfer to Armenia.

1988 Mass protests held in Armenia and Nagorno-Karabakh; Sumgait anti-Armenian riots take place; wave of ethnic cleansing occurs in Armenia and Azerbaijan.

1990 Baku riot is crushed by Soviet troops; Armenian nationalists win Armenian election.

1991 Soviet military cracks down on Karabakh in Operation Ring; the collapse of the Soviet Union leads to Soviet withdrawal and independence of Armenia and Azerbaijan.

1992 Khojaly massacre initiates full-scale war; Azerbaijani Popular Front is voted in by election.

1993 Former Communist Party chief Heidar Aliev takes power in Azerbaijan after coup.

1994 A stable cease-fire is established in May, sealing de facto Armenian military victory.

1998 Armenian President Levon Ter-Petrosian is forced to resign for making concessions in peace talks.

From 1923 until 1991, Nagorno-Karabakh was an autonomous province in the Azerbaijani Soviet Socialist Republic (SSR), one of the constituent units of the Soviet Union. Populated mostly by ethnic Armenians, Nagorno (or "mountainous") Karabakh was separated from the Armenian SSR by only a thin strip of Azerbaijani land. It was this situation—geographically and politically located in Azerbaijan, but ethnically Armenian in population—that made Nagorno Karabakh a bone of contention between the two republics throughout Soviet history and beyond. The Soviet Union's repressive apparatus kept the Karabakh issue off the formal political agenda for decades, but when Mikhail Gorbachev's policy of glasnost opened the door to expression of previously taboo issues, Karabakh quickly emerged as one of the Soviet Union's most explosive problems. In February 1988, protestors numbering in the hundreds of thousands took over the Armenian capital of Erevan to demand the area's transfer to Armenia. Violence quickly followed, most notoriously in bloody anti-Armenian riots occurring in Sumgait, Azerbaijan, at the end of the month. When the Soviet Union broke up in 1991, spurred in no small part by nationalist rivalries among Armenians, Azerbaijanis, and Russians, the Karabakh conflict escalated further, from guerrilla warfare to full-scale conventional combat. By the time a cease-fire was reached in May 1994, the conflict had resulted in the deaths of some 20,000 people, the occupation of 20 percent of Azerbaijani territory by Karabakh Armenian forces, and ethnic cleansing on a scale wide enough to produce a million refugees and displaced persons. At century's end, the conflict remained unresolved.

HISTORICAL BACKGROUND

While the history of the contemporary Karabakh conflict goes back only a century or two, both sides trace its origins deep into antiquity, competing with each other with ever more ancient claims to control over the land.[1] The Armenians, a historically Christian people speaking a unique Indo-European language, first appear in history when they migrated to the southern Caucasus area in the sixth century B.C., where they established a major kingdom under King Tigran in the first century B.C. Armenian ideologues, however, claim to trace their history to a period hundreds or even thousands of years earlier. As for the Azerbaijanis, a Turkic-speaking people who are traditionally Shiite Muslim in religion, they can plausibly claim descent from the Turkic tribes that swept into the area after the eleventh-century invasion of the Seljuk Turks. Azerbaijani ideologues, however, trace their ancestry, and their claim to Karabakh, to their linguistically unrelated predecessors in the region, the Albanians (unrelated to modern Albanians), whose presence predated that of the Armenians.

All of these claims are further complicated by changes in borders over time. Ancient and medieval Armenia, for example, was centered in what is now eastern Turkey; modern Armenia and Karabakh were then, at best, peripheral Armenian lands. Azerbaijan, on the other hand, traditionally refers not only to the contemporary state, but also to the adjacent land in northwestern Iran that is also inhabited by Turkic-speaking Shiite Muslims. Thus the older kingdoms mentioned by Armenian and Azerbaijani ideologues may not even have included Karabakh.

The modern history of the Karabakh conflict begins with the 1813 Treaty of

Gulistan and the 1828 Treaty of Turkmen-chai, under which the Russian empire annexed the territories that later formed the Armenian and Azerbaijani SSRs. The second treaty also sparked a century-long process of migration that turned contemporary Armenia and Karabakh from predominantly Muslim into majority-Armenian lands. A century later came the Armenian "era of massacres," beginning with a series of massacres of Armenians organized by the Ottoman government in 1895–1896, and followed by the 1905–1906 Armeno-Tatar war, a series of battles and massacres between Armenians and (mostly Azerbaijani) Muslims in Russian-controlled lands in which Armenians were both victims and victimizers. The peak of horror was reached in the genocide of 1915, during which the Ottoman government instigated the expulsion or murder of over a million Armenians, virtually the entire population of the Armenian heartland, a tragedy that still dominates the consciousness of the Armenian people.[2]

Armenia and Azerbaijan emerged from the Russian Revolution as independent states in 1918 and quickly went to war over the control of Karabakh and other areas. Annexed by Soviet Russia in 1920, the two countries were made constituent republics of the Soviet Union, with Joseph Stalin fixing their borders and assigning Nagorno-Karabakh to Azerbaijan in the process. Sporadic Armenian protests about that decision, and about mistreatment and discrimination by Azerbaijani authorities, were ignored by the Soviet rulers in the following decades. At the same time, however, official propaganda in both Armenia and Azerbaijan encouraged nationalist feelings that were superficially Soviet, but aimed as much against each other as against the Soviet Union's foreign enemies. This atmosphere spurred a slow-motion exchange of populations in which most Azerbaijanis left Armenia, and most Armenians left parts of Azerbaijan.

THE CONFLICT

In this context, where a spark of mutual hostility was always present, Gorbachev's policy of glasnost provided the oxygen that turned the spark into a flame. Emboldened by the apparent opening, Karabakh Armenians launched petition drives in 1986–1987 calling for the transfer of their region to the Armenian SSR. When Moscow rejected the petitions in February 1988, the Karabakh Armenians tried again, with their local soviets (councils) and the Karabakh legislature also voting to request the transfer. When Moscow again demurred, mass protests in Armenia began. Opposition orators in Erevan, linking the Karabakh issue to other Armenian nationalist symbols, especially the genocide, found it easy to fan popular emotions to white heat in spite of the local Communist leadership's opposition. Their message resonated, and within a few days, they had mobilized as many as one million participants to attend a February 26 rally. Finally, Gorbachev agreed to examine the issue in exchange for an end to the rallies.

The next day, however, encouraged by orators with inflammatory reports of killings of Azerbaijanis and atrocities by Armenians, mobs of Azerbaijanis in Sumgait rampaged through that Azerbaijani city, killing dozens of Armenians—by some accounts hundreds—and raping and beating many more. In the city's atmosphere of ugly national chauvinism, the local police did nothing; in fact, they even released the few rioters arrested. The rioting was not stopped until Soviet Interior Ministry troops were introduced into the city; in the aftermath, most Armenians left Sumgait for good. The Soviet leadership in Moscow announced, a month later, a package of economic and cultural concessions for Nagorno-Karabakh, but the violence had already shown the inadequacy of such measures. Additional rallies in Erevan were prevented only by the deployment of thousands of troops in the city.

The rest of the year saw a continuing escalation of the political conflict and violence. On the political level, the republic legislatures joined in the nationalist causes. Armenia's legislature—responding to yet another mass street rally—voted to endorse Karabakh's request for transfer to Armenia; Azerbaijan's legislature quickly denied the request. Azerbaijanis, meanwhile, began rallying around the cause of the Sumgait rioters, whom some nationalists labeled "heroes" and whose punishment they protested. Later, Karabakh itself became for Azerbaijanis an emotion-laden symbol of Armenian plotting and of attempts to dismember Azerbaijan. By the end of the year, mounting violence and increasing migration reached a massive scale, with some 180,000 Armenians fleeing Azerbaijani cities, and 160,000 Azerbaijanis fleeing from villages in Armenia and Karabakh.[3] Nationalist extremists took over the media on both sides, and Azerbaijani attacks on Armenian commerce slowly evolved into an informal blockade of Nagorno-Karabakh, and later of Armenia itself. Trying to calm the situation, the Soviet government set up a commission, led by Russian politician Arkady Volsky and reporting directly to Moscow, to rule Karabakh. But the commission quickly alienated both sides, and it was disbanded at the end of the year, returning Karabakh to nominal Azerbaijani sovereignty.

The abolition of the commission triggered war. Armenia declared its annexation of Nagorno-Karabakh and appropriated a budget to implement its action. The response in the Azerbaijani capital of Baku was a massive anti-Armenian riot starting on January 12, 1990, and resulting in the ethnic cleansing of the city. After the violence ended, Soviet troops entered Baku to suppress the Azerbaijani nationalists who now controlled it; the result was a second bloodbath. Bands of Armenians and Azerbaijanis now began attacking each other across the Armenia-Azerbaijan border and in and around Karabakh, with Soviet Interior Ministry troops often aiding the Azerbaijanis. In the summer, the increasingly anti-Soviet population of Armenia elected the Armenian Nationalist Movement to take control of the country, and nationalist leader Levon Ter-Petrosian became chairman of the parliament and eventually president. The new government quickly formed an army but never gained complete control of the fighting, which was prosecuted largely by an autonomous Karabakh Armenian army.

The Azerbaijani government, led by Ayaz Mutalibov, still wholeheartedly pro-Soviet, relied instead on the Soviet army. After Armenia decided to boycott the 1991 referendum on preserving the Soviet Union, Moscow retaliated by launching Operation Ring, in which Soviet troops encircled, subjugated, and frequently ethnically cleansed troublesome Armenian villages in and near Nagorno-Karabakh. Horrified, Karabakh Armenian leaders began searching for a way to submit to Baku, but before they could do so, the August 1991 coup in Moscow sounded the death knell of the Soviet Union. After Soviet troops withdrew from the region, and both Armenia and Azerbaijan declared independence, the military momentum in the conflict swung to the side of the better-organized Armenians.

The disintegration of the Soviet army made more and heavier weapons available to both sides, leading to a further escalation of the fighting starting in early 1992. Azerbaijani forces quickly began using their newly inherited equipment to launch rocket and artillery attacks on Stepanakert, the capital of Nagorno-Karabakh. The Karabakh Armenians responded in February by capturing the bases from which the attacks were launched, brutally ethnically cleansing the town of Khojaly, and massacring probably hundreds of Azerbaijani civilians in the process. In the outcry in Baku after the catastrophe, Azerbaijani President Mutalibov was forced to resign, and elections were set. The provisional government that followed was unable to organize a proper defense, and Shusha, the largest ethnically Azerbaijani town in Na-gorno-Karabakh, was captured by the Ar-menians and its population was expelled in early April. In May, the Armenians cap-tured the town of Lachin between Kara-bakh and Armenia, permanently opening a supply corridor between the two.

Meanwhile, the June 1992 elections brought the leader of the nationalist Azer-baijani Popular Front, Abulfez Elchibei, into power as president in Baku. A quick Azerbaijani counteroffensive into northern Karabakh made some progress, but also began to sow the seeds of even worse prob-lems for Azerbaijan. The young hero of the offensive, Colonel Surat Husseinov, an erstwhile wool factory director, was made generalissimo of the Azerbaijani forces fighting in Karabakh; however, he began building an army loyal to himself rather than to the government. When Elchibei tried to fire Husseinov in February 1993, Husseinov pulled back his troops from combat, leaving the way open for an Ar-menian counteroffensive that not only re-versed the Azerbaijani gains of the previ-ous year but also captured the key Azerbaijani town of Kelbajar in April 1993, completing the Armenian occupa-tion of all Azerbaijani territory between Karabakh and Armenia. Elchibei, whose pro-Turkish policy had alienated Moscow, causing Russia to tilt back toward Arme-nia, did not survive the aftershock. Hus-seinov, allegedly directed by Moscow, now led a coup which toppled Elchibei in June, leading to the installation of Heidar Aliev, the Brezhnev-era Communist Party boss of Azerbaijan, as speaker of parliament and acting president; Husseinov was made premier. Although Aliev restored political stability to Azerbaijan, his government was unable to stem the tide of battle. Ar-menian offensives continued to capture Azerbaijani territory east and south of Karabakh, opening a direct link to Iran.

MANAGEMENT OF THE CONFLICT

Until the Soviet collapse in 1991, the government of the Soviet Union under Mikhail Gorbachev was responsible for managing the Karabakh conflict, a task it carried out with consistent ineptitude and intermittent malice. The March 1988 package of economic and cultural conces-sions offered to Nagorno-Karabakh was inadequate, and indeed, the Soviet govern-ment knew it would be: that is why it de-ployed troops to Erevan to head off antic-ipated rallies against it. The Armenians' main concern, especially in the aftermath of the Sumgait riots, was not about eco-nomics but about communal security, a concern the proposed measures did not ad-dress. Indeed, official Soviet efforts to stop the violence and punish violent offenders, Azerbaijani and Armenian, were too often halfhearted and ineffective. A quiet June 1988 proposal to upgrade the status and autonomy of the region, while leaving it inside Azerbaijan, might have been the ba-sis of a workable compromise, but because the details were skewed in favor of Azer-baijani interests, the Armenians rejected it. The 1989 Volsky commission alienated both sides, for example by drastically abridging the local Armenians' self-government, while at the same time re-fusing to protect ethnic Azerbaijanis in Stepanakert.

Soviet behavior in the January 1990 Baku riots was similarly self-defeating. In-stead of restoring order in Baku during the anti-Armenian riots and protecting the Ar-menian victims, the Soviet troops waited until the riots ended, then launched another bloodbath to suppress the Azerbaijani Pop-ular Front, further alienating both sides. Operation Ring in 1991, though presumably aimed at forcing the Armenian government to sign the Union Treaty and remain in the Soviet Union, instead escalated the conflict and reinforced the Armenian determination to secede.

Later, international efforts at mediation were no more successful until the conflict burned itself out; that is, until the Armenians achieved their objectives and the Azerbaijanis gave up trying to reverse the Armenian successes. Thus Russian President Boris Yeltsin and Kazakhstani President Nursultan Nazarbaev induced the two sides to sign an agreement in September 1991, but fighting resumed the next day. A spring 1992 Iranian-mediated cease-fire lasted a week, but it collapsed in the face of Western opposition to Iranian intervention and the unreadiness of either side to stop fighting. A more lasting effort at mediation began later in 1992, when the Conference on Security and Cooperation in Europe (CSCE, later OSCE) created the Minsk Conference on the conflict, which in turn gave rise to the Minsk Group of OSCE members. At the Budapest Summit held in December 1994, the OSCE decided to appoint Minsk Group cochairs who would lead the mediation effort; a year later, the OSCE designated a personal representative of the chairman-in-office to lead a permanent mission in the region.

While the cochairs and the personal representative actively attempted to broker a peace settlement, they made little progress beyond modest confidence-building measures, such as the exchange of prisoners. The most hopeful moment came in September 1997, when Presidents Ter-Petrosian and Aliev accepted a cochair's proposal for a phased approach to peace—one involving an Armenian withdrawal from Azerbaijani lands outside Karabakh, in exchange for an opening of economic ties in the region. The Karabakh authorities, however, adamantly rejected the idea of withdrawal from any territory before the status of Karabakh was settled; in the ensuing backlash, Ter-Petrosian was forced to resign, and he was replaced by Premier and former Karabakh President Robert Kocharian in 1998. Later, a series of bilateral meetings between Kocharian and Aliev in 1999 was undermined by the assassination of an Armenian premier and war hero, Vazgen Sarkisian, whose support for any peace deal would have been pivotal in gaining its acceptance in Armenia.

SIGNIFICANCE

The conflict over Nagorno-Karabakh played a major role in spurring the breakup of the Soviet Union. While the nationalities problem was a growing issue in Gorbachev-era Soviet Union, the outbreak of the Karabakh conflict in February 1988 marked a series of firsts in what was to become the accelerating decline of Soviet official control over the non-Russian republics of the Soviet Union. The votes cast by the Karabakh local and regional legislatures for transfer of the territory to Armenia marked the first time official Soviet legislative bodies openly challenged Soviet policy on a nationalities issue. The Sumgait riot, while not the first major outbreak of ethnic violence—the December 1986 riots in Alma Ata, Kazakhstan, occurred on a similar scale—was the bloodiest ethnic clash up to that time.

Even more important, the continuing conflict and escalating violence turned the Karabakh conflict into the only example of an ongoing ethnic war inside the Soviet Union. The inability of the Gorbachev leadership to control the situation graphically illustrated the Soviet state's weakening control, serving in a way as the death knell of the Soviet state. The Soviet system's weakness was in large measure economic and political, not just ethnic or nationalist, but it was the nationality problem that caused the country to disintegrate. The Karabakh conflict, which both discredited the Soviet state and illustrated its weakness, helped open the door to other strident nationalist demands that literally tore the country apart.

After the Soviet collapse, the conflict over Nagorno-Karabakh remained one of the central facts of political life in the Caucasus. While it has remained unresolved, it has stymied the ability of both Armenia and Azerbaijan to develop economically and politically. It became the dominant political issue in both countries—the emotional symbol of self-defense against genocide for the Armenians, the cause of up to a million refugees and displaced persons for Azerbaijan—crowding other urgent issues of state building, nation building, and foreign relations off the political agenda. The continuing enmity and military spending have prevented both from taking advantage of their different but considerable prospects for economic development. Azerbaijan has oil and gas, and Armenia has access to the capital accumulation of the diaspora; however, investors are deterred by the instability and poverty that comes from the continuing confrontation. Furthermore, the continuing weakness of both states, and their continuing need for military help, has left both vulnerable to manipulation by those parts of the Russian government trying to expand their influence in the region. Armenia also faces a critical demographic problem, as its economic enfeeblement has driven a significant portion of its population into exile in search of work. In short, as long as the conflict remains unresolved, it will continue to be a curse on both countries.

See also Soviet Union: The Ethnic Conflicts in Georgia; Yugoslavia: Ethnic Conflict and the Meltdown in Kosovo; and Yugoslavia: The Deconstruction of a State and Birth of Bosnia.

NOTES

1. Stephan H. Astourian, "In Search of Their Forefathers: National Identity and the Historiography and Politics of Armenian and Azerbaijani Ethnogeneses," in *Nationalism and History: The Politics of Nation Building in Post-Soviet Armenia, Azerbaijan and Georgia,* ed. Donald V. Schwartz and Razmik Panossian (Toronto: University of Toronto Centre for Russian and East European Studies, 1994), 47 ff.
2. Competing views of these events are presented in Christopher J. Walker, ed., *Armenia and Karabagh: The Struggle for Unity* (London: Minority Rights Publications, 1991); and Tadeusz Swietochowski, "National Consciousness and Political Orientations in Azerbaijan, 1905–1920," in *Transcaucasia, Nationalism and Social Change: Essays in the History of Armenia, Azerbaijan and Georgia,* rev. ed., ed. Ronald Grigor Suny (Ann Arbor: University of Michigan Press, 1996).
3. Stuart J. Kaufman, *Modern Hatreds: The Symbolic Politics of Ethnic War*. Ithaca, NY: Cornell University Press, 2001, 67.

SUGGESTED READINGS

Croissant, Michael P. *The Armenia-Azerbaijan Conflict: Causes and Implications.* Westport, Conn: Praeger, 1998.

Goldenberg, Suzanne. *Pride of Small Nations: The Caucasus and Post-Soviet Disorder.* London: Zed Books, 1994.

Goltz, Thomas. *Azerbaijan Diary: A Rogue Reporter's Advantures in an Oil-Rich, War-Torn, Post-Soviet Republic.* Armonk, N.Y.: M. E. Sharpe, 1998.

Kaufman, Stuart J. *Modern Hatreds: The Symbolic Politics of Ethnic War.* Ithaca, NY: Cornell University Press, 2001, chap. 3.

Libaridian, Gerald J., ed. *The Karabakh File: Documents and Facts on the Region of Mountainous Karabakh, 1918–1988.* Cambridge, Mass.: Zoryan Institute, 1988.

Malkasian, Mark. *Gha-ra-bagh! The Emergence of the National Democratic Movement in Armenia.* Detroit: Wayne State University Press, 1996.

Saroyan, Mark. *Minorities, Mullahs and Modernity: Reshaping Community in the Former Soviet Union.* Berkeley: University of California Press, 1997.

Schwartz, Donald V., and Razmik Panossian, eds.

Nationalism and History: The Politics of Nation Building in Post-Soviet Armenia, Azerbaijan and Georgia. Toronto: University of Toronto Centre for Russian and East European Studies, 1994.

Suny, Ronald Grigor. *Looking Toward Ararat: Armenia in Modern History.* Bloomington: Indiana University Press, 1993.

Suny, Ronald Grigor, ed. *Transcaucasia, Nationalism and Social Change: Essays in the History of Armenia, Azerbaijan and Georgia,* rev. ed. Ann Arbor: University of Michigan Press, 1996.

Walker, Christopher J., ed. *Armenia and Karabagh: The Struggle for Unity.* London: Minority Rights Publications, 1991.

Spain

Basque Nationalism and Conflict in Democratic Spain

Roland Vazquez

TIMELINE

1029 Sancho the Elder incorporates the western Basque territory into the kingdom of Navarre.

1200 The separation of Navarre and Basque provinces begins through Castilian conquest.

1379 Basque province of Vizcaya is joined in marriage to the kingdom of Castile.

1512 Navarre is absorbed by Castile.

1545 First book is published in the Basque language.

1717 Royal decree to include Basque imports within a common Spanish tariff system leads to a bloody uprising by Basque peasants, with the original customs stations being returned.

1833 First Carlist War begins; lasts until 1840.

1873 Second Carlist War begins; upon its conclusion in 1876, customs control is moved to state borders.

1895 Basque Nationalist Party (PNV) and movement are founded by Sabino Arana.

1898 Spain's last colonies are lost as a result of the Spanish-American War.

1936 First Basque autonomy statute passes, and Basque government is formed; Spanish Civil War begins.

1939 Spanish Civil War ends, and Francisco Franco assumes power. Nearly 150,000 Basques are forced into exile.

1959 Ekin cultural group splits away from PNV's youth group to form Basque Homeland and Freedom (ETA).

1968 ETA member Txabi Etxebarrieta kills civil guard and is killed; ETA retaliates by killing a police inspector.

1970 In the Burgos trial, 16 are tried and convicted; 6 are sentenced to death, but death sentences ultimately are commuted.

1973 ETA assassinates Spanish Prime Minister Carrero Blanco, the heir apparent to Franco.

1975 Franco dies, and King Juan Carlos is appointed successor.

1979 Basque Autonomy Statute is approved.

1983 Operations of the anti-ETA Antiterrorist Liberation Groups (GAL) paramilitary forces begin.

1995 Corpses of two former ETA members, killed by the GAL, are discovered in a Spanish cemetery.

1997 The assassination of Miguel Angel Blanco leads to the anti-ETA Forum of Ermua; the executive committee of the radical nationalist coalition is imprisoned for its pro-ETA propaganda.

1998 Highest ranking Spanish officials to date are convicted in GAL affair; the ETA declares a cease-fire; and the Lizarra Pact is signed by nationalist parties and other groups.

1999 The ETA resumes attacks.

2000 First new victim dies since resumption of the attacks. Number reached 38 by mid-2002.

Article 2 of the Spanish constitution affirms Spain's indivisibility, while recognizing its peoples' right to self-determination. This juridical paradox has at its heart the long, unfinished process of Spain's state crafting in the face of the sometimes nationalist demands of its non-Castilian peoples. Among these demands, the most virulent for the past century (and, arguably, longer) have been those of the Basques.

In its maximalist expanse, the Basque country comprises seven provinces or historic territories: three to the north of the French-Spanish border and four to the south. The three in France—Labourd, Basse Navarre, and Soule—are subsumed within the *département* of the Pyrénées Atlantiques. The four in Spain account for over four-fifths of the Basque population and Basque territory. Three, Alava, Vizcaya, and Guipúzcoa, make up the Basque Autonomous Community (BAC), the result of a 1979 statute. The fourth, Navarre, is an autonomous community as a result of a subsequent statute. As the "Basque Ulster," its noninclusion in the BAC is a point of contention among nationalists.[1] The insurgent separatist ETA (Basque Homeland and Freedom) remains the best-known Basque acronym, especially in the face of its increased violence after the state's post-Franco transition to democracy.

HISTORICAL BACKGROUND

The much debated ethnic charter for Basque political distinctiveness is rooted in prehistory, with Cromagnon remains in the western Pyrenees Mountains suggesting (albeit not definitively) a direct connection with the historical population. The Basques are distinguished from the Spanish and French populations by different blood-type ratios. Euskera, the Basque language, is a non–Indo European, agglutinative language alone in its family, with the only possible relatives being those of the northern Caucasus. Although only a quarter of the population speaks it, Euskera's distinctiveness is vital to the sense of Basque exceptionalism.

Historically, the Basques were never fully integrated into the Roman system. Similarly, and unlike a majority of the Iberian Peninsula after the eighth-century Arab expansion, Basque territory was not conquered by the Muslims, although they did briefly take the kingdom of Pamplona (later Navarre's capital). By the tenth century, a small but unified Navarre would be a regional power. In 1029 Sancho the Elder incorporated the western Basque territory (roughly coterminous with the BAC) into Navarre—the first time that all Basque-inhabited land south of the Pyrenees was part of a single political sovereignty. The majority of the populations of Navarre, Vizcaya, Guipúzcoa, north across the Pyrenees into Gascogny, and south into Castile (the heart of modern Spain) were Basque speaking. They had no sense of political consciousness as such, however, since the language was rejected as a vehicle for high culture. Nevertheless, from at least the late tenth century (and unmodified since the mid-twelfth century), local and later provincial agreements called *fueros* guaranteed them an exceptional degree of territorial control.

After Sancho's death, his kingdom was split among his three sons, to Navarre's detriment. In the twelfth century, most of the present BAC came under the control of the kingdom of Castille and was thus separated from Navarre. The following two centuries witnessed a sharp recession of Basque-speaking territory.

In 1379 Vizcaya was joined to Castile through marriage. While remaining independent, Vizcaya recognized the crown within the limits of its own local autonomy and custom. The Spanish project was completed in 1512 when King Ferdinand of Aragon conquered Navarre and incorporated it into an expanding imperial state in the process of becoming a colonial power. This was a tenuous balancing act, however, given the kingdom's internal cultural and political pluralism. Among Spanish subjects, the Basques would, through their *fueros,* benefit through singular exemptions and distinct legal status. They would also be major players in the rising Spanish colonial project of conquest and trade.

In 1659 France and Spain signed the Treaty of the Pyrenees, which strictly determined the boundary division. This event was important in a trajectory that would pull apart the two segments of the Basque territory.

Following the War of Spanish Succession (1702–1713), Navarre and the Basque provinces accepted the inheritance of the Spanish crown by a junior branch of the French Bourbon dynasty. The crown, however, soon attempted to override the fiscal exemptions granted by the *fueros* by including Basque imports within a common Spanish tariff system. The reaction, a mass revolt in Vizcaya and Guipúzcoa, was bloodily suppressed, but the former customs borders were restored.

Meanwhile, an essentially cultural development took center stage in shaping the Basque question. Although Basque was and would remain (until the late twentieth century) largely an oral language, the first book was published in 1545. In 1571 Es-

taban de Garibay published a compendium explaining Basque origins, arguing that the area was populated by Tubal (a grandson of Noah), and Euskera was one of the original languages in the Tower of Babel. In the eighteenth century, a Jesuit, Father Manuel Larramendi, advanced theories of Basque exceptionalism, and he published the first Euskera grammar. In 1766 the Basque Society of Friends of the Country was born; this transatlantic economic association was the first to use the term "Basque nation."

When Prince Fernando acceded to the throne on the eve of the French invasion and war of independence (1808–1814), he decreed full restoration of the *fueros;* however, his actions were entirely negated by the liberal constitution of 1812. A generation later, following the disbanding of regional parliaments, the support for Don Carlos's claim to the Spanish throne led to the Carlist War (1833–1840), which was regarded in the Basque country as a defense of their traditions.

From 1873 to 1876, increasing anti-clericalism throughout Spain produced the backlash of another Carlist revolt. As a result of this second defeat, there followed a definitive redrawing of Spain's customs borders and, thus, the sounding of the death knell for the *fueros.*

At least in part because the redrawing of the customs borders significantly hurt the Basques in European markets, a postwar environment of great upheaval ensued. Rapid growth, especially through mid-century Vizcayan industrialization, encouraged widespread Spanish migration. Among the Basques, a sense of cultural displacement arose, especially on the heels of the two unsuccessful wars.

The century's last great event was the Spanish-American War of 1898, as a result of which Spain lost its last colonies. The impact of empire upon Spain and the Basque country alike had been great. So, too, was the effect of its loss on political and economic alignment and sense of national identity. Important sectors of the Basque population realized that postimperial Spain could not be counted upon as their "national" reference point.

From Regionalism to Nationalism

In 1895 Sabino Arana founded the Basque Nationalist Party (PNV). Arana's father had supported Carlism, to his personal detriment. An ardent Catholic and not a Euskera speaker, Sabino devoted himself to Basque studies. He preached a gospel of ethnic and cultural purity mixed with religious zeal after his political epiphany, denying the legitimacy of Spanish rule. A feeble but charismatic figure, Arana was revered by his followers. By the time of his premature death in 1903, Arana had single-handedly founded Basque nationalism as a cult movement, albeit one with a limited infrastructure and following. He remained the movement's saint and martyr.

Of negligible strength in its early years, the movement spread from its urban Bilbao cradle into the countryside. It was beset with major dilemmas that subsequently marked its internal dynamics: to what degree nationalism should be connected to its Catholic roots, and how extreme secessionist demands could or should be. (This second issue continues to mark the political trajectory of Basque nationalism.) Although statewide humiliation over the defeat of Spain's army at the hands of the rebel forces in Spain's Moroccan protectorate was a valuable political weapon for opponents of the constitutional monarchy and provided much of the impetus for Primo de Rivera's subsequent authoritarian regime (1923–1930), disorder and political dissidence were also factors. The regime's ambivalent policy of prohibiting regional political activity while allowing cultural association sowed the seeds for the subsequent eruption of Basque nationalism.

At the beginning of the second republic in 1931, the PNV did not command a Basque majority. Nationalism was one vortex of a political triangle, with the state-centralizing Spanish right and the anticonfessional Spanish left. None of the three could impose its will. In the republic's twilight, nationalists secured an autonomy statute from the left-led state government, resulting in the formation of a regional government amidst increasing statewide unrest.

With the 1936 outbreak of the Spanish Civil War, choosing sides was unavoidable. Basque nationalists again cast their lot with the Spanish left. (Some PNV leaders entertained thoughts of siding with the Spanish right as a result of leftist attacks against the Church.) The war's darkest day for the Basques was April 26, 1937, when the German Condor Legion, allied to General Francisco Franco's cause, bombed Gernika. The attack converted the Basque town into an international symbol of peace and inspired Picasso's painting "Guernica" (the Spanish name for Gernika). When Bilbao fell two months later, it was basically over for the Basques, although the war continued into 1939. In retribution for their pro-republican posture, Vizcaya and Guipúzcoa were declared "traitor provinces." Executions and property confiscation were rampant. The number of Basques in exile approached 150,000. The use of Euskera was prohibited, and the outflow of capital and resources from these industrialized provinces was striking as late as the early 1950s.

The PNV-led Basque government in exile pinned its hopes on external intervention, especially given the international isolation of Franco's regime. Cold War geopolitics, however, led to an about-face of American attitudes in 1947, and U.S. military bases subsequently found their way into Spain.

By the 1950s, its strategy had admittedly failed, and the PNV was increasingly delegitimized in the nationalist community. This time also marked the beginning of two decades of industrial upsurge in Spain and a new wave of Spanish migration into Basque territory. In 1959 the cultural group "Ekin" broke its ties with the party's youth group to form the ETA, at that point an intellectually oriented group which debated the Basque condition. Cultural resurgence began in the early 1960s, perhaps most notably through the clandestine Basque-language primary and secondary schools.

By this time, Franco's Spain had gradually been opening to foreign capital and economic development. It was eager for inclusion on the European and world scenes. As a result, there were corresponding international expectations for civil and political freedoms in Spain. Basque nationalism's political resurgence came in the late 1960s and early 1970s, with the ETA and the PNV building infrastructures.

THE CONFLICT

In 1968, an ETA member, Txabi Etxebarrieta, shot a civil guard to death at a roadblock, and then he was killed. His "heroic" death brought new recruits, and the ETA retaliated by assassinating a police commissioner. A state of emergency was declared in Guipúzcoa and later was extended statewide. Arrests and torture were widespread. Manzanas's death resulted in the 1970 Burgos trial, at which 16 were tried and convicted for ETA activity; six of them were sentenced to death. The trial was an international public relations nightmare for the Franco regime, and the death sentences were commuted.

In 1973 Carrero Blanco, Franco's self-appointed successor, was killed in a bombing. The ETA's most stunning attack to that date potentially changed Spain's political future and marked the type of action for which the organization would become notorious. Most Basques regarded the ETA's violence as less of a threat than that of the security forces, which killed 22 people during demonstrations or at police checkpoints in the four Basque provinces in 1974 and 1975. Opposition groups, while disagreeing with the ETA's methods, accepted that they were in response to greater state violence, and they expected the ETA's violence to cease under any new regime.

Political Transition and Beyond

After Franco's death in 1975, the question of whether to demand separatism or accept reform dominated the Spanish political process. In many quarters, the strong Basque sense of need for separateness galvanized into a separatist desire for independence, and among the Basques in general the hope for change was pervasive among both nationalists and other opposition groups.

A series of post-Franco amnesty decrees was followed by the broad 1978 amnesty law for political prisoners not convicted of blood crimes. On the other hand, by the time of Spain's first post-Franco elections held in mid-1977, Madrid was focusing on pacifying the Basque country, and subsequently the number of Basque political prisoners tripled between December 1978 and January 1981.

Basque nationalist forces were united in their public calls for independence and amnesty. When the Spanish constitution was ratified by referendum in 1978, most Basques followed the PNV's lead and abstained. One year later, the 1979 federalism statute, negotiated by Spanish and PNV leaders, was approved by the Basque electorate, paving the way for the establishment of an autonomous community and government in the Basque provinces.

Meanwhile, as the conflict between Madrid and the Basque provinces subsided after the Basques received their own federal autonomy in post-Franco Spain, intra-Basque conflict intensified, and ETA attacks became increasingly indiscriminate. Both the number of victims and public concern grew, leading to increased condemnation of the ETA by the PNV and other nationalist groups.[2] ETA demanded "revolutionary tax" payments from Basque industrialists and began kidnapping them. In the escalating violence, in 1979, one wing of the ETA bombed two Madrid train stations and the airport on the same day. Although this wing abandoned its arms in 1980 after negotiations with the Spanish government, violent activity increased throughout the 1980s, with 86 deaths in 1980 and 54 as late as 1987. The 1987 Hipercor supermarket bombing in Barcelona resulted in 21 deaths and 40 injuries. Perhaps even more disturbing for the government was the Zaragosa Civil Guard headquarters attack, which left 11 dead and 40 wounded. The 1986 ETA assassination of Dolores González Katarain, or "Yoyes," a former leader and ETA-designated "traitor," upon her return from exile is also noteworthy, serving as it did as notice to others of ETA's intolerance toward anyone who might contemplate following her example.

Nor could ETA claim a monopoly over the use of violence. The most salient post-transition moment occurred with the unsuccessful 1981 military coup in the Spanish parliament led by Colonel Antonio Tejero, which came about largely in response to the post-Franco government's handling of the regional question. It showed the extent to which any Spanish government would have to take a military and right-wing backlash into account in configuring the state.

State antiterrorist activity, both legal and extralegal, also grew harsher. Into the late 1970s, antiseparatist paramilitary forces assassinated several ETA activists. In 1983 the Antiterrorist Liberation Groups (GAL) was formed. The GAL stood came into being after the 1982 accession to state power of the Socialist Party, which had been in the anti-Franco opposition. In addition, the GAL systematically received state funding in an acknowledged political democracy. Through 1986 the GAL was responsible for 24 killings and 25 injuries. The organization withered largely as a result of French government pressure against it (much of the GAL's activity occurred across the border) and a growing French willingness to extradite and expel suspected ETA members, something France was previously reluctant to do given the reputation of the Spanish police for torture.

In 1988 a Spanish police subcommissioner was imprisoned for GAL activity; in 1991, he and his lieutenant were sentenced to over 100 years in prison apiece. The following year, recognizing that the protagonists of the "dirty war" had acted from above, courts ordered the state to indemnify victims. The scandal was revived in 1995 with the identification of the corpses of two former ETA members hidden in a cemetery in southern Spain. They had been tortured, dismembered, and shot in the head. In 1998 José Barrionuevo and Rafael Vera, the Spanish interior minister and the secretary of state during the GAL's high point, were imprisoned. The GAL's legacy has been a backlash of violence, new ETA adherents, and a general Basque skepticism of policy overtures coming from Madrid.

Recent years have witnessed numerous, widely publicized ETA activities. The first was the ETA's July 1997 kidnapping and assassination of an Ermua, Vizcaya, town councilman, Miguel Angel Blanco. This was one of a series of ETA attacks conducted against Spanish Conservatives (particularly against municipal representatives), which escalated after the Conservatives acceded to state power. When the Spanish government refused the ETA's demand that Basque prisoners be transferred to Basque prisons, the kidnappers shot their victim in the head. His brutal death produced a mass outcry and gave rise to the Forum of Ermua, an initiative marked by aggressive rhetoric against negotiating with Basque extremists. In December 1997, the entire radical nationalist coalition executive committee was incarcerated for collaborating with ETA, and its newspaper and radio station were ordered closed down by Spanish courts. Basque nationalism had thus been put on the defensive, and the ETA and radical nationalism have been stigmatized and isolated.

In September 1998, the pendulum swung again. After extended talks, the three Basque nationalist parties and other organizations signed the Lizarra Pact. Nationalists argued that Lizarra was a forum for cooperation. Those not participating (notably, the two major state parties) countered that it was a closing of fronts. A month before the Basque elections were held, citing the Irish agreements, the ETA announced a "total and indefinite truce." The Lizarra Pact ultimately led to a tripartite Basque nationalist coalition government (including hard-liners) in the Basque region.

The tide would turn yet again, however, with mutual accusations of duplicity between Madrid and the Basque provinces following the allegedly fortuitous arrest of

VITORIA, SPAIN, February 22, 2002. Firemen try to extinguish a burning car after a local Socialist Party leader and his bodyguard were killed in a car bombing blamed on the ETA. Photo by David Aguilar, © AFP/CORBIS.

one of the ETA's negotiators in France, public identification of the secret intermediary (a bishop), and government charges that the ETA was rearming. In November 1999, in a victory for its hard-line faction, the ETA broke off its cease-fire. The radical nationalist coalition abandoned parliament, leaving a tainted minority nationalist government. In January 2000, blood once more began to flow.

MANAGEMENT OF THE CONFLICT

The 1998–1999 negotiations between the Spanish government and ETA were the twentieth century's last of a series. The degree of each party's sincerity is open to speculation. The 1990s saw the introduction of new methods of influencing the bargaining process by both parties, with the rise of radical youth street violence creating a weapon not directly traceable to ETA and with the government introducing the questionable penitentiary policy of dispersing imprisoned ETA members in a divide-and-conquer strategy.

Various actors have attempted to extract political capital from the conflict and limit the damage to themselves. Basque terrorism seemed to be the Interior Ministry's only issue (whether the Socialists or Conservatives govern in Madrid), in spite of the increasingly violent street crime and the wave of illegal African immigration, and other issues challenging the skills of those in office. For its part, the degree to which the ETA has maintained its position and regenerated itself owes to its long-standing strategy of "action-repression-action" in attempting to portray itself as the champion of the Basque cause, encourage recruits, and influence public support for independence. Despite their belief in the ETA's usefulness as a pressure mechanism on Madrid into the late 1980s, the PNV and other moderate Basque nationalist groups have increasingly condemned violence because these techniques have become politically burdensome rather than beneficial. Many of these actions and postures reveal that intragroup mobilization strategies and interests within the Basque community are at least as important to political bargaining as the corresponding intergroup dynamics between the Basques and Madrid, which invariably receive the greater attention.

The overall dynamics at the century's end made it likely that the combined support for nationalist parties would dip below a parliamentary majority for the first time in the post-Franco era, potentially facilitating the creation of a coalition Basque government that shuts out the nationalists. On the other hand, given ETA's continuing attacks and the state's hard-line policies, this scenario could be inopportune to resolving the conflict still on going in Spain's Basque country.

SIGNIFICANCE

Aside from Northern Ireland, the Basque conflict has been the most virulent ethnonationalist conflict in Western Europe over the past century. It conjures up images of Balkanization in the very heart of the "civilized" world. Students of politics often note the discrepancy between the political newness of modern nationalist movements and the antiquity of their claims. What all such movements share is some sort of charter or mission that allows them to resonate with a significant segment of the population and acquire a momentum all their own.

The markers of "Basqueness" (ethnicity, language, birthplace, will, political affiliation, place of livelihood) are currently being debated amidst a sea of contention in a changing Basque society: How can an ethnic group be defined, to what extent does this justify a distinct political entity, and what means are necessary or accept-

able? Basque concerns have played a determining role in configuring post-Franco Spain, and the BAC is currently the most politically and financially autonomous region within the European Union.

If violence potentially related to a social cleavage does occur, escalation can be avoided only if there is a mutually acknowledged framework to define it and respond to it in other terms. That at the end of the twentieth century the ETA was no longer able to define violence in "nationalist" terms was a measure of the degree to which the ETA's goals had come to lack legitimacy among Basques, however they define their national identification.[3]

See also Canada: The Nationalist Movement in Quebec; France: Ethnic Conflict and the Problem of Corsica; and United Kingdom: The Conflict in Ulster.

NOTES

1. As in other contested lands, the decision of how to name places is itself part of the polemic. I take a middle ground, using Basque spellings when referring to the BAC, French when referring to territories in France, and Spanish for Navarre.
2. PNV rhetoric would become increasingly obtuse, even more so after its 1986 split, which limited its ability and legitimacy as an arbiter in the conflict.
3. One barometer is identification of the members of ETA as either patriots or idealists; a combined 48 percent of Basque polled in 1978 and 50 percent in 1979 expressed this view; the number fell to 23 percent in 1989, 22 percent in 1993, and 24 percent in 1996. See Francisco J. Llero Ramo, "Basque Polarization: Between Autonomy and Independence," *Nationalism & Ethnic Politics* 5, nos. 3, 4 (Autumn/Winter 1999): 111. The last of these statistics are prior to a probable realignment in public opinion after the death of Miguel Angel Blanco.

SUGGESTED READINGS

Clark, Robert P. *Negotiating with ETA: Obstacles to Peace in the Basque Country, 1975–1988.* Reno: University of Nevada Press, 1990.

Collins, Roger. *The Basques*. Oxford, England: Basil Blackwell, 1986.

Conversi, Daniele. *The Basques, the Catalans, and Spain: Alternative Routes to Nationalist Mobilization*. Reno: University of Nevada Press, 1997.

Díez Medrano, Juan. *Divided Nations: Class, Politics, and Nationalism in the Basque Country and Catalonia*. Ithaca, N.Y.: Cornell University Press, 1995.

Douglass, William A., ed. *Basque Politics: A Case Study in Ethnic Nationalism*. Reno: Basque Studies Program, 1985.

Douglass, William A., et al., eds. *Basque Politics and Nationalism on the Eve of the Millennium*. Reno: Basque Studies Program, 1999.

Jacob, James E. *Hills of Conflict: Basque Nationalism in France*. Reno: University of Nevada Press, 1994.

Linz, Juan J. "Early State-Building and Late Peripheral Nationalism Against the State: The Case of Spain." In *Building States and Nations,* edited by S. N. Eisenstadt and Stein Rokkan, 2: 32–116. Beverly Hills, Calif.: Sage Publication, 1973.

Llera Ramo, Francisco J. "Basque Polarization: Between Autonomy and Independence." *Nationalism & Ethnic Politics* 5, nos. 3, 4 (Autumn/ Winter 1999): 101–20.

Payne, Stanley G. *Basque Nationalism*. Reno: University of Nevada Press, 1975.

Shabad, Goldie, and Francisco J. Llera Ramo. "Political Violence in a Democratic State: Basque Terrorism in Spain." In *Terrorism in Context,* edited by Martha Crenshaw, 410–69. University Park: Pennsylvania State University Press, 1995.

Sullivan, John. *ETA and Basque Nationalism: The Fight for Euskadi 1890–1986*. London: Routledge, 1988.

Valle, Teresa del. *Korrika: Basque Ritual for Ethnic Identity*. Reno: University of Nevada Press, 1994.

Zulaika, Joseba. *Basque Violence: Metaphor and Sacrament*. Reno: University of Nevada Press, 1988.

Sri Lanka

Tamil-Sinhalese Conflict in India's Backyard

Joseph R. Rudolph, Jr.

TIMELINE

ca. 545 B.C. The island's indigenous people are conquered by Buddhists from India, the forebears of contemporary Sri Lanka's Sinhalese majority.

16th century Portuguese take control of the island of Ceylon.

17th century Dutch control displaces Portuguese control of the island.

1796 The British East India Company seizes the coastal towns.

1802 The Dutch cede control of the island to Britain; British control of Ceylon is consolidated by 1814.

1815 Ceylon becomes a British colony.

1920 Local representative institutions are allowed to develop.

1926 During independence struggle, nationalist leader Solomon West Bandaranaike describes Ceylon's future in federal terms.

1948 On February 4, Ceylon gains independence.

1956 The passage of Sinhala Only Act ends status of English as official language, placing Tamils at a disadvantage in obtaining jobs in the civil service.

1957 Prime Minister Bandaranaike agrees to some autonomy for Tamils; Sinhalese backlash to communal violence occurs.

1958 In response to the communal violence, Bandaranaike rejects federalism as devolution option.

1958–1973 Despite intermittent communal violence, language laws and other pro-Sinhalese reforms are enacted.

1972 The country's name is changed to the Republic of Sri Lanka.

1976 Given Sinhalese reluctance to reform state, Tamils adopt a separatist agenda; insurgent activity increases in Tamil north.

1977 Tamil United Liberation Front (TULF) wins all seats in north and east running on a separatist platform.

1978 On August 16, a new constitution is adopted by Sinhalese majority. Parliamentary model is replaced by a presidential system.

1981 Country is shaken by communal violence for the fifth time since the mid-1950s; the government holds informal talks with TULF on ways to defuse communal violence.

1982 Talks break down, and the government's control over the north deteriorates sharply.

1983 *May:* Upsurge of terrorism strengthens hands of both Sinhalese and Tamil extremists; a state of emergency is declared.

July 23: Anti-Tamil riots occur in Colombo, the seat of Sri Lanka's government; many Tamils are driven to the Tamil north.

August: TULF proposal to accept autonomy is blocked by Tamil extremists; India is invited to mediate the conflict.

October: 2,000 government troops are deployed in the northern peninsula as Colombo adopts an increasingly military response to the problem of Tamil separatism.

1984 Fighting intensifies; Colombo's reprisals against guerrilla attacks injure Tamil civilians, straining Colombo's relations with India.

1985 *February:* Representatives of six Tamil groups propose diplomatic solution to the conflict based on an autonomous homeland for Tamils in Sri Lanka.

Summer: Indian Prime Minister Rajiv Gandhi agrees to clamp down on guerrilla training camps in India.

September: Tamil guerrillas kill TULF moderates in an effort to torpedo a diplomatic solution to the conflict.

1986 *August:* Colombo proposes the creation of provincial councils with wide powers when it loses control over the north; sharp divisions appear among Sinhalese over Colombo's willingness to negotiate with Tamils.

November 3: Tamil militants reject Colombo's proposals.

1987 *February:* Reports of government massacres in the north cause India to threaten to suspend mediation efforts.

April 17–21: Nearly 300 Sinhalese are killed in Tamil terrorist attacks inside and outside Colombo.

May 26: Colombo launches 7,000-man assault to regain control of northern (Jaffna) peninsula; civilian Tamil casualties are high.

June 4: India's air force parachutes relief supplies into the Jaffna peninsula

July 29: Leaders of India and Sri Lanka announce an accord in which India agrees to stop secessionist threat in Sri Lanka.

July 30: 6,000 Indian troops are deployed to enforce the pact.

August 4: Colombo agrees to disband paramilitary forces in Jaffna if India enforces peace there; Sinhalese militants do not trust India's neutrality.

September–October: India is unable to disarm the Liberation Tigers of Tamil Eelam (LTTE); intra-Tamil conflict accelerates as does tension between Indian forces and Sri Lankan security forces.

October 10: Indian forces launch major attack on LTTE.

November: Indian peacekeeping force (IPKF) now numbers 20,000 in the north; in the south, the Sinhalese Peoples Liberation Front (JVP) begins a terrorist campaign to destabilize Colombo regime for collaborating with India.

1988 *January:* The IPKF's success in the north forces the LTTE to regroup in the east.

Fall and winter: Casualties mount as fighting is divided between the IPKF and rebels in the north and Colombo's security forces and the JVP in the south.

1989 *Spring:* New government is elected in Colombo with less personal interest in accord than Jayawardene had.

June: India is asked to withdraw troops by July 31.

July: Widespread JVP violence in the south forces the government to mobilize 15,000 voluntary militiamen.

July 4: India agrees to negotiate timetable for its withdrawal.

July 28: India agrees to begin withdrawing IPKF.

1990 Last Indian forces depart, and Colombo begins peace talks with Tamil leadership.

1991 Former Indian leader Rajiv Gandhi is assassinated.

1993 Peace talks stall, and heavy fighting resumes.

1994–2001 Fighting continues, seemingly without end.

2002 Fatigue with war on all sides results in a permanent cease-fire agreement between Tamil Tiger leaders and government, possibly to be policed by international forces.

The crucial events involving the development of the Tamil-Sinhalese conflict in the island state of Sri Lanka unfolded over a period of almost 30 years, touched off in the mid-1950s by the passage of a series of laws highly prejudicial to the interests of the country's Tamil minority. By the early 1980s, the conflict had reached such intensity that neighboring India—with its large, sometimes separatist-inclined, Tamil-speaking minority—concluded that it could no longer ignore developments in Sri Lanka. Eventually, India sent more than 50,000 peacekeepers into Sri Lanka in a futile effort to control the violence there. The story of Sri Lanka's communal conflict is consequently almost as much about the limits of peacekeeping intervention in communal conflicts as it is about the conflict between that island's principal ethnolinguistic communities.

HISTORICAL BACKGROUND

Sri Lanka, formerly Ceylon, lies just off the southern tip of India—a fact of geographical life that has profoundly shaped its demographics, its history, and politics both before and after Ceylon achieved its independence from Britain in 1948.

More than 2,500 years ago, in approximately 545 B.C., the island's indigenous peoples were overrun, and the island was settled by waves of Buddhist peoples from India. Their descendants today make up Sri Lanka's Sinhalese majority, who are concentrated in the island's south and constitute approximately 72 percent of its overall population. The largest minority—approximately 18 percent of the population—can claim an even stronger, continuing connection with India. Territorially concentrated in Sri Lanka's northern Jaffna peninsula and eastern districts where they respectively constitute a majority and plurality of the local populations, they are the island's original people and the ethnic and linguistic cousins of the Tamils who dominate the southern Indian state of Tamil Nadu, less than twenty miles to the north.[1]

When Europe discovered the wealth of India a half millennium ago, Ceylon became a part of the power scramble for possessions in South Asia. The outcome was the same as in India. After passing through the hands of the Portuguese and the Dutch, Ceylon fell under the control of the British from 1796 to 1814. In 1815 Ceylon became a crown colony and, though small in size, it was an important part of the British Empire, providing Britain with significant quantities of tea, rubber, and other tropical goods until it gained independence in 1948, a year after the British withdrawal from India and the subcontinent's partition into India and Pakistan.

In 1926, during Ceylon's nationalist struggle for self-rule, its nationalist leader and future prime minister, Solomon Bandaranaike, spoke of a future Ceylon whose peoples could profit from a federal division of power between the center and the regions reflecting Sinhalese and Tamil living patterns on the island. Once prime minister of independent Ceylon, however, he found himself under intense pressure from Sinhalese elements to move in a quite different direction. Not only did they oppose constitutionally reorganizing the state to give Tamils federal autonomy in Tamil-majority areas, but they demanded that the government redress the fact that though a minority in Ceylon, the Tamils were better educated than the Sinhalese and held a disproportionately large share of the civil service posts in the country.

In 1956 the government bowed to Sinhalese majority wishes and passed the controversial Sinhala Only Act, ending the official status of English in the country and placing Tamils at a disadvantage in obtaining employment in the civil service. In an effort to soften the blow, the following year, Bandaranaike agreed to support some form of devolution of power to the Tamil minority. By this point, however, the protests against the Sinhalese Only Act were beginning to turn violent, and in response to that violence, Bandaranaike further alienated Tamil leaders by disavowing federalism as an option in devolving political power to the Tamils (although it remained the political goal of moderate Tamil leaders until 1976).

Sinhalese-Tamil relations continued to deteriorate from this (1956–1958) point onward, with the government constantly caught in the whiplash of trying to accommodate the Tamil demand for autonomy without alienating the country's Sinhalese majority. This rarely proved possible. Thus, as communal killings began to mount in the late 1950s, the government negotiated a pact with Tamil leaders in which it promised, in vague terms, Tamil autonomy. Under pressure from the Sinhalese majority, however, Bandaranaike not only abrogated the agreement but also, between 1958 and 1973, implemented additional language reforms that further tilted educational and employment opportunities toward the Sinhalese majority.

By 1976 accumulating Tamil grievances, based on their absence of power at the center, failure to make any headway in obtaining regional autonomy, inability even to administer themselves in their own language in Tamil-majority areas, and the barriers erected to block their access to education and jobs, prompted mainstream Tamil leaders to abandon the goal of federal autonomy and adopt a separatist agenda. Almost immediately, insurgent activity increased in the Tamil north. The following year, campaigning on a separatist platform, the Tamil United Liberation Front (TULF) won all seats in the country's north and east areas, and then forfeited them when those elected refused to take the required oath of office against secession. The same election also highlighted the Tamil's inherent weakness at the center when the country's gerrymandered election system gave the Sinhalese United National Party (UNP) 85 percent of the seats in parliament with only 52 percent of the vote—a majority it quickly used to adopt a new constitution built around strong (inevitably Sinhalese) presidential rule, not executive responsibility to a majority in the bicommunal parliament.

Tensions continued to build throughout the early 1980s, beginning in 1981 when the country (officially renamed Sri Lanka in 1972) was rocked for the fifth time since 1956 by a significant wave of communal violence. In response, Sri Lanka's government in Colombo, the island's capital, again extended an olive branch to Tamil leaders, this time by holding informal discussions with the TULF on ways to defuse intercommunal conflict. The discussions broke down within a year, and so too did Colombo's security position in the north. Moreover, tense as Sinhalese-Tamil relations had already become, they sharpened even further in December 1982 when President J. R. (Junius Richard) Jayawardene, following his reelection, proposed holding a referendum on the subject of postponing until 1989 the scheduled assembly elections, which were to be soon held on a proportional representation basis likely to give the Tamils 20 percent of the seats in the legislature. Although Tamil areas voted heavily against the postponement, the referendum passed. In protest, the Tamil representatives from those areas voting "no" resigned from the sitting legislature at the end of their regularly elected term, ending all Sinhalese-Tamil dialogue inside Sri Lanka's parliament.

THE CONFLICT

As late as 1983, though often extremely violent, the conflict in Sri Lanka was still essentially one dimensional: between the minority Tamil community and its leadership on the one side and the Sinhalese majority and the Sinhalese-dominated government in Colombo on the other. Four critical years later, when the Indian Peacekeeping Force (IPKF) was deployed into Sri Lanka, the complexity of strife in the country had increased fourfold, largely as a result of the ripples set in motion by one event that occurred in 1983 and another, in 1987.

The July Riots in Colombo and Their Aftermath

In the spring and early summer of 1983, an upsurge of terrorism strengthened the hand of extremists in both the Tamil and Sinhalese camps. By May, the violence had become so widespread that the government found it necessary to declare a state of emergency throughout the country. Then came the first crucial date, July 23, when in response to the violence being caused by the Tamil insurgents, anti-Tamil riots erupted in Colombo, frequently with the police looking on and doing nothing. The loss of Tamil property was significant, and many Tamils were forced to seek sanctuary in the Tamil-majority area of the Jaffna peninsula. Their migration eliminated whatever moderating effect their presence as "hostages" in the south may have had on the activities of the Tamil guerrillas in the north.

By August law and order had been restored in Colombo, and—in return for the TULF abandoning its separatist goals—Colombo offered amnesty to all Tamil rebels willing to withdraw from the north. The compromise collapsed, however, when the Tamil separatists refused to support it. Running out of domestic options, President Jayawardene turned to the prime minister of India, Indira Gandhi, and requested India's diplomatic intervention in the form of her extending her good offices to mediate the conflict in Sri Lanka. Accepting the proffered "savior mediator" role, India dispatched an emissary to commence the process, just as Sri Lanka amended its constitution to ban even the advocacy of secession.

Far from providing the light at the end of the tunnel, India quickly found itself ensnared in Sri Lanka's conflicts. In October 1983, the TULF dispatched its spokesmen to India to lobby for the Tamil cause and announced that it would talk with Colombo only through Indian intermediaries. For its part, Colombo opted for a military solution and increased the size of its security force in the north in order to crush the separatist guerrillas. Gradually, the pattern emerged that would last until India was finally militarily drawn into the conflict in 1987. Guerrilla attacks on government military targets increasingly begat police and military reprisals that injured growing numbers of Tamil civilians and thereby strained Sri Lanka–India relations, but did little damage to the separatists, who by the end of 1984 were receiving substantial assistance from India's southernmost state, Tamil Nadu.[2]

Between 1984 and 1986, the political picture in Sri Lanka deteriorated on other fronts as well. To the extent that Colombo pursued a military solution to the conflict, it became increasingly difficult for moderate Tamils to accept the proposals put forward by Colombo, or even to follow up their own diplomatic initiatives. For example, in February 1985, the representatives of six Tamil groups advanced a set of four principles as a basis for negotiating with Colombo. The heart of these proposals was the creation of a Tamil homeland and full citizenship for all Tamils in Sri Lanka, including the nearly 100,000 imported from India to work on Ceylon's plantations during the colonial era. Six months later, India-mediated peace talks based on these principles were held in Bhutan among Colombo and the TULF and five Tamil guerrilla groups. As the discussions progressed, however, the representatives of those Tamil groups fighting the government became increasingly disenchanted with the talks, and India was forced to spend as much time trying to narrow the differences between the two moderate and four radical Tamil groups present as between the Tamils and Colombo.

The gap between the moderate and extremist elements within the Tamil camp further widened in September 1985, when Tamil guerrillas killed several moderate TULF officials in an apparent effort to torpedo the talks in Bhutan. Shortly thereafter the talks collapsed completely when the representatives of the militant Eelam National Liberation Front walked out of the negotiations. By May 1986, the rupture inside the Tamil community was complete, and the radical Tamil group LTTE (Liberation Tigers of Tamil Eelam, or simply the Tamil Tigers) was routinely attacking its major rivals within the Tamil movement and had established itself as the spokesmen for Tamil separatism. It had also established itself as the preeminent force in the Jaffna peninsula, where local justice, once administered by the center, had collapsed into the hands of locally organized committees firmly under the control of the Tamil guerrillas.

The government's declining control over the Tamil regions, in turn, contributed to a sharpening of divisions inside the Sinhalese community; in particular, the creation of the Movement for the Defense of the Nation (MDN) by former prime minister Bandaranaike. A militant Sinhalese organization dedicated to retaining Sri Lanka as a Buddhist state, the MDN was explicitly opposed the passage of any legislation that might create an autonomous region for the overwhelmingly Hindu Tamils.

Finally, frustrated Colombo's inability or unwillingness to make significant concessions to the Tamils because of the divisions inside the Sinhalese community, India's relations with Colombo degenerated throughout 1986. Consequently, when in early 1987 stories began to circulate that government security forces were conducting massacres in the east, India quickly threatened to suspend its mediation activities until Colombo restrained its military operations in the guerrilla-held territories. By this time, though, Colombo was thoroughly disenchanted with India because of its inability to control Tamil extremists.

It was against this deteriorating environment that the second crucial series of events unfolded, beginning with a wave of anti-Sinhalese Tamil violence between April 17 and April 21, 1987, which claimed nearly 300 lives. These attacks moved the country still further, if not irrevocably, away from a political solution to its communal conflict and seemingly toward all-out civil war.

In retaliation, on May 26, Colombo launched a 7,000-man assault to regain control of a key portion of the Jaffna peninsula. Despite orders to limit civilian casualties, by June 1, the number of Tamil civilians killed in the assault was mounting and, under pressure from its own Tamil minority, the government of India concluded that it could no longer sit on the sidelines. Without Sri Lanka's official permission, on June 3, India dispatched 20 small boats to provide emergency humanitarian aid to the Jaffna civilian population; however, at the last minute, the government in Colombo, under pressure from the Sinhalese militants, had its navy turn the flotilla back to India. India responded the next day by parachuting relief supplies into the Jaffna peninsula, defining its action as "intermestic" (neither domestic nor international) and essentially redefining its role in Sri Lanka's communal conflict from intermediary to interventionist.

MANAGEMENT OF
THE CONFLICT

Despite the fact that India's relief efforts in the Jaffna peninsula further soured its relationship with Sri Lanka, the Colombo government's deteriorating position in the north and northeast forced it to turn back to India for assistance. Thus, in a surprise announcement on June 29, 1987, India and Sri Lanka announced a peace accord (the Indo–Sri Lankan Accord) under the terms of the which India was granted hegemony over Sri Lanka's foreign policy in return for agreeing to help Colombo defeat the Tamil secessionists. Within twenty-four hours, 6,000 Indian troops were deployed in the Jaffna area to enforce India's part of the pact. Simultaneously, India began to deny the rebels the sanctuary that previously had been available to them in Tamil Nadu.

The use of outside peacekeepers as a means of managing communal conflict was not as common in 1987 as it was to become during the 1990s, but the IPKF was not without precedent. British troops, for example, had been keeping the peace in Northern Ireland for nearly 20 years by that time. On the other hand, in most previous instances, there had been a peace—however tenuous—to keep when the troops arrived. The terrain was far none treacherous in Sri Lanka given the multiple, ongoing political conflicts there. India not only had to resolve the intracommunal conflict between the extremists and moderates in the Tamil camp and disarm the guerrillas, but it had to maintain an aura of neutrality in the Tamil-Sinhalese conflict if it was to be able to cooperate with the government in Colombo, which, under the accord, could expel the IPKF at its pleasure and which itself had to avoid appearing to make too many concessions to the Tamil community lest the Sinhalese moderates be driven into the extremist camp. India's difficulties were further compounded by the fact that it inherited—and had to work around—Colombo's failed strategy in dealing with Tamil demands.

Colombo's carrot-and-stick approach of responding to Tamil demands for autonomy collapsed because Colombo repeatedly conceded too little too late to satisfy the demands of even the Tamil moderates. The four-point compromise advanced by the TULF in 1985 offers a case in point. Because of Colombo's insistence that any compromise on its part be preceded by cease-fires and other concessions by Tamil extremists, it was 12 months before Colombo finally acceded to the minimum demand in those four points and conferred Sri Lankan citizenship on the Tamil Indians long living in the country. Another five months passed before Colombo acquiesced to the TULF's core demand: Tamil autonomy in the north in matters of law and order and the allocation of agricultural land. By that time, the TULF had so lost its credibility within the Tamil community that its continuing negotiations with Colombo acquired a surreal quality, and the effective spokesmen for the Tamil cause had become the Tamil Tigers, who were rejecting anything short of full independence for the country's Tamil-majority north and east.

India's problems as a third-party peacemaker were less self-made than situation-laden. It could not favor the Tamils in their conflict with the Sinhalese without antagonizing the Sinhalese and straining its relations with Colombo. It could not be too severe in repressing the Tigers without appearing to favor the Sinhalese and antagonizing the Tamil majority in southern India. It could not openly favor the moderates in Sri Lanka's Tamil camp without so polarizing the more extremist Tamil organizations that it would be unable to mediate the intra-Tamil conflict.

In practice, India focused on its most basic commitment—disarming the rebels—and threw its support behind the TULF and other moderate Tamil organizations willing to accept regional autonomy for peace. The result was both predictable and perverse. The more India took the moderate side in the intra-Tamil dispute, the less unacceptable India's presence in Sri Lanka became to mainstream Sinhalese, whose first reaction to the accord had been negative.[3] But, the more India took the moderate side, the less it could serve as a mediator in the intra-Tamil power struggle and the more it boxed itself into the position of having to subdue the Tigers militarily—the Sinhalese strategy whose failure had forced Colombo to turn to India in the first place. And, the more the IPKF waged a war against Tamil separatists, with the inevitable civilian casualties, the more the Gandhi government alienated itself from its citizens in Tamil Nadu. Add India's inclination to increase the size of the IPKF in the face of its continuing inability to subdue the insurgents—from the initial 6,000 to 20,000 by November 1987; 50,000 by July 1988; and nearly 80,000 just before the IPKF's withdrawal in the summer of 1989—and the tale of India's two-year excursion into interventionary peacekeeping can be largely written in these terms. The story might have stretched out even longer had it not been for two developments. First, throughout Sri Lanka's south, the Sinhalese Peoples Liberation Front (JVP) used the IPKF's inability to subdue the Tamil extremists and Colombo's inability to protect the state to justify its terrorist campaign against civil servants, the police, and members of parliament in its all-out effort to destabilize the existing government. By the end of 1988, the JVP-Colombo conflict had reached the point where fighting in Sri Lanka was almost evenly divided between the IPKF and the rebels in the north and Colombo's security forces and the JVP in the south. Then came the second development.

In the spring of 1989, Sri Lanka elected a new government—one that had far less personal interest in the Indo–Sri Lanka Accord than its predecessor. Surveying the condition of his state, Sri Lanka's new president, Ranasinghe Premadasa, surprised India in June by asking it to withdraw its troops from Sri Lanka by the end of July. Unfortunately for Colombo, although the last Indian troops were withdrawn during 1990, its success in reestablishing control over Sri Lanka has been, at best, incomplete. The new set of peace talks inaugurated with Tamil leaders in 1990 stalled in 1993, and the fighting which resumed almost immediately in northern Sri Lanka was still heavy when the twentieth century came to its close.

SRI LANKA'S FUTURE? Negotiations in 2002 brought talk of creating an international peacekeeping force in Sri Lanka. Here, a Canadian soldier raises the United Nations flag over the UN's Nicosia base on March 19, 1964, inaugurating the UN's longest running peacekeeping venture. © Bettmann/CORBIS.

Nor was India's venture into the slippery world of peacekeeping cost free. Its military casualties were not trivial; the Tamil Tigers, like many guerrilla groups, proved to be a difficult and expensive enemy to engage. Then there was the political cost. While campaigning in 1991, former Prime Minister Rajiv Gandhi was assassinated by a sympathizer of, if not a member of, the Tamil Tigers.

SIGNIFICANCE

Lessons can be drawn from virtually all stances of ethnic conflict, and usually the more complicated the conflict the greater the number of conclusions and hypotheses to be gleaned from it. Volumes can therefore be written about the immense complexity of the conflicts to be found swirling within and around Tamil-Sinhalese strife in Sri Lanka. Still, three points seem to stand out.

First, the history of communal conflict in Sri Lanka clearly indicates the often overlooked fact that, in matters of managing ethnic conflict, intraethnic group conflict can be as important a target as intergroup conflict. Ultimately it was the intra-Tamil struggle for power that undermined India's peacekeeping operations and forced the IPKF to become ever more involved in the basically military operation of pacifying Sri Lanka's Tamil areas. Meanwhile, the Colombo government's efforts to negotiate a compromise with the Tamil moderates was continuously undermined by the activity of uncompromising factions within the country's Sinhalese majority.

Second, because most ethnonational movements are apt to contain "rejectionist" elements unwilling to compromise on anything short of full independence, it is important—whenever the accommodation path is chosen as the strategy for dealing with minority demands—for leaders in the majority community to support, as early as possible, the moderates in the minority community. The failure of Sinhalese leadership to to do so was, even at the time, as noticeable as it proved to be costly. Unlike areas in which majorities and minorities are intermingled (Beirut, Belfast), in Sri Lanka the territorialized nature of the Tamil community not only made the Tamils' call for territorial autonomy understandable but relatively easy to fulfill without affecting Sinhalese control over the center or the country as a whole.

Finally, the Sri Lanka case dramatizes how very difficult it is for third parties to resolve communal conflicts through peacekeeping operations. Nothing is more essential in peacekeeping than maintaining a posture of neutrality in the dispute. It is, however, almost impossible to do this in an area of communal conflict. Peacekeepers invariably define their task in terms of a status quo, be it boundaries to be policed, laws to be enforced, or pacts or treaties to be implemented. Yet, by their nature, communal conflicts are precisely about the legitimacy of the status quo, and actions approved by one faction in a dispute are highly likely, sooner or later, to antagonize another. It was India's misfortune in Sri Lanka to be perceived as biased by significant portions of both the Sinhalese community, given its semi-open support for the Tamils prior to the signing of the Indo–Sri Lanka Accord, and the Tamil community, against whose separatist wing it fought a two-year-long war.

See also Cyprus: Communal Conflict and the International System; United Kingdom: The Conflict in Ulster; Yugoslavia: Ethnic Conflict and the Meltdown in Kosovo; and Yugoslavia: The Deconstruction of a State and Brith of Bosnia.

NOTES

1. There was also a third important group at the time of the breakdown of Sri Lanka democracy during the 1980s: the Indian Tamils. Approximately

800,000 Tamils were imported from India during the colonial period by the British to work on Ceylon's plantations. Still living in Sri Lanka in the mid-1980s as Indian citizens, they constituted 9 percent of the country's population at the time of India's intervention.

2. It was not until summer 1985 that India's prime minister, Rajiv Gandhi, agreed to tighten India's control over the guerrilla training camps in Tamil Nadu. His action eased the growing tensions between Delhi and Colombo at the time; however, it occurred too late to prevent Sinhalese militants from concluding that, in Sri Lanka's communal conflict, India was pro-Tamil.

3. Even members of the Jayawardene government initially opposed the pact on the grounds that it deprived their country of its independence in foreign policy. As time passed and the rebels in the north refused to disarm, discontent grew.

SUGGESTED READINGS

Hubbell, L. Kenneth. "The Devolution of Power in Sri Lanka." *Asian Survey* 27 (November 1987): 1176–87.

Rothberg, Robert I., ed. *Creating Peace in Sri Lanka: Civil War and Reconciliation.* Washington, D.C.: Brookings Institution, 1999.

Rupesinghe, Kumar. "Ethnic Conflicts in South Asia: The Case of Sri Lanka and the Indian Peace-keeping Force (IPKF)." *Journal of Peace Research* 25 (1988): 337–50.

Wilson, A. Jeyaratnam. *Sri Lankan Tamil Nationalism.* Vancouver, Canada: University of British Colombia Press, 1999.

Sudan

Ethnic Conflict in the Sudan

Ann Mosely Lesch

TIMELINE

1821 Turkish and Egyptian forces conquer northern Sudan.

1885 The Mahdist forces overthrow the Turko-Egyptian regime.

1898 British forces conquer Sudan and establish the Anglo-Egyptian condominium.

1922 Closed Districts Order separates the south and Nuba mountains from the north.

1956 Sudan becomes independent under a parliamentary government.

1958 General Ibrahim Abboud seizes power and escalates the civil war in the south.

1964 A popular uprising overthrows Abboud and restores parliamentary rule.

1969 Colonel Ja'far Numairi seizes power and suppresses the religiously oriented political parties.

1972 The Addis Ababa Accord ends the civil war in the south.

1983 Numairi redivides the south and imposes Islamic law; civil war resumes under the Sudan Peoples Liberation Movement (SPLM).

1985 A popular uprising overthrows Numairi.

1986 After parliamentary elections are held, the Umma Party's al-Sadiq al-Mahdi becomes prime minister.

1988 The SPLM's accord with the Democratic Unionist Party creates the possibility of a negotiated end to the civil war.

1989 Brigadier Omar Hasan Ahmad al-Bashir seizes power, supported by Hasan al-Turabi's National Islamic Front.

1991 Divisions in the SPLM weaken its fighting capacity.

1994 Declaration of Principles issued by the East African Intergovernmental Authority on Development (IGAD) articulates a political framework to end the fighting, but it is rejected by the government.

1995 Opposition groups' National Democratic Alliance (NDA) agrees on common political principles at the Asmara conference.

1996–1997 The government signs political charters with dissident southern groups; Mahdi flees into exile.

1999 Oil exports begin; Egypt and Libya attempt to mediate; Mahdi signs an accord with Bashir; and Bashir ousts Turabi.

2000 Mahdi breaks with the NDA and returns to Sudan; Turabi forms an opposition party; and Bashir stages elections that are boycotted by most parties.

2001 Bashir arrests Turabi.

The Sudan is wracked by political and armed conflicts, rooted in the politicization of ethnic differences as well as the struggle over scarce resources. The sheer size and diversity of the country make it difficult to govern. Its 27 million people, scattered across a million square miles, vary significantly by language, religion, and customs. More than 50 ethnic groups can be identified, which subdivide into at least 570 distinct peoples. Forty percent are Arabized peoples who live in the northern two-thirds of the country; 26 percent are African peoples who also live in the north; and the remaining 34 percent are African peoples, living in the south, who speak more than 100 indigenous languages. About 70 percent of the population are Muslim, 25 percent adhere to indigenous religions, and 5 percent are Christian. Most of the Christians are Africans who, living in the south, became Christian in the twentieth century.[1]

Linguistic and religious differences overlap. Nearly all the Arabized peoples and most African peoples indigenous to the north are Muslim. The south is sharply distinct: simultaneously African and non-Muslim. Moreover, natural resources are unevenly distributed. The south has significant mineral resources (notably oil and copper ore) and potentially rich, rain-fed agriculture, in contrast to the dry savannahs and deserts found in the north. Nonetheless, government development efforts have focused on the north, particularly in the Nile-irrigated cotton schemes and industries located near the capital city, Khartoum. Moreover, the government insists on controlling all the oil resources, which are concentrated in the south.

The domination of the political and economic systems by northern Muslim Arabs exacerbates the perception of systematic discrimination held by African Sudanese. This politicization of ethnic divisions embitters relations among the Sudanese people and plays a crucial role in the civil wars that have engulfed the country for most of its existence as an independent state.

HISTORICAL BACKGROUND

Historical developments have underlined and aggravated these differences. The peoples of the Sudan lived in relative isolation from each other until the Turko-Egyptian invasion of 1821, which brought centralizing military garrisons, telegraph lines, and tax collection to the north. The diverse southern peoples resisted the raiders from the north who enslaved the southerners; they also fended off efforts to impose a centralized administration on their territories. After Mohammed Ahmad Ibn Abdallah called himself the *mahdi* (messiah) and defeated the Egyptian forces in 1885, the south also resisted the subsequent Mahdist religio-political rule. Southerners particularly resisted the renewed slave raids and efforts to convert them to Islam. The historical legacy of slavery and Islamization still weighs heavily on the relationship between the north and the south.

British troops marched down the Nile from Egypt and captured Khartoum from the Mahdists in 1898. After years of violent skirmishes, those troops had subdued the south by the 1920s. Then British officials attempted to seal off the south from the north, arguing that the entirely different southern peoples should be protected from contact with the more sophisticated and alien northern culture and economic life. The British decreed the Closed Districts Order (1922) and other measures that banned northern traders and Muslim preachers from going to the south. The British even banned Arab-style dress and the use of the Arabic language in government offices and schools. Although these measures were designed to protect the southerners, they severed normal contact and exacerbated the inherent differences between northern and southern peoples. Moreover, the British did little to provide schooling and promote economic development in the south. Therefore, when preparations for independence began in the late 1940s, the peoples of the north and the south lived in different worlds, and there was a wide socioeconomic gap between them.

The Muslim Arab politicians in the north, who led the drive for independence, conceived of the Sudan in their own image and hoped to transform the south into that image; in contrast, southern leaders sought to preserve their autonomy and cultural identity. They objected strenuously to policies that centralized administration in Muslim Arab hands, banned Christian missionary activities while promoting conversion to Islam, Arabized the educational system in the south, and concentrated socioeconomic development efforts in the north.

Southerners were deeply suspicious before the country became independent on January 1, 1956. The previous summer, southern troops mutinied and southern workers protested large-scale dismissals by newly appointed northern bosses. Southern politicians sought, unsuccessfully, to create a federal system, in which regional-level governments would have significant power. As civil strife increased in the late 1950s, the southern guerrilla movement argued that the south had exchanged benign British colonizers for new, harsh northern rulers and declared that southern independence was the only solution to the country's cultural divide.

Meanwhile, northern politicians failed to establish a stable democratic system in Khartoum. The first prime minister, Ismail al-Azhari, led a secular political party, but the two major political parties were based on Islamic religious movements. The core of support for the Umma Party came from the adherents of the nineteenth-century Mahdist movement. The Khatmiyya religious order supported a rival political party, now known as the Democratic Unionist Party (DUP). Both parties viewed Sudanese identity as Muslim and Arab.

They formed coalition governments, but then became preoccupied with jockeying for power and ignored the deepening economic problems and social tensions.

In this context of simmering unrest in the south and public disillusionment with parliamentary rule, Commander-in-Chief Major General Ibrahim Abboud seized power in November 1958. He set up a dictatorship and accelerated Islamization, Arabization, and centralization. As fighting escalated in the south, the southern guerrillas coalesced into a broad politico-military movement which demanded separation. Meanwhile, a half million southerners fled into exile, leaving behind their bombed and scorched villages.

Northern politicians and trade unionists also became restive under Abboud's one-man rule, although they did not sympathize with the south's demand for independence. They mounted a general strike in 1964. When young officers refused to fire on demonstrators in Khartoum, senior officers persuaded Abboud to resign. Sudanese hailed this "October revolution" as an exemplary use of moral power by unarmed civilians to overthrow an unjust regime. Nonetheless, the subsequent transitional government, and especially the government elected in April 1965, retained Abboud's emphasis on Sudan's Islamic-Arab identity. The transitional government convened a roundtable conference in March 1965 that enabled northern and southern groups to air their views, but war later intensified in the south. Moreover, the rise of a militant Islamist movement, led by law professor Hasan al-Turabi, increased pressure on the Umma Party and the Khatmiyya order to promulgate a constitution based on Islamic law.

Once again an ineffective parliamentary regime was overthrown by military officers. Young secularist officers, led by Colonel Ja'far Numairi, engineered a coup d'état in May 1969. Numairi cracked down on all three Islamic-oriented parties and adopted a new approach to the south, based on recognizing its historical and cultural differences, rather than on suppressing those differences. In 1972, after more than 15 years of civil war, the government and southern guerrillas negotiated an agreement to grant the south political autonomy as one large region within a united Sudan. That Addis Ababa Accord also provided for the south to control its economy and educational system and have freedom of religious expression. Those measures led to a decade of relative calm and freed the people's energies to promote socioeconomic development throughout the country. For southerners, independence seemed less important so long as their rights and autonomy were upheld.

THE CONFLICT

The hope of realizing unity within diversity was a short-lived one. Although Numairi signed the Addis Ababa Accord in 1972, he unilaterally canceled that accord in 1983. Numairi could not tolerate the idea that revenue from newly discovered oil fields in the south would benefit primarily that region. He also resented the free-wheeling political life in the south. After he reached a political détente with religiously oriented northern politicians, whom he had initially quashed and who strongly opposed the Addis Ababa Accord, he redivided the south into three provinces in June 1983 and then imposed Islamic public and criminal law on the whole country. The militant Islamist Hasan al-Turabi strongly supported Numairi's moves. Not surprisingly, the south erupted again in an even more violent uprising.

Colonel John Garang founded the Sudan Peoples Liberation Movement/Army (SPLM/SPLA) along with other southern army officers in May 1983. In sharp contrast to the earlier uprising, which had demanded secession and independence for the south, the SPLM supported the Sudan's territorial unity. Garang demanded the end to rule by Islamic law and the creation of a decentralized political system that would share power and resources equitably among all the Sudanese peoples.

Most northern politicians were also angry at Numairi, especially for his harsh dictatorship, economic corruption, misuse of Islamic law to consolidate his power, and irresponsible triggering of renewed civil war. Army officers resented the war, which they knew was unwinnable. Only Turabi's militants backed Numairi. After months of grassroots protests, northern politicians and trade unionists, supported by the senior command of the armed forces, overthrew Numairi in a nonviolent uprising in April 1985.

The joint military-civilian interim government that ruled for one year and then the government elected in April 1986 expressed interest in annulling Numairi's decrees and signing a peace accord with the SPLM. Nonetheless, neither government took effective steps to change the legal system or start negotiations with the SPLM. Fighting even spread into the Nuba mountains and Southern Blue Nile province, whose African peoples resented Arab rule and economic discrimination. Umma Party leader al-Sadiq al-Mahdi, who became prime minister in May 1986, called on Arab and Muslim governments to support him against these alleged African attacks on Sudan's Islamic-Arab identity. Mahdi never canceled Numairi's Islamic laws, in part because he was constrained by Turabi, who proclaimed that anyone who restored the secular legal codes was an apostate, a traitor to Islam. As a result, Mahdi merely stated that the government would not enforce Islamic laws in the south. That angered secularists in the north, who wanted a nonreligious constitution, and it further alienated southerners, who sought a uniform legal system and resented this ghettoization.

Although Mahdi remained hostile to the SPLM and was unwilling to grant the south legal equality, some other northern politicians sought to bridge the differences. The SPLM participated in a conference with northern politicians in March 1986 that urged that the legal and political systems be restructured so that they would be fair to all Sudanese citizens. Most important, Mohammed Osman al-Mirghani, head of the Khatmiyya religious order and leader of the conservative Democratic Unionist Party (DUP), signed a path-breaking agreement with Garang in November 1988 that called for freezing Numairi's Islamic decrees. Mirghani and Garang affirmed that political differences must be resolved by democratic dialogue, not war. Freezing Islamic law was a major concession for Mirghani, who led a religiously based political party that had been a staunch supporter of Islamization. Apparently Mirghani's qualms about acknowledging the multireligious character of the Sudan were overridden by his concern about the economic and human costs of the fighting and his fear that polarization over Islamic law would tear the country apart.

The DUP-SPLM accord threatened Prime Minister Mahdi's political primacy and challenged the core ideology of Turabi's National Islamic Front (NIF). Mahdi and Turabi jointly rejected the accord and forced the DUP out of the cabinet. These actions alienated senior officers in the armed forces, who knew that the war could not be won and welcomed the prospect of a negotiated settlement. Those officers compelled Mahdi to endorse the DUP-SPLM accord and open negotiations with the SPLM in the spring of 1989. That diplomatic move, in turn, triggered an Islamist coup d'état in June 1989 whose goal was to prevent the creation of a constitution based on nonreligious legal codes.

Turabi and his NIF cadres engineered the coup, commanded by Brigadier Omar Hasan Ahmad al-Bashir. Bashir immediately denounced the DUP-SPLM accord, closed the parliament, banned political parties and trade unions, instituted harsh martial law, and entrenched all-encompassing Islamic laws. The regime's authoritarianism remained intact over the next decade, even though it established a democratic facade by holding presidential and parliamentary elections in 1996 and promulgating an Islamic constitution in 1999 under which Bashir served as president and Turabi became speaker of the parliament. By then, Bashir and Turabi had redefined the war against the SPLM as a jihad (holy war) against infidels and apostates. They enforced Islamic criminal, commercial, and civil laws on all persons living in the north, irrespective of their religion; in the south, residents were exempted from a few provisions of the criminal code.

MANAGEMENT OF THE CONFLICT

The civil war might have ended in 1989; instead, it intensified after the coup d'état. There was no room for compromise between the secularist SPLM and the Islamist military regime. Two rounds of negotiations, hosted by the Nigerian government in 1992 and 1993, foundered on the core issue of the relationship between religion and the form of government. Bashir's negotiators insisted on maintaining Islamic law, with minor exemptions for persons living in the south. The SPLM insisted on a secular government, based on a uniform legal code. Similarly, four rounds of negotiations in 1994, organized by Sudan's East African neighbors through the Intergovernmental Authority on Development (IGAD), failed to break the impasse.

Meanwhile, some officers split with the SPLM in 1991, dissatisfied with Garang's insistence on a united Sudan. Mounting pressures for secession within the south, as a result of the diplomatic deadlock, led the SPLM to begin to demand the right to self-determination for the marginalized people of Sudan. This meant, in essence, that the south should have the right to secede if an acceptable constitutional arrangement could not be achieved. The return to the idea of secession demonstrated the level of despair, as intense fighting extended into the second decade. By the mid-1990s, nearly half of the south's population had fled their homes under the pressure of government air raids, progovernment militia attacks on—and enslavement of—civilians, and the profound economic and social disruption caused by continual warfare. Some people fled to neighboring countries, and others fled north, despite the overt discrimination that they faced there.

The government responded to the SPLM's call for self-determination by intensifying the war, in line with a senior negotiator's blunt statement that "separation comes from the mouth of the gun," not from negotiations.[2] The government refused to place the issue of self-determination on the agenda of the negotiations held in Nigeria in 1992 and 1993. Subsequently, its delegates became enraged when the IGAD proposed in its Declaration of Principles (DoP) in 1994 that priority should be accorded to territorial unity *only if* Sudan established "a secular and democratic state" with legal guarantees of "complete political and social equalities of all peoples," separation of "state and religion," and "extensive rights of self-administration . . . to the various peoples." The DoP also noted, "in the absence of agreement on the above principles . . . the [southern] people will have the option to determine their future, including independence, through a referendum."[3] The government completely rejected this concept

of conditional unity, which the SPLM warmly embraced.

It was not until 1996 and 1997 that the government signed "political charters" with southern officers who had defected from the SPLM in which the government accepted the south's right to self-determination. Then, during renewed IGAD negotiations in 1997 and 1998, the government agreed that an internationally supervised vote on self-determination could be held in the south at the end of an interim period. Even then, it remained unclear whether the government meant self-determination within a united Sudanese territory or whether it meant that the south could secede. Since the government insisted on controlling the south during the interim period through its political appointees and armed forces, the government expected to manipulate the referendum in order to defeat the proponents of secession.

Meanwhile, the SPLM aligned with the coalition of northern opposition parties, known as the National Democratic Alliance (NDA). Headed by the same Mirghani who had signed the accord with Garang in 1988 and who later lived in exile, the NDA aimed to overthrow the regime by another popular uprising and then restore democracy. In a landmark conference held in Asmara (Eritrea) in 1995, the NDA endorsed the formation of a nonreligious government and acknowledged the south's right to self-determination. In essence, the NDA conceded that the south could secede should an NDA-led government fail to uphold the rights of the African citizens.

Despite this political solidarity, the NDA lacked the strength to overthrow the regime. Security forces quickly crushed grassroots protests, and the NDA's armed forces, bolstered by SPLA units, only captured toeholds in eastern Sudan. When Mahdi fled from Sudan to Asmara in December 1996, he complicated its internal politics, since he viewed himself as the legitimate prime minister and refused to be bound by NDA processes. He angered his colleagues when he negotiated on his own with Turabi and Bashir in 1999, urged Egypt and Libya to mediate a reconciliation among northern political groups, and returned to Khartoum in late 2000. Meanwhile, the government's hand strengthened significantly when oil began to flow in August 1998. Oil revenues enabled the government to double its military expenditure, intensify its bombing raids, and establish military industries with European and Asian investment. Ironically, just before Mahdi split the NDA, a major showdown between Bashir and Turabi resulted in Turabi's expulsion from the governing clique. In December 2000, Bashir held elections, which nearly all political groups boycotted, to consolidate his hold over the executive branch and the parliament. He sidelined Mahdi, arrested key NDA leaders living in Khartoum, and even detained Turabi in February 2001.

SIGNIFICANCE

The impasse between the government and the SPLM is unlikely to end. The ideological antagonism remains deep, and fighting is escalating as the armed forces expel southerners from the areas around the oil fields and intimidate humanitarian agencies by their bombing raids.

The high point for the SPLM and NDA came in 1994–1995, when the IGAD articulated its path-breaking DoP, and the NDA agreed on the fundamentals of an alternative constitutional system. Since then, the IGAD has been unable to transform its negotiating principles into operational agreements, and the NDA has suffered serious internal stress. Despite the crisis between Bashir and Turabi, the government has manipulated the diplomatic scene to its own advantage. The complex interactions among northern and southern politicians

make the government and the SPLM each believe that it can strengthen its bargaining position and avoid conducting serious negotiations. Meanwhile, the fighting devastates the south, and the social fabric of the entire country is being torn by decades of discord.

See also India: Ethnic Conflict and Nation-building in a Multiethnic State; Indonesia: The Struggle to Control East Timor; and Western Sahara: Ethnic Conflict and the Twentieth Century's Last Colonial War.

NOTES

1. Ann Mosely Lesch, *The Sudan: Contested National Identities* (Bloomington: Indiana University Press, 1998): 20.
2. Mohammad al-Amin Khalifa, chief negotiator at the Abuja negotiations in 1992, quoted in Steven Wöndu and Ann Lesch, *Battle for Peace in Sudan* (Lanham, Md.: University Press of America, 2000), 51.
3. The full text of the IGAD DoP can be found in Wöndu and Lesch, *Battle for Peace in Sudan,* Appendix F, 227–29.

SUGGESTED READINGS

Assefa, Hizkias. *Mediation of Civil Wars: Approaches and Strategies—The Sudan Conflict.* Boulder, Colo.: Westview Press, 1987.

Burr, J. Millard, and Robert O. Collins. *Requiem for the Sudan: War, Drought, and Disaster Relief on the Nile.* Boulder, Colo.: Westview Press, 1994.

Deng, Francis Mading. *War of Visions: Conflict of Identities in the Sudan.* Washington, D.C.: Brookings Institution, 1995.

Holt, P. M., and M. W. Daly. *The History of the Sudan.* Boulder, Colo.: Westview Press, 1979.

Human Rights Watch/Africa. *Sudan: "In the Name of God."* New York: Human Rights Watch, 1994.

Hutchison, Sharon E. *Nuer Dilemmas: Coping with Money, War, and the State.* Berkeley: University of California Press, 1996.

Johnston, Douglas H. *Nuer Prophets.* Oxford, England: Clarendon Press, 1994.

Jok, Jok Madut. *War and Slavery in Sudan.* Philadelphia: University of Pennsylvania Press, 2001.

Khalid, Mansour. *The Government They Deserve: The Role of the Elite in Sudan's Political Evolution*. London: Kegan Paul International, 1990.

———. *Nimeiri and the Revolution of Dis-May*. London: Kegan Paul International, 1985.

Kok, Peter Nyot. *Governance and Conflict in the Sudan, 1985–1995*. Hamburg, Germany: Deutsches Orient-Institut, 1996.

Lesch, Ann Mosely. *The Sudan: Contested National Identities*. Bloomington: Indiana University Press, 1998.

Nyaba, Peter Adwok. *The Politics of Liberation in South Sudan: An Insider's View*. Oxford, England: African Books Collective, 1997.

Prendergast, John. *Dare to Hope: Children of War in Southern Sudan*. Washington, D.C.: Center of Concern, 1996.

Sikainga, Ahmad Alawad. *Slaves into Workers: Emancipation and Labor in Colonial Sudan*. Austin: University of Texas Press, 1994.

Simone, T. Abdou Maliqalim. *In Whose Image? Political Islam and Urban Practices in Sudan*. Chicago: University of Chicago Press, 1994.

Wöndu, Steven, and Ann Lesch. *Battle for Peace in Sudan*. Lanham, Md.: University Press of America, 2000.

Woodward, Peter. *Sudan, 1898–1989: The Unstable State*. Boulder, Colo: Lynne Rienner, 1990.

United Kingdom

The Making of British Race Relations

Anthony Mark Messina

TIMELINE

1948 The British Nationality Act confirms that citizens of the colonies and commonwealth are British subjects, resulting in the start of a significant, nonwhite migration to Britain; 492 Jamaicans arrive in Britain on the ship *Empire Windrush*.

1958 Race riots erupt in Nottingham and Notting Hill, London.

1962 Commonwealth Immigrants Act restricting nonwhite immigration is enacted.

1964 Labour government minister unexpectedly loses his parliamentary seat to an overtly racist Conservative challenger.

1965 Race Relations Act is enacted.

1967 Kenya's Asians crisis begins.

1968 In his "Rivers of Blood" speech, maverick Conservative politician Enoch Powell warns of dire social consequences if New Commonwealth immigration is not curbed; Second Commonwealth Immigrants Act is passed.

1971 Immigration Act halts significant new labor immigration.

1976 Third Race Relations Act establishes the Commission for Racial Equality.

1978 Conservative Party leader Margaret Thatcher publicly empathizes with popular fears that Britain is being "swamped" by people with a different culture.

1981 New British Nationality Act narrows the scope of British citizenship. Riots in which ethnic minority youth are prominent erupt in Brixton, Toxteth, and other English cities.

1987 Four nonwhite Labour Party candidates are elected to House of Commons.

1988 Muslims across Britain publicly protest the English publication of Salman Rushdie's *The Satanic Verses*.

1995 Death of black burglary suspect at the hands of police sparks a riot among Afro-Caribbean youth in Brixton.

1997 Nine nonwhite Labour Party candidates are elected to the House of Commons.

1999 Macpherson Report cites "institutional racism" within London Metropolitan police force.

2001 The Race Relations Act is extended to cover public authorities and bodies. Race riots erupt in Oldham, Leeds, and Burnley. Eleven ethnic minorities are elected to Parliament after a general election campaign in which race and asylum seekers are prominent issues.

2002 Prime Minister Tony Blair names Paul Boateng as his chief secretary of the treasury, making Boateng the first black member of the Cabinet in Britain's history.

Although circumscribed by the legacies of the slave trade of the sixteenth, seventeenth, and eighteenth centuries and, more profoundly, by the experience of British imperialism and empire during the nineteenth century, it is nevertheless the case that race relations in Britain began to assume their contemporary shape only during the late 1940s and early 1950s. With the migration to Britain of some 800 immigrant workers from Jamaica between December 1947 and October 1948 and the subsequent settlement of tens of thousands of workers and their families from the West Indies and the Indian subcontinent in England's major cities during the next decade and a half, contemporary British race relations came to assume several enduring features. First, questions of ethnicity and race became inextricably linked to immigration-related concerns and, specifically, to recurrent political pressures for immigration control. Second, race relations and state policies that regulate the immigration of nonwhites have brought to the forefront politically charged issues that have significantly challenged the decision-making capacity of the British political system. Finally, despite their relatively small size—currently an estimated 10 percent of the total population, more than 5 percent of the workforce, and more than 5 percent of the electorate—Britain's new ethnic and racial populations either have precipitated or been the receivers of significant social and political change.[1] This change includes revision of the very concept and the basic rights of formal British citizenship, an incremental overhaul of Britain's immigration laws, the emergence of a multicultural society, and the adoption and implementation of an American-inspired legal framework that proscribes overt racial discrimination in employment, housing, and other areas.

HISTORICAL BACKGROUND

On the surface, Britain's experience with post–World War II immigration was similar to that of other immigration-receiving states in Western Europe. Like many others, Britain suffered from labor shortages during the early postwar period as its economy rebounded from the ravages of World War II and as the great economic boom among the Western countries (1945–1969) spurred domestic production.

Having exhausted the available supply of white European foreign labor during the early 1950s, the economy, with some modest assistance from private employers and the government, began to attract workers from Britain's New Commonwealth, particularly from the West Indies, India, and Pakistan. Although unorganized and spontaneous compared to the experiences of other immigration-receiving states, the size of this wave of nonwhite migration to Britain was nevertheless considerable. Beginning with approximately 2,000 New Commonwealth immigrants in 1953, their numbers grew to 46,800 in 1956, 57,700 in 1960, and 231,000 during the eighteen-month period between January 1961 and July 1962.[2]

The events that forever altered this largely self-regulating pattern of immigration were the British government's publication, on November 1, 1961, of a bill designed to curtail New Commonwealth immigration and its subsequent implementation as the Commonwealth Immigrants Act in July 1962. On the one hand, the act restricted nonwhite immigration by instituting a labor-voucher system, which required immigrants to have a work permit issued by the minister of labor. This provision reduced the number of immigrant workers entering Britain from over 50,000 during the act's first six months of implementation to approximately 13,000 for the whole of 1965.[3] However, to placate the pro-Commonwealth lobby in Parliament and various pro-immigrant interest groups in the country, the 1962 act rather generously permitted the entry of the family members of previously settled workers.

The origins and implications of the 1962 Commonwealth Immigrants Act have been comprehensively discussed in numerous scholarly works. In a nutshell, Britain's hasty efforts to restrict nonwhite immigration in 1962 were driven primarily by political rather than economic motives, as they were governed by the government's fear of rising public hostility toward the presence of nonwhite immigrants in society. Unlike many of its European counterparts, however, the British government could not treat its nonwhite immigrant population, estimated to be 597,000 in 1961, as temporary "guest workers."[4] On the contrary, most nonwhite immigrants were full British citizens, having automatically acquired this status as a result of being subjects of the commonwealth after the 1948 British Nationality Act was passed.

The 1962 Commonwealth Immigrants Act was, in the end, only partially effective. Although it substantially decreased labor migration to Britain, it inadvertently stimulated a wave of secondary or family immigration and significantly accelerated the pace of permanent settlement. It also fell short in another respect. Specifically, it failed to address adequately the status of a special population of Asians holding British passports who were progressively being expelled from the African country of Kenya by that country's government.

As a consequence of the arrival of substantial numbers of Kenya's Asian refugees in Britain during the so-called Kenyan Asians crisis of 1967–1968, the British government again tightened its immigration rules. It executed this objective by passing the 1968 Commonwealth Immigrants Act, which, for the first time, introduced the notion of "patriality," the category of persons with an automatic right of abode in the United Kingdom, into

British immigration and nationality law.[5] The 1968 act and the principle of patriality, in turn, provided the foundation for further immigration controls legislated in the 1971 immigration act. By sharpening the distinction between patrials and nonpatrials and by tearing down the barrier between the categories of aliens and commonwealth citizens, the 1971 immigration act eliminated all preferential treatment for the latter group. It also further distanced Britain from its prior obligations to the peoples and governments of the New Commonwealth.

Even with the aforementioned legislative measures undertaken to reduce the intake of nonwhite immigrants into Britain, the flow did not dramatically decrease. Indeed, between 1969 and 1978 over 535,000 immigrants from the New Commonwealth and Pakistan were admitted for settlement in Britain, or approximately 53,500 per annum, a figure only slightly smaller than the annual intake between 1963 and 1968.[6]

The entry of more than 50,000 nonwhite immigrants annually in Britain during the 1960s and 1970s, set against the backdrop of slow economic growth and, periodically, full-blown recession, laid the groundwork for an anti-immigrant, nativist reaction among whites. First in the incendiary speeches of maverick Conservative Party politician Enoch Powell, during the late 1960s and early 1970s, and later in the street violence and electoral campaigns of the neofascist National Front, racist white Britons discovered their political voice and vehicles for the political representation of their illiberal views. Although these reactionary forces are more quiescent at the dawn of the new century, their previous strength should not be underestimated. At one point during the early 1970s, Powell was the most popular political figure in Britain, and a fifth of the British public wished to see him become prime minister. Moreover, in a public opinion survey conducted at the peak of the National Front's popularity in 1978, one-quarter of all respondents agreed that the National Front expressed the views of "ordinary working people," and 21 percent thought that it would be "good for Britain" if candidates of the National Front gained seats in the House of Commons.[7]

Public hostility toward New Commonwealth immigration and settled immigrants continued to find political expression and contaminate the general social and political environment in Britain until 1982 or so when it quickly began to dissipate. Despite several outbreaks of urban violence, in which alienated ethnic minority youth prominently participated in 1981 and 1985, by the mid-1980s the political salience of nonwhite immigration had significantly declined, Enoch Powell and the National Front had been relegated to the political wilderness, and the British government's immigration and immigrant policies had become models of coherence.

Several factors appear responsible for this sea change. First, the election in 1979 of a Conservative government, which was openly hostile toward the idea of a multicultural society and which was committed to introducing even tighter immigration restrictions, undercut political support for the National Front and other illiberal political forces. Second, the implementation of new immigration restrictions and a new, even more restrictive British Nationality Act during the early 1980s reduced the annual inflow of New Commonwealth and Pakistani immigrants into Britain by half, to approximately 24,000. Further immigration restrictions imposed by a successor Conservative government in 1988 preempted any significant future increase in New Commonwealth immigration by repealing the right of the primary dependents of male immigrants who were settled in Britain before 1973 to enter the country. And finally, by diluting the long-observed principle of *jus soli* (citizenship by virtue of birth within the national territory) in favor of a greater emphasis on *jus sanguinis* (citizenship by virtue of inheriting the nationality of a parent or close relation), the 1981 British Nationality Act rationalized Britain's nationality law and legitimized the 1962–1980 wave of immigration restrictions. In so doing, the new act removed many of the lingering ambiguities in British nationality law and immigration rules so that both became less vulnerable to legal challenge.

THE CONFLICT

Apart from a secondary and, by past standards, relatively minor political conflict over an influx of asylum seekers, Britain has been one of the least conflicted countries in Western Europe with regard to both immigration and immigrant policy since the 1990s. As a consequence of the 1971 Immigration Act and subsequent immigration restrictions, the annual volume of both primary and secondary (kin) immigration are relatively modest. Mostly due to the legacy of the 1948 British Nationality Act, an overwhelming majority of nonwhites in Britain today are full citizens. Thanks to the 1971 Immigration Act, the 1981 British Nationality Act, and subsequent legislation, there is currently little

ENGLAND, UNITED KINGDOM, August 25, 1972. Smithfield Meat Market porters march to the home office to protest about immigration. © Hulton-Deutsch Collection/CORBIS.

confusion about who is and who is not a citizen. Moreover, Britain is only one of a handful of West European countries at the turn of the new century without a politically significant party or movement of the extreme right.

The redefinition of Britain's nationality laws, the declining political salience of immigration-related issues, and the retreat of the political far right do not mean, however, that British race relations have reached some harmonious equilibrium. To the contrary, as overt political conflict over immigration policy has gradually waned, issues associated with the incorporation of Britain's new ethnic and racial minorities into the mainstream of British economic, social, and political life have become more prominent.

With regard to the economic incorporation of Britain's new ethnic and racial minorities, the primary challenge remains high unemployment and a dearth of economic mobility and opportunity—problems that are especially acute among Britain's Afro-Caribbean population. Although successive race relations acts have proscribed overt discrimination in much of the public sector and the private economy, racial prejudice still undisputedly contributes to high black underemployment. A government survey conducted in 1995, for example, found that 21 percent of Caribbean blacks were unemployed compared with 8 percent of whites.[8] Numerous studies of the employment status of ethnic minorities have underscored the facts that, on the whole, nonwhites are employed in less-skilled jobs and at lower tiers of the labor market than whites, and they are disproportionately concentrated in particular industrial sectors.

The picture is a bit brighter with regard to the social incorporation of nonwhites. Although social exclusion and disadvantage stubbornly persist, especially in the form of racially segregated housing patterns and comparatively poor health standards among ethnic minority populations, interracial cohabitation and marriage are relatively common in Britain compared to other countries, including the United States. According to the 1991 census, 40 percent of Afro-Caribbean men between the ages of 16 and 34 and 22 percent of black men between the age of 35 and 59 cohabit with a white partner. Moreover, and perhaps more significantly for the long-term trajectory of race relations, most white Britons are relatively liberal minded about interracial marriages. The results of one study, for example, found that 74 percent of whites expressed the view that they would accept a close relative marrying a black person. Similarly, 70 percent of white respondents said they would not mind a close relative marrying an Asian.[9]

Much as it has during the past 40 years, the process of incorporating the new ethnic and racial minorities into British politics is proceeding at a glacially slow pace. An increasing presence of nonwhite politicians in local government, relatively robust turnout rates among ethnic minority voters (65–83 percent depending upon the specific group) and the inclusion of greater numbers of nonwhites among the formal members of Britain's major political parties obviously signal tangible progress in the political realm. These trends, coupled with the elevation of four nonwhite parliamentary candidates to the House of Commons, Britain's lower legislative house, in 1987, six in 1992, and nine in 1997, provide evidence that Britain's new ethnic and racial minorities are gradually coming of political age.

On the deficit side, however, is the stark fact that ethnic-minority elected officials are still relatively few, and many of the public policy issues that are especially pertinent to this special population remain politically neglected. Moreover, for complex historical and ideological reasons, the definition, articulation, and promotion of the collective interests of nonwhites within

Britain's political party system is primarily being undertaken by only one major political party, the left-of-center Labour Party, whose near monopoly of the ethnic-minority vote is viewed by some observers as politically unhealthy for both nonwhites and the party.

MANAGEMENT OF THE CONFLICT

As has been true during most of the post–World War II period, there are currently two schools of thought with regard to race relations and, more specifically, to the pertinence of public policy for ameliorating race-related conflict in Britain. On the one side, there are those who argue that the role of government in improving race relations should be almost exclusively limited to restricting the number of new nonwhite immigrants and establishing the general macroeconomic conditions that will improve, rather inevitably and automatically it is believed, the prospects for greater economic opportunity and mobility among ethnic and racial minorities and their steady incorporation into the economic, social, and political mainstream. This view assumes that, like many of the groups who previously migrated to Britain, Britain's new ethnic and racial minorities will eventually gain their appropriate place as soon as their population size is stabilized, and they gradually transcend their immigrant origins and adopt the economic, social, and political behavior patterns long prevalent among whites.

On the other side, there are those who insist that Britain's new ethnic and racial minorities confront serious obstacles to their successful incorporation, obstacles that are not likely to be surmounted even over the medium to long term. This side points to public opinion surveys and other empirical evidence of racial prejudice, including overt racially discriminatory practices among employers, judges, poli-

ticians, landlords, the police, and other elites, to justify their prescription of active government intervention to combat prejudice and to reduce disadvantage. Although this camp has succeeded over time in persuading Britain's major political parties to support and enact significant antidiscrimination legislation and other legal protections, it nevertheless remains dissatisfied with the effectiveness of existing measures as well as the breadth, depth, and pace of social change. Thus inspired, these voices advocate yet more aggressive and comprehensive political action, including the adoption in Britain of American-style affirmative action programs, in order to accelerate the incorporation of the new ethnic and racial minorities into the economic, social, and political mainstream.

SIGNIFICANCE

The conflict over which public policy course to adopt in confronting the challenges posed by the emergence of a multicultural society in Britain is not likely to be resolved any time soon. Indeed, apart from the difficult policy dilemmas raised by these challenges, there lurks an ever-present ideological tension over the changes already wrought by nonwhite immigration and the degree to which Britons should embrace further change.

This ideological tension was perhaps best reflected in the social and political turmoil that surfaced during the so-called Salman Rushdie affair during the late 1980s and early 1990s. On one side stood thousands of militantly devout British Muslims who were incensed by the publication in Britain of Rushdie's book, *The Satanic Verses,* which they viewed as blasphemy against their religion. On the opposite side were numerous white Britons who saw in the more militant and sometimes violent Muslim reaction to the publication of Rushdie's provocative book an ominous threat to freedom of speech and the preservation of a liberal and tolerant society. Although the turmoil over the publication of *The Satanic Verses* directly affected only a minority of Britons, white and nonwhite, it nevertheless symbolized the depth of the current ideological divide over what constitutes the good society, a divide that has largely sprung from the experience of significant nonwhite immigrant settlement. Moreover, it underscored the erroneousness of the assumption, previously held by and comforting many white Britons, that the incorporation of Britain's new ethnic and racial minorities would be a relatively seamless process, a process assumed to be driven by the same forces of assimilation that had led to the rather successful incorporation of Jews, Poles, and other minorities into British society in decades and centuries past.

Whatever its future course, it is rather clear that the story of British race relations potentially offers valuable lessons for those West European societies who have begun to grapple more recently with the legacies of their own post–World War II nonwhite immigration. Less a model for other countries to emulate, the British case perhaps better serves as an example of what can and does go wrong when societies and governments only reluctantly, and perhaps rather tardily, address the challenges posed by nonwhite immigration and the race-related conflict it spawns.

See also France: The "Foreigner" Issue; and Germany: The Foreign Worker Issue.

NOTES

1. Alan Travis, "Ethnic Minorities Grow to 1 in 10," *Guardian Unlimited* (February 23, 2001), available online at http://society.guardian.co.uk/race equality/story/0,8150,441925,00.html; and "Race Relations: Integrated but Unequal," *The Economist* (February 8, 1997), available online at http://www.economist.com/archive/view.cgi.

For a broader account of the topic, see Shamit Saggar, *Race and Representation: Electoral Politics and Ethnic Pluralism in Britain* (Manchester, England: Manchester University Press, 2001).

2. Zig Layton-Henry, *The Politics of Race in Britain* (London: George Allen and Unqin, 1984): 23.
3. David Butler and Anne Sloman, *British Political Facts, 1900–1979* (London, Macmillan, 1980): 300.
4. David Butler and Gareth Butler, *British Political Facts, 1900–1994* (London: Macmillan, 1994: 328.
5. Patrials are, by definition, citizens of the Commonwealth and of the United Kingdom born of or adopted by parents who had British citizenship by virtue of their own birth in the United Kingdom.
6. Butler and Butler, 328.
7. See Martin Harrop, Judith England, and Christopher T. Husbands, "The Bases of National Front Support," *Political Studies* 28, no. 2 (June 1980): 271–83.
8. "Race Relations: Integrated but Unequal," op. cit.
9. Ibid.

SUGGESTED READINGS

Blackstone, Tessa. Bhikhu Parekh, and Peter Sanders, eds. *Race Relations in Britain: A Developing Agenda*. London: Routledge, 1998.

Goulbourne, Harry. *Race Relations in Britain Since 1945*. New York: St. Martin's Press, 1998.

Hansen, Randall. *Citizenship and Immigration in Post-War Britain*. Oxford, England: Oxford University Press, 2000.

Layton-Henry, Zig. *The Politics of Immigration*. Oxford, England; Blackwell, 1992.

Messina, Anthony M. *Race and Party Competition in Britain*. Oxford, England: Clarendon Press, 1989.

Paul, Kathleen. *Whitewashing Britain: Race and Citizenship in the Postwar Era*. Ithaca, N.Y.: Cornell University Press, 1997.

Phillips, Mike, and Trevor Phillips. *Windrush: The Irresistible Rise of Multi-Racial Britain*. London: HarperCollins, 1998.

Rich, Paul B. *Race and Empire in British Politics*. New York: Cambridge University Press, 1990.

Saggar, Shamit. *Race and Representation: Electoral Politics and Ethnic Pluralism in Britain*. Manchester, England: Manchester University Press, 2001.

Solomos, John, and Les Back. *Race, Politics and Social Change*. London: Routledge, 1995.

United Kingdom

The Irish Question and the Partition of Ireland

Sean P. Duffy

TIMELINE

1171 Norman Conquest of Ireland is completed; Anglo-Norman rule is established in Dublin. Most Irish kings and princes swear fealty to Henry II. Direct English control over Irish affairs erodes over the following 350 years.

1533–1603 Tudors reconquer Ireland; Protestant Reformation takes place in England; "Old English" aristocracy is replaced with new Anglo-Protestant landowning nobility; plantations of English Protestants begin.

1691 The Treaty of Limerick is signed, in which James II surrenders to William II (of Orange); Anglo-Irish and Catholic Irish aristocrats who supported James lose their lands and titles.

1695 The Penal Law Code is established, which imposes a series of religious, social, and political limitations on Catholics.

1782 Led by Henry Grattan, the Irish Parliament wins restricted political autonomy from Westminster, establishing the golden era of Irish parliamentary democracy.

1791 The Society of United Irishmen is founded by Theobald Wolf Tone.

1795 The Orange Order is founded in Ulster.

1798 A republican insurrection fails.

1800 The Act of Union is passed. Beginning in 1801, Ireland is ruled directly from London.

1829 The Catholic Emancipation Act is passed.

1840s The Young Ireland Movement, which emobdies a nonsectarian nationalism, is started by Thomas Davis.

1844–1848 The potato crop fails, bringing famine and causing waves of mass emigration.

1858 The Irish Republican Brotherhood (IRB) is founded, with a view to gaining Irish independence. It has strong roots and connections in the United States.

1867 Fenian (IRB) uprising in Ireland is crushed.

1867 and 1884 Reform acts in the Westminster Parliament effectively extend the vote to many Catholics in Ireland.

1879 Land League, led by Michael Davitt, spearheads the land wars against landlords who evict their tenants and pushes for land reform legislation.

1880 Charles Stewart Parnell becomes leader of the Irish Parliamentary Party at Westminster. He begins to campaign for Irish home rule.

1884 The Gaelic Athletic Association is founded.

1892 The Gaelic League is founded by Douglas Hyde, a Protestant.

1893 Home Rule Bill is passed in House of Commons, but is blocked in House of Lords.

1899 The Irish National Theatre is established by William Butler Yeats.

1900 Arthur Griffith founds the *Cumann na nGaedhael.*

1905 Ulster Unionist Council is founded to oppose home rule.

1907 Arthur Griffith founds the Sinn Féin League to work toward a modern Catholic state.

1911 Parliamentary reform ends the House of Lords's ability to veto legislation, granting it merely the ability to delay implementation.

1912 400,000 Ulster Protestants sign a Solemn League and Covenant to defend Ulster against home rule.

1913 A second Home Rule Bill is passed in the House of Commons and delayed by the House of Lords. The Ulster Volunteer Force (UVF) is formed to resist further attempts to institute home rule.

1913–1918 World War I is fought. In 1918 conscription is introduced.

1916 An Irish Republic is proclaimed on Easter Monday in Dublin.

1918–1921 The Anglo-Irish War is fought.

1920 The Westminster Parliament passes the Government of Ireland Act, providing for parliaments in Dublin and Belfast subordinate to itself.

1922 The Anglo-Irish Treaty establishes an Irish Free State comprising 26 of Irelands' 32 counties, under the United Kingdom. Aspects of partition are deferred to the Boundary Commission.

1925 The frontier between the Irish Free State and the British province of Northern Ireland is registered at the League of Nations.

1949 The Republic of Ireland is declared; Northern Ireland remains a part of the United Kingdom.

The history of ethnic conflict in Ireland, which has its origins in the twelfth century, persists today. The conflict came to a head in the struggles for Irish independence in the early twentieth century but was not solved at that time. Partition of the island between the Irish Free State, governed from Dublin, and Northern Ireland, governed from Belfast, was an attempt to defuse diverging identities and aspirations (as well as considerable amounts of distrust and fear) which had intensified in the first few decades of the century.

The Irish historical experience could be described as one defined by conquest, colonization, and failed assimilation by and into the greater British identity. This was complicated in the sixteenth and seventeenth centuries by the religious conflict at the heart of the struggle for authority in England, which resulted in successive waves of disenfranchisement and marginalization on the basis of religion of many Irishmen and women, and the settlement of new groups of peoples. The result has been that modern Ireland can be described as one of the few postcolonial societies in Europe. As such, Irish political and social development, driven by the conflicts at the heart of Irish society, has been defined by many of the major movements in European and world history during the last 150 years, including the development of nationalism and anticolonial struggles for land reform and political independence. The culmination of these trends in the first decades of the twentieth century challenged Britain's idea of empire, with far-ranging implications from India to Canada. Partition has become emblematic of the difficulties resulting from colonialist boundary tampering as a solution to more fundamental underlying conflict. The incomplete resolution of these difficulties has been made manifest in the violent conflict in Northern Ireland in recent generations.

HISTORICAL BACKGROUND

While the groundwork for ethnic divergence and conflict was laid as early as the successive conquests and plantations of new settlers in the twelfth, sixteenth, and seventeenth centuries, the development of ethnic identities with identifiably nationalist characteristics began in the 1840s or—at the earliest—in the 1780s. As a result of the seventeenth-century religious wars in England and Ireland, Irish society at the end of the eighteenth century was split into a small, landholding, politically powerful, Anglo-Irish, Protestant elite, on the one hand, and large masses of disenfranchised Catholic peasants, on the other. The Anglo-Irish elite was sufficiently secure in its command of Irish society to win, in 1782, an unprecedented degree of independence for the Irish Parliament in Dublin. At this time, Irish political elites began forming ideas of Irish political autonomy, if not outright independence from Britain. This movement toward a separate national state faltered with the failure of the United Irishmen's uprising in 1798. Two years later, an Act of Union was passed in the British and Irish Parliaments which disbanded the Irish Parliament and instituted direct rule of Ireland from London. By removing political power from Irish soil, this act began a slow decline in nationalist political aspirations among the Anglo-Irish political elites, who followed political power to London, leaving many of their Irish landholdings and interests behind. Nevertheless, the move toward the formation of an identifiably nationalist Irish identity continued in the form of the Young Ireland Movement and its flagship newspaper *The Nation* in the 1840s. This movement, started by Thomas Davis, a Protestant from the middle classes, embodied an explicitly nonsectarian[1] approach to Irish nationalism.

Meanwhile, after a decade-long campaign for Catholic rights, led by Daniel O'Connell, the Catholic Emancipation Act was passed in 1829. This restored to Catholics many of the political and economic rights that had been denied them by the Penal Laws in the aftermath of the defeat of the Catholic King James II by William II of Orange in the 1690s. Reform Acts passed in Parliament in 1867 and 1884 extended the franchise throughout the United Kingdom; in Ireland, this gave the vote to many Catholics for the first time. These developments signaled a beginning to the political and economic rise of Irish Catholics.

The Great Famine of the 1840s, which resulted in waves of emigration that cut the Irish population in half in only 40 years, dealt a staggering blow to Irish culture and society. Ironically, this may have hastened the rise of such organizations as the Society for the Preservation of the Irish Language (1876), the Gaelic Union (1879), and the Gaelic Athletic Association (GAA) (1884), which was the longest lasting.[2] While nonpolitical in nature, the GAA gained mass support for the revival of traditional Irish sports such as hurling and Gaelic football. At the same time, it worked closely with Catholic social and educational institutions. This association, together with a ban placed on athletes who participated in "imported" sports (largely Protestants), increasingly identified this important venue for raising Irish nationalism with the Catholic population of Ireland. While intending to appeal to the broad Irish population, the GAA introduced a "reactionary" form of nationalism that defined itself in a way that excluded many who identified with (or participated in) a larger British culture. While not unique to the GAA, this rising trend in Irish nationalism would have important consequences for the development of conflict in the coming decades.

On the political front, postfamine Irish nationalism continued to be predominantly nonsectarian, yet institutions and movements important to the coming conflict had their origins in this period. The Irish Republican Brotherhood (IRB), a predecessor to the Irish Republican Army (IRA), was founded in 1858, with the explicit aim of gaining Irish independence. The IRB, which had important ties to the large immigrant Irish community in the United States, executed the failed Fenian uprising in Ireland in 1867, which drew its support from both sides of the Atlantic. The rising contributions of the largely Catholic American immigrant community accelerated the association of Irish nationalism with the Catholic community. From 1879, the Land League, led by Michael Davitt, spearheaded the land wars against largely Anglo-Protestant landlords who evicted their tenants. These comprised a series of formal and informal actions, ranging from demonstrations and boycotts (the origin of the term is in these struggles) to assassination and other violence against landowners and their managers. By bringing pressure to bear through these "wars" and on the parliamentary front, the Land League contributed to significant land reform in the ensuing decades, beginning with the Land Act of 1881. Meanwhile, the Irish Parliamentary Party became a significant, moderate voice for political reform at Westminster in the 1880s. Led by Charles Stewart Parnell, a Protestant landowner, the Irish in Parliament began their push for Irish home rule, a degree of political autonomy that would reverse the Act of Union within the context of the United Kingdom. In 1893 the first of three Home Rule Bills was passed in the House of Commons, but it was blocked in the House of Lords. For the next 25 years, the Irish were to use their leverage in Parliament to advance the cause of Irish political autonomy in this fashion, only to be defeated by the much more conservative House of Lords.

With the founding of the Gaelic League (1892), the establishment of the Irish National Theatre (1899), and the foundation of the Cumann na nGaedhael (1900), the cultural and political groundwork was laid by the end of the century for a vibrant, and increasingly assertive, Irish nationalism.[3] However, the largely nonsectarian nature of these movements had eroded, and the more demanding brands of nationalism were increasingly identified with Irish Catholicism. This sectarianization of Irish nationalism was to form the basis for increasing conflict in the early decades of the twentieth century.

THE CONFLICT

It is commonplace to define the Irish conflict (in the early twentieth century as well as in Northern Ireland today) as a religious conflict. This is, in fact, an oversimplification of many varied divisions in Irish society which are historical, often "tribal," and quite economic and political in nature. Nevertheless, the religious dimension closely overlaps many of these divisions, and the Irish themselves have used religion as an abbreviation for various aspects of Irish social and political cleavage.

Social order in Ulster, the northern province of Ireland, has never been easily achieved or maintained. It is here, perhaps, that the roots of Irish domestic conflict find most fertile ground. The implanting of Scottish Presbyterians from Scotland's lowlands in the seventeenth century substantially changed the social landscape, and the subsequent Cromwellian and Williamite attempts to resolve the resulting tribal conflict between native Irish and newcomers were never fully successful. Nevertheless, it was in Ulster that the Protestants were least in the minority, making up roughly half the population of the province, and it was thus there a separate, Protestant, society was most strongly asserted and defended, linking ethnoreligious identity with political power and economic access. While the roots of modern Irish nationalism lie in the foundation of the Society of United Irishmen in Belfast by Theobald Wolf Tone (a Church of Ireland Protestant) in 1791, only four years later, the roots of modern Irish conflict could be said to lie in the foundation of the Orange Order, following another round of conflict between Protestants and Catholics in Ulster. By explicitly invoking the Williamite (Orange) conquest of Irish Catholic power, the Orange Order became an important cultural and political referent for Ulster Protestants who felt the continual need to defend their social, economic, and political position in Ireland. With the increasing identification of Irish nationalist aspirations with the Catholic community by the turn of the twentieth century, these tensions again came to the fore.

In 1905 the Ulster Unionist Council (UUC) was formed to oppose home rule. Five years later, it formed a committee to buy arms to resist home rule with violence, if necessary. During the same period, Arthur Griffith founded the Sinn Féin League (1907). Literally "ourselves alone," Sinn Féin was dedicated to the formation of a modern Catholic state in Ireland, and it became increasingly identified with the more radical politics of the IRB. Griffith himself was a member of both organizations. By 1912, 400,000 Ulster Protestants had signed a Solemn League and Covenant to defend Ulster against home rule, which was explicitly associated with "Rome rule." A year later, after another attempt to pass a home rule bill was delayed in the House of Lords, the Ulster Volunteer Force (UVF), a militia ostensibly intended to protect all of Ireland, was formed to resist any attempts to institute home rule.

These more sectarian and nationalist elements of divergence were undergirded by very real economic differences as well. The southern and western three-quarters of Ireland remained largely agricultural in nature. While land reform during the preceding decades had effectively ended the old landlord-controlled land tenure system, the rural nature of most Irish society at this time facilitated the rising nationalist contrast (made by Sinn Féin and others) between rural, Celtic, Catholic society and corrupt, exploitative, urban British control. The regions of Ulster around Belfast, however, differed from this pattern. In addition to being predominantly Protestant, the northeastern corner of Ireland was also much more industrialized. The industries of the Belfast region tied the largely Protestant industrial working class to the larger British economic identity and interests. Ulster commercial and industrial elites also feared that an Irish state would heavily tax the northern industries to pay for a more ambitious economic statism. The Catholic populations involved in industrial production, organized around the turn of the century by James Connolly and James Larkin into the Irish Socialist Republican Party and the Irish Transport and General Workers Union, were largely ignored by the trade union movement and rising Labour Party in Britain, and increasingly associated the socialist project of labor with the nationalist movement. Irish nationalism thereby became combined with a drive for economic self-sufficiency and the prospects of state-led economic development for Irish interests, while Unionism maintained a closer identification of economic interest with the British industrial, free-market economy of which it was a part and regarded Irish nationalism as an economic threat.

Thus twin movements were born: one aiming toward a more radically nationalist, politically independent, and culturally Catholic Irish state; and the other waging a more conservative, reactionary battle to prevent the development of such a state. The Unionist movement, largely Protestant in its membership and concentrated in the northeastern part of Ireland, saw continued union with Britain as its best and most reliable defense against an increasingly assertive and exclusionary Catholic Irish nationalism. Throughout the home rule debates in the 1880s and 1890s, a coalition of Ulster political groupings worked with Tory (Conservative Party) allies in Westminster to defeat home rule in the House of Lords. When British parliamentary reform ended the ability of the House of Lords to block permanently home rule for Ireland in 1911,[4] Unionists were ready and willing to use force to prevent the devolution of political power to Dublin. In 1912 the UUC proclaimed a provisional government for Ulster to provide the administrative base to resist home rule, and the UVF was founded the following year to provide the military muscle against an assertion of home rule from Dublin. In reaction, Eoin Mac Neill founded a corresponding Catholic militia, the Irish Volunteers, which quickly gained membership from the increasing numbers of nationalists willing to use force to defend their aspirations. In 1914 British officers in Ireland implied that they might disobey orders to suppress Protestant unrest in Belfast. This made it increasingly clear that increased political autonomy for Ireland, no matter how established, was unlikely to be achieved easily or peacefully. The threatened violence and implementation of home rule were delayed, however, by the onset of World War I.

In 1916 the more radical elements in the Irish nationalist struggle made a bid for outright Irish independence. On Easter Monday, in Dublin, a small group of idealists seized several government buildings and proclaimed an Irish Republic. The uprising was ended quite decisively five days later when the British sailed gunships up the Liffey River and shelled the city. Although the uprising initially had virtually no support from the population, the British authorities' long, drawn-out series of executions of the participants slowly changed the tide of public opinion. In 1918 British Prime Minister Lloyd George introduced conscription. The conscription of Irishmen to fight "English battles" was almost universally unpopular. In December 1918, the transition from a more moderate parliamentary (home rule) movement to a more radical independence movement was made when as Sinn Féin succeeded in replacing the Irish Parliamentary Party as the main political actor in Ireland. Sinn Féin captured 73 Irish seats in the Westminster Parliament; the Parliamentary Party won 6, and the Unionists won 22. The following year, those Sinn Féin members of Parliament (MPs) who were not imprisoned boycotted the Westminster Parliament and met instead in Dublin, where they passed resolutions confirming support for the 1916 Proclamation of the Republic and declared themselves the legislative assembly of Ireland.

The Irish leaders' aspirations for addressing Irish self-determination in the context of the Versailles Peace Conference were dashed when President Woodrow Wilson was unwilling to press the issue on Britain, a U.S. ally in the war. Shortly thereafter, the Irish Volunteers, renamed the Irish Republican Army, conducted an all-out guerrilla war against British authority in Ireland. British attempts to regain control in the Irish countryside resulted in a full-scale war that lasted until 1921 and the signing of the Anglo-Irish Treaty a year later. Some of the nastiest fighting took place in Ulster, where Protestant militias ruthlessly suppressed Catholic unrest. Hence, the Anglo-Irish war was complicated throughout by the political and paramilitary pressures asserted by Irish Unionists in an attempt to resist or prevent Irish political autonomy.

MANAGEMENT OF THE CONFLICT

British forces were unable to win this guerrilla war. In 1920, in an effort to find an acceptable solution short of recognizing the presumptive Irish government, Prime Minister Lloyd George pushed the Government of Ireland Act through Parliament. This act finally granted home rule to Ireland in the form of two legislatures: one in Dublin, and the other in Belfast. This implicit division of Ireland, as well as the limited nature of the home rule granted, was unacceptable to Sinn Féin and the IRA. Faced with difficult situations elsewhere in their empire, and increasing diplomatic pressures from the United States, the British called for a truce in December 1921, and invited Sinn Féin representatives to London for talks. These talks had to deal with the difficult nature of Ulster-based Unionism and the very real division that had developed in Ireland, reflected in the two power centers of Belfast and Dublin.[5] The resulting treaty deferred to a Boundary Commission the questions of partition and the precise borders of the two political entities. It also granted to Ireland fiscal and domestic autonomy within the dominion, where the crown retained ultimate sovereignty and Britain managed external affairs. While a majority of the Irish cabinet (4 to 3) accepted the treaty, profound differences of opinion over the terms of the treaty led to two years of civil war. The grounds for the differences—Irish status within the dominion and the partition of Ireland—became the central components of Irish politics, north and south, for the rest of the century. In 1925 the Irish government ostensibly dropped its support of the Boundary Commission's efforts to renegotiate the line of partition, and the boundary was registered with the League of Nations. Subsequent developments of the Irish State (specifically the constitution of 1937) failed to recognize the border or partition as political facts at all.

SIGNIFICANCE

Partition as a solution to the Irish ethnoreligious conflict has always been an incomplete and problematic remedy. It satisfied neither group: nationalists considered it a hindrance to their goals, and Unionists in Ulster begrudgingly accepted local rule there as better than complete home rule from Dublin. In essence, the accomplishment was to create two incomplete statelike entities, each predicated on an exclusive ethnoreligious identity, under the overall sovereignty of the United Kingdom. The Irish Free State in the south adopted a strongly exclusionary, Catholic-Celtic basis for national identification that, when finally ensconced in the constitution of 1937, provided a major stumbling block to the highly vaunted aspirations for reunification. Likewise, the Parliament established in Belfast provided the means for the creation in Ulster of a "Protestant state for a Protestant people." This Protestant state became notorious for its economic and political repression of the significant Catholic minority. By the late 1960s, the province became virtually ungovernable as it decayed into political unrest and violence and economic stagnation. In effect, while temporarily solving the problem of intercommunal violence in the context of all-out guerrilla warfare, partition also allowed for the solidification of exclusively ethnoreligious bases for identification in Ireland. Both the province of Northern Ireland and the Republic of Ireland were formed on the basis of chauvinistic, exclusionary ideas of identity. Each included in its very definition terms that were to be undesirable, indeed unacceptable, to a significant minority of its desired citizenry. The boundaries of Northern Ireland were drawn specifically to create a permanent Protestant majority in the province, with no thought for the status of the Catholic minority living there. When the Republic of Ireland claimed, in its 1937 Constitution, jurisdiction over the entire island, its definition of itself as a Catholic, Celtic country continued to make it unacceptable to the Protestant majority living in the north, who would form a minority in a united Ireland. These tensions are only now beginning to be addressed, after a century of continued ethnoreligious conflict.

See also Czechoslovakia: The Peaceful Breakup of a State; Middle East: The Arab-Jewish Struggle for Palestine to 1948; United Kingdom: The Conflict in Ulster; and United States: The United States–Puerto Rico Relationship.

NOTES

1. By *sectarian* and *nonsectarian,* I refer to the religious nature of the movement. In Ireland, sectarianism has largely been based on the Catholic-Protestant distinction deriving from the seventeenth-century religious wars and subsequent settlements. In Ireland, three identifiable religious groups can be noted: Catholics (the majority on the island as a whole), Church of Ireland Protestants in the Anglican Communion (largely the landowning and politically powerful elites), and Presbyterian Protestants (concentrated in the northeastern corner of the island and largely working-class people).

2. In fact, it still exists today.
3. Approximately translated as "society of the Gales," *Cumann na nGaedhael* was largely a cultural and educational association oriented to the de-Anglicization of Irish society. The name was later used by the political movement that favored the Anglo-Irish Ireaty of 1922, and became the *Fine Gael* political parts.
4. In 1911 the Liberal Party (with the support of the Irish Home Rule Party) passed legislation that ended the Lords' veto power over legislation, and substituted in its place the ability to delay the implementation of legislation for two sessions.
5. A parliament had been established in Belfast, according to the Government of Ireland Act, and was already running affairs in Ulster.

SUGGESTED READINGS

Bew, Paul. *Ideology and the Irish Question: Ulster Unionism and Irish Nationalism 1912–1916.* Oxford, England: Clarendon Press, 1994.

Collins, Peter, ed. *Nationalism & Unionism: Conflict in Ireland 1885–1921.* Belfast: Institute of Irish Studies, Queens University, 1994.

Gallagher, Michael. "How Many Nations Are There in Ireland?" *Ethnic and Racial Studies* 18, no. 4 (1995): 715–39.

Irish Times. "The Path to Peace." Ongoing. http://www.ireland.com/special/peace/.

Kiberd, Declan. "White Skins, Black Masks? Celticism and Negritude." *Eire-Ireland* 31 (1996): 163–75.

Lee, Joseph. *The Modernisation of Irish Society, 1848–1918.* Dublin: Gill and Macmillan, 1973.

Suzman, Mark. *Ethnic Nationalism and State Power: The Rise of Irish Nationalism, Afrikaner Nationalism and Zionism.* New York: St. Martin's Press, 1999.

United Kingdom

The Conflict in Ulster

Sean P. Duffy

TIMELINE

1880s Several attempts are made to pass home rule for Ireland in Westminster Parliament. Attempts are met with increasing resistance from the Protestant Unionists concentrated in northeastern Ireland. Last tries are made in early 1910s.

1916 Easter uprising declares an Irish Republic, but it is put down in five days.

1918–1921 The Anglo-Irish war takes place.

1922 The Anglo-Irish Treaty establishes an Irish Free State, comprising 26 of Ireland's 32 counties, under the United Kingdom.

1925 The frontier between the Irish Free State and the British province of Northern Ireland is registered at the League of Nations.

1936 Edward VII abdicates; Irish Free State does not acknowledge the accession to the throne of George VI.

1937 Ireland ratifies a new constitution, defining its jurisdiction as all 32 counties of the island of Ireland.

1938–1945 World War II is fought. Ireland declares a policy of neutrality; Northern Ireland, as part of the United Kingdom, enters the war against Germany.

1949 The Republic of Ireland is declared; Northern Ireland remains a part of the United Kingdom.

1956 The Irish Republican Army (IRA) campaign begins but is called off in 1962 owing to a lack of support. Internment without trial is introduced.

1966 The Ulster Volunteer Force (UVF) is re-established.

1968–1969 The Catholic civil rights movement begins.

1969 British troops are deployed in Londonderry and Belfast.

1971 Internment without trial is resumed; a UVF bomb kills 15.

1972 *January:* Bloody Sunday. Fourteen are killed when British troops fire on peaceful Catholic demonstraters.

March: Stormont Parliament is disbanded; British establish direct rule and suspend civil liberties.

1972–1974 First attempt is made at a power-sharing executive in a new Northern Ireland Assembly. Assembly collapses after Protestants refuse to participate and Protestant working classes engage in a general strike. Direct rule resumes.

1981 IRA prisoners go on hunger strike in Maze Prison over their political status. Bobby Sands is the first of ten to die, on May 5.

1985 Anglo-Irish Agreement establishes the basis for a limited sharing of governmental responsibilities between the British and Irish governments over Northern Ireland.

1989–1991 Talks take place among four main political parties to establish the conditions under which peace talks could occur, accompanied by a short-lived cease-fire by the UVF and Ulster Freedom Fighters, both Protestant paramilitary organizations. Talks take place from June 17 to July 3, 1991, and periodically in 1992.

1994 IRA cease-fire is established, followed by a cease-fire from the Combined Loyalist Military Command. First official meeting between government officials and Sinn Féin is held. Decommissioning issue becomes the major obstacle to inclusion of Sinn Féin in the all-party talks.

1996 Mitchell Report lays down six principles of nonviolence for entry into all-party talks. The IRA's 16-month cease-fire ends with a bomb explosion in Canary Wharf, London.

1997 The IRA renews the cease-fire. International decommissioning body is set up to oversee the handover of weapons. Sinn Féin enters the talks, joined by the Ulster Unionists but not the Democratic Unionists.

1998 Good Friday Agreement is reached, setting the conditions for a new power-sharing government, accompanied by cross-border and regional political bodies; approved by parallel referenda in both the Republic of Ireland and Northern Ireland. The Republic of Ireland renounces its explicit constitutional claim to the six counties of Northern Ireland.

1999 The Ulster Unionist Party (UUP), the largest political party in Northern Ireland, boycotts the new Assembly over the scheduling of IRA arms decommissioning, effectively delaying the establishment of the Northern Ireland Executive. The Patton Commission report on policing in Northern Ireland is published; its implementation becomes another bone of contention between the nationalist and unionist communities and the British government.

2000 The British secretary of state for Northern Ireland, Peter Mandelson, suspends the Northern Ireland Assembly after a threat by First Minister David Trimble (UUP) to resign over the IRA decommissioning issue. Direct rule from London is re-established. The IRA subsequently agrees to put its weapons "completely and verifiably beyond use," and to international monitoring of its weapons dumps. The Northern Ireland Assembly is restored.

2001 David Trimble tenders his resignation as first minister over the issue of IRA decommissioning. In order to forestall elections, the secretary of state for Northern Ireland (now John Reid) suspends the assembly for a day (twice) to initiate consecutive six-week periods for negotiation. After additional moves by the IRA, Trimble withdraws his resignation, allowing the Assembly and executive to continue without new elections. United Kingdom parliamentary elections indicate a loss of strength in Northern Ireland for the moderate nationalist party—the SDLP—and the pro-agreement unionist party—the UUP. Both Sinn Féin and the Democratic Unionist Party (DUP) record gains, foreboding difficult times following the Ulster elections scheduled for the spring of 2003.

2002 Isolated sectarian violence erupts in Belfast—predominantly around "interface zones" between Catholic and Protestant communities in the North and East sections of the city. Alex Maskey becomes the first Sinn Féin Lord Mayor of Belfast.

The conflict in Ulster, specifically that concentrated in the six counties that make up the territory of Northern Ireland, has origins and dimensions that are difficult to summarize. It is often portrayed as a religious conflict, although this is somewhat misleading. While religion is a useful marker for the different communities—or perspectives—represented, the conflict could be as easily summarized as one between ethnicities (Gaelic Irish vs. Anglo-Scottish), political ideologies (republicanism vs. loyalism), political allegiance (Irish nationalist vs. British unionist), or historical identity (native vs. settler). The difficult thing about the conflict is that all these dimensions overlap, and they are compounded by recent and ancient histories of animosity, political domination, and economic inequality.

It is also difficult to identify the scope—or context—of the conflict. Many have preferred to view it as a conflict internal to Northern Ireland, between two separate communities within the territory. Alternatively, its origins can be seen in social, political, and economic divisions in Ireland as a whole, which resulted in a conflict that was incompletely solved by partition of the island between 1922 and 1925. Finally, the conflict can be seen as one that encompasses the relations between Ireland and Great Britain—relations begun hundreds of years ago, continued in the context of empire, and now existing largely between two sovereign nation-states in the context of a unifying Europe and an international system no longer dominated by Britain. All three contexts are part of the story; nevertheless, the proximate cause of the current "Troubles" in the six counties of Northern Ireland is undisputedly the partition of Ireland, which was made a political fact of life between 1922 and 1925. The partition established two separate governments in Ireland: a nationalist government oriented toward Irish independence, based in Dublin, and a unionist government in Belfast, dedicated to the preservation of traditional privileges and associations within the United Kingdom. Both political entities encompassed minorities opposed to their

orientations; however, in the north the sizable Catholic nationalist minority was never assimilated into the Northern Irish political identity. Thus, the conflict in Ulster, in a very real sense, also represents the ultimate crisis of governance in Northern Ireland, Ireland, and indeed throughout the British Isles.

Recently, there has been a movement toward a potential resolution of the conflict, which claimed some 3,400 lives from 1968 through 1998, injured over 20,000, and personally affected up to 80 percent of the population in some areas.[1] The 1990s saw the ending of formal hostilities via a series of interrelated cease-fires agreed to by rival paramilitary organizations, the establishment of a power-sharing executive in Northern Ireland and the promise of regional governmental institutions, and changes in the Republic of Ireland's constitutional and economic positions. These changes hold out real hope for the eventual solution of these difficulties on three fronts: the creation of effective local institutions of governance, the resolution of issues of political sovereignty and individual identity, and an effective reconstruction of regional political dynamics and relationships.

HISTORICAL BACKGROUND

Partition has its origins in the Government of Ireland Act of 1920. This act was passed by the British Parliament to defuse the conflict that had erupted between it and the Irish nationalists, who had been promised some measure of local control, but who were increasingly fighting for complete independence from Great Britain. One of the major difficulties that had emerged in the resolution of the British-Irish conflict was the fact that a significant portion of the Irish population wished to retain its ties to Great Britain. These Unionists feared that any degree of local government would eventually lead to complete independence and the subordination of Protestant, loyalist Irishmen and women to a Catholic, Celtic nationalist identity. In the interests of granting home rule before the political pressures for complete independence became too great, the British Parliament allowed for the establishment of two local parliamentary assemblies, one in Dublin and the other in Belfast. The Belfast assembly was to have jurisdiction over the six most heavily unionist (and Protestant) counties in the northeast of the island, and the Dublin parliament was to have jurisdiction over the rest of Ireland.

The political tide continued to push events, however, and the Irish uprising continued for another year and a half. While the Belfast assembly began meeting in 1920, parliamentarians in the rest of Ireland refused to act in the context of the Government of Ireland Act, and they continued fighting through 1921. In December 1921, the Articles of Agreement for a Treaty between Great Britain and Ireland were signed, establishing the Irish Free State as a British dominion. The treaty allowed the six counties in the north to "opt out," which they did, and to continue to be governed by the assembly in Belfast. The boundary between these political entities was to be provisional on ratification by a Boundary Commission, which was charged with determining the border in the fairest, most just manner possible. This political solution satisfied neither Irish nationalists nor the Unionists in the six counties. The nationalists split over the terms of the treaty, with partition chief among the contested issues. For the nationalist movement in its extreme, nothing short of complete independence for all of Ireland could be accepted. Unionists in the north not only had to abandon to the nationalist parliament in Dublin all unionists in the rest of Ireland, but they also had to accept home rule of their own—the very form of limited self- government they had resisted for Ireland as a whole.

In 1925 the border was registered with the League of Nations. Nevertheless, the political situation on the island of Ireland was such that Northern unionists perceived themselves as being under siege by a chauvinistic, irredentist, nationalist Irish state to the south. This context led to the establishment of a highly exclusionary unionist government in Belfast, dedicated to preserving a Protestant state for a Protestant people. A Council of Ireland, intended by the Government of Ireland Act to bring parliamentarians from north and south together in one forum, received no support from the regional governments, and they never met. From the beginning, there was little to no cooperation between the rival governments on Irish soil.

In 1936 the British government was convulsed by a crisis initiated by the abdication of King Edward VII. The British crown passed to Edward's younger brother, who became George VI. The abdication and recognition of George as king were both ratified by the Westminster Parliament, and all subordinate parliaments in the British dominions. The Irish Parliament in Dublin, the Dáil, recognized the abdication, but never acquiesced to the succession of George VI. Instead, in 1937, Ireland passed a new constitution, which defined its jurisdiction as "the whole island of Ireland, its islands and the territorial seas."[2] Nationalist Ireland's ambitions were finally realized in 1949, with the declaration of the Republic of Ireland. This declaration was supported by the Ireland Act in the Westminster Parliament, which officially declared the republic no longer a part of the British dominions. Northern Ireland, while officially claimed as part of the republic, remained a territory of the United Kingdom of Great Britain and Northern Ireland. For most of the island, this chain of events realized the ultimate goals of Irish nationalists; however, it also confirmed the ultimate fears of Irish unionists in the north. Ireland was now governed by a completely independent administration in Dublin that was dominated by a fierce nationalism and a strong affiliation with the Catholic Church. This Irish government was both explicitly and implicitly hostile to the ultimate continuation of partition and unionist government in the north. Although, with time, this hostility became less and less overt, the constitutional claims and (until the 1980s) strong involvement of the Church in Irish politics perpetuated the conditions for a siege mentality in the north.

Under these circumstances, northern residents, mostly Catholics, who identified with nationalist aspirations to become a part of the Free State (later Republic) were never fully trusted by the unionist administration in Belfast. The administration moved early to remove local political power from Catholic nationalists and created a highly gerrymandered electoral system to ensure almost total Protestant, unionist control over the government. This government retained exclusive control over political (and economic) power in Northern Ireland until it was disbanded in March 1972. In the meantime, Protestant supporters of the government exerted an effective monopoly over the best housing, employment, and public services in the north. The Irish Republican Army (IRA), outlawed in the republic itself, began its first campaign in the north in 1956. The same year, the administration introduced internment (imprisonment) without trial as a way of combating nationalist insurgency. Due to a lack of support, the IRA campaign was called off in 1962. The use of internment, the effective suspension of civil liberties, was an unpleasant indicator of things to come, as it was to be reintroduced in later years as a way of dealing with the loss of political authority that came with the "Troubles."

THE CONFLICT

The "Troubles," as the conflict in Northern Ireland became known, began in earnest in 1968. Inspired by Martin Luther King, Jr.'s movement for African American civil rights in the United States, Catholics began to march for their own rights in the cities of Northern Ireland. These peaceful demonstrations were met with rioting and violence on the part of Protestant mobs, who regarded the Catholic assertiveness as the ultimate threat to their continued economic, social, and political dominance of the province. In 1969 British troops were deployed in Londonderry,[3] and their presence increased in Belfast. This was the beginning of the militarization of the conflict, and of Northern Ireland. While initially introduced to protect Catholic demonstrators, the British military was increasingly regarded by Catholics and nationalists as the real manifestation of their oppression, and the symbol of continued British rule in Ireland. Violence continued to escalate. In 1971 the Protestant Ulster Volunteer Force (UVF) (reestablished in 1966) planted a bomb that killed 15 civilians, the first large death count of the conflict. As a response to the increase in violence, the administration reinstituted internment without trial. In January 1972, on what was to become known as "Bloody Sunday," British troops fired on unarmed Catholic demonstrators, killing 14 of them.[4] From this point, nationalists advocating the use of violence through such paramilitary organizations as the IRA and the Irish National Liberation Army (INLA) gained influence, and the conflict became dominated by violence from opposing Catholic, nationalist/republican and Protestant, unionist/loyalist paramilitary forces.

The year 1972 also saw the end of the social and political status quo in Northern Ireland. As the conflict escalated, neighborhoods and regions once generally integrated in terms of religion gave way to increasing segregation between Catholics and Protestants. The two religious groupings, always educated separately, were increasingly isolated from those of the opposing denomination. In March 1972, in response to the increasing loss of civic order, the unionist government was disbanded; direct rule from London was accompanied by a further suspension of civil liberties in the province.

In 1973 the government was reconstituted at Stormont Castle outside Belfast in an attempt to create a power-sharing arrangement in the province. The new assembly was constructed to guarantee both Protestant (unionist) and Catholic (nationalist) representation in the legislative and executive functions of government. This attempt ultimately failed, however. Protestant (unionist) hard-liners regarded this situation as a threat to their continued dominance of the province and, after declaring guaranteed minority representation in government undemocratic, they boycotted the assembly. This boycott was reinforced with a general strike by Protestant industrial workers in Belfast, which created a province-wide economic crisis. In 1974 the assembly collapsed, and direct rule was resumed.

By the 1980s, many of the conditions that had given rise to the civil rights demonstrations in the late 1960s had been addressed by the British government. There remained, however, a very real and significant incompatibility between the aspirations and identities of the two communities in the north: those who identified with a Catholic, Celtic culture considered themselves part of an Irish nation and aspired to eventual inclusion in the Irish Republic; those who identified with a Protestant culture regarded themselves as part of the British nation willing to defend their continued affiliation with the United Kingdom. Each group fundamentally views movement toward the accommodation of the other as the denial of their own aspirations. At the heart of the conflict, of course, remains the original Irish dilemma over who is going to control the political and economic power in Ireland, and to what end. In addition, the tit-for-tat, violent nature of the conflict seemed to have created a permanent condition of paramilitary terror in the poorest and most polarized regions of the province.

The conflict continued of its own logic through the 1980s and early 1990s. In a significant development, republican prisoners in Maze Prison, which was constructed purely for the purpose of interring fighters from both sides of the conflict, went on a hunger strike to promote their rights to be treated as political prisoners, not mere criminals. Ten prisoners died before the hunger strike was called off. In addition to bringing considerable worldwide attention to the conflict, the strike signaled a resumption of political battle on the part of nationalists. While on hunger strike, Bobby Sands (the first to die) was elected to Parliament from an open district. Although he never took his seat at Westminster, his election rejuvenated Sinn Féin, the political party allied with the IRA, which indicated that there was electoral support for the republican movement.

MANAGEMENT OF THE CONFLICT

Early attempts to manage the conflict were based on the view that it was internal to British sovereignty. Local government was suspended, law enforcement was militarized (including basing thousands of British troops in the province), and local civil liberties were suspended through the Internment and the Prevention of Terrorism Act. Believing the troubles to be a challenge to British political authority, the government responded by viewing the crisis as a breakdown of public order. Unfortu-

DERRY, NORTHERN IRELAND. Loyalist mural on Bond's Street in the Waterside area of Londonderry, Northern Ireland. Photo courtesy of Dr. Martin Melaugh.

nately, this approach largely supported the loyalist/unionist perspective on the conflict, and it left little room to bring the nationalist perspective into more productive play. During the 1980s, this approach began slowly to change. In 1985 the British and Irish governments came together to discuss how they could *jointly* move toward managing the conflict. The Anglo-Irish Agreement that emerged established the basis for a limited sharing of governing responsibilities. This signaled a new direction, as it acknowledged the all-Ireland, as well as British, aspects of the conflict— both causes and consequences. The agreement was built on the explicit recognition of the legitimate aspirations of *both* communities in Northern Ireland. It began by "recognizing and respecting the identities of these two communities in Northern Ireland, and the right of each to pursue its aspirations by peaceful and constitutional means."[5] An intergovernmental confer-

ence was set up, which gave to nationalists a formal means by which they could air their concerns via the Irish government. In retrospect, it was the progress made by this step and its surrounding climate of cooperation that made the more recent progress possible.

Changes in the international environment during the 1980s and 1990s also had an important effect on the conflict. The increasing integration of both Ireland and Britain into the European Community had the effect of widening the economic (and later political) context for the conflict, as well as the identities at its core. The end of the Cold War in 1989 changed the disposition of other external actors to the conflict and their willingness to become involved. In particular, the United States, which had always previously considered the conflict an internal matter of an important ally (Britain), now began to exert subtle pressure on the British and Irish governments to move toward a new solution. Significantly, in 1993, the Clinton administration issued a visa to Gerry Adams, the leader of Sinn Féin, to visit the United States, thus ending his pariah status. Finally, Irish society itself changed during the 1980s and early 1990s. Once an adamantly Catholic and somewhat provincial society, the Irish became much more secular and cosmopolitan. While earlier Irish identity was predicated on a more exclusive vision of what it means to be Irish, the Irish began to envision a new form of identity based on what Mary Robinson, seventh president of the Republic of Ireland and a human rights activist, referred to as its "imaginative possessions," based particularly on the Irish diaspora and the consequent diversity of Irish experience in the world.[6]

The Good Friday Agreement of April 1998 built on the foundation established by these developments. Its approach toward solving the conflict relies on the recognition of the aspirations of both communities in the north as legitimate. It also addresses the local, all-Ireland, and regional aspects of the conflict. Institutionally, it reestablishes a legislature with a power-sharing executive arrangement. This Northern Ireland Assembly moves beyond a simple majoritarian philosophy and toward a principle of joint consensus for important decisions—giving the minority community a stake in its own government and holding out the hope that government will not be used as a tool of domination. Another institution, the North/South Ministerial Council, was established between the governments of Northern Ireland and the Republic of Ireland to handle issues of mutual concern. This begins to address the all-Ireland dimension of the conflict by recognizing an island-wide basis for administrative authority, transcending the limitations placed on culture, identity, and economic interaction by institutions that enforce a strict territorial concept of political authority. At the same time, the Republic of Ireland has (following a referendum held in May 1998) dropped its territorial claim to the six counties in Northern Ireland, recognizing that unification of the island under one government shall take place only with the consent of majorities in both administrative entities. Finally, a British-Irish Council is to be established to create a regional context for governance. This council will be a forum for the governments of Ireland and Britain, joined by territorial governments in Northern Ireland, Wales, and Scotland, to pursue issues of common interest. This also has the potential of blurring the correspondence among identity, territory, and political sovereignty in a way that could defuse the difficult issues at the heart of the conflict in Ulster.

SIGNIFICANCE

The institutional structures established by the Good Friday Agreement, paired with more relaxed attitudes toward identity, sovereignty, and the politics of blame, hold out real hope for the final resolution of the conflict. However, there are still a number of difficult and significant issues to be resolved, and movement on these issues continues to be highly political and emotional. Decommissioning[7] and demilitarization are issues yet to be solved, and misunderstandings concerning the decommissioning process have already caused the suspension of the Assembly more than once. In a related issue, effective reconstitution of Northern Ireland's police force is imperative to reestablish trust in the nationalist community. Finally, traditional expressions of communal pride continue to provide the context for intercommunal harassment and intimidation. Protestant (Orange) parades commemorating defeats of the Catholic community several hundred years ago all too often cross the line from the celebration of heritage to a real tool of political and cultural intimidation. These are issues that will take a considerable amount of good will, in addition to political institutions, to transcend. Nevertheless, the peace process that has evolved over the last two decades in Northern Ireland has held out great hope for that territory, and many others confronting similar ethnic and sectarian conflict. The conflict in Ulster is indeed complex, combining complete communal polarization reinforced by historical conditions and political and institutional structures, all summed up in the constitution of identity, sovereignty, and territoriality. The most recent attempts at solution have tried to finesse and broaden all these aspects in an approach that seeks to emancipate the individuals involved from the tyranny of their historical, social, and political structures. The prognosis is good, but far from assured.

See also Canada: The Nationalist Movement in Quebec; Czechoslovakia: The Peaceful Breakup of a State; Spain: Basque Nationalism and Conflict in Democratic Spain; and United Kingdom: The Irish Question and the Partition of Ireland.

NOTES

1. Joseph Ruane and Jennifer Todd, *The Dynamics of Conflict in Northern Ireland* (Cambridge, England: Cambridge University Press, 1996), 1.
2. Article 2 of the 1937 Constitution. This was recently amended as part of the Good Friday Accords to relax the territorial claim.
3. This city's name is one of the more politicized place names in the north. Unionists refer to it by its (later) name, Londonderry. Nationalists refer to it as Derry, its more ancient name.
4. The British government has recently reopened investigations into the events of Bloody Sunday. Many have claimed that not only were the demonstrators unarmed, but the troops may have been given prior orders to fire, and may have been using banned ammunition. Current investigations also will investigate whether, and to what degree,

there was a cover-up in the initial government report.
5. From the preamble to the Anglo-Irish Agreement, 1985.
6. See Mary Robinson, "Imaginative Possessions: John Galway Foster Lecture," *Critical Quarterly* 39, no. 4 (1995): 3–8.
7. Decommissioning refers to the effective "disarmament" of the numerous paramilitary organizations (particularly the IRA). It has become a major issue for the Unionist political parties. Sinn Féin voices concern with the continued presence of British military troops in the province, a majority of whom are quartered in heavily Catholic neighborhoods or regions.

SUGGESTED READING

Anderson, James, and Liam O'Dowd. "Contested Borders: Globalization and Ethno-national Conflict in Ireland." *Regional Studies* 33 (1999): 681–96.

Brewer, John D., and Gareth L. Higgins. "Understanding Anti-Catholicism in Northern Ireland." *Sociology* 33, no. 2 (1999): 235–55.

Delanty, Gerard. "Northern Ireland in a Europe of Regions." *Political Quarterly* 67 (1996): 127–34.

Fraser, T. G. *Ireland in Conflict: 1922–1998*. New York: Routledge, 2000.

Hennessey, Thomas. *The Northern Ireland Peace Process: Ending the Troubles?* New York: Palgrave, 2001.

Irish Times. "The Path to Peace." Ongoing. www.ireland.com/special/peace/.

MacGinty, Roger, and John Darby. *Guns and Government: The Management of the Northern Ireland Peace Process*. New York: Palgrave, 2002.

McKittrick, David, and David McVea. *Making Sense of the Troubles*. New York: Penguin Books, 2001.

O'Leary, Brendan. "Introduction: Reflections on a Cold Peace." *Ethnic and Racial Studies* 18, no. 4 (1995): 695–713.

Robinson, Mary. "Imaginative Possessions: John Galway Foster Lecture." *Critical Quarterly* 39, no. 4 (1995): 3–8.

Roche, Patrick J., and Brian Barton, eds. *The Northern Ireland Question: Nationalism, Unionism and Partition*. Brookfield, Vt.: Ashgate, 1999.

Ruane, Joseph, and Jennifer Todd. *The Dynamics of Conflict in Northern Ireland*. Cambridge, England: Cambridge University Press, 1996.

United Kingdom

Scotland and Scottish Nationalism

Robert J. Thompson

TIMELINE

1603 James VI, king of Scotland, succeeds Elizabeth I as James I, sovereign of England and Wales.

1707 Act of Union creates the United Kingdom of England, Wales, Scotland, and Ireland.

1715 First major Scottish uprising occurs.

1745 Second major Scottish rebellion takes place.

1746 The position of Scottish secretary is eliminated.

1828 The Home Secretary Office is made responsible for Scottish matters under the supervision of the lord advocate.

1885 The Scottish Office is created and the secretary of state for Scotland post is restored.

William Gladstone supports home rule for Ireland and Scotland.

1886 The Scottish Home Rule Association is founded.

1923 The National Party of Scotland (NPS) is formed.

1934 The Scottish National Party (SNP) is established, combining the NPS and other nationalist groups.

1945 The SNP wins by-election seat for Motherwell, but loses it in general election a few months later.

1967 The SNP wins by-election seat for Hamilton.

1970 In the general election, the SNP wins one seat and 11.4 percent of the Scottish vote.

1973 Report on the Royal Commission on the Constitution is issued.

1974 In the February general election, the SNP wins seven seats and 21.9 percent of the Scottish vote. In the October general election, the SNP wins 11 seats and 30.4 percent of the Scottish vote.

1979 In the first referendum, 51.6 percent vote in favor of assembly, but the measure fails to secure the mandated approval of 40 percent of the total electorate.

1996 The Stone of Scone, the ancient coronation chair of Scottish kings, is returned to Edinburgh from Westminster Cathedral in London.

1997 In the second referendum, 74 percent vote their approval of a Scottish Assembly.

1998 The Scotland Act is passed by Parliament.

1999 Elections are held, and the first Scottish Cabinet is formed.

Scotland is an important example of contemporary ethnonational conflicts because of the manner in which Scottish nationalism has manifested itself over the years and the ways in which the political system of the United Kingdom has responded to it. In one way or another, three examples of ethnic politics—Ireland, Scotland, and Wales—have been consistent, major issues on the political agenda of the United Kingdom for the last 700 years. While Scottish and Welsh nationalisms have fluctuated in their political intensity, they have never taken on the violent dimensions of the conflict in Northern Ireland. Moreover, Scottish and Welsh nationalism has lacked the resounding issues and rallying points that characterize many other ethnonational conflicts. Nonetheless, the presence of these nationalist movements, especially that in Scotland, has threatened the nature of the political party system and even the nature of parliamentary sovereignty in the United Kingdom.

HISTORICAL BACKGROUND

Britain is a comparatively small island composed of three constituent countries: England, Wales, and Scotland. While they share a great deal in common, each country has its own distinctive historical and cultural features. As is true of many other small countries, it is difficult to discuss the development of Scottish nationalism without discussing Scotland's relations with its larger, more powerful neighbor: England. Prior to unification, Scotland and England engaged in periodic conflicts from pre-Roman times; however, even given those conflicts—and partly in response to them—the royal families, nobility, and leading families of both countries became highly intertwined over the years. In fact, the current political union of England, Scotland, and Wales stems from the succession of James VI of Scotland to the throne of England and Wales in 1603 after the death of Elizabeth I. James Stuart ruled Scotland as James VI and England as

James I. The Act of Union united these two separate kingdoms in 1707, thereby creating the United Kingdom of England, Scotland, and Wales. Dissatisfaction with this union and loyalty to the displaced Stuart line from the throne led to the uprisings in 1715 and 1745.

The Act of Union created the basis for the political setting within which the United Kingdom operates even today. Scotland was guaranteed the separation of its religious, legal, and educational institutions. Scotland was also assured, as a region, that it would have political representation in Parliament. England, Scotland, and Wales would have one monarch and one parliament governing them. The requirement for maintaining Scottish legal institutions, however, meant that separate legislation would have to be adopted by parliament for Scotland and that some variations in laws was permitted.

Over time, Scotland became highly integrated into the British state, culture, and economy. English as a language became the predominant tongue. Scottish Gaelic faded from usage. Thus, while Scotland as a country maintained a genuine sense of identity, that distinctiveness became based more on a sense of history and place than on religion or language. Scotland became the site of a dual identity with many of its citizens seeing themselves as Scots *and* as British. They did not, however, consider being British as the equivalent of being English.[1]

Political agitation for increased governmental autonomy for Scotland and Wales has been active since the mid-nineteenth century, but it did not attain electoral prominence until the mid-1960s. In both cases, a political party scored electoral successes that enabled those parties to claim and be recognized as the political representatives for Scottish and Welsh nationalism. The Scottish National Party (SNP), though, was much more successful than the Welsh nationalist party. In the October 1974 general election, the SNP won 11 parliamentary seats with 30.4 percent of the popular vote, making it the second largest party in Scotland. The Welsh Nationalist Party, the Plaid Cymru (PC), on the other hand, was able to elect only three members of parliament (MPs) with 10.8 percent of the Welsh vote at that highwater moment in its electoral history. The SNP electoral victories were followed by polls in Scotland showing high public support for the devolution of governmental power to a Scottish Assembly, although not for the SNP's stated goal of independence. Support for that option reached a high of 24 percent in the mid- to late 1970s, but generally stayed nearer the 15 percent mark. Broader structural changes less drastic than independence, however, consistently found support among a majority of Liberal, Labour, and SNP voters. Moreover, a substantial majority of Conservative identifiers also supported devolution.

Both major British parties—Labour and Conservative—responded to the SNP's and the PC's agenda after the PC's initial success in the 1960s, but lost interest when the nationalists failed to make as large an impact in the 1970 general election as had been feared. Not until the SNP threatened the Labour Party's precarious position in the 1974 elections did devolution become a serious issue. The Labour government then began its four-year-long push to secure passage of devolution legislation granting assemblies to Scotland and Wales, which culminated in the holding of referendums on home rule in the two countries.[2]

The decision to use a referendum to determine whether the Scottish and Welsh devolution bills would be implemented was not the Labour government's choice. The government was forced to accept the referendum in exchange for the support of some of its own backbenchers—members of Parliament not a part of the government—in passing the acts. Furthermore,

during the parliamentary debate of the bills, an amendment was imposed requiring that a majority of those voting and 40 percent of the total eligible electorate vote affirmatively in the referendum in order for the legislation to be implemented. If such affirmative majorities were not secured, then the secretaries of state for Scotland and Wales were required to resubmit the legislation to Parliament. This amendment generated intense controversy, especially in Scotland, as there was considerable uncertainty about how many persons should be counted as eligible to vote given the inevitable errors in the voting rolls. The Labour government, however, did indicate that it would seek to resecure Parliament's approval for the legislation if the 40 percent figure were not met, as long as there was a sufficiently wide affirmative margin among those actually voting.

The positions of the major political actors in the referendum were somewhat confusing. There were no government-funded umbrella organizations participating in the campaign, in contrast to Britain's mid-1970s referendum on continued membership in the European Community. As a result, the campaigns were very much free-for-all contests with each group responsible for raising its own funds. The SNP and the PC both campaigned for approval of the Labour government's devolution proposal. The Labour Party, though, was divided on the issue despite the Labour government's position, and individuals were permitted to campaign according to their personal preferences. Thus, an odd situation developed in the Labour Party with some of its affiliated unions contributing money to the pro-devolution campaign, while some Labour MPs played major roles for the opposing side. The Conservatives were similarly divided, although to a lesser degree since more of their supporters opposed the bills. Still, some prominent Conservatives, particularly in Scotland, campaigned for devolution.

The campaigns reflected this uncertainty of overlapping political loyalties. The anti-devolutionists, who got off to a much earlier start, developed a well-organized campaign that tended to override the campaign of the pro-devolution groups. The pro-devolution forces, consequently, were put in the position of addressing the agenda established by the anti-devolutionists. The pro-devolution groups also had substantial problems campaigning for the same objective. The Labour Party in Scotland, for example, had difficulty explaining why its supporters should support something desired by the SNP when it had campaigned vigorously against the nationalists only months before in several parliamentary by-elections. The pro-devolution forces also assumed that the substantial lead in the public opinion polls for some form of devolution would lead to a sufficiently large turnout and positive vote in favor of these particular devolution bills. This, faulty as it turned out, assumption was present in Scotland, where support for devolution had consistently held a large margin in the public opinion polls. Furthermore, in both regions, the entire process was complicated by the fact that a general election was obviously going to take place in the near future and that the outcome of the referendums would be an important factor in how the Labour government would face the electorate in Scottish and Welsh constituencies.

The results of the March 1, 1979, referendum were not at all favorable from the nationalist perspective. The Welsh vote was overwhelmingly negative. Only 20.3 percent of those voting supported the devolution act. The Scottish vote was affirmative, but only by a small margin: 51.6 percent to 48.6 percent. Measured in terms of the eligible electorate, however, the Scottish margin fell substantially below the 40 percent requirement because only 32.8 percent of registered Scottish voters

voted in favor of devolution. These results left the Labour government little discretionary room for interpretation. Even so, before it could decide to act, the SNP withdrew its support from Prime Minister James Callaghan's minority government, triggering a series of events that eventually led to a parliamentary vote of no confidence and the 1979 general election, which was won by the Conservative Party. In the subsequent parliament, the SNP's representation fell from eleven to three MPs and that of the PC fell from three to two. The new Conservative government repealed the devolution acts shortly after taking office.[3]

After the failure of the referendum and the Conservative victory, Scottish nationalism entered a new phase in its development, one that illustrates its reciprocal dependence on the fortunes of the Labour Party. The Conservative governments of Margaret Thatcher and John Major basically ignored Scottish nationalism. Scotland was not electorally important to their prospects except as a thorn in the side of the Labour Party. During the 1980s and through the mid-1990s, Labour became increasingly dependent on the seats it secured in Scotland. As a consequence, there was no incentive for the Conservatives to act; moreover, the SNP's vote-getting power seemed to have stagnated between 10 and 15 percent of the Scottish vote. Labour, on the other hand, could not avoid the devolution issue or the influence of the SNP. If it failed to support Scottish interests, it stood to lose even more seats in Parliament, as the SNP would pull votes away from its candidates. At the same time, general interest in the concept of independence seemed to grow, and interest in devolution shifted from an assembly with limited powers to a parliament with more general authority.

Labour's response to its electoral dilemma and the growing general support for Scottish self-government evolved over time. In the 1992 general election, the party pledged to legislate on Scottish and Welsh devolution within its first year in office if elected. While Labour was not successful in 1992, support for devolution continued to build. The pledge was repeated in the May 1997 general election. Within three months of the winning that election, the new Labour government issued white papers on devolution, and a second Scottish referendum was scheduled for September 1997. As pledged, this time around, the referendum was held prior to the development of the full details of the legislative proposals. With a turnout of 60 percent of the Scottish electorate, 74 percent of the voters supported the idea of creating a Scottish Parliament, and 63 percent endorsed granting the new parliament taxation powers.[4]

Legislation was subsequently introduced in Parliament on December 17, 1997. It secured Royal Assent in 1998, with the first elections scheduled for May 6, 1999. The Labour Party emerged from those elections with a large plurality with 53 of the assembly's seats, but not the majority needed for governing. The SNP came in second with 35 seats, followed by the Conservatives with 18 seats and the Liberal Democrats with 17. With the new Parliament having a total of 129 seats, 65 seats were needed for a governing majority. Donald Dewar, the longtime leader of Scottish interests within the Labour Party and former secretary of state for Scotland, consequently formed a coalition government—with the Liberal Democrats—to form the first Scottish Cabinet. He was sworn in as first minister on May 17, 1999, and the Scottish Parliament assumed its full powers six weeks later on July 1, 1999.[5]

The powers of the Scottish Parliament are extensive, but not fully defined. Unlike the 1979 effort, the 1998 legislation listed the powers reserved to Westminister and left the remaining powers to the new par-

liament. Reserved to Westminister are those powers dealing with the constitution, foreign policy, national security, immigration, system-wide economic policy, social security and employment, and commerce. The Scottish Parliament, in turn, can legislate on almost all aspects of domestic policy, including health, education, local government, job training, social work, housing, economic development, forestry, fishing, sports, the arts, agriculture, civil law, the criminal justice system, and the environment. In many ways, the range of powers granted to the new parliament is not unlike those granted to states in a federal system. The Scottish Parliament, however, cannot change its own authority. That power continues to reside in Westminister.

THE CONFLICT

The key issues at the heart of Scottish nationalism are not easy to identify in a satisfactory manner. There have been no clearly resounding issues around which the political forces have rallied. As noted, Scottish cultural, religious, linguistic, and institutional factors are present, but they are not politically very significant. Neither has independence served well as a political objective around which to form masses of voters. While Scottish nationalists find these factors important, they alone do not motivate voters or activists.

One economic factor that influenced the political situation of the 1970s was the discovery and development of the North Sea oil fields at the same time that the British economy in general was having serious problems. Scotland had a lower growth rate and higher unemployment than England as a whole, particularly the southeastern region around London. For some of the more fervent Scottish nationalists, the claim that the oil was Scotland's provided a basis for arguing about past mismanagement of the Scottish economy and a resource base for promising better times ahead under a separate Scottish government. For their opponents, the oil-revenues issue was an example of the narrow self-interest base and lack of economic realism of the nationalists. In general, though, the potential economic benefits of the oil provided a serious context for the major British parties to reconsider the SNP's potential political significance in the 1970s. This significance continued past the high point of the oil's impact.

At the heart of much of the debate about Scottish nationalism, however, lay a general sense on the part of many Scottish voters in all of the major political parties that the central political institutions in London and, hence, Britain's central economic decision-making process was just not sufficiently appreciative of Scotland's needs and could not be under existing constitutional-institutional arrangements. The cultural elements and history noted above acted to confirm this sense of a lack of effective representation in any decision making affecting Scotland. The Labour Party's advocacy of the establishment of an assembly reflected Scotland's desire for more representation both among the nationalists and within Labour's own ranks. It also reflected the genuine sense of most Scots of being both Scottish and British.

MANAGEMENT OF THE CONFLICT

The management of the conflict generated by Scottish nationalism is a fascinating example of the striking of a democratic balance of political interests. All of the principal political leaders, activists, and parties have sought to deal with the issues raised by Scottish nationalism within the existing political structures of the United Kingdom while seeking to modify those structures in some basic ways. Over the past 125–150 years, the major political parties have consistently sought to deal with the issues through study and minimal institutional change. At times the political institutions moved slowly, and at other times they moved with surprising speed. In one sense, it is as if the institutions were seeking to determine the lasting power of nationalist issues and the magnitude of their constituencies in Scotland (and Wales). The Royal Commission on the Constitution studied the issue of devolution and recommended a limited assembly in the early 1970s. A Conservative study group had made a similar recommendation in the late 1960s. In some ways, both efforts were building on the nineteenth-century themes of Scottish home rule. Both were also laying the groundwork for the acceptance of the contemporary idea of a Scottish Parliament.

In a similar way, the political parties have been responsive to their constituencies. The Conservatives recognized early on that there was electorally little they could reap from supporting Scottish nationalism and that it was inconsistent with their overall commitment to the unity of the United Kingdom. So they chose to ignore the issue as much as possible. As noted, the Labour Party could not afford to avoid the issue. Moreover, supporting the idea of Scottish self-government was a long-standing tradition within the party, even as it ran counter to those other traditions of the Labour Party (for example, welfare statism) positing the presence of a strong centralized government in London. Failure to support devolution would have also likely confined the Labour Party to continued minority status in Westminister; therefore, a compromise eventually leading to the newly established Scottish parliament was acceptable. Even the SNP worked within this framework. Its leaders knew a hard-line push for independence would not likely succeed. They, consequently, worked within the system to build acceptance for the idea of more direct Scottish control over its own government. They still seek independence, but will continue to do so within the framework of the existing institutions.

In the end, by 1997 the establishment of the new Scottish Parliament seemed a foregone conclusion. The political system had debated the issue for almost twenty-five years, and the fears of disastrous consequences had eroded over time. The United Kingdom and parliamentary sovereignty could survive the transition.

SIGNIFICANCE

Scottish nationalism is worth considering as an example of ethnopolitical conflict because of the range of contemporary ethnic conflicts within the United Kingdom. It is also worth considering because of its other political dimensions. The United Kingdom is a unitary political system with a strong tradition of centralized government and parliamentary sovereignty. This means that the politics of the United Kingdom's ethnic conflicts, as with other political issues, tend to focus on central government actions. Thus, the issues raised by the conflicts in Scotland, Wales, and Northern Ireland potentially threatened the very existence of the United Kingdom as it has developed constitutionally. In particular, any potential devolution of constitutional authority to a regional government based in Edinburgh raised serious questions about the meaning of parliamentary sovereignty as the basic organizing principle of government.

Scotland is also worth including in this volume because of the changing nature of the self- and other-conception of its political identity. In the historical, English/majority perspective, the United Kingdom was a homogeneous country with Scotland, Wales, and Northern Ireland joining England in its imperial glory. The cultural differences among these regions were largely dismissed as holdovers from the past that would vanish with the passage of time. In addition, the United Kingdom was

a major world power with colonies and, later, the center of the British Commonwealth. That self-definition, however, has changed dramatically with the loss of Britain's position as a world power, the rise of the regional nationalist movements inside the United Kingdom, the immigration of large numbers of nonwhites into the country, and the United Kingdom's entrance into the European Community. The English still dominate the political system and culture as they are the major population group, but even English politicians can no longer ignore the regions as being unimportant. In fact, what becomes ever more clear is that they did not entirely ignore the regions beforehand. There has been substantial variation and diversity within the political structures affecting the regions and England over the years.

Finally, Scotland warrants inclusion in this study because of the effects this conflict has had on the nature of party politics in the United Kingdom, especially the internal politics of the Labour and Conservative parties. While each party has responded differently to the issues raised by the various national conflicts in the United Kingdom, both major parties have been significantly affected by them. The ways in which they have dealt with them illustrate very well how minority groups can affect the political options of the majority without political violence.

See also Czechoslovakia: The Peaceful Breakup of a State; France: Ethnic Conflict and the Problem of Corsica; Spain: Basque Nationalism and Conflict in Democratic Spain; United Kingdom: The Irish Question and the Partition of Ireland; and United Kingdom: The Decline and Revival of Welsh Nationalism.

NOTES

1. See H. J. Hanham, *Scottish Nationalism* (Cambridge, Mass.: Harvard University Press, 1969); and Christopher Harvie, *Scotland and National-*

ism (London: George Allen and Unwin, 1977) for a discussion of the historical development of Scottish identity.

2. See Keith Webb, *The Growth of Nationalism in Scotland* (Glasgow: Molendinar Press, 1977); and Jack Brand, *The National Movement in Scotland* (London: Routledge and Kegan Paul, 1978) on the development of the SNP.

3. See Robert J. Thompson, "Referendums and Ethnoterritorial Movements: The Policy Consequences and Political Ramifications," in *Ethnoterritorial Politics, Policy, and the Western World* ed. Joseph R. Rudolph, Jr., and Robert J. Thompson (Boulder, Color.: Lynne Reinner Publishers, 1989); and John Bochel et al., eds., *The Referendum Experience: Scotland 1979* (Aberdeen: Aberdeen University Press, 1981).

4. Robert Hazell, Meg Russell, Ben Seyd, and David Sinclair, "The British Constitution, 1998–99: The Continuous Revolution," *Parliamentary Affairs* 53, no. 2 (April 2000): 245–47.

5. Michael O'Neill, "Great Britain: From Dicey to Devolution," *Parliamentary Affairs* 53, no. 1 (January 2000): 69–95.

SUGGESTED READINGS

Bogdanor, Vernon. *Devolution*. Oxford, England: Oxford University Press, 1979.

Brown, Alice, et al. *Politics and Society in Scotland*. Basingstoke, Hants, England: Macmillan, 1998.

Kellas, James G. *The Scottish Political System*. Cambridge; England: Cambridge University Press, 1973, 1975, 1984.

Levy, Roger. *Scottish Nationalism at the Crossroads*. Edinburgh: Scottish Academic Press, 1990.

Patterson, Lindsay. *A Diverse Assembly: The Debate on a Scottish Parliament*. Edinburgh: Edinburgh University Press, 1998.

Scottish Parliament's homepage: http://www. Scottish.parliament.uk.

Scottish politics homepage: http://www.alba.org.uk.

SNP homepage: http://www. SNP.org.uk.

United Kingdom

The Decline and Revival of Welsh Nationalism

TIMELINE

1276–1282 Wales is conquered by Edward I of England.

1400–1410 Rebellion of Owen Glendower occurs.

1536, 1543 Acts of Union with England are established.

1881 Sunday Closing (Wales) Act is passed: first separate legislation for Wales.

1886 Cymru Fydd cultural movement founded.

1896 Attempt to merge Cymru Fydd and the Welsh Liberal Party collapses.

1921 Anglican Church is disestablished in Wales.

1925 Plaid Cymru (PC) (Party of Wales) is founded.

1964 The Welsh Office is created to oversee education, local government, infrastructure, environmental policies for Wales.

1966 Gwynfor Evans captures first House of Commons seat for PC.

1967 Welsh Language Act allows use of Welsh in legal proceedings and public administration.

1979 Referendum on March 1 for Welsh devolution fails with 20.3 percent in favor and 79.7 percent opposed.

1982 Fourth BBC channel in Wales (S4C) is established as a Welsh-language channel.

1993 Welsh Language Act puts Welsh on an equal footing with English in the conduct of all public business.

1997 A government white paper, *A Voice for Wales,* calls for a National Assembly of 60 members to take over responsibilities of Welsh secretary.

1997 Referendum on September 18 on a Welsh Assembly passes with 50.3 percent voting in favor, a majority of just 0.6 percent (or 6,721 voters) on a turnout of just over 50 percent.

1998 Government of Wales Act is passed by British Parliament.

1999 Elections held on May 6 for National Assembly; Labour Party wins plurality.

1999 Powers are formally transferred on July 1 from the secretary of state for Wales to the National Assembly for Wales.

The British Isles is a multiethnic area historically dominated by the English. Irish and Scottish resistance to that domination has resulted in some of the most dramatic moments in British history. Welsh nationalism is relegated to the footnotes; however, Wales has as much claim to nationalistic resentment as Scotland, if not Ireland. Wales was conquered by the English and swallowed up by English political and cultural institutions—a point perfectly encapsulated in a notorious Victorian-era *Encyclopedia Britannica* entry: "for Wales, see England."[1] More than the Scots, the Welsh have maintained a separate language, perhaps the most basic element of national identity. Why, then, has Welsh nationalism been such a minor issue in British political history? Conversely, insofar as 1999 saw the establishment of the National Assembly of Wales, the first independent political body in centuries, why are we are presented with the dual paradox of a historically quiescent nationalism that suddenly burst forth in institutional form at a time of economic prosperity and political stability?

HISTORICAL BACKGROUND

Unlike Scotland, Wales was not a united kingdom prior to its incorporation under the English crown. In the Middle Ages, Wales was divided among warring factions and the Norman "Marcher lords" along the English border. A briefly unified principality under Llywelyn ap Gruffydd was engulfed by the English conquests of Edward I (1276–1282), after which Welsh laws and customs were, often brutally, subsumed under English law. A rebellion led by Owen Glendower (Owain Glyn Dwr), which occurred in the first decade of the 1400s, established Glendower briefly as the last independent prince of Wales. English military superiority again won in the end, and Glendower vanished. Thereafter, the idea of Welsh independence became largely unthinkable, particularly after the rise of the Welsh Tudwrs (anglicized to Tu-

dor) in the person of Henry Tudor (Henry VII) to the English throne. Wales was fully incorporated under the English crown under Henry VIII through the Acts of Union in 1536 and 1543. Administratively and constitutionally, Wales was indistinguishable from England, and the Welsh gentry tied their fortunes to assimilation. British scholars might be forgiven for ignoring Welsh history, for while Scotland and Ireland were tumultuous, Wales was passive. The ways of Celtic Wales continued among the peasantry, but those seeking advancement adopted English language and manners.

The nationalist revival of the nineteenth century can trace its roots to the religious revival of the eighteenth century. Nonconformist religious sects (i.e., those that did not conform to Anglican doctrine) found fertile ground in the Welsh valleys. Choral societies and nonconformist chapels, whose ministers preached in the vernacular, proliferated the language. The emergent cultural nationalism manifested itself in the birth of the *eisteddfod* (poetic and choral competitions) and the founding of Welsh cultural societies, most significantly the *Cymru Fydd* (Wales to Be),[2] and in the incorporation of Welsh into the school curriculum in Wales.

In 1884 the franchise was extended to all adult males, eroding the social and political dominance of the gentry and clergy. Despite problems similar to those in Ireland, agrarian and political reforms were achieved through normal politics, obviating demands for home rule.[3] Lacking a separatist bent, nationalism translated into issues of nonconformity (e.g., temperance, disestablishment)—goals the Welsh sought to achieve through their overwhelming support for the reformist Liberal Party. In short, nineteenth-century Welsh nationalism was not about seeking political independence from the British Empire, but rather about establishing a distinct cultural identity within it.

David Lloyd George, who sought to merge Cymru Fydd with the separate North and South Wales Liberal Federations, attempted this marriage of cultural and political nationalism in 1896. The northern group agreed, but the southerners were adamantly opposed. South Wales, rich with coal, was industrializing rapidly. Except for the northeast, which bordered industrial northern England, the rest of Wales remained rural. Economic change also begat demographic change as rural Wales saw an outflow of people, and the south experienced an influx of English and Scottish workers.[4] The south became industrial and Anglicized, but the north and west remained agricultural and Welsh speaking. The "Welsh" began to be defined by ethnicity and language, not just residence in Wales. To those in the south, nationalism offered an alien language, the promotion of farm over factory interests, and the imposition of Puritan values. Nationalism thus proved to be a divisive rather than an integrative force, and this Welsh/Anglo-Welsh division shaped Welsh nationalism throughout the twentieth century.

With the collapse of Cymru Fydd, Lloyd George shifted his focus to London-based politics, and so did Wales, becoming the most redoubtable stronghold of the Liberal Party through World War I. Indeed, the war led Lloyd George to the premiership, and in 1921 he was able to deliver the Holy Grail of Welsh nationalism: disestablishment of the Anglican Church in Wales. Victory for Welsh liberalism was short-lived, however. Liberalism and nationalism were tied to such issues as agrarian reform, religion, and the language—all of which were rapidly diminishing in importance in Welsh life. A class division was replacing the liberal-unionist division that shaped Welsh politics. By 1922 the Labour Party[5] had replaced the Liberal Party as the dominant party of Wales, a position Labour retains. The new Welsh politics, focused on the industrial working class, sought salvation through socialist centralization. It could not countenance a bourgeois nationalism that celebrated the language and ignored the needs of the masses.[6] The other major party, the Conservatives, stood for an unbreakable union, leaving the Welsh to choose between socialist and conservative versions of control from London. On top of this, use of the Welsh language and religious practice were plummeting. The social bases of Welsh nationalism were eroding.

The movement might have disappeared were it not for a small cadre of academics and cultural activists who banded together in the Plaid Genedlaethol Cymru (Welsh Nationalist Party) in 1925, later shortened to Plaid Cymru (Party of Wales or PC). The PC's first leader, Professor Saunders Lewis, pushed for a Welsh-only policy and national independence, but it was an electoral nonstarter—the PC's first candidate for the House of Commons received just 1 percent of the vote.[7] The party was perceived in the interwar era as being socially authoritarian, envisioning a fascistic Wales that excluded English speakers.[8] The majority of voters, especially in south Wales, were alienated, and the party languished.[9] The war only made things worse. Mobilization brought thousands of non-Welshmen into the region as soldiers and workers. After losing another by-election in 1943, Lewis left the party, disillusioned, and retired from public life. For nearly four decades, no PC candidate came close to winning a seat in the Commons.

The postwar creation of the welfare state reinforced Labour's dominance in Wales. The economic boom brought unprecedented prosperity and foreign (largely American) products and ideas. Larger social forces were overcoming "Welsh Wales." The PC focused on defending the last ditch of Welsh identity: language. Yet this only further distanced them from the majority of voters. Evocations of English dominance and oppression fell on prosperous, hence deaf, ears. Welsh nationalism seemed perennially relegated to the fringe of British politics.

The Welsh nationalist story since 1945, however, has not been so straightforward. The movement languished for another two decades before breaking into Parliament in 1966, and it managed to attract double-digit electoral support in the 1970s. On the cusp of revival came the humiliating defeat of the 1979 devolution referendum. Devolution seemed as dead as the Druids when British politics took a radical turn under Margaret Thatcher, which ultimately opened the door for the nationalists' greatest triumph: the establishment of a National Assembly at Cardiff in 1999. To comprehend this strange course of events, it is necessary to examine the nature of the postwar conflict and its management.

THE CONFLICT

From the defeat of Owen Glendower until the reign of Queen Victoria, there was, for all intents are purposes, no Welsh nationalist movement. A movement developed in the late 1800s, but modern Welsh nationalism lacked a precipitating event. The stages through which the conflict progressed, moreover, overlap. It is nonetheless possible to discern three eras, each distinguished by the changing priorities of the Welsh nationalist movement.

The first era, that of nonconformist nationalism, began in earnest with the establishment of Cymru Fydd in 1886 and ran into the 1920s. During this period, Welsh nationalists sought to carve out a separate Welsh cultural space within the British polity. Nationalism and nonconformity were as one, with the chapels providing the cadre and issues for the nationalist movement. Despite its brief flirtation with the Liberal Party, the movement was more cultural than political. This phase was primarily about establishing Welsh identity and seeking social and cultural equality within the United Kingdom. It peaked with the 1921 disestablishment of the Anglican Church in Wales.

The second era, running from the establishment of the PC in 1925 to the defeat of the referendum on a national assembly in 1979, was a period of linguistic nationalism. Liberalism and nonconformity died together. Language preservation replaced nonconformity as the raison d'etre for Welsh nationalists. But the Wales they sought to defend was transforming. South Wales became industrialized and Anglicized. Class politics and the Labour Party dominated Welsh politics, marginalizing the nationalists for decades. A breakthrough finally occurred when Gwynfor Evans won the Carmarthen by-election for Plaid Cymru in July 1966. The party's percentage of votes broke into double digits in the 1970s and gained three seats in the Commons in 1974.[10] But 1979 saw the failed referendum on a Welsh assembly. After languishing for decades, why the sudden success? And, in the wake of the electoral breakthrough, why the disaster of the referendum?

One answer can be found in the fact that the elements that had hindered the PC after 1950 began to benefit Welsh nationalists. The welfare state and economic planning made the case for—and often put into practice—treating Wales as a separate entity. The postwar boom also created a materially secure generation open to cultural concerns, like the rapid disappearance of the Welsh-speaking Welshman in postwar Wales. By the mid-1960s the postwar economic dynamo was slowing, coming to a full stop with the 1973 oil crisis. Labour had become entrenched and immobile. Welsh voters were desperate for alternatives. By grafting economic concerns onto the linguistic message, the nationalists were able to reap electoral dividends.

The harvest nevertheless was modest. The PC was still a language-based party, adopting bilingualism only in 1968. On economic policy, they could offer voters only a slightly more activist socialism than Labour. Plus, PC support was still minuscule nationally. Labour then stole a march by offering devolution[11] for Scotland and Wales to counter rising nationalist sentiment in Scotland. Wales was tacked on largely for good measure. Many Labour members of Parliament (MPs), led by future leader Neil Kinnock, were flatly opposed to the move because Welsh nationalism went against the centralism inherent in their brand of social democracy. The result was an overwhelming defeat for the referendum to establish a Welsh chamber, with four-to-one opposition to the plan. Two decades later, however, a referendum would pass (albeit barely), and a National Assembly for Wales would sit in Cardiff. What changed?

The short answer is Margaret Thatcher. The period from the 1979 referendum to the present can be dubbed the era of political nationalism because the Welsh political elite and populace moved to support autonomy. The causes were numerous. Thatcher's free-market policies devastated the Welsh economy for years, reinforcing the region's peripheral economic position. More important was the "democratic deficit." Wales turned back Labour majorities, but the Conservatives won nationally—Wales voted Labour and got Thatcher. To make matters worse, Welsh secretaries were often Englishmen who represented English constituencies. By the 1990s, much of Conservative administration was conducted through appointed "quangoes,"[12] leaving the population feeling further that the Westminster political system was unresponsive to Wales.[13] Concurrently, European integration heightened the feasibility of an independent Wales within the European Union (EU).

Conservatives opposed devolution, and the PC remained inconsequential nationally. The Labour Party could deliver, save for their previous hostility to devolution. When both elite and popular sentiment in Wales warmed to the nationalist agenda and the Labour Party abandoned top-down socialism in favor of the decentralized New Labour of Tony Blair during the 1990s,[14] the result was the establishment of a National Assembly.

MANAGEMENT OF THE CONFLICT

Welsh nationalism has been managed by four methods. The least significant method has been separate legislation for Wales. The two best examples are the Sunday Closing Act (1881) and the disestablishment of the Anglican Church in Wales (1921). In dealing with nonconformist issues, separate legislation was practical because it did not upset basic constitutional arrangements. Separate legislation also required, however, that its use be limited. In a legal, constitutional, and bureaucratic sense, Wales was part of England. If Parliament passed numerous laws to the contrary, it would upset the constitutional order. Separate legislation could be used only to resolve specific grievances.

Administrative devolution within the British bureaucracy was a second option. The first Welsh bureaucratic entity was the Welsh Department of the Board of Education, established in 1907. By 1950 some 17 departments had established administrative units for Wales, albeit haphazardly.[15] The big change came with the creation of a cabinet-level Welsh Office in 1964 to administer health, education, economic development, agriculture, an so on for the nation. Further institutions, such as the Welsh Water Authority and the Welsh Development Agency, supplemented this. Administrative devolution offered bureaucratic coordination and greater cabinet

WALES, UNITED KINGDOM. Portrait of a Nationalist Party in a developed democrary. The members of the Plaid Cymru (Welsh Nationalist Party) in the Welsh National Assembly. Photo courtesy of the Plaid Cymru.

representation, but little more. These agencies, which were controlled by the national government, were intended to implement its policy. They did not provide an independent voice for Wales.

A third method was enhancement of the Welsh language. Welsh had no legal standing, and the use of Welsh has been in steady decline (see table). If "Welshness" were based on language, four-fifths of the population today would be excluded. Policies have, therefore, been implemented to boost the number of Welsh speakers and alter the legal status of the language. Welsh instruction was incorporated into state schools in the 1800s, but as a supplement to instruction in English. The first Welsh-language schools, which were private schools, opened in the 1930s. The 1944 Education Act directed local councils to educate children according to parents' wishes, opening the way for primarily Welsh instruction in state-run schools. Since Welsh activists drew largely from the professional middle classes, this encouraged high academic quality at these institutions, which attracted English-speaking students. English-speaking children are also introduced to the language through the Mudiad Ysgolion Meithrin (Welsh Nursery Schools Movement), about half of whose children come from English-speaking households.

Welsh has also been integrated into the public sector, where it had previously been banned. Spurred by a Saunders Lewis radio lecture in 1962, the newly formed Cymdeithas yr Iaith Gymraeg (Welsh Lan-

Percentage of Welsh Speakers in Wales

1891	55%
1901	50%
1911	44%
1921	37%
1931	29%
1951	28%
1961	25%
1971	21%
1981	19%
1991	19%
2000	18%

Denotes those able to speak Welsh, not solely or primarily Welsh speakers.

guage Society) used protest and direct action—especially desecrating English road signs—to secure official recognition of Welsh. This led to the 1967 Welsh Language Act, which guarantees the right to use Welsh in court and allows its use in public administration. A further Welsh Language Act in 1993 expanded this principle, making Welsh equal to English throughout the public sector and requiring public agencies to deliver services in Welsh. The state-owned mass media also contributed. The BBC's Radio Cymru began broadcasting in 1977, and a fourth television channel, S4C, was created as a Welsh-language channel in 1982. Bilingualism is not required in the private sector, however, and businesses and the private media remain predominantly English. There is, for example, no Welsh language daily newspaper in the country. That being said, these policies halted the decline in Welsh speakers . . . and deprived the nationalists of the issue. Indeed, because language and nationalism go hand in glove, the stabilization of Welsh in the population could alter the social foundations of nationalism long term.[16]

The final and most important method of managing the conflict has come through the devolution of political authority. Two proposals have been offered for Welsh devolution: the one put forward in 1979, which failed, and the one advanced in 1997, which succeeded. In both instances, devolution was driven by the interests of the Labour Party rather than by any grand constitutional scheme. In the late 1970s, with a narrow Commons majority dependent upon nationalist MPs, the Labour government proposed the creation of Scottish and Welsh governments. Opposition came from Conservative and Labour ranks, and the opponents gained two deadly provisos: that referendums be held in Scotland and Wales and that they receive a favorable vote from at least 40 percent of the registered electorate. The latter requirement mattered in Scotland, where 53 percent of those voting—but only 32 percent of the electorate—favored devolution. In Wales the result was hardly close. Devolution was rejected four to one by those who voted; only 12 percent of the eligible electorate voted in favor, causing one historian to declare, "Welsh politics had ceased to exist. Wales had finally disappeared into Britain."[17]

Or so it seemed. The intervening Conservative years changed everything. After Tony Blair's New Labour landslide in 1997, devolution was first on the agenda. Wales would get a National Assembly, but the powers envisioned were limited (although little different from the 1979 scheme). A 60-member chamber, 40 from single-member districts and 20 elected through proportional representation, would sit for a four-year term. Primary legislative authority remained in London; the assembly was limited to secondary legislation; that is, to the enactment of regulations to fulfill the goals mandated by acts of Parliament.[18] It was also denied tax-raising power. On the other hand, it was given the power to control the £8 billion Welsh Office budget, and in both its debate and publications, the assembly was to be bilingual.

As in 1979, referenda were held before any legislation was passed, but this time it required only simple majorities. Scotland voted overwhelmingly in favor; support for a Welsh Assembly was tepid, yet sufficient. On September 18, 1997, with a turnout of just barely over half of the electorate, 50.3 percent voted yes while 49.7 percent voted no. When the last votes were counted, the referendum had passed by only 6,721 votes. The Blair government duly passed the Government of Wales Act (1998), creating a National Assembly for Wales. The elections held on May 6, 1999, garnered only a 46 percent turnout. Labour's showing was below expectations, winning only a plurality of seats (28 out of 60). Plaid Cymru exceeded expectations, capturing 17 seats and emerging for the first time as a potential party of government. Labour formed a minority administration with the tacit consent of the Liberal Democrats, and powers were formally transferred to the National Assembly on July 1, 1999. At the end of the twentieth century, the Welsh Assembly

was still in its infancy, after setting off to a somewhat rocky start as a result of struggles over leadership and funding from London. Nevertheless, for the first time since Owen Glendower, Wales has its own government.

SIGNIFICANCE

Welsh nationalism is a paradox, both in its absence and its curious revival. Historically, Wales was much more quiescent than Ireland or Scotland. Being completely subsumed into the social, economic, and political institutions of England, much of the population saw their interest as one with the United Kingdom and its empire. Language served to divide rather than unite the people of Wales, pitting the Anglo-Welsh of the industrial south against the "Welsh" Welsh of the north. The dominant parties of Wales, both Liberal and Labour, were always distracted by larger national interests. No individual or event, moreover, sparked nationalist sentiment. There was no equivalent of Scotland's oil, Owen Glendower was no *Braveheart,* and the bookish Saunders Lewis was hardly a Welsh de Valera. The only Welsh political giant, Lloyd George, chose London over Cardiff. With wet logs and no kindling, Welsh nationalism never ignited.

All this actually makes for an interesting and cautionary tale. Welsh nationalism neared extinction at numerous points, carried on by only a few eccentric professors. It has never been a major political force, even in Wales, and it generally has eschewed separatism. The irony is that the policies intended to sate this trifling nationalist appetite—policies often driven by Scottish imperatives—may serve to whet it over the long term. Linguistic policies are creating a new generation of Welsh speakers potentially more receptive to nationalist appeals. The establishment of a National Assembly creates a separate sphere of Welsh politics where none had previously existed. Greater control of public policy and direct linkages with the EU may decrease the perceived necessity of a continued union. All this could instill a deeper, more widespread Welsh identity that might supercede British identity (as already seen in Scotland). Numerous exogenous factors (e.g., Edinburgh's relations with London and trends in European integration) will affect the final outcome; however, whatever the outcome the Welsh case clearly highlights the potential pitfalls and costs to central governments that seemingly innocuous policies of ethnoregional recognition may entail.

See also Canada: The Nationalist Movement in Quebec; Czechoslovakia: The Peaceful Breakup of a State; France: Ethnic Conflict and the Problem of Corsica; and Spain: Basque Nationalism and Conflict in Democratic Spain.

NOTES

1. Kenneth O. Morgan, *Rebirth of a Nation: Wales 1880–1980* (Oxford, England: Oxford University Press, 1981), 3.
2. Welsh nationalism was distinctly limited at this point: the Cymru Fydd was founded in London, and the *eisteddfod* was held in English. Charlotte Aull Davies, *Welsh Nationalism in the Twentieth Century*, (London: Praeger, 1989), 13, 23.
3. Vernon Bogdanor, *Devolution in the United Kingdom* (Oxford, England: Oxford University Press, 1999), 146–47.
4. Gwyn A. Williams, *When Was Wales? A History of the Welsh* (London: Black Raven Press, 1985), 178–81.
5. Keir Hardie, the first Labour MP, was elected to a Welsh constituency in 1906.
6. Welshman Aneurin Bevan, the conscience of the left, ridiculed the idea of a separate interest for the Welsh and English working classes during the first "Welsh Day" debate in 1944. See Williams, *When was Wales?* 274.
7. Lewis Valentine for Caernarvonshire in 1929. See Morgan, *Rebirth of a Nation,* 254.
8. The PC's Ambrose Bebb wrote, "It is a Mussolini that Wales needs!" In fairness, Plaid in the 1930s was a party of nationalist Christian democrats, not fascists. But opposing "England's im-

perialist war" in 1939 further alienated voters. See Morgan, *Rebirth of a Nation,* 254–58.
9. To jump-start the movement in 1936, Lewis and two others burned down the RAF bomber school at Pen-y-Berth and promptly turned themselves in. Tried in London, the three were convicted after refusing to testify in English. The outcry in Wales was immense. Welsh nationalism now had martyrs, but the PC was unable to parlay the public outcry into votes.
10. In fact, the party peaked at 11.5 percent in 1970.
11. Devolution refers to policies that transfer (devolve) political authority to lower levels.
12. "Quasi-autonomous non-governmental organizations"—government appointed but independent agencies.
13. No Conservatives won seats in Wales or Scotland in the 1997 general election.
14. Labour transformed to a devolutionist party with the resignation of (Welshman) Neil Kinnock and his replacement by (Scotsman) John Smith. His untimely death in 1994 led to the leadership of the (English) Tony Blair, who inherited and actively advanced Smith's commitment to devolution.
15. Bogdanor, *Devolution in the United Kingdom,* 157–58.
16. Sixty-one percent of Welsh speakers voted for devolution in 1997; only 24 percent of non-Welsh speakers did so. Geoffrey Evans and Dafydd Trystan, "Why Was 1997 Different?" in *Scotland and Wales: Nations Again,* ed. Bridget Taylor and Katrina Thomsom (Cardiff: University of Wales Press, 1999), 101.
17. Williams, *When Was Wales,* 297.
18. Because the division between primary and secondary legislation is unclear, the Assembly powers depend on how tightly legislation is drawn for Wales.

SUGGESTED READINGS

Bogdanor, Vernon. *Devolution in the United Kingdom.* Oxford, England: Oxford University Press, 1999.

Davies, Charlotte Aull. *Welsh Nationalism in the Twentieth Century.* London: Praeger, 1989.

Davies, Norman. *The Isles: A History.* Oxford, England: Oxford University Press, 1999.

Davies, Ron. *Devolution: A Process Not an Event.* Cardiff: Institute of Welsh Affairs, 1999.

Laffin, Martin, and Alys Thomas. "Designing the National Assembly for Wales." *Parliamentary Affairs* 53, no. 3 (July 2000): 557–76.

McAllister, Laura. "Changing the Landscape? The Wider Lessons from Recent Elections in

Wales." *Political Quarterly* (April, 2000): 211–22.

Morgan, Kenneth O. *Rebirth of a Nation: Wales 1880–1980*. Oxford, England: Oxford University Press, 1981.

Taylor, Bridget, and Katrina Thomsom, eds. *Scotland and Wales: Nations Again*? Cardiff: University of Wales Press, 1999.

Williams, Gwyn A. *When Was Wales? A History of the Welsh*. London: Black Raven Press, 1985.

United States

The Struggle for Survival and Equality of the First Americans

Joseph R. Rudolph, Jr.

Accursed be the race that has seized our country and made women of our warriors! Our fathers from their tombs reproach us as slaves and cowards. I hear them now in the wailing winds.

Tecumseh[1]

TIMELINE

turely cutting many tribes free from federal assistance.

1959 Alaska and Hawaii are admitted to the union as states.

1961 The Keeler Commission recommends that the termination process be halted.

1968 Congress enacts the American Indian Civil Rights Act, extending to Native Americans in statutory form many Bill of Rights guarantees. The American Indian Movement (AIM) is founded.

1969–1971 Indian occupation of Alcatraz Island by transtribal Native American organization occurs.

1971 Congress passes Alaskan Native Claims Settlement Act, recognizing the land claims of Native Indians, Aleuts, and Inuits.

1972–1997 Civil rights demonstrations conducted by Native Americans become violent.

1973 AIM activists occupy Wounded Knee, South Dakota, in response to efforts of reservation leaders to challenge the AIM's influence on the Pine Ridge Reservation.

1978 Longest Walk staged by Native American activists to protest pending federal legislation. The American Indian Religious Freedom Act is passed, guaranteeing Native Americans the right to visit their sacred sites and use sacred objects in their ceremonies. The Indian Child Welfare Act is passed by Congress to regulate placement of Indian children in adoption families or foster homes.

1988 The Indian Gaming Regulatory Act permits Native American tribes to operate gambling facilities on tribal lands.

Under the Constitution of the United States, the only group(s) allowed territorial autonomy based on ethnic origin within the federal system were (and are) the country's first involuntary members, the Native Americans (including the Native Alaskans). The saga of their search for survival and political rights in the continent they lost to the United States's predominantly European settlers is not a pretty story. Nor, significantly, does it cover a statistically important part of the U.S. population—a fact of political life that explains much of the history of the country's tribal peoples and the strategies that the Native Americans have adopted in their efforts first to survive and then to achieve the rights that others possess under the U.S. Constitution.[2] Their story is nevertheless worth examining as both an example of the limits of forced assimilation policies directed at even the smallest and weakest of ethnopolitical groups and as a study of the tendency for even oppressed minorities to splinter into internal factions when there is political power to control.

HISTORICAL BACKGROUND

The struggle of Native Americans to survive in an increasingly explored and colonized continent long predated the birth of the United States. As an eminent American historian phrased it, "The English-American empire builders went first for the land cleared and cultivated by the First Americans."[3] Likewise, most of the historical turbulence in Native American history under the U.S. government—the tribal wars against the federal government and the forced, westward relocation of numerous tribes—occurred prior to the twentieth century. Indeed, the struggle of the Native Americans for rights and liberty in the country's constitutional democracy began with the ratification of the U.S. Constitution.[4]

From Wardship to the Reservations

As adopted in 1789, the U.S. Constitution bestowed upon the tribes the unique status of being the only cultural minority granted territorial autonomy by the federal government. At the same time, it seriously limited their right to self-rule by making them the wards of that government. In that wardship system, members of tribes initially lacked federal and state citizenship and hence the protection which the federal Constitution accorded other Americans and several state constitutions guaranteed to their citizens. On the other hand, within the wardship system, the tribal nations (Cherokees, Apaches, and so on) were to enjoy a limited right to self-government, free from state interference.

The rationale for this arrangement was explained in several U.S. Supreme Court decisions authored before 1832 by Chief Justice John Marshall. Marshall believed in the right of the Indians to preserve their traditional ways, and he viewed the wardship system as a useful arrangement that would permit them to do so. To him, the system rested on three premises: the weakness and helplessness of the Native Americans, the degree to which their condition could be traced to their prior dealings with the federal government, and the government's resultant obligation to protect them.

In practice, the policies adopted toward the native Americans built more on the pattern of relations with the tribes established by Europeans prior to the adoption of the U.S. Constitution than on the benevolent guardianship role of the federal government outlined in Marshall's decisions. For hundreds of years, the French, Portuguese, Spanish, English, and Dutch had militarily subdued the Native Americans, denigrated their cultures, and confiscated their lands and wealth. Early government policies in the United States continued the trend, with little attention to the often highly developed levels of social and political life within the tribes.

Almost from the outset, the federal government's trusteeship responsibilities collided with the public and government's Manifest Destiny agendas, which called for spreading the polity from coast to coast and populating it with nonnative peoples. The first Americans were more often than not perceived as primitive, if not savage, obstacles to the achievement of these goals; their right to self-government was distinctly expendable when it conflicted with these designs. Thus, when the Marshall Court continued to adopt a protective line toward Native American rights in the Cherokee Cases of the 1830s, and, in the central 1832 case of *Worcester v. Georgia,* struck down as unconstitutional the state of Georgia's seizure of Indian lands, President Andrew Jackson refused to enforce the decision. Indeed, at the time Jackson was himself fashioning a land confiscation and Indian removal policy based upon the concept of "Indian Territory" and designed to push the tribes westward to ever newer and ever contracting sets of tribal lands physically remote from those inhabited by the settlers.

In theory, Indian Territory would enable the tribes to preserve their way of life. In practice, removal was usually at gunpoint, and the journey to Indian Territory was invariably harsh: most memorably in the winter of 1838–1839, when 4,000 of the 16,000 Cherokees driven from their homeland died on what has become known as the "Trail of Tears." Thereafter, losing wars (like Red Cloud's War of the Bozeman Trail in 1866), suffering periodic massacres (like the Sioux massacre in Mankato, Minnesota, in 1862, and the misnamed Battle of Wounded Knee in 1890), and enduring forced removals of the Trail of Tears variety marked the nineteenth-century history of the first Americans. In this world, the right to self-rule was a hollow one, and the struggle for physical survival left neither the tribe nor its members the luxury of pressing for other collective or individual rights.

The forced migration to Indian Territory did leave the tribes with a territorial base for self-rule; however, it was no longer *their* historical land. Most of the tribes originally living in the eastern half of the country were driven into the western half, just as those traditionally living in the west were invariably relocated to other areas in that region. Within half a century (1835–1883), the ability of the tribes to practice their traditional ways on their traditional land was irrovocably destroyed. Thus, although Native Americans have subsequently expressed a dual identity (American and Cherokee, for example), not unlike that found among ethnoterritorial groups in other developed states (being British and Welsh, for example), the "indigenous homeland" element, which has led to strong ethnoterritorial, home rule movements abroad, vanished for most Native Americans with the federal government's nineteenth-century relocation policies.

Reservations and Forced Assimilation

When even the most remote areas were opened to European immigrants, the Indian Territory policy was abandoned in favor of settling the tribes into the contained borders of reservations. By this time, even the U.S. Supreme Court had ceased to oppose the continued denigration of the first Americans' lifestyle. Rather, it was persistently upholding the federal government's right to rescind, by ordinary legislation, those rights accorded the tribes by prior treaties and refusing to accord Native Americans the protection given other federal citizens by the Bill of Rights.[5]

During the 1880s, the confinement policy utilizing reservations was augmented by a frequently cruel policy of forcefully assimilating the members of the tribes into the broader political community from which they had been constitutionally and physically removed. Concerned about the loyalty of Indians, the federal government began to send school-age Native Americans away from their reservations to boarding schools, which enforced extremely rigid codes of conduct. There, tribal ways were ridiculed, and the use of

native tongues in class could result in beatings. Meanwhile, a severe, secular rule was intrusively applied on the reservation by the agents of the federal Bureau of Indian Affairs (BIA). The right to wear traditional attire was often restricted, and the visible practice of indigenous religions vanished in administrative regulations forbidding ceremonies of "threatening unchristian primitivism." Perhaps most devastating, a direct attack on tribal territory was mounted via the General Allotment Act of 1887, which broke up tribal land into individual 160-acre allotments given to naive Native Americans who were often easily deprived of their land by unscrupulous land-grabbers.

Belated Citizenship

Only with World War I did these policies soften. By this time, however, the combination of forced removal, reservation confinement, and coerced assimilation had taken its toll. It is estimated that, as a result of contact with European diseases and the harsh life increasingly forced on Native Americans as a by-product of government-instigated and privately launched land-grabs, the number of identifiable Native Americans in the country declined from an estimated 1,500,000 in 1830 to fewer than 250,000 by 1890.[6] In addition, by the time of the Great Depression in the 1930s, Indians had lost two-thirds of the 140,000,000 acres owned in joint tenure by American tribes when the General Allotment Act became law in 1887.[7]

Despite its destructive effect on Native American life, a quarter century after its inception, the assimilation policy had also failed to achieve its goals. On the reservation, ethnic pride and self-expression had been stripped away, but poverty persisted, along with high levels of depression, alcoholism, disease, and low life expectancy. Children educated off the reservation and treated as outcasts in the broader society returned to their tribes

OKLAHOMA. Founded in 1882, the Presbyterian School for Indian Girls was moved to this Tulsa location in 1907. Like many schools created in the nineteenth century to educate Native Americans, this structure subsequently acquired a different mission, becoming the University of Tulsa cornerstone building in 1921. Photo courtesy of the University of Tulsa Archive.

with skills inappropriate to reservation life. Throughout, the traditional ways, which had endured among the tribes for hundreds of years, survived the intense, 25-year effort to eradicate them. Nevertheless, the goal of assimilating Native Americans into the American nation continued to inspire government policy as late as the Indian Citizenship Act of 1924, which bestowed federal citizenship on all Indians but without removing their tribal citizenship, without changing their wardship status (states could continue to deny them state citizenship and Fourteenth Amendment protection), and without giving them the Bill of Rights guarantees enjoyed by other Americans.

Restoration

Relief from the assimilation process and a return to the original policy of tribal self-rule did not come until the Great Depression. Even then, the policy shift came about largely as a result of the efforts of one man, John Collier, who in 1933 became head of the Bureau of Indian Affairs.

Relying on executive orders, Collier almost immediately restored religious freedom on the reservations and encouraged BIA agents to respect bilingualism and cultural diversity among Native Americans. Collier urged the Congress to restore the system of "shared governance," which originally characterized the wardship system between the federal government and the tribes, and proposed ending the allotment system, downsizing the BIA's presence on the reservation, reorganizing tribal governments, and subsidizing Indian culture and development.

Collectively, his proposals inaugurated a new era of Indian politics in the United States, but they did not go unchallenged. Opposition to Collier's agenda was intense, especially among those groups coveting Indian lands and the resources they contained. Lobbyists initially succeeded in excluding Native Alaskans and some of the largest tribes in the country from many Indian Reorganization Act (IRA) provisions. The assimilationists also achieved some of their objectives. When it was finally passed in 1934, the IRA did not contain many of Collier's suggestions for subsidizing a renaissance of individual tribal cultures. Moreover, while the IRA embraced the philosophy of the Marshall Court decisions recognizing the right of Indians to territorial autonomy and self-government, the IRA departed from Marshall's image of native self-government in an important way. The IRA proposed reestablishing a system of autonomy in which the tribes would be encouraged, though not required, to adopt governing institutions of a representative, democratic nature, whatever their traditional form of government had been.

Tribal reorganization proceeded slowly but steadily under the IRA, only to be disrupted by the communist scare in post–World War II America. In this setting, the IRA became vulnerable. The goal of assimilating the Indians had never been fully abandoned by its proponents. Moreover, the IRA had critics both on the reservations, where reorganization threatened traditional power structures, and in those segments of the broader society who attributed to the reservation system the high infant mortality, low life expectancy, poverty, drunkenness, and diseases afflicting Native Americans. The fear of a Communist menace lurking on the reservations provided the leverage that critics of the IRA needed to shift public policy in the direction of ending the tribes' special legal status.

In 1953 Congress approved a resolution calling for the eventual termination of the wardship system. Dismantlement began almost immediately despite the nearly unanimous opposition of reservation Indians and numerous non–Native American civil rights organizations. In response to their appeals, federal policy shifted again during the presidencies of John F. Kennedy (1961–1963) and Lyndon B. Johnson (1963–1969). Notably, the man leading this charge was a Native American with substantial status in both the white and Native American communities, W. W. Keeler, a vice president of the Phillips Petroleum Corporation and a chief of the Cherokee Nation.

Appointed by President Kennedy in early 1961 to chair a task force examining the termination policy, Keeler, within six months, issued a terse report recommending that, instead of terminating the existing legal relationship with the separate tribes, Washington boost its spending on the 360,000 Native Americans then living on the reservations and pursue the long-term goal of raising the social, economic, and political status of Native Americans to the point where a federal trusteeship would become unnecessary. Only where no harm would accrue did the Keeler Commission recommend reducing federal services to tribal communities. In July 1961, the secretary of the interior accepted the commission's recommendations; however, by then more than a hundred tribes had lost their ward status under the termination policy. More important, despite having acquired formal citizenship in 1924, the members of the tribal communities still living on the reservations as wards of the federal government continued to lack the constitutional rights and protection of other American citizens.

THE CONFLICT

By the time the Keeler Commission had issued its report, the Red Scare had largely passed, and the public and the government were beginning to focus their attention elsewhere. The conditions and civil rights of African Americans quickly took center state, and Native Americans benefited from the public's shifting interests. The attention that the civil rights of black Americans received during the 1960s also illuminated the diminished rights and the vulnerability of Native Americans in twentieth-century American society.

The political struggle involving the Native Americans that subsequently emerged had two broad dimensions. To the general public, the more visible front was the Native Americans' struggle for equality and progress in a political system that had long consigned the Iroquois, Cherokee, Shawnee, Apache, Navajo, and hundreds of other Native American tribes to second-class status in a country whose territories once were theirs. Less visible but equally important in explaining Native American politics in the civil rights era was the second front—the struggle between the leaders of the Native American organizations, which emerged from the reservations in the 1960s, and the traditional leadership of the reservation communities.

The Struggle for Constitutional Rights and Economic Progress

The general status of Native Americans in the civil rights–conscious era of the 1960s placed their spokesmen in a good position to piggyback on the African American and women's rights movements of the time. Both of these groups were comparatively much better off than twentieth-century Native Americans as a group—especially those exercising their qualified right to self-government on the tribal reservations, who constituted the poorest, least healthy, least educated, least long lived, and least constitutionally protected of all American ethnic groups. At the same time, the continuing, depressed social and economic conditions of Native Americans both on and off the reservations appeared to many young, educated, urbanized Native Americans as a graphic indictment of the ineffectiveness of the traditional leaders in representing Native American interests. As a result, Native American politics altered substantially during the late 1960s as pantribal organizations, such as the American Indian Movement (AIM), founded in Minneapolis in 1968, began to emerge and to shift the Native Americans' political agenda from its previous stress on the status of reservation Indians to an emphasis on improving the general status of Native Americans in American society.

As the agenda shifted, so too did the tactics of Native American spokesmen—from relying on lobbying the BIA to conducting public protests, marches, and other forms of direct-action politics. The 1969–1971 occupation of federally owned Alcatraz Island by a Native American group calling itself "Indians of All Tribes," ostensibly in support of a century-old Sioux claim to that island, heralded the beginning of a decade of television-covered protests; the February 1978 "Longest Walk" march from San Francisco to Washington, D.C., in protest of pending federal legislation essentially marked the end of that decade. In part, this changing approach to politics reflected the impatience of the leaders of AIM and other emerging transtribal organizations with the slowness of the policymaking process in Washington. To a greater extent, however, it reflected the fact that such organizations as AIM only began to emerge at the end of the 1960s and consequently had to work hard to sustain the momentum they inherited from those groups who had previously relied on public protest in order to raise the public's awareness to their causes.

The Leadership Struggle Within

From the outset, the founders of AIM pinpointed tribal governments as much as federal authorities as obstacles to improving the lives of Native Americans. According to AIM, the BIA enforced unjust laws, and tribal leaders collaborated with them to protect their own corrupt hold on power. Thus, the February 1973 protest held at Wounded Knee, South Dakota, which led to a confrontation between 300 federal agents and 200 AIM activists in a small (population 400) trading-post town, actually began several months before when AIM's leadership publicly criticized Richard Wilson, a recently elected tribal chairman on South Dakota's Pine Ridge Reservation. In response, Wilson did his best to undercut AIM's influence on his reservation. AIM then, in turn, countered by seizing the trading post at Wounded Knee in order to force the federal government to come to Wilson's defense and thereby demonstrate anew that the traditional leaders depended on federal protection for their power and could therefore not be trusted to press aggressively for Native American interests.

The resultant confrontation at Wounded Knee was the most violent manifestation of the brewing conflict between traditional reservation leadership and the younger, self-nominated spokesmen for Native America. It was not, however, the only one. In fact, these conflicts multiplied during the 1970s as more and more federal legislation was enacted for the special benefit of the reservation dwellers rather than the general benefit of those of Native American descent. By the late 1970s, relations between the spokesmen for these two groups had deteriorated to the point where the symbolic significance of the Longest March was vastly undermined by the conspicuous and pointed absence from the crowd gathering in Washington of any of tribal America's traditional leaders.

The conflict itself involved more than the different perspective of the two groups with respect to the status of Native Americans in the United States. The growing responsiveness of government policy to Native American issues during the 1960s and 1970s increased the rewards of being a Native American and, especially, of being a spokesperson for Native America. Unfortunately for the causes of the Native Americans, the resultant battle for influence inside the Native American community along generational and residential (on or off the reservations) lines further fragmented Native Americans who historically had been divided from one another on the basis of tribal identity and the cultural, linguistic, and historical differences involved in these tribal identities. In the short term, the emergence of an energetic, new set of Native American leaders worked to the advantage of Native Americans by giving their causes a greater visibility than otherwise would have occurred. In time, however, the new divisions severely undercut the Native American voice in the American political process. As a result, by the 1980s, Native American activists had shifted their tactics from holding loud demonstrations in the streets to filing legal suits and quietly lobbying the Congress for assistance.

MANAGEMENT OF THE CONFLICT

Given the environment in which Native American spokesmen had to function after 1968—which included a political process dominated by international issues (the Vietnam War) and domestic political scandal (Watergate) between 1968 to 1973 and handicapped by more than a decade of staggering budgetary deficits thereafter—the gains achieved by Native Americans since the late 1960s are impressive. They are also, to no small degree, a product of the general, accommodation-oriented approach to dealing with minority demands which Washington adopted during the mid-1960s and which it has largely continued to follow since that time.

To be specific, in 1968, Native Americans secured the passage of the American Indian Civil Rights Act, complete with an Indian Bill of Rights, which finally extended—albeit in statutory form—most of the rights other Americans were constitutionally granted in 1791. Substantial gains were also achieved in the areas of property rights, education, and family law. Thus, in the 1971 Alaska Native Claims Settlement Act, 80,000 Native Alaskans (Native Indians, Aleuts, and Inuits) were accorded two-thirds of the 60 million acres they collectively claimed, plus nearly a billion dollars in a cash settlement for the other lands lost. The following year, through the Indian Education Act of 1972, Congress made federal grants available throughout the country to schools educating significant numbers of Native Americans. A series of other laws granting Native Americans greater educational opportunity quickly followed; for example, the 1975 Indian Development and Education Assistance Act and the 1978 Tribally Controlled Community College Assistance Act. Even during the years of large budgetary deficits, important legislation was passed, though principally in the form of low-cost enabling legislation—for example, the 1988 Indian Gaming Regulatory Act, which granted tribes the right to operate casinos and bingo parlors on tribal lands in order to raise revenue—and protective family rights legislation. Indeed, in terms of protecting the Native Americans' traditional culture, no legislation has been more important than the 1978 Indian Child Welfare Act, which was passed to end the widespread state court practice of placing Indian children in foster homes exclusively on the legal grounds that such children would thereby have greater opportunities in life than if they remained in the economically deprived, reservation-bound surroundings of their parents.

SIGNIFICANCE

The gains harvested by Native Americans during the 1960s and early 1970s can be overstated. First, it is necessary to place them into historical perspective. The big battles involving the Native Americans—over land preservation and constitutional rights—were fought and lost in the nineteenth century, leaving Native American leaders a diminished agenda to pursue in the twentieth century. Moreover, many of the gains they achieved during the second half of the twentieth century initially appeared larger than they later proved to be. Subsequent U.S. Supreme Court decisions, for example, significantly reduced the rights bestowed on Native Americans via the 1968 Indian Bill of Rights by preventing federal courts from enforcing most of those rights against tribal institutions. Supreme Court opinions have likewise gutted the 1978 American Indian Religious Freedom Act by severely downgrading the relative importance of the free exercise of religion by Native American when that exercise is in conflict with legitimate state interests.

Nor did a benevolent concern with Native American interests necessarily lie behind the initial passage of many of the acts which did benefit them. The Alaska Native Claims Settlement Act, for example, awarded Native Alaskans a share of the profits from the oil and mineral resources developed on the federal lands they claimed; however, the settlement largely reflected the interest-group politics that led to the act's passage. In 1966 the secretary of the Department of the Interior championed the claims of the Native Alaskans and froze all further leasing of federal territories in Alaska until Congress compensated them for lands lost to the federal government. When oil was found in Alaska the following year on lands opened for exploration prior to 1966, the oil and gas industry joined the Native Alaskans in lobbying for a settlement of those claims—but one that was distinctly pro-industry in terms of the profits that Native Alaskans might receive from future resource finds. The act capped the maximum receivable royalty at 2 percent of all profits derived from such developmental ventures, or a maximum of $500 million—an amount soon dwarfed by the profits that American oil companies derived from the Prudhoe Bay oil venture alone following the 1977 opening of the Trans-Alaskan Pipeline.

Perhaps most important, the Native Americans' acquisition of greater control over their own affairs, through such legislation as the Indian Rights Act and 1968 American Indian Civil Rights Act (which gave tribal courts the power to incarcerate those convicted of criminal offenses), did not attack the persisting problem of the poverty and misery experienced by reservation Indians, or the socioeconomic disparity separating Native Americans living off the reservation from mainstream American society. Estimates continue to place the number of Native Americans living below the poverty level at nearly 45 percent for those living on the reservation and 22 percent for those living off the reservation. Unemployment rates among Indians have persistently been at least three times that of the population as a whole. In part, these figures bespeak of a Third World lifestyle and reflect the graver social problems besetting the Indians: alcoholism rates more than 400 percent greater than the national average; above average suicide, homicide, and accident rates; education statistics that indicate that nearly half of Indian adults fail to graduate from high school in a country where high school completion rates have persistently been in the 75 to 80 percent range for the population as a whole; and college education

figures indicating that less than 6 percent of all Native Americans have completed college, and most of these attended college in small Midwestern or Southwestern universities where they were exposed to high incidents of campus racism.[8]

Given the small number of Native Americans (0.8 percent of the population), the dispersion of the reservation tribes over hundreds of reservations generally containing considerably less than 1,000 people each, the Native Americans' internal divisions across ethnotribal, socioeconomic, residential, and generational lines, and the fact that the Indian civil rights movement largely unfolded after the civil rights–conscious 1960s and during the stagflation/tight budget period of the 1970s, it is not surprising that the Native American movement was notably less successful in achieving gains from the Congress than was the African American movement which preceded it. In any democratic process, critical mass and unity of purpose are important to the advancement of minority interests, even where governments have adopted accommodation as their modus vivendi in responding to the demands of minorities.

On the other hand, through the protests they conducted during the 1970s and the lobbying and litigation efforts they made during the 1980s and early 1990s, Native Americans did adroitly appeal to and receive benefits from federal policy makers. Consequently, the principal threat to the Native American way of life by the end of the twentieth century was no longer hostile or indifferent public policies but the accelerated pace at which members of numerous tribes were being voluntarily assimilated into the broader society through economic and social success (for example, W. W. Keeler) and intermarriage with non–Native American partners. Both developments have steadily eroded the *ethno*-class nature of Native American politics in the American political process. In fact, studies of households made during the 1980s indicated that self-identifying "Indians are actually more likely to marry whites than they are fellow Indians!"[9] The children of these unions have been able to select their own group and have tended to blur into the white population. Thus, of the estimated 20 million American citizens with some Indian blood,[10] only approximately 2.5 million identified themselves for census purposes in 2000 as Indians (more than 800,000 of these were living in Arizona, California, New Mexico, Oklahoma or Texas).[11] Approximately 80 percent of these 2 million lived off the reservations[12]—a number that reflects the fact that the tribes themselves have also become increasingly marginal to and invisible in both the American political process and American society.

See also Central Europe: The Romany, a Stateless Minority in a World of States; Indonesia: The Struggle to Control East Timor; and Western Sahara: Ethnic Conflict and the Twentieth Century's Last Colonial War.

NOTES

1. Chief Tecumseh, in a speech to the 1811 gathering of the Muskogee Grand Council, cited in Brewton Berry and Henry L. Tischler, *Race and Ethnic Relations* (Boston: Houghton Mifflin, 1978), 395.
2. In a country of more than a quarter of a billion people, only approximately 400,000 Native Americans still live on the reservations allotted to them, plus perhaps another 80,000 Native Alaskans (Indians, Inuits, and Eskimos). Combined, their total is no larger than the number of illegal aliens estimated to be living in New York City alone.
3. William Appleman Williams, *Empire as a Way of Life* (New York: Oxford University Press, 1980), 31.
4. For a detailed treatment of the struggle of Native Americans for their constitutional rights, see John R. Wunder, *"Retained by the People": A History of American Indians and the Bill of Rights* (New York: Oxford University Press, 1994).

5. The key case was *Talton v. Mayes* (1896), which explicitly denied Native Americans the protection of the Bill of Rights. The reasoning was that Indians are wards of the federal government, not federal citizens.
6. See Francis Paul Prucha, *American Indian Policy in Crisis: Christian Reforms and the Indian, 1865–1900* (Norman: University of Oklahoma Press, 1976).
7. D'Arcy McNickle, *The Indian Tribes of the United States: Ethnic and Cultural Survival* (New York: Oxford University Press, 1962), 49.
8. See Terry E. Huffman, "The Experiences, Perceptions, and Consequences of Campus Racism Among Northern Plains Indians," *Journal of American Indian Education* (January 1991): 25–33, 27; Alexander W. Astin, *Minorities in Higher Education: Final Report of the Commission on the Higher Education of Minorities* (San Francisco: Jossey-Bass, 1982), 2; Harvey Markowitz, ed., "Civil Rights and Citizenship," *Ready Reference: American Indians* (Pasadena, Calif.: Salem Press, 1995), I: 175–76.
9. Stephan Thernstrom, "American Ethnic Statistics," in *Immigration in Two Democracies: French and American Experience*, ed., Donald L. Horwitz and Gerard Noiriel, 80–111 at 101. (New York: New York University Press, 1992). Of those classifying themselves as Native Americans in the 1980 census, only 48 percent of the married males and 46 percent of the married females had Indian spouses.
10. For a thorough discussion of various estimates of the numbers of those with Native American blood in the United States' population, and of the chronic difficulty of counting their number, see Brian W. Dippie, *The Vanishing American: White Attitudes and U.S. Indian Policy* (Middletown, Connecticut: Wesleyan University Press, 1982): xv–xvi, 236–41, and 346–49.
11. Stella U. Ugunwole, *The American Indian and Alaskan Native Population: 2002—Census 2000 Brief* (Washington: United States Census Bureau, 2002): 3–4.
12. Ibid., 3–12. See also "American Indian Population by Reservations and Jurisdictional Areas," available online at http://www.ovc.edu/missions/indians/indesju.html.

SUGGESTED READINGS

Deloris, Vine, Jr., and Clifford Lytle. *American Indians, American Justice*. Austin: University of Texas Press, 1983.
McNickle, D'Arcy. *The Indian Tribes of the United States: Ethnic and Cultural Survival*. New York: Oxford University Press, 1962.

Nichols, Robert L. *The American Indian: Past and Present*. New York: McGraw Hill, 1992.

Norgren, Jill, and Serena Nanda. "Native Americans, Law and Land." In *American Cultural Pluralism and Law*. New York: Praeger, 1996.

Pevar, Stephen L. *The Rights of Indians and Tribes: The Basic ACLU Guide to Indian and Tribal Rights*. Carbondale: Southern Illinois University Press, 1992.

Prucha, Francis Paul. *The Great Father: The United States Government and the American Indians*. Lincoln: University of Nebraska Press, 1986.

Spicer, Edward H. *The American Indians: Dimensions of Ethnicity*. Cambridge, Mass.: Harvard University Press, 1980.

Wilkinson, Charles F. *American Indians, Time, and the Law: Native Societies in a Modern Constituional Democracy*. New Haven, Conn.: Yale University Press, 1987.

Wunder, John R. *"Retained by the People:" A History of American Indians and the Bill of Rights*. New York: Oxford University Press, 1994.

United States

Racial Violence in the United States: 1900–1919

James N. Upton

TIMELINE

1619 Slavery begins in British North America.

1680–1730 Indian slave trade supports economy in Carolina.

1712 First major slave revolt occurs in New York City.

1775 Pennsylvania Society for Abolition of Slavery is founded.

1777 Northeast states abolish slavery.

1793 First Fugitive Slave Act is passed by Congress.

1804 Ohio limits the rights of blacks in North.

1807 Congress prohibits further importation of African slaves.

1810 The Underground Railroad is founded.

1820 The Missouri Compromise overcomes division in Congress on slavery issue.

1830 Proslavery arguments are launched.

1831 Nat Turner's slave insurrection takes place.

1850 The Great Compromise sidesteps the division on the slavery issue.

Second Fugitive Slave law is enacted.

1853 The National Council of Colored People is founded.

1855–1858 Slavery issue leads to "Bleeding Kansas."

1857 Dred Scott decision on slavery is made by U.S. Supreme Court.

1863 Abraham Lincoln writes the Emancipation Proclamation.

1865 Ku Klux Klan is founded; Civil War ends.

1866 Race riots occur in Memphis and New Orleans.

1868 The Fourteenth Amendment is ratified.

1883 U.S. Supreme Court strikes down the Civil Rights Act of 1875.

1903 Rioting occurs in Belleville, Illinois.

1904 Rioting takes place in Springfield, Ohio.

1906 Riots happen in Brownsville, Texas, and Chattanooga, Tennessee.

1913 Anti-Defamation League of B'nai B'rith is founded.

1917 The Immigration Act of 1917 begins to shut the door on immigrants.

1919 Riots take place in Omaha, Nebraska, and Chicago, Illinois.

1920–1930 The Great Migration of Southern blacks to North and Midwest occurs; new aggressiveness is noted in black community; incident-driven riots occur in several American cities.

1943 Race riots take place across United States.

1954 U.S. Supreme Court invalidates segregation in public education.

1955 Montgomery bus boycott is staged.

1957 Desegregation crisis occurs in Little Rock, Arkansas.

1964 The Civil Rights Act of 1964 is passed.

1965 Rioting and violence occur in ghetto in Watts, California.

1967 Race riots in Detroit lead to Kerner Commission Report.

1968 Assassination of Martin Luther King, Jr., leads to rioting.

1971 Busing debate divides Americans.

1972 Equal Employment Opportunity Act is passed by Congress.

Racial conflict in the United States has been so prevalent and commonplace that whites and blacks, who have been living with this conflict since the seventeenth century, have come to accept it as a basic feature of the American way of life. Since the end of the Civil War, the United States has been faced with the unique challenge of promoting the ideals of civil liberty for all—without providing national *minority group* rights. A contradiction is apparent in this endeavor between an egalitarian American creed, on the one hand, and a history of violence against national minority groups, on the other. In many ways, this contradiction is the "American Dilemma."[1]

Martin Luther King, Jr., emphasized the significance of this dilemma by referring to it as "schizophrenic behavior." In 1967 King wrote,

Ever since the birth of our nation, white America has had a schizophrenic personality on the question of race. She has been torn between selves—a self in which she proudly professed the great principles of de-

mocracy and a self in which she sadly practiced the antithesis of democracy.[2]

According to King, the one indispensable element of a great nation that the United States lacks is racial justice.[3] This is the context in which race relations in the United States must be understood.

HISTORICAL BACKGROUND

The pre– and post–World War I time periods in race relations between whites and blacks in the United States are significant because they chronicle the migration of blacks from the South, which led to the urbanization of the black population. This urbanization of the Southern black population during the first two decades of the twentieth century helped create the conditions that were necessary for a social movement toward resisting white aggression. Moreover, it was the industrialized labor demands that initiated the black migration to urban centers throughout the United States and that transformed the black laborer from an agricultural worker to an industrial worker. Industrialization had the long-term effect of indirectly changing the structure of power relationships between blacks and whites. This timeframe illustrates the development of an urban black community and highlights the causes and conditions that characterized race relations in the United States.

A sequence of events in the first two decades of the twentieth century shows the transformation of black Americans' response to violent attacks. They moved from a defenseless position to an organized stance. These events illustrate the thesis that "interracial riots in the early years of the century were essentially pogroms in which the Negroes were victims of white aggression."[4]

Racial violence in the twentieth century is commonly grouped into three stages: communal riots, commodity riots,

Select Communal Riots: 1900–1919

Place	Year	Race of Aggressor	Race of Victim	Causes	Characteristics
Belleville, IL	1903	White	Black (1)	Inadequate law enforcement; role of mass media	Death by hanging
Springfield, OH	1904	Unknown	Black (1), White (1)	Role of mass media; inadequate law enforcement	Death by hanging
Brownsville, TX	1906	Unknown	White (1)	Role of mass media; inadequate law enforcement	Ecological conflict over contested area
Chattanooga, TN	1906	White	Black (1)	Inadequate law enforcement; role of mass media	Death by hanging
Omaha, NE	1919	White	Black (1)	Inadequate law enforcement; role of mass media	Death by hanging
Chicago, IL	1919	White	White (15), Black (23)	Black migration; competition for jobs	Insufficient housing; ecological conflict over contested area

and political violence.[5] This chapter considers only the anatomy of communal riots. Communal clashes characterized the first two decades of the century. During that time, racial riots occurred on the boundaries of expanding black and white neighborhoods. In such circumstances, whites—more often than blacks—were the aggressors.

Racial Violence and Black Victimization: Before World War I

At the turn of the twentieth century, white aggression against blacks (outside the South) demonstrated itself in white-dominated riots. Between 1900 and 1917, more than 1,100 blacks were lynched in the United States.[6] In most instances of interracial violence during that time, blacks were the victims. It was not uncommon to witness the entire white adult population of certain communities—in both the South and the North—collectively violating the law by attacking entire communities of blacks. The one-sided nature of this racial violence characterizes these race riots more as "one-way terrorization" than as two-way riots.[7] White law officials not only failed to enforce the law, they often joined white mobs in killing blacks.

Numerous riots have been documented between 1900 and 1910; however, major riots occurred in Chattanooga, Tennessee, and Brownsville, Texas.[8] These riots are all examples of the one-way terrorization that characterized the riots. The immediate causes of the riots are difficult to determine, but the concentration of blacks in segregated ghettos was a frequent pattern in all of the cities involved in the riots. A brief look at two of the riots in that decade shows that the "anatomy" of the riots can provide a chart of their underlying causes.

In Springfield, Ohio, in 1904, a black man shot and killed a white policeman. It was not determined whether the black man responded in self-defense. The white mob did not ponder the immediate or legitimate causes. An intense hatred of blacks led the white mob to hang the black man, riddle his body with bullets, and destroy the black section of the city of Springfield. Two generations after the Civil War, racial hatred overrode the American creed that proclaimed "due process and equal justice for all."[9]

The riot in Brownsville, Texas, in August 1906 involved the black Twenty-Fifth Regiment, which had fought gallantly at El Caney, Cuba, during the Spanish-

American War. A fight broke out in the town between the soldiers and a mob of white residents. The riot that followed left one white resident dead by a gunshot wound. It was never determined which soldier had fired the shot. However, by the stroke of a pen, President Theodore Roosevelt "dismissed the entire battalion stationed there without honor and disqualified its members for service in either the military or the civil service of the United States."[10]

The pattern of American race riots in the first decade of the twentieth century had been firmly established by the time of the 1906 riots in Chattanooga, Tennessee. At this time, a black man had only to be accused of raping a white woman to be viciously murdered by a white mob without ever appearing before a judge and jury. In March 1906, a black man, Ed Johnson, was charged with raping a white woman. Johnson was one of the few accused black men in this era to receive a trial. The trial court, however, denied him the aid of counsel and a petition for a writ of habeas corpus. The U.S. Supreme Court granted Johnson the right of appeal and a stay of execution until the case could be reviewed:

> On March 19, 1906, the sheriff and his deputy in Chattanooga left the jail unguarded; a mob seized Johnson and hanged him. The Supreme Court of the United States, on November, 1909, sentenced six members of the mob to short prison terms for contempt of the court.[11]

Records indicate that this was a rare case in which the courts punished whites for murdering a black person.

During this time, major newspapers rarely published a detailed description of a lynching unless it was very brutal or contained some unusual element. The *New York Times* probably provided a public service in 1903 when it published a graphic description of a black man who was lynched on the charge of rape in Belleville, Illinois:

> The mob hanged Wyatt to a telephone pole in the public square. Even while his body was jerking in the throes of death from the strangulation, members of the mob began building a fire at the bottom of the pole. . . . When it had begun burning briskly, the Negro still half alive, was cut down, and after being covered with coal oil . . . cast into the fire.[12]

In a halfhearted attempt to speak out against such inhuman acts of violence, the *New York Times* placed the primary responsibility for the lynching on the local sheriffs. The article called for an end to lynching, but in doing so also argued that, given the nature of American federalism, the prevention of lynching could best be achieved by a sheriff who was brave enough to defy cowardly mobs. The *New York Times* opposed federal intervention, but—forecasting the future—warned:

> If conditions became much worse, some action would have to be taken. The *Times* reported the background of race riots and the spark which inflamed them; it pointed out that the police and troops usually sided with whites by disarming Negroes and allowing whites to roam the streets beating and killing Negroes and burning their homes.[13]

Racial hatred in the early part of the twentieth century was plagued by allegations of the rape of white women by black men. This appealed to a sort of sexual psychosis and too often became a tactic of newspaper editors deliberately to provoke whites to attack blacks. There was no evidence to associate blacks with the accusations against them, but under those conditions, evidence was not required to associate a black man with a sexual violation. The diagnosis of sexual psychosis emerged after scholars had analyzed patterns in race relations of the era that had been exacerbated by dishonest journalists.

Racial Violence and Black Counterviolence: After World War I

After World War I, mob violence against blacks continued at an alarming rate and rapidly became a national phenomenon. Ironically, at the same time that this violence was occurring at home, more than 350,000 black men were serving in segregated units of the U.S. Army, winning medals and sacrificing their lives to "make the world safe for democracy." The dilemma between egalitarian principles and the values that promoted lingering racial hatred continued to plague white Americans' understanding of justice.

Black soldiers returning home after World War I were mobbed for attempting to use facilities open to white soldiers. In the year after the war ended, 83 black men were lynched in the United States. Some were in uniform. One such lynching took place in Omaha, Nebraska, in 1919:

> A white mob in this city demanded that the local authorities turn over to them a Negro soldier accused of raping a white woman. . . . The mob then moved to the jail, beating and stomping any Negro who happened to be in the crowd. After seizing the accused Negro, the mob shot him, hanged him, burned his body, and hung it in the public square.[14]

The summer of 1919 was the bloodiest, most brutal period of interracial disorder and violence in American history. Major race riots in 1919 accounted for approximately 400 black and white deaths, with significantly more black casualties. The race war of 1919 was marked by naked aggression and carried out by the worst elements of white America. As more than one analyst of the black movement in this era has observed,

> [Perhaps] the white mobs were driven by a will to lynch. If so, these were social orgies of cruelty in which certain classes in the community expressed their hatred of a race they considered to be inferior, their contempt for the law, and their sense of Anglo-Saxon superiority.[15]

Foremost among the causes of the racial violence that flared up in 1919 was the competition for jobs between black and white workers. The advent of World War I in 1914 saw both a great advancement in industrialization in the United States and a growing need for additional laborers in Northern industrial areas. Meanwhile, the sharecropping system and white violence were on the rise in the South. The South suffered an economic recession in 1914 and a boll weevil attack on cotton crops in 1915. As a result, hundreds of thousands of blacks found themselves out of work, and they headed North and to the Midwest looking for employment. Between 1910 and 1920, the black population in the North increased from 850,000 to 1.4 million.[16]

In the North, however, white labor unions were on the rise, and they were demanding better working conditions. There is ample evidence that big business was manipulating the white and black labor forces in such a manner as to keep the cost of labor at a minimum. Big business recruited tens of thousands of semiskilled and unskilled black workers, primarily from the South, to be used as scab workers and strikebreakers, while discouraging their participation in white unions and encouraging a false sense of racial superiority among white workers.

A second effect of this large-scale migration to the North can be seen in housing disputes. With a large migration of Southern blacks and no new housing accommodations, previously white neighborhoods were overcome by black workers and their families. Whites began to feel threatened by blacks, whom they viewed as taking over not only their jobs, but also their neighborhoods. The Chicago riot of 1919 illustrates this point. The underlying factor that hastened this riot was the mass influx of blacks into Chicago from the South between 1910 and 1915. This decade saw the black population of Chicago increase by 50,000, and this population growth resulted in increased violence. Fifty-eight house bombings occurred between July 1, 1917, and March 1, 1921,[17] and 26 of these took place before the 1919 riot. As the violence escalated, so did the resistance in the black community. With the atmosphere for violence and resistance intensifying on both sides, the events that took place on July 27, 1919, provided the breaking point.[18]

The 1919 Chicago riot is probably the closest example of a clash between blacks and whites on an equal basis of violence. Approximately 15 whites and 23 blacks were killed, and the strong commitment of many Chicago blacks to meet white violence with counterviolence was evident.[19] At the same time, it is also clear that most of the 1919 riots were white dominated and directed against black migrants from the South. The violent struggles between 1917 and 1919 are evidence of some of the first signs of retaliation, or counterviolence, on the part of blacks.

Many historians have characterized blacks prior to World War I as having been spiritually crippled by the failures and disappointments of Reconstruction, the period immediately following the Civil War and the end of slavery. The combination of the Great Migration and the entrance of the United States into World War I, however, generated a new fighting spirit within the black community. As a result of being veterans of the battlefields of France or of the racial conflicts in a great metropolis, blacks had become comparatively more sophisticated and definitely more militant. Black Americans no longer automatically panicked in the face of a white mob; now they would often stand and fight for their rights. Moreover, by this time, blacks had realized that they could not expect protection from the federal government and that they thus had to defend themselves as best they could. They had witnessed local governments giving in to white lynch mobs. They had observed the onslaught of racist attacks by the white press. Indeed, never before in the history of the country had there been more distrust of whites by blacks than after World War I. The despair felt by blacks was amplified in the 1919 writings of W.E.B. Du Bois, a renowned black scholar and philosopher. Du Bois proposed a "league of nations" to curb the antiblack policies of the United States and South Africa. He argued that, unless such an international power were created, "We are doomed eventually to fight for our rights."[20]

Communal riots indicate the inequality that exists between the ethnic and racial groups. They have explosive and destructive characteristics which make generalizations very difficult. As a form of "collective behavior," their development is not easily recorded or analyzed. In addition, their history in the United States has been hidden in a system of law enforcement that has denied blacks due process and equal protection of the law and, in some instances, has weakened the legitimacy of the legal system itself.

The forms and extent of collective racial violence are expressions of the social structure and the means of their change and control. Thus, the roles of the police and the mass media affect the patterns of collective urban violence and are crucial in accounting for actual occurrences of urban communal violence. Consequently, the manner in which racial conflicts are handled and controlled deeply influences race relations and subsequent patterns of violence. For instance, both law enforcement agencies and the mass media can be directly linked to rioting; in many cases, they are the elements that give rise to and hasten rioting and the perpetuation of riots—usually as a result of inadequate protection for minorities and inaccurate reporting of community problems. Consequently, social tensions generated by discrimination, prejudice, and poverty offer limited explanations for communal violence in the United States.[21]

THE CONFLICT

Racial violence in the United States is as old as the nation itself. In fact, racial clashes throughout the twentieth century can be traced to these early decades. The pattern of racial violence at the beginning of the twentieth century is characterized here as "communal" clashes or riots. Communal riots occur as a result of struggles between black and white civilians over areas of unclear racial domain. Usually, the contested area centers on neighborhood housing or other public places, such as a beach or park. In response to World War I, large numbers of both black and white persons migrated to the cities, and because of legal segregation and a shortage of housing, they were pitted against one another. The following lists contain suggestions of probable underlying causes and characteristics of the communal riots that occurred during the first two decades of the twentieth century.

Summary of Underlying Causes

- Relatively large numbers of new migrants (both black and white) lived in segregated groups in urban centers, under conditions in which older patterns of acceptance were not effective.

- Inadequate law enforcement agencies often conspired with white rioters against the black population.

- Newspapers frequently published inflammatory reports, such as "Black Man Rapes White Woman." Since the riots lasted for several days, news reports served to recruit white activists from other parts of the city and even from out of town.

- Big business manipulation—recruiting blacks as strikebreakers while discouraging their participation in white unions—contributed to a false sense of racial superiority among white workers, thereby intensifying racial discrimination and racial prejudice.

- There was poverty.

- There was a shortage of housing for both blacks and whites.

- Police brutality in maintaining racial segregation was common.

Summary of Underlying Characteristics

- Ecological warfare (a struggle for living space) occurred over contested areas. Hastening incidents included small-scale struggles between black and white civilians, often in a public place such as a beach or in an area of unclear racial domain, and were characterized by minor but persistent outbursts of violence. The Chicago riot of 1919, for example, was preceded by two years of residential bombing.

- Death (most often by hanging) and injuries resulted from direct confrontations between black and white citizens.

- Whites invaded black neighborhoods, contributing to insufficient housing for blacks. Much of the violence occurred on the fringes of black and low-income white neighborhoods. Moreover, violence occurred on main transfer points, when blacks attempted to return home or to seek some sort of refuge. These areas were usually central business districts where whites outnumbered blacks.

- Weapons included bricks, rocks, and blunt sticks; hand-to-hand combat was common. A limited number of handguns and rifles were used in the riots.

In short, the pattern of racial violence during the first two decades of the twentieth century was characterized by conflict, and it reflected an attempt being made by blacks to alter their position of racial subordination, and an attempt being made by whites to maintain their racial domination. Violence during this period was an expression of the white population's fear of black competition for jobs. The frequency of race riots was a negative response to those fears.

MANAGEMENT OF THE CONFLICT

The Role of State and Local Government

Prior to 1919, violent confrontations between blacks and whites had been hastened and managed by the local police and the local media. In many cases, the local police may even have been responsible for provoking racial violence by restricting legitimate forms of civil protest activity. Indeed, any form of organized black protest was frequently considered an internal threat to national security. Some newspapers were also blamed for provoking white attacks against black citizens. Often, after the violence had begun, the newspapers published inflammatory stories that fueled the intensity of the riots.

The year 1919 became a key moment in the expression of interracial violence in the United States because black Americans began to respond to violence in an organized fashion. The federal government had long tacitly condoned lynching or pogroms (organized massacres) against blacks as almost legal. State and local government control of interracial violence was based on a system of racial hierarchy. However, two new forces began to emerge in 1919:

an uneasy and tentative commitment by some elements in American society to a value system tied to "making the world safe for democracy" and therefore to racial equality; [and] an increasing feeling of power, prosperity, and dignity among Negroes.[22]

Response to the Conflict in the Black Community

Gradually, the lynchings instigated and fueled by local and state governments were replaced by "riots," in which blacks were sufficiently organized to fight back when attacked. Large numbers of black men had been recruited to fight in Europe in World War I. Their return to unemployment and poverty prompted them to seek action to relieve their troubles. Their participation in the war, among other factors, had given black people renewed pride in their race and new courage to fight against oppression and violence.

The black press became a key factor in announcing the appearance of this new aggressiveness among blacks. At a conference held in 1918, which had been called by the War Department to secure the support of the black press for the war, 31 black editors solemnly directed the government's attention to the upsurge in lynching and mob violence in a nation supposedly fighting to make the world safe for democracy. Moreover, early in 1919 the National Association for the Advancement of Colored People (NAACP) published a study, *Thirty Years of Lynching in the United States: 1889–1918,* which documented approximately 3,224 lynchings of blacks during that period.[23]

The renewed spirit and the enhanced organizational response of the black community to violent attacks by local police departments and white mobs served to change the way in which the police (state, local, and national) responded to racial conflicts. The response by black citizens to meet violence with violence "spawned a fear of violence in the society at large which had the effect of giving form to the early seeds of the American 'state' on race relations."[24] This resulted in the establishment of a neutral police force—from a previously nonneutral position in relationship to blacks—because the action of the local police had been associated with the length and severity of the riots. With the establishment of a neutral police force, order was more quickly restored during interracial rioting, especially when federal troops were called. These events signaled some meager beginnings for the use of "creative disorder" to solve racial conflict situations. For instance, in 1919, some black leaders began calling for work boycotts by black laborers and service workers. The NAACP was strengthened by its efforts to protect black people who were arrested or victimized in the 1919 riots. The NAACP and many blacks began to look to the federal government for protective legislation and help. The riots of 1919 caused blacks (and many whites) to push for a national police force or for "neutral" local and state police.

SIGNIFICANCE

The interracial violence that took place in the United States from 1900 to 1919 allows us to view how the management of this conflict was transformed from private, local, and state governments to the federal government. Prior to 1919, interracial conflict in the United States was managed and even caused by a series of local systems of order (private, local, and state governments) based on a system of racial hierarchy. That is, state and local governments usually joined white mobs in their attacks on black communities. Prior to 1919, the federal government did not attempt to intercede. This changed when the black community began to defend itself violently against such attacks. The black community's success in defending itself during what was called the "bloody

summer" of 1919 (especially because of the Chicago riots) startled white America and the federal government. As a result, the federal government began to build up a peacetime military presence in the country and, consequently, created a monopoly on the legitimate/legal means of violence. The black community's willingness to fight local and state governments with violence created an "internal" national security threat in the country, which forced the federal government to oversee state and local governments' use of violence in interracial conflicts. The federal government's control and management of interracial violence led to more neutral state and local police behavior, as well as the option for direct federal intervention in interracial violence. Paradoxically, the federal government's intervention in interracial conflicts increased black Americans' claims for citizenship rights and channeled the demands for equality into a type of peaceful creative disorder. This included such tactics as sit-ins, boycotts, strikes, and marches, all of which were designed to protest against a system of racial hierarchy and to replace it with a new system of order which would be more in alignment with the democratic principles of racial equality. These new creative disorder tactics were successfully employed throughout the rest of the twentieth century.

See also Central Europe: The Romany, a Stateless Minority in a World of States; United Kingdom: The Making of British Race Relations; United States: The Struggle for Survival and Equality of the First Americans; United States: Race and the Civil Rights Struggle in Post–World War II America.

NOTES

1. Gunnar Myrdal, *An American Dilemma* (New York: Harper and Brothers, 1944), 567.
2. Martin Luther King, Jr., *Where Do We Go from Here: Chaos or Community?* (Boston: Beacon Press, 1967) 68.

3. Ibid. 109.

4. Hugh Davis Graham and Ted Robert Gurr, eds., *The History of Violence in America* (New York: Bantam Books, 1969), 396–97.

5. Morris Janowitz, "Patterns of Collective Racial Violence," in Graham and Gurr, *History of Violence in America,* 412–13.

6. James S. Olson, *The Ethnic Dimension in American History* (New York: St. Martin's Press, 1994), 195.

7. Myrdal, *An American Dilemma,* 567.

8. Rayford W. Logan, *The Betrayal of the Negro* (New York: Macmillian 1965).

9. Ibid., 349–50.

10. Ibid., 350.

11. Ibid., 348.

12. Ibid., 391–92.

13. Ibid., 392.

14. Robert H. Brisbane, *The Black Vanguard: Origins of the Negro Social Revolution 1900–1960* (Valley Forge, Pa.: Judson Press, 1970), 78.

15. Ibid., 71.

16. Olson, *Ethnic Dimension,* 197; and Emmett J. Scott, *Negro Migration During the War* (New York: Oxford University Press, 1920; reprinted Arno Press and the *New York Times,* 1969).

17. Chicago Commission on Race Relations, *The Negro in Chicago: A Study of Race Relations and a Race Riot* (Chicago: University of Chicago Press, 1922), 122.

18. William M. Tuttle, *Race Riot: Chicago in the Red Summer of 1919* (New York: Athenuem, 1970), 159.

19. Arthur I. Waskow, *From Race Riot to Sit-in* (Garden City, N.Y.: Doubleday, 1966), 10.

20. Brisbane, *Black Vanguard,* 74.

21. Janowitz, "Patterns of Collective Racial Violence," 417–18.

22. Waskow, *Race Riot to Sit-in,* 22.

23. Brisbane, *Black Vanguard,* 75.

24. Waskow, *Race Riot to Sit-in,* 294–99.

SUGGESTED READINGS

Brisbane, Robert H. *The Black Vanguard: Origins of the Negro Social Revolution 1900–1960.* Valley Forge, Pa.: Judson Press, 1970.

Chicago Commission on Race Relations. *The Negro in Chicago: A Study of Race Relations and a Race Riot.* Chicago: University of Chicago Press, 1922.

Graham, Hugh Davis, and Ted Robert Gurr, eds. *The History of Violence in America.* New York: Bantam Books, 1969.

King, Martin Luther, Jr. *Where Do We Go From Here: Chaos or Community?* Boston: Beacon Press, 1967.

Logan, Rayford W. *The Betrayal of the Negro.* New York: Macmillan, 1965; reprint, 1997.

Myrdal, Gunnar. *An American Dilemma.* New York: Harper and Brothers, 1944.

Olson, James S. *The Ethnic Dimension in American History.* New York: St. Martin's Press, 1994.

Report of the National Advisory Commission on Civil Disorders. New York: Bantam Books, 1968.

Scott, Emmett. J., *Negro Migration During the War.* (New York: Oxford University Press, 1920; reprinted New York: Arno Press and the *New York Times,* 1969).

Tuttle, William M. *Race Riot: Chicago in the Red Summer of 1919.* United States Kerner Commission. New York: Athenuem, 1970.

Waskow, Arthur I. *From Race Riot to Sit-in.* Garden City, N.Y.: Doubleday, 1966.

United States

Race and the Civil Rights Struggle in Post–World War II America

Kevin J. Mumford

TIMELINE

1664 Miscegenation laws are passed in Chesapeake and New England.

1776 American Revolution leads to independence from colonial rule; Northern states emancipate slaves but Southerners retain their "peculiar institution."

1787 The Three-Fifths Clause in the U.S. Constitution defines slaves as partial citizens.

1840s Suffrage is restricted or denied to African Americans in the North.

1856 South Carolina passes the Slave Codes.

1863 Emancipation Proclamation frees slaves in rebelling states.

1865 The Thirteenth Amendment to the U.S. Constitution prohibits slavery.
     South Carolina passes the Black Codes, which severely restrict the freedom of former slaves.

1868 The Fourteenth Amendment to the U.S. Constitution incorporates citizenship and guarantees legal process rights to former male slaves.

1870 The Fifteenth Amendment grants suffrage to former male slaves.
     The Enforcement Act promises national government enforcement of voting rights.

1871 The Ku Klux Klan Act authorizes federal intervention in response to violence committed against African Americans.

1883 The Civil Rights Cases overturn federal legislation that had elaborated the constitutional provisions for equal rights.

1896 *Plessy v. Fergusson* sustains racial segregation: separate facilities are permitted if equal—the final blow to Reconstruction.

1908 The National Association for the Advancement of Colored People (NAACP), the first national civil rights organization, is founded.

1910s The Great Migration begins—1.5 million African Americans migrate to Northern cities by 1930.

1940s Double V Campaign: African American newspapers sustain protests against Northern segregation and win equal accommodations legislation in many states.

1941 A. Philip Randolph, black labor leader, threatens march and wins federal commission to monitor equal employment in some industries.

1946 President Harry S. Truman signs executive order to desegregate the military.

1948 In *Shelley v. Kramer,* U.S. Supreme Court prohibits restrictive covenants, which restricted sales of real estate to white buyers, enforcing neighborhood segregation.

1954 *Brown v. Board of Education* orders the integration of public education, overturning the separate-but-equal doctrine.

1955 Rosa Parks refuses to stand on a segregated bus; the Montgomery bus boycott spawns numerous protest activities for civil rights.

1957 The Civil Rights Act of 1957 establishes the Civil Rights Commission and reaffirms the right to vote.

1960 The Civil Rights Act of 1960 establishes the Civil Rights Commission and Office of the Attorney General for Civil Rights, especially voting. In Greensboro, North Carolina, college students sit in at a segregated diner. The increase of youth involved in the civil rights struggle leads to the establishment of the Student Non-Violent Coordinating Committee.

1962 President John F. Kennedy signs executive order pertaining to discrimination in housing.

1964 The Civil Rights Act of 1964 prohibits discrimination in public accommodations or employment. The Twenty-first Amendment to the U.S. Constitution prohibits the poll tax, protecting the right to vote.

1965 President Johnson signs the Voting Rights Act of 1965, aimed at Southern intransigence and authorizing federal protection of voting.

1968 The Civil Rights Act of 1968 builds upon federal legislation; housing discrimination is specifically prohibited.

1972 The Equal Employment Opportunity Act is passed by Congress, inaugurating an Affirmative Action program aimed at hiring groups historically discriminated against in hiring decisions.

1980 The election of Ronald Reagan to the presidency shifts the focus of the civil rights debate to the reverse discrimination nature of affirmative action programs and marks the end of the 1945–1980 civil rights movement.

White ethnic conflict in the United States, arising from the massive European immigration between the seventeenth century and the early twentieth century, affected every facet of American political culture. The political system, however, granted all white immigrants equal civil rights. It was black Americans who suffered the exclusion or the withdrawal of civil rights based on perceptions of racial difference. If and when African American civil status improved depended to a large extent on the unique formula for the distribution of power through American federalism—that is, both the shifting allocation of authority over citizenship as exercised by the states or local governments, and the authority of the national government. Federal civil rights policies frequently contrasted with or contradicted politics and practices in the states, particularly the laws of the Southern states. Yet, significant as this resultant structural tension in federalism was in determining the course of civil rights, the rise, decline, and revival of the political activities of various African Americans were equally significant in affecting the course of integration and the struggle for equality in the United States.

HISTORICAL BACKGROUND

From the onset of the British settlement of America in the seventeenth century, the legal status of black people, African and African Americans, was different from that of Europeans, with restrictions governing such diverse areas as accommodations, trade, gun ownership, baptism, and marriage with whites. During this time, New World slavery was expanding, and the mainland colonies increasingly employed slave and indentured labor for the production of staples. During the American Revolution, popular ideas of liberal or republican independence ignited a strong emancipationist movement in the Northern colonies, leading to the abolition of slavery there. Southern colonies, however, retained the institution. With the creation of the U.S. Constitution in 1787, regional conflict over slavery required formal political compromise, particularly concerning the national representation of slaves who were defined as three-fifths of a citizen; however, free African Americans received equal civil rights in many states.

Over the course of the nineteenth century, the status of a slave was increasingly interrelated with second-class citizenship. One historian has characterized the free black population as little more than slaves without masters. Similarly, when Northern states adopted universal manhood suffrage for whites, special legislation appended property qualifications to black suffrage or totally prohibited it. This deepening discrimination against black Americans was sharply diverted by the outbreak of the Civil War. When Southern slaveholders seceded from the Union, Northerners embraced free labor nationalism and declared war to prevent secession. The Northern victory finally resolved long-standing tensions between the North and South; Northern troops captured slaves during the war, and what remained of the national government after Southern secession emancipated the slaves and prohibited slavery in the U.S. Constitution.

Reconstruction

The period of regional reunification that followed, known as Reconstruction, was a historic milestone in civil rights. Reconstruction differed from emancipation in other countries both in speed and scope. In the United States, black slaves received citizenship rights in 1868, three years after emancipation and much earlier than slaves in Caribbean nations; for example, although slavery was abolished in Jamaica in the 1830s, black people there lacked universal suffrage until the 1940s.

In part, the relatively swift extension in the American case was a product of the radical idealism of leading statesmen dating back to the abolitionist movement, and in part democracy grew from Republican efforts to strengthen their political standing in the South by protecting the black electorate. Toward the goal of incorporating equal citizenship for the black freedmen, the Constitution was amended three times: the Thirteenth Amendment (1865) enforced emancipation by prohibiting slavery; the Fourteenth Amendment (1868), considered by legal scholars to be the most significant constitutional mechanism for preserving civil rights, extended all privileges and immunities of citizenship to black men; and the Fifteenth Amendment (1870) extended the franchise to all men regardless of creed or color. White women were disappointed by their efforts to link woman's suffrage to black male enfranchisement, which caused lasting rifts between black and feminist progressive social movements. The Republican Party consequently commanded the undivided loyalty of black voters for next 60 years.

A LONG MARCH. Former slaves at Freedmen's Village in Alexandria, Virginia, freed by President Lincoln's Emancipation Proclamation. The photograph was taken in 1863, more than a century before the passage of the landmark Civil Rights Act of 1964. © Corbis.

In the final analysis, historians do not agree on the significance of post–Civil War national reunification for the former slaves. White Southerners never accepted the federal measures. The deliberations over emancipation did not encompass fundamental economic redistribution or compensation, such as the transfer of land or homesteading. Moreover, during the final phase of unification, the majority political party, the Republicans, lost influence within the Southern states. Factions of white Southerners violently resisted the extension of civil rights to African Americans and blocked their exercise of the suffrage. Eventually federalism—that is, the intervention of the federal government—was necessary to ensure that the intention of the Congress in this regard would be fulfilled; in this case, through national military intervention. In 1870 the Congress passed the Enforcement Act, which authorized prosecution of any individual who interfered with the Fifteenth Amendment, or the right to vote; the federal government could send election commissions to recalcitrant Southern states. White racist violence was prohibited in the Ku Klux Klan Act of 1871 in response to the founding of white vigilante groups. Southern states elected moderate to reactionary governments, while the national Congress continued to pursue liberal civil rights policies. The question of segregation, or the separation of the races, which the freedmen had resisted almost from beginning of Reconstruction, was forbidden by the federal government in one final act of congressional prohibition: the Civil Rights Act of 1875, which prohibited discrimination on the basis of color or creed.

It is often forgotten that Reconstruction also significantly affected the status of African Americans in the North. When Northern state governments ratified the Fourteenth and Fifteenth Amendments, they repealed discriminatory legislation which had prohibited African Americans from voting, had segregated public accommodations, or had enforced second-class education. The Northern state of New Jersey, for instance, in 1882, removed the term "white" from its statutory provisions on voting; all men enjoyed the right to vote. In 1884 the state explicitly prohibited any sort of discrimination in accommodations on the basis of race or color. Though only 10 percent of African Americans resided in Northern states, they enjoyed tenuous equality with whites from the 1880s until approximately the 1910s.

Within 20 years after the Civil War, the party of union—the Republican Party—had declined to a minority in the national government. Political reconciliation had been achieved through a political compromise known as nonintervention; both Northern Republicans and Southern Democrats granted the states increased authority over race relations. In the final analysis, the consistent tension between the unionist national government and the former rebellious states had produced extensive democratic freedom for the subordinates of the conquered regime. But when the pressure from the federal government was relieved after reunification, the Southern governments capitulated to white supremacy. This tendency worsened with the acceleration of modernization, particularly the rise of cities, and Jim Crow facilities, such as separate parks, restrooms, and water fountains, redefined the infrastructure of the New South. Worse, the U.S. Supreme Court narrowly interpreting the intentions of the framers of the Fourteenth Amendment, began to curb national liberal policy. In 1883 the Supreme Court decided the Civil Rights Cases, which nullified the equal accommodations provisions of the Civil Rights Act of 1875. In *Pace v. Alabama,* the Court held that a state law that prohibited interracial marriage was constitutional under the equal protection clause of the Fourteenth Amendment. The national backlash against Reconstruction culminated in the Court's decision in *Plessy v. Ferguson* (1896), which permitted separate facilities as long as they were substantively equal.

In the 1890s, though the federal government again debated anti–Ku Klux Klan legislation and new enforcement measures to protect black voters, liberals overwhelmingly lost in the U.S. Senate. The guardianship over citizenship rights having by then shifted toward the states, the Southern governments were permitted to disenfranchise African Americans by blocking their exercise of the suffrage. From the perspective of political discourse, African Americans represented second-class citizens within the national constitution—a recognized exception to supposedly universal principles of liberal democracy.

The Great Migration and the First Civil Rights Movement

The next phase in the struggle for civil rights could not have emerged without the Great Migration. In response to World War I shortages in labor and attracted by the promise of urban freedom, Southern black workers began to migrate from Southern towns to major Northern cities. In 1909 black intellectual W.E.B. Du Bois founded the first national civil rights organization in New York City, the National Association for the Advancement of Colored People (NAACP). Local black self-help and reform organizations confederated in the National Urban League in 1913. Scattered across Northern cities were local literary societies, labor unions, and fraternal orders. Together these organizations formed a foundation for a black-led civil rights movement by the beginning of World War I.

The first phase of the movement focused on the problems of poverty and employment discrimination, as well as segregation, intermarriage, and lynching. Except for the black nationalism of Mar-

cus Garvey, which flourished in the 1920s, most black leaders and intellectuals championed civil rights and linked equality to the goal of integration. Historians of black migration continue to emphasize that Northern cities were not the promised land. Extralegal mechanisms enforced neighborhood segregation, excluded black children from equal schools, and constrained economic mobility. In New Jersey, though state compliance with Reconstruction had produced equal protection legislation in the nineteenth century, local practices varied greatly. As the Great Migration proceeded, towns in southern New Jersey passed local ordinances prohibiting integrated high schools and elementary schools. Proprietors of restaurants, hotels, and theaters informally practiced segregation; and municipal institutions also practiced either exclusion or segregation. Much of this was de facto segregation, and it has proven to be the most difficult form of racism to combat.

The Great Depression and World War II

Another important turning point was the Great Depression of the 1930s. In response to this economic disaster, the federal government reversed laissez-faire acquiescence to social problems, building the largest state structure in the history of the country. This newly discovered bureaucratic power eventually rescued African Americans. In 1941 black labor leader A. Philip Randolph threatened President Franklin D. Roosevelt with a disruptive march on the capital if he did not immediately address the problem of federal segregation. The president responded by signing Executive Order 8802, which established a bureaucratic organization to monitor employment discrimination in wartime industries. It subsequently served as a prototype for new state agencies that would regulate discrimination.

The next phase of the civil rights struggle was more catalyzed by ideology and events than by federal legislation; that is, by American involvement in World War II. Drawing on wartime propaganda, which promoted patriotism and democracy, black activists and newspapers promoted antiracism at home as the necessary ideology with which to combat fascism abroad. More than 3 million black Americans read black newspapers and joined sporadic demonstrations against segregation. By the 1940s, many Northern states had passed equal employment legislation or had established antidiscrimination agencies. Still Southern intransigence prevailed. Then the momentum returned to the federal government. The Allied victory against fascism led President Harry S. Truman to integrate the armed forces, a major symbolic protest against the validity of racism at home. When the president proposed the Civil Rights Act of 1948, including desegregation and antilynching measures, the Southern wing of his party bolted and blocked the legislation by filibustering. Truman's liberal wing retreated from an active federal stance, despite the fact that the number of Southern lynchings totaled 3,842 between 1889 and 1941.[1]

THE CONFLICT

By the end of the 1940s, the recurrent divergence between Northern racial liberalism and Southern segregation had produced numerous tensions and contradictions. The federal government, however, was not compelled to intervene and impose a liberal constitutional interpretation on the South. In 1942 a new civil rights organization, the Congress of Racial Equality (CORE) targeted segregated accommodations for direct-action protest tactics. The NAACP embarked on a massive legal campaign against discrimina-

tion, led by Charles Hamilton Houston and Thurgood Marshall. In cases heard before the U.S. Supreme Court, the team won against the white primary in *Smith v. Allwright* (1948), and against restrictive covenants, which incorporated a racial preference clause in deeds of sale of houses, in *Shelley v. Kramer* (1948). Marshall also triumphed against unequal school facilities in *Sweatt v. Painter* (1950) and against unequal or differential treatment of African American students in *McLaurin v. Oklahoma* (1950). The historic decision in *Brown v. Board of Education* (1954), which overturned *Plessy,* explicitly prohibited separate-but-equal facilities. Although some constituencies within black political circles criticized the legalistic approach or promoted direct-action protest tactics, the two strategies are probably best seen as complementary, even mutually dependent. African American civil rights leader Martin Luther King, Jr.'s first protest against bus segregation in Montgomery, Alabama, was reinforced by Thurgood Marshall's victory in *Gayle v. Browder* (1956). Without this kind of legal legitimation, the protests that sprang up around the South would have been turned back by local courts as well as the police. Still, during the 1950s, the federal government did not actively assist protesters or consider effective federal legislation. Although President Dwight D. Eisenhower ordered federal troops to protect Southern black students who were integrating public schools and colleges, the president's Civil Rights Act of 1957 was comparatively weak.

It could be said that the escalation of the civil rights movement responded not only to intractable segregationist policies but also to federal indifference. By testing Jim Crow legislation and challenging racist law enforcement, black activists exposed themselves to enormous physical danger in the name of demonstrating their righteousness and the evils of the white South. In 1960, for instance, Martin Luther King, Jr., was arrested three times during a week of demonstrations held in Albany, Georgia, protesting segregated waiting rooms in an interstate bus terminal. At the same time, local black student activists resented King's fame and feared that his charisma would sap the confidence of local black residents if they credited King, rather than themselves, with victories over white segregationists. King was later arrested during an antisegregation protest in Birmingham, Alabama, and he wrote a letter from prison on toilet paper. He reasserted his commitment to nonviolence, which had grown from his continual interchange with Mahatma Gandhi and the eclectic practice of *satyagraha* (nonviolent, or passive, resistance).

MANAGEMENT OF THE CONFLICT

As early as 1963, President Lyndon B. Johnson warned of a rising tide of discontent among African Americans, and he proposed a new agenda to respond to the conflict in the South. The president maneuvered through the Congress the Civil Rights Act of 1964. The federal government prohibited discrimination in voting and permitted the registration, as well as the collection of voting statistics or supervision of elections, by the federal government. The most important statutes were the prohibition of employment discrimination (Title VII) and provision for injunctive relief from discrimination in accommodations (Title II). This federal legislation, including the laws pertaining to accommodations and employment practices, was similar to that passed by the Northern states in the midst of the renaissance of democracy and black activism there after World War II. The fact that it

was *subsequently* written into federal statutory law underscores the extent to which the momentum of federalism was often *bilateral*. Meanwhile in the South, when black demonstrators attempted to conduct a protest march from Selma to Montgomery, Alabama, they were attacked by armed police, reminiscent of the KKK obstruction of black citizenship in the days of Reconstruction. The Selma demonstration, televised to a shocked nation, moved congressional leaders to pass the Voting Rights Act of 1965, which appointed federal examiners to enforce the right to vote.

Meanwhile, what was happening in the North? Informal practices of segregation in Northern neighborhoods, though illegal and challenged by black residents, had proceeded on a such large scale that major ghettos had formed in American cities. Economic dislocation compounded the segregation. By the 1960s, the poverty index located black women as the poorest class in the nation. It was this social distress that led to the great urban upheaval and crises of the late 1960s; for example, the 1965 rioting in Watts, California, and in 1967 in Newark, New Jersey, and Detroit, Michigan. Here black protesters renounced nonviolence, demanded political representation, and temporarily reclaimed cities. At approximately the same time that the *Kerner Commission Report* was identifying racism in the press, ineffective city government, and excessive police force as serious problems affecting race relations, President Johnson was signing into law the Civil Rights Act of 1968, which prohibited discrimination in housing, including rental, finance, or purchase. But the specter of black uprisings in Newark, Detroit, and Milwaukee, Wisconsin, had caused a conservative reaction among many white suburbanites, and the Civil Rights Act also targeted individuals or groups who had collaborated in riots or civil disobedience. Out of this setting, a new ideology of black power developed—one that escalated the demands on the federal government beyond formal civil rights to include urban renewal, education programs, and retraining or employment programs. This upstart black radicalism peaked at the end of the 1970s, when the cultural nationalists promoted the black arts movement and black studies in universities, toward the goals of fostering antiracism and a rediscovery of black identity. For their part, the militant Black Panthers agitated for black neighborhood survival, published newspapers, and campaigned for elected office.

SIGNIFICANCE

Black social protest, affected by the revival of mainstream liberalism at the end of the 1960s, gradually declined in the 1970s. The question of the radicalism of the civil rights movement continues to stir debate. Recent federal revision of voting districts, despite black appeals for actual representation, continues to raise the issue of racist disenfranchisement; procedural measures which flowed from the civil rights movement, particularly affirmative action, are less popular than the federal legislation which inspired them. Though many Americans believe that large segments of the African American population remain disadvantaged and unequal, it is unlikely that such a major civil rights movement will again emerge.

See also France: The "Foreigner" Issue; United Kingdom: The Making of British Race Relations; and United States: Racial Violence in the United States: 1900–1919.

NOTE

1. On lynchings, see Jessie Carnie Smith and Carrell Peterson Horton, eds., *Historical Statistics of Black America, Volume I* (New York: Gale, 1995), 488–90.

SUGGESTED READINGS

Bond, James Edward. *No Easy Walk to Freedom: Reconstruction and the Ratification of the Fourteenth Amendment*. Westport, Conn.: Praeger, 1997.

Carson, Clayborne. *In Struggle: The SNCC and the Black Awakening of the 1960s*. Cambridge, Mass.: Harvard University Press, 1981.

Dallek, Robert. *Flawed Giant: Lyndon Johnson and His Times, 1961–1973*. New York: Oxford University Press, 1998.

Foner, Eric. *Reconstruction: America's Unfinished Revolution, 1863–1877*. New York: Harper & Row, 1988.

Garrow, David. *Bearing the Cross: Martin Luther King, Jr., and the Southern Christian Leadership Conference*. New York: William Morrow, 1986.

Graham, Hugh. *The Civil Rights Era: Origins and Development of National Policy, 1960–1972*. New York: Oxford, University Press, 1998.

Grossman, James. *Land of Hope: Chicago, Black Southerners, and the Great Migration*. Chicago: University of Chicago Press, 1989.

Jones, Charles E. *The Black Panther Party Reconsidered*. Baltimore: Black Classic, 1998.

Klinker, Philip A., and Rogers M. Smith. *Unsteady March: The Rise and Decline of Racial Equality in the United States*. Chicago: University of Chicago Press, 1999.

Kulter, Stanley I. *The Supreme Court and the Constitution: Readings in American Constitutional History*. New York: Houghton Mifflin, 1969.

Lawson, Steven F. *Running for Freedom: Civil Rights and Black Politics in America Since 1941*. New York: McGraw-Hill, 1991.

Lawson, Steven F., and Charles Payne. *Debating the Civil Rights Movement, 1945–1968*. New York: Rowman and Littlefield, 1998.

Leuchtenberg, William. "The White House and Civil Rights from Eisenhower to Carter." In *Have We Overcome?*, edited by Michael V. Manorato, 147–71. Jackson, Miss.: University Press of Mississippi, 1979.

Mumford, Kevin J. "After Hugh: Statutory Race Segregation in Colonial America, 1630–1725." *American Journal of Legal History* 18, 3 (1999): 280–305.

———. "Double V in New Jersey: Rising Consciousness Against Jim Crow." *New Jersey History* 119, no. 3–4 (Spring 2001): 22–56.

Panetta, Leon, and Peter Gall. *Bring Us Together: The Nixon Team and the Civil Rights Retreat.* Philadelphia: Lippincott, 1971.

Shull, Steven. *The President and Civil Rights Policy: Leadership and Challenge.* New York: Greenwood Press, 1989.

Sugrue, Thomas J. *The Origins of the Urban Crisis: Race and Ethnicity in Postwar Detroit.* Princeton, N.J.: Princeton University Press, 1996.

Sullivan, Patricia. "Civil Rights Movement." In *Africana: The Encyclopedia of the African and African American Experience,* edited by Kwame Anthony Appiah and Henry Louis Gates Jr. New York: Basic Civitas Books, 1999.

United States

The United States–Puerto Rico Relationship

Lynn-Darrell Bender

TIMELINE

1493 Christopher Columbus discovers Puerto Rico on his second trip to the Americas.

1815 Spain issues the Real Cédula de Gracias, a decree establishing free trade, opening Puerto Rico's ports to all countries and allowing non-Spanish immigration to the island.

1898 The United States invades and occupies Puerto Rico during the Spanish-American War. Puerto Rico is ceded to the United States in the Treaty of Paris.

1900 Under the Foraker Act, a civilian government controlled by the United States replaces military rule. Puerto Rican natives are classified as "nationals" of the United States.

1917 The Jones Act grants U.S. citizenship to the "citizens of Puerto Rico." It increases local participation in the island's government, but the island fundamentally is still under direct U.S. control. It also exempts Puerto Rico from the income tax provisions of the recently approved Internal Revenue Code.

1922 In the case of *Balzac v. Porto Rico,* the U.S. Supreme Court decides that the island is a territory rather than part of the Union.

1930 Puerto Rico's population of 1 million in 1898 reaches 1,544,000 due to improved health and economic conditions. Nevertheless, the average Puerto Rican remains in poverty.

1933 The United States responds to the Great Depression by creating the Puerto Rican Emergency Relief Administration, which spends $230 million between 1933 and 1941 for relief measures.

1935 Federal funds directed toward economic development are channeled through the Puerto Rico Reconstruction Administration.

1938 The Popular Democratic Party (PDP) emerges under the leadership of Luis Muñoz Marín.

1941 Rexford G. Tugwell is named governor of Puerto Rico by President Franklin D. Roosevelt. He serves in this post until 1946.

1942 The government of Puerto Rico creates the Government Development Company (later known as Fomento) and the Government Development Bank.

1945 Large numbers of Puerto Ricans begin to migrate to the United States in search of jobs and better living conditions.

1946 President Harry S. Truman appoints Jesús Piñeiro as the island's first Puerto Rican governor.

1948 Muñoz becomes Puerto Rico's first elected governor.

1950 Social Security is extended to the residents of Puerto Rico.

1951 Law 600 authorizes a process to establish a constitution for Puerto Rico based on the principle of self-determination.

1952 The new constitution of the commonwealth of Puerto Rico goes into effect.

1967 A plebiscite is held on the question of Puerto Rico's political relationship with the United States. Voters overwhelmingly support the continuation of the commonwealth (commonwealth, 60 percent; statehood, 39 percent; independence, 1 percent).

1968 Luis A. Ferré, founder of the statehood-seeking New Progressive Party (NPP), wins the governorship.

1976 Congress approves Section 936 of the Federal Internal Revenue Tax Code, which allows U.S. companies operating in Puerto Rico to repatriate profits free of federal taxes. This leads to extensive U.S. investment in capital-intensive industries, which become the backbone of Puerto Rico's economy.

1993 Another status vote takes place, and commonwealth wins by a small margin (commonwealth, 48.6 percent; statehood, 46.3 percent; independence, 4.4 percent).

1995 Congress decides to phase out Section 936. Federal expenditures and tranfer payments play an increasing role in sustaining Puerto Rico's economy. The island's population reaches nearly 4 million.

1999 A growing problem develops over the U.S. Navy's continued use of Puerto Rico's Vieques Island as a practice range.

2001 By nearly a 70 percent majority, residents of Vieques Island approve referendum option 2, which called for the immediate withdrawal of U.S. Navy ships from Vieques; Navy spokesmen immediately reject the demand, but President George W. Bush subsequently agrees to withdraw U.S. forces from the island by May 2003.

2002 On July 26, Puerto Rico officially celebrates the fiftieth anniversary of its acquisition of commonwealth status, despite dissatisfaction among many Puerto Ricans with the arrangement.

The Spanish-American War of 1898 marked a transition for Puerto Rico from 400 years of Spanish rule to life under U.S. sovereignty. In the ensuing century, this encounter bonded two cultural traditions and historical experiences into what has become a fluid, dynamic, and highly controversial relationship. At its core is the persistently unresolved issue of the island's political "status" with the United States, culminating neither in complete separation nor assimilation.

Puerto Ricans themselves are almost hopelessly divided on what should be the ultimate political destiny of their people. Americans, in official circles and as individuals, are mostly just perplexed, and thus more inclined to passivity and noncommitment. Is there ethnic conflict? Perhaps so, but this takes on an entirely new dimension in the United States–Puerto Rico context. *Puertorriqueños,* no matter how "Americanized" they may have become, genuinely feel and consider themselves to be different from *americanos;* yet such sociological resistance to cultural absorption rarely manifests itself in overt anti-Americanism. This curious juxtaposition of values and circumstances continues to fascinate scholars and laymen alike.

HISTORICAL BACKGROUND

Largely unknown is the fact that an economic relationship of considerable significance had developed between Puerto Rico and the United States prior to the

Spanish-American War. As soon as Puerto Rico was officially allowed to engage in international trade (via the Real Cédula de Gracia) in 1815, the United States quickly replaced Spain as the island's major trading partner. It became Puerto Rico's leading customer for sugar and a major provider of imported goods for the island, especially foodstuffs and agricultural implements. American merchant ships came to outnumber those of other nations, and many trading houses were established to facilitate the evolving trade pattern.

The growing economic relations also produced a small yet highly influential American migration to Puerto Rico— American sugar planters who took their capital and then their slaves to the island, American ship captains and seamen, U.S. consular officers and staff, and business opportunists, as well as simple adventurers. Many were transients, but others stayed initiating a cultural interchange on the personal level that continues to the present day. Americans in great numbers have taken up residence on the island since 1815. Thousands do today. Like so many elements of the United States–Puerto Rico relationship, this has hardly been a one-way road: many more Puerto Ricans, for sundry reasons, have sought new opportunities and lives in the United States. Rarely does this mean, however, that migrants forever abandon their respective homelands. The ease of modern transportation and communications greatly facilitates staying in touch.

Puerto Rico came under sovereign U.S. control in the wake of the Spanish-American War, along with other former Spanish colonies ceded by Spain via the Treaty of Paris. Unhappy with life under Spanish colonial rule, most Puerto Ricans actually viewed the American arrival as a harbinger of freedom and prosperity. Indeed, the island's political elite traditionally divided into opposing camps, temporarily united in seeking statehood for the

island. They were as confused about American intentions as the Americans themselves. Unfamiliar and perhaps even uncomfortable with responsibility for an "alien" people, the U.S. government vacillated: neither statehood nor independence. It opted, instead, for direct colonial rule. This was placed in the hands of military authorities until enactment of the Foraker Act (1900), which created a temporary civilian government headed by an American governor and his resident administrative staff. No civil rights were enumerated in the law, and Puerto Ricans had only limited participation in their own local affairs. Moreover, subsequent U.S. Supreme Court interpretations of this legislation defined Puerto Rico as an "unincorporated" territory of the United States—a possession subject to Congress under the territorial clause of the U.S. Constitution. This "temporary" political arrangement lasted until mid-century with few significant alterations. The most significant event of the period was the decision of Congress to confer U.S. citizenship on the "citizens of Puerto Rico" via the Jones Act of 1917.

Economically and socially, how did the Americans find Puerto Rico in the early decades of the twentieth century? Long neglected by the Spaniards (who for centuries regarded the island mainly as a strategic garrison), Puerto Rico lacked even the most basic conditions for economic development. There were no exploitable minerals, few roads, and only 159 miles of railroad on the 3,421-square-mile island whose population was already approaching 1 million people. Public education was limited to a few urban-based schools, and there was no university. Nearly 90 percent of the people were illiterate and lived practically on a subsistence level. The largely untrained and unskilled workforce engaged in rudimentary agricultural pursuits for pay only a few months each year. The new U.S. authorities gave first priority to basic social needs: public works, health, sanitation, and education. A public school system became a reality, followed by the creation in 1903 of an institution of higher learning whose initial purpose was to train people for the teaching profession. It became the University of Puerto Rico. Simultaneously, the influx of U.S. capital was rapid and dramatic. Much of Puerto Rico's sugar, tobacco, and needlework industries came under its domination, thus tightly linking the island's economy to American interests. Regardless, Puerto Rico remained what former Puerto Rican Governor Rexford G. Tugwell called "a stricken land."

This dreary panorama began to change in the early 1940s with the victory of the Popular Democratic Party (PDP) under the charismatic leadership of Luis Muñoz Marín and the arrival of Governor Tugwell. A one-time proponent of independence for Puerto Rico, Muñoz came to the realization that the welfare of his people should come first. By emphasizing that Puerto Ricans could decide their own future by creating an economy with social justice, he astutely struck the chord of Puerto Rican nationalism without attacking the U.S. government. Tugwell largely supported the implementation of Muñoz's state economic development program under the aegis of the Government Development Company (later known as Fomento) and the Government Development Bank. A key element was full tax exemption (income, property, excise, and municipal) for new industries established on the island. The response was immediate and pronounced, mostly from U.S. industries. This initiative marked the beginning of Operation Bootstrap. In 1948 Muñoz and the PDP swept the elections with 61 percent of the popular vote, thus making him the island's first elected governor.

Muñoz had concluded that Puerto Rico's separation from the United States would be an economic disaster. He chose a middle ground between outright assimilation and independence: an arrangement that would allow Puerto Rico maximum autonomy in close association with the United States. This concept became a reality between 1950 and 1952 with the creation of the Commonwealth of Puerto Rico (Estado Libre Asociado) through a process that involved U.S. congressional legislation authorizing a constitutional convention and popular referenda in Puerto Rico. This legislation (Public Law 600 and the Federal Relations Act) still defines the legal relationship between the United States and Puerto Rico. It also let the United States off the hook with the United Nations, which had required yearly reports on the well-being of Puerto Rico as a "non-self-governing territory." In 1953 the UN General Assembly decided (Resolution 748, VIII) that the commonwealth had produced "self-government" for the people of Puerto Rico.

THE CONFLICT

Status is the linchpin of Puerto Rican politics. Without it, the wheel that propels Puerto Rican politics would fall off. While under Spanish rule, Puerto Rico's body politic splintered around what relationship the island should have with the metropolitan power. A familiar tripartite division developed: yesterday's assimilationists, autonomists, and separatists have become, respectively, today's statehooders, commonwealthers, and *independentistas*. The autonomists, who sought a large measure of self-government in political association with Spain, achieved a degree of success on the eve of the Spanish-American War. Fearful that the insurrection in Cuba would reverberate in neighboring Puerto Rico, the Spanish government granted the island a charter of autonomy in 1897. But even these minimal, new local powers were never put to a test, being cut off by the U.S. occupation only a few months later.

Now, despite the 50-year experience with commonwealth and an extremely large measure of material progress for the island residents, the status debate rages on. The statehood option (New Progressive Party, or NPP) has gained considerable acceptance, with about 45 percent of the electorate now supporting it. The independence movement, slivered into various factions, is electorally represented by the Puerto Rican Independence Party (PIP) which, although quite vocal and capable of mobilizing strong demonstrations in support of its causes, rarely garners more than 5 percent of the popular vote at election time. Although diminished, support for the PDP (the so-called *populares*) is still quite solid, preferred by no less than 45 percent of Puerto Rican voters. None of the parties, including the PDP, is happy with the status quo.

The NPP statehooders demand the full rights and privileges of U.S. citizenship through the incorporation of Puerto Rico as a state of the Union. They believe the present commonwealth arrangement is undignified, and they are willing to forego special privileges (for example, the island's current fiscal autonomy and federal tax exemption) for complete equality. However, they believe that Spanish should—and would—remain as the island's principal language and that arrangements can be made to retain a separate identity in such contests as Miss Universe and the Olympic Games. Statehood itself, many of them think, will be enough to raise Puerto Rico's economy and its citizens' economic well-being to U.S. levels. A major hindrance is how to pay federal taxes without in some way severely reducing insular taxes and the island's massive governmental bureaucracy.

Proponents of independence emphasize the benefits of nationhood, and the sovereign power Puerto Rico will have to make its own decisions. With statehood, they believe, the Puerto Rican "nation"

will eventually disappear within the "melting pot" that still largely characterizes American society. The PIP advocates a democratic socialism as an ideological guide for Puerto Rico as an independent republic. They believe that close ties with the United States will continue, including open access to the United States for its people and products. Party leaders stress that it is constitutionally feasible for the United States to allow Puerto Ricans to retain U.S. citizenship, and they openly support the concept of dual citizenship as a distinctive feature of the "sovereign" Puerto Rico republic.

Supporters for the continuation of the commonwealth argue that this carefully crafted arrangement gives Puerto Rico the benefits and security embodied in statehood without the loss of Puerto Rico's unique culture. It is, indeed, a middle ground between the extremes of statehood and independence that has worked remarkably well. Puerto Ricans (on the island) enjoy the rights and privileges of all Americans, but they cannot vote in national elections for president and vice president. In turn, island residents are exempt from paying most federal taxes. Representation in the U.S. Congress is limited to one nonvoting (except in committee) resident commissioner popularly elected by island voters for a four-year term. Party ideologues insist that the commonwealth was

SAN JUAN, PUERTO RICO. The Puerto Rico Capitol building in February 2000. © Corbis.

founded on the basis of a "compact" between the U.S. government and the people of Puerto Rico that cannot unilaterally be altered. Moreover, the time has come, they assert, for negotiations leading to "improvements" in the current arrangements in the interest of expanding Puerto Rican autonomy. They cite specific areas for expanded local authority: immigration, commerce, communications, environmental control, labor relations, and, above all, the legal ability to limit the application of certain federal laws. (Unless specifically omitted, all federal statutes apply equally to Puerto Rico—even when they are contrary to provisions of the Commonwealth Constitution, e.g., the death penalty for certain crimes committed in violation of federal law.) Puerto Rico would continue to share a common citizenship, currency, and defense, with exemption from federal taxes. A party slogan is "The best of both worlds." Critics call it "Fantasy Island," in that it is wholly unlikely that the United States would, or even could, accede to surrendering such essential attributes of its sovereignty.

Another option, currently gaining certain acceptance, champions the idea of making Puerto Rico an "associated republic," with sovereign power freely, and in full equality, to sign a treaty that defines in detail a relationship of mutuality. This meets one of the decolonization standards set by the United Nations (the other two are independence and full integration into the metropolitan political system). The United States already engages in this type of relationship with the Marshall Islands, the Federated States of Micronesia, and Palau, all formerly part of the Trust Territory of the Pacific Islands administered by the United States. Its proponents in Puerto Rico believe most elements of the commonwealth could be retained, such as common market, currency, and defense, many federal social programs, and the right to enter the United States to work or

establish residence. The key to this option, perhaps, is whether Puerto Ricans would willingly relinquish U.S. citizenship. Free association would certainly put to rest the question of self-determination and Puerto Rico's place in the world community.

MANAGEMENT OF THE CONFLICT

Several plebiscites have taken place over the years to gauge public support on a preferred status alternative. Although the commonwealth system wins the most votes, statehood has made significant gains, and independence (with only 5 to 8 percent support) is relegated to the role of sentimental favorite. With no clear-cut winner, the United States is quite logically reluctant to impose a "solution." In fact, without a crystal-clear signal from the Puerto Rican people in the form of an overwhelming approval of one option, Congress is unlikely to consider the vote a true expression of self-determination. A major defect in the plebiscitary process has been the practice of allowing the local parties to provide their own definitions of the option they espouse, without regard to what the U.S. Congress might be willing to grant. Then when Congress attempts to set down a more realistic and politically feasible statement of what the options could be from the U.S. perspective, the parties balk (particularly the PDP).

Another difficulty is the inability of Congress to make a firm commitment to abide by the choice of the Puerto Rican people. For example, there is no constitutional imperative that could obligate a future Congress to grant statehood to Puerto Rico based on a prior agreement that "guarantees" this outcome. There is also the thorny issue of who should be allowed to vote: only Puerto Ricans on the island, ethnic Puerto Ricans anywhere, or all normally qualified island voters, regardless of ethnic background? Hispanics in the

United States are likewise conflicted on the Puerto Rico issue. Accustomed to minority group politics within the context of American civil rights, their natural inclination is to view it as a struggle for equality under the U.S. Constitution. They may wonder why Puerto Ricans are so unhappy with their lot, but they certainly empathize with the desire for self-identification and the preservation of the island's ethno-distinctive culture.

SIGNIFICANCE

It is easy to see why the contentious issue of Puerto Rico's status seems to have a life of its own. There would be no such issue, of course, if the island were fully assimilated into the U.S. federal system and there were no striving for a political expression commensurate with a sense of cultural distinctness. As it is, in the end, it must be the Puerto Ricans themselves who decide their destiny as a people.

Whether the United States–Puerto Rico relationship is viewed as good or bad, boon or bane, democratic or authoritarian, liberating or restraining, the only sure truth is that the American presence in Puerto Rico has been the dominant fact of the island's history for more than 100 years. The history of the island and its people is intimately intertwined with the United States on every imaginable level. Although still lagging behind U.S. norms, Puerto Rico's social and economic indices far exceed those of neighboring islands and republics. It enjoys political stability and the trappings of modernity. The primary language is still Spanish (spoken and used more correctly today than in 1898 due to universal public education), but the thoughts, feelings, and values underlying the spoken or written word reveal evidences of deep-seated American influences.

Indeed, "Americanization" permeates every aspect of Puerto Rico's physical and psychic environment—not only such things as lifestyles, employment, living and working conditions, and transportation, but also choices of entertainment, moral and ethical views, political and legal values, and aspirations for the future. From this standpoint, most Puerto Ricans would likely feel more comfortable living in Iowa than in most localities in Spanish-speaking Latin America.

Still, Puerto Rico has not yet become truly "American." Stores, malls, highways, schools, vehicles, and businesses identical to those in the United States abound, even in the far corners of the island's rurality. Yet, nothing is quite the same. Everything becomes "Puertoricanized." By far the vast majority of American companies on the island are now largely staffed and run by Puerto Ricans. And no less than 90 percent of those who read the local English-language newspaper and listen to the English-language radio station are Puerto Ricans whose first language is Spanish. Even the federal government workforce is almost entirely made up of Puerto Ricans—from postal workers to federal judges.

Puerto Rico is an open society that has drawn people of diverse nationalities and backgrounds. Overt xenophobia is rare. Some rancor is displayed toward the rather large Dominican and Cuban communities, but this almost never translates into open hostility. Even some of their own (people of Puerto Rican descent born and reared off island) are oftentimes treated with condescension. Racism exists in a subtle yet pungent form. Puerto Ricans are also used to all types of Americans, from transient tourists, soldiers, business people, and government employees to those who for diverse reasons decide to make the island their permanent home. The latter freely interact with Puerto Ricans at all levels as equals. Yet, seldom is an American fully accepted as a "Puerto Rican"—even those who live on the island for decades, speak fluent Spanish, work in Puerto Rican employment situations, or marry into an island family.

Puerto Rico is increasingly integrated into the larger scope of U.S. and even world dynamics. In areas such as the economy, the military and public administration, the distinction between *americanos* and *puertorriqueños* has become blurred over time. Notably absent, however, is any such fusion in the arena of local politics and arts, where the feeling of separateness finds its fullest expression.

Despite the common tie of U.S. citizenship, Puerto Ricans show little interest in the inner workings of American politics—even though many of its outcomes bear directly on them and their society. Furthermore, the issues that fire public debate and political partisanship in the United States resonate weakly in Puerto Rico's political culture. Ideological battles of liberals versus conservatives, states' rights versus federal authority, welfare versus workfare are pertinent only to the extent that they may affect Puerto Rican interests. Moreover, local politics is truly a local preserve, a place where few outsiders dwell: elective offices and appointments to key governmental positions go almost exclusively to Puerto Ricans.

A similar phenomenon occurs in the arts and cultural circles of the island. These are the bastions of *puertorriquenidad,* the exaltation of a unique cultural heritage linguistically, racially, and historically separate from that of the United States. These are the cultural elites and intellectuals who view Puerto Rico as a nation, in the sense of a distinct cultural-linguistic unit, that must be defended and preserved. This sentiment predominates in their artistic creativity. Puerto Rican literature, for instance, more often than not simply ignores the effects of the American presence on island society over the past century. This diversion from reality is quite prevalent even in the more popular culture, where Americans and U.S. institutions and policies are typically portrayed—if mentioned at all—in stereotypical characterizations.

The analysis offered in this study highlights the contacts between two peoples with different cultures and values whose relationship is still far from settled. With the American invasion in 1898, Puerto Rico had to begin yet another process in a continuing endeavor to find a satisfactory solution to relations with a metropolitan power. The search continues today, sometime leading to conflict with Washington, as in the case of the U.S. Navy using Puerto Rico's Vieques Island for target practice, and sometimes producing tranquility, as in July, 2002, when the island celebrated its fiftieth year of commonwealth status.

See also Czechoslovakia: The Peaceful Breakup of a State; and United Kingdom: The Irish Question and the Partition of Ireland.

SUGGESTED READINGS

Anderson, Robert. *Party Politics in Puerto Rico.* Stanford, Calif.: Stanford University Press, 1965.

Bender, Lynn-Darrell, ed. *The American Presence in Puerto Rico.* San Juan, P.R.: Publicaciones Puertorriqueñas, 1998.

Berbusse, E. J. *The United States in Puerto Rico, 1898–1900.* Chapel Hill: University of North Carolina Press, 1966.

Cabán, Pedro A. *Constructing a Colonial People: Puerto Rico and the United States, 1898–1932* Boulder, Colo.: Westview Press, 2000.

Cabranes, José. *Citizenship and the American Empire: Notes on the Legislative History of the U.S. Citizenship of Puerto Ricans.* New Haven, Conn.: Yale University Press, 1979.

Carr, Raymond. *Puerto Rico: A Colonial Experiment.* New York: Vintage Books, 1984.

Dietz, James L. *The Economic History of Puerto Rico.* Princeton, N.J.: Princeton University Press, 1987.

Duffy Burnett, Christina, and Marshall Burke, eds. *Foreign in a Domestic Sense: Puerto Rico, American Expansion and the Constitution.* Durham, N.C.: Duke University Press, 2001.

Fernández, Ronald. *The Disenchanted Island*. New York: Praeger, 1996.

Freidrich, Carl J. *Puerto Rico: Middle Road to Freedom*. North Stratford, N.H.: Ayer, 1975.

Maldonado, Alex W. *Teodoro Moscoso and Puerto Rico's Operation Bootstrap*. Gainesville: University of Florida Press, 1997.

Meléndez, Edgardo. *Puerto Rico's Statehood Movement*. New York: Greenwood Press 1989.

Negrón Muntaner, F., and Ramón Grosfoguel, eds. *Puerto Rican Jam: Rethinking Colonialism and Nationalism*. Minneapolis: University of Minnesota Press, 1997.

Rivera-Baliz, Francisco L., and Carlos E. Santiago, eds. *Island Paradox: Puerto Rico in the 1990's*. New York: Russel Sage Foundation, 1998.

Scarano, Francisco A. *Puerto Rico*. Oxford, England: Latin American Histories, Oxford University Press, 2001.

Trias Monge, José. *The Trials of the Oldest Colony in the World*. New Haven, Conn.: Yale University Press, 1997.

Western Sahara

Ethnic Conflict and the Twentieth Century's Last Colonial War

Stephen Zunes

TIMELINE

1884 Spaniards declare protectorate over much of the Western Sahara.

1934 Spaniards control much of the interior for the first time.

1956 In March, Morocco becomes independent from France.

1973 In May, the Polisario Front is formed as the leading nationalist movement of the Western Sahara.

1974 Armed clashes between the Polisario and the Spanish colonial forces begin.

1975 *May:* visiting UN mission notes that the overwhelming majority of the population supports independence under Polisario rule.

September: Spain promises independence to the Polisario by February 1976.

October: International Court of Justice affirms ruling affirming primacy of the principle of self-determination over irrendentist claims of Morocco and Mauritania. Morocco launches Green March into Western Sahara to assert its claim to territory, soon followed by the Moroccan army.

November: UN Security Council deplores Morocco's actions and calls for withdrawal; the Madrid Accord is signed, provisionally partitioning territory between Morocco and Mauritania.

1975–1976 Large-scale exodus of Sahrawi population occurs in face of Moroccan attacks.

1976 In February, Polisario declares Sahrawi Arab Democratic Republic.

1979 In August, Mauritania is defeated by the Polisario and renounces claim over its southern third of the territory, which is promptly seized by Morocco.

1980s Large-scale French and American military assistance lead to a reversal of strategic situation, including the creation of a wall sealing most of the territory from the Polisario.

1982 Successive victories by the Polisario gives it control of 85 percent of the territory, leaving Morocco with control of the far northwestern corner and a few garrison towns.

1990s Disputes on voter identification indefinitely delay implementation of the referendum; continued French and U.S. support for Morocco discourages compromise.

1991 In April, the UN accepts plans for a referendum on the fate of the territory, and a cease-fire goes into effect between Morocco and the Polisario.

1997 The Houston Agreement, negotiated by UN special envoy and former U.S. Secretary of State James Baker, between Morocco and the Polisario appears to break the impasse, but Morocco refuses to follow through.

1999 King Hassan II of Morocco, architect of the takeover, dies and is replaced by his son, King Mohammed VI.

2001 Pressure builds to drop planned referendum and impose limited autonomy for Western Sahara under Moroccan sovereignty.

Morocco has occupied Western Sahara, a desert country about the size of Colorado on the northwestern coast of Africa, since late 1975. While most of the international community regards this situation as a case of an illegal military occupation, Morocco has annexed the territory and considers it an integral part of its own country. Most of the indigenous population, known as Sahrawis, have rejected Moroccan efforts at assimilation; indeed, most of the population lives in exile in self-governing refugee camps in neighboring Algeria. While the conflict in many respects is more that of territorial conquest of one country by another than a classic ethnic conflict, important issues regarding ethnicity have made the conflict one of the longest-running disputes in the world.

Unlike most ethnic minorities, the Sahrawis are represented by a government, known as the Sahrawi Arab Democratic Republic (SADR), which has been recognized by more than 75 countries and is a full member of the Organization of African Unity (OAU). Indeed, most Sahrawis do not see themselves as an ethnic minority within Morocco, but as an occupied people in what many consider Africa's last colony. Because it is one of the few remaining non-self-governing territories recognized by the United Nations, the fate of the territory has significant implications.

HISTORICAL BACKGROUND

Just prior to the scheduled end of Spain's colonial administration in 1976, the territory—then known as Spanish Sahara—was partitioned between Morocco and Mauritania. Spain had promised the country independence, but pressure from Morocco forced the Spanish government, in the midst of its own delicate transition period to democratic rule, to back away from its commitment.

Instead, in November 1975, Spain signed the Madrid Accord, which granted to Morocco the administration of the northern two-thirds of the colony and to Mauritania the remainder. The United States played a major role in pressuring the reluctant Spain to sign the agreement, given its concern about the possible leftist orientation of an independent Western Sahara and fear that Spain's failure to meet Moroccan territorial demands might result in the overthrow of Morocco's King Hassan II, a strong American ally.

The Western Sahara Polisario Front, the nationalist movement that had until then been battling Spain for independence, rejected the accord, so Morocco seized the territory by force. The invasion was widely condemned throughout the international community. Thomas M. Franck of the New York University Law School stated before Congress at the time that Morocco's invasion constituted "a particularly destabilizing precedent for Africa and indeed the whole world."[1]

The United Nations Security Council passed a resolution deploring the invasion and called for the withdrawal of Moroccan forces and a negotiated settlement. In addition, the UN reaffirmed the "inalienable right of the people of Spanish Sahara to

WESTERN SAHARA. A parade of military force by the Polisario Front, commemorating the tenth anniversary of the Polisario's February 27, 1976, declaration of the Sahrawi Arab Democratic Republic. Photo courtesy of the Polisario and Western Sahara Online, www.wsahara.net.

self-determination" and insisted on an end to the fighting and a referendum to decide the fate of the territory. As a result of French and American objections, however, no enforcement mechanisms, such as military or economic sanctions, were included.

During Morocco's invasion, widespread attacks on civilians forced the majority of the population into exile in a desert region of neighboring Algeria. Nearly 150,000 Sahrawis now live in a series of refugee camps spread out over a broad expanse of territory southeast of Tindouf where they have been granted effective autonomy under Polisario rule by the Algerian government. Guerrillas of the Sahrawi People's Liberation Army (SPLA) continued their war against the Moroccan occupation forces for the next sixteen years.

In 1976 the Polisario Front proclaimed the creation of the Sahrawi Arab Democratic Republic (SADR). In addition to widespread international recognition, a landmark ruling by the International Court of Justice in 1975 also confirmed Western Sahara's right to self-determination.

In 1979, after a series of losses on the battlefield, Mauritania signed a peace treaty with the Polisario and renounced sovereignty over its share of Western Sahara. Morocco then simply annexed the Mauritanian share as well.

By 1981, thanks in part to substantial military aid from Algeria, the Polisario had driven Moroccan forces back until the occupation forces controlled a bare 15 percent of the territory. The Polisario even began to conduct strikes in Morocco itself; however, since Morocco had long been considered an important Western ally, a bulwark against communism, France and the United States—while stopping short of formally endorsing Morocco's takeover—came to Morocco's assistance.

Under President Ronald Reagan, the already substantial U.S. support for the Moroccan war effort, launched under President Jimmy Carter, was greatly expanded to include direct assistance in counterinsurgency operations. These efforts effectively reversed the tide of the war in Morocco's favor. Part of Morocco's military successes was the construction—with U.S. support—of a series of heavily fortified sand walls, now 1,500 miles long, to prevent Polisario penetration into virtually all of Western Sahara.

The wall led to a war of attrition. By the time a cease-fire went into effect in 1991, more than 10,000 people had been killed. Meanwhile, the Moroccan government had sent tens of thousands of Moroccan settlers into the occupied territory as part of its effort to incorporate it into Morocco. Sahrawis are now a minority in their own country.

The Moroccan monarchy and virtually the entire political establishment enthusiastically embraced the takeover as a nationalist victory against Spanish colonialism. Though heavy Moroccan casualties from the 16-year war and the enormous financial costs of maintaining the occupation has lessened the enthusiasm somewhat, among Moroccans, popular support for the incorporation of "the Sahara provinces" remains high.

THE CONFLICT

Western Sahara has been long subjected to irredentist claims from both Mauritania and Morocco. The disputed region, which encompasses 127,000 square miles in northwestern Africa, has historically consisted of three subethnic groups: the Requibat, the Teknas, and the Oulad Delim, whose ancestors have been inhabiting the land for more than a millennium. Although, as groups, they have all main-tained ties with people in the neighboring countries, they have collectively exhibited a history of independent governance and a fierce resistance to colonialism. The ancestors of the Sahrawis resisted attempted conquests by Romans, Vandals, and Byzantines. As a distinct people, the Sahrawi date from the fourteenth century with the intermarriage of desert Berbers with the Maquil Arabs.[2]

Like the Moroccans, the Sahrawis are an Arab Muslim people. Were it not for the continued Spanish repression and the resulting sense of nationalism that emerged, Western Sahara might have been integrated into Morocco as a hinterland of traditional peoples with minimal contact with, but essentially loyal, to the government. The nomadic peoples of southern Algeria, for example, have this relationship with the government in Algiers, despite occasional acts of resistance by the Tuaregs and others.

Spain traditionally emphasized the cultural and ethnic distinctiveness of the Sahrawis, though this was undoubtedly influenced by the desire to resist Moroccan and Mauritanian irredentism during their colonial rule.[3] At the same time, the Sahrawis' distinct identity was hardly an artificial creation. The pastoral nomadism of the Sahrawis, as well as their clothing, diet, dialect, style of poetry, pigmentation, and facial features, clearly distinguish them from their Moroccan counterparts. As Sahrawi nationalism grew, however, Morocco continued to view the territory on its southern border as its own, basing its claim on the traditional fealty of the region's nomadic leaders,[4] which at most seems to have been a recognition of the sultan's religious authority.[5] The Moroccans, largely a sedentary people with a long history of centralized government, often see themselves as representing a higher form of civilization than the nomadic and anarchic Sahrawis. Having traditionally looked down on the desert peoples as dark-skinned savages, many Moroccans regard their Saharan conquest as a kind of *mission civilisatriste* (civilizing mission). This sentiment has been used to help fuel the transformation of the territory through the migration of tens of thousands of Moroccan colonists and hundreds of millions of dollars worth of ambitious development projects.

Differentiating themselves from Israeli efforts to settle the West Bank, the Moroccans emphasize that they are sending trained people into the territory to the develop it, unlike the Israelis, who enacted measures to discourage economic initiatives to improve the Palestinians' standard of living. Indeed, Morocco has totally transformed Sahrawi society. The transformation of Al Aioun from a shantytown of 30,000 at the end of the Spanish colonialism to a modern city of 100,000 complete with factories, modern port facilities, schools, a stadium, an international conference center, and modern hospitals is an example of what Morocco is willing to do to maintain its control over the territory. The few foreign observers who have strayed two blocks beyond the showpiece main avenues of Al Aioun, however, have witnessed enormous poverty, filth, dilapidated shacks, and mud streets, as well as evidence that Morocco has built up its military infrastructure in the territory at the expense of the civilian infrastructure.[6]

The Moroccan settlers pay no taxes and live in heavily subsidized housing, consume duty-free items,[7] and make twice the wages of comparable jobs in Morocco. There are no taxes in Western Sahara; fresh meat and vegetables are flown in daily and sold for one-quarter of what they would be sold for in Morocco; physicians and other professionals are given exceptionally high salaries; and free housing is given to former nomads.[8] Three-quarters of Al Aioun is now Moroccan.[9] Indeed, throughout Western Sahara, settlers and civil servants outnumber the local popu-

lation by at least three to one, with the total number of settlers in early 1991 totaling approximately 100,000. Such population transfers are contrary to international law. The enormous cost Morocco has incurred over the years of building up such an infrastructure, providing incentives for Moroccans to emigrate, and maintaining the kinds of services to win the hearts and minds of the remaining Sahrawi population makes the prospects of Morocco's abandoning the territory voluntarily extremely remote.

The nomadic lifestyle for many Sahrawis was a matter of choice and cultural right. Even educated Sahrawis with urban jobs typically return to a tent in the desert for part of the year.[10] Moroccan occupiers have forcefully sought to alter that lifestyle, imposing nearly totalitarian control over the remaining Sahrawi population under its control, including a prohibition against Sahrawis speaking in their native dialects, wearing traditional costumes, listening to radio other than official state broadcasts, and meeting in groups of more than three.[11] The Polisario has charged that Morocco initially forced many Sahrawis into concentration camps closed to outsiders, with the result that these previously nomadic people were forced to live in makeshift housing. Additionally, large numbers of Sahrawi children have been shipped to Morocco and have not been returned to their parents in an attempt to assimilate them into Moroccan society.[12] There have been reports of widespread repression of ethnic Sahrawis in southern Morocco in patterns similar to those in the occupied territories, with the central government encouraging people to speak with a Moroccan dialect, creating artificial shortages of traditional foods, and discouraging the use of traditional clothing and other cultural attributes. Despite Moroccanization efforts in Western Sahara and southern Morocco, however, observers have noted how the Sahrawis tend to hold on to their desert culture and traditions.[13]

MANAGEMENT OF
THE CONFLICT

By the early 1990s, both sides were exhausted by the war. Algeria, facing a serious internal crisis, was unable to continue providing the Polisario with its high level of financial and military support. The fighting was costing the Moroccans, heavily indebted to foreign lenders, over a million dollars a day. Neither side could reasonably hope for a military victory. Thanks to negotiations brokered by the United Nations, a cease-fire and a peace plan went into effect in April 1991.

Both sides, with UN backing, agreed to a referendum that would give the Sahrawi population the choice of independence or incorporation into Morocco. The United Nations would provide funding and personnel for implementation and logistics. Refugees were to be repatriated to take part in the voting along with Sahrawis still living in the territory. The roster of eligible voters was to have been based on a 1974 Spanish census. However, disputes between the two parties erupted over Morocco's insistence that large numbers of Moroccans with tribal links to Western Sahara be allowed to vote as well. In addition, Moroccan harassment of UN personnel and ongoing political suppression of pro-independence Sahrawis made further progress difficult.

The long-running diplomatic stalemate appeared to have been broken through the efforts of UN special envoy and former U.S. Secretary of State James Baker in September 1997, in Houston, in an agreement between representatives of Morocco and the Polisario Front. The parties agreed on the identification process for voters and a code of conduct for the long-awaited plebiscite to determine whether the territory would become independent or be integrated into Morocco. Yet again, however, disputes erupted over Moroccan objections regarding voter identification.

France and the United States, both of which have veto power in the UN Security Council, are strong supporters of the Moroccan monarchy. They fear that a vote for independence would create a political backlash against young King Mohammed VI, who is considered a strong ally of the West and a bulwark against extremist Islamic movements in the region. As a result, they have made it difficult for the United Nations to enforce its resolutions and allow a fair referendum to go forward.

In response to the frustrating stalemate, Baker and other officials, in the summer of 2001, began to advocate dropping the proposed referendum and replacing it with a plan that would offer limited autonomy for Western Sahara under Moroccan sovereignty. The Polisario rejected the idea, citing the highly centralized nature of the Moroccan state, the ongoing Moroccan colonization of the territory, and the Sahrawis' strong legal case for total independence.

SIGNIFICANCE

The struggle over Western Sahara is regarded by many as a case where realpolitik, the perspective that military power can win out over such principles as international law and the right of self-determination, has at least for the time being triumphed. This is quite disturbing for advocates of these principles who fear that, should Morocco succeed in holding onto the territory for an indefinite period, the outcome in Western Sahara may constitute a very dangerous precedent. This is particularly true in Africa, given the number of African states that have irredentist claims on their neighbors and the arbitrary nature of many of the colonially imposed boundaries between African states.

There is also a risk of the resumption of open warfare between Moroccan occupation forces and the Polisario Front, and the danger of it becoming a wider regional war involving Algeria and perhaps other countries. The dispute has already retarded efforts at attaining greater regional integration and sustainable economic development. Given the refusal of the majority of Sahrawis, including those who have lived under Moroccan control for over a quarter century, to assimilate into Moroccan society, it is unlikely that even the eventual international recognition of Moroccan sovereignty will prevent future conflict.

While Western Sahara has generous mineral resources and rich fishing grounds off its coast, Morocco's takeover has been based on nationalistic more than economic grounds, particularly in light of the enormous financial drain the war and occupation have meant for the kingdom of Morocco. In many respects, however, this makes it far less likely that Morocco will willingly give up the territory, given its strong ideological and political significance to the Moroccan state. Indeed, Morocco's takeover of Western Sahara was the only successful manifestation of the nationalist dream of *Le Grand Maroc*— Greater Morocco—which included all or parts of several other northwestern African countries.

The conflict has received enormous attention from the Organization of African Unity, the United Nations, and other intergovernmental organizations. However, the geopolitical concerns of France and the United States have prevented the international community from forcing Morocco to live up to what are widely recognized as its legal obligations.

The markedly similar conflict between Indonesia and East Timor ended in 1999 with an Indonesian withdrawal from that island nation, leading to eventual independence. This came about only because of belated international pressure, largely resulting from pressure on governments by such nongovernmental organizations as human rights groups, the churches, and others. It may take a similar movement to resolve the conflict over Western Sahara. Whether such a movement will be forthcoming remains to be seen.

See also Cyprus: Communal Conflict and the International System; and Indonesia: The Struggle to Control East Timor.

NOTES

1. Thomas Franck, U.S. Congress. House Committee on International Relations, Subcommittees on Africa and on International Organizations, *Hearings on the Question of Self-Determination in Western Sahara,* 95th Cong., 1st sess., October 12, 1977 (Washington, D.C.: U.S. Government Printing Office, 1977), 19.

2. Barbara Harrell-Bond, *The Struggle for the Western Sahara* (Hanover, N.H.: *American Universities Field Staff Reports,* 1981): 3.

3. Ibid., 1.

4. Maurice Barbier's *Voyages et explorations au Sahara Occidental* (Paris: L'Harmattan, 1985) raises serious doubts concerning the legitimacy of even this claim.

5. It should be noted, however, that under Islam the distinction between religious and political ties is vague and, within Moroccan historical tradition, this would indeed constitute sovereignty.

6. Personal observation by the author during field research, June 1990.

7. Henry Kamm, "In Western Sahara, Distrust and Dislocation," *New York Times,* February 7, 1984, A8.

8. Pranay B. Gupte, "Morocco, Backed by U.S., Spurs Economic Buildup in West Sahara," *New York Times,* May 4, 1982, 2.

9. See Teresa Smith de Cherif, "Al-Mukhtufin: A Report on Disappearances in Western Sahara," *WSC* (Washington, D.C.: Western Sahara Committee Pamphlet of February 1985).

10. Henry Kamm, "In Western Sahara, Distrust and Dislocation," *New York Times,* February 7, 1984, A8.

11. "Dateline," *West Africa,* no. 3279 (May 26, 1980): 948.

12. Majid Abdullah, Polisario representative to the United Nations, in a talk given at the Institute for Policy Studies, Washington, D.C., May 12, 1982.

13. Smith de Cherif, "Al-Mukhtufin," 18.

SUGGESTED READINGS

"Desert Dawn: War and Peace in Western Sahara." Special issue of the *New Internationalist* (Hertford, England) 297 (December 1997).

Hodges, Tony. *Western Sahara: The Roots of a Desert War*. Westport, Conn.: Lawrence Hill, 1983.

Pazzanita, Anthony, and Tony Hodges. *Historical Dictionary of Western Sahara*. Edison, N.J.: Metuchen, 1994.

Zoubir, Yahia, and Daniel Volman, eds. *International Dimensions of the Western Sahara Conflict*. Westport, Conn.: Praeger, 1993.

Zunes, Stephen. "The U.S. and the Western Sahara Peace Process." *Middle East Policy* 5, no. 4 (January 1998): 131–46.

Yugoslavia

Ethnic Conflict and the Meltdown in Kosovo

John C. Scharfen

TIMELINE

1389 Ottoman Turks defeat the Serbs at Kosovo Polje.

ca. 1389–1912 Ottoman Turks rule Kosovo until Serbs retake Kosovo amid the wreckage of the Ottoman Empire.

1945 Federal Republic of Yugoslavia (FRY) is established as a Communist state under Marshal Josip Broz Tito. Kosovo province is established as an integral part of the Serb Republic of the FRY.

1989 Following widespread unrest and disaffection of the Albanians in Kosovo, Slobodan Milosevic, chief of the Serbian Communist Party, rallies the Serbs to his support. Kosovo's autonomous status within the FRY is abrogated.

1990 Kosovar Albanians defy Belgrade by establishing a shadow, separatist government.

1991–1995 Four of the six republics of the Federal Republic of Yugoslavia secede; three of the secessions—Slovenia, Croatia, and Bosnia—are accompanied by war.

1992 Pacifist Albanian Ibrahim Rugova is elected president of a Kosovo shadow government.

1993 The Kosovo Liberation Army (KLA) is organized.

1995 NATO bombs positions above Sarajevo, leading to the Dayton Peace Accords, which bring the war in Bosnia to a close.

1997 KLA guerrilla operations against FRY police (MUP) and army become a factor.

Albania implodes, leading to a period of anarchy making weapons available to the KLA.

1998 The MUP mounts attacks against the KLA and conducts an ethnic cleansing of Albanian Kosovars from the province. The UN High Commission for Refugees (UNHCR) estimates nearly 300,000 Kosovar refugees have been created. The United States, United Kingdom, Germany, Russia, and France join in a Contact Group on Kosovo to resolve the crisis.

March: the United States delivers terms to the FRY that must be accepted to avoid allied intervention.

May 28: NATO announces its Kosovo objectives.

October: a meeting of representatives of major allied powers is held at London's Heathrow airport to seek a solution to the Kosovo crisis.

1999 *January 28:* NATO notifies Milosevic that it is prepared to commit military forces to halt the FRY's ethnic cleansing in Kosovo.

February: An unsuccessful conference of Western allies with representatives of the FRY and Albanian Kosovars is held at Rambouillet, France, to resolve the Kosovo crisis.

March 24: NATO launches Operation Allied Force, a 78-day air offensive against the FRY and its military and police forces. The number of Kosovo refugees soars.

March 25: The European Union expresses support for the NATO air operations.

March 26: Russia, India, Belarus, and Namibia float a UN resolution calling for a halt to the air strikes.

April 3: President Clinton writes to Russian President Boris Yeltsin reaffirming NATO's terms for an end to the air offensive.

April 10: Clinton states for the first time that a ground attack in the FRY would be considered.

May 27: Milosevic and four Serbian leaders are indicted by the UN War Crimes Tribunal. U.S. B-52s support the KLA against FRY forces in the battle of Mount Pastrick.

June 9: A military technical agreement to cease hostilities is signed by NATO and Belgrade representatives.

June 20: Operation Allied Force is officially terminated. UN Security Council Resolution 1244 authorizes the creation and deployment of a Kosovo Stabilization Force (KFOR) and the United Nations Interim Administration Mission in Kosovo (UNMIK).

2000 In October, municipal elections held in Kosovo select Rugova's moderate Democratic League of Kosovo (LDK) party.

2000–2001 The security of Serbian minorities from attacks by Albanian Kosovars and widespread criminal activity in Kosovo are major concerns. Kosovar Albanian guerrillas attack Macedonia in the name of Albanian minority rights in the one part of the FRY that had previously achieved independence peacefully.

2002 In July, noting Kosovo's steady progress toward reducing ethnic conflict and developing stable democratic institutions, the United States announces that it will reduce its forces in Kosovo by 20 percent in November 2002.

Prior to the breakup of the Socialist Federal Republic of Yugoslavia (FRY), the country consisted of six republics and two autonomous provinces, Kosovo and Vojvodina, which were constituents of the Republic of Serbia. Between 1992 and 1995, four of the republics seceded from the FRY. At the turn of the twenty-first century, only the republics of Serbia (including Kosovo and Vojvodina) and Montenegro remained within the federation, and the ties to the FRY are strained in the case of Montenegro and at breaking point for Kosovo. During the 1990s, the FRY embarked upon an ethnic cleansing campaign to purge the Albanians from Kosovo. A United Nations (UN) and North Atlantic Treaty Organization (NATO) diplomatic intervention ended in a 1998–1999 war. As a result of the conflict, the FRY capitulated, leading to a UN stewardship of Kosovo.[1]

HISTORICAL BACKGROUND

Kosovo was settled by the Slavs in the seventh century and occupied by Bulgaria in the ninth century. By the twelfth century it was dominated by Serbia. In 1389 the Turks defeated the Serbs and their Balkan allies at Kosovo Polje. Although the battle had minor strategic significance, it is romanticized in Serbian lore. Today, Kosovo remains hallowed ground for the Serbs. Ironically, Albanians also revere Kosovo as the birthplace of Albanian nationalism.

From 1389 to 1913, Kosovo was ruled by the Ottoman Turks. In 1913 it was partitioned between Serbia and Montenegro.

After World War I, it was incorporated into Yugoslavia. Following World War II, it became a province of Serbia in Marshal Josip Broz Tito's Communist Yugoslavia. Tito, father of the Balkan FRY, fearing that a dominant Serbia would threaten the stability of the nation, gerrymandered the Serbian Republic and created within it the noncontiguous provinces of Kosovo and Vojvodina. Although Kosovo had representation in the federal parliament and in its own assembly, the Kosovars nevertheless aspired to full republic status free from Serb oversight.

The case for a fully independent Kosovo, objectively, is at best moot. At 4,203 square miles, Kosovo is slightly smaller than the state of Connecticut with about half the population (1.6 million). A 1991 estimate indicated that 90 percent of Kosovar citizens were Albanian and 8 percent were Serbs. The remaining minorities were from other Balkan ethnic groups. With the Serbs' migration out of the province during the 1998–1999 war, plus the higher Albanian birthrates, the Albanian majority in Kosovo today probably exceeds 90 percent. Kosovo has few natural assets. Before the 1998–1999 crisis,[2] the annual income was about one-third that of the rest of the FRY. At century's end, it was even less than that.

THE CONFLICT

During the 1980s, the Albanian majority in Kosovo protested old grievances. They campaigned for status as a republic and demanded better living conditions. The minority Kosovo Serbs, threatened by the increasingly hostile attitude of the Albanians, petitioned Belgrade to dismiss the Kosovar Albanian leadership.

The chief of the Serbian Communist Party, Slobodan Milosevic, capitalized on the crisis. When called upon to subdue a mob of rioting Serbs, he instead further incited them by invoking the myth of the battle of Kosovo Polje, which centuries before had made the land Serb. He replaced senior officials in the Kosovo Communist Party and, in 1989, declared a state of emergency in the province. The subsequent rioting in Kosovo resulted in several deaths shortly thereafter. Belgrade imposed on the province a new constitution that abrogated its autonomous status.

Kosovar Serbs, living an uneasy existence as minorities in Kosovo, were at the time leaving in alarming numbers. Milosevic imposed measures to counter this exodus and to encourage Serbs to immigrate to Kosovo. From primary to university levels, school curricula were purged of Albanian history, language, and culture. The university system was underfunded and suspected "separatist" university professors were dismissed. Belgrade also dismissed the bulk of the Albanians from the Kosovo police (MUP).

In 1990 the Albanian Kosovars responded by creating a separatist government and a constitution independent of Belgrade. In 1992 Ibrahim Rugova was elected president. A parliament (which failed to meet for fear of the Serbian police) was also elected. Belgrade, embroiled in war in Bosnia Herzegovina, chose to ignore these separatist initiatives and, internationally, Albania was the only state to recognize the contrived republic.

The shadow Kosovar parliament, drawing on financial support from Albanian expatriates, instituted a de facto system covering both education and health care. Notwithstanding Belgrade repressive techniques, Rugova and his party, the Democratic League of Kosovo (LDK), were dedicated to nonviolence. In fact, Rugova was criticized for his lack of aggressiveness, and many contended that had he been more forceful during the 1990s war in Bosnia, the Kosovars could have won their independence while Belgrade was distracted. Contrastingly, the Kosovo Liberation Army (KLA), active since

1993, rejected the pacifist approach and launched a series of attacks upon the Serb-dominated Kosovo police. By 1997 the KLA was engaged in a guerrilla war against the Serbs in Kosovo.

In early 1998, the MUP mounted operations against the KLA. The attacks had little effect other than to rally the Albanian population to the guerrillas' cause and to undermine Rugova's strategy of nonviolence. The FRY army and police tactics were simple: seal off routes of egress from a town and then shell it continuously for a period of days. The double objective was to inflict casualties and to drive out the Albanians through the escape routes that were left open. Once it appeared that all residents who would evacuate had left, the Serbs would sweep the area and assemble those remaining for a processing that often resulted in torture, rape, and murder. Towns and villages were plundered, livestock killed, and homes destroyed. Once an area had been cleared, the Serb forces would move to another sector leaving a cadre behind to harass and intimidate any Kosovars who remained or returned. Many Kosovars did not return. By the fall of 1998, the United Nations High Commission for Refugees (UNHCR) estimated that there were nearly 300,000 Kosovar refugees. Two-thirds of those remained in Kosovo; 20,000 had fled to enclaves in Serbia. More than 20,000 Kosovars fled to Albania, nearly 42,000 to Montenegro, and some 7,000 to Bosnia. Smaller numbers fled to Turkey and Slovenia.[3]

Following the failure of peace initiatives in 1998 and early 1999, and in an action designed to halt FRY actions in Kosovo, on March 24, 1999, NATO launched air strikes that lasted 78 days. Belgrade declared a state of war in Yugoslavia. On June 20, FRY forces had essentially withdrawn from Kosovo, and Operation Allied Force was declared a success and was terminated. NATO then deployed an international peacekeeping force (KFOR) to provide stability and security for all Kosovars. The following year, municipal elections were held in Kosovo in October. A month later, in November 2000, elections in the FRY installed Vojislav Kostunica as president, replacing Milosevic, and several of the economic sanctions that had been imposed upon the FRY over the past decade were lifted.

MANAGEMENT OF THE CONFLICT

The 1995 Dayton Conference on Bosnia was important to events in Kosovo because it reinforced U.S. confidence that aerial bombing could coerce the FRY and decisively influence the FRY's policies toward Kosovo. Because the May 1995 Western bombing of the Serb positions in the hills above Sarajevo had pushed the Serbs to sue for peace in the war over Bosnia's independence, NATO was confident that such coercion would be effective again in Kosovo. The Dayton conference also had a second influence on the Kosovo drama: during those negotiations, the pressing question of Kosovo was never considered. Dayton negotiators were loathe to endanger diplomatic negotiations over Bosnia by broaching the complicated issues involving Kosovo. As a result, many Kosovar Albanians felt that Rugova's policy of passive resistance was bankrupt and that they had been abandoned. The lifting of some of the economic sanctions imposed upon the FRY only reinforced that conviction.

Other international events also significantly influenced events in Kosovo. The 1997 implosion of Albania provided arms for the KLA. The immediate cause of the country's collapse was the crash of a national Ponzi scheme that financially ruined many Albanians. As the country plunged into anarchy, armories were thrown open to a looting public, and hundreds of thousands of weapons fell into KLA hands.

In early 1998, both the guerrilla war and the Serb/FRY ethnic cleansing of Kosovo increased. The United States, United Kingdom, Germany, Russia, and France joined in a Contact Group on Kosovo aimed at ending the conflict there. In March, the United States delivered terms (essentially an ultimatum) that the Serbs had to accept in order to avoid intervention: the presence of international observers in Kosovo, a stop to the purging of Albanians, and the return of an "enhanced" provincial status for Kosovo. Two months later, on May 28, NATO announced its objectives: (1) to help achieve a peaceful resolution of the crisis by the international community and (2) to promote stability and security in neighboring countries.

In June, NATO directed the military to develop options for operations in Kosovo, and in October, NATO authorized an air campaign against the FRY forces if Milosevic failed to respect the "repeated political and humanitarian demands of the UN."[4] Later in October, the U.S. secretary of state announced that Milosevic had complied with the NATO demands to the extent that, at this time, an air campaign was unwarranted. In turn, Milosevic agreed to allow 1,800 international observers into Kosovo, to withdraw his troops from the province, and to permit overflight observations of the withdrawal. The KLA misread the NATO signals as supportive of its guerrilla war and intensified offensive operations, and—in response—the Serb forces countered by escalating their operations against the KLA and the Kosovar Albanians. The October agreement collapsed.

Noting that Belgrade had failed to comply with UN Security Resolution 1199, which demanded that the FRY "cease all action by the security forces affecting the civilian population,"[5] on January 28, 1999, NATO notified Milosevic that it was prepared to commit military forces immediately. A February conference attended by the Western allies was held in Rambouillet, France, led by the United States and including representatives of the FRY and the Albanian Kosovars. If no settlement was achieved within two weeks, NATO threatened to launch an air attack against the FRY.

The settlement proposed had several parts. FRY forces were to withdraw from Kosovo, and the KLA was to cease its guerrilla operations and disarm. For its part, NATO would deploy peacekeeping forces, and all parties were to abide by a three-year political moratorium before deciding on the political future of the Kosovo-Belgrade relationship. The FRY objected to the agreement as an assault on its national sovereignty and rejected the implied premise of Kosovo independence in three years. The Kosovars objected that the agreement failed to give them immediate independence. The deadline for the NATO bombing was extended for two weeks.

A fortnight later, the conference reconvened in Paris where the Kosovars, under intense pressure from the West, agreed to the terms. Milosevic demurred. On March 22, U.S. Ambassador Richard Holbrooke went to Belgrade to make a final attempt to secure agreement from Milosevic. Reportedly, Holbrooke asked Milosevic if he understood the consequences of his demurring, and the Serb is said to have answered, "You are going to bomb us." Holbrooke reports that he replied, "That's right."[6]

Operation Allied Force—employing international military intervention as a tool for resolving the conflict—started two days later. An air campaign that NATO anticipated would last three days extended to weeks and then months. Military commanders criticized the restraints imposed on them during the early stages of the campaign, contending that massive initial strikes would have been more effective than gradual escalation. Initially, the force included 400 aircraft. At the end, more than 1,000 were in the task force. Nineteen nations contributed to the operation.

The first flights struck the outskirts of Belgrade. The Pentagon mandated that attack aircraft fly only at night at an altitude at or above 15,000 feet, an altitude that acknowledged the accuracy of the FRY air defense and a concern for the domestic political fallout that would result from U.S. casualties. Multiple passes on targets were prohibited. The targets within the FRY were military or military support installations and vital infrastructure. Within Kosovo, they were generally limited to troop concentrations, barracks, and the headquarters of the 40,000 FRY troops in the province. Milosevic declared the FRY was in a state of war and urged his countrymen to stay calm. He claimed that what was at stake was "not only Kosovo, but also the freedom of the whole country."[7] In support of the FRY, Moscow curtailed its cooperation with NATO, but on March 25, the European Union (EU) declared its support for the NATO air operations. The next day, Russia—supported by India, Belarus, China, and Namibia—floated a UN resolution calling for a halt to the air strikes.

Throughout the operation, NATO took extreme care to limit collateral damage. Lawyers examined each target list for legality under the Geneva Conventions. Inevitably, however, noncombatants suffered casualties. NATO officials identified 15 strikes that hit civilians or nonmilitary structures. The Serb authorities alleged that 2,000 civilians were killed during the air campaign, a figure that NATO challenged. Most unfortunate was the May 14 strike against an Albanian Kosovar refugee convoy. An embarrassing mistake was the accidental bombing of the Chinese Embassy in Belgrade on May 7, resulting in three deaths and 20 wounded.

Operation Allied Force was suspended on June 10 following a June 9 military technical agreement signed by the KFOR commander and Belgrade representatives. The air offensive officially terminated on June 20. The end of the campaign followed the departure of virtually all FRY military and police from Kosovo.

The Serbian offensive against the Albanian Kosovars did not abate during the bombing. If anything, in retaliation for NATO's bombing of Belgrade, the efforts to cleanse Kosovo of Albanians increased during this period. The ethnic cleansing of Kosovo was not haphazard. Indications are that the massive expulsion of Albanians from Kosovo was formalized in a FRY plan called Operation Horseshoe. During Operation Allied Force, tens of thousands of Albanians were deported by trains, vehicles, and on foot. Some 850,000 refugees were forced out of Kosovo, and perhaps as many more fled their homes for refuge in the forests and mountains. Belgrade, at worst, institutionalized and, at least, condoned a brutal process of intimidation.

Negotiations to terminate the war were vigorously pursued before and throughout the bombing campaign. In October 1998, a meeting of representatives of major powers was held at London's Heathrow airport to discuss whether the use of outside force was justified to halt the violence in Kosovo. The Russian representative adamantly asserted that Russia would veto any recommendation to the United Nations to use military force in Kosovo. The Russian declaration bolstered Milosevic and perhaps gave him false hopes that Russia would support the Serbs. After the bombs began to fall, Milosevic broke off diplomatic relations with the United States, the United Kingdom, Germany, and France. At this stage, the Italian government, never enthusiastic about Operation Allied Force, proposed a pause to reinitiate diplomatic initiatives. The Italian proposal was rejected by NATO. A week after the start of the bombing, the Russian prime minister, foreign minister, and defense minister met with Milosovic in Belgrade. While the Russians, aligned with Belgrade through historical precedents and religious ties, were favorably disposed to the Serbs, they failed to find common grounds to halt the bombing. On April 3, President Clinton wrote to Russian President Boris Yeltsin relating the Serb atrocities, reaffirming NATO's terms for ending the air offensive, and pledging that NATO would exact a "very high price" for Serb intransigence.

In the first week of April, Clinton stated that it was NATO's intent to inflict such damage upon Belgrade that Milosevic would "change his calculations." Milosevic declared a unilateral cease-fire for April 11 and declared his willingness to reopen negotiations with Rugova. NATO rejected the offer as meaningless. The Serbs hoped that a divided NATO would be unable to pursue a united Kosovo strategy. A second Serb miscalculation was overestimating the impact of Russian diplomatic support. On March 30, the Russian prime minister delivered a Milosovic offer to reduce his troop numbers in Kosovo in return for an end to the bombing. Again, NATO found the offer unacceptable. On April 9, Yeltsin further encouraged the Serbs by announcing on television that NATO ground operations in Kosovo (being encouraged by the British) would elicit a Russian response, flagging the specter of a world war. Nevertheless, the Russians ultimately joined with a group of seven industrialized nations to form a G8 consortium that agreed upon the principles for settling the conflict. Following a suspension of strikes during the Orthodox Easter, April 10–11, Clinton stated for the first time that a ground attack in the FRY would be considered. Some believe that it was this threat that finally pushed Milosevic to sue for peace.

On May 27, Milosevic and four Serbian leaders were indicted by the UN War Crimes Tribunal. The indictment accused the FRY president of murder, persecution,

and deportation. The indictment was one of a series of personal setbacks for the Serb. His home had been bombed, Russian support had not developed, and the possibility of a protected (extradiction-proof) exile seemed to be foreclosed. Belgrade was suffering the effects of economic sanctions and the bombing campaign.[8] While the FRY army was able to control the population centers and main routes in Kosovo, the KLA was successfully attacking isolated FRY units. Furthermore, the KLA had now initiated a major offensive supported by Albanian artillery and, as the month of May came to an end, U.S. B-52s, in support of the KLA, bombed Serb forces in the battle of Mount Pastrick. On June 1, the FRY announced that it would acquiesce to the G8 conditions and petitioned for an end to the NATO bombing. Four days later, NATO-Serb talks started in Macedonia. The meetings addressed the protocols for the withdrawal of FRY forces from and the deployment of the KFOR into Kosovo. On June 9, the agreement was signed.[9] It provided, in part, "To establish a durable cessation of hostilities, under no circumstances shall any Forces of the FRY and the Republic of Serbia enter into, reenter, or remain within the territory of Kosovo."

The following day, NATO suspended Operation Allied Force. On the same date, the UN Security Council approved Resolution 1244 authorizing the creation of KFOR and UNMIK (the United Nations Interim Administration Mission in Kosovo) to secure and administer Kosovo on behalf of the international community.[10]

SIGNIFICANCE

There are two salient sources of conflict in the Balkans in general and in Kosovo in particular. The first is remote; the second, proximate. The remote cause of the Kosovo conflict stems from a combination of the historical myths, wrongs,

RAHOVEC, KOSOVO, 2001. In a now nearly 100 percent Albanian Kosovar village, a sadly common sight throughout contemporary Kosovo: The minaret of a Muslim mosque, badly scarred by Serbian fire. Photo courtesy of the author.

victories, and defeats of the different ethnic groups over the centuries. There is the Serbian devotion to the myths of the 1389 Battle of Kosovo countered by the Albanian devotion to a Kosovo they believe is the site of Albanian nationalism. History is not just an academic subject in Kosovo; rather it provides the rationale and justification for the present and the future. National, ethnic pride is deeply ingrained in the ethos of both the Serbs and the Albanian Kosovars.

Nevertheless, the principal source of Kosovo's ethnic conflict lies in the proximate causes. The passions of the Kosovars, both Albanian and Serb, can be traced to the personal experiences of victims who have had their homes burned; family members slain; sisters, mothers, and wives violated by hoodlums who were unconstrained and in some cases encouraged by political authorities. Revenge for contemporary outrages trumps the milder passions aroused by legend or religious differences.

To the degree that the NATO/UN intervention in Kosovo stemmed the purging of the Albanians by Milosevic and the KLA killing of Serbs, the crusade was a success. But the UNHCR has certified that 848,100 ethnic Albanians were purged during the period.[11] Many thousands more were driven from their homes and took refuge in the mountains and forests. There are thousands of documented incidents of pillage, assault, murder, and rape, and many of the atrocities took place during Operation Allied Force. The question remains: Could an early introduction of NATO ground forces have restrained the FRY from the ethnic cleansing that took place from March to June 1999? Some analysts agree that the United States, in particular, acted timidly and was unwilling to accept the casualties that might have resulted from an early introduction of ground forces.[12]

Throughout the crisis, two political factions competed for the support of the Albanian Kosovars. Both sought a Kosovar independent from Belgrade. One, the KLA, advocated that such independence must be won through the force of arms. The other, under the leadership of Rugova, argued for a peaceful resolution. Municipal elections held in October 2000, more that a year after the NATO operation, heavily favored Rugova's moderate LDK party. Following the October elections, it appeared that the majority of the Kosovars supported Rugova and the LDK.

Whereas the protection of the Albanians was a principal Western objective in 1999, the protection of the Serbian minority became a major concern of the new century. There are no accurate counts of the Serb casualties that have been sustained in the postwar period. By early 2000, however, estimates provided by the Yugoslav authorities placed the numbers at 793 murders, of which 630 were Serbs or Montenegrins.[13] Trained police are in short supply in Kosovo, and crimes for profit have become as prevalent as those which are ethnically motivated. Meanwhile, in early 2001, nationalist guerrillas at least nominally committed to the ideal of a Greater Albania drew neigbhoring Macedonia—with its Albanian minority—into the regional conflict.

NATO powers were obviously relieved by the results of the national elections of September 24, 2000, in which Vojislav Kostunica defeated Milosevic. The EU signaled its approval by lifting sanctions on October 9 and taking economic and political initiatives to resurrect the FRY. For its part, the FRY Republic of Montenegro continues to maneuver for a nonviolent secession from Belgrade. Should Montenegro be successful, it would encourage Kosovo in its search for independence.

Much was invested by NATO in this war. Had the FRY endured for an extended period, and Milosevic succeeded in testing the perseverance of the allies to the point of sparking serious dissension over continuing the offensive, NATO may not have been torn asunder, but it would certainly have become less relevant in Europe.

As the new century entered its second year, Kosovo remained a province of the FRY. Nevertheless, UN Resolution 1244 gave hope to the Albanian separatists as it tasked UNMIK to prepare the province for "substantial autonomy and self government" while "pending a final resolution."

See also Soviet Union: The Ethnic Conflicts in Georgia; Soviet Union: The Nagorno-Karabakh Conflict; and Yugoslavia: The Deconstruction of a State and Birth of Bosnia.

NOTES

1. For a more complete history of Yugoslavia and the Serb Republic see Tim Judah, *The Serbs: History, Myth and the Destruction of Yugoslavia* (New Haven, Conn.: Yale University Press, 1997). For the history of the 1988–1999 Kosovo conflict, see Ivo H. Daalder and Michael F. O'Hanlon, *Winning Ugly: NATO's War to Save Kosovo* (Washington, D.C.: Brookings Institution, 2000).

2. Spatial dimensions are taken from *The New Encyclopedia Britannica, Volume 6* (Chicago, Illinois: Encyclopedia Britannica, Micropaedia, 15th Edition, 1989): 969. The data pertaining to population, which is estimated because the 1990 census was boycotted by Kosovo's Albanian population, is taken from the official census data of the Socialist Republic of Yugoslavia, available online at http://www.albanian.com/main/countries/kosovo/population.html.

3. See the report by the University of the West of England (Bristol, England), "Kosovo Background—Campaign by the Serbian/FRY Forces," Part IIIA, available online at http://www.ess.uwe.ac.uk/Kosovo/Kosovo-Background12C.html.

4. G. Richard Jansen, "Albanians and Serbs in Kosovo, An Abbreviated History," Colorado State University (Fort Collins, Colorado) online, June 5, 1999, available at http//lamar.colostate.edu/~grjan/kosovohistory.html.

5. University of the West of England, *op. cit.*

6. Tim Judah, *War and Revenge* (New Haven, Connecticut: Yale University Press, 2000): 227.

7. Judah, op. cit., 238.

8. For an analysis of the efficacy of sanctions to achieve national security objectives, see John C. Scharfen, *The Dismal Battlefield: Mobilizing for Economic Conflict* (Annapolis, Md.: Naval Institute Press, 1995).

9. Military Agreement for Ending the War in Kosovo, Military Technical Agreement, 9 June 1999. See www.kforonline.com/resources/documents/mta.htm.

10. See UN Resolution Ending Kosovo War, United Nations Resolution 1244 (1999), S/RES?1244, 10 June 1999, adopted by the Security Council at its 4011th meeting. See www.un.org/docs/scres/1999/99sc1244htm.

11. Judah, op. cit. 250.

12. An analysis of the efficacy of bombing alone to achieve objectives in conflicts such as Kosovo is presented in Robert A. Pape, *Bombing to Win: Air Power and Coercion in War* (Ithaca, N.Y.: Cornell University Press, 1996). Also relevant is Anthony H. Cordesman, *The Lessons and Non-Lessons of the Air and Missile Campaign in Kosovo* (Westport, Conn.: Praeger, 2001).

13. World: Europe, BBC Online, "Kosovo one year on," March 16, 2000, available at http://news.bbc.co.uk/low/english/world/europe/newsid_676000/676196.stm.

SUGGESTED READINGS

Anderson, Scott. "The Curse of Blood and Vengeance." *New York Times Magazine,* December 26, 1999: 28f.

Cordesman, Anthony H. *The Lessons and Non-Lessons of the Air and Missile War in Kosovo: Report to the USAF XP Strategy Forum, Center for Strategic and International Studies*. Washington, D.C.: Center for Strategic and International Studies 1999. See at http://www.csis.org.

Daalder, Ivo H. and Michael F. O'Hanlon. *Winning Ugly, NATO's War to Save Kosovo*. Washington, D.C.: Brookings Institution, 2000.

Holbrooke, Richard. *To End a War*. New York: Random House, 1999.

Judah, Tim. *The Serbs: History, Myth and the Destruction of Yugoslavia*. New Haven, Conn.: Yale University Press, 1997.

Malcolm, Noel. *Bosnia, a Short History*. London: PAPERMAC, 1996.

Mertus, Julie A. *Kosovo: How Myths and Truths Started a War*. Berkeley: University of California Press, 1999.

Silber, Laura, and Alan Little. *Yugoslavia, Death of a Nation*. New York: Penguin, 1995.

Ullman, Richard, ed. *The World and Yugoslavia's Wars*. New York: Council on Foreign Relations, 1996.

West, Rebecca. *Black Lamb and Grey Falcon: The Record of a Journey Through Yugoslavia in 1937*. 2 vols. New York: The Viking Press, 1943.

Woodward, Susan. *Balkan Tragedy: Chaos and Dissolution after the Cold War*. Washington, D.C.: Brookings Institution, 1995.

Yugoslavia

The Deconstruction of a State and Birth of Bosnia

Joseph R. Rudolph, Jr.

TIMELINE

19th century Origins of modern Yugoslav state occur as a result of nineteenth-century pan-Slavic movements, chiefly in Serbia.

1878 Serbia, including Montenegro, achieves independence from Ottoman rule.

1908 Austria-Hungary annexes Bosnia, leading to Balkan wars of 1912–1913; Serbia gains northern and central Macedonia but Austria forces Serbia to yield Albania.

1914 Serb animosity against Austrian empire peaks when a radical Serb assassinates Austrian Archduke Francis Ferdinand.

1918 Kingdom of the Serbs, Croats, and Slovenes is formed following World War I.

1929 King Alexander I renames the country Yugoslavia and assumes near dictatorial powers.

1934 King Alexander is assassinated.

1945–1947 Marshal Josip Broz Tito assumes power in postwar Yugoslavia and makes it into a Communist state comprising six republics.

1948 Tito asserts Yugoslavia's independence from Moscow.

1966–1971 The dismantling of the repressive secret police leads to major outbursts of nationalism in Kosovo and Croatia.

1974 New constitution gives autonomy to two Serb provinces: Kosovo and Vojvodina.

1980 Tito dies. The continuing fear of the Soviet Union holds country together temporarily, but nationalism increases among all groups in Yugoslavia.

1989 Slobodan Milosevic, fanning flames of Serbian nationalism, emerges as the state's strongman.

1990 Revolutions sweep the Soviet Union and Eastern Europe; four Yugoslav republics elect non-Communist governments.

1991 Western countries encourage Croatia and Slovenia to secede; both declare independence on June 25. Civil war is brief in Slovenia but heavy in Croatia by winter.

1991–1992 The Soviet Union collapses.

1992 *January 15:* The European Community (EC) recognizes Croatia and Slovenia.
February: Bosnia-Herzegovina votes for independence, but the republic's Serbs vote against it; the United Nations creates a peacekeeping force for Croatia.

March: A cease-fire is achieved in Croatia; the EC proposes breaking Bosnia up into a series of small, political districts.

April 7: The United States recognizes the three breakaway republics and the EC recognizes Bosnia; war starts in Bosnia.

May 7: Serbs and Croats agree to divide Bosnia without consulting the 44 percent Muslim plurality there.

May 22: The United Nations admits Slovenia, Croatia, and Bosnia.

May 30–31: The United Nations imposes mandatory economic sanctions on Yugoslavia for militarily aiding Bosnian Serbs.

August–September: London Peace Conference fails; peacekeepers are deployed in Bosnia.

September 19: UN Security Council votes 12–0 to expel Yugoslavia for supporting Serb aggression in Bosnia.

October 9: The UN bans military flights over war zones.

December 11: UN Security Council votes to deploy preventive peacekeeping force in Macedonia.

1993 *January 2:* Vance-Owen plan for dividing Bosnia-Herzegovina into 10 cantons is unveiled in Geneva.

February 22: UN Security Council unanimously authorizes an international tribunal to prosecute war crimes.

May: Bosnian Serbs reject Vance-Owen Plan; UN Security Council creates six "safe havens" in Bosnia.

1994 *September:* Croatian and Bosnian Muslim leaders agree to begin constructing a joint federation.

1995 *February 13:* UN Yugoslav War Crimes Tribunal orders arrest of 21 Bosnian Serbs for wartime atrocities.

May 30: United States agrees to permit use of U.S. ground forces to protect peacekeepers.

June: France, United Kingdom, and Holland create an armored rapid reaction force to protect peacekeepers in Bosnia.

July: Serbs launch major offensive against safe-haven areas; Srebrenica and Zepa fall; the rapid reaction force is deployed in Sarajevo.

August: Croatia launches all-out offensive against rebellious Serb region in Croatia; Serb attack on Sarajevo produces NATO air response.

November 21: Presidents of Bosnia, Croatia, and Serbia meet under U.S. auspices in Dayton, Ohio, and reach an agreement to end the war in Bosnia.

1996–Present Dayton Accord's implementation proceeds slowly as difficulties in implementing details are faced

To the Western European architects of the post–World War I settlement in the Balkans, the union of numerous southern European Slavic groups into Yugoslavia in 1918 fulfilled the victor's wartime pledge to honor the principle of national self-determination in drawing postwar boundaries in the region. The entities merged together had petitioned for just such a solution, and their union seemed to give the Slavs a state of their own. By the 1930s, however, it was apparent that Yugoslavia was not a nation-state built on the principle of national self-determination, but a multinational state whose component nations—Serbs, Croatians, Slovenes, Macedonians, Muslims, Montenegrins, and Albanians—at best coexisted uneasily inside the state. The same was also true by then of the Slovaks and Czechs in Czechoslovakia, that Slavic union to the north that also had been created in the name of national self-determination after World War I. And, with one difference, like Czechoslovakia, Yugoslavia ceased to exist in the early 1990s. That difference, however, was huge. Czechoslovakia peacefully divided into two states on January 1, 1993. By that date, Yugoslavia had already split into five different countries, in most instances violently.

HISTORICAL BACKGROUND

Yugoslavia was born in Central Europe's heartland, at the point of intersection of two great empires that—being on the losing side—collapsed at the end of World War I: the Austrian-Hungarian Empire to the north and the Turkish/Muslim Ottoman Empire to the south. By the nineteenth century, when pan-Slavic nationalism could be heard throughout much of this region, all of the territories later joined to form Yugoslavia were under the rule of one or the other of these empires, and in most cases that rule left marks that significantly influenced their twentieth-century history.

Those living under Austrian and Hungarian rule (the Slovenes, who were ruled by the Austrian Habsburgs from 1278 to 1918, and the Croats, who fell under Hungarian control in 1102 and were ruled by Budapest until 1918), were much more economically advanced than their Ottoman-ruled Slavic cousins and the non-Slavic minorities who found themselves in Yugoslavia after 1918. On the other hand, although ruled by the Ottomans for most of the period from 1459 until its independence in 1878, Serbia was much further advanced politically than Yugoslavia's other areas in 1918 because it was the first to gain a large measure of self-government. Least economically and politically advanced of all were those peoples dwelling south of the Serbs and under tight Ottoman rule until 1918. These included both the Albanians (the majority in Serbia's Kosovo area) and the Slavs who became Muslims in what is today Bosnia.

From Independence to Communist Rule: 1918–1945

By the time the Kingdom of the Serbs, Croats, and Slovenes (renamed Yugoslavia in 1929) was born, Central Europe had experienced more than half a century of uprisings against outside rule, and political violence had become a firmly established means of expressing political dissent. The most famous of its practitioners was Gavrilo Princip, the fervent Slavic nationalist who assassinated Austrian Archduke Francis Ferdinand in Sarajevo in June 1914 in the hope his act would free more Slavs from Austrian-Hungarian rule. Many, however, followed in his footsteps during the interwar period, including representatives from the country's minorities, the Macedonians, Albanians, and Muslims. The principal travelers, however, tended to be Croatian autonomists, who resented their economically more advanced region being—in their view—exploited by the Serbs. Though only a plurality (approximately 40 percent) in the Yugoslav population, the Serbs dominated the country's political and administrative process, which seemed to be constantly evolving in an ever more centralized and dictatorial direction. As a consequence, the "short, twenty-three year life span of the first Yugoslavia was strewn with assassinations and failed attempts to create a viable parliamentary monarchy."[1] World War II significantly exacerbated matters.

In 1939 continuing Serbo-Croatian tensions prompted the government to reorganize Croatia administratively into a single autonomous province. Unfortunately, the move had little time in which to work to ease ethnic tensions. In June 1941, Nazi Germany bombed Yugoslav's capital of Belgrade, and shortly thereafter overran and dissolved the country, dismembering Serbia into segments occupied by Germany, Hungary, Bulgaria, and Italy and establishing a separate Croatian state governed by German collaborators. The latter soon absorbed Bosnia and spent a good part of the war repressing the Serbs, Jews, and Romany (Gypsies) who fell under its control.

Although German occupation intensified the Serbo-Croatian conflict, opposition to the Germans also united vast portions of the country's people and produced Yugoslavia's postwar leader, Josip Broz (Marshal Tito). By 1944, in a brutally successful underground campaign that took the lives of 800,000 Germans and another

350,000 (disproportionately Croatian) collaborators, the Communist resistance led by Tito had liberated all of Yugoslavia, and was beginning to fashion the federalism-communism-based government that Tito hoped would hold postwar Yugoslavia.

Postwar Yugoslavia: Disintegration of a Multinational State

Tito's scheme essentially had three elements, one of which was Tito himself, who replaced the monarchy with a Communist regime and the king with himself as the country's postwar symbol of unity. The second element, designed to abate minority fears of Serbian domination, was the federal structure in which Slovenia (91 percent Slovene), Croatia (78 percent Croat), Bosnia-Herzegovina (38 percent Muslim Slav, 22 percent Croat), Montenegro (68.5 percent Montenegrin), and Macedonia (67 percent Macedonian) became autonomous republics. Finally, there was the glue that was expected to hold the country together: Yugoslavia was to be a one-party Communist state—independent from Moscow—in which the multinational Yugoslav Communist party would hold power at both the center and in each republic.

By 1948 the new state was in place and—perhaps because of collective desire among all groups not to reopen the wartime wounds—was running reasonably smoothly.

Beneath the surface, however, old concerns and rivalries simmered among the Serbs (who were minorities in all republics except Serbia and who felt they were losing control even of *their* country) and the minorities (who still equated Belgrade-rule with Serb-rule). Hence, when the repressive national secret police network was dismantled in the name of political liberalization in 1966, the accommodative gesture backfired. By 1968 Belgrade faced strong nationalist movements among the Albanian majority in Serbia's Kosovo re-

gion; three years later, Croat nationalists were demanding greater autonomy for Croatia. Tito nonetheless stayed with his game plan, adopting a new constitution in 1974 that provided for a rotating (among the republics) Yugoslav presidency and gave the Albanian majority in Kosovo and the large Hungarian minority in Vojvodina provincial autonomy inside Serbia.

The 1974 constitution further alarmed Serb nationalists, who regarded it as yet another step away from Serb control of Yugoslavia, but there were few further shocks to the state until 1980, when the system began to unravel with Tito's death. Gradually ethnic conflict again boiled into view, fueled by historical grievances, ethnonational desires for greater republic and provincial autonomy, and dissatisfaction with the still significant economic disparities separating the republics (per capita income in Slovenia was nearly three times that of Serbia, whose per capita income was at least 50 percent greater than that of Bosnia-Herzegovina's). Still, as late as 1984, Bosnia's multinational city of Sarajevo, the host of the Winter Olympics, appeared to the world to be a model of interethnic harmony.

The weakening hold of the Communist Party over the Soviet Union and its Eastern European empire during the late 1980s was paralleled in Yugoslavia by the eroding cohesiveness of its Communist Party. Croat Communists, for example, became champions of greater republic autonomy during this period, signaling a breakdown of discipline inside the party and Belgrade's control over the state. Bosnia was both the victim and beneficiary of that meltdown, for its minorities were the least shrill and nearly the last to call for the restructuring or dissolution of the Yugoslav state.

Yugoslavia's final days essentially began with the 1988–1989 nationalist protests in Kosovo in response to Belgrade's decision to rescind Kosovo's provincial autonomy, and the subsequent emergence of Slobodan Milosevic as the dominant voice of Serbian nationalism and the Yugoslav government. Abandoning accommodation, Milosevic allied himself with the Serb nationalists, pledged to preserve the centralized Yugoslav state whose bureaucracy and military were still Serb-dominated, and began to speak of a Greater Serbia, which to Yugoslavia's minorities implied bringing all republics with Serb minorities under the firm control of Serbia/Belgrade. The pendulum did briefly swing back in 1990 when Milosevic—whose power was increasingly associated with the state's military, not its Communist Party— watched as the Yugoslav Communist Party yielded its monopoly over national political power and inaugurated a new set of economic reforms. By then, however, the centrifugal forces in Yugoslavia were at the point where such concessions were much more likely to be exploited by the nationalists than prop up Belgrade's rule.

Although it was not until 1992 that Yugoslavia fully disintegrated, it was the rapidly unfolding sequence of events in 1990 that made its collapse—peaceful or otherwise—inevitable. Early in the year, the Slovenes voted their Communist Party out of office in Slovenia's parliamentary elections and installed a pro-independence cabinet. Given Slovenia's very small (3 percent) Serb minority, this development did not, however, significantly increase ethnic conflict in Yugoslavia. The same was not true of elections held a few months later, when Croatia's predominantly Croat voters elected a republic parliament favoring a confederate relationship with Belgrade in which vast power would be in the hands of the republics. That vote triggered a significant political backlash among the nearly 600,000 Serbs living in southern Croatia, many of whom feared that Croat grievances dating from World War II would encourage a confederate Croatia's majority to attack their culture.

In August, the Serbs in Croatia held a referendum in which 99 percent of the Croat voters endorsed full political autonomy from Zagreb. Soon thereafter, the Serb National Council (local Serb political parties in Croatia) declared the Serb majority areas autonomous, and extremist Serb groups began to form paramilitary groups in Croatia. By the year's end, when Slovenia's parliament overwhelmingly voted for independence, a major Serb-Croat conflict was already brewing in Croatia.

The next step toward war ironically occurred on the diplomatic front in early 1991, when Western countries—under the mistaken belief that Milosevic had his hands full in Kosovo and would accept a fait accompli in the Serb minority areas to his west—encouraged Croatia and Slovenia to secede. When both declared their independence on June 25, 1991, however, Belgrade's response was war, although it was a brief one on the Slovenia front where the Slovene contingent in the Yugoslav army confronted their former comrades and where the small number of Serbs in Slovenia deprived Belgrade of an internationally marketable justification for a long campaign.

The situation was, again, significantly different in Croatia, where a large Serbian population qualified parts of southern Croatia for membership in Greater Serbia. During the winter of 1991–1992, as the Soviet Union imploded to the east, Belgrade sustained a major offensive against Croatia despite the European Community's belated, January 15 diplomatic recognition of Croatia and Slovenia. Meanwhile in Bosnia, a February vote on independence produced predictably mixed results. Its Serbs, concentrated in Bosnia's north and east, voted solidly against independence while the Muslims and Croats throughout Bosnia voted equally overwhelmingly in favor of it. With an overall majority favoring the action, Bosnia shortly thereafter declared its independence. By late May it, Croatia, and Slovenia not only had been admitted to the United Nations as independent states, but Bosnia had become the recipient of a lightly armed UN peacekeeping force. In the interval, the Bosnian Serbs organized their own paramilitary units, and Belgrade had begun to supply them with arms even before any of the breakaway republics had taken their UN seats.[2]

THE CONFLICT

The conflict in Bosnia, as in Croatia, had two broad dimensions—ethnic and territorial—and multiple variations, with its centerpiece shifting over time. At its most basic level, the conflict was about who would govern whom and who would control what territory. In this context, it primarily pitted the Croats and Muslim Slavs on the one side, united by their desire to escape Belgrade's rule, against Bosnia's Serbs and Belgrade, which by 1993 was the capital of a Yugoslavia reduced to Serbia and Montenegro. Less basically, as the United Nations obtained a cease-fire in Croatia and that conflict wound down, enabling Belgrade to pour more resources into the war in Bosnia but also allowing the international community to focus their mediation efforts on pressuring Belgrade to accept Bosnia's independence, the ethnoterritorial conflict in Bosnia became far more complicated.[3] Indeed, on May 7, while Bosnia was still negotiating admission to the United Nations, the struggle for political power and territory inside Bosnia was already producing strange and revolving bedfellows; in this instance, Serb-Croat agreement to divide Bosnia internally, reached without consulting Bosnia's then 44 percent Muslim plurality. It was a harbinger of things to come.

During the course of the more than three-year war in Bosnia, the Croats and Muslims at times fought each other as well as the Bosnian and Yugoslav Serbs. In the process, the fighting escalated to ever nastier instances of civilian shelling, the proliferation of extremist paramilitary groups, acts of atrocity by all sides, the use of rape as a tool of combat, ethnic cleansing, and mass migrations and mass graves as one group sought to rid a territory of another. By 1993 the model multinational city of Sarajevo had turned into a murderers' row—its main street a sniper's alley and its citizens forced to live underground as much as possible. The changing nature of the war frequently drew UN observers and peacekeepers into the combat when they tried to enforce cease-fires against armies temporarily on the losing side in a war which ebbed and flowed over time in terms of its winners and losers on the ground. On other occasions, UN forces found themselves too underarmed to halt the genocide being committed before their eyes. Above all, as the battle ensued, for want of broad cross-national support, one peace plan after another put forward by outside mediators collapsed, and the fighting ended only when NATO stepped in militarily to create a sufficient enough peace for a diplomatic settlement to be reached.

MANAGEMENT OF THE CONFLICT

Given the ethnic composition of trinational Bosnia, as well as its location between Croatia and Serbia, it was perhaps inevitable that—even if its leaders had not decided to piggyback on the separatist momentum elsewhere in the state—it would have been drawn into the conflicts triggered by Slovenia's and (especially) Croatia's secession. Consequently, had any conflict-management effort successfully accommodated Yugoslavia's other minorities to the point where separatism would not have ensued elsewhere in the early 1990s, it might have also prevented the war in Bosnia. However, as noted, even when inclined to try accommodation, Serb leaders tended to offer too little too late. Nor was this approach ever pursued for very long before being preempted by the preferences of Serb nationalists concerned with maintaining a centralized Yugoslav state.

The inability of the country's Croat, Slovene, Kosovo Albanian, Bosnian Muslim, and Serb leaders to agree on accommodation formulas to avert the events of the 1990s also made it almost impossible to settle the conflict at the diplomatic table once the wars began. Not only did the increasingly ugly nature of the conflict further dissuade the various sides from trusting one another, but with proliferation of paramilitary groups and roving bands of essentially warrior-thugs emerging in all communities, the number of "leaders" who would have had to agree to any peace accord multiplied, and many of these had uncompromisable agendas. Consequently, the early failure of the mediation efforts of former U.S. Secretary of State Cyrus Vance and former British Minister David Owen was followed by a series of other diplomatic failures as the conflict escalated in intensity and propelled hundred of thousands of refugees into neighboring states.

Eventually the conflict in Bosnia, like the conflict in Croatia before it, reached the United Nations. Its initial responses, however, also fell largely into the too little, too late category. In both separatist republics, its peacekeeping missions were too small and often too ill equipped to halt the carnage, much less create any kind of peace which could be kept. Faced with the impossibility of ending the conflict, even with the limited resources that NATO began to put at its disposal, the United Nation basically compromised by establishing, in May 1993, six "safe havens" to be monitored continuously by its observers, as well as by the rapid deployment force

created by Britain, Holland, and France in June 1995 to supplement the UN forces in Yugoslavia. The assumption was that the refugees who reached these havens—Srebrenica, Zepa, Bihac, Tuzla, Gradzde, and Sarajevo—would be safe, because none of the combatants would be willing to attack civilians in full view of the international community.

On July 11, 1995, that assumption exploded when Bosnian Serb forces seized Srebrenica, forcing approximately 40,000 civilians to flee and, despite the presence of a small Dutch force in the city, committing one of the war's worst acts of mass murder. Within a week, Zepa also fell, producing another 35,000 refugees. Then the Serbs politically miscalculated and began to train their heavy artillery on Sarajevo. Motivated as much by the audacity of the Serbian attacks as the emerging stories of atrocities, both the United Nation and NATO reassessed their options in Bosnia. The result was a major policy shift from trying to manage the conflict by keeping a nonexistence peace to taking the military action—in particular, lethal NATO strikes against Serbian artillery—necessary to end the fighting.

On November 21, 1995, the presidents of Bosnia, Croatia, and Serbia met under U.S. auspices in Dayton, Ohio, and agreed to accept an independent Bosnia composed of two entities: a Croat-Muslim Federation in the center and a Serb Republic in the heavily Serb areas to the north and east. Democratic governments were to be established at the local, entity, and national levels, and displaced people living abroad and in Bosnia were to be returned to their homes. Implementation of the Dayton Accord was still proceeding very slowly at century's end.

SIGNIFICANCE

No area in the world better exemplifies the staying and destructive power of

BOSNIA, 2002. SFOR still on patrol, a familiar sight throughout Bosnia since the 1995 Dayton Accord. Photo courtesy of United States Army, 1st Lt. Tracy Sullins.

twentieth-century ethnic conflict than the Balkans. The 1914 assassination of Archduke Francis Ferdinand in Sarajevo in 1914 set in motion the chain of events that culminated in World War I. Violent Serb-Croat conflict tainted the history of interwar Yugoslavia. In response to Croatian collaboration with the Nazis in World War II, Yugoslavia's largely Serb underground resistance killed hundreds of thousands of Croats before the war ended, leaving a legacy of heightened intercommunal distrust that lingered throughout Tito's Yugoslavia. A decade after Tito's death, civil war and interethnic strife finally, violently, dismembered the state, claiming the lives of at least 200,000 Bosnian Muslims, Croats, and Serbs (approximately 1 in 16)[4] and creating an international "humanitarian crisis" as even greater numbers of refugees fled their homes in response to the siege

warfare and ethnic-cleansing tactics employed by the warring sides.[5]

Viewed from this perspective, the first, unavoidable conclusion to be drawn from ethnic conflict in Bosnia is an unpleasant and sobering one: protracted communal conflicts in even the most seemingly civilized of settings can quickly strip away the veneer of civilization and replace it with acts of torture and mass murder. From this conclusion, two corollaries follow: (1) it is imperative that, insofar as possible, ethnic conflict be kept in the bottle and (2) if it is not and the international community decides to intervene, little short of superior military power is apt to lower the carnage to the point where a peace in the field can be sustained. Regrettably in the case of Yugoslavia, far from urging Slav, Croat, and Serbs inside the state to try to hold Yugoslavia together, Germany and other countries irresponsibly encouraged Croatia and Bosnia to pursue independence without providing them with the tangible support necessary to go their separate ways securely. Equally regrettably, when the bloodletting escalated, the international community responded reluctantly and incrementally. Thus, UN action evolved from monitoring the cease-fires in Slovenia and Croatia, to launching a large, humanitarian mission in Bosnia, to deploying peacekeepers to protect its humanitarian programs, but it never extended to amassing the level of military force necessary to stop the violence.

Nevertheless, out of the sad tales of intercommunal strife in Bosnia and elsewhere in the former Yugoslavia, two precedents have been set that *may* deter similar levels of excess in the future. First, because ethnic wars tend to be so violent and generate such large numbers of refugees in adjacent countries, ethnic civil wars are now being viewed under international law as *international* threats to the peace and hence not domestic civil wars beyond the reach of international intervention. Second, in responding to the conflict in Bosnia on February 22, 1993, the UN Security Council unanimously authorized the creation of an international tribunal to prosecute war crimes. Reorganized with an expanded mandate after the war, the court now functions as a permanent war crimes tribunal in the Hague, with the roster of those having to appear before it extending all the way to the top in 2001, when the new government in Belgrade surrendered Milosevic to its jurisdiction.

See also Czechoslovakia: The Peaceful Breakup of a State; Soviet Union: The Ethnic Conflicts in Georgia; Sri Lanka: Tamil-Sinhalese Conflict in India's Backyard; United Kingdom: The Irish Question and the Partition of Ireland; and Yugoslavia: Ethnic Conflict and the Meltdown in Kosovo.

NOTES

1. David A. Dyker and Ivan Vejvoda, *Yugoslavia and After: A Study in Fragmentation, Despair and Rebirth* (New York: Addison Wesley Longman, 1996), 10. The assassinated included King Alexander in 1934.

2. By the end of 1992, Macedonia had also proclaimed its independence, and the United Nations had established a small, preventive peacekeeping force along its border to discourage a Serbian attack upon it as well. Until Albanian extremists in Kosovo sparked a conflict between its Macedonian majority and Albanian minority in 2001, Macedonia was Yugoslavia's only separatist republic to escape war.

3. Reciprocally, as the Serbs encountered NATO resistance in Bosnia during the summer of 1995 and diplomatic efforts focused on Bosnia, the Croatian government seized the opportunity to launch an all-out offensive against its rebellious Serb region on the assumption that Belgrade would be too tied down in Bosnia to assist Croatia's Serbs.

4. Janez Kovac, "Bosnia: Ten Years on," Institute for War and Peace Reporting, April 15, 2002, available online at http://www.iwpr.net.

5. Only one year into the war, it was estimated that already more than 3 million of the former Yugoslavia's 20 million people needed humanitarian assistance, and that without it more than 400,000 Bosnian Muslims would die of starvation in the winter of 1992–1993, most as refugees and displaced persons. "Bosnian Deaths May Top 400,000 This Winter." *The Sun* (Baltimore, MD), November 4, 1992: A3.

SUGGESTED READINGS

Dyker, David A., and Ivan Vejvoda. *Yugoslavia and After: A Study in Fragmentation, Despair and Rebirth*. New York: Addison Wesley Longman, 1996.

Honig, Jan Willem, and Norbert Both. *Srebrenica: Record of a War Crime*. New York: Penguin Books, 1997.

Ramet, Sabrina P. *Balkan Babel: The Disintegration of Yugoslavia from the Death of Tito to Ethnic War*. Boulder, Colo.: Westview Press/HarperCollins, 1996.

Ramet, Sabrina P. *Nationalism and Federalism in Yugoslavia, 1962–1991*. Bloomington: Indiana University Press, 1992.

Silber, Laura, and Allan Little. *Yugoslavia: Death of a Nation*. New York: Penguin Books, 1997.

APPENDIX: CONTENTS BY REGION

INDEX

ABOUT THE CONTRIBUTORS

LYNN-DARRELL BENDER is a professor of political science at the Inter American University of Puerto Rico. The editor of *The American Presence in Puerto Rico,* Bender continues to be involved in the United States Presence in Puerto Rico Project.

JOHN S. BENDIX is a Western Europe comparativist and the author of *Importing Foreign Workers: A Comparison of German and American Policy.* He has taught at Lewis and Clark, Reed, Bryn Mawr, and Haverford Colleges and now lives, teaches, and translates social science texts in Germany.

TERRENCE C. CASEY recently completed his doctorate and is currently an assistant professor of political science at the Rose-Hulman Institute of Technology. His dissertation received the Beer Prize for the best dissertation on British politics, awarded annually by the American Political Science Association's British Studies Group, and has now been published as *The Social Context of Economic Change in Britain: Between Policy and Performance.*

MAYA CHADDA is a professor of political science at William Paterson University. Her scholarship includes *Ethnicity, Security, and Separatism in India* and *Building Democracy in South Asia: India, Nepal and Pakistan.* A member of the Council on Foreign Relations, she is the U.S. editor of the *Global Review of Ethnopolitics.*

SUE ELLEN CHARLTON is a professor of political science at Colorado State University and former chair of her department. Her areas of specialization are comparative politics and international relations. She coedited *Women, the State, and Politics,* and her most recent book is *Comparing Asian Politics.*

DAVID W. DENT is a professor of political science at Towson University. His work includes the *Encyclopedia of Modern Mexico, The Legacy of the Monroe Doctrine: A Reference Guide to U.S. Involvement in Latin America and the Caribbean,* and the *Historical Dictionary of Inter-American Organizations.*

SEAN P. DUFFY is an assistant professor of political science at Quinnipiac University. He coauthored the *Atlas of Irish History,* and his recent work includes *Ireland in the Middle Ages* and *An Illustrated History of Ireland.*

AMY L. FREEDMAN is an assistant professor in the Department of Government at Franklin and Marshall College. She is the author of *Political Participation and Ethnic Minorities: Chinese Overseas in Malaysia, Indonesia and the United States,* as well as several articles on Chinese overseas.

DEBORAH J. GERNER is a professor of political science at the University of Kansas. She is the author of *One Land, Two Peoples: The Conflict over Palestine* and recently edited *Understanding the Contemporary Middle East.* In 1996 she held a Fulbright appointment at Birzeit University, a Palestinian institution located in the West Bank.

MICHAEL M. GUNTER is a professor of political science at Tennessee Technological University. He has held Fulbright appointments to China, Turkey, and Israel, and he is the author of eight books and more than 70 articles or chapters in journals and books.

STUART J. KAUFMAN is an associate professor in the Department of Political Science at the University of Kentucky. His most recent book is *Modern Hatreds: The Symbolic Politics of Ethnic War.*

KATHERINE PALMER KAUP in an assistant professor of political science at Furman University and recently authored *Creating the Zhuang: Ethnic Politics in China.* She is currently editing a text, *Understanding the Contemporary Asia Pacific.*

ANN MOSELY LESCH is a professor of political science at Villanova University and past president of the Middle East Studies Association. Her recent work includes *The Sudan: Contested National Identities* and *Battle for Peace in Sudan: An Analysis of the Abuja Conferences, 1992–93*, with Steven Wŏndu.

ANTHONY MARK MESSINA is an associate professor of government and international studies at the University of Notre Dame. The author of *Race and Party Competition in Britain* and coeditor of *Ethnic and Racial Minorities in Advanced Industrial Democracies* (1992), he just completed editing *West European Immigration and Immigrant Policy in the New Millennium.*

KEVIN J. MUMFORD is currently an assistant professor of history at Towson University. His research focuses on African American history and the civil rights movement. His article on race in colonial America is forthcoming in the *American Journal of Legal History.*

SAUL NEWMAN is an associate professor of government at American University. He is the author of *Ethnoregional Conflict in Democracies* and articles on nationalism and ethnic conflict is such journals as *Comparative Politics, World Politics,* and *Ethnic and Racial Studies.* He is currently researching a comparative study of settler nationalism.

JAMES A. REILLY is a historian of the modern Middle East. He is head of the Department of Near and Middle Eastern Civilizations at the University of Toronto.

JOSEPH R. RUDOLPH, JR., is a professor of political science at Towson University. The author of numerous works on the politics of nationalism, he is currently focusing on third-party management of ethnic conflict and concluding his study *Ethnicity and Politics.*

JOHN C. SCHARFEN, a retired colonel in the U.S. Marine Corps, has served in a number of strategic planning assignments in Europe and the Pacific. In addition to numerous publications on national security affairs, he is the author of *The Dismal Battlefield: Mobilizing for Economic Conflict.*

MARTIN SMITH is a writer who specializes in Burmese and ethnic nationality affairs. He is the author of *Burma: Insurgency and the Politics of Ethnicity, Ethnic Groups in Burma: De-velopment, Democracy and Human Rights,* and *Fatal Silence? Freedom of Expression and the Right to Health in Burma.*

RICHARD STAHLER-SHOLK is an associate professor of political science at Eastern Michigan University. He is the associate editor of *Latin American Perspectives* and a member of the board of directors of Witness for Peace. He has participated in human rights work in Chiapas, Mexico, since 1994.

ROBERT J. THOMPSON is a professor of political science and vice chancellor for academic affairs at East Carolina University. A political scientist and coeditor of *Ethnoterritorial Politics, Policy, and the Western World,* he is a longtime student and scholar of Scottish politics.

JAMES N. UPTON is an associate professor of African American and African studies at Ohio State University. The author of *Urban Riots in the 20th Century: A Social History,* his research focuses on urban violence and riots, civil rights, and African American political thought and social movements.

ROLAND VAZQUEZ, formerly at the Center for Basque Studies at the University of Nevada, is now an assistant professor of social science and anthropology at Upper Iowa University. He is currently creating an ethnography of Basque politics focusing on the Basque National Party.

ROBERT BRUCE WARE is an associate professor at Southern Illinois University. He conducts field work in the Caucasus and has authored numerous articles on ethnicity, religion, and political stability in the region.

STEPHEN D. WRAGE is an associate professor of political science at the U.S. Naval Academy in Annapolis, Maryland. His research and writing focuses on international politics and U.S. foreign policy.

JAMES S. WUNSCH is a professor of political science, chair of the Department of Political Science and International Studies, and director of the African Studies Program at Creighton University. He has conducted field research throughout West, East, and Southern Africa. His research interests include field administration and local government in Africa as well as ethnicity.

MARIE-JOELLE ZAHAR is an assistant professor of international relations at the University of Montreal. A recipient of a U.S. Institute for Peace fellowship, her research focuses on civil wars, conflict resolution, and post-conflict reconstruction in the Middle East and in the Balkans.

STEPHEN ZUNES is an associate professor in the Department of Politics at the University of San Francisco. His articles have appeared in such journals as *Middle East Policy,* and he recently coedited *Nonviolent Social Movements: A Geographical Perspective.*